VICTORIA CROSS BIBLIOGRAPHY

Second Edition

John Mulholland & Alan Jordan

VICTORIA CROSS BIBLIOGRAPHY

Second Edition

John Mulholland & Alan Jordan

Editors
John Mulholland
Alan Jordan

Associate Editors
Derek Hunt
W. James MacDonald

First published in Great Britain in 1999 by Spink and Son Ltd, London

Second Edition published in Great Britain in 2019 by Spink and Son Ltd, London

British Library Cataloguing-in-Publication Data

A catalogue record for this book is available from the British Library.

ISBN 1 902040 21 X (First Edition)
ISBN 978-1-912667-03-1 (Second Edition)

CONTENTS

Preface   *vii*

Acknowledgements   *ix*

Foreword by Lord Ashcroft KCMG PC   *xi*

Explanatory Notes   *xiii*

Abbreviations   *xvii*

Part 1   VC books and booklets   1

Part 2   Books written by VC recipients on non-VC subjects 299
   -         Section A (Non-fiction)
   -         Section B (Fiction)

Part 3   Other Sources of Information   327

Index   VC recipients cross-referenced to books and   331
           booklets in Parts 1 and 2

PREFACE TO SECOND EDITION

Prior to 1999, Victoria Cross researchers must have been surprised, like myself, to discover that no comprehensive bibliography of VC books had ever been published. The identification of printed material concerning VC recipients and the VC in general was largely a process of trial and error for researchers. In 1994, Jim MacDonald of Nova Scotia published a booklet listing nearly 300 VC books, which generated interest and correspondence with him from around the world. The outcome was the formation of the Victoria Cross Research Group (VCRG) – an informal group of VC researchers who felt that a comprehensive annotated and cross-referenced VC bibliography was sorely needed.

The First Edition was the result of the VCRG's collaborative effort inspired by Jim MacDonald, whose encouragement and contribution helped to realise his vision. My co-author, Alan Jordan, made an immense contribution based on his extensive knowledge and concise drafting skills. Spink published the First Edition in 1999 and this was well received and is often quoted as a source in VC publications.

However, over the last 20 years there has been a significant increase in the number of new VC titles published which prompted us to produce a Second Edition. Since the First Edition, the size of Part 1 of the bibliography has more than doubled from 636 to over 1,300 titles. Most of the new titles are those published since 1999 but some pre 1999 titles have come to our notice and these have been added.

As a team we have specifically excluded journal articles, auction catalogues, newspapers and websites. Part 3 provides pointers on these sources. It is estimated that there are over ten thousand journal and magazine articles on the VC and VC recipients. This would require several volumes of a bibliography if written to the same format of this Second Edition.

This Second Edition has been compiled by a small dedicated team, most of whom were involved in the First Edition. Alan Jordan, my co-author, has made a very significant contribution without which this edition would not have reached fruition. His efforts and expert knowledge combined with a detailed eye have made an enormous contribution to the scope and detail. Jim Macdonald, whose idea and own publication of 1994 inspired the bibliography, has retained his enthusiasm over the years and provided many useful details, particularly in tracing volumes not previously identified. Derek Hunt, with whom I have collaborated in writing two VC titles, has been an excellent contributor and editor. His eye for detail and knowledge of the VC and its recipients have been very welcome.

It should be stated that this bibliography does not meet the exacting standards of describing the technical details of each book such as type of binding, dust jacket details, book weight and size. These are omitted purposely to focus on the content of each book and to identify useful volumes for anyone researching particular VC recipients. We recognise this approach will not satisfy some bibliophiles but we hope it meets the needs of VC researchers and authors who, in the main, see the books primarily as a means to an end, rather than an end in itself.

The Explanatory Notes section provides a guide and explanation to the entries including the title description to a standard format and inclusions and exclusions. We suggest readers take the time to read these notes as they may speed up the research process.

The Index has the names and *London Gazette* date of every VC with the relevant books given for each recipient. This will enable a rapid identification of printed volumes related to a particular VC recipient.

In writing this volume, we hope it will help VC researchers to readily identify VC titles that may accelerate their searches. We also hope it will stimulate VC authors to use the efforts of others as a basis to launch their own primary research to discover new or more relevant information rather than simply re-using existing material already in print.

As the Index shows, some VC recipients like Guy Gibson, Lord Roberts or VC recipients of Rorke's Drift have numerous volumes dedicated to them. But the Index also shows that many VC recipients have relatively little written about them and they are worthy of further research, possibly leading to new and informative titles. We hope this Second Edition will stimulate this process so that all VC recipients get the attention they so richly deserve.

John Mulholland

Sheffield   2019

ACKNOWLEDGEMENTS

I would particularly like to thank Jim MacDonald for his original idea of an annotated VC bibliography. In turn, the original team of researchers, which included Jim, produced the First Edition in 1999. Thanks also go to Lydia Bradley for drafting the First Edition and Rear Admiral JAL Myres CB, past President of the Orders and Medals Research Society, for the Foreword to the First Edition.

In the preparation of this Second Edition I would like to acknowledge the contribution of the late Erling Breinholm of Denmark for advice on Scandinavian texts related to VC titles. Also I acknowledge the considerable efforts of Gail Balfour since 1999 in redrafting numerous drafts and for her enduring patience and dedication.

In the search for new titles the databases of libraries, archives and publishers across the world have been searched on-line. I would like to express our thanks to these sources which are too numerous to list. Thanks also go to Chris Lindsay for seeking out rare titles.

I would like to thank Brian Best, former editor of *The Journal of the Victoria Cross Society*, for his support over the years and we have included all 28 volumes of the *Journal* in Part 1.

Also I would like to thank Emma Howard, Head of Books, at Spink for supporting this Second Edition. And thanks go to David Erskine-Hill for his invaluable advice, support and guidance since 1999. I am most grateful to Lord Ashcroft KCMG PC for writing the Foreword to this Second Edition.

Finally my thanks go to my long-suffering wife, Shelley, for her help and patience over the years. My co-author thanks his wife, Judith, for her unstinting support, and his brother, Neil, for his sterling efforts in identifying and sourcing an extensive range of VC titles.

For all others who have helped, we offer our sincerest thanks.

John Mulholland

FOREWORD

When Queen Victoria created the Victoria Cross (VC) in January 1856, it was impossible to imagine quite how popular the decoration would become over future decades. By instituting, through a Royal Warrant, such an egalitarian award, the Queen created something that captured the public's imagination like no gallantry award before or since.

The results of such a popular decoration have included a number of offshoot 'industries', not least the 'publishing industry'. For more than 160 years, millions of words have been written about the VC, many in the form of books written either specifically about the decoration, or in which the VC plays a significant role.

It had been impossible for anyone to keep tabs on quite how many books there were on the VC and exactly which area, or areas, they all covered. That was until John Mulholland and Alan Jordan came up with the splendid idea of writing a book restricted to this very subject. And so, in 1999, *Victoria Cross Bibliography* was born: as its name suggests, it was a comprehensive list of all of the hundreds of books that had been written about the VC, some of them, of course, by VC recipients themselves.

Since 1999, the interest in the VC has grown again, partly because of the interest around the 150th anniversary of the decoration's creation and partly because wars in Iraq and Afghanistan led to the awards of further VCs to servicemen. To date, the VC has been awarded 1,363 times including three bars, four awards of the VC for Australia and one award of the VC for New Zealand. An on-going public fascination with gallant deeds, particularly the VC, led to a plethora of new publications in recent years. So, with admirable determination and energy, the two authors set about the task of updating the first edition of their book written with the help of Jim MacDonald and Derek Hunt. The result of their latest endeavours is the *Victoria Cross Bibliography: Second Edition*.

This updated book is an indispensable guide for anyone – be they author, historian or researcher – wanting to delve into a particular area of the VC. For someone like me, with a passion for bravery that has led me to build the world's largest collection of VCs and to write six books on gallantry, it is a precious tool.

I commend the authors for the diligence of their research and for producing a book that is a wonderful asset for anyone who wants to take a serious look at the VC, its recipients and all that they have come to represent. This will be a 'must read' for enthusiasts of the VC for many, many years to come.

Lord Ashcroft KCMG PC

EXPLANATORY NOTES

1. Aim

This bibliography aims to assist VC researchers by endeavouring to list all known published books and booklets relating to the VC and its recipients.

2. Partitioning of Bibliography

The publication is divided into two main parts and is supplemented by a cross-referenced index.

Part 1

This part lists and describes those VC books and booklets which meet any of the following criteria:

- the publication is wholly related to the VC or to one or more VC recipients
- a chapter, or specific part of the publication, is devoted wholly to the VC or to one or more VC recipients
- significant coverage of a VC recipient or VC action is otherwise contained within the work.

This list includes conventionally printed books and booklets by mainstream, private and self-publishers. The criteria for inclusion is not restricted to the ability to purchase a title (new or second-hand) but whether the volume can be consulted in a reference library. This applies mainly to desk-top published titles on small print runs. Publishers have a legal responsibility to deposit copies of every publication with an ISBN in the six UK legal depositories which include the British Library. However, our experience shows that this does not always happen.

Part 2

This part lists those books written or edited by VC recipients where the subject matter does not relate to the VC. It is arranged into two sections:

> Section A covers non-fictional works
> Section B covers fictional works.

Section A is produced in a similar format to that used for Part 1 (see above) with the VC authors listed in alphabetical order. Section B is simply a listing of book titles by author and indicates the year of publication. Titles in Part 2 are listed by VC author in alphabetical order and do not have a specific reference number (e.g. A12). However, authors with works in Part 2 are cross-referenced in the Index.

Part 3

Part 3 includes pointers to some of the following sources specifically excluded from the bibliography:

- unit histories
- *Who's Who, Dictionary of National Biography* and similar works
- school and memorial registers
- articles in magazines, journals and newspapers
- medal auction catalogues of VC sales

- pamphlets concerning the VC
- memorial service programmes related to VC recipients
- campaign histories not related specifically to a VC action
- books containing part-factual and part-fictional VC content unless they have particular merit on the factual element
- novels or plays relating to the VC or VC actions or to fictitious VC recipients
- electronic books which do not have a printed version
- websites

Index

The Index is a comprehensive list of VC recipients. It is arranged alphabetically by surname (and by forename if like surnames apply), against which the Gazette date announcing the recipient's VC award is recorded. Most Gazette references refer to *The London Gazette* but recent awards of the Victoria Cross for Australia and the Victoria Cross for New Zealand refer to the Gazettes of these nations.

The references shown against each name relate to the item 'Reference Number' in Part 1, where the publication covers or makes significant mention of the VC winner. To qualify for this cross-reference, the book must contain at least 300 words about the recipient. This will enable researchers to quickly identify appropriate publications.

3. Format of Entries in Part 1 and Section A of Part 2

Sequencing of entries

Entries in Parts 1 and 2 are arranged alphabetically by author's surname or by the name of the publisher, if no author is credited.

Reference Number

In Part 1 each book has been allocated a reference number (e.g. A55, B20). The prefix letter refers to the first letter of the author's surname (or the name of the publisher if the author is unknown). Numbers, whilst sequential within each letter, are not necessarily consecutive. Gaps have been left to accommodate the incorporation of further titles in future editions of the bibliography and minimise the need for significant change to cross references in the Index. On a few occasions, where there is no further room for references, an A, B or C suffix is added to avoid significant disruption to the cross reference system, e.g. C113, C113A, C113B, C113C and C113D.

Books listed in Part 2 are listed by VC author in alphabetical order, and do not have a reference number. However, VC authors with titles in Part 2 are referred to in the Index.

Book Description

The title, rank and decorations of the author (or editor or compiler) are recorded as indicated on the title page of the book. Where a book is not accredited to an individual, the publisher's name is stated.

A book title might differ on the dust jacket, spine, front board and title page. As a general rule, the title recorded in capitals in this bibliography is the main title as shown on the book's title page. Any subtitle on the title page is also recorded but is not capitalised. Where a book has been republished under a different title, the distinction between the original and subsequent title(s) is indicated.

The publisher details recorded usually omit 'Co.', 'Ltd.', and '& Sons' and so forth, as the style used might differ between books produced by the same publisher.

Edition

Normally, entries refer to only the first edition of a title. However, in cases where the work has been revised, or reformatted substantially, one or more subsequent editions may also be indicated. No reference is usually made to softback versions of books published originally in hardback form unless the contents are significantly different.

Abbreviations

The following abbreviations are used for book descriptions in Part 1 and Section A of Part 2:

fp   **frontispiece**
           This term is often used in relation to facsimile copies referring to the title page   of a first edition. The term is also used for an illustrated page opposite the title   page.

cr   **cross referenced**
           The publication reference number is cross-referred within the Index to the bibliography (see 'Partitioning of Bibliography' above).

ncr   **not cross referenced**
           The publication does not qualify for indexed cross referencing to any particular VC winner. For example, S62 *The Story of the Victoria Cross* by Sir John Smyth VC contains only brief mentions of the many VC recipients covered.

tbc   **to be checked**
           The publication has not yet been accessed by the editors to determine the cross reference status (i.e. 'cr' or 'ncr'). This may be because the title is yet to be published. For example, O21 in the series by Paul Oldfield.

pp   **number of pages**
           This shows the total quantity of numbered pages but excludes any Roman-numbered pages preceding the main body of the book.

nd   **no date (c: circa)**
           If no publication date is shown in the work, an approximate publication date is given where such a date can be derived.

np   **no publisher**
           This means that no publisher's name is identified in the work. In these cases, the printer's name is recorded, if known.

photo(s)   **photograph(s)**
           'photo' means a single photograph.
           'photos' means more than one photograph.
           Colour photos are highlighted.
           This distinction applies similarly to maps, drawings, artist's impressions, sketches and line drawings.

hb   **hardback publication**
sb   **softback publication**
           This includes both card covers and paper covers.

index	index

This means an index is included at the back of the book. The existence of any detailed contents listing at the front of the book is ignored.

sic   **author or publisher error**

(*sic*) indicates an apparent error by the publisher or author but quoted exactly as it appears in the title. For example see title of A12B.

A full glossary of abbreviations used is shown in Abbreviations section. Not included are abbreviations of rank. For example, Wg Cdr for Wing Commander, as these are self evident.

Annotation

The purpose of the annotation is simply to describe the scope of the book's contents and to indicate the extent of coverage given to VC topics and recipients. It is not intended to critically appraise a work or to comment on its accuracy and quality unless the editors consider this important. However, if a title is of particular significance this is usually reflected in the length of the annotation. Some annotations occasionally have critical comments, such as a book title not reflecting the scope of the contents. Or if a title is particularly well-illustrated or well-researched, this is sometimes highlighted.

Incomplete Title Details

Most of the 1,300 titles in Part 1 have been reviewed by the editors as hard copies. However, there are titles which have not been obtained. In these cases the editors have decided to include the titles but with incomplete details which are indicated.

Titles to be published

At the time of publication of this bibliography there are planned titles which have not yet been published. Such titles, known to the editors, are included. It is hoped they will be published as some titles are advertised ahead of publication but fail to reach fruition.

Value

No attempt has been made to value books. Values vary with time, the edition, scarcity and condition of the volume. However, the current value of more common titles are readily available via websites such as **www.amazon.co.uk/books** and **www.abebooks.co.uk** .

Additions and corrections

Whilst the editors have attempted to include every known VC publication within the scope of this bibliography, readers will be able to identify other works that meet the inclusion criteria. Readers may also wish to advise the editors on incomplete titles. Furthermore, newly-published titles will arise. It is, therefore, intended to publish a Third Edition of the complete bibliography within ten years, which will enable additions and corrections to be incorporated.

Any additions or corrections to this Second Edition would be gratefully received by the editors who can be contacted by email at **j.a.mulholland@btinternet.com** or via the publisher.

The editors have made every effort to provide accurate and fair descriptions of the publications covered in this bibliography. However, they accept no responsibility for any issues arising from the details recorded.

ABBREVIATIONS
(used in Parts 1 and 2)

AAAV	Australian Army Advisers Vietnam
ACM	Air Chief Marshal
AFC	Air Force Cross
AFM	Air Force Medal
AIF	Australian Imperial Force
AM	Air Marshal *or* Albert Medal *or* Member of the Order of Australia
ANZAC	Australian and New Zealand Army Corps
AOC	Air Officer Commanding
AOC in C	Air Officer Commanding in Chief
AVM	Air Vice Marshal
AVSM	Ati Vishisht Seva Medal
Bdr	Bombardier
BEF	British Expeditionary Force
BEM	British Empire Medal
BSc	Bachelor of Science
CAE	Air Efficiency Award (Canada)
CB	Companion of the Order of the Bath
CBE	Commander of the Order of the British Empire
CC	Companion of the Order of Canada
CD	Canadian Forces Decoration
CdeG	Croix de Guerre
CIE	Companion of the Order of the Indian Empire
C-in-C	Commander-in-Chief
CGM	Conspicuous Gallantry Medal
CM	Medal of Canada
CMB	Coastal Motor Boat
CMG	Companion of the Order of St Michael and St George
CO	Commanding Officer
CPO	Chief Petty Officer
CSI	Commander of the Order of the Star of India
CSM	Company Sergeant Major
CStJ	Cross of the Order of St John of Jerusalem
CV	Cross of Valour (Canada)
CVO	Commander of the Royal Victorian Order
DBE	Dame Commander of the Order of the British Empire
DCL	Doctor of Civil Law
DCM	Distinguished Conduct Medal
DFC	Distinguished Flying Cross
DFM	Distinguished Flying Medal
DL	Deputy Lieutenant

DSC	Distinguished Service Cross
DSM	Distinguished Service Medal
DSO	Distinguished Service Order
EGM	Empire Gallantry Medal
EM	Edward Medal
FLS	Fellow of the Linnean Society
FM	Field Marshal
FRCPath	Fellow of the Royal College of Pathology
FRCP(C)	Fellow of the Royal College of Physicians (Canada)
FRGS	Fellow of the Royal Geographical Society
FRHistS	Fellow of the Royal Historical Society
FRS	Fellow of the Royal Society
GC	George Cross
GCB	Knight Grand Cross of the Order of the Bath
GCIE	Knight Grand Commander of the Indian Empire
GCMG	Knight Grand Cross of the Order of St Michael and St George
GCSI	Knight Grand Commander of the Order of the Star of India
GCVO	Knight Grand Cross of the Royal Victorian Order
GHQ	General Headquarters
GM	George Medal
GOC-in-C	General Officer Commander-in-Chief
HAC	Honourable Artillery Company
HEIC	Honourable East India Company
HQ	Headquarters
IOM	Indian Order of Merit
IWM	Imperial War Museum, London
KBE	Knight Commander of the Order of the British Empire
KCB	Knight Commander of the Order of the Bath
KCMG	Knight Commander of St Michael and St George
KCSI	Knight Commander of the Star of India
KG	Knight of the Order of the Garter
KP	Knight of the Order of St Patrick
KPM	King's Police Medal
KSLI	King's Shropshire Light Infantry
LG	*London Gazette*
LLD	Doctor of Laws
MA	Master of Arts
MB	Bachelor of Medicine
MBE	Member of the Order of the British Empire
MC	Military Cross
MD	Doctor Medicine
MM	Military Medal
MP	Member of Parliament
MVO	Member of the Royal Victorian Order

NAM	National Army Museum, London
NCO	Non-Commissioned Officer
NZC	New Zealand Cross
NZEF	New Zealand Expeditionary Force
OBE	Officer of the Order of the British Empire
OC	Officer of the Order of Canada *or* Officer Commanding
OM	Order of Merit
PC	Privy Councillor
POW	Prisoner of War
PVSM	Param Vishisht Seva Medal
QARANC	Queen Alexandra's Royal Army Nursing Corps
QGO	Queen's Gurkha Officer
QMG	Quartermaster-General
RA	Royal Artillery
RAAF	Royal Australian Air Force
RAF	Royal Air Force
RAMC	Royal Army Medical Corps
RAN	Royal Australian Navy
RCAF	Royal Canadian Air Force
RCN	Royal Canadian Navy
RCNVR	Royal Canadian Naval Volunteer Reserve
RCT	Royal Corps of Transport
RD	Royal Naval Reserve Decoration
RE	Royal Engineers
RFC	Royal Flying Corps
RMC	Royal Military College
RN	Royal Navy
RNAS	Royal Naval Air Service
RND	Royal Naval Division
RNLI	Royal National Lifeboat Institution
RNR	Royal Naval Reserve
RNVR	Royal Naval Volunteer Reserve
RNZAF	Royal New Zealand Air Force
RRC	Royal Red Cross
RSA	Republic of South Africa
SAS	Special Air Service
SOE	Special Operations Executive
TD	Territorial Decoration / Efficiency Decoration
VC	Victoria Cross
VD	Volunteer Officer's Decoration
VSM	Vishisht Seva Medal
WAAF	Women's Auxiliary Air Force
WW1	World War 1
WW2	World War 2

WO	Warrant Officer
WO1	Warrant Officer Class 1
WO2	Warrant Officer Class 2

PART 1

VC Books and Booklets

A1 ABBOTT, P.E. and TAMPLIN, J.M.A.
BRITISH GALLANTRY AWARDS
[1] Guinness Seaby, London, 1971 (expanded and reformatted: Nimrod Dix, London, 1981)
359 pp, photos, index, hb, cr
[2] Nimrod Dix, London, 1981 (expanded and reformatted) 316 pp, hb [VC: p263-295]

This standard reference work on British gallantry awards documents in a separate chapter for each award, the award's origin and development, physical description (including illustrations), verification sources, numbers awarded and an illustrative account. The 1971 edition covers 34 separate awards whereas the 1981 edition covers 44 awards. The Victoria Cross is featured as Chapter 34 (pages 310-330) and as Chapter 44 (pages 283-295) in these editions, respectively. The illustrative VC account relates to the VC deed and subsequent career of Daniel Cambridge and also traces the sales of his VC group.

A5 ADKIN, Mark
THE LAST ELEVEN?: Winners of the Victoria Cross since the Second World War
Leo Cooper, London, 1991
220 pp, photos, maps, index, hb, cr

A collection of biographical sketches and detailed accounts of the VC deeds of the then eleven post-WW2 recipients of the VC. The book is arranged in four parts, covering the conflicts and VC actions in Korea (Muir, Curtis, Carne and Speakman), Borneo (Rambahadur Limbu), Vietnam (Wheatley, Badcoe, Simpson and Payne) and the Falkland Islands (Jones and McKay). The text is supported by battle maps.

A6 ADKIN, Mark
GOOSE GREEN: A Battle is Fought to be Won
Leo Cooper, London, 1992
305 pp, photos, sketches, maps, index, hb, cr

A detailed study of the battle for Goose Green, the first land battle of the Falklands conflict in 1982. It recounts vividly the actions of both British and Argentine forces in the battle and, in particular, the role played by Lt-Col 'H' Jones VC OBE. In addition, the work considers the character of Jones, chronicles his career and appraises his posthumous VC action.

A9 *AFTER THE BATTLE* MAGAZINE (*publisher*)
PILOT'S FLYING LOG BOOK No. 2: W/CMDR G.P. GIBSON, DFC
After the Battle Magazine, London, 1976
Unnumbered pages, photo, hb, cr

A facsimile of *RAF Form 414 - Pilot's Flying Log Book* of Wing Commander GP Gibson VC for the period 15 November 1940 to 16 September 1944. Apart from identifying the publisher and the Crown Copyright ownership, this facsimile is identical in every respect to the original log book compiled in Gibson's own hand. It records every flight that he made within the log period. The 102 entries cease halfway through the log book, three days before he was killed in action. The entry immediately after the Dams Raid is "Awarded VC 23.5.43".

A10   AGAR, Captain Augustus, VC DSO
BALTIC EPISODE: A Classic of Secret Service in Russian Waters
Hodder & Stoughton, London, 1963
255 pp, photos, maps, hb, cr

A comprehensive account of the Royal Navy's coastal motor boat operations in the Baltic Sea in 1919 which were led by the author. It describes the achievements of his CMB flotilla and in particular the raids on the Russian fleet which won him the VC. It also documents the deeds of Cdr CC Dobson and Lt GC Steele during these raids for which they were also awarded the VC.

A11   AGAR, Captain Augustus, VC RN
SHOWING THE FLAG
Evans Brothers, London, 1962
304 pp, photo, maps (on inside covers), index, hb, cr

This book relates the role of the Royal Navy between the two world wars. The author draws on his own experiences to describe life in the Navy's ships on stations on which he served in the Pacific, the Mediterranean, the Caribbean, South America and Canada. He discusses the part these stations played, in combination with the colonial administrators, in consolidating the Commonwealth.

A12   AGAR, Captain Augustus, VC RN
FOOTPRINTS IN THE SEA: The Autobiography of Captain Augustus Agar VC RN
Evans Brothers, London, 1959
336 pp, photos, map, index, hb, cr

This autobiography is arranged in four parts. Part 1 covers Agar's family background and naval service up to 1918. Part 2 describes his coastal motor boat operations in the Baltic in 1919 (recounted in detail in A10). Part 3 covers his inter-war naval service (described more fully in A11). Part 4 chronicles his WW2 service up to his retirement from the Royal Navy. Appendix A is an extended account of the raid on Krondstaat, written by Lt GC Steele VC, during which Steele and Cdr Dobson won the VC.

A12B   AIKENHEAD, Charles (*compiler*)
LADYSMITH'S 20 VC's (*sic*): The awards of the Victoria Cross for the defence and relief of Ladysmith 1899-1900, covering the engagements, their locations and memorials.
Privately published, (c2009)
81 pp, (65 numbered), photos (some colour), maps, sb, cr

A4-sized book about the VCs awarded for the Defence and Relief of Ladysmith in 1899-1900. It is profusely illustrated with many maps and photos, some in colour, recording the VC actions and memorials to the 20 VCs associated with Ladysmith. Entries include brief biographical details. Chapter 12 (pages 60-64) covers the posthumous VC awarded to Freddie Roberts and the process by which this occurred. The last chapter provides brief biographies of three British commanders in the Boer War who were holders of the VC - Sir George White, Sir Redvers Buller and Sir Frederick Roberts. Reviewed in V64.

A13   ALI, Colonel Khan Badahur Sardar Asghar
OUR HEROES OF THE GREAT WAR: A Record of the VCs won by the Indian Army during the Great War
The Times Press, Bombay, India, 1922
119 pp, photos, sb, cr

This work comprises photographs and citations of Indian Army VC recipients of WW1. However, the text concerns mainly the service of the recipients' regiments.

A14   ALLAWAY, Jim
HERO OF THE UPHOLDER: The Story of Lieutenant Commander M.D. Wanklyn VC DSO - The Royal Navy's Top Submarine Ace**
Airlife Publishing, Shrewsbury, 1991
191 pp, photos, maps, index, hb, cr

A biography of Wanklyn from his childhood to his death with his crew in the loss of the *Upholder* in the Gulf of Tripoli on 14 April 1942. It chronicles in detail his naval service and, in particular, his command of HM Submarine *Upholder*. It also tells the story of his crew and describes life on board a submarine during hostilities. Appendix 2 provides an academic analysis of Wanklyn's handwriting to describe his character and personality.

A15   ALLIGHAN, Garry
THE FIRST THIRTEEN: These Gripping Dramas of Epic Adventure and Deathless Glory Pinpoint the Entire Range of British Bravery which Won the First VCs of This War
John Long, London, nd (c1941)
96 pp, sb, cr

Despite the book's title, the contents cover the first 14 VCs of WW2 as it treats Garland and Gray together in a single chapter. VCs covered are: Warbuton-Lee, Ervine-Andrews, Garland, T Gray, Stannard, Nicholls, Learoyd, Annand, Gristock, Mantle, Hannah, ECT Wilson, Nicholson and Fegen.

A15A   ALRING, Michael
A SHORT HISTORY OF GREAT DANES (*English version*)
BERØMTE DANSKERE – KORT FORTALT (*Danish version*)
Aschehoug, København, Sweden, 2002
80 pp, photos, hb, cr

A series of short biographies of 23 famous Danes from history and up to modern times. Four pages are devoted to Anders Lassen VC MC**.

A16   ANAND, Vidya
INDIAN HEROES AND HEROINES OF WORLD WAR II: A Brief History
Institute for Media Communication, New Delhi, 1995
196 pp, photos, index, hb, cr

The first part of this book (up to page 64) summarises the involvement of Indian troops in the various theatres of WW2. Pages 65-104 relate to a biographical sketch of Assistant Section Officer Inayat Khan GC MBE CdeG WAAF who was shot at Dachau in 1944. Pages 105-170 concerns the VCs awarded to Asians during WW2 and, typically, includes a brief account of the VC deed for each of the 27 Indian and Gurkha recipients and of the sole Fijian VC. Portrait photographs accompany the text.

A19   ANDERSON, Ken
HEROES OF SOUTH AFRICA
Purnell, Cape Town, 1965 (1983 edition: Donkers)
407 pp, (1983 edition: 230 pp.), photos, sketches, hb, cr

This book has 36 chapters: 35 chapters describe 35 South African heroes and Chapter 36 entitled *The Victoria Cross* lists 28 South Africans who were awarded the VC. There are individual chapters on the following VC recipients: AW Beauchamp-Proctor, JRM Chard, QGM Smythe, E Swales, HG Moore and JD Nettleton. Each chapter has approximately ten pages.

A20   ANDERSON, Captain T. Carnegy (*compiler*)
THE ORDER OF THE VICTORIA CROSS: "For Valour"
Wyman Brothers, Calcutta, 1867
21 pp, hb, ncr

This brief booklet erroneously describes the VC as an order in its title. It is dedicated by the author to Col DM Probyn CB VC (*sic*) who was a schoolboy friend. The publication reproduces the first warrant and LG citation of 28 VC holders of the Bengal Army.

A25   ANGELL, Granville, S., MEd BSc BA
THE VICTORIA CROSS FREEMASONS BAND OF BROTHERS
Published by the author, 2002
Full version: 61 pp, photos, hb, cr
Condensed version: 24 pp, photos, sb, cr

This book contains biographical sketches of the nine VC recipients who were Freemasons in the Province of Hampshire and Isle of Wight. About one-third of the textual content of the book is devoted to Vice Admiral Sir WNW Hewett, who was the first Freemason to be invested with the VC. The other sketches are, typically, one page in length. All sketches include both military and Masonic career details. Both versions of the book contain the same biographical text and portray similar photographs but are as full-page coloured plates in the hardback version. The latter also includes facsimile reproductions of various Masonic documents.

A26   ANGELL, Granville, S., MEd BSc BA
THE VICTORIA CROSS FREEMASONS BAND OF BROTHERS
Published privately, 2006
60 pp, portrait photos and drawings, sb, cr

The author, the Freemasons Prestonian Lecturer for 2006, prepared this book for presentation at the 2006 Lecture. At the time of writing, the author had identified 142 VC recipients who were Freemasons and of these, the life and deeds of 13 recipients, from the Crimean War up to WW2, are recalled in this book. Each biographical account documents the recipient's family background, early years, military service, later life and death. Full details of their Masonic service are provided. The VCs featured are WW Hewett, H Rowlands, TH Kavanagh, S Mitchell, NJA Coghill, T Melvill, GM Samson, RWF Addison, BC Freyberg, RG McBeath, NA Finch, J MacGregor and W Reid. The biographical details vary in length with BC Freyberg given 8 pages and Addison only 1 page. There are several appendices including all the VCs listed in the *London Gazette* of 24 February 1857 and all those who received the VC from Queen Victoria at the first VC investiture on 26 June 1857.

A27   ANGELL, Granville
THE GREAT WAR 1914-18: Victoria Cross Freemasons
Masonic Publishing Company, Glasgow, 2015
528 pp, photos (some colour), maps, hb, cr

This volume records the 91 WW1 VC recipients the author verified at the time of publication as having been accepted as Freemasons. A ten-page introduction outlines the early history of the VC. The biographies of the recipients are arranged alphabetically and, typically five pages long, provide details of their background, early years, military service, including an account of their VC deed supported by a full VC citation, and later life. Their Masonic membership is fully-documented.

A28   ANGELL, Granville
       THE VOLUME OF VALOUR
       Privately published, Cannock, Staffordshire, 2017
       704 pp, photos, hb, cr (partial)

Produced to coincide with the tercentenary of the formation of the United Grand Lodge of England, this well-illustrated volume comprises biographical accounts of the VC recipients who the author has verified were Freemasons (at the time of writing, 13% of all VCs). The biographies, which are arranged alphabetically by surname, include full details of their Masonic membership. The volume was produced as a limited de-luxe edition of 125 copies, most of which the author donated to Grand Lodges worldwide. This volume is not available for sale and only accessible via Grand Lodges. This volume is cross-referenced to the 91 VCs of WW1 featured in A27. At the time of publication the identity of the remaining Freemason VCs is unknown and can only be accessed through this volume.

A32   ANON
       BRIGADIER-GENERAL R.B. BRADFORD VC MC AND HIS BROTHERS
       Privately published, nd (c.1919); facsimile reprint by Ray Westlake, Newport, Gwent, nd (c1993)
       146 pp, photos, hb, cr

An account of four gallant brothers who served with distinction in WW1. The family background and careers of three of the four Bradford brothers are featured in pages 1-33. Lt Cdr GN Bradford received a posthumous VC for the action at Zeebrugge in 1918, 2nd Lt JB Bradford MC was killed in action in 1917 but Capt TA Bradford DSO survived WW1. However, the main subject of the book is Brig-Gen RB Bradford VC MC whose life and service career is chronicled on pages 34-146. He was killed in France in 1917. See M120.

A33   ANON
       THE DEATHLESS STORY OF AN ESSEX VC: Pte H.G. Columbine, Machine Gun Corps of Walton-on-the-Naze
       Weston (Printers), Walton and Frinton, Essex, nd (c1918)
       12 pp, photo, sb, cr

A small booklet of 12 unnumbered pages containing three letters to Columbine's mother after his death, an eyewitness account of the VC action, the LG citation and a photograph.

A34   ANON (by *A Quartermaster*)
       FIELD MARSHAL LORD ROBERTS VC, GCB, GCSI, GCIE
       Thrilling Stories' Committee, Manchester, nd (c1899)
       16 pp, photo, sb, cr

A concise account of the life of Lord Roberts up to the early 1890s.

A35   ANON (by *An Average Observer*)
       THE BURDEN OF PROOF: England's Debt to Sir Redvers Buller
       Grant Richards, London, 1902
       123 pp, hb, cr

This book is an attempt to reinstate the reputation of Sir Redvers Buller VC after his setbacks and criticisms of his command during the Boer War. The volume was republished in 1902 which provides additional and up-dated material not in the first edition.

A36 ANON
FAMOUS SCOTTISH FREEMASONS
William Anderson & Sons, Glasgow (*printers*), for the Grand Lodge of Scotland, 2010
184 pp, photos, drawings, hb, cr

This book features brief biographical accounts of 121 prominent Scottish Freemasons arranged in five categories: Arts & Science (37), Industry & Commerce (8), Awarded the Victoria Cross (23), Public Figures (44) and Sports & Entertainment (9). Each account, supported by a photograph, includes details of the individual's membership of the Freemasons.

A55 ANTHONY, Gordon and MACADAM, John
AIR ACES
Home & Van Thal, London, 1944
40 pp. (text) and 32 pp. (plates), hb, cr

A collection of brief biographical sketches of thirty-two of the RAF's most famous contemporary pilots including three VCs: Cheshire, Gibson and Learoyd. A full page photographic portrait of each pilot supports the text.

A58 ARMY HEADQUARTERS (*publisher*)
NEW ZEALAND HONOURS AND AWARDS: The Victoria Cross
Army Headquarters, Wellington, New Zealand, 1969
23 pp, sb, cr

This typescript booklet records biographical notes of the 21 members of New Zealand's armed forces who have won the VC. In each case a full citation is given. The biographical notes cover the recipients' service career, pre-service and post-service details, burial place and composition of medal group.

A60 ARTHUR, Max
THERE SHALL BE WINGS – The RAF: 1918 to the Present
Hodder & Stoughton, London, 1993
412 pp, photos, index, hb, cr

This narrative history of the RAF is told through the personal experiences of over 150 of its past and present members, who were interviewed by the author. Each account is recorded in the interviewee's own words. The four surviving RAF VCs (at the time of publication) recall their experiences on pages 195-196 (Cruickshank), 198-201 (Learoyd), 226-231 (Reid) and 231-235 (Jackson).

A61 ARTHUR, Max
SYMBOL OF COURAGE: A Complete History of the Victoria Cross
Sidgwick & Jackson, London, 2004
686 pp, photos, maps, index, hb, cr

This book covers every VC recipient from 1854 to 2004. The entries are listed chronologically by date of VC action in separate chapters covering each war, campaign or engagement. Some VC entries are as short as two lines, and the longest (Hitch VC) is four pages. A total of 51 entries exceed one page and are cross-referenced. A 64-page appendix lists every VC alphabetically with full details of *London Gazette* date, page number and supplement (if any). Another appendix (58 pages) provides another alphabetical list of VC holders with brief details including dates of birth/death, place of burial/cremation and other honours received. Reviewed in V54.

A62   ARTHUR, Max
DAMBUSTER: A Landmark Oral History
Virgin Books, London, 2008
339 pp, photos, map, index, hb, cr

This book is a compilation of eye witness accounts of those who were connected or participated in the Dams Raid of May 1943. There are also accounts of Germans involved at the receiving end of the raid. Sources included oral sound archives and personal written accounts in the IWM, RAF Museum and Lancaster Museum, Alberta, Canada.

A63   ASBURY-BAILEY, Jock
BENJAMIN HANDLEY GEARY, VC 1891-1976: An Account of His Life
Privately published, Canterbury, 1997
26 pp, photos, maps, sb, cr

A short account of the life of 2nd Lt (later Major) BH Geary who received his VC for action at Hill 60 in April 1915. Five pages give a biographical sketch and 16 pages of appendices include the LG citation, Geary's own account of his VC action (recorded shortly after the event) and a report of his Commanding Officer.

A65   ASHCROFT, Michael
VICTORIA CROSS HEROES
Headline Review (inprint of Headline Publishing Group), London, 2006
335 pp, photos, index, hb, cr

This book has a Foreword by HRH The Prince of Wales. In Chapter 1 Ashcroft describes his passion for collecting VCs, how it began and his plans for displaying the Collection to the public. The book then gives brief accounts of the exploits of VC recipients from the Crimea to Iraq (2004). Many of the VCs covered are represented by the VCs in the Ashcroft Collection but some are not. An Appendix lists the VCs in the Ashcroft Collection at time of publication. It also states how they were acquired and the year of acquisition. Reviewed in V59.

A66   ASHCROFT, Michael
VICTORIA CROSS HEROES: Volume II
Biteback Publishing, London, 2016
376 pp, photos, index, hb, cr

This is a follow-up volume to A65 which describes the stories behind 58 VC recipients whose decorations are now in the Ashcroft VC Collection. The first chapter provides a short history of the VC and how the Ashcroft Collection has developed. Pages 21 to 357 contain the 58 VC biographies in the subsequent six chapters set in chronological order from the Crimean War to WW2. The Foreword is by L/Sgt Johnson Beharry VC.

A67   ASHCROFT VC TRUST
THE VICTORIA CROSS COLLECTION: 16ᵀᴴ - 25ᵀᴴ APRIL 2008
Spink, London, 2008
54 pp, photos, sb, cr

This brochure describes the 50 VC groups belonging to the Ashcroft VC Trust which were displayed at Spink's London office between 16 and 25 April 2008. One page is dedicated to each VC including a colour photograph of the VC group and the *LG* citation. Some also include photographs of the recipients.

A68   ASHCROFT, Michael
HEROES OF THE SKIES: Amazing True Stories of Courage in the Air
Headline Publishing Group, London, 2012
380 pp, photos, index, hb, cr

The author describes the deeds of 86 heroic airmen who won gallantry awards in WW1, WW2 and in subsequent conflicts up to 2007. In most cases, their awards are held in Lord Ashcroft's collection in the IWM. Chapter 2 (pages 13-37) is devoted to six WW1 VCs: WB Rhodes-Moorhouse, JA Liddell, WL Robinson, T Motteshead, E Mannock and A Jerrard. Two of the six chapters on WW2 heroes including accounts of six VCs: NC Jackson, LT Manser, HG Malcolm, DSA Lord, AL Trigg and RAB Learoyd. Individuals' accounts vary in length but average five pages.

A69   ASHE, Major Waller and WYATT-EDGELL, Captain The Hon. E.V.
THE STORY OF THE ZULU CAMPAIGN
Sampson Low, Marston, Searle & Livingston, London, 1880
(Facsimile reprint: N & S Press, Cape Town, South Africa, 1989)
418 pp, index, hb, cr

A contemporary account of the Anglo-Zulu war of 1879. In particular, substantial references are made to the services and VC deeds of Major (Lt Col) RH Buller, Capt Lord Gifford and Capt Lord William Beresford. Additionally, the services of Brig-Gen HE Wood VC, who commanded a flying column in the campaign, are documented throughout the book.

A70   ASHER, Michael
GET ROMMEL: The Secret British Mission to Kill Hitler's Greatest General
Weidenfeld and Nicolson, London, 2004
303 pp, photos, maps, index, hb, cr

This book describes in detail the story of Operation *Flipper*: the British plot to kill Rommel, led by Lt Col Geoffrey Keyes, who was awarded a posthumous VC for his part in the operation. On the eve of Operation *Crusader*, commandos embarked from a British submarine and marched into the desert to attack Rommel's HQ. However, because of poor planning and intelligence the operation was a failure and only a handful of survivors escaped.

A71   ATTWOOD, Rodney
THE MARCH TO KANDAHAR: Roberts in Afghanistan
Pen & Sword, Barnsley, 2008
214 pp, photos, maps, index, hb, cr

This volume provides a background on the history and politics of Afghanistan in the 19th century. The book then focuses on the role of FS Roberts VC in the Second Afghan War and detailing the celebrated 100 mile march from Kabul to Kandahar in 1880.

A72   ATTWOOD, Rodney
THE LIFE OF FIELD MARSHAL LORD ROBERTS
Bloomsbury Academic, London, 2014
368 pp, hb, cr

A biography of Lord Roberts VC charting his career from the Indian Mutiny (VC), his strategic defence of India and contribution in the Boer War. His army reforms and campaigns for National Service are described prior to WW1. Roberts's role as a tactican in Afghanistan, Burma, NWF, South Africa and Europe are examined.

A73   ATTWOOD, Rodney
ROBERTS AND KITCHENER IN SOUTH AFRICA 1900 - 1902
Pen & Sword Military, Barnsley, 2011
322 pp, photos, maps, index, hb, cr

The author compares and contrasts the careers, achievements and personalities of Lord Roberts and Lord Kitchener. The Boer War operations under their command are examined and the tactical and strategic decisions made by the two commanders are appraised.

A74   AUSTIN, Wendy
TRING PERSONALITIES
Privately published, 2000
77 pp, photos, hb, cr

Biographical profiles of 20 personalities from Tring, Hertfordshire and its surrounding villages. Pages 14 to 17 are devoted to James Osborne VC from Wiggington. See A75.

A75   AUSTIN, Wendy
MORE TRING PERSONALITIES
Privately published, 2003
119 pp, photos, hb, cr

A companion volume to A74 contains biographical profiles of a further 21 Tring personalities. Pages 25 to 28 relate to Pte E Barber VC.

A76   AUSTRALIAN WAR MEMORIAL
THIS COMPANY OF BRAVE MEN: The Gallipoli VCs
Australian War Memorial, Australia, 2010
16 pp, photos, sb, cr

This A4 booklet was produced to accompany a 2010 tour of Australia of VCs held by the Australian War Memorial. Between March and December 2010 the exhibition visited Perth, Darwin, Adelaide, Melbourne, Brisbane and Hobart in Tasmania. Each VC is given one page and features Jacka VC, Throssell VC, Shout VC, John Hamilton VC, Keysor VC, Symons VC, Burton VC, Tubb VC and Dunstan VC.

A80   AUTEN, Lieutenant Commander Harold, VC RNR
"Q" BOAT ADVENTURES: The Exploits of the Famous Mystery Ships by a "Q" Boat Commander
Herbert Jenkins, London, 1919
289 pp, photos, hb, cr

A memoir of the author's service in *Q* ships from 1915 (as one of the first *Q* ship officers appointed) to 1918, during which period he won the VC. Two chapters record the exploits of Cdr Gordon Campbell VC and one chapter concerns the VC action of Lt WE Sanders on HMS *Prize*.

A100   AVIATION SALES COMPANY INCORPORATED (publisher)
BRITS
Aviation Sales Company Incorporated, Miami, USA, nd,
46 pp, photos, paintings, casebound, cr

This unusual publication has a case cover (hb) containing four documents (sb) each of which is a fold out of 12 pages. The first document covers the RFC in WW1, the second covers Hawker VC, the third McCudden VC and the fourth Mannock VC. The photos are black and white but aircraft and other illustrations are in colour. Each VC has biographical details and a colour portrait.

B1   BAILEY, Roderick Dr
FORGOTTEN VOICES OF THE VICTORIA CROSS
Ebury Press (in association with the Imperial War Museum), London, 2010
382 pp, photos, index, hb, cr

This volume is a compilation of transcripts from sound archives of interviews with VC recipients and/or by those who knew them and some who witnessed VC acts. Because the sound archives at IWM started in the early 1970s there is more material on WW2 recipients than for WW1. Each chapter begins with an overview of the campaign, battle or action; each VC recipient featured has a brief biographical introduction. Some WW2 recipients were self-effacing so the testimonies of comrades provide a fuller picture of their acts. The final chapter is by combat veterans on the nature of courage and cowardice and observations on the conduct of fellow combatants under fire. Reviewed in V67.

B1A   BAIRD, Catherine
"LITTLE DOCTOR" VC
Salvationist Publishing and Supplies, London, 1944
17 pp, sketches, sb, cr

A short biography of Capt HJ Andrews who won a posthumous VC in 1919 for action on the North West Frontier of India. He had previously served for 30 years as a medical missionary with the Salvation Army.

B2   BAKER, David
WILLIAM AVERY "BILLY" BISHOP – The man and the aircraft he flew
Outline Press, London, 1990
127 pp, photos, sketches, sb, cr

This well-illustrated book (No. 2 in the *Famous Flyers* series) concentrates on Bishop's flying service in WW1. His aerial combats are narrated in detail and are supported by combat reports, many of which are replicated in full. In other instances, extracts of combat reports are used to describe the action and his VC deed. Chapter 6 includes a complete and detailed list of his combats relating to both his official score of 72 victories and his unofficial score of 79 victories.

B2A   BAKER, David J. and LAKE, Roger E.
PARADOX: The Story of Colonel G. V. Fosbery, Holland & Holland and the Paradox Rifled Shot and Ball Gun - Volume 1
Privately published, Llandysul, Ceredigion and Livermore, California, USA, 2010
281 pp, 308 colour photos, 84 b+w photos, drawings, hb, cr

This lavishly-illustrated first of two volumes on the evolution and production of the Paradox gun is arranged in two sections. Section 1 (pages 1-56) [written by David J. Baker] is an in-depth study of Colonel George Vincent Fosbery VC, the gun's inventor. The extensively-researched biographical information traces his family background, early years, military service and later years and is supported by previously unpublished photographs supplied by the Fosbery family. His inventions are discussed in detail and are depicted in photographs and design drawings. Appendix 1 lists the 41 patents issued for Fosbery's inventions from 1866 to 1896 and records the patent number, date, patent title and, where applicable, the co-patentee or agent. Section 2 (pages 57-268) [written by Roger E. Lake] examines the Paradox's evolution, development and production, the author's research for which included extensive access to Holland & Holland's records.

B3   BALL, Tom, ISO
HENRY KELLY VC MC: A Manchester hero and one of the most decorated soldiers of the First World War
Privately published, 1997
12 pp, photos, sb, cr

A biographical sketch of Major Henry Kelly. In 1922, after gallant service in the Great War, he became a major in the Irish Free State Army and in 1936 was a Commandante-Generale in the International Brigade taking part in the Spanish Civil War.

B4   BALLANTINE, Brigadier D.E., OBE MC
"SERGEANT ROGERS' DAY"
Royal Gloucestershire, Berkshire & Wiltshire Regiment, Salisbury, nd (c.1989)
12 pp, photos, map, sb, cr

A brief biographical account of Sgt MAW Rogers VC, which is arranged in three sections: pre-war years; 1939-1942; and 1942-1944. The latter section details his posthumous VC action. The account concludes with the transcription of the CO's speech in 1944 proposing a toast to the memory of Rogers. Photographs include a portrait of Rogers in uniform and a painting of his VC action. This painting is reproduced in colour on the front cover of V57.

B5   BANCROFT, James W.
LOCAL HEROES: The Light Brigade at Balaclava
The House of Heroes, Eccles, Manchester, 2001
62 pp, photos, sb, cr

This well-illustrated volume in the author's *Local Heroes* series contains biographical sketches of the 35 men from North-West England (Manchester, Liverpool, Cheshire and Cumbria) who served with the Light Brigade in the Battle of Balaclava. Pages 30-31 feature Joseph Malone VC of the 13th Light Dragoons.

B6   BANCROFT, James W.
LOCAL HEROES – BOER WAR VCs
The House of Heroes, Eccles, Manchester, 2003
51 pp, photos, map, index, sb, cr

This volume in the author's *Local Heroes* series is devoted to biographical sketches of the 16 Boer War VCs from Lancashire (including Liverpool and Manchester) and Cheshire. Each biographical sketch includes a portrait photograph of the recipient. Additionally, the work includes a complete chronological roll of all Boer War VCs.

B7   BANCROFT, James W.
ZULU WAR HEROES: The Defence of Rorke's Drift
The House of Heroes, Eccles, Manchester, 2004
51 pp, photos, sketch, map, index, sb, cr

The second volume in the *Zulu War Heroes* series provides biographical tributes to six of the defenders of Rorke's Drift. These sketches relate to four of the eleven VCs (JRM Chard, JL Dalton, JH Reynolds and FC Scheiss) and two other gallant defenders (Clr Sgt FE Bourne and Rev G Smith).

B9   BANCROFT, James W.
      GALLANTRY AWARDS AT RORKE'S DRIFT
      Published by the author, Eccles, 2007
      52 pp, photos, sb, cr

      This book describes the men who were awarded for the action at Rorke's Drift in January 1879. This includes
      the 11 VC awards.

B10   BANCROFT, James W. (*compiler*)
      THE VICTORIA CROSS ROLL OF HONOUR
      Aim High Publications, Eccles, Manchester, 1989
      123 pp, index, hb, ncr

      This book lists every recipient of the VC. The list is categorised by service, regiment or corps, within which
      recipients are listed chronologically by year of deed. The index is arranged by conflict, listing recipients
      alphabetically by surname.

B11   BANCROFT, James W.
      RORKE'S DRIFT: The Terrible Night at Rorke's Drift
      Spellmount, Tunbridge Wells, 1988 (co-published in 1988 by Bok Books International, Durban,
      RSA)
      168 pp, photos, sketches, maps, hb, cr

      This profusely-illustrated study of the defence of Rorke's Drift in January 1879 chronicles the battle and the
      deeds which earned 11 VCs. Chapter 9 (pages 123-155) contains biographical sketches of these VCs and is
      supported by photographs of the recipients and their memorials. A two-page bibliography lists sources and
      other reference material.

B12   BANCROFT, James W.
      DEVOTION TO DUTY: Tributes to a Region's VCs
      Aim High Publications, Manchester, 1990
      129 pp, photos, drawings, index, hb, cr

      A collective work of biographical sketches of the 51 VC recipients from Manchester and its surrounding
      area. Typically, each sketch records the recipient's family background, service career, the VC action set in the
      context of the conflict or battle and recording in full the VC citation, post-service career, marital details and
      death. Photographs of most recipients and some modern artists' impressions of their VC actions are included.

B13   BANCROFT, James W.
      THE ZULU WAR VCs
      James Bancroft, Eccles, 1992
      147 pp, photos, sketches, index, hb, cr

      This book provides short biographies of the 23 VCs awarded for the Zulu War of 1879 in the actions at
      Isandlwana, Rorke's Drift, Ntombe River, Hlobane Mountain and Ulundi, Typically, each account records the
      recipient's family background, service career, the VC action, post-service career, marital details and death.
      Photographs of most recipients, and in some cases their graves, are included. Artists' impressions (in colour)
      illustrate some VC actions.

B14 BANCROFT, James W.
DEEDS OF VALOUR: A Victorian Military and Naval History Trilogy
The House of Heroes, Eccles, 1994
149 pp, photos, sketches, hb, cr

The publication is in three parts: Part 1 is a chronology of Victorian VCs (up to 1904) arranged by campaign (35 pages) and incorporating a 5-page analysis of citations. Part 2 is a biographical account of a Sgt H Gallagher 2/24th Regiment, who fought at Rorke's Drift. Part 3 is a miscellany of first-hand accounts of Victorian naval battles and disasters including a chapter (pages 126-134) recording an account written by Gunner Israel Harding about his VC action at Alexandria in 1882.

B15 BANCROFT, James W.
ZULU WAR HEROES: 24th Regiment VCs
[1] The House of Heroes, Eccles, 2001
52 pp, photos, drawings, index, sb, cr
[2] The House of Heroes, Eccles, 2003 [revised edition], 52 pp, sb, cr

This first volume in the series *Zulu War Heroes'* is devoted to biographical accounts of the 24th Regiment's ten VCs of the Anglo-Zulu War of 1879. The accounts appeared in the author's earlier work, *The Zulu War VCs* (see B13) but have been revised and updated.

B15A BANCROFT, James W.
THE VICTORIA CROSSES OF THE CRIMEAN WAR: The Men Behind the Medals
Frontline Books, (Pen & Sword Books), Barnsley, 2017
234 pp, photos, index, hb, cr

This volume describes the exploits of the 111 men who won the VC in the Baltic and Crimea campaigns of 1854-55. Chapter 1 gives a brief history of the VC. Chapters 2 to 16 describes, chronologically, the context of VC action as well as the actions themselves followed by brief biographical details of each VC recipient involved. Some recipients are covered in one third of a page with longer entries of up to five pages. Chapter 2 begins with the Baltic Fleet resulting in the award of three VCs and ends with Chapter 16 and the actions on the Sea of Azov covering nine recipients. Chapter 17 titled *The Most Victoria Crosses for a Single Action* argues the case that it was for the first attack on the Great Redan at Sebastopol on 18 June 1855 for which 20 VCs were awarded with a list of recipients and LG dates. Chapter 16 gives a chronological roll of the Crimean War VCs and they are also listed alphabetically, by surname, in the index. (See G63).

B15B BANCROFT, James W.
THE RORKE'S DRIFT MEN: Heroes of the Zulu War
Spellmount, Stroud, 2010
222 pp, photos, maps, index, hb, cr

This volume is a collection of biographical accounts of all the defenders of Rorke's Drift on 22/23 January 1879. The biographies, which are arranged by unit and are of varying length, record individual's background, military service, medals awarded, later life, marital details and death. In each case the individual's involvement in the defence is documented. Eleven men were awarded the VC.

B15C BANCROFT, James W and DICKSON, Geoffrey
MENDIP VICTORIA CROSSES
JWB, Eccles, 2015
36 pp, photos (some colour), drawings, map, hb, cr

Written by James Bancroft with illustrations and photographs provided by Geoffrey Dickson, this A5-sized booklet comprises biographical accounts of six VCs who were associated with the Mendip district in Somerset: CM Douglas, J Crimmin, HG Crandon, WD Fuller, AHH Batten-Pooll and HW Le Patourel. The volume has drawings of VC actions by Geoffrey Dickson and a two page description of the VC. Each biography is supported by at least a portrait photograph of the recipient and a drawing depicturing his VC action.

B15D BANCROFT, James W.
ZULU WAR VCs: Victoria Crosses of the Anglo-Zulu War 1879
Frontline Books (Pen & Sword Books), Barnsley, 2018
Published privately, 2006
184 pp, photos, index, hb, cr

This volume provides biographical accounts of the 23 VC recipients of the Anglo-Zulu War of 1879. The first two chapters concern the evolution of the VC up to 1879 and a brief history of the rise of the Zulu nation. The VCs' biographies are arranged within six chapters, each relating to a key event the historical background of which is described. the chapters and related VCs are: The Disaster at iSandlwana (Coghill, Melvill and Wassall); the Defence of Rorke's Drift (Chard, Bromhead, Allan, Hitch, Hook, R Jones, W Jones, J Williams, Reynolds, Dalton and Schiess); the iNtombe River Massacre (AC Booth); Hlobane Mountain (Butler, Leet, Lysons and Fowler) and Operations at Ulundi (Beresford, D'Arcy and O'Toole). The Appendices list all recipients of gallantry awards for the Anglo-Zulu War 1879.

B15E BANCROFT, James W.
THE DEFENCE OF RORKE'S DRIFT: a Graphic Account
James W. Bancroft, Eccles, 2014
40 pp, photos, illustrations, sb, cr

A concise account of the defence of Rorke's Drift in January 1879, which resulted in the award of 11 VCs.

B16 BANNISTER, Chris
HENRY WARD VC 1823-1867
C.J. Bannister, Malvern, Worcestershire, nd (c.2001)
39 pp, photos, maps, index, sb, cr

This booklet describes the life and exploits of Henry Ward who won his VC at Lucknow in September 1857. The book is well illustrated with two colour photographs including one of his VC group.

B16A BARBARY, Carmel
REGINALD ROY RATTEY - OUR HUMBLE HERO
Blurb, Australia, 2008
263 pp, photos, maps, hb, cr

This beautifully produced and lavishly illustrated book, written and compiled by the daughter of Reg Rattey VC and his wife, Aileen, reproduces a significant amount of newspaper cuttings, photographs and memorabilia including official letters and invitations, bequeathed to her by her parents and also from her own collection. There are nearly 300 illustrations, which are arranged chronologically and supported by biographical and background information.

B17   BARBER, Laurie and TONKIN-COVELL, John
FREYBERG: Churchill's Salamander
Century Hutchinson, Auckland, 1989
310 pp, photos, maps, index, hb, cr

A detailed study of Freyberg's generalship between 1941 and 1945 recounting his military operations in command of the New Zealand Expeditionary Force and reassessing his command capabilities and competencies. The extensive sources used for the book are documented.

B18   BARCLAY, Vera Charlesworth
THE FACE OF A KING: Group Captain Cheshire VC champions the Holy Shroud
Century Art Press, Bognor Regis, 1955
99 pp, photos, sb, cr

Part 1 of this book is an account of Group Captain Leonard Cheshire's life and, in particular, his significant interest in the Holy Shroud of Turin. Part 2 is the story of the Shroud.

B19   BARCLAY, Brigadier C.N., CBE DSO
ON THEIR SHOULDERS: British Generalship in the Lean Years 1939-1942
Faber & Faber, London, 1964
184 pp, photos, maps, index, hb, cr

This book appraises the achievements of eight British generals who held command in the early years of WW2. Chapter 3 (pages 36-49) relates to Field Marshal Gort VC, as C-in-C BEF in 1939-40. The other generals covered are Wavell, O'Connor, Wilson, Auchinleck, Cunningham, Percival and Hutton.

B19A   BARKER, Keith
GENERAL SIR REDVERS BULLER VC: A Brief Biography
Publisher unknown, 2010
18 pp, photos, sb, cr

A concise biography of Sir Redvers Buller VC.

B20   BARKER, Ralph
THE SHIP BUSTERS: The Story of RAF Torpedo-Bombers
Chatto & Windus, London, 1957
272 pp, photos, maps, index, hb, cr

Flt Lt Barker narrates detailed accounts of heroic low-level strikes against enemy shipping by the RAF's torpedo-carrying aircraft. The posthumous VC actions of Fg Off K Campbell and Lt Cdr E Esmonde are covered fully in Chapters 3 and 5 respectively.

B21   BARKER, Ralph
THE ROYAL FLYING CORPS IN FRANCE: From Mons to the Somme
Constable, London, 1994
237 pp, photos, maps, index, hb, cr

A history of the Royal Flying Corps in France during the period 1915-1916. The VC recipients of this period and beyond are mentioned throughout the text and, in particular, Ball, McCudden and Hawker are given significant coverage. Other VCs included are Liddell, Rhodes-Moorhouse and Rees. In 2001, Robinson, London, published a softback (507 pp.) combining B21 and B22.

B22 BARKER, Ralph
THE ROYAL FLYING CORPS IN FRANCE: From Bloody April 1917 to Final Victory
Constable, London, 1995
265 pp, photos, maps, index, hb, cr

This history follows on from B21 and covers the period 1917-1918 and the birth of the Royal Air Force. The exploits of all the RFC/RAF VCs of this period and theatre are covered (Ball, Bishop, Robinson, McCudden, McLeod and Mannock). In particular, the fighter tactics of McCudden and Mannock are examined in Chapter 17 (pages 168-175). In 2001, Robinson, London, published a softback (507 pp.) combining B21 and B22.

B23 BARKER, Ralph
STRIKE HARD STRIKE SURE: Epics of the Bombers
Chatto & Windus, London, 1963
210 pp, photos, maps, index, hb, cr

The VC exploits of ten Bomber Command recipients are detailed in nine of the book's ten chapters and covers Nettleton, Thompson, Garland and Gray, Edwards, Middleton, Gibson, Jackson, Aaron and Reid. The tenth chapter relates to the non-VC Amiens raid.

B24 BARKER, Ralph
THAT ETERNAL SUMMER: Unknown Stories from the Battle of Britain
Collins, London, 1990
241 pp, photos, index, hb, cr

The book recalls in separate chapters the deeds of 12 less well-known Royal Air Force heroes of 1940, three of whom are VC winners: Learoyd, Nicolson and Hannah.

B24A BARNES, B. S.
OPERATION SCIPIO: The 8th Army at the Battle of Wadi Akarit 6th April 1943
Sentinel Press, Market Weighton, York, 2007
352 pp, photos, map, index, cr

An account of Wadi Akarit with many accounts of participants of the battle. There are short chapters on the three VC recipients of the battle: Subadar Lalbahadur Thapa, Pte E Anderson and Lt Col LM Campbell.

B24B BARNES, John
SO I FEAR NOTHING: The Story of Paddy Bugden VC
Dragonwick Publishing, 2011
62 pp, photos, map, index, sb, cr

The title of this book is derived from a letter sent home by Paddy Bugden on 9 January 1917. At the age of 20 Bugden won the VC at Polygon Wood as a member of the 31st Battalion, AIF. His early life and military service is described and much of the book uses his letters he sent home during his active service. A memorial to Bugden was unveiled on 28 September 1997 at Alsonville, Queensland, Australia depicting Bugden assisting three comrades from a trench.

B25 BARNETT, Lieutenant Gilbert, RAF
VCs OF THE AIR: The Glorious Record of Men of the British Empire Air Force awarded the Victoria Cross for Valour, with an additional chapter on Heroes of America
Ed. J. Burrow & Co., London; Simkin, Marshall, Hamilton, Kent and Co, London, nd (c.1918)
36 pp, sketches, hb & sb, cr

This book provides, typically, a two-page description of the VC deed of each RFC/RNAS/RAF recipient in WW1. A painting depicting the action accompanies the text, which does not include any biographical information.

B26 BARNETT, Senator Guy
OUR HEROES: Tasmania's Victoria Cross Heroes
Privately published, Launceston, Tasmania, 2008
36 pp, photos, sb, cr

A booklet describing the 13 VC recipients with a connection with Tasmania. Most recipients have one page dedicated to them along with a photo and the full LG citation. A pdf file of the whole publication is available on www.guybarnett.com. Recipients featured are Bisdee, W Brown, Cherry, Dwyer, Gaby, S Gordon, H Murray, Newland, Statton, McGee, Whittle and Wylly.

B26A BARRIS, Ted
DAM BUSTERS: Canadian Airmen and the Secret Raid against Nazi Germany
Patrick Crean Editions, HarperCollins, Toronto, Canada, 2018
434 pp, photos, hb, cr

This account of 617 Squadron's raid on the Ruhr dams on 16/17 May 1943 led by Wg Cdr Gibson, focuses on the 30 Canadians who took part, 14 of whom lost their life and of the 16 survivors, seven were decorated, including two RCAF members of Gibson's crew, Plt Off T Taeron (navigator) and Flt Sgt GA Deering (front gunner). Sources include personal accounts and flight logs.

B26B BARTLETT, W. B
THE DAM BUSTERS: In the Words of the Bomber Crews
Amberley Publishing, Stroud, 2011
320 pp, photos, index, hb, cr

The author chronicles the Dams Raid on 16/17 May 1943 from the operation's inception to its execution and aftermath. Chapters are arranged chronologically. The four appendices identify (by aircraft) the aircrews and their fate on the raid; explain all the operations codewords; list all the W/T messages received or sent on the raid and provide a transcription of the raid questionnaires and responses made by each pilot who returned from the raid.

B26C BARTLETT, W. B.
THE NIGHT OF THE DAM BUSTERS
Amberley Publishing, Stroud, 2014
126 pp, sb, cr

This book in the *Great Tales from British History* series, charts the history of 617 Squadron's raid on the Möhne, Eder and Sorpe Dams on 16/17 May 1943 led by Wg Cdr Gibson.

B27   BASHOW, Lieutenant Colonel David L.
KNIGHTS OF THE AIR: Canadian Fighter Pilots in the First World War
McArthur & Company, Toronto, Canada, 2000
210 pp, photos, drawings, paintings, maps, index, hb, cr

The author, a Canadian Air Force fighter pilot and Assistant Professor of History at the Royal Military College of Canada, charts the evolution of the Canadian fighter and scout pilot during WW1. The exploits of many of the 171 Canadian fighter or scout aces are recalled in chapters relating to each year of the war. Chapter 4 (pages 99-127) is devoted to Billy Bishop VC and reassesses the controversy over his claims. This large format book is illustrated with 100 photographs, over 20 sketches and aircraft profiles and 10 original full colour paintings including a new depiction of Bishop's dawn raid.

B28   BATCHELOR, Peter F. and MATSON, Christopher
VCs OF THE FIRST WORLD WAR: THE WESTERN FRONT 1915
[1] Sutton Publishing, Stroud, 1997
224 pp, photos, sketches, maps, index, hb, cr
[2] The History Press, Stroud, 2011
287 pp, photos, sketches, maps, index, sb, cr

Arranged chronologically by date of VC deed, this book provides a biographical account of each of the 67 soldiers who won the VC on the Western Front in 1915 and recounts each action in detail. The volume is organised into the six main battles (Neuve Chapelle, Hill 60, Ypres, Aubers Ridge, Festubert and Loos), a description of which precedes the related VC accounts. Sources used in respect of each recipient are identified. This book is part of the series *The VCs of The First World War*. See G31 annotation, second paragraph. This volume was re-issued in a revised paperback edition by The History Press in 2011. The text has been updated but there are fewer photos within the text and there are 16 pages of photos near the centre of the book. This pocket book has the same format as the hardback edition.

B30   BATEMAN, Alex
No 617 'DAMBUSTER' SQN
Osprey, Oxford, 2009
128 pp, photos (some colour), drawings, index, sb, cr

This profusely-illustrated book, No 34 in Osprey's *Aviation Elite Units* series, traces in its eight chapters, the operational history of 617 Squadron during WW2. Two chapters deal with the squadron's formation and command under Wg Cdr Gibson, including coverage of the Dams Raid, and two chapters relate to period in which Wg Cdr Cheshire led the Squadron. The five Appendices include detailed lists of the Squadron's WW2 targets, Squadron Commanders, bases, battle honours, aircraft and aircrew losses. Colour plates include side profile drawings of the Squadron's aircraft in various markings.

B31   BATES, Thomas, BRISSET, Jean and LUMMIS, Eric
NORMANDY: THE SEARCH FOR SIDNEY
Bates Books (UK), Dumfries, 2000
201 pp, photos, maps, hb, cr

This bilingual book (English/French) describes the search for the location where Corporal Sidney Bates won a posthumous VC with the 1st Royal Norfolk Regiment on 6th August 1944 in Normandy. One of the authors, Thomas Bates, landed with the 1st Norfolks on D-Day. The text is well supported by 150 illustrations and maps.

B32   BATTEN-POOLL, A.H.H., VC MC
A WEST COUNTRY POT-POURRI
Privately published, Bath, 1969
346 pp, map, hb, cr

This work consists of 84 short chapters on West Country personalities and events. Chapter 50 (pages 221-224) relates to Rear Admiral J Bythesea VC; Chapter 54 (pages 229-231) covers Brigadier General PA Kenna VC and Chapter 57 (pages 234-235) is in respect of Lance Corporal F Room VC.

B33   BEASLEY, A. W.
ZEAL & HONOUR: The Life and Times of Bernard Freyberg
Winter Productions, Khandallah, Wellington, New Zealand, 2015
232 pp, photos, maps, index, sb, cr

A full biography of Bernard Freyberg VC from his birth and childhood in the UK to becoming New Zealand's most distinguished soldier. He was awarded the VC for action at Beaucourt-sur-Ancre on 13 November 1916 and wounded a number of times. His role as commander of the NZ Division in the ill-fated WW2 campaigns in Greece and Crete is fully covered and his triumphs in North Africa and Italy. He was Governor General of New Zealand from 1946 to 1952.

B34   BECKETT, Ian W.
JOHNNIE GOUGH VC: A Biography of Brigadier-General Sir John Edmond Gough VC KCB CMG
Tom Donovan Publishing, London, 1989
244 pp, photos, maps, index, hb, cr

A full and detailed biography supported by extensive notes of sources. A biographical summary of key events, service appointments and awards precedes the text which gives a thorough account of Gough's military service. Also, his distinguished family background is recorded, supported by simplified genealogical tables of the Gough and Keyes families showing the relationship between their VC recipients.

B35   BEETON, S.O. (*editor*)
[1] **OUR SOLDIERS AND THE VICTORIA CROSS** (*original title*)
Ward, Lock & Tyler, London, nd (c1867)
[2] **BRAVE BRITISH SOLDIERS AND THE VICTORIA CROSS** (*subsequent title*)
Ward, Lock & Co., London, nd (c1875)
383 pp, sketches, hb, cr

This book originated from a series of articles published in the 'Boys Own' Magazine in the mid-1860s. The first ten chapters of this work cover the history of the Guards, Engineers, Welsh and Highland Regiments and also the pipers of the Highland Regiments. The subsequent 17 chapters relate to the campaigns (Crimea, India Mutiny, Maori wars) in which the VC was won. VC winners given significant coverage include: EWD Bell, GF Day, AT Moore, JG Malcolmson, WA Kerr, H Ward, AC Bogle, J Jee, VM McMaster, TA Butler, TH Kavanagh, TJ Young, W Hall, N Salmon, W Peel and HE Wood.

B36   BEHARRY, Johnson, VC, with COOK, Nick
BAREFOOT SOLDIER: A Story of Extreme Valour
Sphere (imprint of Little Brown), London, 2006
370 pp, photos (colour), maps, hb, cr

This is a full autobiography of Johnson Beharry VC, written with help from Nick Cook. Beharry won his award for two acts of bravery in Iraq on 1 May and 11 June 2004. A short prologue describes an engagement with insurgents in Al Amarah in April 2004. The book has four parts sub-divided with chapters within each part. The bulk of the book is in Parts 1 to 3. In Part 1 Beharry describes his childhood and time in Grenada up to the age of 19 when he moved to London. Part 2 describes his time in the UK joining the army, his training and deployment to Kosovo and service elsewhere. Part 3 describes Beharry's service in Iraq including his VC actions, his severe wounding and evacuation to the UK. A shorter Part 4 describes his gradual recovery, the announcement of his VC award and the investiture at Buckingham Palace and ends with the hero's visit to Grenada in August 2005. Reviewed in V59.

B37   BEHARRY, Johnson, VC, with ELDRIDGE, Jim
HERO: The Incredible True Story of Courage Under Fire
Scholastic Children's Books, London, 2014
218 pp, maps, sb, cr

This collaborative autobiography is aimed at younger readers. It describes Beharry's childhood and schooling in Grenada, his move to London and experience serving in the British Army. Beharry provides a detailed account of his service in Iraq in 2004, including the action in which he was severely wounded and that led to his award of the VC. He recalls his experiences recovering from his wounds while remaining in the army.

B38   BELL DAVIES, Richard, VC CB DSO AFC
SAILOR IN THE AIR: The Memoirs of Vice Admiral Richard Bell Davies VC CB DSO AFC
Peter Davies, London, 1967
245 pp, photos, index, hb, cr

A detailed personal account of Bell Davies's distinguished naval and flying career. From joining the Royal Navy as a naval cadet in 1901 he saw service in WW1 as a Wing Commander RNAS, Lieutenant Commander RN and Lieutenant Colonel RAF. During WW2, having retired as a Vice Admiral, his service continued on convoy duties and culminated in 1944 as captain of a trials carrier, which concludes the memoir. Although he makes no mention of the award of the VC, an editor's note provides the full citation.

B39   BENNETT Lieutenant Colonel Ian H.W.
EYEWITNESS IN ZULULAND: The Campaign Reminiscences of Colonel W.A. Dunne CB, South Africa, 1877-1881
Greenhill Books, London, 1989
192 pp, photos, contemporary engravings, maps, index, hb, cr

A narrative of the campaign experiences of Colonel Dunne based on his papers and on additional material sourced by the author. Dunne was the senior commissariat officer at Rorke's Drift and was recommended for (but was not awarded) the VC. The part played in the battle by VC winners Bromhead, Chard and Dalton, in particular, are narrated in detail. The Appendix (pages 169-182) contains transcripts of correspondence relating to the Rorke's Drift VC awards. Additionally, there are many references to Brig-Gen HE Wood VC and his involvement in South Africa.

B40   BENNETT, Tom
617 SQUADRON: The Dambusters at War
Patrick Stephens, Wellingborough, 1986
272 pp, photos, hb, cr

The author, a former navigator with 617 Sqn's marker force and, at the time of writing, the Squadron's official archivist, recalls the Squadron's wartime operations under the command of Wg Cdrs Leonard Cheshire and Willie Tait and of the tales of bravery and devotion to duty displayed by the unit's members.

B40A   BERESFORD, Charles
THE CHRISTIAN SOLDIER: The Life of Lieutenant Colonel the Rev Bernard William Vann VC, MC & Bar, Croix De Guerre avec palme
Helion & Company Ltd, Solihull, 2017
326 pp, photos, maps, index, hb, cr

This biography, printed on good quality art paper, tells the story of Lt Col the Rev Bernard William Vann VC, MC & Bar, Croix de Guerre avec palme. He was one of only three Anglican clergymen to command an infantry battalion on the Western Front during the First World War, and the only one of them to have been awarded the VC. The book covers his early life and sporting success, ordination, war record and untimely death while leading his battalion into action in October 1918.

B40B   BERREY, R. Power
THE BOY'S BOOK OF BRAVERY: Deeds of Daring on Land and Sea
C. Arthur Pearson, London, 1902
318 pp, hb, artists' impressions, hb, sb

The tales of soldiers' and sailors' heroism in this book span the Peninsular War 1812 to the Boer War. VC deeds are narrated in the context of the battles being fought and are featured in Chapter II (*Some Heroes of the Victoria Cross*) and specific chapters relating to the Indian Mutiny, Rorke's Drift, the storming of Dargai, the Boer War and Kumassi.

B40C   BERTRAND, Luc
TROIS HISTORIES DE BRAVOURE: le Canada Francais et la Croix De Victoria
Les Presses de L'Universite Laval, Quebec, Canada, 2015
204 pp, photos, maps, index, sb, cr

The French text covers the lives of Quebec's three VCs: Jean Brilliant for action at Meharicourt on 27 September 1917, Joseph Kaeble for action at Neuville-Vitasse on 8/9 June 1918 and Paul Triquet for action at Casa Beradi on 14 December 1943. Busts of the three recipients are on display at the Citadel in Quebec City.

B41   BESLIÈVRE, June (*compiler and editor*) and RUSSELL, Peter F. (*editor*)
STILL THE CANDLE BURNS: An Anthology of Reminiscences and Reflections on "GC" Group Captain Leonard Cheshire VC OM DSO DFC
Jersey Cheshire Home Foundation, St Helier, Jersey, 1997
194 pp, photos, sb, cr

A compilation of memories of Lord Cheshire VC, wartime hero and extraordinary peacetime humanitarian, by those from around the world who knew him. Chapter Seven entitled *The Pathfinder Remembered* recalls his association with the RAF. A full list of contributors features on pages 192-194.

B42   BEST, Brian
THE VICTORIA CROSSES THAT SAVED AN EMPIRE: The story of the VCs of the Indian Mutiny
Frontline Books, (Pen & Sword Books), Barnsley, 2016
236 pp, photos (some colour), index, hb, cr

This book describes the Indian Mutiny and briefly covers each of the 182 VCs awarded. Each of the eleven chapters provides a background to a battle, siege or operations and then describes the associated VC actions and recipients. Many VCs are covered in four to ten lines. Longer entries, like Thomas Kavanagh VC, are covered in more detail. Reviewed in V77.

B43   BEST, Brian
THE VICTORIA CROSS WARS: The Battles, Campaign and Conflicts of All the VC Heroes
Frontline Books, (Pen & Sword Books), Barnsley, 2017
574 pp, photos, index, hb, cr

Sixty-one chapters cover every war or campaign for which the VC was awarded. Chapter 1 starts with the Crimean War, 1854-56, and Chapter 61 ends with the Second Iraq War, 2003-11. Each chapter is preceded by a list of the number of VCs awarded, which is sub-divided into awards to officers/other ranks and also awards to each service. There is a short background to each war/campaign, followed by biographies of a few of the VC recipients. For example, the Indian Mutiny has five biographies (out of 181 VCs awarded), each covered in fewer than five pages, and the First World War, 1914 has just two biographies (Garforth and Yate).

B44   BEST, Brian
THE FORGOTTEN VCs: The Victoria Crosses of the War in the Far East During WW2
Frontline Books, (Pen & Sword Books), Barnsley, 2018
196 pp, photos, index, hb, cr

This volume features biographical sketches of the 48 VCs of the Far East theatre in WW2. Arranged by campaign or battle, each biography includes a detailed account of the VC action. The final chapter, *Australia's War*, also deals with the war in the Pacific.

B45   BEST, Brian
THE DESERT VCs: Extraordinary Valour in the North African Campaign in WWII
Frontline Books, imprint of Pen & Sword Books Ltd, Barnsley, 2018
199 pp, photos, index, hb, cr

Short biographies of 43 VC recipients for the Mediterranean theatre in WW2 including North Africa, East Africa, Greece, Syria, Crete, Operation *Torch* (Peters VC), other naval VCs and one airman. The VCs are grouped around operations which are described to provide a background before detailing each VC recipient. Some VCs are covered in two pages while others get up to 12. The title and sub-title of the volume is misleading as the geographical scope is much wider than desert VCs in the North African campaign.

B46   BEST, Brian
THE VICTORIA CROSS IN 100 OBJECTS
Frontline Books (Pen & Sword Books), Barnsley, 2019
248 pp, photos, sb, **tbc**

To be published.

B48 BHARGAVA, Yogebsa Candra
VIKTORIYA A KROSA: Bhavat iya sainikom ki sacitra bsauryagatha
Nai Dilli, Basanti Prakabsana, India, 1998
143 pp, **tbc** (Hindi text)

A short introduction, in Hindi text, of a selection of Indian soldiers who were awarded the VC in WW1 and WW2.

B49 BICE, R.Z. (*editor*)
A VICTORIA CROSS ON BOUGAINVILLE, 24ᵗʰ JULY 1945 AND EVENTS VIEWED BY A WITNESS
Privately published, McGraths Hill, New South Wales, Australia, nd (1990s)
26 pp, photo, maps, sb, cr

'Zachey' Bice served with Private Frank Partridge as a private in the 8th Australian Infantry Battalion, AIF and witnessed Pte Partridge's VC action on Bougainville. In his own words, he records in detail the VC action and the events that led to it. He also includes the transcript of an interview with a fellow witness.

B50 BIGGS, Maurice (*editor*)
THE STORY OF GURKHA VCs
Gurkha Museum, Winchester, 1993
83 pp, photos, line drawings, sb, cr

This book provides a brief biographical sketch of each of the 26 VC recipients who at the time of deed was serving with a Gurkha regiment. Each sketch incorporates a short account of the VC deed and replicates the VC citation in full. The book also includes, in a similar format, a biographical sketch of three Gurkha recipients of the GC, IOM or EGM.

B55 BILL, Stuart
MIDDLETON VC
S & L Bill, East Bentleigh, Victoria, Australia, 1991
201 pp, photos, maps, sb, cr

A biography of Pilot Officer Middleton VC, RAAF, supported by memories of his friends and colleagues. The appendices include the full transcripts of the VC recommendations of his Wing Commander, Station Commander and AOC. Honour recommendations for his crew are also recorded.

B60 BILLS, Leslie William
A MEDAL FOR LIFE: Biography of Capt Wm Leefe Robinson VC
Spellmount, Tunbridge Wells, 1990
148 pp, photos, sketches, maps, hb, cr

A biography of WL Robinson VC covering his family background, early years and WW1 service through to his death from influenza in 1918 hastened by ill treatment as a POW. His VC action in shooting down a Zeppelin is chronicled in detail. Chapter 18 covers the sale of his VC and medals to support a charity for children with leukaemia. A family tree traces his lineage from 1769.

B63   BINGHAM, Commander The Hon Barry, VC RN
FALKLANDS, JUTLAND AND THE BIGHT
John Murray, London, 1919
155 pp, photos, maps, hb, cr

The author describes his naval service throughout WW1 and, in particular, his experiences of naval battles at the Falklands, Jutland and the Bight. He chronicles his command of HMS *Nestor*, on which his VC deed occurred, and also his time in captivity following the sinking of the ship.

B65   BIRD, Andrew D.
HEROES OF COASTAL COMMAND: The RAF's Maritime War 1939-1945
Frontline Books (Pen & Sword Books), Barnsley, 2017
256 pp, photos, maps, hb, cr

An account of notable airmen of RAF's Coastal Command in WW2. The book includes details of three Coastal Command VCs: A Trigg, K Campbell and J Cruickshank.

B66   BIRRELL, Dave
BAZ: Squadron Leader Ian Bazalgette VC DFC. A Canadian Victoria Cross Recipient
[1] Nanton Lancaster Society, Nanton, Alberta, Canada, 1996
77 pp, photos, hb, cr
[2] Nanton Lancaster Society, Nanton, Alberta, Canada, 2009
109 pp, photos, sb, cr
[3] Nanton Lancaster Society, Nanton, Alberta, Canada, 2014
209 pp, photos, sb, cr

A biography of Sqn Ldr Bazalgette who won a posthumous VC in 1944 on a Pathfinder squadron sortie over France. It also narrates the story of the dedication of Lancaster FM159 to the memory of Bazalgette. This aircraft is a constituent of the Nanton Lancaster Society Air Museum in Alberta. The 2009 edition has an additional 32 pages and more photographs.

B67   BIRRELL, Dave
FM159: The Lucky Lancaster
Nanton Lancaster Society, Nanton, Alberta, Canada, 2002
60 pp, photos, sb, cr

This well-illustrated book records the history of Avro Lancaster B.X, serial FM159 which is displayed in the Nanton Lancaster Air Museum. On 27 July 1990, it was formally dedicated as the Ian Bazalgette Memorial Lancaster and bears Sqn Ldr Bazalgette's aircraft code 'F2-T'.

B69   BISHOP, Arthur
OUR BRAVEST AND OUR BEST: The Stories of Canada's Victoria Cross Winners
McGraw-Hill Ryerson, Whitby, Ontario, Canada, 1995
211 pp, photos, index, hb, cr

Written by the son of AM WA Bishop VC, this book comprises biographical sketches of the 95 Canadian VC winners. Each account describes the recipient's VC deed, the events surrounding the action and provides biographical information supported by a photographic portrait. Appendix 1 identifies the 16 VCs (not otherwise covered), who were domiciled in or associated with Canada. Appendix 2 records for each of the 95 VCs the locations of their VC and burial place.

B70   BISHOP, Diana
LIVING UP TO A LEGEND: My adventures with Billy Bishop's ghost
Dundurn, Toronto, Canada, 2017
213 pp, photos, sb, cr

The author, granddaughter of AM WA Bishop VC, reviews her grandfather's legacy and examines its influence over her life and that of her father, Arthur, Billy Bishop's only son. In addition to appraising Billy Bishop as a person and a national hero, she also scrutinises the attempts to discredit him. Family photographs depict Billy Bishop at various stages in his life.

B71   BISHOP, William Arthur
THE COURAGE OF THE EARLY MORNING: The Story of Billy Bishop
[1] McClelland & Stewart, Toronto, 1965
211 pp, map, index, hb, cr
[2] Heinemann, London, 1966
206 pp, map, index, hb cr

The author, the son of AM WA Bishop VC, wrote this biography as a result of a promise he made to his father. The book reveals the story of the man behind the legend and describes in detail his military career and achievements spanning the two world wars. A significant proportion of the book concerns Bishop's aerial combats and a list of victories is included.

B72   [1] BISHOP, Major W. A, VC DSO MC
WINGED WARFARE: Hunting the Huns in the Air
Hodder & Stoughton, London, 1918
301 pp, hb, cr
[2] BISHOP, Lieutenant Colonel William A., VC DSO MC (*Editor*: ULANOFF, Stanley. M)
WINGED WARFARE
Bailey Brothers & Swinfen, Folkstone, 1975
281 pp, photos, hb, cr
[3] BISHOP, Lieutenant Colonel William A., VC DSO MC (*Editor*: ULANOFF, Stanley. M)
WINGED WARFARE
Arco Publishing, New York, 1981
281 pp, photos, hb, cr

Bishop's memoirs of his experiences in the RFC in WW1 in which he gives a detailed account of his aerial combats. The new edition includes appendices covering lists of aces, line drawings of aircraft flown by Bishop and a list of his confirmed victories.

B73   BISHOP, Air Marshal William A., VC CB DSO MC DFC
WINGED PEACE
MacMillan, Toronto, 1944 / Viking Press, New York, 1944
175 pp, photos, maps, hb, cr

In this book Bishop describes the past, present and future of flight. In Part 1, he traces how conquest of the air has affected the global geography. Part 2 describes the pioneering flights leading to the development of military aviation in WW1. In developing the theme he recalls some of his own aerial combat experiences. Part 3 concerns the development of civil aviation during the inter-war years and military aviation during the early years of WW2. He concludes with his predictions for aviation in the future and, in particular, the era of the rocket and the jet.

B74   BISHOP, Patrick
3 PARA: Afghanistan, Summer 2006, This is War
Harper Press, London, 2007
289 pp, photos, maps, index, hb, cr

An account of the deployment of 3 Para in the Helmand Province of Afghanistan and the actions resulting in the award of a posthumous VC to Corporal Bryan Budd in December 2006.

B75   BISHOP, Patrick
TARGET TIRPITZ: The Epic Hunt for Hitler's Last Battleship
Harper Collins, London, 2012
390 pp, photos, maps, index, hb, cr

A detailed examination of attempts made by *X craft*, the Fleet Air Arm and the RAF to sink the German battleship *Tirpitz*. Cameron VC and Place VC are covered extensively in the section on *X craft*.

B75A   BLAKE, David and HISSEY, Terry
REVEREND THEODORE HARDY VC DSO MC
Published by authors, Harrow, 2018
15 pp, colour photos, sb, cr

An A5 desktop published booklet commemorating the centenary of the death of Rev TH Hardy VC DSO MC. The publication provides a concise biography including a poem dedicated to Hardy with photos of his VC, decorations and medals, his VC paving stone and other memorials.

B76   BLANCH, John
GOWRIE, VC
Barbara Blanch, Hawthorn, Victoria, Australia, 1998
192 pp, photos, index, sb, cr

This first full biography of Alexander Hore-Ruthven VC (later the Earl of Gowrie) was published privately a year after the author's death and almost 50 years after Blanch was originally contracted to ghost-write Gowrie's autobiography. The book is based on a number of interviews with Gowrie at Windsor Castle in the early 1950s and from documents supplied by Gowrie. It covers his campaigning in the Sudan where he won his VC (1898), service in WW1 and concentrates on his public career as Governor of South Australia and New South Wales and as Governor-General of Australia.

B76A   BLANCH, Craig and PEGRAM, Aaron
FOR VALOUR: Australians awarded the Victoria Cross
New South, New South Wales, Australia, 2018
512 pp, photos, artwork, hb, cr

This book describes the 100 Australians who have been awarded the VC. It begins with Captain Neville Howse in 1900 and ends with Cpl C Baird in 2013. The recipients received their awards for the Boer War, WW1, North Russia, WW2, Vietnam and Afghanistan. The battles are described along with biographical profiles of each recipient. The Foreword is by Daniel Keighran VC and the volume includes new archival research and artworks provided by the Australian War Memorial.

B77   BLASCHE, Herbert
INTONATION UND LAUTEGEBUNG IN DER ENGLISCHEN AUSSPRACHE DES LORD ROBERTS
Walter de Gruyter & Co, Berlin, 1939
113 pp, sb, cr

This German text analyses the written text of a political speech by Lord Roberts and a photographic recording. The text is followed by numerous graphs and tables. The analysis includes the quantity of vowels and consonants, the influence of pitch in vowel quality, the innotation of syllables and the pitch of the attack and release of phonic groups.

B78   BLATHERWICK, Surgeon Commander Francis John CM CD BSc DPH MD FRCP(C)
1000 BRAVE CANADIANS: The Canadian Gallantry Awards 1854-1989
The Unitrade Press, Toronto, 1991
415 pp, photos, indexes, sb, ncr

This book is divided into two parts: Part 1 (pages 11-172) covers British gallantry awards including a section on each of 94 Canadian VC winners (pages 13-88). The following information is recorded for each recipient: VC action date, LG date, location of VC action, some biographical notes and location of VC and medals. Part 2 (pages 173-413) covers Canadian decorations for bravery.

B78A   BLISS, James, Major
FREYBERG'S FAILURE AT CRETE: A Close-Run Thing
University of New England, Armidale, NSW, Australia, 2002
159 pp, maps, sb, cr

This is a thesis for a Master's Degree by Major James Bliss of the NZ Army. It examines Freyberg's role in the loss of Greece and Crete to German forces in WW2 when he commanded the NZ Division. The author concludes Freyberg made errors prior to and during the battle for Crete but could not be held capable for its loss. Also published by Fort Leavenworth, Kansas, 2006.

B79   BOILEAU, John
VALIANT HEARTS: Atlantic Canada and the Victoria Cross
Nimbus Publishing, Halifax, Nova Scotia, 2006
276 pp, photos, index, sb, cr

This book provides profiles of 21 Victoria Cross recipients who came from Canada's Atlantic region or who had connections with the area. The region comprises four provinces: Nova Scotia, New Brunswick, Prince Edward Island and Newfoundland/Labrador. Reviewed in V58.

B80   BOND, Geoffrey
REMEMBER MAZOE
Pioneer Head, Salisbury, Rhodesia, 1973
164 pp, photos, maps, sketches, hb, cr

A vivid reconstruction of the Mazoe patrol in which its commander, Captain RC Nesbitt, was awarded the VC. In June 1896, a patrol of 13 men under Nesbitt's command successfully rescued a party of miners in a series of running fights with rebels in the Mazoe Valley near Salisbury.

B81   BONNER, Robert
WILFRITH ELSTOB VC DSO MC, THE MANCHESTER REGIMENT
Fleur de Lys Publishing, Knutsford, 1998
34 pp, photos, map, index, sb, cr

A well-illustrated biographical account of Lt Col Elstob recalls his early years and then focuses on his Great War service with the Manchester Regiment, which culminated in the posthumous award of the VC. Details of the tributes and memorials to him conclude the work.

B83   BONNER, Robert
VOLUNTEER INFANTRY OF ASHTON-UNDER-LYNE 1859-1971
Fleur de Lys Publishing, Knutsford, Cheshire, 2005
181 pp, photos, maps, index, hb, cr

This book records the history of the 9th Battalion, The Manchester Regiment since the raising of volunteer companies to form the 23rd Lancashire Rifle Volunteers in 1859. Included in the chapter on Gallipoli is a 20-page illustrated biography of Lieutenant William Forshaw who was awarded a VC for his gallant defence of the Vineyard between 7 and 9 August 1915. Reviewed in V57.

B84   BONNER, Robert (*not designated*)
THE KING'S REGIMENT, 8th, 63rd, 96th: For Valour
Fleur de Lys Publishing, Cheshire, nd (c.1996)
47 pp, photos, sb, cr

This pocket-sized booklet records the 23 VC recipients of the Manchester and King's Regiments. There is a portrait photograph, citation and basic biographical details relating to each recipient. (The booklet does not have a title as such: the cover has a colour photograph of a memorial wood carving inscribed with the title shown above).

B84A   BONNER, Robert
ISSY SMITH - The Manchester Regiment: A Soldier of the Jullundur Brigade
Fleur de Lys Publishing, Knutsford, Cheshire, 2014
32 pp, photos, map, index, sb, cr

A concise biography of Issy Smith VC, 1st Bn Manchester Regiment who won the VC at St Julien, Belgium on 26 April 1915. This A4-sized publication traces his birth and childhood in the East End of London. His military service is recorded including a detailed account of his VC action. Reviewed in V75.

B85   BOON, Kevin
BERNARD FREYBERG
Nelson Price Milburn Ltd., Petone, New Zealand, 1993
20 pp, photos, index, sb, cr

A short biography in large-print text of Bernard Freyberg VC in the *People in New Zealand History* series.

B86   BOON, Kevin
CHARLES UPHAM
Kotuku Publishing, Wellington, New Zealand, 1994
24 pp, photos, sb, cr

A short biography in large-print text of Charles Upham VC and bar in the *People in New Zealand History* series.

B86A   BOOT, Richard OBE DL (*compiler and editor*)
TEN HEROES: One City at War
Published by the author, Kidderminster, Worcestershire, 2018
64 pp, illustrations, sb, cr

Biographical sketches of the ten soldiers from Birmingham who were awarded the VC in WW1: W Amey, NA Finch, A Gill, WH James, AJ Knight, JN Marshall, J Tombs, TG Turrall, A Vickers and A Wilcox. A brief introduction to the VC and an insight into life in Birmingham during WW1 are also given.

B86B   BOOTH, Ron
ANTHONY CLARKE BOOTH VC 1841-1899: Hero of The Intombe River in the Zulu War
Ron Booth, Ravenshead Graphics, 2004
43 pp, photos, drawings, maps, documents, sb, cr

This detailed biography of Clr Sgt Anthony Booth, who won the VC in the Zulu War, is the product of family research undertaken by the author, whose great-great-grandfather was the brother of Anthony's grandfather. Extensive use has been made of family records and official records from which there are transcriptions or photocopies of various census information, a detailed record of his army service and birth, marriage and death certificates. A family tree is included.

B86C   BOOTH, Jeffrey (*editor*)
"ALL IS WELL WITH ELLIS TONIGHT": Letters of Ellis Wellwood Sifton VC
The Elgin Military Museum, Canada, 2007
85 pp, photos, sb, cr

A spiral-bound booklet which provides edited letters of Sgt Ellis Sifton VC from 1 November 1914 to 5 April 1917. Ellis was killed in action on 9 April 1917 at Vimy Ridge while serving with the 18th Canadian Battalion. The volume contains several black and white photographs and brief biographical details. Sifton wrote numerous letters to his sisters starting on 1 November 1914. His last letter was dated 5 April 1917. The author has inserted portions of 18th Battalion War diary to provide a context to Sifton's service.

B87   BOWER, Tom
HEROES OF WORLD WAR II: The Men and Women Who Won the War
Boxtree, London, 1995
144 pp, photos, hb, ncr

This volume has short accounts of over 100 men and women who performed heroic deeds during WW2. Presented in chronological order, with many photographs, the accounts include 67 VC and 4 GC recipients.

B88   BOWMAN, Martin W.
RAF BOMBER STORIES: Dramatic first-hand accounts of British and Commonwealth airmen of World War 2
Patrick Stephens, imprint of Haynes Publishing, Sparkford, Somerset, 1998
192 pp, photos, index, hb, cr

An anthology of 23 accounts of RAF bomber missions over occupied Europe in WW2, which are recalled by, or relate specifically to, a participant in the mission. Chapter 10 (pages 86-95) is devoted to Flt Lt W Reid and the raid in which he won the VC.

B88A   BOWMAN, Martin W
THE DAM BUSTERS: A Pocket History
Amberley Publishing, Stroud, 2009
127 pp, photos, sb, cr

This well-illustrated pocketbook is a brief history of 617 Squadron during WW2. Chapter 1 (pages 12-57) concerns Operation *Chastise*, the attack on the dams led by Wg Cdr Gibson. Chapter 2 (pages 58-82) relates to the Squadron's service after the raid during which time Wg Cdr Cheshire was a Squadron Commander. Chapter 3 covers the unit's service from D-Day to VE-Day and Chapter 4 (pages 100-125) recalls the making of the 1954 film *The Dam Busters*.

B89   BOWYER, Chaz
FOR VALOUR: The Air VCs
[1] William Kimber, London, 1978
548 pp, photos, index, hb, cr
[2] Grub Street, London, 1992 (*revised and updated*)
[3] Grub Street, London, 1992 (*revised and updated*) De-Luxe Limited Edition with de-luxe binding (100 copies produced)

This definitive reference work on the air VCs of both world wars records detailed biographies of each of the 51 recipients and fully describes their VC deed. The text is accompanied by a full-plate portrait photograph of each recipient. There are, in addition, in excess of 300 other photographs relating to the recipients.

B90   BOWYER, Chaz
EUGENE ESMONDE VC DSO
William Kimber, London, 1983
222 pp, photos, index, hb, cr

A profusely illustrated biographical study of Lieutenant Commander E Esmonde VC DSO, which describes his family background and details his flying career in the RAF, Imperial Airways and the Fleet Air Arm. The action for which he won a posthumous VC is documented thoroughly.

B91   BOWYER, Chaz
CHESHIRE: Man and Legend
Leonard Cheshire Foundation, London, nd (c1995)
11 pp, photos, sb, cr

The booklet describes Leonard Cheshire's wartime experiences. The text is similar to that contained in the chapter on Cheshire in B89.

B92   BOWYER, Chaz
BOMBER BARONS
William Kimber, London, 1983
222 pp, photos, index, hb, cr

An account of the careers and achievements of 19 distinguished WW2 pilots of Bomber Command, each of whom has a dedicated chapter. Four VC winners are included: Edwards (pages 63-69), Middleton (pages 151-158), Gibson (pages 159-165) and Cheshire (pages 167-173). B93 is a companion volume.

B93   BOWYER, Chaz
FIGHTER PILOTS OF THE RAF 1939-45
William Kimber, London, 1984
223 pp, photos, index, hb, cr

Continuing the theme of B92, the author provides a study of some 20 RAF fighter pilots of WW2 which describe their courage, prowess and character. Separate chapters are devoted to 17 of these men. Chapter VIII (pages 81-88) relates to James Nicolson VC DFC.

B94   BOWYER, Chaz
ALBERT BALL VC
[1] William Kimber, London, 1977
208 pp, photos, map, index, hb, cr
[2] Bridge Books, Wrexham, 1994 (*reformatted and extended*)
197 pp, photos, maps, index, hb, cr

A full biography of Capt Ball VC DSO** MC. Appendices detail aircraft flown by him, Ball's award citations, combat record and a list of memorabilia relating to him.

B95   BOYLE, Vice Admiral W.H.D.
GALLANT DEEDS
Gieves, Portsmouth, 1919 (reprinted 1985)
61 pp, hb, cr

A record of the circumstances under which the VC, Conspicuous Gallantry Medal or Albert Medal was won by petty officers, non-commissioned officers and men of the Royal Navy, Royal Marines and the naval reserve forces during WW1. Several of the deeds described recall the circumstances in which officers also won the VC in the action.

B99   BOYLE, Andrew, and other authors
HEROES OF OUR TIME
Victor Gollancz, London, 1961
192 pp, photos, hb, cr

A compilation of chapters on modern heroes by different authors. A chapter is included by Andrew Boyle on Group Captain Leonard Cheshire VC DSO DFC titled: *He looked on Nagasaki* describing Cheshire's role of one of two official UK eye-witnesses of the dropping of the A-bomb and its effects on him.

B100   BOYLE, Andrew
NO PASSING GLORY: The Full and Authentic Biography of Group Captain Cheshire VC DSO DFC
Collins, London, 1955
384 pp, photo, index, hb, cr

A detailed biography of Leonard Cheshire. It describes fully his family background, early years, life as an undergraduate, distinguished RAF service and his religious beliefs. There are several mentions of Jack Randle (later VC), who was Cheshire's closest friend during their undergraduate days at Oxford.

B103   BOYS' BRIGADE (*publisher*)
HEROES OF THE BOYS' BRIGADE: Officers and Old Boys who Won the Victoria Cross in the Great War, 1914-1919
Boys' Brigade, London, nd (c1919)
27 pp, photos, sb, cr

This small booklet contains brief biographical sketches and portrait photographs of 11 VC winners: FW Holmes, JHS Dimmer, WP Richie, J Caffrey, EK Myles, R Shankland, JB Hamilton, H Strachan, EF Beal, JCR Richardson and F Lester.

B104   BRADBURY, Charles Kinder
BRADBURY HERITAGE
Braykc Publishing, Cupar, Scotland, 2013
311 pp, photos, drawings, maps, index, hb, cr

This lavishly-produced volume contains biographical sketches with photographs (generally two pages in length) of notable Bradburys over the ages and worldwide. They are arranged by generic occupation. Within *The Forces* category, pages 62-65, are devoted to Captain Edward Kinder Bradbury VC and include his portrait photograph and photographs of his WW1 memorial plaque, his headstone and a plaque in Altrincham. Pages 58-59 relate, respectively, to the former Bradbury Barracks, Germany and Bradbury Lines, Hereford, reputed to have been named after him. Page 92 is devoted to his father, His Honour James Kinder Bradbury.

B105   BRADDON, Russell
CHESHIRE VC: A Story of War and Peace
Evans Brothers, London, 1954
217 pp, photos, hb, cr

A full biography of Group Captain GL Cheshire VC DSO DFC covering his early years, war service and religious convictions. It also describes the evolution of the Cheshire Homes.

B110   BRADFORD, Admiral Sir Edward E., KCB CVO
LIFE OF ADMIRAL OF THE FLEET SIR ARTHUR KNYVET WILSON, Bart VC GCB OM GCVO
John Murray, London, 1923
257 pp, photos, sketches, index, hb, cr

This biography describes Wilson's family background and early years but is concerned predominantly with his distinguished naval career. Each chapter relates to a rank or appointment and chronicles his service in that capacity making extensive use of his diaries and private letters.

B111   BRADLEY, P.E.
FOR VALOUR: A South African Victoria Cross
Privately published, Eastbourne, 1987
29 pp, photos, sketches, sb, cr

A short biography of Captain FH Bradley VC VD who won his VC for action in the Boer War. In addition to describing his military career, the book includes a statement of his military service, a list of his medals detailing the inscriptions and a photograph of his VC and medals.

B112   BRAGA, Stuart
JOHN PATON VC: Hero of Lucknow
St. Andrew's Anglican Church, Summer Hill, NSW, Australia, 2007
38 pp, photos, maps, index, sb, cr

A short biography of John Paton VC (1834-1914) who received his reward for gallantry in the India Mutiny. Most of the booklet covers Paton's service in India at the time of the Mutiny and his later life in Australia. The back cover has a colour photograph of Paton's VC and medal group. As a member of the 93rd Regt, he was a witness of the Charge of the Light Brigade.

B113   BRAGA, Stuart
ANZAC DOCTOR: The Life of Sir Neville Howse VC
Hale and Iremonger, Alexandria, NSW, Australia, 2000
392 pp, photos, maps, index, hb, cr

A detailed and well-researched biography of Sir Neville Howse VC KCB KCMG who was the first Australian to win the VC. The book is profusely illustrated with many maps and end notes charting the extraordinary career of a country doctor who volunteered as a medical officer in the Boer War and won the VC. Chapter 5 (pages 64-78) is dedicated to the VC action and the presentation. Howse was responsible for evacuating the wounded at the Anzac landings in Gallipoli in April 1915. Later he was promoted to Major General and appointed Director of Medical Services for the AIF. He was later a cabinet minister in the Australian Government and died in 1930.

B114   BRAHAM, Michael
MEN OF VALOUR: Canada's Victoria Cross Winners
CreateSpace Independent Publishing Platform, 2016
231 pp, photos, sb, cr

This book comprises biographical sketches of 100 VC recipients associated with Canada by birth, residence or service in Canadian forces or whose VC deed was performed in Canada (pre-Confederation). The biographies, which are arranged alphabetically within each category, are laid out in standard format: birth details, VC citation, gravesite, medal location and postscript providing additional information.

B115   BRANCH, Newton
THE BOYS' BOOK OF VC HEROES
Publicity Products, London, 1957
93 pp, photos, sketches, hb, cr

This book (written for the younger reader) recounts the exploits of a selection of VC winners. The VC actions of Keyes and E Esmonde are illustrated in cartoon format. Narrative text describes the deeds of the other VCs, namely: G Campbell, RED Ryder, SH Beattie, WA Savage, D Cameron, BCG Place, IE Fraser, JJ Magennis, A Ball, JTB McCudden, E Mannock, GP Gibson and GL Cheshire.

B116   BRASCH, Nicolas
EXTREME BRAVERY: AUSTRALIA'S VICTORIA CROSS RECIPIENTS
Book 1: World War I
Book 2: Boer War, North Russia Campaign, World War II, Vietnam War
Echinda Books, Port Melbourne, Victoria, Australia, 2003
32 pp./32 pp, photos, map, index, hb, cr

These two volumes cover all of Australia's VC recipients. For each recipient, brief personal details are given together with a short account of the VC action. A portrait photograph is also included. Book 1 covers the 64 Australian VCs of World War 1; Book 2 covers the Australian VCs of the Boer War (6), the North Russian campaign (2), World War 2 (20) and the Vietnam War (4).

B116A   BRASCH, Nicolas
FOR VALOUR: Australia's Victoria Cross Heroes
Black Dog Books (Walker Books Australia), 2013
32 pp, photos, index, sb, cr

This large-sized and well-illustrated book tells the stories of 22 Australian VC recipients representative of the country's 99 VC recipients (at the time of writing). Arranged by conflict, from the Boer War to Afghanistan, each recipient's story provides basic biographical information and a brief account of the VC deed. A photograph of the recipient accompanies the text. Full lists of all Australian VCs by conflict are given.

B117   BRAZIER, Kevin
THE COMPLETE VICTORIA CROSS: A Full Chronological Record of All Holders of Britain's Highest Award for Gallantry
Pen & Sword Military, Barnsley, 2010
406 pp, photos, hb, index, ncr

Chapters 1 and 2 cover a short history of the VC and the VC warrants. Chapter 3 lists VC recipients in chronological order of date of VC action with burial location and location of the VC (where known). Chapters 4 to 13 list VC recipients by date of VC action from Crimea and Persian Wars (Chapter 4) to the Post-War Period 1950 - 2009 (Chapter 13). Each entry is between 40 and 100 words but longer for those listed in the Post-War Period. Chapter 14 shows VC burial location by country listed alphabetically and cross-referenced to the VC entry in Chapters 4 to 13. Chapter 15 lists VC recipients alphabetically by surname with cross-reference to the VC entry.

B118   BREMNER SMITH, R.J.
SIR REDVERS BULLER VC
London Publishing Company, London, 1900
16 pp, sb, cr

A short biography of Sir Redvers Buller VC and No. 2 in the series *Soldiers of the Queen Library*. (See B119 and L58).

B119   BREMNER SMITH, R.J.
SIR GEORGE STEWART WHITE VC
London Publishing Company, London, 1900
16 pp, line drawings, sb, cr

A short biography of Sir George White VC and No.3 in the series *Soldiers of the Queen Library*. (See B118 and L57).

B120   BRICKHILL, Paul
THE DAM BUSTERS
[1] Evans Brothers, London, 1951
269 pp. photos, index, hb, cr
[2] Evans Brothers, London, 1977 (*reset and updated*)
238 pp, photos, index, hb, cr (*reprinted 1978*)

The story of 617 Squadron, RAF during WW2. The first half of the book relates to Wg Cdr Gibson's command of the squadron from its formation and details the preparation for and the attack on the Ruhr dams, for which Gibson received the VC. Group Captain Cheshire's subsequent command of the squadron is also covered extensively. The 1977 (reset) edition incorporates additional material relating to the bomb used in the raid. It was also re-published in 2017 as part of Pan's 70th anniversary.

B121 BRIDGLAND, Tony
SEA KILLERS IN DISGUISE: The Story of the Q-Ships and Decoy Ships in the First World War
Leo Cooper, Barnsley, 1999
274 pp, photos, maps, index, hb, cr

This study traces the development, exploits and successes of armed disguised merchant auxiliaries in the British and German navies during WW1. Amongst the many *Q*-ship actions recalled in detail are those that culminated in the award of the VC and, in particular, the adventures of Captain Gordon Campbell are covered extensively. The VC deeds described include those relating to Lt H Auten, Mstr A Bissett-Smith, Skpr T Crisp, PO E Pitcher, Lt W Sanders, Lt R Stuart and Smn W Williams. In addition the *Baralong* incident (see C97), which involved Lt G Steele (later a VC) is reappraised.

B122 BRIGGS, James C, MB BS DPath FRCPath
THE SEARCH FOR LT COL F.W. BELL, VC
Privately published, Westbury-on-Trym, Bristol, 1998
22 pp, sb, cr

This booklet is the result of Dr Briggs' search for the reason why Lt Col Bell VC, an Australian, is buried in Westbury-on-Trym, Bristol. It traces Bell's family history, military service (Boer War, Somaliland and WW1), subsequent career in the colonial service and his later life. Much information has been obtained from Bell's relatives.

B123 BRIGHTON, Terry
THE LAST CHARGE: The 21st Lancers and the Battle of Omdurman 2 September 1898
Crowood Press, Marlborough, 1998
128 pp, photos, colour plates, maps, index, hb, cr

A well-illustrated account of the charge of the 21st Lancers at Omdurman which resulted in the award of three VCs: Capt PA Kenna, Lt R de Montmorency and Pte T Byrne. The volume was produced to commemorate the centenary of the charge and describes fully the deeds of the VC recipients.

B124 BRISCOE, Walter A.
THE BOY HERO OF THE AIR: From Schoolboy to VC
Humphrey Milford / Oxford University Press, London, 1921
108 pp, photo, line drawings, hb, cr

Written for children, this biography of Captain Ball VC covers his schooldays, RFC service and death. It mentions some exploits and letters not contained in the author's earlier biography of Ball (B125).

B125 BRISCOE, Walter Alwyn and STANNARD, H. Russell
CAPTAIN ALBERT BALL VC OF THE ROYAL FLYING CORPS: The Career of Flight-Commander Ball VC DSO
Herbert Jenkins, London, 1918
320 pp, photos, hb, cr

This biography makes extensive use of Ball's letters to his parents, sister and fiancée and much of this correspondence intersperses the authors' text. After describing Ball's parentage and early life, the book then concentrates on his military and flying service and, in particular, his aerial combats. His last flight, death and tributes are documented.

B126　*BRITAIN AT WAR* MAGAZINE (*editor*: GREEHAN, John)
ZEEBRUGGE 1918: The Greatest Raid
Key Publishing, Stamford, Lincolnshire, 2018
98 pp, photos, drawings, maps, sb, cr

This lavishly-illustrated 'bookazine' tells the story of the raid on Zeebrugge and Ostend on 23 April 1918 and recounts the operation's origin, planning, preparation, execution and outcome. Tales of heroism include a six-page section on HM Sub *C3's* action for which for Lt Sandford was posthumously awarded the VC. Many of the photographs are contemporary portrayals of the ships, the men, the damage and memorials.

B130　BROEHL, Jnr, Wayne G.
CRISIS OF THE RAJ:　The Revolt of 1857 through British Lieutenants' Eyes
University Press of New England, Hanover, New Hampshire, USA and London, 1986
347 pp, photos, maps, index, hb, cr

This book tells the story of the Indian Mutiny through the personal experiences of four army lieutenants: Frederick Roberts VC, George Cracklow, Arthur Lang and Thomas Watson. The author intertwines excerpts from their letters with the essential historical background and some later accounts. The different personalities of the lieutenants colour their observations and writing styles.

B132　BROOKE-HUNT, Violet
LORD ROBERTS: A Life for Boys (*original title*)
LORD ROBERTS: A Biography (*revised edition*)
James Nisbet, London, 1901 (revised: James Nisbet, London, 1914)
346 pp. (1914 edition: 362 pp.), photos, hb, cr

The life of Field Marshal Lord Roberts VC from his early days. All the campaigns in which Roberts took part are covered. The author was in the Cape Colony, Orange Free State and the Transvaal during the most critical phases of the campaign in 1900 and recalls her own memories of Lord Roberts during that period. The revised edition is expanded with two chapters that cover the period 1901 up to his death in 1914.

B134　BROWN, Duncan
MY HERO, MY SOLDIER LADDIE
The Carman Centre, Renton, Dunbartonshire, 2010
274 pp, photos, paintings, sb, cr

The author, who is also the artist of all the paintings in this work, recalls the life and deeds of Lanarkshire's 14 VC recipients. Pages 19 to 173 are devoted to Private David MacKay and pages 175-227 relate to the other 13 VCs. As part of each recipient's account, there is a full-page colour painting depicting his VC action. The work concludes with a comprehensive listing of all 172 Scottish VC winners.

B135　BROWN, Eunice P. (*editor*)
YOUR LOVING SON, DON: Letters home to North Otago from Sgt Donald Brown VC
Otago Heritage Books, Dunedin, New Zealand, 1998
48 pp, photos, index, sb, cr

This book is a compilation of transcripts of 17 letters sent home by Sgt Donald Brown VC of 2nd Battalion, Otago Infantry Regiment, NZEF, in 1916 during his time in Egypt and France. He won his VC on the Somme in September 1916 and was killed on 1st October 1917. A further 10 letters are included, which were sent to his father to pay tribute to his bravery.

B136   BROWN, Gordon
WARTIME COURAGE: Stories of Extraordinary Courage by Ordinary Men and Women in World War Two
Bloomsbury, London, 2008
238 pp, maps, index, hb, cr

The author, a former British Prime Minister, recalls in 11 schematic chapters, the courageous deeds of 18 men and women in WW2, five of whom are VC recipients. *Command under Pressure* concerns Stannard and Place; *Press Home Your Attack* relates to Manser; *The Bravest of Brothers* is devoted to Derek Seagrim VC and his brother, Hugh Seagrim GC. SE Hollis is covered under *D-Day Heroes*.

B137   BROWNE, General Sir Sam, VC GCB KCSI
JOURNAL OF THE LATE GENERAL SIR SAM BROWNE VC GCB KCSI FROM 1840 TO 1878
William Blackwood, Edinburgh and London, 1937
80 pp, photo, hb, cr

This journal, edited by General Browne's son for private circulation, contains extracts from his father's diary featuring campaigns in the Sikh Wars and Indian Mutiny (VC). Browne was an outstanding light cavalry leader and invented the 'Sam Browne' belt as a consequence of losing an arm. Included is a copy of a letter from General Browne to the War Office, providing advice on the pistol pouch when considering the introduction of the belt to general service.

B138   BRUYÉRE, Franck
HENRY JAMES NICHOLAS VC MM
Mon Petit Editeur, Paris, France, 2011
177 pp, photos, maps, index, sb, cr

A French-language account of Sergeant Nicholas' war service with the New Zealand Expeditionary Force in France and Belgium from 1916 to 1918 when he was killed in action. The exploits for which he was awarded the VC and MM and the action in which he was killed are recalled in the context of the battles. The commemorations and memorials for him are described.

B140   BRYANT, George
WHERE THE PRIZE IS HIGHEST: The Stories of the New Zealanders who won the Victoria Cross
Collins, Auckland, 1972
181 pp, photos, map, hb, cr

This book covers the 28 VC winners who came from or had close links with New Zealand. It includes the four New Zealanders who served in the Australian Imperial Force (Cooke, Stuart, Storkey and Weathers) and also covers Rhodes-Moorhouse because his mother was half Maori. A chapter is devoted to each recipient and gives a detailed account of the VC deed and background to the action. Some biographical information is included in the text, which is accompanied by a full-plate portrait photograph of the VC recipient.

B143   BRYCE, David
ORANGEMEN OF VALOUR: Orange VCs
Published by the author, Glasgow, Scotland, 2015
28 pp, photos, sb, cr

This book provides biographies of members of the Royal Orange Institution who were awarded the VC. Recipients included are: A Acton, JW Foote, RH Hanna, GT Lyall, R Quigg, WL Rayfield and G Richardson.

B145   BUCHAN, John
        FRANCIS AND RIVERSDALE GRENFELL: A Memoir
        Thomas Nelson, London, 1920
        240 pp, photos, index, hb, cr

        The author (later Lord Tweedsmuir) describes the life and death of the Grenfell twins, Francis Octavius (VC) and Riversdale Nonus, both of whom were killed in action in 1914/15. Pages 1-185 cover the period 1880 up to 1914. Thereafter, the book relates to their war service.

B148   BUJAK, Philip
        [1] UNDEFEATED: The Extraordinary Life and Death of Lt. Col. Jack Sherwood Kelly VC, DSO, CMG
        Forster Consulting, [no location], 2008
        254 pp, photos, index, sb, cr
        [2] THE BRAVEST MAN IN THE BRITISH ARMY: The Extraordinary Life and Death of Lt. Col. Jack Sherwood Kelly VC (*revised and reformatted*)
        Pen & Sword Military, Barnsley, 2018
        199 pp, photos, index, hb, cr

        A biography of Lt Col Jack Sherwood Kelly VC, CMG, DSO from his birth in South Africa in 1880 to his lonely death in a London nursing home in 1931. He served in South Africa, 1899-1902, Gallipoli, the Western Front, where he was awarded the VC (Marcoing, France 1917) and the North Russia campaign in 1919. He led a rebellious life, often at odds with his military superiors, and his clashes with Winston Churchill over the situation in Russia resulted in his court martial – for which he received a severe reprimand.

B149   BURGESS, Colin
        AUSTRALIA'S DAMBUSTERS: The Men and Missions of 617 Squadron
        Australian Military History Publications, Loftus, Australia, 2003
        173 pp, photos, maps, diagrams, index, hb, cr

        This profusely-illustrated work covers the exploits of 617 Squadron throughout WW2. Part 1 (pages 1-58) documents the squadron under Wg Cdr Guy Gibson's command and the Dams Raid on which Gibson won the VC. Part 2 (pages 59-157) relates to the subsequent missions under the commands of Leonard Cheshire (who also won the VC with 617 Sqn) and 'Willie' Tait. Aircrew lists are given for each aircraft participating in the squadron's principal missions and all 95 operations carried out by 617 Sqn between May 1943 and April 1945 are listed. All Australian aircrew are identified.

B150   BURKE, Edmund
        GUY GIBSON VC
        Arco Publications, London, 1961
        128 pp, hb, cr

        This biography in the *Modern Heroes* series recalls Wg Cdr Gibson's early years but, predominantly, concerns his wartime RAF service up to his death in 1944.

B152   BURTON, Doris
        BRAVE WINGS: More Heroic Christians of Our Day
        Burns and Oates, London, 1957
        191 pp, hb, cr

        A collection of 10 heroes from a Roman Catholic background. Chapter 5 (pages 85-99) covers Flying Officer Donald Garland VC. Chapter 9 (pages 154-172) covers Captain Michael Allmand VC.

B155   BUTLER, Captain Lewis
SIR REDVERS BULLER VC
Smith, Elder & Co., London, 1909
120 pp, photos index, hb, cr

Concise biography of Sir Redvers Buller VC based on a text previously published in *The King's Royal Rifle Corps Chronicle* to which the author has incorporated some additional information. A facsimilie of a letter dated 3 March 1909 from Buller to his wife, written from Ladysmith, is an insert.

B160   BUTLER, Ruth, and GILBERT, Don
FOR VALOUR: Kidderminster's Four VCs
Veldonn Printers, Kidderminster, Worcestershire (*printer*), nd (c2000)
24 pp, photos, maps, sb, cr

Biographical sketches of three VCs who were born in Kidderminster and the one VC who was born in nearby Stourbridge. They are BTT Lawrence, E Jotham, EF Baxter and JF Young. The booklet is illustrated with 37 photographs.

C5   CAIRNES, Captain W.E.
LORD ROBERTS AS A SOLDIER IN PEACE AND WAR: A Biography
Hodder & Stoughton, London, 1901
331 pp, maps, hb, cr

A concise biography of Lord Roberts VC which concentrates on his military career from Sandhurst to the Boer War (1900).

C6   CAMERON, Alison
JOHN ERSKINE VC OF DUNFERMLINE
Privately published, Dunfermline, 2003
33 pp, photos, maps, sb, cr

This desktop produced A5-sized booklet briefly describes the life, VC action and death of Sgt John Erskine who won his VC at Givenchy in June 1916 while serving with the Cameronians. He was killed in action near Arras in April 1917. The publication includes reproductions of documents, maps and photographs, some of which are in colour.

C7   CAMPBELL, Commander A.B.
ZEEBRUGGE: St George's Day 1918
Oxford University Press, London, 1940
40 pp, drawing, sb, cr

This volume within the *Great Exploits* series is devoted to the raid on Zeebrugge on 23 April 1918. Short accounts of the associated VC deeds are given in the context of the operation but particular focus is on the role of HMS *Vindictive* and its commander, Capt AFB Carpenter, who also won the VC.

C8   CAMPBELL, Arthur F., MC
THE SIEGE: A Story from Kohima
George Allen & Unwin, London, 1956
212 pp, photos, maps, hb, cr

This book describes the siege of Kohima and, in particular, the involvement of the 4th Battalion Royal West Kent Regiment. Chapter 2 (pages 23-35) entitled *John Harman* and Chapter 9 (pages 96-108) entitled *John Harman Dies* concern L/Cpl J Harman's participation in the battle which resulted in him winning a posthumous VC.

C9   CAMPBELL, Christopher
ACES AND AIRCRAFT OF WORLD WAR I
Blandford Press, Poole, 1981
144 pp, photos, drawings, hb, cr

This profusely-illustrated volume, which analyses the development of air fighting during WW1, features detailed accounts of the life and career of 29 prominent WW1 fighter pilots representing Great Britain and the Empire, Belgium, France, Italy, Russia, USA, Germany and Austria-Hungary. Each biography gives extensive coverage of the individual's military service and awards and is supplemented by photographs and artist drawings, which include a full-colour profile of their aircraft. Five VC recipients are featured: Hawker (pages 52-55), Ball (pages 56-60), Bishop (pages 80-83), McCudden (pages 113-115) and Barker (pages 136-139).

C10   CAMPBELL, Rear Admiral Gordon, VC DSO
[1] MY MYSTERY SHIPS
Hodder & Stoughton, London, 1928
300 pp, photos, sketches, maps, hb, cr
[2] WIR JAGEN DEUTSCHE U-BOOTE (*German edition*)
C. Bertelsmann, Gütersloh, Germany 1937
234 pp, photos, sketches, maps, hb, cr (*German text*)

Gordon Campbell relates his experiences in *Q* ships in WW1 and gives a full account of his ships' engagements with the enemy. He also describes the day-to-day life on board *Q* ships. Maps, sketches and photos support the accounts relating to the key actions. The decorations awarded for each action are listed and the Appendix contains full *London Gazette* extracts describing the VC actions of Campbell, CG Bonner, W Williams, EH Pitcher, RN Stuart. A German edition was published in 1937. Also a French edition was published in Paris.

C11   CAMPBELL, Rear Admiral Gordon, VC DSO MP
NUMBER THIRTEEN: Being the Autobiography of Rear Admiral Gordon Campbell VC DSO MP
Hodder & Stoughton, London, 1932
352 pp, photos, index, hb, cr

In this autobiography Campbell describes his early days and then concentrates on detailing his naval career. In particular, he recalls his experiences in *Q* ships during WW1 and then recounts his post-war naval service at home and overseas. Stationed in the West Indies and, later, in South Africa allowed him to travel extensively. On retiring from the Navy, he embarked on lecturing in the USA and Canada, an account of which concludes the book.

C12   CAMPBELL, Vice Admiral Gordon, VC DSO MP
SAILORMEN ALL
Hodder & Stoughton, London, 1933
301 pp, photos, sketches, index, hb, cr

A selection of stories of stirring naval adventures of particular vessels and the gallant deeds of their men, which span the sixteenth century up to WW1. Chapter IX (pages 117-125) describes the VC exploits of Lt WE Sanders in the *Q* ship HMS *Prize*. Chapter XVIII (pages 254-264) relates to the VC action of HM Submarine *E11* commanded by Nasmith. Chapter XIX (pages 265-280) covers the Zeebrugge raid in April 1918 and in particular the VC action of HMS *Vindictive* commanded by Capt AFB Carpenter.

C15   CANADIAN SCOTTISH REGIMENT (PRINCESS MARY'S) REGIMENTAL MUSEUM
FOR VALOUR
The Canadian Scottish Regiment (Princess Mary's) Regimental Museum, Vancouver, 1998
16 pp, sb, cr

A booklet to commemorate a VC exhibition at the museum 9-15 November 1998. There are short biographies and photos of the following VCs: WH Metcalf, WJ Milne, CW Peck, JC Richardson, J MacGregor, GR Pearkes. In addition there is a short biography and photo of Field Marshal Viscount Byng of Vimy whose orders, decorations and medals were also on display.

C17   CANVET PUBLICATIONS
         VICTORIA CROSS
         Canvet Publications Ltd, Kanata, Ontario, Canada, 2014
         96 pp, photos (some colour), paintings, maps, sb, ncr

This A4 magazine-format publication, from the publishers of Legion Magazine, is dedicated to 98 Canadian VCs. The publication comprises mainly photos, paintings and maps with some text. Following an Introduction there are eight chapters covering the VC recipients with three maps showing locations of awards. There are specially commissioned head and shoulder portraits of each recipient. These are shown throughout the text and summarized on pages 94 and 95. There is also a two-sided fold-out colour wall poster at the back of the publication.

C18   CARDOZO, Major-General Ian, AVSM SM
         THE BRAVEST OF THE BRAVE: The Extraordinary Story of Indian VCs of World War I
         Bloomsbury Publishing India, Pvt Ltd, New Delhi, 2016
         118 pp, photos, map, hb, cr

This volume comprises principally biographies of the 11 Indian VC recipients of the Indian Army in WW1. The first two chapters (up to page 36) relate the history of the VC awarded to Indian soldiers and an overview of India's participation in WW1. Each of Chapters 4 to 14 is devoted to an individual recipient, the biography for whom provides a detailed account of his VC action (including the gazetted citation), his record of military service and an account of his early and later life. Annexure 5 records the Indian winners of the VC in Waziristan (1) and in WW2 (28). Annexure 6 gives brief details of the eight British personnel of the Indian Army awarded the VC in WW1 and of the nine British Army recipients of the VC in WW1 who were subsequently appointed to the Indian Army.

C19   CAREW, Tim
         THE GLORIOUS GLOSTERS
         Leo Cooper, London, 1970
         175 pp, photos, maps, index, hb, cr

In this history of the Gloucestershire Regiment from 1945-1970, substantial coverage is given to Colonel Carne's command of the 1st Battalion in Korea (pages 43-119) during which he won the VC and DSO. Detailed accounts of the Battalion's operations under his command are chronicled, including the posthumous VC action of Lt PKE Curtis who was serving with 'A' Company during this period.

C20   CAREW, Tim
         KOREA: The Commonwealth at War
         Cassell, London, 1967
         307 pp, photos, maps, index, hb, cr

This book gives an overview of the major actions involving British units in the Korean War. Much of the text is based on interviews with participants. The actions of the four VC winners (Carne, Muir, Curtis and Speakman) are documented.

C21   CARPENTER, Captain A.F.B., VC RN
         THE BLOCKING OF ZEEBRUGGE
         Herbert Jenkins, London, 1921
         295 pp, photos, sketches, maps, index, hb, cr

The story of the naval operation in April 1918 to block the port of Zeebrugge. Carpenter was the commander of HMS *Vindictive* which played a key role in the action for which he received the VC. The book describes in detail both the rationale for the operation and each of its phases. Brief references are made to the other VCs awarded for the operation. Reviewed in V52.

C22   CARR, William Guy
BY GUESS AND BY GOD: The Story of British Submarines in the War
Hutchinson, London, 1930
288 pp, photos, index, hb, cr

Written by a submarine navigation officer, the book describes Royal Navy Submarine Service operations during WW1 and recounts life on board submarines on active service. Amongst the numerous submariner actions described are the exploits (including the VC deeds) of Boyle, Holbrook, Nasmith and Sandford.

C23   CARR, William Guy
OUT OF THE MISTS: Great Deeds of the Navy in the Last War and Her Role Today
Hutchinson, London, nd (c1941)
176 pp, photos, index, hb, cr

This book describes the work of the RNAS and Harwich Flotillas in the North Sea in 1917/1918. Chapter 3 (pages 43-47) describes the action for which Skipper T Crisp DSC RNR won the VC. It also contains a 15 page glossary of names and phrases used at sea by the RN and Merchant Navy.

C25   CARTON DE WIART, Lieutenant General Sir Adrian, VC KBE CB CMG DSO
HAPPY ODYSSEY: The Memoirs of Lieutenant General Sir Adrian Carton De Wiart VC KBE CB CMG DSO
Jonathan Cape, London, 1950
287 pp, photo, index, hb, cr

An autobiography of Carton de Wiart's early life and military career. He describes his many active service experiences in the Boer War, WW1 in Somaliland and Europe and WW2 including his time as a POW and his subsequent service in China. In recalling his time in captivity he refers to his fellow POW and VC holder, General Neame. Reviewed in V61.

C26   CARVER, Field Marshal Sir Michael (*editor*)
THE WAR LORDS: Military Commanders of the Twentieth Century
Weidenfeld & Nicolson, London, 1976
624 pp, photos, index, hb, cr

This work comprises biographical portraits of 43 of the great commanders of WW1 and WW2. The main criterion for their inclusion is that they have exercised command of a considerable force in an important campaign. The 42nd chapter (pages 582-595) is devoted to Lt Gen Lord Freyberg VC whose distinguished service and achievements spanning the two world wars are discussed.

C30   CAVE, Joy B.
TWO NEWFOUNDLAND VCs
Creative Printers & Publishers, St John's, Newfoundland, 1984
95 pp, photos, maps, sb, cr

This book covers in detail the lives of John B Croak VC and Thomas R Ricketts VC. In particular, it documents fully the VC deeds and the background to the action. Ricketts survived the war, but Croak was killed in action. A poem dedicated to Ricketts is included.

C32   CAVE, Colonel Terry, CBE
CEMETERIES AND MEMORIALS IN BELGIUM WHERE VCs ARE BURIED OR COMMEMORATED (MILITARY FACT SHEET No 3)
The Western Front Association, 1984
6 pp, sb, ncr

This publication has two tables with brief details of 41 VC recipients with memorials in Belgium. The first has the names in alphabetical order with rank, unit, brigade, division and the cemetery/memorial. The second table lists the cemeteries/memorials in alphabetical order with the name of the VC, the place and date of action and the date of death (see S24, S25, S26 and S27).

C33   CAWDRON, Hugh, FRIBA FRSA
BASED AT BURN (*republished as* **BASED AT BURN Mk II**)
The 578 Burn Association, Staines, nd (c1995) (Mk II, 2001)
First edition 431 pp. (Mk II edition: 497 pp.), photos, drawings, plans, paintings, index, hb, cr

A history of No 578 Squadron, Royal Air Force, which was formed in January 1944 and was stood down in March 1945. Based at RAF Station Burn, North Yorkshire, the Squadron flew Halifaxes and during its 14 months' operational service earned one VC, two DSOs, 143 DFCs and 79 DFMs. The history includes recollections of former squadron and station personnel. A separate chapter (pages 132 to 154) is devoted to the life and service of Pilot Officer CJ Barton who earned a posthumous VC with the Squadron, the deed for which is described in detail. Additionally, significant references to Barton and to his VC action are also made within the recollections elsewhere in the book. The Mk II edition of the work contains considerable additional research and recollections.

C34   CAWTHORNE, Nigel
[1] **HEROES: The True Stories Behind Every VC Winner Since World War Two** (*original edition*)
John Blake Publishing, London, 2007
287 pp, sb, cr
[2] **VC HEROES: The True Stories Behind Every VC Winner Since World War Two** (*updated edition*)
John Blake Publishing, London, 2012
303 pp, sb, cr

The original (2007) edition features biographies of the 14 post-WW2 VCs up to 2007. Arranged by campaign, the biographies are in the form of individual chapters and one joint chapter: Korea (Muir, Carne & Curtis, Speakman); Malaya (Limbu); Vietnam (Wheatley, Badcoe, Simpson, Payne); Falklands (Jones, McKay); Iraq (Beharry); and Afghanistan (Budd, Apiata). The updated (2012) edition features two further VCs for Afghanistan: Donaldson (2008) and Roberts-Smith (2010). Chapters vary in length (10-27 pages) but most comprise about 20 pages.

C35   CAWTHORNE, Nigel
TOO BRAVE TO LIVE, TOO YOUNG TO DIE: Teenage Heroes from World War I
Metro Publishing (John Blake Publishing), London, 2015
287 pp, hb, cr

Each of the 28 chapters of this book is devoted to a WWI VC recipient who at the time of his VC deed was under the age of 20 years old. The chapters arranged chronologically by date of deed, provide recipients' biographical information and details of their VC deed set in the context of the battle or action.

C36   CHADDERTON, H. Clifford, OC CAE
HANGING A LEGEND: The National Film Board's shameful attempt to discredit Billy Bishop VC
War Amputations of Canada, Ottawa, 1986
371 pp, photos, sketches, maps, sb, cr

This book was written to rebuff *The Kid Who Couldn't Miss* - a film made by the National Film Board of Canada in which it was alleged that Billy Bishop lied about his score of combat victories. The book argues well Bishop's case and includes 24 research documents in support. See M1B.

C37   CHALMERS, Bradley A.
"NEXT TO IMPOSSIBLE": The remarkable life of Albert Chalmers Borella VC
Published by author, Australia, 2015
510 pp, photos, maps, index, hb, cr

This is a very detailed biography of AC Borella who was awarded the VC for gallantry at Villiers-Bretonneux on 16 September 1918, during which he led his men against superior numbers, capturing a trench and two large dug-outs. The volume traces Borella's early life and his time as a surveyor in the Northern Territory of Australia. Borella travelled 1,000 miles to enlist in the AIF in Darwin. He was part of the ANZAC force at Gallipoli before being evacuated to France where he won the MM near Baupame in 1917. He was commissioned before winning the VC. The volume includes a detailed history of the Borella family. Reviewed in V77.

C40   CHAMBERLAIN, W.M.
VICTORIA CROSS WINNERS OF NEW ZEALAND
Military Historical Society of Australia, Ormond East, Victoria, Australia, 1967
41 pp, photos, map, sb, cr

All 23 New Zealander VCs are featured. The text (which is in typescript) comprises for each recipient the full citation only and is accompanied by poorly-reproduced portrait photographs. Additionally, the 23 recipients of the New Zealand Cross are listed and a brief account of each associated deed is given.

C43   CHAPMAN, David Ian
ONE CROWDED HOUR: Jack Cornwell, The Boy VC
Leyton & Leytonstone Historical Society, 2006
20 pp, photos, sb, cr

This *Occasional Publication No 4* of the Society is, predominantly, a short biography of Boy 1st Class JT Cornwell. After documenting his family background, early years and schooling, it then concentrates on his service in the Royal Navy and the Battle of Jutland in which he performed his VC deed. His funeral and reburial in Manor Park Cemetery are described and details of some memorials to him are recorded. The booklet also covers three other locally-associated VCs: five pages are devoted to GA Mitchell who attended the same school as Cornwell and two pages are shared between P Mullane and EK Myles.

C44   CHANCELLERY OF HONOURS
        PRO VALORE: Canada's Victoria Cross
        Chancellery of Honours, Ottawa, Canada, 2008
        34 pp, (English) and 34 pp, (French), photos (some colour), sb, ncr

This bi-lingual publication describes the Canada Victoria Cross, instituted in 1993 and similar in constitution to the Victoria Cross for Australia and the Victoria Cross for New Zealand. There is a 15-page un-numbered chapter listing Canada's VC recipients between the Boer War and the end of WW2. The second chapter describes the manufacturing process to develop Canada's VC which has *Pro Valore* to replace *For Valour*. By February 2019 no awards had been made. The final chapter lists alphabetically Canada's VC recipients between 1900 and 1945.

C45   CHAPMAN, Commander, Paul, DSO OBE DSC* RN
        SUBMARINE TORBAY
        Robert Hale, London, 1989
        187 pp, photos, sketches, maps, index, hb, cr

The book describes the wartime exploits of HM Submarine *Torbay* and its commanding officer, Cdr (later Rear Adml Sir) ACC Miers who during his service in her was awarded the VC. The author was second-in-command of *Torbay*. The submarine's main area of operation was the Mediterranean and it landed Geoffrey Keyes (VC) on the North African coast for the ill-fated attack on Rommel's HQ. Miers was later accused of giving an order to gun down some marooned Germans, an account of which is documented. In a later book (see I60) these accusations were said to be false.

C46   CHAPMAN, Roger
        BEYOND THEIR DUTY: Heroes of the Green Howards
        The Green Howards Museum, Richmond, North Yorkshire, 2001
        92 pp, photos, maps, sb, cr

This book was published to coincide with a VC and GC exhibition in 2001 of all 18 VCs and 3 GCs won by the Green Howards. A chapter is dedicated to each recipient with photos, maps and specially commissioned pen and ink drawings illustrating each act of valour. Endnotes include all the LG citations with source material held by the Museum and other bodies. Reviewed in V52. See also G62.

C47   CHARTERED INSTITUTE OF BUILDING, The
        THE HISTORY OF ENGLEMERE
        The Chartered Institute of Building, Ascot, Berkshire, 1997
        12 pp, photos, sb, cr

This booklet tells the story of the history of Englemere, the HQ of the Institute of Building. The house, in Ascot, was the home of Field Marshal Lord Roberts VC from 1904 to 1914. Pages 6 to 9 cover Lord Roberts' time at the house. Page 12 has a photo of the unveiling of a plaque in 1997 in honour of Lord Roberts.

C48   CHATTERTON, E. Keeble
        Q SHIPS AND THEIR STORY
        Hurst & Blackett, London, 1923 (reprinted: Conway Maritime Press, 1972)
        276 pp, photos, sketches, maps, index, hb, cr

An account of the Royal Navy's *Q* ships, between 1915 and 1918 and a description of the bravery of their officers and men. The exploits of G Campbell VC and H Auten VC are covered extensively.

C50   CHESHIRE, Leonard, VC
[1] **THE FACE OF VICTORY**
Hutchinson, London, 1961
180 pp, photos, hb, cr
CHESHIRE, Leonard (translated into French by JOUAN, R)
[2] **L'ENVERS DE LA VICTOIRE** (*French edition*)
Editions France-Empire, Paris, 1961,
280 pp, sb, cr
CHESHIRE, Leonard (translated into German text by NOSTITZ, Oswalt von)
[3] **ES BEGANN IN DER LUFT: Aust Meinem Leben** (*German edition*)
Bluchdruckare Raber, Luzerne, 1962
205 pp, hb, cr

Group Captain Cheshire's war service is chronicled (pages 9-51) as a prelude to the main thrust of the book which details his search for the true religion culminating in his conversion to Roman Catholicism. The work also explains how the Cheshire Homes were established.

C51   CHESHIRE, Squadron Leader Leonard, DSO DFC
BOMBER PILOT
[1] Hutchinson, London, 1943
136 pp, photos, hb, cr
[2] Hutchinson, London, (*Services edition*)
127 pp, photos, hb, cr
[3] CHESHIRE, Group Captain Leonard, VC DSO DFC
Hutchinson, 1955
191 pp, photos, hb, cr
[4] CHESHIRE, Group Captain Leonard (translated into French by JOUAN, R)
PILOTE DE BOMBARDIER (*French edition*)
Presses Pocket, Paris, 1958
187 pp, photos, sb, cr

A chronicle of the author's 52 bombing flights over enemy territory between 1940 and 1943, which he wrote as a 24-year old Squadron Leader before his VC award. He also documents the day-to-day life as a bomber pilot flying Whitleys and Halifaxes. (See O68).

C52   CHESHIRE, Leonard
THE LIGHT OF MANY SUNS: The Meaning of the Bomb
Methuen, London, 1985
138 pp, photos, sketches, maps, index, hb, cr

The first part of this work is an account of events leading up to the dropping of the two atomic bombs on Japan. Group Captain Cheshire was the official British observer for the dropping of the second bomb at Nagasaki. Some personal details of Cheshire's early career are included. The second part relates to his views on the moral and ethical aspects of nuclear warfare.

C53   CHESHIRE, Group Captain Leonard G., VC OM DSO DFC
THE HIDDEN WORLD
Collins, London, 1981
154 pp, photos, maps, hb, cr

In this personal memoir, Cheshire describes his efforts to establish and develop his homes for the disabled and provides a significant insight into his mission and motivation.

C55　　CHORLTON, Martyn
BOMBER COMMAND: The Victoria Cross Raids
Countryside Books, Newbury, Berkshire, 2014
192 pp, photos, index, sb, cr

This volume has 23 chapters each describing the exploits of Bomber Command VCs of WW2. VCs featured are D Garland, D Grey, R Learoyd, J Hannah, H Edwards, J Ward, A Scarf, J Nettleton, L Manser, R Middleton, H Malcolm L Trent, G Gibson, A Aaron, W Reid, C Barton, N Jackson, A Mynarski, L Cheshire, I Bazalgette, R Palmer, G Thompson and E Swales. Reviewed in V75.

C58　　CHRISTIE, MANSON & WOODS (*publisher*)
AN EXHIBITION OF THE VICTORIA CROSS GROUP TO CAPTAIN WILLIAM LEEFE ROBINSON, ROYAL FLYING CORPS
Christie, Manson & Woods, London, 1988
32 pp, photos, sb, cr

This well-illustrated catalogue relates wholly to the exhibition of Captain WL Robinson's VC and medal group and memorabilia prior to their sale by Christie's on 22 November 1988. The text provides a biographical sketch of Robinson and is supported by transcripts of several letters of significance written by him. There are 30 photographs including one of his VC medal group.

C59　　CHURCH LADS' BRIGADE (*publisher*)
THE CHURCH LADS' BRIGADE AND THE VC
Church Lads' Brigade HQ, London, 1916
30 pp, photos, sb, cr

This small booklet is a record of seven VC recipients with a connection with the Church Lads' Brigade (EN Mellish, WRF Addison, E Barber, DW Belcher, J Hutchinson, AH Proctor and J Upton). Mellish and Addison were padres while the others were former cadets. The VC citation is given in each case and is accompanied by a portrait photograph of the recipient and a mention of their particular CLB company.

C60　　CITIZENS COMMITTEE, BELFAST CITY COUNCIL (*original publisher*)
THE GREAT WAR: A Tribute to Ulster's Heroes 1914-1918
Citizens Committee, Belfast City Council, 1919 (facsimile edition: Pretani Press, Belfast, 1991)
124 pp, photos, hb, cr

This book, reproduced on the 75th anniversary of the Battle of the Somme, remembers the courage of the Ulster regiments and Ulster men and women displayed during the Great War. A chapter (pages 103-119) is devoted to the Ulstermen who were awarded the VC: Nelson, Morrow, FW Hall, Somers, Sinton, Bingham, Cather, McFadzean, Quigg, ENF Bell, T Hughes, Dunville, Emerson, Gourley, Hanna, J Duffy, deWind, RA West. The information provided is limited to the recipients' VC citation and, typically, parents' names and place of residence.

C62   CLARK, Major Frank, A.O.
THROUGH HELL TO IMMORTALITY: A Story of the Crimean War and of the First Suffolk Soldier to Win the Victoria Cross
Leiston Press (Printer), Leiston, Suffolk, 1997
122 pp, photos, sb, cr

A biography of Sgt A Ablett VC DCM, who won his VC whilst serving with the Grenadier Guards in the Crimea. It provides a glimpse of the war and the part played in it by the Brigade of Guards and Ablett, in particular. His entire military career, subsequent service with the Millwall Docks Police, life in retirement and death are documented. Appendix 2 summarises the military career of Anthony Palmer VC, as replicated from his discharge papers.

C65   CLARK, R. KING-
GEORGE STUART HENDERSON: The Story of a Scottish Soldier 1893-1920
Campbell Bros (Printers) Ltd, Cumbernauld, 1975
169 pp, photos, maps, sb, cr

A biography of Capt GS Henderson VC DSO MC who was killed at Hillah, Iraq, during the Arab rebellion in 1920 and was awarded a posthumous VC. It recalls his early years and chronicles extensively his military career which commenced at RMC Sandhurst in 1912.

C70   CLARKE, Robert Sterling and SOWERBY, Arthur de C.
THROUGH SHÊN-KAN: The Account of the Clark Expedition to North China 1908-9
T. Fisher Unwin, London, 1912
414 pp, photos, drawings, maps, sb, cr

This volume describes a 16-month expedition across North China in 1908/09. A group of 36 men was led by Robert Sterling Clark (1877-1956) heir to the Singer Sewing Machine Company. The scientific expedition travelled over 2,000 miles. A key member of the expedition was HEM Douglas VC who won his award on 11 December 1899 at Magersfontein. He went as the expedition's doctor and meteorologist. The team travelled mainly on horses and mules collecting zoological and botanical specimens while recording meteorological data and mapping this then unchartered area of China. The volume was reprinted in 2013.

C75   CLAYTON, Ann
CHAVASSE - DOUBLE VC
Leo Cooper, London, 1992
261 pp, photos, sketches, maps, index, hb, cr

A comprehensive study of Capt Noel Chavasse VC and bar MC, spanning his early years, his time as an undergraduate qualifying as a doctor and his military service in WW1 during which he was killed in action. The author had access to family and other papers, including Chavasse's letters from the front, which are quoted extensively. The study also covers the background of his family whose genealogical table is included.

C76   CLAYTON, Ann
MARTIN-LEAKE DOUBLE VC
Leo Cooper, London, 1994
250 pp, photos, maps, index, hb, cr

This companion volume to C75 is a comprehensive biography of Lt Col Arthur Martin-Leake VC and bar, who served in the Boer War (VC), the Balkans and WW1 (bar to VC). The author has drawn much on the many letters written by Martin-Leake, extracts of which are replicated in the study. Martin-Leake's family background is documented and is supported by a family tree.

C77   CLAYTON, Ann (*editor*)
LIVERPOOL HEROES BOOK 1: The Stories of 16 Liverpool Holders of the Victoria Cross
Noel Chavasse VC Memorial Association, Liverpool, 2006
108 pp, photos, sb, cr

This book was published to raise funds for the Noel Chavasse VC Memorial. The Introduction and chapter on the VC were written by the late Sid Lindsay who had researched the Liverpool VCs and printed his findings in L42. The editor and her team drew on Sid Lindsay's material for 16 of the VCs. The VCs featured are NG Chavasse, J Kirk, AS Jones, W Connolly, F Whirlpool, C Anderson, G Hinkley, EW Alexander, A White, RN Stuart, W Ratcliffe, CE Gourley, HM McKenzie, PA Kenna and GG Coury. See C78.

C78   CLAYTON, Ann (*editor*)
LIVERPOOL HEROES BOOK 2: The Stories of 18 Liverpool Holders of the Victoria Cross
Noel Chavasse VC Memorial Association, Liverpool, 2007
110 pp, photos, maps, sb, cr

This is a sequel to C77 and contains short biographies of 18 more VC holders with a connection with Liverpool. There are also amendments to C77 based on more accurate information and three appendices, one of which gives a short history of the VC. The chapter on AHL Richardson reveals an imposter based in Aberdeen and only after he had been given a funeral with military honours did the real Arthur Richardson come forward and as a result was reunited with his estranged family. Other VCs featured are EF Baxter, ENF Bell, CH Cowley, ES Dougall, W Dowling, A Evans, DD Farmer, JV Holland, AM Lafone, F Lester, RG Masters, P Mylott, TP Neeley, GE Nurse, AH Procter, J Prosser and JA Sinton. Reviewed in V60.

C79   CLAYTON, Ann (*editor*)
LIVERPOOL HEROES BOOK 3: 17 Liverpool Heroes of the Victoria Cross
Noel Chavasse VC Memorial Association, Liverpool, 2009
112 pp, photos, maps, sb, cr

This is the third volume on Liverpool VCs (see C77 and C78). Pages 7 to 46 contain short biographies of PE Bent, CG Bonner, C Bushell, WN Cosgrove, WLa. Congreve, EC Cookson, JT Counter, JT Davies, CC Foss, IE Fraser, CW Gunn, H Hampton, HJ Knight, JS Knox, A Moynihan, JO'Neill and E Unwin. An Addendum provides additional information on some recipients in C77 and C78 and also corrects some errors. Appendix 1 describes the background to the book and a short history of the VC. Appendix 2 describes with photographs the Noel Chavasse VC* memorial unveiled on 17 August 2008.

C80   CLAYTON, Ann (*editor*)
LIVERPOOL HEROES Book 4: 17 holders of the Victoria Cross with Merseyside Connections
Noel Chavasse VC Memorial Association, Liverpool, 2010
120 pp, photos, maps, sb, cr

This is the fourth volume on Liverpool VCs (see C77, C78 and C79). The geographical scope goes beyond Liverpool to Merseyside and into parts of Lancashire and Cheshire. Brief biographics include H Ackroyd, DMW Beak, HP Boughey, WA Sandys-Clarke, E Esmonde, N Harvey, WE Heaton, TA Jones, J Lucas, J Molyneux, T Mottershead, W Norman, J Readitt, OA Reid, AE Sephton, J Tombs and Lt T Wilkinson. Pages 101 to 114 contain an Addendum which provides additional information to recipients covered in the previous three volumes in the series.

C80A   CLAYTON, Carl
KIPPER VC: The Life and Times of Rear Admiral Eric Robinson VC 1882-1965
Published by the author, 2015 (revised 2017)
38 pp. text and 6 pp. (illustrations), photos, drawings, sb, cr

This biography describes his early years and then charts his naval career after joining HMS *Britannia* as a cadet in 1897. In particular, it provides full coverage of his service in China in 1900, WW1, Russia in 1917-19, the inter-war years and WW2. It concludes with his life in retirement up to his death in 1965.

C81   CLIFF, Dr K. S.
MR LOCK THE HATTER: Victoria Cross Holders 1856 - 1919
Published by the author, 2012
44 pp, photos, sb, ncr

The author is a member of the famous hat maker, James Lock & Co Ltd, of St James's Street, London, which has been trading since 1676. The author researched ledgers between 1856 and 1919 and identified 27 VCs. For each recipient there is a brief biography, VC citation and details of headwear supplied. Also included is a history of the hatting business and the origins of the VC. Reviewed in V70.

C82   CLIFFORD, Hugh
THE HOUSE OF CLIFFORD: From Before the Conquest
Phillimore, Chichester, 1987
320 pp, photos, index, hb, cr

The author, the 13th Lord Clifford of Chudleigh, OBE DL, traces the lineage and provides biographical accounts and, where available, portraits of the Barons Clifford of Chudleigh, and their forebears and issue from 1066. Chapter 45 relates to Maj Gen Sir Henry Clifford VC (of the 27th generation and son of the 7th Baron) and details his issue.

C83   CLIMO, Percy L.
LET US REMEMBER: Lively Letters from World War One
Privately published, Ontario, Canada, 1990
374 pp, photos, index, hb, cr

The first part of this book is a print of *With the First Canadian Contingent*, originally published by Hodder & Stoughton and The Musson Book Company, Toronto in 1915. The second part contains letters, primarily from servicemen from the Coburg area of Ontario. The third part is mainly devoted to the exploits and later life of Captain CS Rutherford VC MC MM.

C84   COATES, Thomas F.G.
SIR GEORGE WHITE VC: The Hero of Ladysmith
Grant Richards, London, 1900
290 pp, photos, hb, cr

A concise biography of General Sir George White VC up to April 1900. After describing his family background and characteristics, this narrative then concentrates on detailing his distinguished military career from 1853 up to his return home from the South African War.

C85 COBBAN, J. MacLaren
THE LIFE AND DEEDS OF EARL ROBERTS VC KG KP GCB GCSI GCIE, FIELD MARSHAL AND COMMANDER-IN-CHIEF
Blackwood, Le Bas & Co, London, 1901 / TC & EC Jack, Edinburgh, 1901
Four volumes: 863 pp. (Vol 1: 243 pp.; Vol 2: 228 pp.; Vol 3: 192 pp.; Vol 4: 200 pp.), photos, sketches, maps, hb, cr

A comprehensive and well-illustrated biography in 4 volumes:
Volume 1: To the End of the Indian Mutiny (covers his family background, early years and service in the Indian Mutiny)
Volume 2: To the Abdication of Yakub Khan (covers his continuing service in India, and his campaigns in Abyssinia and Afghanistan)
Volume 3: To the End of Lord Roberts' Indian Career (covers his continuing role in the Afghan War up to the end of his 41 years in India)
Volume 4: To Lord Roberts' Reign in Pall Mall (relates to his service in the South African War and to his return to the UK).

C86 COETZER, Owen
THE ANGLO-BOER WAR: The Road to Infamy 1899-1900
Arms & Armour Press, London, 1996 / William Waterman Publications, South Africa, 1996
294 pp, photos, sketch, map, index, hb, cr

An investigative study into the controversial strategies, directives, opinions and reports of the Boer War generals, particularly Lord Roberts VC, Sir George White VC and Sir Redvers Buller VC. Details of the resultant Commission of Enquiry and parliamentary debate are featured. There is also a chapter (pages 96-102) on the VC heroes of 1899-1900 with predominant coverage of Lt Hon FHS Roberts.

C90 COGHILL, Patrick (*compiler*)
WHOM THE GODS LOVE: A Memoir of Lieutenant Nevill Josiah Aylmer Coghill VC, the 24th Regiment, 1852-1879
Privately published, Halesowen, Worcestershire, 1968
126 pp, photos, index, hb, cr

A memoir of Lt Coghill VC compiled by his nephew and based on his letters, diaries and family papers and traditions up to his death in 1879.

C92 COLBOURNE, Roger
CHARLES HARRY COVERDALE 1888-1955
OMRS North, 2002
6pp, photos, sb, cr

A short biography of Captain CH Coverdale VC MM, West Riding Home Guard, late Manchester Regiment. This booklet was prepared as part of a display for the first official Orders and Medals Research Society event of the OMRS Diamond Jubilee Year.

C94 COLE, Christopher
McCUDDEN VC
William Kimber, London, 1967
224 pp, photos, sketches, maps, index, hb, cr

A detailed biography of one of the most successful Allied fighter pilots in WW1. The book also gives an in-depth account of air fighting from 1914 to 1918. The appendices include details of McCudden's air combat victories, aircraft flown and aircraft markings.

C95 COLEMAN, E. C.
NO PYRRHIC VICTORIES: The 1918 Raids on Zeebrugge and Ostend - A Radical Reappraisal
Spellmount (The History Press), Stroud, 2014
318 pp, photos, drawings, maps, sb, cr

A comprehensive re-examination of the raids on Zeebrugge and Ostend on 23 April 1918 and on Ostend on 9/10 May 1918. It documents the raids' rationale and challenges, the planning and the preparation. The execution of the attacks and the outcome are described thoroughly. Chapter 13 includes an examination of the recommendations for awards. The Epilogue contains biographical sketches of notable staff and decorated personnel, including the eleven VC recipients.

C97 COLES, Alan
SLAUGHTER AT SEA: The Truth Behind a Naval War Crime
Robert Hale, London, 1986
220 pp, photos, index, hb, cr

A detailed account of the attack, in 1915, on the German U-boat U27 by the *Q* ship *Baralong*, disguised as a US merchantman. The attack caused an international diplomatic furore and resulted in allegations that the crew of the *Baralong* murdered in cold blood some of the U-boat survivors. Lt G Steele (later VC) was in charge of a gun crew of the *Baralong* during the attack and, as the last known survivor, reveals his version of the affair.

C99 COLLISTER, Peter
'HELLFIRE JACK!' VC: The Life and Times of General Sir William Olpherts VC GCB 1822-1902
British Association for Cemeteries in South Asia, London, 1989
182 pp, photos, sketches, maps, sb, cr

A biography of General Olpherts VC and, in particular, covering his life and his distinguished military career in the Crimea and the various campaigns in India and on its frontier.

C100 COLMAN, Mike
PAYNE VC: The Story of Australia's most decorated soldier of the Vietnam War
ABC Books, Sydney, Australia, 2009
244 pp, photos, index, sb, cr

A full and authoritative biography of Keith Payne VC whose war service induced Korea, Malaya, Vietnam and Dhofar. This biography covers his early life, service career in detail and his life after army service and deals with his triumph over a decade of alcohol and prescription drug abuse, caused by post traumatic stress. The last chapter covers the sale of Payne's VC and the public reaction to the sale of VCs in general. Reviewed in V65.

C101 COLQUOHOUN, Frank, MA
THE AIR PILOT'S DECISION: The Story of Cyril Barton VC
Pickering and Inglis, London, nd (c1944)
25 pp, photo, sb, cr

This small booklet, No 28 in the *WSMU Series for officers and others*, relates the short life of Pilot Officer Cyril Barton who won the VC posthumously. In addition to recalling his RAF service and VC action, the booklet also reviews his life as a committed Christian.

C102   COLVILLE, J.R.
MAN OF VALOUR: The Life of Field Marshal The Viscount Gort VC GCB DSO MVO MC
Collins, London, 1972
285 pp, photos, maps, index, hb, cr

A full biography of Gort who won the VC, DSO and two bars and the MC in WW1 and in 1939 was appointed C-in-C BEF in France. The book documents, in particular, his service in WW1, the inter-war years, BEF command and Dunkirk and his subsequent appointments as Governor of Gibraltar, Governor of Malta and finally High Commissioner of Palestine. Chapter 3 (pages 40-48) entitled *The Victoria Cross*, describes Gort's VC action.

C103   COMMONWEALTH DEPARTMENT OF VETERANS' AFFAIRS (*publisher*)
ORDER OF SERVICE: CORPORAL JOHN ALEXANDER FRENCH, 2/9TH BATTALION
Commonwealth Department of Veterans' Affairs, Canberra, 1995
12 pp, photos, sketches, sb, cr

This Order of Service booklet was produced for the wreath laying ceremony at Milne Bay on 9 July 1995. The text on Cpl French's VC action is authored by Dr Richard Reid of the Australian War Memorial. The booklet is part of the *Australia Remembers 1945-1995* series (see C104).

C104   COMMONWEALTH DEPARTMENT OF VETERANS' AFFAIRS (*publisher*)
ORDER OF SERVICE: TWO VICTORIA CROSSES, PAPUA NEW GUINEA, 1945
Commonwealth Department of Veterans' Affairs, Canberra, 1995
12 pp, photos, sketch, sb, cr

This Order of Service booklet was produced for the plaque unveiling ceremony to commemorate Pte E Kenna VC and Lt A Chowne VC MM at Mission Hill, Wewak, 8 July 1995. The text on the VC actions is authored by Dr Richard Reid of the Australian War Memorial. The booklet is part of *The Australia Remembers 1945-1995* series (see C103).

C105   COMMONWEALTH WAR GRAVES COMMISSION (*publisher*)
RECIPIENTS OF THE VICTORIA CROSS AND RECIPIENTS OF THE GEORGE CROSS IN THE CARE OF THE COMMONWEALTH WAR GRAVES COMMISSION
Commonwealth War Graves Commission, Maidenhead, 2004
136 pp, index, sb, ncr

The first part of the document is a listing of all 373 VCs whose grave or memorial is in the care of the Commission (261 for WW1 and 112 for WW2). The list is arranged alphabetically by country and location of grave or memorial. For each recipient, basic personal details are included together with place and date of death, parents' names and address and the plot/panel reference of the grave/memorial. An extract of the VC citation in *The London Gazette* is also provided. The second part of the document similarly lists 71 recipients of the George Cross. This addendum added in 2004 is a supplement to a 1997 edition which covered only VC recipients.

C105A   COMMONWEALTH WAR GRAVES COMMISSION (*publisher*)
RECIPIENTS OF THE VICTORIA CROSS IN THE CARE OF THE COMMONWEALTH WAR GRAVES COMMISSION
Commonwealth War Graves Commission, Maidenhead, 1997
97 numbered pages, plus 6 pages of unnumbered index, sb, ncr

This book lists all 376 VCs whose grave or memorial is in the care of the CWGC (263 for WW1, 112 for WW2 and one non-world war casualty). The format is the same as C105 and this is an earlier and shorter version of that book.

C106   COMPTON-HALL, Richard
SUBMARINES AND THE WAR AT SEA
Macmillan, London, 1991
345 pp, photos, index, hb, cr

A history of submarine warfare in WWI, focusing on tactics, exploits and personalities. Detailed accounts of the VC deeds of Nasmith, Holbrook and Sandford are narrated in the context of the campaign.

C107   CONGREVE, Commander Sir Geoffrey Cecil (Edited by Mrs MA Hodson and Major ACJ Congreve)
THE CONGREVE FAMILY
Privately printed, 1980
144 pp, photos, hb, cr

A family history of the Congreve family from 1315 to 1980. There are three pages devoted to WN Congreve VC for whom there are also three photographs. There is only a brief mention and one photograph of William La Touche Congreve VC.

C108   COOK, Graeme
WINGS OF GLORY: Stories of Air Adventures
Hart-Davis, McGibbon, London, nd (c1976)
151 pp, photos, index, hb, cr

This book's ten chapters focus mainly on the exploits of well-known aviators of WW1 and WW2. Five chapters relate wholly to VC recipients: Chap 1 (pages 14-26) - Ball; Chap 2 (pages 27-42) - Warneford and Robinson; Chap 5 (pages 77-84) - Esmonde; Chap 9 (pages 124-136) - Gibson; Chap 10 (pages 137-149) - Hannah, Jackson and Hornell.

C108A   COOK, Graeme
AIR ADVENTURES: Landmarks in the True Story of Flight
Macdonald & Janes, London, 1973
203 pp, drawings, hb, cr

A selection of stories about notable aviators and aviation events. Individual chapters are devoted to three VC recipients: Ball (Chapter 1), Mannock (Chapter 4) and Gibson (Chapter 13). The deeds of six other VC recipients are narrated in thematic chapters: RAJ Warneford, WL Robinson, EJB Nicolson, J Hannah, NC Jackson and DE Hornell.

C109   COOK, Graeme
SURVIVAL AGAINST THE ODDS
Harwood-Stuart Publishing, Lewes, Sussex, 1975
146 pp, hb, ncr

This work recalls the exploits of six Allied servicemen in WW2 who survived desperate situations in which death seemed inevitable and were decorated for their bravery. Chapter 3 (pages 40-57) is devoted to the VC action of Sqn Ldr Nettleton.

C110   COOK, Graeme
NONE BUT THE VALIANT: Stories of War at Sea
Rupert Hart-Davis, London, 1972
151 pp, photos, hb, cr

A selection of stories of gallant sailors and the battles in which they fought during the two world wars. The stories are arranged in ten chapters, six of which relate to specific VC actions: Chapter 1 (Nasmith), Chapter 2 (Sanders and Campbell), Chapter 6 (Warburton-Lee), Chapter 8 (Ryder and Beattie), Chapter 9 (Cameron and Place), Chapter 10 (Esmonde).

C111   COOK, Graeme
SILENT MARAUDERS: British Submarines in the Two World Wars
Hart-Davis, MacGibbon, London, 1976
159 pp, hb, cr

An account of the war exploits of notable submariners and *X-craft* crews and, in particular, those who won the VC. The book has three parts: Part 1 covers WW1 submariners (Holbrook, Boyle, Nasmith and Sandford); Part 2 - WW2 submariners (Wanklyn, Linton, Miers, Roberts and Gould). Part 3 - Midget submarines (Cameron, Place, Fraser and Magennis). The VC actions are described in detail.

C112   COOK, Graeme
MISSIONS MOST SECRET
Harwood-Smart Publishing, Blandford, Dorset, 1976
186 pp, hb, cr

A collection of true stories of courageous men who, during WW1 or WW2, risked their life on daring secret missions into enemy territory. Chapter 4 (pages 109-144) is devoted to Cdr Gordon Campbell VC and his *Q* ship service. Chapter 5 (pages 145-185) describes Agar's VC action and service in the Baltic Sea in 1919.

C113   COOKE, Arthur Owens
THE STORY OF LORD ROBERTS
Oxford University Press/Hodder and Stoughton, London, 1915
95 pp, hb, cr

A brief biography of Lord Roberts VC, in the *Herbert Strang's Readers* series for the young.

C113A   COOKE, Walter
CONTEMPT FOR DANGER: Legends of Victoria Cross Recipients and other Canadian Military Heroes
Published by author, Toronto, Canada, 2005
241 pp, sb, cr

A collection of short biographical sketches of Canadian military heroes including 92 VCs awarded to Canadians serving in either Canadian forces or with other Commonwealth countries. The entries vary in length and only those in excess of 300 words are cross referenced.

C113B COOKSEY, Jon
3 PARA MOUNT LONGDON: The Bloodiest Battle
Pen & Sword Military, Barnsley, 2004
109 pp, photos, maps, drawings, index, sb, cr

This lavishly-illustrated volume in the *Elite Forces Operations* series is the story of the 3rd Bn, Parachute Regiment's struggle for Mount Longdon in the 1982 Falklands conflict. During the battle Sgt Ian McKay won the VC posthumously. His exploit is fully described. See C113D.

C113C COOKSEY, Jon
OPERATION CHARIOT: The Raid on St Nazaire
Pen & Sword Military, Barnsley, 2005
128 pp, photos, illustrations (some colour), maps, index, sb, cr

This volume in the *Elite Forces Operations* series, describes the raid on the dry dock at St Nazaire on 27/28 March 1942. A total of five VCs were awarded for the operation: SH Beattie, RED Ryder, AC Newman, WA Savage and TF Durrant.

C113D COOKSEY, Jon
FALKLANDS HERO: Ian McKay - The Last VC of the 20th Century
Pen & Sword, Barnsley, 2012
262 pp, photos, index, hb, cr

A well researched and detailed biography of Ian McKay VC. The book traces McKay's family background and upbringing in South Yorkshire, his enlistment in the Parachute Regiment in 1970. Chapter 5 describes McKay's involvement in the Blood Sunday episode in Londonderry in January 1972 and subsequent enquiry. Chapters 8 to 11 describe McKay's involvement in the Falklands conflict including the battle to take Mount Longdon on 11/12 June 1982 for which he was awarded a posthumous VC. The volume includes detailed Notes, Appendices, Bibliography and Index. See C113B. Reviewed in V70.

C114 COOKSLEY, Peter G.
VCs OF THE FIRST WORLD WAR: THE AIR VCs
[1] Sutton Publishing, Stroud, 1996
204 pp, photos, index, hb, cr
[2] The History Press, Stroud, 2014
256 pp, photos, index, sb, cr

Arranged chronologically by date of VC deed, this book provides biographical accounts of the 19 air VCs of WW1. Many of the photographs and illustrations included are previously unpublished. Some technical details are included on aircraft types and markings. This book is part of the series *VCs of The First World War*. See G31 annotation, second paragraph.

C114A COOKSLEY, Peter G.
OPERATION THUNDERBOLT: The Nazi warships' escape 1942
Robert Hale, London, 1981
190 pp, photos, maps, index, hb, cr

This work tells the story of the dash through the English Channel by the German warships *Scharnhorst, Gneisenau* and *Prinz Eugen* in 1942 and the British attempts to destroy the vessels before they escaped. Detailed accounts describe the Beaufort and Swordfish attacks for which Fg Off K Campbell and Lt Cdr Esmonde were awarded the VC posthumously.

C115   COOPER, Alan W.

THE MEN WHO BREACHED THE DAMS: 617 Squadron *'The Dambusters'*

William Kimber, London, 1982

223 pp, photos, sketches, map, index, hb, cr

An account of 617 Squadron's raid on the Möhne, Eder and Sorpe dams in May 1943 for which its commander, Wg Cdr Guy Gibson, received the VC. The book describes in detail Barnes Wallis's idea of the bouncing bomb, the formation of 617 Squadron, the preparation for the raid, the raid itself and the outcome. The appendices record the aircraft participating in the raid, the awards gazetted and the service, promotions and awards of each participating crew member. See C116.

C116   COOPER, Alan W.

BEYOND THE DAMS TO THE TIRPITZ: The Later Operations of 617 Squadron

William Kimber, London, 1983

253 pp, photos, index, hb, cr

A companion volume to C115, this book chronicles 617 Squadron operations from July 1943 up to the end of the war. Wg Cdr Cheshire VC commanded the Squadron from November 1943 to July 1944 during which period he received the VC. Appendices include a list of 617 Squadron's WW2 targets, roll of honour, a list of recipients of gallantry awards and a list of the squadron's aircraft and summary of service.

C117   COOPER, Alan

BORN LEADER: The Story of Guy Gibson VC

Independent Books (London), Bromley, 1993

192 pp, photos, sketches, maps, hb, cr

A full biography of Wg Cdr Guy Gibson VC DSO* DFC* to his death in 1944. The final chapter concerns his memorials and the making of the film *The Dam Busters*. Appendix I summarises his service history; Appendix II identifies the crews for Operation *Chastise*; Appendix III lists all aircraft flown by Gibson; and Appendix IV summarises his wartime operations.

C117A   COOPER, Alan W.

THE DAM BUSTER RAID: A Reappraisal, 70 Years On

Pen & Sword Aviation, Barnsley, 2013

216 pp, photos, index, hb, cr

Written in tribute to the Dambusters aircrews, this history of Operation *Chastise* reviews the raid. Following a description of the dams and of Barnes Wallis' development of *Upkeep*, there is detailed coverage of 617 Squadron's formation, the raid's planning and preparation, the pre-raid briefing, the attacks on the Möhne, Eder and Sorpe Dams, the raid's results and the crews who failed to return. The Squadron's post-raid events and Germany's restorative work on the dams are described and the fate of those crews who survived the raid is recorded.

C117B   COOPER, E. D.

EDWARD COOPER V.C.: The Life of a Stockton Lad

Published by the author, Stockton-on-Tees, 2017

226 pp, photos (some colour), maps (some colour), sb, cr

A biography of Edward Cooper VC, KRRC, from Stockton-on-Tees, who won his VC on 16 August 1917 at Langemarck, Belgium. The author is related to his subject.

C118   CORVI, Steven J. and BECKETT, Ian F. W. (*editors*)
VICTORIA'S GENERALS
Pen & Sword Military, Barnsley, 2009
226 pp, photos, maps, index, hb, cr

An in-depth study of eight famous British generals of the late-Victorian period: Garnet Wolseley, Evelyn Wood VC, Redvers Buller VC, George Colley, Lord Chelmsford, Charles Gordon, Frederick Roberts VC and Herbert Kitchener. Each biography, in which they are critically-appraised as individuals and as military leaders, includes a chronological list of their appointments and promotions.

C119   COSGROVE, Edmund
CANADA'S FIGHTING PILOTS
Clarke, Irwin and Co., Toronto, Canada, 1965
173 pp, index, hb, cr

This book contains 9 chapters covering outstanding Canadian fighter pilots of WW1 and WW2. Chapter 2 is devoted to Barker VC, part of Chapter 3 is devoted to McLeod VC, Chapter 4 covers Bishop VC and part of Chapter 7 is devoted to Mynarski VC.

C120   COSTAIN, A.J.
[1] **A BOY'S LIFE OF LORD ROBERTS: His Life-story told for Boys** (*original title*)
[2] **LORD ROBERTS: His Life-story told for Boys** Charles H Kelly, London, 1915
229 pp, photo, index, hb, cr
J. Alfred Sharpe (The Epworth Press), London, 1925
229 pp, photo, index, hb, cr

A concise biography of FM Earl Roberts VC from his early years up to his death. In particular, his campaign service and military commands are described.

C121   COULTHARD-CLARK, Chris
THE DIGGERS: Makers of the Australian Military Tradition
Melbourne University Press, Melbourne, 1993
369 pp, photos, index, hb, cr

This book contains 207 edited entries from the Australian Dictionary of Biography for the period 1890 to 1939. It includes 34 biographies of Australian VC recipients from the Boer War and WW1.

C122   COULTHARD-CLARK, Chris
McNAMARA VC: A Hero's Dilemma
Air Powers Studies Centre, RAAF, Australia, 1997
128 pp, photos, maps, index, sb, cr

A full biography of AVM FH McNamara VC CB CBE - the only Australian airman to win the VC in WW1 – for landing his aircraft under fire to rescue a fellow officer forced down in enemy territory. The book describes McNamara's early years, WW1 service (VC), inter-war years in the RAAF, senior posts in both the RAAF and RAF in WW2, post-war years and his death. The author had assistance from McNamara's family and sources are listed.

C125 CRAMP, K.R., MA (*compiler*)
AUSTRALIAN WINNERS OF THE VICTORIA CROSS: A Record of the Deeds that Won the Decoration during the Great War 1914-1919
McCarron, Stewart & Co., Sydney, New South Wales, Australia, 1919
80 pp, photos, sb, cr

All 63 Australian WW1 VCs are featured. The text comprises their VC citation (in full) and is supported by their portrait photograph.

C126 CRAWFORD, Captain, M.L.C., DSC* RN (Ret'd)
HM S/M UPHOLDER (Warship Profile 16)
Profile Publications, London, 1972
24 pp. (pp 73 to 96), photos, plans, sb, cr

This publication, No. 16 in the *Warship Profile* series, is devoted to HM Submarine *Upholder*, which through her two-year life (1940-1942) was commanded by Lt Cdr MD Wanklyn VC DSO. The author had served in *Upholder* as first lieutenant. In addition to detailing the submarine's design characteristics, the profile chronicles her operational service and particularly each of her 25 patrols, the last on which she was sunk with the total loss of her crew. The illustrations include coloured profile plans of *Upholder* and 36 photographs.

C130 CREAGH, The late Sir O'Moore, VC GCB GCSI and HUMPHRIES, E.M. (*editors*)
[1] **THE VC AND DSO** (*original title*)
Standard Art Book Co., London, 1924
Three vols: 1154 pp. (VC volume: 337 pp.), photos, index, hb, cr
[2] **THE VICTORIA CROSS 1856-1920**
JB Hayward & Son, Polstead, Suffolk
337 pp, (*facsimile*), photos, index, hb, cr

This work covers all VC recipients from 1856 to 1920 and the recipients of the DSO from 1886 to 1923. The original version is in three volumes:
• Volume I - The Victoria Cross (1856-1920)
• Volume II - The Distinguished Service Order (1886-1915)
• Volume III - The Distinguished Service Order (1916-1923)
The 1985 reprint is in two unrelated volumes:
• The Victoria Cross 1856-1920
• The Distinguished Service Order 1886-1923

For each recipient, the *London Gazette* citation is reproduced in full. Many entries include brief biographical information which, for officers, is supplemented by military service details usually sourced from Hart's Army List or the official Army List. Some of the VC accounts are described in greater detail replicating text in *Deeds that Thrill the Empire*. A total of 722 photographs of recipients are reproduced. This title included contributions from VC recipients and families of recipients. Some entries are very short while others are extensive. While extensive in scope, the book contains many inaccuracies which have been reproduced in subsequent books since 1925.

C131 CREAGH, General Sir O'Moore, VC GCB GCSI
THE AUTOBIOGRAPHY OF GENERAL SIR O'MOORE CREAGH VC GCB GCSI
Hutchinson, London, 1925
304 pp, photos, hb, cr

This detailed autobiography covers Creagh's life and military career up to 1914 when he was Commander-in-Chief in India. At the time of his death in 1923 the manuscripts had been completed and required only minor revision. Footnotes were added by Major General Sir Charles E Caldwell KCB.

C140   CREEDON, Cónal
THE IMMORTAL DEED OF MICHAEL O'LEARY
Cork City Libraries, Cork, 2015
305 pp, photos, sb, cr

The author, an Irish playwright, describes the life of Michael O'Leary VC, his background and the history of the area where he was born and raised. O'Leary's military service and VC action is described and the media's response to his award. It also covers O'Leary's later life in Canada, USA and UK and service in WW2.

C141   CRIDDLE, Roy
A MAN CALLED STAN: Arthur Stanley Gurney VC 1942
Published by author, Western Australia, 2015
139 pp, photos (some colour), sb, cr

A biography of AS Gurney VC covering his early years in Western Australia. After college he worked at Perth City Electricity and Gas Department. He later became a professional road racing cyclist and was a prominent figure in cycle club and league administration. He volunteered for the AIF in 1940 and was killed in North Africa in 1942 and won a posthumous VC.

C142   CROFT, Melba Morris
THE STORY OF TOMMY HOLMES VC 1898-1950
Simcoe Forresters, Owen Sand, Ontario, Canada, 1986
22 pp, photos, sb, cr

This biographical sketch of Canada's youngest VC recipient was published in commemoration of the naming of the Tommy Holmes Armoury, home of the Grey and Simcoe Forresters on 20 September 1986.

C145   CROOK, Michael J.
THE EVOLUTION OF THE VICTORIA CROSS: A Study in Administrative History
Midas Books in association with the Ogilby Trusts', Tunbridge Wells, 1975
321 pp, photos, index, hb, ncr

A detailed and well-researched book tracing the history of the development of the VC. It describes the origins of the award, the design of the Cross, selection of recipients, criteria for award, the Royal Warrant and its amendments, awards to civilians, posthumous awards, eligibility, bars, misconduct and forfeiture. This study focuses on the administration of the award rather than on the recipients or their deeds. However, some recipients are referred to as illustrative examples in the development of the VC. Primary sources were used extensively and are quoted in the book.

C147   CROSS, Craig
PIPER FINDLATER VC: The Hero of Dargai
The Ducat Press, Edinburgh, 2007
91 pp, photos, maps, sb, cr

This book is based on newspaper reports and letters by Findlater after he returned wounded from his VC action in the Tirah campaign of 1897. After his army discharge he enjoyed fame playing his pipes in music halls which was viewed negatively by the military authorities.

C148   CROUCHER, Matt, GC
THE ROYAL BRITISH LEGION 90 YEARS OF HEROES
Collins, London, 2011
256 pp, photos, index, hb, cr

In celebration of the RBL's 90th anniversary, tributes are paid to ninety heroes representing each decade from World War I to 2011. Two pages are devoted to each individual, 23 of whom are VC recipients, and feature photographs, brief biographical details and an account of their deed. Recipients of each of the other British gallantry awards are represented.

C149   CROWDY, Terry (*editor*)
DONALD DEAN VC: The Memoirs of A Volunteer & Territorial From Two World Wars
Pen & Sword, Barnsley, 2010
178 pp, photos, maps, index, hb, cr

This book, based on Donald Dean's own recollections, recounts his wartime exploits in two world wars. In the First World War he served in the Artists' Rifles and the Royal West Kent Regiment, and was awarded the VC in September 1918 for an action near Lens, France. In the Second World War he served in the Pioneer Corps, seeing action in France, Madagascar, Sicily and Italy. The editor has made use of Colonel Dean's typed manuscripts, papers and diary entries, and also included extracts from letters to his wife and official documents. Reviewed in V67.

C150   CRYSTAL PALACE PRESS (*publisher*)
THE VICTORIA CROSS: Descriptive Catalogue of the Picture Gallery, Crystal Palace (*various years*)
Crystal Palace Press, London, 1862-1899
40-44 pp. (typically), portraits, sb, cr

This publication contains black and white and colour reproductions of 44 paintings by Chevalier LW Desanges illustrating the VC deed of 56 VC winners as exhibited in the Victoria Cross Gallery at the Crystal Palace Exhibitions between 1862 and 1899. A new catalogue was produced for each annual exhibition. (See also D16, D17, H15 and W42). In 1900, Lord Wantage presented the paintings to the town of Wantage.

C160   CURRIE, Jack, DFC
THE AUGSBURG RAID
Goodall Publications, London and St Albans, 1987
140 pp, photos, sketch, hb, cr

Sqn Ldr Currie, a former Lancaster pilot, tells the story of one of the most dramatic and dangerous raids performed by Bomber Command in WW2. He reveals new information and examines the enigmas about this operation for which Sqn Ldr Nettleton DFC received the VC. The part played by Nettleton is related in detail and the recommendation for his VC is contained in the Appendix.

D1 DABBS, Mark
MIDLAND HEROES: Victoria Cross winners from the West Midlands
Privately published, Walsall, nd (c2016)
71 pp, photos, sb, cr

This book comprises biographical sketches of 33 VC recipients associated with the West Midlands by birth, residence, military unit or were laid to rest in the region. Each biography provides details of the recipient's birth and family background, military service, VC deed, later years and death. In addition to a portrait photograph, grave and other memorials are depicted.

D5 D'ARCY, Patricia
WHAT HAPPENED TO A VC
Dundalgen Press (W. Tempest), Dundalk, nd (post-1964)
107 pp, photos, sketches, map, sb, cr

A biography of Captain Henry Cecil Dudgeon D'Arcy VC written by a descendant and based on family documents, copies of despatches and miscellaneous papers. The family history is detailed in Part 1. The rest of the book concerns D'Arcy's exploits in the Zulu War. The Appendix lists all the members of the Frontier Light Horse (as at 1 Sep 1880) showing commission / enlistment / resignation and discharge dates as well as South Africa Medal (1877-79) clasp entitlements.

D7 DAVIES, N.G. (*publisher*)
THE GREAT WAR - TASMANIA'S HEROES: Awards for Valour
NG Davies, 'The Mercury' Office, Hobart, Tasmania, 1918
30 pp, photos, sb, cr

This small booklet has two pages dedicated to each of Tasmania's nine VCs of WW1 and includes a portrait photograph (in uniform), VC citation and biographical notes. VC winners are HW Murray, JE Newland, PH Cherry, JW Whittle, JJ Dwyer, L McGee, SR McDougall, WE Brown and PC Statton. Pages 22-29 list Tasmania's recipients of other gallantry awards.

D10 DAYBELL, Peter
WITH A SMILE AND A WAVE: The Life of Captain John Aidan Liddell VC MC
Pen and Sword, Barnsley, 2005
303 pp, photos, maps, index, hb, cr

This is a full and detailed biography of one of the early air VCs of the Great War. The author had full access to family letters, diaries and photographs. The volume covers Liddell's early life, his education at Stonyhurst and Balliol College, Oxford. Liddell won an MC for his handling of his machine guns at Le Maisnil in October 1914 and experienced the Christmas truce of 1914 before being invalided out of the trenches. He had learned to fly before the war and decided to join the RFC. He was awarded the VC for his second and last reconnaissance patrol with No 7 Squadron when he was severely wounded. The book is lavishly illustrated with 91 photos, most of which are published for the first time. Reviewed in V57.

D11   De COSSEN, Major E.A.
DAYS AND NIGHTS OF SERVICE WITH SIR GERALD GRAHAM'S FIELD FORCE AT SUAKIN (*original title*)
FIGHTING THE FUZZY-WUZZY: Days and Nights of Service with Sir Gerald Graham's Field Force at Suakin (*reprint title*)
John Murray, London, 1886 (reprinted facsimile: Greenhill Books, London, 1990)
343 pp, (sketches only in reprint version) hb, cr

A detailed account of the Suakin Expedition of 1885 commanded by Lt Gen Sir Gerald Graham VC KCB about whom extensive references are made.

D12   DECALUWÉ Carl and TERMOTE, Tomas
THE RAID ON ZEBRUGGE - 23rd APRIL 1918, as seen through the eyes of Captain Alfred Carpenter VC
Pen & Sword Military, Barnsley, 2015
145 pp, photos, hb, cr

This lavishly-illustrated volume features 67 photographs from a collection of photographic glass plates depicting the raid on Zeebrugge. The plates once belonged to Captain Carpenter VC, the captain of HMS *Vindictive* on the raid, who after the war had used them to illustrate a series of lectures about the raid (one of two complete sets is now owned by Tomas Termote). The introductory text provides a succinct account of the raid and is supported by an additional 15 contemporary photographs. Eight full-page colour photographs depict the raid's memorials in Zeebrugge, including the bow section of the HMS *Vindictive*.

D13   De La BILLIÈRE, General Sir Peter, KCB KBE DSO MC*
SUPREME COURAGE: Heroic Stories from 150 Years of the Victoria Cross
Little, Brown, London, 2004
387 pp, photos, index, hb, cr

The author starts this book with a history of the decoration and a chapter on courage. There are then chapters on Chavasse, John Byrne, Ball, Jacka, Wanklyn, Gibson, Upham, the Bradford brothers and Lassen. There are also chapters on Gurkha/Indian VCs and on Canadian VCs. The book ends with a chapter on VC imposters. Reviewed in V55.

D14   De WATTEVILLE, Lieutenant Colonel H., CBE MA
LORD ROBERTS
Blackie, London, 1938
176 pp, photos, maps, index, hb, cr

A concise biography of FM Earl Roberts VC covering his early life and military career and campaigns up to his death in France in 1914.

D15   DENT & SONS A. J. (*publisher*)
"FOR VALOUR"
J.M. Dent & Sons Limited, London, nd (c1917)
48 pp, sketches, sb, ncr

This is an introduction to the VC for children and was published as an aid to reading as Intermediate No. 2 in a series of *Dent's School Pamphlets*. There are very brief descriptions of VC actions from the Crimean War to 1915.

D16 DESANGES, Chevalier L.W. (*painter*)
CATALOGUE OF A SERIES OF HISTORICAL PICTURES ILLUSTRATING ACTIONS WHICH HAVE WON THE VICTORIA CROSS
Nassau Steam Press – W.S. Johnson, London, 1861
16 pp, sb, ncr

A catalogue of the 47 paintings by Desanges that formed the VC gallery and which were exhibited in Egyptian Hall, Piccadilly, in 1861. In each case, the VC citation (or extract from the relevant despatches) is given. (See also C150, D17, H15 and W42).

D17 DESANGES, Chevalier L.W. (*painter*)
CATALOGUE OF THE PICTURES OF THE VICTORIA CROSS GALLERY
Nichols (printers), Wantage, 1900; reprinted: Wantage Town Council, 2000
23 pp, photos, sb, cr

A catalogue of the pictures of the Victoria Cross Gallery painted by Chevalier LW Desanges and presented to the town of Wantage by Lord Wantage VC KCB in 1900. The paintings are reproduced with details of the circumstances under which the VCs were won. (See also C150, D16, H15 and W42).

D18 DICKENS, Captain Peter, DSO MBE DSC RN
NARVIK: Battle in the Fjords
Naval Institute Press, United States of America, 1974
184 pp, photos, maps, index, hb, cr

This book describes British naval actions off Norway in April 1940 and focuses on the exploits of Captain BAW Warburton-Lee which resulted in the award of a posthumous VC, the first to be gazetted in WW2. There are many photos of the battle and portraits of those who commanded ships in the action.

D18A DIDLY, Doug
DAMBUSTERS: Operation *Chastise* 1943
Osprey, London, 2010
80 pp, photos, maps, paintings, sb, cr

An account of the Dambuster raid in the *Raid* series by Osprey, in which Guy Gibson VC receives detailed coverage.

D19 DIMMOCK, F. Haydn (*editor*)
THE SCOUTS' BOOK OF HEROES: A Record of Scouts' Work in the Great War
C Arthur Pearson, London, 1919
320 pp, photos, sketches, hb, cr

This book records the deeds of many former Boy Scouts who, during WW1, won a gallantry award or were killed in action. A short account of their war deed is given, although a longer account applies in respect to Cornwell (pages 128-146). Their former Scout troop is identified and, in some cases, brief biographical information is included. Eleven VC winners are covered (D Laidlaw, GE Cates, R Haine, RP Hallowes, RE Cruickshank, JM Craig, JHS Dimmer, GB McKean, DJ Dean, AM Toye, JT Cornwell). The appendix (pages 257-320) is a list of ex-Scouts who were awarded a British or foreign decoration or medal for gallant or distinguished service.

D20   DINESEN, Lieutenant Thomas, VC
[1] NO MAN'S LAND: En Dansker med Canadierne Ved Vestfronten (*original Danish version*)
C.A. Reitzels Forlag, København, Denmark, 1929
205 pp, hb, cr (*Danish text*)
[2] MERRY HELL!: A Dane with the Canadians
Jarrolds, London, 1929
254 pp, hb, cr (*English text*)
[3] MERRY HELL!: A Dane with the Canadians
The Naval & Military Press, Uckfield, 2005
254 pp, sb, cr (*English text*)

The autobiography of the Dane, Thomas Dinesen VC, which was first published in Denmark in 1929. Dinesen came from a wealthy family and was the brother of Karen Blixen, author of *Out of Africa*. The volume describes how, at the outbreak of WW1, he offered his services to the French and British but was turned down. He later travelled to the USA, who were on the point of joining the allied cause, where he was also turned down. Crossing the border into Canada he joined the 42nd Battalion Quebec Regiment (Royal Highlanders of Canada). Dinesen finally reached the Western Front in March 1918 and on 12 August 1918 he won the VC. Reviewed in V56.

D20A   DIXON, Ed
'HOODOO' KINROSS, VC: The Pride of Lougheed
Privately published, Alberta, Canada, 2005
26 pp, photos, sb, cr

This A4-sized comb-bound biographical sketch of Cecil John Kinross VC reveals his family background, early years, military service and later years. Some of the memorials for him are depicted. Appendix 1 confirms his date and place of birth and Appendix 2 examines his nickname 'Hoodoo'

D21   DODDS, Ronald
THE BRAVE YOUNG WINGS
Canada's Wings Inc., Ontario, Canada, 1980
302 pp, photos, index, hb, cr

This book describes the exploits of the Canadians in the RFC and RAF in the First World War. There are individual chapters on VC recipients Billy Bishop and WG Barker. Appendix A lists 780 Canadian fatalities in the British Flying Services, Appendix B lists honours and awards and Appendix C lists Canadian aerial victories.

D22   DOHERTY, Richard
IRISH MEN AND WOMEN IN THE SECOND WORLD WAR
Four Courts Press, Dublin, 1999
319 pp, photos, index, hb, cr

This book describes Ireland's contribution to British forces during WW2. A total of 12 chapters cover the war in the air, sea and on land with dedicated chapters to Irish chaplains, doctors and women. The exploits of the following Irish VC winners are described: HM Ervine-Andrews (pp 70-71), JJB Jackman (pp 72-76), ESF Fegen (pp 79-84), E Esmonde (pp 85-96), DE Garland (pp 98-103) and JJ Magennis (pp 226-229).

D23 DOHERTY, Richard and TRUESDALE, David
IRISH WINNERS OF THE VICTORIA CROSS
Four Courts Press, Dublin, 2000
272 pp, photos, index, hb, cr

An account of the 207 Irishmen who won the VC. Of these, 166 were Irish-born and had at least one Irish parent. The remainder were Irish-born to non-Irish parents. The text (up to page 187) is arranged chronologically by date of VC deed within campaign or theatre and gives a brief account of the deed. Some biographical information is included in many cases. Appendix 1 (pages 189-234) is an alphabetical list of the 207 VCs showing name, rank, unit, action location and date, date and location of birth and death, memorials and remarks (including location of VC). Reviewed in V56.

D24 DONALDSON, Mark, VC
THE CROSSROAD: A story of life, death and the SAS
Pan Macmillan Australia, Sydney, NSW, 2013
422 pp, colour photos, hb, cr

The detailed and frank autobiography of Mark Donaldson VC, the Australian who won his VC with the Australian SAS in Afghanistan in 2008. Donaldson describes his early life in a rural area of New South Wales. After his father died, his mother befriended a male work colleague. One day she disappeared and the police suspected she was murdered. After a chance meeting with a former member of the SAS, Donaldson joined the army and was selected for the SAS. His service in Afghanistan is recounted in detail, as is the VC action. Reviewed in V74.

D24A DOOLEY, Michael Kevin
"OUR MICKEY": The Story of Private James O'Rourke VC MM 1879 - 1957 (CEF - 7th Battalion)
Privately published, Ottawa, 2000
25 pp, photos, sb, cr

A brief biography of James O'Rourke VC MM including his early life, service in the First World War and a troubled period towards the end of his life in which he applied for a disability pension for his poor physical and mental condition caused by his war service.

D24B DÖRFLINGER, Michael (translated by BROOKS, Geoffrey)
DEATH WAS THEIR CO-PILOT: Aces of the Skies
Pen & Sword Aviation, Barnsley, 2017
208 pp, photos, hb, cr

This volume examines the evolution of the WW1 fighter ace and describes the organisation of fighter units of Great Britain, France and Germany. Biographies of numerous WW1 aces who were killed during the war recount their exploits and circumstances of their death. The aces covered include VC recipients Albert Ball, Edward Mannock and James McCudden. The book has 70 b&w illustrations. The book was first published as *Der Ted fliegt mit* by GeraMond Verlag GmbH, München in 2014 (German text).

D25 DORRIAN, James
STORMING ST. NAZAIRE: The Gripping Story of the Dock-Busting Raid, March, 1942
Leo Cooper, London, 1998
304 pp, photos, maps, index, hb, cr

The full story of Operation *Chariot*, the British attack on the dry dock at St Nazaire in 1942. The attack resulted in the award of five VCs: SH Beattie, WA Savage, RED Ryder, AC Newman and TF Durrant, whose services and deeds are documented fully.

D26 DOUGLAS, Tom
GREAT CANADIAN WAR HEROES: The Victoria Cross Recipients of World War II
Altitude Publishing, Alberta, Canada, 2005
128 pp, photos, sb, cr

Brief stories of each of the 16 Canadians who were awarded the VC in WW2.

D26A DOWNER, Martyn
THE QUEEN'S KNIGHT: The extraordinary life of Queen Victoria's most trusted confidant
Bantam Press, London, 2007
452 pp, photos, colour illustrations, index, hb, cr

This is a detailed biography of one of Queen Victoria's most trusted confidants: Sir Howard Elphinstone VC. Elphinstone won his VC with the Royal Engineers at the Great Redan, Sebastopol, on 7 June 1855. He joined the royal household as a governor to Queen Victoria's favourite son, Prince Arthur. The author was able to source primary sources in letters and diaries as his wife is Elphinstone's great great granddaughter. The biography describes tales of intrigue, rivalries and tragedies in the royal household as well as references to key figures in the Victorian era. Elphinstone had an untimely death at sea in 1890. Reviewed in V60.

D27 DOYLE, Arthur T.
HEROES OF NEW BRUNSWICK
Brunswick Press, Fredericton, New Brunswick, Canada, 1984
133 pp, photos, sb, cr

A series of short biographies of heroes from New Brunswick. Six pages are devoted to Milton F Gregg VC.

D27A DOYLE, N. E.
VICTORIA CROSS HOLDERS FROM WARE HERTFORDSHIRE
Privately published, Tottenham, London, 2016
109 pp, photos, sb, cr

This booklet concerns the two Ware-related VC recipients. Eight pages are devoted to Arthur Martin-Leake VC* who was born in High Cross near Ware and is buried locally and one page provides brief details of Irish-born Dudley Stagpool VC DCM who died in Ware.

D28 DREW, Lieutenant Colonel George A.
CANADA'S FIGHTING AIRMEN
MacLean Publishing, Toronto, Canada, 1931
305 pp, photos, sketches, hb, cr

The story of 12 Canadian pilots of WW1 and a description of Canada's role in aviation during that period. VC recipients covered are Bishop (43 pages), Barker (78 pages) and McLeod (20 pages).

D29 DRIJVERS, Hubert, SJ
UN HÉROS DE LA R.A.F. – LEONARD CHESHIRE
Foyer-Notre Dame, Brussels, Belgium, 1954
16 pp, sb, cr (*French text*)

A short booklet, in French, describing the life of Leonard Cheshire VC up to 1954. This includes his war service in the RAF and the establishment of the Cheshire Homes.

D30   DRURY, Ken
FOR VALOUR: The Story of Reverend Noel Mellish VC MC Vicar of Great Dunmow 1928-1948
Great Dunmow Historical and Literary Society, Great Dunmow, Essex, 2008
40 pp, photos, sb, cr

A short biography of Rev Noel Mellish VC who served as a trooper in the Boer War and won the VC and MC in the Great War as an army chaplain attached to the 4th Bn Royal Fusiliers. The publication was produced to mark the unveiling of a memorial plaque to Mellish in 2008 in Great Dunmow where he was a vicar between 1928 and 1948. Reviewed in V62. See M105.

D31   DUCKERS, Peter
THE VICTORIA CROSS
Shire Books, Princes Risborough, Buckinghamshire, 2005
72 pp, photos, sb, cr

A title in the Shire series providing an introduction and overview to the VC. The book has over 100 illustrations, mainly in colour, and depicts a number of VCs in groups, obverse and reverse as well as artists' impressions of actions for which the VC was awarded. Reviewed in V57.

D32   DUCKERS, Peter
THE VICTORIA CROSS TO THE SHROPSHIRE REGIMENTS
Shropshire Regimental Museum, Shrewsbury Castle, 2007
36 pp, photos, drawings, maps, sb, cr

This A4-sized spiral-bound work features biographical accounts of the VC recipients of, predominantly, the 53rd Regiment (Dynan, Ffrench, Irwin, J Kenny, Pye) and the King's Shropshire Light Infantry (Whitfield, Eardley and Stokes). Each account, supported by photographs, records the recipient's background, early years, military service, VC action details, later years, death, memorials and medal group composition. Further biographical accounts relate to two VC recipients with close connections with the Shropshire Regiments (Dalton and Meynell) and five other VC recipients who were born in Shropshire (Brunt, Price-Davies, TOL Wilkinson, WC Williams and Yate).

D35   DUDGEON, James M.
"MICK": The Story of Major Edward Mannock VC DSO MC, Royal Flying Corps and Royal Air Force
Robert Hale, London, 1981
208 pp, photos, index, hb, cr

A comprehensive biography of Major 'Mick' Mannock VC. Following an account of his family background and early years, the book documents his distinguished but short military service. The appendices provide full citations for his decorations and a table detailing his combats and victories.

D36   DUFFUS, Louis
BEYOND THE LAAGER: An Inspiring Record of Gallantry
Hurst & Blackett, London, nd (c1950)
168 pp, photos, index, hb, cr

A collection of tales of valour displayed by South Africans during WW2. Chapter VI (pages 87-103) entitled *Ordeals of a VC* is a biographical account of Capt Quentin Smythe VC which also describes his VC action. One of the three photos of Smythe depicts him being presented with the VC by Major General Piennar.

D37   DUNPHIE, Christopher and JOHNSON, Garry
GOLD BEACH: Inland from King
Leo Cooper, Pen and Sword Books, Barnsley, 1999
160 pp, photos, maps, index, sb, cr

This book is part of the *Battleground Europe* series of battlefield guides. It describes the landings on D-Day in King Sector of Gold Beach by the British 50th Division and subsequent operations in the Battle of Normandy. CSM Stanley Hollis of 6th Green Howards won the only VC for D-Day and his actions are described in detail on pages 47 to 58. Hollis's gallantry at Cristot on 11 June 1944 is also covered on pages 84 to 92.

D38   DURAND, Sir Mortimer
THE LIFE OF FIELD-MARSHAL SIR GEORGE WHITE VC GCB GCSI GCMG GCVO GCIE OM DCL LLD
William Blackwood, London and Edinburgh, 1915
Two volumes - 776 pp. (Vol I: 448 pp.; Vol II: 328 pp.), photos, sketches, maps, index, hb, cr

A comprehensive biography of Sir George White. Volume 1 covers his ancestral background, early life and military career up to 1898, spanning service in the Indian Mutiny, other Indian campaigns, Afghan War, Sudan campaign and the Burmese War. It concludes with the cessation of his post as C-in-C India. Volume 2 relates to his subsequent appointment as QMG, his distinguished campaign service in South Africa, followed by Governorships of Gibraltar and then the Royal Hospital Chelsea, culminating in his death in 1912. There are extensive references to Lord Roberts VC and Sir Redvers Buller VC.

D40   DUSKIN, Gerald L and SEGMAN, Ralph
IF THE GODS ARE GOOD: The Epic Sacrifice of the HMS *Jervis Bay*
Naval Institute Press, Annapolis, Maryland, USA, 2004
270 pp, photos, maps, index, hb, cr

A detailed and stirring account of the sea-fight between the armed merchant cruiser HMS *Jervis Bay* and *Admiral Scheer*, one of Germany's most feared warships. The *Jervis Bay*'s captain, ESF Fegen, won the VC posthumously for the action.

E1   EARDLEY, Roy H.
EARDLEY VC MM KSLI
Rothley Publishing, Congleton, Cheshire, 1997
110 pp, photos, maps, hb, cr

This well-illustrated biography of Sgt GH Eardley VC MM, written by his younger son, chronicles his early years, military service in WW2 and up to 1950 and his subsequent civilian life. His VC deed is narrated in detail. The book uses, extensively, information from the original official records and from the family files from which many of the photographs are also sourced. A full-page colour plate depicts his VC and medal group. The book also recalls the tragic accident in 1964 in which his wife was killed and he sustained severe injuries. He died in 1991.

E2   EARDLEY, Roy H.
FOR VALOUR VC MM
Rothley Publishing, Oswestry, 2003
69 pp, photos, sb, cr

This A5 comb-bound production is written by the younger son of Sgt GH Eardley VC MM. It starts at the beginning of WW2 and describes his father's service and exploits. The later chapters describe a memorial to Eardley in his home town of Congleton and some family differences resulting from Eardley's three marriages. Reviewed in V54.

E2A   EARDLEY, Roy H.
CONGLETON VC MEMORIAL
Rothley Publishing, Oswestry, 2004
34 pp, photos, map, sb, cr

This comb-bound publication contains 34 un-numbered pages and describes the VC action of Sgt GH Eardley VC MM. It contains photos and text describing a visit by Eardley's son and widow to the Dutch National War and Resistance Museum at Overloon where Eardley is commemorated. A copy of the map used by KSLI during the VC attack is included.

E2B   EARDLEY, Roy H.
THE VC.s (*sic*) **LETTER: Sergeant G. H. Eardley VC MM**
Rothley Publishing, Prestatyn, Denbighshire, 2009
120 pp, photos, map, sb, cr

The text of E2 has been adapted for this significantly-expanded and reformatted biography of George Eardley. It addition to including many more photographs, one of which depicts his medal group, it also reproduces official documents relating to the award of his MM and VC, as well as the feature on him in the boys' comic *The Victor*.

E3   EDWARDS, Bernard
CONVOY WILL SCATTER: The Full Story of Jervis Bay and Convoy HX84
Pen & Sword Maritime, Barnsley, 2013
184 pp, photos, drawing, index, hb, cr

An account of the naval action on 5 November 1940 in the Atlantic which resulted in a posthumous VC for Commander ESF Fegen who commanded the lightly-armed merchant cruiser HMS *Jervis Bay*. He was escorting 38 merchantmen when they encountered the German pocket battleship *Admiral Hipper*. Fegen steered his vessel head-on at the enemy battleship, enabling the ship in the convoy to scatter. Fegen fought on for three hours and went down with his ship. A total of 33 merchantmen reached port.

E4   EDWARDS, Commander Kenneth, RN
      SEVEN SAILORS
      Collins, London, 1945
      255 pp, photos, hb, cr

      A study of seven distinguished naval commanders (Royal Navy and Royal Canadian Navy). The fifth study (pages 177-197) concerns Capt Sherbrooke VC whose war services, including his VC action, are narrated.

E5   EDWARDS, E.
      LT. MOANA NGARIMU VC
      James G. Harvey (*printer*), Palmerston North, New Zealand, 1943
      8 pp, photo (on cover), sb, cr

      A bi-lingual text in English and Maori describing Ngarimu's early life, military service and circumstances leading to his award of the VC in North Africa. The cover shows a photo of the recipient.

E6   EDWARDS-STUART, Lieutenant Colonel Ivor A.J.
      A JOHN COMPANY GENERAL: The Life of Lieutenant-General Sir Abraham Roberts
      New Horizon, Bognor Regis, 1983
      237 pp, photos, maps, index, hb, cr

      General Sir Abraham Roberts, the father of Lord Roberts VC, had a distinguished military career which became overshadowed by his famous son. This biography also recounts the early years and early military career of Lord Roberts including his award of the VC.

E6A   EGE, Lennart
      Krigsflyvningens "Esser"
      Det ny Lademann, København, 1989
      125 pp, photos, sb, cr

      The title of this Danish-text book means "The Aces of War Aviation". The book contains a selection of brief accounts of the exploits of twelve air aces of WW1, WW2, the Korean War and the Vietnam War. One chapter is devoted to William Barker VC.

E7   EISINGER, Larry (*editor*)
      SKY FIGHTERS OF WORLD WAR I
      Fawcett Publications, Greenwich, Connecticut, USA, 1961
      144 pp, photos, sb, cr

      An anthology of biographical sketches and combat experiences of ten flying aces of WWI. A separate chapter is devoted to each pilot. Edward Mannock VC and William Barker VC are featured on pages 65-78 and 105-116 respectively. The other stories relate to Garros, Guynemer, Luftbery, Fonk, Udet, Springs and Luke.

E8   ELDER, John F.
      THE LAST HEROES: The story of three Victoria Cross winners and their World War II exploits
      Vantage Press, New York, 1980
      278 pp, photos, hb, cr

      The book is divided into three parts covering three VCs of WW2: Place VC (93 pages), Porteous VC (83 pages) and Chapman VC (88 pages). Their VC exploits are detailed and biographical notes are included.

E9 ELDRIDGE, Jim
MY TRUE STORY: Standing Alone - Jack Cornwell VC Battle of Jutland 1916
Scholastic Children's Books, London, 2011
157 pp, sb, cr

Narrated in the first person and based on factual details and events, this children's book in the form of a personal diary chronicles Jack Cornwell's life from 5 Aug 1914 when he was 14 years old to 1 Jun 1916, the day before he died. He records his home life, his employment after leaving school and his longing to join the Royal Navy, which he achieves on 27 Jul 1915. He provides details of his basic and gunnery training, his service on HMS *Chester* and his part in the Battle of Jutland in which he was mortally wounded and awarded the VC posthumously. Jack's brother, George, takes up the narrative, covering Jack's death, funeral, burial and re-burial. A concluding chapter provides a brief account of the Battle of Jutland. The Appendix contains a transcript of Jack's last letter to his father, Eli Cornwell, written just before the battle.

E10 ELIAS, Gillian
ALBERT BALL VC
Nottinghamshire County Council, West Bridgeford, nd (c1995)
38 pp, line drawings, sb, cr

This booklet gives a brief account of the life of Capt Albert Ball VC DSO** MC.

E10A ELKIN, Peter
TAMWORTH'S FORGOTTEN HERO: Samuel Parkes VC
Wonderworks Studios, Nantwich, 2004
155 pp, photos, hb, cr

A biography of Samuel Parkes VC who was awarded the VC for the Charge of the Light Brigade in October 1854. The author is a great-great-nephew of Samuel Parkes. Reviewed in V55.

E11 ELLIOTT, Major W.J.
THE VICTORIA CROSS IN AFGHANISTAN: And On the Frontiers of India During the Years 1877, 1878, 1879 and 1880. How it was Won.
Dean, London, 1882
248 pp, line drawings, map, index, hb, cr

This work, within the *Deeds of Daring Library* series, contains a chapter devoted to each VC action set in the context of the related battle or campaign in Afghanistan or on the Indian Frontiers between 1877 and 1880. The deeds of the following VC winners are covered: J Cook, Hart, EP Leach, Creagh, WRP Hamilton, EH Sartorius, JW Adams, Dick-Cunyngham, Sellar, Vousden, Hammond, Mullane, Collis, Chase, Ashford, GS White, A Scott, Ridgeway. The line drawings include portraits of some VC recipients.

E12   ELLIOTT, Major W.J.
THE VICTORIA CROSS IN ZULULAND AND SOUTH AFRICA (*original title*)
VICTORIA CROSS IN ZULULAND (*1990 facsimile reprint*)
Dean, London, 1882 (single volume), c.1882 (two volumes); facsimile reprint (Vol 1 only) by Grant Christian, Pietermaritzburg, South Africa, 1990
Single volume - 268 pp.; two volumes - 245 pp. (Vol 1 - 112 pp.; Vol 2 - 133 pp.), line drawings, maps, hb, (1990 reprint - sb), cr

This work, within the *Deeds of Daring Library* series, covers all of the Victoria Crosses won in the Zulu War of 1879 and the Basuto War. The VC deeds are described in the context of the conflict or battle. In the two-volume edition, Vol 1 is subtitled *Isandhlwana and Rorke's Drift* and Vol 2, subtitled *The End of the War*, covers the subsequent events in Zululand and the Basuto War. The 1990 reprint (a limited edition of 300 copies) is a facsimile of Vol 1 only. Line drawings include portraits of some VCs.

E15   ELLIOTT, Keith, VC with ADSHEAD, Rona
FROM COWSHED TO DOGCOLLAR
AH & AW Reed, Wellington, 1967
167 pp, photos, hb, cr

The autobiography of the Rev Keith Elliott VC, who grew up on a farm in New Zealand during the Depression. He became a hard-fighting NCO during WW2 and later was ordained into the Anglican Church.

E16   ELLIS, Phil
A ROUGH DIAMOND: The Story of William Bees VC
North West Leicestershire District Council, Coalville, Leicestershire, 1996
18 pp. (8 numbered), sb, cr

This booklet covers Bees' early life, service history, VC action in South Africa, later life as a road sweeper and death. It was thought that Bees was born in Loughborough but recent research has proved he was born in Midsomer Norton. See V66.

E17   ELMES, Jenny
M-MOTHER: Dambuster Flight Lieutenant John 'Hoppy' Hopgood
The History Press, Stroud, 2015
270 pp, photos, index, hb, cr

This biography of Flight Lieutenant John Vere Hopgood DFC* recalls his early years, his time at Marlborough College and his service in the RAFVR from 1940. Posted to 617 Sqn on 31 Mar 1943, he served as Wg Cdr Gibson's deputy leader for the attack on the Möhne Dam on 16/17 May 1943. Piloting Lancaster AJ-M in the first trio of the first wave, led by Gibson, his aircraft was severely flak-damaged and after he released his *Upkeep* mine, which bounced over the dam, his aircraft crashed and he and some of his crew were killed. Pages 214 onwards document the Dams Raid and the aftermath.

E20 ELPHINSTONE, Captain H.C., RE (VC), JONES, Major General Sir Harry D., KCB DCL RE and REILLY, Edmund M.
JOURNAL OF THE OPERATIONS CONDUCTED BY THE CORPS OF ROYAL ENGINEERS AND AN ACCOUNT OF THE ARTILLERY OPERATIONS
HMSO, Longmans & Co for the Secretary of State for War, London, 1859
Three volumes - 1310 pp. (Vol 1 - 299 pp.; Vol 2 - 638 pp.; Vol 3 - 373pp.), sketches, maps, hb, cr (author only)

Captain HC Elphinstone VC RE was employed from September 1857 by the topographical department of the War Office to help in the compilation of this monumental work covering the involvement of the Royal Engineers in the siege of Sebastopol. The work consists of three volumes and a separate case of maps containing 15 folding maps including a sheet of views and a large plan. In addition, six maps are bound at the back of Part 1. Capt Elphinstone wrote Part 1 (From the Invasion of the Crimea to the close of the Winter Campaign 1854-55). Part 2 (From February 1855 to the fall of Sebastopol, September 1855) was written by Major General Sir Harry Jones.

E40 ENSOR, David
WITH LORD ROBERTS THROUGH THE KHYBER PASS
Frederick Muller, London, 1963
143 pp, photos, sketches, maps, index, hb, cr

This book in the series *Adventures in Geography* is intended for secondary school pupils. It follows the travels and adventures of Lord Roberts and, using his journeys as a framework, describes the geography of the countries through which he passed.

E60 ESHEL, David
BRAVERY IN BATTLE: Stories from the Front Line
Arms and Armour Press, London, 1997 (reprinted Brockhampton Press, 1999)
240 pp, photos, maps, index, hb, cr

The author describes, in dedicated chapters, 23 heroic actions in battles ranging from Omdurman through to the Golan Heights in 1973. Chapters devoted to VC actions are: Chapter Two (pages 18-24) concerning Lt FH McNamara; Chapter 4 (pages 31-41) on the St George's Day raid on Zeebrugge; Chapter Six (pages 49-57) relating to the attack on the Maastricht Bridges involving Fg Off Garland and Flt Sgt Gray; and Chapter Eleven (pages 92-105) on the Channel Dash in which action Campbell and Esmonde won the VC.

E69 EULER, Helmuth
ALS DEUTSCHLANDS DÄMME BRACHEN: Die Wahrheit über die Bombardierung der Möhne-Eder-Sorpe-Staudämme 1943
Motorbuch-verlag, Stuttgart, Germany, 1979
224 pp, drawings, photos, maps, hb, cr

A German-text history of 617 Squadron's raids on the Möhne, Eder and Sorpe Dams on 16/17 May 1943. It describes in detail the aftermath and effect of the deluge resulting from the Möhne and Eder breaches and the effort to repair the dams. The raid was led by Wg Cdr Guy Gibson who was awarded the VC.

E70   EULER, Helmuth
WASSERKRIEG: 17. Mai 1943: Rollbomben gegen die Möhne-, Eder-und Sorpestaudämme
Motorbuch-verlag, Stuttgart, Germany, 2013
257 pp, photos, drawings, maps, hb, cr (*German text*)

This profusely-illustrated book with German text covers all aspects of 617 Squadron's raid on the Möhne, Eder and Sorpe Dams on 16/17 May 1943. The first half of the book records the history of the reservoirs, Barnes Wallis' experiments against dams and the planning, preparation and execution of the RAF attack. The second half concerns the aftermath from British and German viewpoints. The devastation caused by the breaches is described and supported by many eye-witness accounts and photographs. The reconstructive work on the Möhne and Eder Dams and the measures taken by the Germans to prevent repeat attack are covered. The book concludes with the reminiscences of surviving aircrew 45 years after the attack. See E72.

E71   EULER, Helmuth
THE DAMS RAID THROUGH THE LENS
Battle of Britain International Ltd., London, 2001
240 pp, photos, drawings, maps, index, hb, cr

This book in the *After the Battle* 'Through the Lens' series recounts the story of 617 Squadron's raid on the Ruhr Dams on 16/17 May 1943 led by Wg Cdr Gibson who won the VC. The book incorporates a lot of new information and photographs not available at the time of the author's earlier works on the subject. It fully documents the background to the operation, the raid itself and the aftermath, particularly from a German perspective. Over 400 captioned photographs are included.

E72   EULER, Helmuth
THE DAMBUSTER RAID: A German View
Pen & Sword Aviation, Barnsley, 2015
267 pp, photos, drawings, maps, hb, cr

This profusely-illustrated book was originally published in German as *Wasserkrieg* in 2007, republished in 2013 (see E70). It covers all aspects of 617 Squadron's raid on the Möhne, Eder and Sorpe Dams on 16/17 May 1943. The first half of the book records the history of the reservoirs, Barnes Wallis' experiments against dams and the planning, preparation and execution of the RAF attack. The second half concerns the aftermath from British and German viewpoints. The devastation caused by the breaches is described and supported by many eye-witness accounts and photographs. The reconstructive work on the Möhne and Eder Dams and the measures taken by the Germans to prevent repeat attack are covered. The book concludes with the reminiscences of surviving aircrew 45 years after the attack.

E80   EVANS, Bob (*editor*)
THE CONWAY HEROES
Countyvise, Birkenhead, 2009
241 pp, photos, sb, cr

Compiled by Old Conways, this book features biographical sketches and stories of the deeds of heroes who trained in HMS *Conway*. Chapter 1 (pages 1-24) concerns former cadets who were awarded the VC (4), Albert Medal/George Cross (5) or George Medal (1). Pages 1-18 contain biographies for the four VCs: PE Bent, CG Bonner, IE Fraser and E Unwin. Chapter 2 recalls the stories about those who served in the Falklands in the 1914 and 1982 campaigns. Chapter 3 relates to Conway notables. Chapters 4 and 5 list alphabetically all those Old Conways decorated in WW1 and WW2, respectively and record their *London Gazette* entry (including award citation).

E82   EVERETT, Valerie
THOMAS LESLIE AXFORD, VC, MM: A life remembered
Published by author, Perth, Western Australia, nd (c2010)
48 pp, photos, illustrations, sb, cr

A short biography of TL Axford VC MM who enlisted in the AIF at Kalgoorlie in 1915. After training he was shipped to Egypt and then to France in 1916 where he was awarded the MM and later the VC for action at Vaire and Hamel Woods on 4 July 1918. He returned to Australia where he worked in Perth and died in 1983.

F1   FALCONER, Jonathan
THE DAM BUSTERS: Breaking the Great Dams of Western Germany 16-17 May 1943
Sutton Publishing, Stroud, 2003
242 pp, photos, maps, index, hb, cr

This profusely-illustrated large format volume provides detailed coverage of the Dams Raid in May 1943 led by Wg Cdr Guy Gibson. It documents the training for the raid, the planning of the operation, the raid itself and the aftermath for Germany and Britain. A biographical sketch of each of the key men involved in the operations planning is given. The final chapter describes the making of the legendary *The Dam Busters* film. The appendices detail the aircraft and aircrews that failed to return and what happened to the surviving aircraft and aircrews.

F2   FALCONER, Jonathan
FILMING THE DAM BUSTERS
Sutton Publishing, Stroud, 2005
160 pp, photos, index, hb, cr

The story of the making of the classic 1955 film *The Dam Busters*, which immortalised 617 Sqn's raid on the Rühr dams in May 1943. After describing the raid itself and the inspiration for the film, the book provides a detailed account of the cast and its selection, the men and machines used, the aerial filming, the main filming and post-production work. Appendices list the film credits and the aircraft used in the film. Supporting photographs include over 100 stills from the film. See R5.

F2A   FALCONER, Jonathan
THE DAM BUSTER STORY
Sutton Publishing, Stroud, 2007
116 pp, photos (some colour), maps, hb, cr

A concise account of the Dams Raid on 16/17 May 1943 for which Guy Gibson was awarded the VC. There are a large number of photographs, with some in colour. The author describes the bouncing bomb, the planning and execution of the raid and the aftermath. An appendix provides a listing of aircraft and aircrew which participated in the raid and their fates.

F3   FALK, Quentin
MR MIDSHIPMAN VC: The Short Accident-Prone Life of George Drewry, Gallipoli Hero
Pen & Sword Maritime, Barnsley, 2018
161 pp, photos, map, index, hb, cr

A full biography of Lt GL Drewry VC RNR who, as a midshipman, won his award for the landings at V Beach, Cape Helles at Gallipoli in which he was wounded. The book traces his family backgtround and recalls his early years and schooling, during which time he survived two accidents. His service and experiences in the Merchant Navy are documented. Serving as an apprentice on a sailing vessel, he survived falling off the rigging in 1910 and being shipwrecked on a deserted island off Cape Horn in 1912. Later, after becoming a P&O Cadet, promoted 4th Officer, he joined the RNR in Aug 1914 as a midshipman. Promoted Lieutenant in Mar 1918 in command of of his first ship, HM Trawler *William Jackson*, he was accidentally killed at Scapa Flow.

F3A   FAREHAM, John
GUY GIBSON VC
Bretwalda Books, Epsom, 2012
128 pp, photos, index, sb, cr

This book in the *Heroes of the RAF* series recalls the life and exploits of Wg Cdr Gibson VC. Focussing mainly on his wartime service, the Dams Raid, which he led, is covered in detail. Later chapters concern his final year, his legacy and a discussion about his final flight in which he was shot down and killed.

F4   FARQUHAR, Murray
DERRICK VC
Rigby, Adelaide, 1982
205 pp, photos, maps, hb, cr

A biography of Lieutenant Derrick VC DCM, an Australian Infantry officer (and former NCO) whose life and military exploits in North Africa, New Guinea and Borneo are recounted in detail. Derrick, who was killed in action in Borneo, maintained a diary which helped the author to reconstruct events.

F5   FARRAR-HOCKLEY, Captain Anthony, DSO MC
THE EDGE OF THE SWORD
Frederick Muller, London, 1954
275 pp, photos, maps, index, hb, cr

The author describes his experiences at the Imjin battle in Korea (April 1951) for which his CO, Colonel Carne, was awarded the VC (pages 11-70). The author and Colonel Carne were taken prisoner after the battle.

F6   FARSET YOUTH AND COMMUNITY DEVELOPMENT (*publisher*)
IRELAND'S VCs: A comprehensive list of Irishmen who were awarded The Victoria Cross
Farset Youth & Community Development, Belfast, nd (c1995)
97 pp, photos, index, hb, ncr

Each recipient is listed, showing rank, name, regiment, date and place of birth, location of VC action, date and location of death, Irish town connection and full VC citation. Portrait photographs of varying quality, some not published previously, are included for most recipients. Much of the information is taken from T10.

F7   FARWELL, Byron
EMINENT VICTORIAN SOLDIERS: Seekers of Glory
Viking, Harmondsworth, Middlesex, 1986
367 pp, photos, maps, index, hb, cr

This book contains, as separate chapters, biographical accounts of eight of the most renowned Victorian generals: Hugh Gough (Viscount), Charles Napier, Charles Gordon, Frederick Roberts VC, Garnet Wolseley, Evelyn Wood VC, Hector MacDonald and Herbert Kitchener. Roberts and Wood are dealt with in Chapter 4 (pages 147-191) and Chapter 6 (pages 239-266), respectively.

F8   FAULKNER, Andrew
      ARTHUR BLACKBURN VC: An Australian hero, his men and their two world wars
      Wakefield Press, Kent Town, South Australia, 2008
      498 pp, photos, maps, index, sb, cr

A full biography of Arthur Blackburn who enlisted in the AIF and received a battlefield commission at Gallipoli. He received the VC for actions at the Somme and later played a key role in the Palestine campaign. In WW2 as a Brigadier, he was taken prisoner by the Japanese and survived the Burma Railway. Includes previously unpublished photos by Blackburn.

F9   FEAST, Sean
      HEROIC ENDEAVOUR: The remarkable story of one Pathfinder Force attack, a Victoria Cross and 206 brave men
      Grub Street, London, 2006
      190 pp, photos, index, hb, cr

This book is arranged in two parts: Part One is a detailed narrative of the daylight raid on the marshalling yards near Cologne on 23 December 1944 and Part Two is an appraisal of the raid and also survivors' recollections. On the raid, Sqn Ldr RAM Palmer DFC* (109 Sqn), in Lancaster V, was Oboe Leader in the first formation's B Flight which also included Capt Edwin Swales (582 Sqn, SAAF) as captain of Lancaster T. Half of the formation's aircraft, including Palmer's, failed to return. He was awarded the VC posthumously and Swales (awarded the VC in 1945) was awarded the DFC. Their deeds are narrated in detail. Appendix V lists Palmer's 110 bombing and marking operations. See F10.

F10   FEAST, Sean
      MASTER BOMBERS: The Experiences of a Pathfinder Squadron at War 1944-1945
      Grub Street, London, 2008
      223 pp, photos, index, hb, cr

This history of No 582 Squadron focuses on the exploits and experiences of its personnel. The Squadron, part of No 8 (Pathfinder) Group, was based at Little Staughton and flew Lancasters. It formed on 1 April 1944 and disbanded on 10 September 1945. Pages 171-178 tell the story of Captain E (Ted) Swales of the Squadron's B Flight. He was awarded the DFC for his gallantry on 23 December 1944 in the attack on marshalling yards near Cologne, as part of the formation under Sqn Ldr RAM Palmer (posthumously awarded the VC). Swales was master bomber of a Lancaster force that attacked Pforzheim on 23 February 1945 and was killed when his crippled aircraft crashed; he was awarded the VC posthumously. See F9.

F11   FELL, Captain W.R., CMG CBE DSC RN
      THE SEA OUR SHIELD
      Cassell, London, 1966
      232 pp, photos, sketches, maps, index, hb, cr

These war memoirs of Capt Fell include an account of his service in midget submarine operations, initially as Training Officer (in 1943) and from 1944 as Commanding Officer of HMS *Bonaventure*, which parented midget submarines. He provides a detailed description of Operation *Source* (pages 166-181) and Operation *Struggle* (pages 208-226) in which operations the VC was won by Cameron and Place and Fraser and Magennis respectively.

F11A   FELTON, Mark
THE SEA DEVILS: Operation STRUGGLE and the last great raid of World War Two
Icon Books, London, 2015
334 pp, photos, maps, index, sb, cr

An account of the *X-craft* raid at the end of WW2 for which VCs were awarded to IE Fraser and JJ Magennis.

F11B   FELTON, Mark
CASTLE OF THE EAGLES: Escape from Mussolini's Colditz
Icon Books, London, 2017
308 pp, photos, hb, cr

This book describes the POW camp at Vincigliata Castle in the Italian Tuscan hills which held high-ranking allied prisoners during WW2. They were guarded by over 200 Italian soldiers. Two of the POWs were WW1 VCs: Adrian Carton de Wiart and Philip Neame. Both generals escaped via a tunnel.

F12   FERGUSON AND OSBORN (*publisher*)
CAPT. A. J. SHOUT, VC
Ferguson & Osborn, Wellington, New Zealand, nd (c1919)
12 pp, sb, cr

A small booklet describing the life and VC exploit of Captain AJ Shout VC.

F13   FERGUSON, Harry
OPERATION KRONSTADT: The greatest true tale of espionage to come out of the early years of MI6
Hutchinson, London, 2008
363pp, photos, maps, index, hb, cr

The author, a former SIS agent, describes the audacious operation to rescue the SIS operative, Paul Dukes, from Krondstadt during the civil war in Russia in 1919. Lieutenant AWS Agar operated a courier service from his secret base at Terrioki on the Finish shore north of Kronstadt. He ferried secret agents and information in and out of Krondstadt Harbour in his shallow draught, 35-knot, Coastal Motor Boat, *CMB4*. For his bravery on 16/17 June 1919, Agar was awarded the DSO for his role on the attack in the harbour on 18 August 1919 in which CC Dobson and GC Steele were awarded the VC. Agar was awarded his VC for a solo raid in *CMB4* into Kronstadt Bay on 16/17 June 1919. Reviewed in V62.

F14   FERGUSON, Ian
AUSSIE WAR HEROES: They Shall Not Grow Old
Brolga Publishing, Melbourne, Victoria, Australia, 2012
266 pp, photos, index, sb, ncr

This book is an assortment of Australian heroes and heroines from the Boer War to Afghanistan. All Australian VCs to 2012 are briefly recorded.

F15   FINCASTLE, Lieutenant Viscount, VC and ELLIOT-LOCKHART, Lieutenant P.C.
A FRONTIER CAMPAIGN: A narrative of the Malakand and Buner Field Forces on the North West Frontiers of India 1897-1898
Methuen, London, 1898 (reprinted: RJ Leach, London, 1990)
232 pp. (1990 reprint: 229 pp.), sketches, maps, hb, cr

An account of the punitive expeditions on the North West Frontiers of India between 1897 and 1898 during which Fincastle won his VC. All officers killed or wounded are listed.

F19   FITZ-GIBBON, Spencer
NOT MENTIONED IN DESPATCHES.... The History and Mythology of the Battle of Goose Green
Lutterworth Press, Cambridge, 1995
208 pp, line drawings, maps, index, hb, cr

A detailed re-examination of the Battle of Goose Green in the Falklands conflict, 1982, and of the part played by Colonel 'H' Jones VC. It reappraises the command style adopted during the battle, tackles the myths that surrounded the action and exposes the lessons learnt. The VC deed of Jones is narrated in detail.

F20   FITZHERBERT, Cuthbert (*editor*)
HENRY CLIFFORD VC: His Letters and Sketches from the Crimea
Michael Joseph, London, 1956
288 pp, photos, sketches, maps, index, hb, cr

The book, primarily, reproduces the letters of Major General Hon Sir Henry Hugh Clifford VC written between May 1854 and April 1856 when he was on active service in the Crimea (during which he won the VC). Sketches drawn by Clifford during the War are reproduced in colour and in black and white. A 31-page biographical note on Clifford prefaces the main text. The introduction erroneously states Clifford was educated at Stonyhurst but he was at Prior Park.

F22   FLEMING, George
MAGENNIS VC: The Story of Northern Ireland's only winner of the Victoria Cross
History Ireland, Dublin, 1998
224 pp, photos, maps, hb, cr

This well-illustrated book documents Magennis' early life during the Depression in Belfast in the 1930s, his enlistment in the Royal Navy as a boy seaman in 1935 and his service in WW2 culminating in the award of the VC for gallantry in a midget submarine in Singapore Harbour in 1945. The latter part of the book explores his post-war life and struggles.

F23   FLETCHER, Joseph Smith
ROBERTS OF PRETORIA: The Story of His Life
Methuen, London, 1900
126 pp, photo, hb, cr

A short biography of Lord Roberts VC.

F24   FLOWER, Stephen
(1) A HELL OF A BOMB: The Bombs of Barnes Wallis and How They Won the War
Tempus Publishing, Stroud, 2003
320 pp, photos, maps, sb, cr
(2) BARNES WALLIS' BOMBS: Tallboy, Dambuster and Grand Slam
Tempus Publishing, Stroud, 2004
496 pp, photos, drawings, index, hb, cr

This book traces the development and operational use of Barnes Wallis' bombs in WW2 and appraises their effectiveness. Their use against high-profile targets are described in detail and aircrews participating in these operations are listed. Eighty pages are devoted to *Upkeep* developed for the Dams Raid led by Wg Cdr Guy Gibson. Other principal bombs covered include *Highball*, *Tallboy* and *Grand Slam*.

F25   FLOYD, Thomas Hope
AT YPRES WITH BEST-DUNKLEY
John Lane, London, 1920
234 pp, fold-out map, hb, cr

A vivid personal account of the fighting and suffering of the 2/5th Lancashire Fusiliers on the Ypres Salient in 1917. During this period the battalion was commanded by Capt (T/Lt Col) Bertram Best-Dunkley, in which capacity he was awarded the VC posthumously. These memoirs are based on the author's private diary and the letters he sent home. The services of Lt Col Best-Dunkley are described throughout the book and the author also gives his own personal impressions of him and reveals his character and personality.

F27   FORBES, Archibald, LLD
BARRACKS BIVOUACS AND BATTLES
Macmillan, London, 1891
328 pp, hb, cr

A miscellany of 16 military essays by the author, each of which had previously appeared in various contemporary periodicals. The seventh essay entitled *Bill Beresford and his Victoria Cross* (pp 129-150) is a personal account of Lt Col Lord William Beresford and how he won the VC in the Zulu War.

F28   FORD, Ken
RUN THE GAUNTLET: The Channel Dash 1942
Osprey Publishing, Oxford, 2012
80 pp, photos, colour illustrations, maps, index, sb, cr

In February 1942 some major vessels of the German fleet, the battle cruisers *Scharnhorst* and *Gneisenau* and the heavy cruiser *Prinz Eugen* left Brest to return to Germany. Passing through the straits of Dover they were attacked by the RAF and Royal Navy. In a running battle the Germans succeeded in getting through. A posthumous VC was awarded to Lt Cmdr E Esmonde. This publication is Volume 28 in Osprey's *Raid* series.

F29   FORREST, G.W., CIE
SEPOY GENERALS: Wellington to Roberts
William Blackwood, Edinburgh & London, 1901
478 pp, photos, index, hb, cr

A collection of biographical studies of nine Generals who distinguished themselves in India. Pages 319-466 relate to a study of Lord Roberts VC, which is based on official records and Roberts' own despatches. The other generals studied are Wellington, Baird, Edwardes, Napier, Munro, Lockhart, Stewart and Jacob.

F30 FORREST, Sir George, CIE
THE LIFE OF LORD ROBERTS KG VC
Cassell, London, 1914
380 pp, photos, index, hb, cr

A full biography of Lord Roberts VC from his early years to his death in 1914 and covering all the military campaigns in which he took part.

F32 FORRESTER, Larry
SKYMEN: Heroes of Fifty Years of Flying
Collins, London, 1961
256 pp, photos, hb, cr

A collection of stories portraying the background, character and career of 67 of some of the world's most famous flyers told in the context of their contribution to aviation. Amongst the many highly decorated personalities included are nine VCs (Ball, McCudden, Mannock, Bishop, Cruickshank, Gibson, Middleton, Edwards and Ward).

F35 FORTESCUE, John (Published as J. W. F.)
GENERAL THE RIGHT HONOURABLE SIR REDVERS BULLER VC
Publisher unknown, nd (c1906)
12 pp, sb, cr

This biography of Sir Redvers Buller VC was published anonymously with an author's initials as JWF, later identified as John Fortescue. A copy is held at Oxford University.

F36 FOSTER, Charles
BREAKING THE DAMS: The Story of Dambuster David Maltby and His Crew
Pen & Sword Aviation, Barnsley, 2008
208 pp, photos, map, index, hb, cr

This biography of Squadron Leader David John Maltby DSO DFC, the author's uncle, recalls his early years and life before WW2 and his wartime career in the RAFVR which he joined in 1940. Posted to 617 Sqn on 25 Mar 1943, he flew on the Dams Raid on 16/17 May 1943 as pilot of Lancaster AJ-J in the first wave attack on the Möhne Dam. His aircraft's *Upkeep* mine, the fifth dropped, caused the substantial second breach. Promoted Squadron Leader, he was appointed 'A' Flight Commander. He was killed on 15 Sep 1943 when his aircraft crashed into the North Sea heading for an attack on the Dortmund-Ems Canal.

F37 FOSTER, Charles
THE COMPLETE DAMBUSTERS: The 133 men who flew on the Dams Raid
The History Press, Stroud, 2018
320 pp, photos, index, sb, cr

The story of the Dams Raid in May 1943 is well known, particularly the part played by Wg Cdr GP Gibson VC, but little is known of many of the individual bomber crew members. This is the first book to tell the stories of all the men who flew on the Dams Raid. Crews are listed under their respective Lancaster bombers, beginning with AJ-G, Gibson's aircraft. There are numerous references to Gibson throughout the book, which also covers selecting the aircrews, training and the attacks on the dams.

F39   FOWLER, Gene
THE JERVIS BAY GOES DOWN
Random House, New York, 1941
24 pp, hb, cr

The Jervis Bay Goes Down is a poem about HMS *Jervis Bay*, an armed merchantman commanded by Captain ESF Fegen RN, and its fight against the *Admiral Scheer* during which Fegen won a posthumous VC. A three-page account of the battle is also included.

F40   FOWLER, T. Robert
VALOUR IN THE VICTORY CAMPAIGN
General Store Publishing Company, Burnstown, Ontario, 1995
235 pp, photos, maps, index, sb, cr

This book describes major actions and awards to the 3rd Canadian Division in Belgium, the Netherlands and Germany in 1944-45. Chapter 4 is dedicated to the action at Mooshof, Holland on 25/26 February 1945 in which Sgt A Cosens won the VC.

F41   FOWLER, T. Robert
[1] COURAGE REWARDED: The Valour of Canadian Soldiers under Fire
Trafford Publishing, Victoria, British Columbia, Canada, 2009
369 pp, photos, maps, index, sb, cr
[2] COURAGE REWARDED: The Valour of Canadian Soldiers under Fire 1900-2011
(revised edition)
CreateSpace Independent Publishing Platform, 2013
376 pp, photos, maps, index, sb, cr

This book investigates the nature of courage and how it is recognized in the context of Canadian soldiers at War from South Africa in 1900 to Afghanistan in 2007. The revised edition (2013) extends the coverage up to the Canada's withdrawal from Afghan operations in 2011. The author charts gallantry awards and analyses the mechanisms for awards and distribution. A total of 14 Canadian VC recipients and their awards are covered .

F41A   FOX, Robert
EYEWITNESS FALKLANDS: A Personal Account of the Falklands Campaign
Methuen, London, 1982
337 pp, photos, maps, index, hb, cr

The author was a BBC reporter with British troops during the Falklands conflict of 1982. Lt Col "H" Jones VC OBE, CO of 2nd Battalion, The Parachute Regiment, and the Battle of Goose Green which led to his posthumous VC, are covered extensively in the book.

F42   FRANKI, George and SLATYER, Clyde
MAD HARRY: Australia's Most Decorated Soldier - Harry Murray VC CMG DSO and Bar DCM CdeG
Kangaroo Press, New South Wales, Australia, 2003
276 pp, photos, maps, index, sb, cr

This is a complete biography of Murray covering his early years and his enlistment as a private in the 16th AIF. By the end of WW1 he had been decorated five times, was four times mentioned in despatches, held the rank of Lieutenant-Colonel and commanded a machine gun battalion. Pages 17-146 cover Murray's service in WW1 and pages 147-180 cover the years 1919 to 1966 when he died. A large Appendix, pages 189-250, reproduces Murray's articles in *Reveille* magazine between 1929 and 1939 and provides Murray's vivid recollections of his experiences in the Great War. Reviewed in V52.

F43 FRANKS, Norman L.R.
SE5/5a ACES OF WORLD WAR I
Osprey Publishing, London, 2007
96 pp, photos (many colour), index, sb, cr

In the last 18 months of WWI in France the SE5/5a aircraft were the workhorses of the RFC/RAF. This book describes almost 100 aces who flew those aircraft including VC recipients: Ball, Mannock, McCudden, Beauchamp-Proctor and Bishop. There are 11 pages of colour plates of aircraft containing 37 illustrations.

F44 FRANKS, Norman L.R., and SAUNDERS, Andy
MANNOCK: The Life and Death of Major Edward Mannock VC DSO MC RAF
Grub Street, London, 2008
192 pp, photos, maps, index, hb, cr

This biography of the highest scoring ace of WW1 examines his life and circumstances surrounding his death which is shrouded in mystery. An examination is made of his victory claims and the whereabouts of his remains and a quest to persuade the CWGC to accept the authors' findings. The volume contains a list of Mannock's victories and many previously unpublished photographs.

F44A FRANKS, Norman
FALLEN EAGLES: Airmen who survived the Great War only to die in peacetime
Pen & Sword Aviation, Barnsley, 2017
244 pp, photos, index, hb, cr

This volume features biographies of the 93 pilots from Great Britain and the Empire who were decorated for bravery in the Great War and lost their life while flying during the inter-war years. The biographies are arranged in five chapters: 1918-19 (20 pilots), 1920-21 (15), 1922-23 (16), 1924-28 (21) and 1929-40) (21). Two VC recipients are included: Capt AFW Beauchamp-Proctor and Lt Col WG Barker. It also includes Capt HT Fox-Russell MC (died 18 Nov 1918), brother of Capt John Fox-Russell VC MC. The book has 150 b&w plates.

F45 FRASER, Edward
ROMANCE OF THE KING'S NAVY
Hodder & Stoughton, London, 1908
312 pp, photos, hb, ncr

This book has 35 chapters covering the Royal Navy from Elizabethan times to the Victoria era. Chapter 2 is titled *How the Navy's VCs have been won*. In 29 pages the author briefly covers 45 VCs won by the RN and RM up to 1907.

F46 FRASER, Ian
FROGMAN VC
Angus & Robertson, London, 1957
216 pp, photos, hb, cr

This autobiography of Lt Cdr Fraser VC DSC RD traces his naval career in the Merchant Navy and on active war service in the RNR. After serving as a midshipman in destroyers, he became a submariner and eventually commanded *XE-craft*. His exploits in *XE3*, for which he and Magennis won the VC, are described in detail. On release from naval service, he established Universal Divers Ltd and proceeded with a civilian career which he documents.

F47   FREMONT-BARNES, Gregory
GOOSE GREEN 1982
Spellmount (The History Press), Stroud, 2013
160 pp, photos, maps, index, sb, cr

The fight for Goose Green was the first major land engagement of the Falklands conflict in 1982 fought between British and Argentine forces. This book describes the 14 hour battle in which British forces (2 Para) were attacking well-dug in Argentine positions over boggy ground. Profiles are given of the British and Argentine commanders and their personalities. Detailed maps of the battle are provided and the part played by Lt Col "H" Jones who won a posthumous VC in the action as CO of 2 Para.

F48   FRERE-COOK, Gervis
THE ATTACKS ON THE TIRPITZ
Ian Allan, London, 1973
112 pp, photos, maps, index, hb, cr

Lt Cdr Frere-Cook, a former submarine commander, describes the efforts made by the British to destroy the German battleship *Tirpitz*. Chapter 3 (pages 37-69) details the attack on the *Tirpitz* by *X-craft* for which Cameron and Place were awarded the VC. This book is No. 8 in the *Sea Battles in Close-Up* series.

F50   FREYBERG, Paul
BERNARD FREYBERG VC: Soldier of Two Nations
Hodder & Stoughton, London, 1991
627 pp, photos, maps, index, hb, cr

The definitive biography of Lt Gen Lord Freyberg VC, written by his eldest son, the 2nd Baron (MC). Supported by extensive notes and sources, the book is comprehensive in its coverage of General Freyberg's military career spanning two world wars and of his subsequent appointments as Governor General of New Zealand and Deputy Constable and Lieutenant Governor of Windsor Castle.

F59   FROST, E.T. (Edward Thorneycroft)
COLOUR SERGEANT McKENNA'S VICTORIA CROSS: A True Tale of the Maori Wars
Steran Press, Canberra, 1945
15 pp, sb, cr

A short account of Col Sgt Edward McKenna of 65th Regt who won the VC on 7 September 1863 near Cameron Town, New Zealand.

F60   FROST, Major General John
2 PARA FALKLANDS: The Battalion at War
Buchan & Enright, London, 1983
192 pp, photos, line drawings, index, hb, cr

A history of the 2nd Battalion The Parachute Regiment during the Falklands conflict of 1982. Lt Col 'H' Jones VC OBE, the Battalion's commander up until his death in the Battle of Goose Green, is covered extensively. The appendices include a summary of the Brigade Log for the Battle of Goose Green and also a list of all honours and awards to the battalion.

F61   FRY, Eric
AN AIRMAN FAR AWAY: The Story of an Australian Dambuster
Kangaroo Press, Kenthurst, New South Wales, Australia, 1993
242 pp, photos, drawings, maps, index, hb, cr

This volume is a biography of Queensland-born Flying Officer Charles Rowland Williams DFC. He joined the Royal Australian Air Force in 1941 and after qualifying as a Wireless Operator/Air Gunner was sent to the UK in October 1941 to serve with RAF Bomber Command. Posted to 617 Squadron in March 1943, he flew as Wireless Operator on Lancaster AJ-E (pilot Flt Lt RNG Barlow) in the second wave for the attack on Sorpe Dam on 16/17 May 1943 but over Germany his aircraft struck high tension cables and crashed, killing the crew.

F62   FULLER, Reginald C. (*editor*)
CROSSING THE FINISHING LINE: Last Thoughts of Leonard Cheshire VC
St Paul's Publications, London, 1998
80 pp, photos, sb, cr

A record of Leonard Cheshire's deeply-held convictions, as told by him to Fr Reginald Fuller during June and July 1992. He describes how he came to terms with his illness, his reflections on his faith and his final thoughts on matters important to him. Lord Cheshire died shortly after, on 31 July 1992.

F65   FURNEAUX, Rupert
THE ZULU WAR: ISANDHLWANA AND RORKE'S DRIFT
JB Lippincott, Philadelphia, USA, 1963
210 pp, maps, index, hb, ncr

An appraisal of the battle of Isandhlwana and the defence of Rorke's Drift in 1879. In addition to describing the fighting, the author also examines the causes and effects in a historical perspective. A brief account of the VC deeds of the two actions is incorporated within the text.

G2   GALLAGHER, Thomas
AGAINST THE ODDS: Midget Submarines against the Tirpitz
McDonald, London, 1971
170 pp, photos, maps, index, hb, cr

The full story of the *X-craft* operation against the German battleship *Tirpitz* in 1943 during which the commanders of *X6* (Lt Cameron) and *X7* (Lt Place) won the VC. The part played by Cameron and Place in the action is given significant coverage.

G4   GARRETT, Richard
SKYHIGH: Heroic Pilots of the Second World War
Weidenfeld & Nicolson, London, 1991
185 pp, photos, hb, cr

The author examines the life and exploits of some well-known WW2 combat pilots. Typically, a chapter is devoted to each pilot; the exception is a chapter concerning several American Pacific aces. Chapter 2 (pages 21-45) relates to Guy Gibson VC and Chapter 7 (pages 113-135) concerns Leonard Cheshire VC. Other chapters relate to George Beurling, Donald Bennett, Adolph Malan, Adolf Galland, Douglas Bader and Pierre Clostermann.

G10   GARRS, Mike
VALIANT HEARTS: The Story of the Uppingham School VCs
Privately published, Lincoln, 2010
76 pp, photos, sb, cr

This publication includes short biographies of VC recipients educated at Uppingham: JG Collings-Wells, AM Lascelles, GA Maling, THB Maufe and WAS Clarke.

G11   GEDDES, John
SPEARHEAD ASSAULT: Blood, Guts and Glory in the Falklands Frontlines
Century, London, 2007
261 pp, photos (some colour), illustrations (some colour), maps, hb, cr

A first-hand account of 2 Para's battle for Goose Green fighting against well-entrenched Argentinean positions in May 1982. The battalion had 17 soldiers killed including the CO, Lt Col 'H' Jones who was awarded a posthumous VC. The author participated in the battle with 2 Para.

G12   GASSON, James
TRAVIS VC: Man in No-Man's Land
AH & AW Reed, Wellington, 1966
128 pp, photos, hb, cr

The biography of Sgt RC Travis VC DCM MM of the Otago Mounted Rifles, NZEF. His early years and family background are documented. Born Dickson Cornelius Savage, Dick Travis's military service and exploits from 1914 until 1918, when he was killed, are narrated in detail.

G15   GIBBS, Gary
THE BRIGADE OF GUARDS: VICTORIA AND GEORGE CROSS [*sic*] **WINNERS**
The Guards Museum, London, 2012
56 pp, photos (many in colour), sb, cr

This A4 size publication records the VC recipients of the five Regiments of the Brigade of Guards (in order of regimental seniority), with one VC per page (two pages for Viscount De L'Isle). Biographical details include background, military service history, VC action, *London Gazette* citation, location of VC group (with colour photo of group) and post-war activities, where relevant. All 45 Guards VCs up to 2012 are included (so does not include JTD Ashworth VC). The Foreword is by The Duke of Edinburgh. Limited edition of 500 copies.

G20   GIBSON, Wing Commander Guy, VC DSO DFC
ENEMY COAST AHEAD
[1] Michael Joseph, London, 1946; 302 pp, hb, cr
[2] Michael Joseph, London, 1993, 302 pp, hb, [*50th anniversary of Dams Raid edition*]
[3] Bridge Books, Wrexham, 1995 [*reformatted and updated*]; 240 pp, photos, hb, cr
[4] **ENEMY COAST AHEAD – UNCENSORED: The Real Guy Gibson**, Crecy Publishing, Manchester, 2003 (*uncensored and reformatted*); 288 pp, photos, hb, cr
[5] **IN ZOEKLICHT EN AFWEERVUUR** (*Dutch edition*), (*translated by LEE, C, Joanita and RUDENKO, Flight Lieutenant, W., DFC*) G.W. Breughel, Amsterdam, nd (late 1940s); 319 pp, photos?, sb, cr
[6] **CAP SUR L'ENNEMI** (*Belgian edition*), Gerard & Co., Verviers, Belgium, 1959; 155 pp, sketches, sb, cr (*French text*). Translated by Henri Daussy.

The war memoirs of Gibson up to 1944 when he was killed. Gibson describes his service flying Hampdens against German naval targets in 1939, then as a night fighter pilot and subsequently as a squadron commander in Bomber Command. His most famous exploit, the Dams Raid of 617 Squadron, is documented. The 1995 reformatted version of the book updates the details of the raid which, due to censorship, had been omitted from the original version. Whilst retaining Gibson's text, it is annotated by Chaz Bowyer and contains photographs.

G23   GIBSON, Mary
WARNEFORD VC
Fleet Air Arm Museum, Yeovilton, 1979
128 pp, photos, sketch, maps, index, hb, cr

A well-illustrated biography of Flight Sub-Lieutenant RAJ Warneford VC RNAS written by his second cousin. It charts the history of three generations of the Warneford family, and describes Warneford's early life in India and in the Merchant Navy. It then documents his short time in the RNAS during which he won his VC for shooting down a Zeppelin on 7 June 1915. Warneford was killed in a flying accident ten days later.

G24   GIESE, Toby
THE MEN OF THE 24th: The Zulu War of 1879
Published by author, Missouri, USA, 1987
96 pp, photos, line drawings, maps, sb, cr

A well-illustrated account of the battles of the Zulu War and, in particular, those at Isandhlwana and Rorke's Drift. Melvill, Coghill, ES Browne and Rorke's Drift VCs receive significant coverage.

G25   GILLIATT, Edward, MA
HEROES OF THE INDIAN MUTINY (*1914 edition*)
DARING DEEDS OF THE INDIAN MUTINY (*1922 edition*)
Seeley, Service & Co, London, 1914 & 1922
345 pp. (1914 ed), 254 pp. (1922 ed), artists' impressions, hb, cr

Both of these volumes are compiled from extracts of various books on the Indian Mutiny. Chapters VI and VII (pages 125-178, both volumes) provide a concise account of FS Roberts, who won the VC during this period, and is based on R50 and Malleson's *Indian Mutiny*. Brief mention is made to the following VCs: Peel, DC Home, Salkeld, Hawthorne, Kavanagh and Hills. The eleven chapters of the 1922 edition are extracted from the larger 1914 edition.

G28   GLANFIELD, John
BRAVEST OF THE BRAVE: The Story of the Victoria Cross
Sutton Publishing, Stroud, 2005
182 pp, photos, index, hb, ncr

This book gives an overview of VC recipients selected from the Baltic / Crimea up to Iraq in 2004. Each VC recipient is given brief coverage. Chapter 2 is entitled *Valour's Cross* and provides the background to the institution of the VC and pages 23 to 36 of the chapter provides significant new insights into the source of metal from which the VCs were manufactured. Reviewed in V57.

G29   GLEESON, Joe
IRISH ACES OF THE RFC AND RAF IN THE FIRST WORLD WAR: The Lives Behind the Legends
Fonthill Media, Stroud, 2015
245 pp, photos, index, hb, cr

This work features full biographical accounts of 29 Irish fighter pilots of the RFC and RAF in WWI who were credited with five or more aerial victories. A chapter is devoted to each ace. After describing their family background and early years, their military careers and achievements, including aerial victories and awards, are examined. Where relevant, details of their later life are given. In addition to recording their death, memorials to them are identified. Chapter 17 (pages 127-148) is devoted to Major Mannock VC.

G30   GLIDDON, Gerald
[1] **VCs OF THE SOMME: A Biographical Portrait** (*original title*)
Gliddon Books, Norwich, 1991
212 pp, photos, sketches, maps, index, hb, cr
[2] **VCs OF THE FIRST WORLD WAR: THE SOMME**
Alan Sutton Publishing, Stroud, 1994
212 pp, photos, sketches, maps, index, hb, cr
[3] **VCs OF THE FIRST WORLD WAR: THE SOMME**
The History Press, Stroud, 2011
268 pp, photos, sketches, maps, index, sb, cr

This book comprises biographical accounts of the 51 VC recipients who won their Cross on the Somme between July and November 1916. Each account contains information about the recipient's family background, early years, military career, post-service life (if applicable) and death. It also describes their VC deed in the context of the operation. The text is supported by 250 illustrations and maps. The republished title is part of the series *VCs of The First World War*. See G31 annotation, second paragraph.

G31   GLIDDON, Gerald
       VCs OF THE FIRST WORLD WAR: 1914
       [1] Alan Sutton Publishing, Stroud, 1994
       230 pp, photos, sketches, maps, index, hb, cr
       [2] The History Press, Stroud, 2011
       278 pp, photos, sketches, maps, index, sb, cr

This book comprises biographical accounts of the 46 VC recipients of 1914. Each account contains information about the recipient's family background, early years, military career, post-service life (if applicable) and death. It also describes their VC deed in the context of the operation. The text is supported by 120 illustrations and maps. The book is part of the series *VCs of The First World War*.

Gliddon's eight volume series of the *VCs First World War* (G30 to G37) was republished by The History Press starting with G31 in 2011 in softback. For the new series the author revised and updated the text. There are fewer photographs in the text but there are 16 pages of photos near the centre of the book. The cover was redesigned but content format remained the same. Also in this series are five volumes by other authors. See B28, C114, S75, S76 and S77.

G32   GLIDDON, Gerald
       VCs OF THE FIRST WORLD WAR: SPRING OFFENSIVE 1918
       [1] Sutton Publishing, Stroud, 1997
       213 pp, photos, index, hb, cr
       [2] The History Press, Stroud, 2013
       287 pp, photos, maps, index, sb, cr

Arranged chronologically by date of VC deed, this book provides biographies of the 57 men who won the VC during the German Spring offensive on the Western Front between March and July 1918. Each account contains information about the recipient's family background, early years, military career, post-service life (if applicable) and death. It also describes their VC deed in the context of the operation. Over 130 photographs and maps are included. The book is part of the series *VCs of The First World War*. See G31 annotation, second paragraph.

G33   GLIDDON, Gerald
       VCs OF THE FIRST WORLD WAR: ARRAS & MESSINES 1917
       [1] Sutton Publishing, Stroud, 1998
       222 pp, photos, maps, index, hb, cr
       [2] The History Press, Stroud , 2012
       270 pp, photos, maps, index, sb, cr

Following a similar format to the author's earlier titles in this series, this book contains biographical accounts of the 50 men who won the VC at Arras or Messines and spans the period January-July 1917. The text is interspersed with over 140 illustrations. This book is part of the series *VCs of the First World War*. See G31 annotation, second paragraph.

G34   GLIDDON, Gerald
       VCs OF THE FIRST WORLD WAR: THE ROAD TO VICTORY 1918
       [1] Sutton Publishing, Stroud, 2000
       218 pp, photos, maps, index, hb, cr
       [2] The History Press, Stroud, 2014
       312 pp, photos, maps, sb, cr

Following a similar format to the author's earlier titles in this series, this book contains biographical accounts of the 64 men who won the VC in the final offensive across France in the period of 8 August to 26 September 1918. The text is interspersed with over 114 illustrations and 29 maps. See G35. This book is part of the series *VCs of the First World War*. See G31 annotation, second paragraph.

G35   GLIDDON, Gerald
      VCs OF THE FIRST WORLD WAR: THE FINAL DAYS 1918
      [1] Sutton Publishing, Stroud, 2000
      218 pp, photos, maps, index, hb, cr
      [2] The History Press, Stroud, 2014
      288 pp, photos, maps, index, sb, cr

This is a continuation of G34 containing biographical accounts of the 56 men who won the VC in the last weeks of WW1 (27 September – 6 November 1918). The text is well illustrated and is in a similar format to the author's other titles in this series. This book is part of the series *VCs of the First World War*. See G31 annotation, second paragraph.

G36   GLIDDON, Gerald
      VCs OF THE FIRST WORLD WAR: CAMBRAI 1917
      [1] Sutton Publishing, Stroud, 2004
      263 pp, photos, maps, drawings, index, hb, cr
      [2] The History Press, Stroud, 2012
      286 pp, photos, maps, drawings, index, sb, cr

This book covers all the VCs of the Western Front not covered by earlier titles in the series *VCs of the First World War*. It contains biographies of 43 men who won the VC between February 1916 and December 1917. The text is well illustrated with several maps. The biographies vary in length; the longer ones include J Sherwood Kelly and R Gee. This book is part of the series *VCs of the First World War*. See G31 annotation, second paragraph. Reviewed in V54.

G37   GLIDDON, Gerald
      VCs OF THE FIRST WORLD WAR: THE SIDESHOWS
      [1]Sutton Publishing, Stroud, 2005
      238 pp, photos, maps, index, hb, cr
      [2] The History Press, Stroud, 2012
      286 pp, photos, maps, drawings, index, sb, cr

This book covers all the VCs not covered by the other volumes in the series. A total of 46 VC recipients are described by campaigns in Africa, India, Italy, Mesopotamia, Palestine and Salonika. The Gallipoli VCs are excluded as these were covered in S75. Each VC has three to four pages but some entries are longer. This volume is part of the series *The VCs of the First World War*. See G31 annotation, second paragraph. Reviewed in V56.

G38   GLIDDON, Gerald (*editor*)
      VCs HANDBOOK: The Western Front 1914-1918
      Sutton Publishing, Stroud, 2005
      218 pp, photos, map, sb, ncr

This book lists each of the 491 VCs awarded for the Western Front from 1914 to 1918. The awards are listed in chronological order with details of birth, background, unit, how each VC was won, LG announcement details, date and place of death and memorials. The account of each VC action is either a summary of the LG citation or, in the case of short citations, an expanded description. Reviewed in V57.

G39   GLIDDON, Gerald (*editor*)
FOR VALOUR: Canadians and the Victoria Cross in the Great War
Dundurn, Toronto, Canada, 2015
488 pp, photos, maps, index, sb, cr

This volume, written by the editor with contributions from Peter F Batchelor and Stephen Snelling, covers the Canadian VCs in WW1. A total of 67 recipients are described along with five others with a Canadian connection. This book is divided into five sections covering 1914/15, 1916, 1917, 1918 and recipients with Canadian connections. On average each recipient is given six pages. The authors were responsible for writing most of the series *VCs of the First World War* published by Sutton Publishing between 1994 and 2005. See G31 annotation, second paragraph.

G41   GLOVER, Michael
RORKE'S DRIFT: A Victorian Epic
Leo Cooper, London, 1975
146 pp, photos, sketches, maps, index, hb, cr

A detailed historical account of the defence of Rorke's Drift in January 1879 and of the deeds that resulted in the award of 11 VCs. Chard, Bromhead, Hook and Hitch are featured prominently.

G43   GOLDING, Harry, FRGS (*General editor*)
THE WONDER BOOK OF DARING DEEDS: True Stories of Heroism and Adventure
Ward, Lock & Co., London, nd (c1937, revised c1947)
256 pp, photos, hb, cr

This well-illustrated book for the younger reader devotes a chapter to each of the 33 true stories that it recalls, six of which are devoted to VCs: Findlater, Cornwell, Earl Roberts, Stuart/Williams (HMS *Pargust*), Holbrook and Warneford. There is also a chapter relating to the VC actions at Zeebrugge in April 1918 and at Rorke's Drift. The c1947 edition includes a chapter on Learoyd and Gibson.

G44   GOMERSALL, Mike
THOMAS BRYAN: The Forgotten VC of Whitwood and Castleford
Privately published, Castleford, 2015
cr

A limited publication covering the life of Thomas Bryan VC. The publication describes his early life when his family moved from Stourbridge to Castleford where his father found employment at Whitwood pit. After schooling Bryan became a miner and played rugby league for Castleford. At the age of 33 joined the Northumberland Fusiliers. At Arras in April 1917 Bryan won the VC and was presented his decoration by King George V at a ceremony at St James' Park Football ground in Newcastle-upon-Tyne before a crowd of 40,000 spectators. After WW1 Bryan returned to the pits and later ran a grocery business. He died in 1945.

G45   GOOD, Mabel Tinkiss
MEN OF VALOUR
MacMillan, Toronto, 1948
137 pp, line drawings, hb, cr

Stories of gallant service by Canadians in WW2. VC winners covered are: Merritt, Osborn, Hornell, Topham, Mynarski, Triquet, Foote, Gray and Smith. The book is written in a dramatized style throughout and is aimed at younger readers. Other non-VC actions are also included.

G47   GORDON, Brian and STUPPLES, Peter
       CHARLES HEAPHY
       Pitman, Pentone, New Zealand, 1987
       46 pp, sketches, sb, cr

       This large-format book depicts the paintings and line drawings of Charles Heaphy VC. There are 22 pages of text and 24 pages of coloured paintings and black and white line drawings of the native Maori. The entire text is on Heaphy's life and work as an artist. His landscapes of New Zealand are some of the earliest produced.

G48   GOSS, Squadron Leader Chris
       MALCOLM CLUBS R.A.F.
       Privately published, 2004
       87 pp. (unnumbered), photos, sb, cr

       An illustrated history of the RAF's Malcolm Clubs from 1943 up to the organisation's disbandment in 1999. Named after Wg Cdr Hugh Malcolm, who was awarded the VC posthumously in Apr 1943 for his actions over Tunisia in Nov-Dec 1942, the first Club was opened in Algiers on 25 Jul 1943 by ACM Sir Arthur Tedder, C-in-C Mediterranean Allied Air Forces. Following a ten-page biographical sketch of Malcolm, Chapters 2-4 trace the Malcolm Club history as an organisation and a full list of the individual Clubs, over 100, records their opening date. Reminiscences feature in Chapter 5. Many of the Clubs are depicted in the book's 108 b&w half-page photographs.

G49   GOUGH, General Sir Hugh, GCB VC
       OLD MEMORIES
       William Blackwood, Edinburgh and London, 1897
       236 pp, sketches, hb, cr

       The memoirs of Sir Hugh Gough VC covering his military experience during the Indian Mutiny in which he won the VC. He confined his writings to the aspects of his service that he considered would interest his family and friends. There are several references to his brother, Sir Charles Gough VC. This volume was republished by the Naval & Military Press and the National Army Museum.

G50   GOURLEY, Colin (*compiler*)
       SGT. C. E. GOURLEY V.C., M.M. 1893-1982
       BookPOD Pty Ltd., Vermond South, Victoria, Australia, 2017
       46 pp, illustrations (some colour), facsimiles (chiefly colour), maps (some colour), portraits (some colour), sb, cr

       A short biography of CE Gourley VC MM compiled by his nephew.

G51   GOVERNMENT OF CANADA VETERANS AFFAIRS (*publisher*)
       FOR VALOUR: The Citations
       Government Department of Canada Veterans Affairs, Ottawa, nd (c1995)
       32 pp. (16 pp. English text/16 pp. French text), line drawings from photos, sb, cr

       This bilingual publication covers all 16 Canadian VC winners of WW2. A portrait, full citation and brief personal details of each recipient are included with a photograph of the appropriate cap badge. The work is in large format (340 x 240 mm) and is accompanied by a large double-sided bilingual poster portraying the recipients.

G52 GOVERNMENT OF WESTERN AUSTRALIA (*publisher*)
THE GALLANT COMPANY OF BRAVE MEN: Western Australia's Victoria Cross and George Cross Recipients
Government of Western Australia, West Perth, Western Australia, 2015
42 pp, photos, sb, cr

This publication has short biographies and photos of the 17 VC recipients of Western Australia. Each recipient is covered in two pages with details of their background, military service and the exploit resulting in the award of the VC. Two GC recipients are also included.

G53 GRAHAM, Arthur S.
LIEUTENANT (ACTING LIEUTENANT COLONEL) JAMES NEVILLE MARSHALL VC MC AND BAR IRISH GUARDS (SPECIAL RESERVE) ATTACHED LANCASHIRE FUSILIERS
Privately published, Birmingham, nd
57 pp, photos, maps, hb, cr

A short biography of JN Marshall VC. This A4-typed transcript is held in the archives section of Birmingham City Library. The text includes letters, documents and recollection from those who knew the recipient. It covers his birth, background, education, war service from September 1914 to his death in action on 4 November 1918.

G54 GRAHAM, Arthur
JAMES NEVILLE MARSHALL VC, MC and bar
Privately published, 1998
57 pp, photos, map, sb, cr

An appraisal of the life of Lt (A/Lt Col) JN Marshall, who won the VC posthumously in 1918. The author's extensive research, which included access to family and regimental papers, has uncovered significant anomalies in the records of Marshall's pre-service life and military service, some of which remain mysterious. A detailed account of Marshall's participation in WWI is documented within the context of the associated operations. An A4 correction sheet was issued by the author in January 1999.

G55 GRANT, Ian
JACKA VC: Australia's Finest Fighting Soldier
MacMillan, South Melbourne, Australia, 1989
196 pp, photos, index, sb, cr

A biography of Captain Albert Jacka VC MC and bar who was the first member of the Australian Infantry Forces to be awarded the VC in WW1. It tells the story of his early years, his military service in WWI, his civilian life (during which he was Mayor of St Kilda) and his death.

G56 GRAVES, T.B.A.
'I SAW A RARE CHANCE': The Combat Diary of Billy Bishop
MvR Publications, Liskeard, Cornwall, 1988
92 pp, photos, sb, cr

The author examines the following question: "What is the evidence and is there sufficient available to support a rational and unbiased assessment of Bishop's combat record in WW1?" Bishop's combat reports are reproduced and after each report the author attempts, through research, to accept or reject the claims found in the report.

G57   GRAVES, T.B.A.
'SCATTERED WITH THE WINDS': The Personal Papers of Captain Albert Ball
MvR Publications, Liskeard, Cornwall, 1988
52 pp, one photo, sb, cr

This comb-bound typescript publication in the series *Aces of the Great War* records the military career and death of Capt Ball VC DSO and two bars MC. The text is interspersed with photocopied reproductions of many of Ball's actual combat reports. In other instances, typed transcripts are included. Additionally, the author uses extracts from Ball's letters to his family describing his experiences.

G58   GRAY, Edwyn
BRITISH SUBMARINES IN THE GREAT WAR: A Damned un-English Weapon
Leo Cooper, Barnsley, 2001 (first published Charles Schribner's Sons, 1971)
261 pp, photos, index, hb, cr

An account of the development and exploits of the Royal Navy's submarines in WW1. Five submarine commanders won the VC and their actions are described in detail (Boyle, Holbrook, Nasmith, Sandford and G White).

G59   GRAY, John and PETERSON, Eric
BILLY BISHOP GOES TO WAR
Talonbooks, Vancouver, Canada, 1981
102 pp, photos, sb, cr

This book is predominantly the script of the musical play, *Billy Bishop Goes to War*, which was first produced by the Vancouver East Cultural Centre, British Columbia, on 3 November 1978. The play was directed by John Gray and starred Eric Peterson who played Billy Bishop VC, as well as seventeen other characters. It relates Billy Bishop's experiences in WW1.

G59A   GRAY, John H.
QUID NON PRO PATRIA: The Short Distinguished Military Life of Henry James Nicholas VC MM
Christchurch City Council, Christchurch, New Zealand, 2007
74 pp. (text) + 27 pp. (appendices), photos (colour), maps (colour), sb, cr

A monograph of Christchurch's only VC recipient of WW1. The biography covers his early years, military service, his VC episode and death in action on 29 Oct 1918. There are 74 numbered pages of text and 27 un-numbered pages of maps, photos and letters. Included is a description of the efforts to get a statue of Nicholas placed at the Bridge of Remembrance, Christchurch in New Zealand, which was dedicated on 7 March 2007.

G60   GREAVES, Adrian
RORKE'S DRIFT
Cassell, London, 2002
446 pp, photos, maps, index, hb, cr

A major reappraisal of the action at Rorke's Drift on 22-23 January 1879, at which 11 VCs were won. Using rare documentary and archaeological evidence, Dr Greaves sheds new light on many aspects of the battle and on the personalities involved. Biographical sketches, particularly military career and award details, are provided in respect of defenders of Rorke's Drift and also of the commanders. The appendices contain full transcripts of the associated official reports, particularly those by Lieutenant Chard, Lieutenant Bromhead and Surgeon Reynolds, all of whom were awarded the VC.

G60A   GREAVES, Dr Adrian FRGS (*editor*)
REDCOATS AND ZULUS: Myths, Legends and Explanations of the Anglo-Zulu War 1879
Leo Cooper, Barnsley, 2003
224 pp, photos, maps, index, hb, cr

This volume is a compendium of research to 2004 on the Anglo-Zulu War of 1879, compiled by the founder of the Anglo-Zulu War Society and editor of its journal. It considers the facts, history, myths and fallacies surrounding the war. There is some coverage of the 23 VCs awarded for the conflict.

G60B   GREAVES, Adrian and KNIGHT, Ian
WHO'S WHO IN THE ZULU WAR 1879
Pen & Sword Military, Barnsley, 2006
Two volumes, 437 pp, (Vol 1 196 pp; Vol 2 241 pp); portrait photos, hb, cased, cr

This book contains brief biographies of the main people involved in the Anglo-Zulu War of 1879, including politicians and administrators, military leaders, soldiers and civilians. The 27 VC recipients associated with the conflict are included. Vol 1 concentrates on British figures and Vol 2 relates to colonial, foreign and Zulu figures.

G61   GREENHOUS, Brereton
THE MAKING OF BILLY BISHOP: The First World War Exploits of Billy Bishop VC
The Dundurn Group, Toronto, Canada, 2002
232 pp, photos, maps, index, hb, cr

A major reappraisal of Billy Bishop VC focusing on his WW1 exploits. This powerful biography exposes and examines the myths about him and provides strong evidence to distinguish between fact and fiction. After extensive research, the author refutes many of Bishop's aerial victories claimed after flying alone. In particular, he argues that the raid for which Bishop was awarded the VC could not have taken place. The author also compares and contrasts his findings with those in earlier books on Bishop. Reviewed in V51.

G62   GREEN HOWARDS REGIMENTAL MUSEUM (*publisher*)
FOR VALOUR 1914-1918: The Green Howards
Green Howards Regimental Museum, Richmond, 1964
27 pp, photos, sketches, sb, cr

This illustrated booklet records the VC citations of the 12 WW1 VC awards to the Green Howards (W Clamp, H Tandey, EF Beal, W McNally, OCS Watson, W Anderson, SW Loudon-Shand, DS Bell, WH Short, ACT White, DP Hirsch, T Dresser). See also C46.

G62A   GREEN, Neville
FREDERICK BELL: Western Australia's First Victoria Cross
Western Australia Focus Education Services, Perth, Western Australia, 2016
84 pp, photos (some colour), colour map, sb, cr

A biography of FW Bell VC who was born in Western Australia in 1875 and served in the Boer War winning the VC in May 1901. He joined the British Colonial Office in 1905 and served in Africa for 15 years. During WW1 he served in France and was later the commandant of an army recuperation camp in England. Bell was forced into retirement from the Colonial Office in 1925 after giving unpopular evidence to a Kenyan Commission of Enquiry. He died in Bristol in 1954.

G63   GREHAN, John
THE FIRST VCs: The Stories Behind The First Victoria Crosses of The Crimean War and The Definition Of Courage
Frontline Books (Pen & Sword Books), Barnsley, 2016
287 pp, photos, maps, index, hb, cr

The Crimean War and all the actions in which VCs were awarded, on land and at sea, are told from a variety of sources, including official documents and eye witness accounts. The stories of the 111 VC deeds are recounted in detail and a separate chapter gives brief biographical information (average 3.5 biographies per page) of the recipients' lives after the war and the location of their VC and medals. The book also includes the background to and the introduction of the VC. (See B15A).

G64   GRIBBLE, Leonard R.
HEROES OF THE FIGHTING RAF
George Harrap, London, 1941
204 pp, photos, hb, cr

The author examines, in individual chapters, the heroic deeds of 13 pilots of the RFC, RNAS and RAF, 11 of whom won the VC in WW1 or WW2. VC-specific chapters relate to Ball, Bishop, Warneford, WL Robinson, Rees, Bell Davies, Hawker, Insall, McLeod, McCudden and Mannock. A further chapter covers, briefly, the VC exploits of Garland and Gray, Learoyd, Hannah and Nicolson.

G65   GRIBBLE, Norah (*compiler*)
THE BOOK OF JULIAN (Volume 1)
FRAGMENTS THAT REMAINED FROM THE BOOK OF JULIAN (Volume 2)
Women's Printing Society, London, nd (c.1920)
Two volumes - 396 pp. (Vol 1: 350 pp.; Vol 2: 46 pp.), photos, sketches, hb, cr

Volume 1 contains a 90-page monograph of the life of Captain Julian Gribble VC, who died in 1918 as a POW. The rest of this volume reproduces letters written by him during his pre-school years and throughout his military career. There are many photographs from his early life onwards. Volume 2 contains his miscellaneous writings from the age of 6 to 19 years. Both volumes were compiled by Captain Gribble's mother.

G66   GRIFFITH, Kenneth
THANK GOD WE KEPT THE FLAG FLYING: The Siege and Relief of Ladysmith 1899-1900
Hutchinson, London, 1974
398 pp, photos, maps, index, hb, cr

Kenneth Griffith, the well-known actor and documentary film maker, narrates a comprehensive history of the siege and relief of Ladysmith's garrison commanded by Sir George White VC. The parts played by White, Sir R Buller VC and Lord Roberts VC are covered extensively. See M8B.

G67   GRIMSHAW, Captain Roly (Edited by Col J. Wakefield and Lt Col J.M. Weippert)
INDIAN CAVALRY OFFICER 1914-15
Costello, Tunbridge Wells, 1986
224 pp, photos, sketches, index, hb, cr

This work comprises, predominantly, the war diary of Captain Grimshaw, 34th Poona Horse which spans the period August 1914 to June 1915 on the Western Front. Additional notes written by the editors expand the chronicle. Grimshaw also documents the exploits of his fellow officer, Lt de Pass whose posthumous VC action is recorded vividly.

G68 GRIMWOOD, Ethel St Clair, RRC
MY THREE YEARS IN MANIPUR AND ESCAPE FROM THE RECENT MUTINY
Richard Bentley, London, 1891
333 pp, photos, sketches, map, hb, cr

A first-hand account of the Mutiny in Manipur, Burma in which the author's husband, the Political Agent, was killed. The book's penultimate chapter (XIX, pages 289-315) is a reprint by Major CJW Grant describing his small force's gallant march which was recognized by his award of the VC. Much detail is also included of life in Manipur prior to the uprising.

G69 GRODZINSKI, Captain J.R.
THE BATTLE OF MOREUIL WOOD
Publisher unknown, Canada, 1993
32 pp, maps, sb, cr

This booklet, published on the 75th anniversary of the Battle of Moreuil Wood, describes the Canadian forces' capture of a strategic position. During the action Lieutenant GM Flowerdew led a desperate charge at enemy positions and was awarded a posthumous VC. In the same action Lieutenant FMW Harvey VC was awarded the MC.

G70 GROSER, Horace G.
FIELD MARSHAL LORD ROBERTS VC KP GCB GCSI GCIE: A Biographical Sketch
Andrew Melrose, London, nd (c1900) (republished: Pilgrim Press, London, 1914)
144 pp, photo, hb, cr

A concise biography of Lord Roberts VC sketching his early life and his military career up to December 1899.

G71 GROVE, Eric
SEA BATTLES IN CLOSE-UP: WORLD WAR 2 (Volume 2)
Ian Allan, Shepperton, Surrey, 1993
224 pp, photos, maps, index, hb, cr

A profusely-illustrated compilation of detailed accounts of nine sea battles of WW2 which, in common with its companion volume (published in 1988), were rewritten from an earlier series of *Sea Battles in Close-Up* monographs. Chapter One (pages 7-35) relates the Battle of Narvik and, in particular, the VC actions of Lt Cdr Roope and Capt Warburton-Lee. Chapter Six (pages 116-139) concerns the *X-craft* attack on the battleship *Tirpitz* in which Lt Cameron and Lt Place won the VC. See also F48.

G73 GUÉRIN, Jean-Paul
MISSION À CASA BARARDI: MAJOR PAUL TRIQUET, VC
Société des Journalistes, Montreal, Canada, 1944
24 pp, photos, sb, cr (*French text*)

A short account, in French, of the VC exploits of Paul Triquet VC.

G75   GUMMER, Canon Selwyn
THE CHAVASSE TWINS
Hodder & Stoughton, London, 1963
255 pp, photos, index, hb, cr

A biography of Captain Noel Godfrey Chavasse VC and bar and of his twin brother, the Rt Rev Christopher Maude Chavasse OBE MC (Bishop of Rochester). The first 70 pages cover both brothers up to 1917, when Noel was killed. Thereafter, the text relates to Christopher Chavasse.

G80   GURNEY, Gene
FLYING ACES OF WORLD WAR 1
Scholastic Book Services, New York/Toronto, 1965
186 pp, photos, maps, index, hb, cr

This book features eight flying aces of WW1 with chapters on Albert Ball VC (pages 40-57) and Edward Mannock VC (pages 100-114). The other aces featured are Coppens (Belgium), Rickenbacker (USA), Lufbery (France), Guynemer (France), Von Richtofen (Germany) and Ingalls (USA).

G90   GUTTMAN, Jon
DEFIANCE AT SEA: Stories of Dramatic Naval Warfare
Arms & Armour Press, London, 1995
192 pp, photos, index, hb, cr

A selection of 14 true stories of valiant sea fights in the face of daunting odds spanning the Elizabethan age up to the Falklands conflict in 1982. Chapter 7 (pages 88-95) is devoted to the exploits of HM Submarine *B11* on 13 December 1914 for which action her commander, Lt Cdr Holbrook, was awarded the VC.

H1   HACKER, Carlotta
         BRAVERY
         Fitzhenry & Whiteside, Markham, Ontario, Canada, 1989
         64 pp, photos, sb, cr

         This book contains biographical details of three Canadian VCs: Chapter 2 on William Hall VC, Chapter 3 on GR Pearkes VC and Chapter 4 on A Mynarski VC.

H2   HAINES, Keith
         SOMTYME IN CHIVACHIE IN FLAUNDRES: EDMUND de WYND VC
         Privately published, Belfast, 2000
         25 pp, photos (some colour), map, sb, cr

         This desktop-published document outlines the life and exploits of Edmund de Wind VC. The author, a member of the East Belfast Historical Society and one time Head of History at de Wind's old school, cites over 100 sources in this brief biography which also contains over 20 photographs, mainly in colour. The monograph's title is derived from the Prologue to Chaucer's *The Canterbury Tales*.

H3   HALCK, Jørgen
         DANMARKS FØRSTE VICTORIA-KORS: Sergent Jørgen Chr. Jensen
         Aschehoug, København, 1958
         47 pp, photos, sb, cr

         A Danish-text biography of Jørgen Christian Jensen VC.

H4   HALCK, Jørgen
         EN DANSK SOLDAT: Major Anders Lassen VC MC
         Thaning & Appels Forlag, København, 1947
         48 pp, photos, maps, sb, cr

         A Danish-text biography of Anders Lassen VC MC.

H5   HALL, Sheldon
         ZULU: With Some Guts Behind It - The making of an epic movie
         Tomahawk Press, Sheffield, 2005, revised 2006
         431 pp, photos (some colour), drawings, index, hb, cr

         This is a profusely-illustrated and very detailed account of the making of the 1964 film *Zulu*. The filming took place in South Africa between March and July 1963 and the book contains interviews previously unpublished, documents, letters and photos. It includes John Prebble's screen play and describes the film's conception, planning, filming and editing. This volume covers every aspect of the film in detail including the actors representing the defenders who were awarded the VC.

H6   HALLAM, Vic
LEST WE FORGET: The Dambusters in the Derwent Valley
Vic Hallam, nd (c1993)
48 pp, photos, sb, cr

This well-illustrated book commemorates 617 Squadron which used the Derwent Valley for training in preparation for the Dams Raid in May 1943. It traces the Squadron's history and provides short biographical sketches of Wg Cdr Gibson, Sir Barnes Wallis, Sqn Ldr Shannon and other Dambusters personalities. The Dams Raid commemorations and memorials in the Derwent Valley conclude the work.

H7   HALLAM, Vic
SILENT VALLEY AT WAR: Life in the Derwent Valley, 1939-1945
Sheaf Publishing, Sheffield, 1990
48 pp, photos, sb, cr

The first 32 pages of this well-illustrated booklet recall life in the Derwent Valley during WW2. Pages 33-48 relate to 617 Squadron's training in the Derwent Valley in preparation for Operation *Chastise*, followed by an account of the raid itself and concluding with the raid's commemorations at Ladybower Reservoir.

H9   HALLET, Mary
WITHOUT HESITATION: The Story of Christopher Cox VC
[1] Privately published, Kings Langley, Hertfordshire, 2003
119 pp, photos, maps, sb, cr
[2] Fourbears Publishing, Horsham, 2007
131 pp, photos, maps, sb, cr

This photocopied, comb-bound document provides a biographical sketch of Pte C Cox VC, who won his award serving as a stretcher bearer with the 7th Bn The Bedfordshire Regiment in March 1917. The first chapter covers Cox's early life and marriage. Chapters 2, 3, 4 and 5 cover each of the years 1914, 1915, 1916, and 1917/18. The final chapter covers the years from 1919 to 1959 when he died. The appendices include copies of seven eyewitness accounts by his comrades which were submitted with the recommendation for the VC. Reviewed in V52.

H10   HALLIDAY, Hugh A.
VALOUR RECONSIDERED: Inquiries into Victoria Cross and other awards for extreme bravery
Robin Brass Studio, Canada, 2006
245 pp, photos, index, sb, ncr

This book explores the way in which the VC is awarded and considers why some recommendations were successful and others not. It examines factors such as service politics, changing regulations, evolving perceptions of extreme danger and the role of personalities who sponsored or opposed recommendations.

H11   HAMILTON (*author's forename not specified*)
IN MEMORIAM
Privately published, 1880
31 pp, photos, hb, cr

A memoir of Lieutenant Walter Richard Pollock Hamilton, Corps of Guides, who fell at Kabul, Afghanistan, on 3 September 1879 and was awarded the VC posthumously. Written by one of his brothers, the book was produced for distribution to family and friends. It records the subject's short life, particularly his army service, and contains three portrait photographs of him. It also includes full transcripts of the significant letters of condolence sent to his father.

H12   HAMILTON, Robert
VICTORIA CROSS HEROES OF WORLD WAR ONE
[1] Atlantic Publishing, Croxley Green, Hertfordshire, 2015
348 pp, photos (some colour), maps, index, hb, cr
[2] Abridged edition, 2017, 175 pp, sb, cr

This is a large format pictorial history of the 628 VC recipients of WW1. There are 1,500 photographs with typically four or five per page. The reproduction quality is good on art quality paper. The VCs are listed chronologically by date of the VC deed with a head and shoulders portrait of each recipient. Typically three recipients are covered in a single page with a short description of the VC action. The significance of this book is the number and quality of the photos which are sourced from the archives of Associated Newspapers (*Daily Mail Picture Library*) and a number are published for the first time. They are well captioned and a number were taken in London at investitures or other VC events after the war, such as at the VC Garden Party in 1920 or the House of Lords VC Dinner in 1929.

Some VCs get more attention with a full page or two pages dedicated to them including AV Smith, Rendle, Mellish, Warneford, Angus and WL Robinson. Some VCs are treated in themed groups such as *Six VCs Before Breakfast* featuring the Lancashire Fusiliers at Gallipoli and the *Zeebrugge VCs*. The book has a introduction and each year of the war is prefaced with a chapter describing the main events of the particular year. Of the 628 VCs featured a total of 82 are cross-referenced as they receive significant coverage. Reviewed in V77.

H13   HAMILTON, John
[1] **THE PRICE OF VALOUR: The triumph and tragedy of a Gallipoli hero**
Hugo Throssell VC (*original title published in Australia in 2012*)
Macmillan (Pan Macmillan Australia), Sydney, 2012
393 pp, photos, map, index, hb, cr
[2] **GALLIPOLI VICTORIA CROSS HERO: The Price of Valour: The Triumph and Tragedy of Hugo Throssell VC**
Frontline Books (Pen & Sword Books), Barnsley, 2015
304 pp, photos, map, index, hb, cr

Hugo Throssell was one of the most controversial and tragic of the Great War VCs. At the beginning of the war he joined the Australian Light Horse which fought in a dismounted role at Gallipoli. He took part in the Battle of Hill 60 where his courage and leadership resulted in his being awarded the VC. Throssell later became an outspoken opponent of war and was widely condemned for his socialist views. As a consequence, employment became difficult and his debts mounted as his health deteriorated, and he took his own life in 1933 aged 49. The story is told in two parts: *Triumph* tells of Throssell's heroism and VC award and *Tragedy* tells of his sad decline and untimely death. Reviewed in V76.

H15   HANCOCK, Irene
THE VICTORIA CROSS GALLERY: The Origin of the Gallery in Wantage
Privately published, Wantage, 2000
16 pp, photos, sb, cr

The booklet gives a brief account of the formation and history of the exhibition and eventual dispersal of the Desanges VC paintings that were presented by Lord Wantage VC KCB to Wantage Town Council in 1900. A list of the 46 paintings is included. (See C150, D16, D17 and W42).

H18 HANNAH, Henry Bathurst
LORD ROBERTS IN WAR: A Study for The Day
Simkin, Marshall & Co., London, 1895
64 pp, hb, cr

A short description and analysis of the campaigns of Lord Roberts VC.

H20 HANNAH, W.H.
BOBS - KIPLING'S GENERAL: The Life of Field Marshal Earl Roberts of Kandahar VC
Leo Cooper, London, 1972
263 pp, photos, maps, index, hb, cr

A full biography of the life and distinguished military career of Lord Roberts VC. The author examines Roberts' achievements and his command and leadership qualities that enabled him to succeed to the post of Commander-in-Chief of the British Army.

H22 HARDEN, Julia
ERIC HARDEN VC (RAMC Attached 45 RM Commando): My Family's Story
Menin House (imprint of Tommies Guides), Eastbourne, 2011
95 pp, photos, maps, sb, cr

This is a biography of Eric Harden VC written by his daughter. Lance Corporal Harden was awarded a posthumous VC for attempting to rescue wounded comrades in 45 RM Commando in The Netherlands in January 1945. The book covers Harden's early life in Northfleet, Kent and after school becoming a butcher and serving as a member of the St John's Ambulance Brigade. The author also describes the difficulty in growing up in post war Britain. See S74.

H23 HARDER, Thomas
ANDERS LASSENS KRIG: 9 April 1940 - 9 April 1945
Informations Forlag, København, 2010
592 pp, photos, drawing, maps, index, hb, cr

A Danish-text of a full and well-illustrated biography of Major Anders Lassen VC MC**. The book's Danish title means "Anders Lassen's War", and the subtitle has the dates of 9 April 1940 (when Denmark was occupied by Germany and Lassen became personally engaged in the war) and 9 April 1945 (when Lassen was killed in action in Italy, winning a posthumous VC). This thoroughly researched biography details Lassen's life and character, his Danish background and early years, his experiences as a seaman and his wartime career as a member of the Small Scale Raiding Force and the Special Boat Squadron. The author has chosen to tell the story of the British commando forces and general conduct of the war in parallel with the biographical chapters, thus placing Lassen's struggle in a wider context.

H25 HARDY, Mary
HARDY VC: An Appreciation
Skeffington, London, nd (c1920)
94 pp, painting, hb, cr

A family memoir based on letters, recollections and diaries of relatives, friends and men who served with Hardy at the front. The Rev TB Hardy VC DSO MC was the most decorated of the forces' chaplains. This book provided much of the material for R11.

H26　HARE-SCOTT, Kenneth
FOR VALOUR
Peter Garnett, London, 1949
178 pp, photos, map, hb, cr

The author traces the origins, influences and characteristics which moulded the life of 22 VC recipients of WW2. A biographical sketch and a detailed account of the VC deed is provided for each recipient. Individual chapters cover 14 VCs: Wanklyn, Upham, Keyes, Ryder and Savage, Derrick, Cheshire, Triquet, Norton, Hollis, Cain, Lord, Fazal Din and Hornell. A postscript chapter records a brief account of the VC deed of eight recipients (Cairns, Warburton-Lee, Sherbrooke, Place and Cameron, Fraser and Magennis and Randle).

H28　HARGEST, Brigadier James, CBE DSO MC
FAREWELL CAMPO 12
Michael Joseph, London, 1945
184 pp, photo, map, hb, cr

This war memoir of Brigadier Hargest CBE DSO and two bars MC recounts his capture in November 1941 at Sidi Aziz, his subsequent imprisonment as a POW in Italy and his escape from Camp Concentramento 12 in 1943. He was one of the highest ranking Allied escapers of WW2. Also in the camp were other Generals, including two VCs, Neame and Carton de Wiart, whose life and exploits in captivity and escape attempts are recorded in detail. Hargest was killed in NW Europe in 1945.

H30　HARPER, Glyn, and RICHARDSON, Colin
IN THE FACE OF THE ENEMY: The Complete History of the Victoria Cross and New Zealand
HarperCollins (New Zealand), Auckland, New Zealand, 2006 (revised 2007)
272 pp, photos, index, sb, cr

This book covers all VC recipients who came from New Zealand or who had a close connection with the country. The book begins with a history of the VC and describes the wars and campaigns in which NZ VCs were awarded. Chapter 4 provides an insight into why few VCs were awarded to New Zealanders in WW1 with a similar analysis in Chapter 10 for WW2. There is also a two-page description of Queen Victoria's scarf and its connection with the VC. The Appendix provides full citations for each VC. There is also a chapter on GC and Albert Medal awards. Reviewed in V58. A children's version of this title (175 pp) was published in 2006.

H35　HARRIS, Barry
BLACK COUNTRY VCs: From the Crimea to World War II
Black Country Society, Dudley, 1985
36 pp, photos, sb, cr

This booklet contains biographical sketches of the 15 VCs associated with the Black Country, an area of the West Midlands in England. Generally, each sketch comprises two pages of text and is accompanied by a portrait photograph of the recipient. The VCs covered are: Barratt, Berryman, Carless, Colley, JJ Davies, Onions, RE Phillips, WA Savage, Wassall, Bonner, AC Booth, J Thompson, Bryan, Elcock and Sephton.

H36   HARRIS, John Norman
KNIGHTS OF THE AIR: Canadian Aces of World War 1
Macmillan, London, 1958
256 pp, drawings, hb, cr

This book, No 18 in the series *Great Stories of Canada*, recalls the exploits of the principal Canadian fighter aces of WW1, including three VCs: WG Barker, WA Bishop and AA McLeod. Chapters 3-7 (pages 23-79) are devoted to Barker and Chapters 10 (pages 103-130) and 13 (pages 149-156) relate to Bishop and McLeod, respectively.

H37   HARRIS, Clive, and WHIPPY, Julian
THE GREATER GAME: Sporting Icons who fell in the Great War
Pen & Sword Military, Barnsley, 2008
199 pp, photos, hb, cr

This book describes 14 sporting heroes who died while serving in the allied cause in WW1. There are two chapters on VC recipients: DS Bell, a footballer and J Harrison, a rugby player.

H38   HARRISON, Major M.C.C., DSO MC and CARTWRIGHT, Captain H.A., MC
WITHIN FOUR WALLS
Edward Arnold, London, 1930
306 pp, photos, sketches, maps, hb, cr

A detailed account of the authors' experiences as POWs, culminating in their successful escape from Ströhen in company with Lt GSM Insall VC who received the MC for his escape.

H39   HARRISON, Simon
DAMBUSTERS: The 60th Anniversary
J & KH Publishing, Hailsham, East Sussex, 2003
158 pp, photos, drawings, maps, hb, cr

This official RAF Museum publication provides an in-depth account of the planning, trials and execution of Operation *Chastise*, the Dams Raid in May 1943 on which Guy Gibson won the VC. The author also describes the reaction to the raid and gives an assessment of its degree of success. Appendices include details of the aircrews and a chronology of events from the raid's inception.

H40   HARRISON, Bill, Heritage Archival Curator Scouts Australia, Queensland Branch
MEMBERS OF THE SCOUTING MOVEMENT, FROM SIX COUNTRIES WITHIN THE BRITISH COMMONWEALTH, WHO HAVE BEEN AWARDED THE VICTORIA CROSS
Scouts Heritage Queensland, Toowong, Queensland, Australia, 2001
55pp, printed one side of A4 paper and spiral bound with acetate cover, small black & white photos, sb, ncr

Every known Commonwealth VC recipient is recorded in this privately produced booklet, with one page for each VC. After brief details of birth, death (if applicable), location of VC deed and name of Scout Group, the *London Gazette* VC citation is quoted in full.

H43   HART, Sydney
SUBMARINE UPHOLDER
Oldbourne, London, 1960
208 pp, photos, maps, hb, cr

The story of HM Submarine *Upholder*, her crew and her Captain, Lt Cdr Wanklyn VC DSO and two bars, who won his VC for exploits in the Mediterranean. It chronicles Wanklyn's command of the *Upholder*, from her commissioning in 1940 to her loss with her crew, in 1942, and gives an in-depth account of her patrols. It also provides a biographical sketch of Wanklyn which is based on information from his relatives. The appendices list the crew of the *Upholder* and also identify their gallantry awards.

H44   HART, Sydney
DISCHARGED DEAD: A true story of British Submariners at War
Odhams Press, London, 1956
208 pp, photos, hb, cr

This memoir of the author's four years' service as a stoker in HM submarines during WW2, provides a lower deck view of submarine life. He served in the most critical phases of the war – in the North Sea, the Atlantic and the Mediterranean. On his first patrol in HM Submarine *Thrasher*, Lt PSW Roberts and PO TW Gould won the VC and Chapter 16 (pages 137-146) relates wholly to this episode.

H52   HARVEY, David
MONUMENTS TO COURAGE: Victoria Cross Headstones and Memorials
[1] Kevin and Kay Patience, Bahrain, 1999
Two volumes – 843 pp. (Vol 1: 410 pp.; Vol 2: 433 pp.), photos, maps, index, hb, cr (contributors only)
[2] Naval and Military Press, Uckfield, 2008
Single volume, 814 pp, photos, maps, index, sb, cr

This major reference work, which contains over 5,000 photographs, records by date of VC deed every VC recipient, 1,322 of whom were deceased at the time of publication. The entry for each recipient comprises, typically, their portrait photograph, a photograph of their headstone or memorial (where applicable), a photograph of any other memorial to them and details relating to their birth, death, and final resting place, VC deed and known memorials. The final resting place details provide (where applicable) their accurate location, indicating whether a headstone or other memorial exists. In this form, the location of the 300 unmarked graves is also identified. Additional photographs include representative VC medal groups and a selection portraying particular recipients, VC memorials or cemeteries. The appendices contain a gazetteer of VC resting places, maps of the main VC-related cemeteries, a miscellany of statistical and summary information and drawings depicting the various types of headstone. Reviewed in V50 and V62.

H53   HARWOOD, Commodore John
WILLIAM HALL VC
Publisher unknown, 1987
16 pp, maps, sb, cr

A small booklet describing the life of William Hall VC from his early days in Nova Scotia, his service in the Indian Mutiny, during which he won the VC, and his return to Nova Scotia.

H55   HASTINGS, Macdonald
MEN OF GLORY
Hulton Press, London, 1958
159 pp, sketches, hb, cr

This book is a compilation of stories describing the deeds of brave men, on both sides, in the two world wars. Written by the *Eagle Special Investigator*, each chapter had, originally, been featured as an article in the *Eagle* paper for boys. Of the 24 chapters, 18 relate specifically to the following 21 VC winners: HM Ervine-Andrews, BAW Warburton-Lee, JA Cruickshank, Lord Lyell, ESF Fegen, BCG Place and D Cameron, CH Upham, GCT Keyes, WE Sanders, NC Jackson, ND Holbrook, A Ball, E Mannock, PSW Roberts and TW Gould, RW Annand, JT Cornwell, J Hannah, Fazal Din and MD Wanklyn. A further chapter relates to the action in which ME Nasmith won his VC.

H56   HASTINGS, Macdonald
MORE MEN OF GLORY
Hulton Press, London, 1959
176 pp, line drawings, hb, cr

This book continues the theme of H55 and is a compilation of stories originally featured in the *Eagle* boys' paper. Of the 33 short chapters, 18 are devoted to VC actions relating to the following VC winners: MJ Dease, SF Godley, WL Robinson, G Campbell, RN Stuart, W Williams, RWL Wain, FWO Potts, HB Wood, GC Steele, AWS Agar, CC Dobson, GB Roope, RB Stannard, PJ Gardner, Lt T Wilkinson, DE Hornell, GQM Smythe, A Lassen, E Esmonde, ACC Miers, IE Fraser, JJ Magennis and TP Hunter.

H57   HASTINGS, Macdonald
PASSED AS CENSORED
George Harrap, London, 1941
159 pp, hb, cr

A narrative by a war correspondent for *Picture Post* describing his experiences in the early part of WW2. There is an illustrated six-page chapter on Captain HM Ervine-Andrews who won a VC near Dunkirk. The author was a contemporary of Ervine-Andrews as pupils at Stonyhurst College, and father of the celebrated author and war correspondent Sir Max Hastings. See H58.

H58   HASTINGS, Sir Max
WARRIORS: Portraits from the Battlefield
Harper Collins, London, 2005
384 pp, photos, hb, cr

Portraits of 14 men and one woman from the 19th and 20th centuries who have distinguished themselves in battle. Chapter 4 covers John Chard VC and Chapter 10 describes Guy Gibson VC. The book's title was later renamed *Extraordinary Tales from the Battlefield*. The author is the son of Macdonald Hastings (see H55, H56 and H57).

H60   HATWELL, Jeff
NO ORDINARY DETERMINATION: The Story of Percy Black and Harry Murray of the First AIF
Fremantle Arts Centre Press, Fremantle, Western Australia, 2005
303 pp, photos, maps, index, sb, cr

This book describes the lives of two Australian heroes in WW1 - Lieutenant-Colonel H Murray VC CMG DSO* DCM CdeG and Major Percy Black DSO DCM CdeG. Both landed at Anzac Cove on 25 April 1915 and distinguished themselves at Gallipoli and on the Western Front.

H65 HAWKER, Lieutenant Colonel Tyrell M., MC
[1] HAWKER, VC: The biography of the late Major Lanoe George Hawker VC DSO
Mitre Press, London, 1965
253 pp, photos, hb, cr
[2] HAWKER VC - RFC ACE: The Life of Major Lanoe Hawker VC DSO 1890 - 1916
Pen & Sword Aviation, 2013 (*republished edition*)
253 pp, photos, hb, cr

A biography of L Hawker VC written by his younger brother. Part I describes his ancestral background, his childhood years, during which he was a constant companion of the author, his short time as a naval cadet and his service with the Royal Engineers. Part II concerns his pioneering years in the RFC during which he was one of the earliest pilots to specialise in air combat, and provides a detailed account of his VC deed. Part III relates to his command of 24 Sqn and his loss in action. The text is supported by 53 photographs.

H66 HAYDON, A.L.
THE BOOK OF THE VC
Andrew Melrose, London, 1906 (revised: 1908)
294 pp, photos, sketches, hb, ncr

This book contains brief descriptions of many VC actions from the Crimea to Tibet (1904). Appendices contain award statistics and a complete alphabetical list of VC recipients up to 1904.

H68 HEATHCOTE, T.A.
THE BRITISH FIELD MARSHALS 1736-1997: A Biographical Dictionary
Leo Cooper, Barnsley, 1999 (reprinted Pen & Sword, Barnsley, 2012)
368 pp, index, sb, cr

This book contains biographies of 138 Field Marshals since 1736 when the rank was created until 1997, when, due to the shrinking size of the British Army, the rank disappeared. The biographies vary in length but on average are 2.5 pages long. There were four VC field marshals: Lord Roberts, Viscount Gort, Sir George White and Sir Evelyn Wood.

H69 HEATHCOTE, T. A.
THE BRITISH ADMIRALS OF THE FLEET 1734 - 1995: A Biographical Dictionary
Leo Cooper, Barnsley, 2002
338 pp, hb, cr

This book contains biographies of Admirals of the Fleet between 1734 and 1995. The biographies vary in length and include three VC recipients: Commerell, Salmon and AK Wilson.

H70 HEINEMANN (publisher) / "HIS MOTHER" (editor)
FROM DARTMOUTH TO THE DARDANELLES: A Midshipman's Log
William Heinemann, London, 1916
174 pp, hb, cr

A chronicle of the experiences of an unnamed midshipman during ten months of WW1. It was compiled by his mother, from a narrative written during her son's sick leave in December 1915. Leaving Dartmouth in August 1914, he eventually served on HMS *Goliath* in the period during which Cdr HP Ritchie (Second-in-Command) won the VC. The VC episode is chronicled in detail. There is evidence to suggest that the unnamed author was Midshipman WBC Weld-Forester, later Lt Cdr (OBE).

H75 HERCUS, Alan
FREYBERG - Lt General Sir Bernard Freyberg VC GCMG KCB KBE DSO LLD
AH & AW Reed, Wellington, New Zealand, 1946
60 pp, photos, hb, cr

A brief biography of Lt Gen Freyberg VC describing his service in both world wars and the awards that he received.

H78 HIS MAJESTY'S STATIONERY OFFICE (*publisher*)
V.C.
His Majesty's Stationery Office, London, 1942 (updated: 1943)
39 pp. (1943 version: 70 pp.), photos, drawings, sb, ncr

The scope of the original (1942) work is all WW2 VCs that had been gazetted up to 17 April 1942. The 1943 version expands the coverage up to 30 June 1943. Typically, a page is devoted to each recipient, which includes an artist's impression of the VC deed, a brief account of the deed and a portrait of the recipient. The book was also published in French and Hindi versions.

H79 HER MAJESTY'S STATIONERY OFFICE (*publisher*)
VICTORIA CROSS CENTENARY EXHIBITION 15TH JUNE - 7TH JULY 1956: The Stories of the Winning of the Victoria Crosses which are represented in the Exhibition
Her Majesty's Stationery Office, London, 1956
143 pp, sb, ncr

This publication records the full citations of the 640 Victoria Crosses on display at the VC Centenary Exhibition at Marlborough House in 1956. (See also H80 and H81).

H80 HER MAJESTY'S STATIONERY OFFICE (*publisher*)
VICTORIA CROSS CENTENARY EXHIBITION 1856 - 1956
Her Majesty's Stationery Office, London, 1956
39 pp, photos, sketches, maps, sb, ncr

A catalogue of items representing the 640 VC medal groups on display at the exhibition. Other display items referred to in the text include paintings depicting VC deeds, portraits, drawings and photographs of display recipients. The original Warrant instituting the VC was on display and is replicated in part. (See also H79 and H81).

H81 HER MAJESTY'S STATIONERY OFFICE (*publisher*)
VICTORIA CROSS CENTENARY: Review of Holders of the Decoration by HM The Queen, Hyde Park 26 June 1956
Her Majesty's Stationery Office, London, 1956
10 pp, sb, ncr

A souvenir programme detailing the order of events of the review and listing, by country, every VC recipient on parade. A card insert lists additions and changes. (See also H79 and H80).

H82   HIGGS, Colin and VIGAR, Bruce
VOICES IN FLIGHT: The Dambuster Squadron
Pen & Sword Aviation, Barnsley, 2013
196 pp, photos, index, hb, cr

The authors present exclusive interviews with nine aircrew members who flew and fought with 617 Squadron during WW2. Three flew on the Dams Raid led by Wg Cdr Gibson (Les Munro, Grant McDonald and George 'Johnny' Johnson) and others flew with the Squadron when it was commanded by Wg Cdr Cheshire. They describe the operations in which they took part. The Appendix lists the locations of 617 Sqn targets.

H83   HILLIER, Kenneth
"COME ON THE TIGERS!": The Story of Phillip E. Bent VC DSO
Ashby-de-la-Zouch Museum, Leicestershire, 2017
66 pp, sb, cr

A biography of PE Bent VC DSO who was born in Halifax, Nova Scotia but moved to Scotland with his family at the age of 12. In 1914 he enlisted in the British Army and served with the 9th Leicestershire Regiment, nicknamed "The Tigers". As a 26 year old Lt Col Bent was killed on 1st October 1917 in a German counterattack at Polygon Wood in Belgium and received a posthumous VC.

H84   HISCOCK, Anthea
CAPTAIN HENRY REYNOLDS VC MC
Blurb, for Whilton Local History Society, Whilton, Northamptonshire, 2017
151 pp, photos (some colour), maps, index sb, cr

This is a profusely illustrated biography of Captain H Reynolds VC MC. It contains many photos and documents from his family roots, upbringing in Whilton, Northamptonshire. His military service is covered including separate chapters on his MC and VC actions. Reynolds won his VC on 20 September 1917 near Frezenberg, Belgium whilst serving in the 12th Bn The Royal Scots.

H85   HISLAM, Percival A.
HOW WE TWISTED THE DRAGON'S TAIL
Hutchinson, London, 1918
96 pp, photos, hb, cr

A short account of the Zeebrugge and Ostend raids in April and May 1918, based on Admiralty documents. The book is well illustrated and contains in the appendix a full list of casualties sustained in the raids and a full list of honours awarded (showing citations, where applicable) in respect of the raids.

H86   *HISTORY OF WAR*
DAM BUSTERS: Inside the most daring raid of World War II
Future Publishing, Bournemouth, Dorset, 2018
145 pp, photos, drawings, maps, sb, cr

This profusely-illustrated *History of War* 'bookazine' published in commemoration of the 75th Anniversary of the Dams Raid on 16/17 May 1943, covers all aspects of Operation *Chastise* from its origination and planning to its execution and aftermath. Numerous contemporary technical drawings, maps, official documents, Flying Log Book extracts (including Gibson's and Hopgood's logs), newspaper reports, dam damage reports and the Squadron's Operations Record Book pages recording the operation are reproduced. Many contemporary photographs are included.

H87 HODDER & STOUGHTON (*publisher*)
JACK CORNWELL: The Story of John Travers Cornwell VC, Boy-1st Class
Hodder & Stoughton, London, 1917
78 pp, photos, hb, cr

This book describes the short life of Jack Cornwell who won a posthumous VC at the battle of Jutland on 31 May 1916. It recalls his time in the Royal Naval Training Establishment as a Boy 2nd Class followed by his sea service in HMS *Chester* on which he was killed in action. The anonymous author is recorded as "the author of *Where's Master?*", under which description he wrote other titles for Hodder and Stoughton between 1910 and 1920. Republished by Naval & Military Press.

H89 HODDER, Edwin
HEROES OF BRITAIN IN PEACE AND WAR
Cassell, London, nd (c. 1892)
Two volumes - 648 pp. (Vol 1: 320 pp.; Vol 2: 328 pp.), line drawings, index, hb, cr

This well-illustrated work tells the story of many of Britain's 'heroes' of the 18th and 19th centuries. The diverse categories include pioneers, engineers, missionaries, inventors, discoverers, reformers, scientists, philanthropists, soldiers and sailors. Three chapters relate specifically to *Heroes of the Victoria Cross* in the Crimea (Vol 1 pages 152-162); in India (Vol 1 pages 292-320), and in the Colonies and elsewhere (Vol 2 pages 164-185). A selection of VC deeds is narrated briefly in the context of the battle and for some includes line drawings depicting the deed.

H89A HOLLAND, James
DAM BUSTERS: The Race to Smash the Dams, 1943
Bantam Press, London, 2012
437 pp, photos, drawings, map, index, hb, cr

This comprehensive study of the Dams Raid on 16/17 May 1943 is arranged in four parts: Part I (p21-118) recalls the politics, development of the bouncing bomb and the personalities involved; Part II (p123-277) concerns the forming of 617 Sqn, target selection and the training and preparation for the operation; Part III (p281-345) gives detailed coverage of the dams' attack; and Part IV (p349-398) analyses the raid's aftermath and legacy. The Operation *Chastise* timeline and a full list the codewords conclude the work.

H90 HOLLEDGE, James
FOR VALOUR: The Story of Australia's VCs
Horwitz, Sydney, Australia, 1965
129 pp, drawings, sb, cr

A compilation of brief accounts of the VC action of every Australian recipient of the VC prior to 1965 (ie excluding Vietnam). The accounts vary in length and detail; some are based solely on the VC citation, others are framed in the context of the particular campaign or battle. Despite the book title, Upham VC, a New Zealander, is covered in a 22-page account.

H91 HOLLOWAY, S.M., MA(Oxon)
THE THREE OLD PORTMUTHIAN VCs
Portsmouth Grammar School, Portsmouth, 1998
24 pp, drawing, map, photos, sb, cr

A small booklet with short biographies of the three old boys of Portsmouth Grammar School who won the VC: WH Nickerson, N Holbrook and FJW Harvey. There is a total of eight photographs and a short introduction on the history of the VC.

H92   HOLME, Norman
SILVER WREATH: Being the 24th Regiment at Isandhlwana and Rorke's Drift, 1879
Samson Books, London, 1979
95 pp, sketches, hb, cr

This book provides biographical details of the officers and men of the 1st and 2nd Battalions, 24th Regiment who participated in the actions at Isandhlwana and Rorke's Drift and, in particular, covers the following VCs: Coghill, Melvill, Chard, Hitch, Hook, Bromhead, Allan, R Jones, W Jones and John Williams. The details relating to these VCs are based on their record of service and are accompanied by their portrait photograph. The book also contains full accounts, written individually, by some of the Rorke's Drift defenders, including Chard, Hitch and Hook.

H93   HOLME, Norman
THE NOBLE 24ᵀᴴ: Biographical Records of the 24ᵗʰ Regiment in the Zulu War and the South African Campaigns 1877-1879
Savannah Publications, London, 1999
384 pp, photos, hb, cr

This work contains biographical, service and casualty details and medal entitlements of the 2500 officers and men of the 1st and 2nd Battalions of the 24th Regiment who fought in the South African campaigns during 1877 to 1879. A section (pages 265-372) relates to the defence of Rorke's Drift and, in addition to containing the aforementioned comprehensive details, includes full transcripts of Lt Chard's despatch and contemporary accounts by some VCs (Chard, Pte Hitch, Pte Hook, Pte R Jones, Pte W Jones), as well as an examination of the sources appertaining to the defence.

H94   HOLMES, Richard
DUSTY WARRIORS: Modern Soldiers at War
Harper Press, London, 2006
385 pp, photos (some colour), maps, index, hb, cr.

The author, a noted military historian and broadcaster, was also the Colonel of the Prince of Wales's Royal Regiment. In this capacity he visited the regiment during their seven month tour in Iraq which included the action in which Johnson Beharry performed his VC exploit. The author draws on the testimonies of soldiers in the danger zone and provides and describes the regiment's tour in detail. Reviewed in V59.

H95   HOME, Surgeon General Sir A.D., VC KCB
SERVICE MEMORIES
Edward Arnold, London, 1912
340 pp, photo, index, hb, cr

Edited by Colonel CH Melville, RAMC, this publication narrates the reminiscences of the author's military career and campaign service, spanning the Crimean War, the Indian Mutiny (VC), the China War (1860), Canada (1861-62) and culminating with the New Zealand War (1864). His subsequent military service up to retirement completes the memoir.

H96 HOPE, Robert
A STAFFORDSHIRE REGIMENT IN THE ZULU AND SEKUKUNI CAMPAIGNS 1878-1879: 80th Regiment of Foot
Churnet Valley Books, Leek, 2007
384 pp, photos, drawings & engravings, maps, tables, sb, cr

This highly-detailed and well-illustrated chronicle of the 80th Regiment's involvement in South Africa from 1876 to 1880 focusses on the Sekukuni Campaigns of 1878 and 1879 (pages 57-83) and the Zulu War of 1879 (pages 85-189). The actions for which the VC was awarded to Sgt AC Booth and Pte S Wassall are described in detail. Significant coverage is given to: Colonel H. Rowland VC as Commandant of Troops in Transvaal during the Sekukuni Campaigns and Commanding No 5 Column in the Zulu War; and to Colonel H.E. Wood VC, Commanding No 4 Column in the Zulu War. A sub-chapter concerns Rorke's Drift and the actions of Lts Bromhead and Chard and Chapter Seven, concerning the VC, includes biographies of Booth and Wassall. The Regiment's full medal roll of the South Africa Medal and brief accounts of the recipients are contained in Chapter Eight. The volume features over 100 illustrations.

H97 HOPE, Robert
THE ZULU WAR AND THE 80ᵀᴴ REGIMENT OF FOOT
Churnet Valley Books, Leek, Staffordshire, 1997
192 pp, photos, maps, sb, cr

A detailed examination off the involvement of the 80th Regiment (the Staffordshire Regiment at time of publication) in the Zulu War of 1879. Chapter 8 (pages 82-97) is devoted to their two VCs, Clr Sgt AC Booth and Pte S Wassall, for whom biographical accounts and associated photographs are provided. Brief details are included about the Staffordshire Regiment's 13 VCs. Clr Sgt Booth's VC deed is described in greater detail in Chapter 7 (pages 69-81), which relates to the 'Intombi River Incident'.

H98 HOPE, Robert
VIVID COURAGE: Victoria Crosses Antecedent and Allied Regiments of the Staffordshire Regiment
Helion & Company Ltd, Solihull, 2016
247 pp, photos, sb, cr

This volume provides short biographies of VC recipients connected with the Staffordshire Regiment, its antecedant and allied regiments. VCs are included if they won their award before joining the Staffordshire Regiment or after they had left. Pages 26 - 54 provides a *Brief History of the Victoria Cross* which includes a reproduction of all the Royal Warrants and a list of wars/campaigns in which all VCs were awarded. The VC biographies are shown chronologically with a brief introduction of each war or campaign to provide the context. Pages 59 to 237 provide the biographies of 36 recipients.

H99 HOPTON, Richard
A RELUCTANT HERO: The Life of Captain Robert Ryder VC
Pen & Sword Maritime, Barnsley, 2011
224 pp, photos, maps, index, hb, cr

This biography tells the story of Robert Ryder from his childhood in India to his death in 1986, aged 78. He joined the Royal Navy in 1926 and served pre-war in Hong Kong waters and took part in in an Antarctic expedition. During the Second World War he served on board a *Q* ship and later played a major part in Operation *Chariot*, the raid on St Nazaire, where his gallantry and leadership earned him one of the five VCs awarded for this operation.

H100   HOSIE, Father Bernard
CHESHIRE VC
Justin D. Simonds, Archbishop of Melbourne, Australia, 1965
31 pp, sb, cr

This booklet describes Cheshire's war time service including the award of the VC and how witnessing the bombing of Nagasaki changed his life. It charts Cheshire's post-war foundation of the Cheshire Homes.

H101   HOWARD, Grant
GUNNER BILLY: Lieutenant-Commander W.E. Sanders VC DSO RNR
Royal New Zealand Navy Museum, Auckland, New Zealand, 2007
193 pp, photos, sb, cr

A biography of the only New Zealander to be awarded a naval VC. The volume covers his humble origins and experience in coastal boats as he worked his way up the ranks of RNR. Sanders was in command of the *Q* ship HMS *Prize* when he was awarded the VC in 1917 for sinking a submarine. Later in the year he was killed in action on board the same ship.

H102   HOWARD, Keble (pseudonym of BELL, 2nd Lt J Keble, RAF)
THE GLORY OF ZEEBRUGGE AND THE "VINDICTIVE": With the official Narratives of the Operations at Zeebrugge and Ostend
Chatto & Windus, London, 1918
64 pp, photos, sketches, maps, sb, cr

The story of the naval raids on Zeebrugge and Ostend in April and May 1918 and, in particular, of the role played by HMS *Vindictive*. The story is recalled from first-hand accounts given by some of the participants, notably Capt AFB Carpenter (who won the VC at Zeebrugge). A transcript of the Admiralty's Official Narratives of the raids is provided on pages 43-64.

H103   HOWARD, Liz
THOMAS ALFRED JONES VC DCM
Countryvise, Birkenhead, 2014
38 pp, photos, sb, cr

A short biography of 'Todger' Jones VC DCM who was born in Runcorn on 25th December 1880. There is a brief description of his civilian life before he joined the Cheshire Regiment. Most of the publication covers his service in WW1, including his VC action on 25 September 1916 at Morval, France. After the war he returned to Runcorn and worked at the salt works at Weston Point until his retirement in 1949.

H104   HOWARD, Peter
UNDERWATER RAID ON TIRPITZ
Ian Allan Publishing, Horsham, 2006
96 pp, photos, drawings, maps, sb, cr

A profusely-illustrated account of Operation *Source*, the midget submarine raid against the *Tirpitz* on 22 September 1943 for which VCs were awarded to D Cameron and CG Place. The publication, part of Osprey's *Secret Operations* series, gives a brief history of the *Tirpits* and then a detailed account of the *X-Craft*, the operation, the attack and the crews involved. Cut-away drawings of the *X-Craft* and numerous contemporary photographs support the text. The final chapter concerns the RAF attacks which sank the Tirpitz.

H105   HOWARTH, David
HEROES OF NOWADAYS
Collins, London, 1957
255 pp, sketches, hb, cr

A collection of short biographies of modern military and civilian heroes from different backgrounds. One chapter (pages 39-76) is devoted to Major Lassen VC MC and two bars. Other chapters (all non-VC) range from Sherpa Tenzing to Albert Schweitzer.

H107   HOWELL, Georgina
DAUGHTER OF THE DESERT: The Remarkable Life of Gertrude Bell
Pan Macmillan, London, 2006
518 pp, photos, maps, index, hb, cr

A biography of Gertrude Bell who came from a privileged background and was the first woman to take a first in modern history at Oxford in 1888. She was fluent in Persian, Arabic and Turkish and worked as a cartographer and archaeologist. She worked alongside TE Lawrence in military intelligence and helped to found the modern state of Iraq, becoming to Oriental Secretary in the British Administration in Iraq in 1920. Between 1913 and 1915 she had a love affair with CHM Doughty-Wylie who was killed in action at Gallipoli and was awarded a posthumous VC.

H108   HOWELL, Chris
NO THANKFUL VILLAGE: The Impact of the Great War on a group of Somerset villages – a microcosm
Fickle Hill, Bath, 2002
224 pp, photos, hb, cr

This book describes the impact of WW1 on a group of villages around Midsomer Norton and Radstock in Somerset. The author has compiled letters, diaries, newspaper articles, interviews and official reports without accompanying narrative. Oliver Brooks VC is featured in four chapters and George Prowse VC is covered in pages 195-198. Reviewed in V51.

H110   HOYLE, Arthur, DFC
HUGHIE EDWARDS VC DSO DFC: The Fortunate Airman
sb: privately published, Canberra, Australia, 1999; hb: Australia Military History Publications, Loftus, Australia, 2000
211 pp, photos, index, sb/hb, cr

A full biography of Air Cdre Sir Hughie Edwards VC KCMG CB DSO DFC. Much of the book concerns his distinguished RAF career after which he served briefly as Governor of Australia until retiring because of ill health.

H115 HUDSON, Miles Matthew Lee (*editor and author*)
TWO LIVES 1892-1992: The Memoirs of Charles Edward Hudson VC CB DSO MC and Miles Matthew Lee Hudson also some poems by Charles Edward Hudson
Privately published by Wilton 65, Bishop Wilton, York, 1992
286 pp, photos, index, hb, cr

This book is divided into three parts: the first part (pages 4-202) is the memoirs of CE Hudson who saw action on the Western Front and was awarded the VC for gallantry at Asagio, Italy in June 1918 as the 26-year-old CO of the 11th Sherwood Foresters. Hudson was also awarded the DSO and bar, MC, Croix de Guerre (France) and Italian Silver Medal for Valour and was Mentioned in Despatches six times. He acted as a Brigade Major in Archangel during the allied intervention in Russia in 1919. Hudson's memoirs, edited by his son, conclude with Dunkirk and home service in WW2. The second part of the book (pages 204-271) is an autobiography of Miles Hudson who served in Malaya before becoming Political Secretary to Sir Alec Douglas-Home when he was Foreign Secretary. The third part of the book (pages 272-286) covers 12 poems by CE Hudson and a short story by Miles Hudson. (See H116).

H116 HUDSON, Miles
SOLDIER, POET, REBEL: The Extraordinary Life of Charles Hudson VC
Sutton Publishing, Stroud, 2007
243pp, photos, maps, index, hb, cr

A full biography of Charles Hudson VC CB DSO* MC written by his son who had access to family letters, archives and photographs. The book covers Hudson's education, family background and WW1 services at the Somme and Italy when he was awarded the VC. Hudson was involved in the intervention in Russia in 1919 and a description is given of the interwar years, his WW2 service, including Dunkirk, and retirement as a Brigadier in 1946. Hudson was also a poet and several of his poems appear in the text. An appendix reproduces LG citations for his VC DSO* and MC. (See H115).

H120 HUGHES, Cledwyn
LEONARD CHESHIRE VC
Phoenix House, London, 1961
106 pp, photos, index, hb, cr

This book for youngsters (in the series *Living Biographies for Young People*) is a biographical sketch of Leonard Cheshire VC.

H123 HUMPHRIES, Harry
LIVING WITH HEROES: The Story of the Dam Busters
Erskine Press, Banham, Norwich, 2003
129 pp, photos, hb, cr

The author was selected by Guy Gibson to be the adjudant of 617 Squadron from its inception until 1945 when he was posted to the Far East. This book gives a rare insight into 617 Squadron by one who was there. Gibson and Cheshire are covered in detail.

H125　　HUNT, Derek (*not designated*)
THE WINDSOR VICTORIA CROSS EXHIBITION: The Story of the Windsor VCs
Privately published by Derek Hunt, Windsor, 1998
24 pp, photos, sb, cr

A souvenir programme for an exhibition of VC winners associated with Windsor. The exhibition took place on 16-31 May 1998 and commemorated the centenary of the deed of one of the three VCs on display, Captain Alexander Hore-Ruthven VC (1st Earl of Gowrie). The other VCs featured were Lt Col H Greenwood VC and Lance Sergeant Oliver Brooks VC.

H126　　HUNT, Derek
VALOUR BEYOND ALL PRAISE: Harry Greenwood VC
Derek Hunt, Windsor, 2003
148 pp, photos, maps, index, cr

This is the first full biography of Lt Col Harry Greenwood VC DSO* OBE MC. This well-illustrated book covers his early life and post-war career. The Great War period, in which he won the VC at Ovillers, France in October 1918, is well documented. This was a limited edition of 500 copies. Reviewed in V53.

H127　　HUNT, Derek, and MULHOLLAND, John
A PARTY FIT FOR HEROES: His Majesty's Garden Party for Recipients of the Victoria Cross, 26 June 1920
Naval & Military Press, Uckfield, 2007
124 pp, photos, map, sb, cr

This book describes the first reunion for VC recipients, a garden party hosted by HM King George V and Queen Mary at Buckingham Palace on 26 June 1920. There is a description of the preparations, the lunch at Wellington Barracks, the march around St. James's Park to the Palace, the inspection and presentations. There are 53 photographs and three appendices cover the marching order, the order of presentation, by LG date, to the King and Queen, and a full list in alphabetical order of VCs who were present on the day. The Foreword is by Bill Speakman VC. Reviewed in V60.

H128　　HUNT, Derek, and MULHOLLAND, John
BEYOND THE LEGEND: Bill Speakman VC
The History Press, Stroud, 2013
256 pp, photos, maps, index, sb, cr

A full and authorized biography of Bill Speakman VC - one of four VCs awarded for the war in Korea. The book is partly based on interviews with Speakman and those involved in the VC action of 4 November 1951. The profusely illustrated book covers his early life, army career and post army life until 2013. Reviewed in V72.

H129　　HUNT, Derek and MITCHELL, Dr Brigitte
WINDSOR IN THE GREAT WAR
Windsor Local History Group, Windsor, 2014
359 pp, photos, index, sb, cr

A history of Windsor's contribution in the Great War published at the centenary of its outbreak. It includes letters from the front, links to the royal family, military units based in Windsor barracks, schools, hospitals and Eton College. Chapter 18 covers the Windsor VCs: H Greenwood, O Brooks and A Hore-Ruthven (1st Earl of Gowrie). Reviewed in V74.

H130   HUTCHESON, Bellenden Rand
AN AMERICAN PHYSICIAN IN CANADA AND FRANCE: Captain Bellenden Seymour Hutcheson VC MC
Paul A. Fraser, Goleta, California, USA, 2005
138 pp, photos, maps, hb, cr

A biography of BS Hutcheson VC which covers his early life, military service, accounts of his VC action and copies of letters of congratulations from military leaders. It is a compilation of articles, appreciations and accounts by his comrades. Included is a list of foreign-born VC recipients including six from the USA, two from Germany, one Swiss, one Belgian, three Danish and a Russian. Also included is an article on VCs to medical services by Edwin Rye.

H140   HUTCHINSON (*publisher*)
WONDERFUL STORIES OF WINNING THE VC IN THE GREAT WAR
Hutchinson, London, nd (c1916)
280 pp, sketches, hb, cr

This book describes numerous WW1 VC actions that occurred between 1914 and 1916. Some deeds are depicted by artists' impressions published previously in *Deeds That Thrill The Empire* (S90).

H150   HYNES, James Patrick
FLIGHT LIEUTENANT DAVID LORD, VICTORIA CROSS: An Arnhem Hero
Privately published, 2018
70 pp, photos, drawings, map, sb, cr

After describing his early years (pages 2-5), this biography of Flt Lt DSA Lord VC DFC then provides an in-depth account of his service in the RAF from 1936 up to his death in his posthumous VC action in Operation *Market Garden* at Arnhem in 1944. The book concludes with details of the memorials to him.

I5   IMPERIAL WAR MUSEUM (*publisher*)
ILLUSTRATED HANDBOOK OF THE VICTORIA CROSS AND GEORGE CROSS
Imperial War Museum, London, 1970
40 pp, photos, sb, ncr

This booklet records superlatives and statistics relating to the VC, in particular, and to the GC. The lists cover first awards by service and country, family VCs, youngest and oldest winners, double VCs, civilian winners, deeds not in the presence of the enemy, forfeitures, elections etc. It also analyses VCs awarded by campaign and by service and country. Similar treatment is given in respect of the GC. Forty photographs of recipients or artists' impressions of their deeds, in particular, are included.

I6   IMPERIAL WAR MUSEUM FOR THE LORD ASHCROFT GALLERY
THE VICTOR
Originally published by DC Thomson & Co Ltd, London (various dates)
Imperial War Museum, London, 2010
16 pp, colour drawings, sb, cr

Reproduction pages from the boys' comic *The Victor*, plus two pages of GC material from *The Hornet*. The two page features were originally the front and back covers of the comics. The VCs included are: NC Jackson, IE Fraser & JJ Magennis, AE McKenzie, Abdul Hafiz, E Unwin, F Lester and JN Randle.

I10   INDIA COMMAND (*publisher*)
THE VICTORIA CROSS: India's VCs in two World Wars
OFFICERS AND MEN OF THE INDIAN ARMY WHO HAVE BEEN AWARDED THE VICTORIA CROSS FOR VALOUR IN THE FIELD (*alternative title*)
The Civil & Military Gazette, for the Public Relations Directorate, GHQ, India, Lahore, nd (c1946)
32 pp, photos, sketches, sb, cr

A compilation of short accounts of the VC deed of each of the 31 recipients who won their award during WW2 whilst serving with the Indian Army or Gurkhas. Each account is accompanied by an artist's impression depicting the VC action and a portrait photograph of the recipient (except in three cases). Indian Army and Gurkha VCs of WW1 and other campaigns are listed only. Also published in Hindi.

I15   INGLETON, Roy
KENT VCs
Pen & Sword, Barnsley, 2011
160 pp, photos, map, index, hb, cr

This book tells the stories of 51 VC recipients connected with the county of Kent through birth, family, residence, death or burial. There are six chapters covering different conflicts from the Crimean War to the Second World War, each beginning with a brief history of the war/conflict and followed by short biographies of the VCs awarded within that timescale (average three pages per VC). Reviewed in V69.

I17   INNES, David J.
BEAUFIGHTERS OVER BURMA: No 27 Squadron, RAF, 1942-45
Blandford Press, Poole, 1985
128 pp, photos, maps, hb, cr

The author was an Australian pilot who served with 27 Sqn in Burma in 1943/44. The book includes a list of casualties, decorations and awards. It includes information on Wg Cdr EJB Nicolson VC DFC who served in Burma and went missing on a Liberator over the Indian Ocean on 2 May 1945. Nicolson was the only fighter pilot to win the VC in WW2 - an award for the Battle of Britain. Between August 1943 and August 1944 Nicolson was CO of 27 Sqn flying Beaufighters over Burma and was awarded the DFC.

I20   INSALL, A.J.
OBSERVER: Memoirs of the RFC 1915-18
William Kimber, London, 1970
208 pp, index, hb, cr

The author was an observer in the RFC and brother of Group Captain G Insall VC. The volume covers the author's experiences as an observer in WW1 and describes the development of aerial combat and air photography. Chapter 8 relates to his VC brother's RFC service and subsequent period as a POW. Part of Chapter 9 concerns Albert Ball VC and Chapter 10 is devoted to Lanoe Hawker VC.

I25   IRELAND, Walter
THE STORY OF STOKEY LEWIS VC
JW Hammond (*printer*), Haverfordwest, nd (c1986)
76 pp, photos, sb, cr

A biography of Sgt HW Lewis VC who received his VC for action in Salonika in WW1. It details his family background, early years, military service, civilian life and his death in 1977.

I40   IRWIN, Mike
VICTORIA CROSS – ANZAC TO ARCHANGEL: The Story of Sgt Sam Pearse VC MM
The Sunnyland Press, Red Cliffs, Victoria, Australia, 2003
144 pp, photos, sb, cr

A biography of a Welsh immigrant who arrived in Australia in 1911. Sam Pearse served with the AIF in Gallipoli and later won his MM on the Western Front at the Battle of the Menin Road in September 1917. After the armistice he was discharged but later volunteered for the North Russian Expeditionary Force. He won a posthumous VC while serving with the 45th Bn City of London Royal Fusiliers near Archangel. This book is lavishly illustrated with over 80 photographs and draws on family archives. Reviewed in V53.

I60   IZZARD, Brian
GAMP VC: The wartime story of maverick submarine commander Anthony Miers
Haynes Publishing, Yeovil, 2009
272 pp, photos, maps, index, hb, cr

Despite the sub-title, this is a full biography of Anthony Miers VC who was a controversial character in terms of his personality and attitude. He was one of three VC submarine commanders in the Mediterranean theatre and landed Keyes VC in the North African coast on an ill-fated attempt to kill Rommel (see C45). Throughout his career, and later, Miers attracted controversy, being accused of war crimes during his service in the Mediterranean. This book sets out to prove the accusations were false. (See C45). Reviewed in V65.

I61   IZZARD, Brian

GLORY AND DISHONOUR: Victoria Cross Heroes whose Lives ended in Tragedy or Disgrace

Amberley Publishing, Stroud, 2018

287 pp, photos, index, hb, cr

Short biographies of 26 VC recipients selected on the basis of the author's evaluation that their lives ended in tragedy or disgrace. The eight forfeited VCs are included and some VCs had tragic endings to their lives, such as the suicides of Throssell VC and Boyes VC. But the inclusion of some recipients do not appear to fit the sub-title: Evelyn Wood is included because he was deemed a poor General and Gordon Steele because he was present at the *Baralong* affair. Nettleton VC was accused of rape but not convicted. Other VCs who were convicted criminals or committed suicide are not included.

J1   JACKMAN, S. W.
THE MEN AT CARY CASTLE: A series of portrait sketches of the Lieutenant-Governors of British Columbia from 1871 to 1971
Morris Printing Company, Victoria, British Columbia, 1972
207 pp, hb, cr

A collection of biographical essays (arranged as chapters) on the 21 Lieutenant-Governors of British Columbia from Joseph William Trutch appointed in 1871 to John Robert Nicholson, appointed in 1968. Pages 180-188 are devoted to Major General Pearkes VC, the 20th Lieutenant-Governor, who was sworn into office on 13 October 1960 and served until July 1968. Each biography is, typically, eight pages in length and includes a hand-drawn portrait of the subject. A full list of the Lieutenant-Governors records their date of commission and gazetting, effective appointment date and the date sworn into office. The final chapter provides a history of Cary Castle which after rebuilding became officially known as Government House and is the official residence of the Lieutenant-Governor.

J2   JACKSON, Robert
FIGHTER PILOTS OF WORLD WAR I
Arthur Barker, London, 1977
152 pp, hb, cr

The stories of 14 fighter pilots, from both sides, who fought in WW1. A chapter is devoted to each pilot, five of whom were VC winners: Chapter 5 (pages 45-53) relates to Mannock, Chapter 6 (pages 54-65) to Ball, Chapter 7 (pages 66-75) to McCudden, Chapter 8 (pages 76-84) to Barker and Chapter 9 (pages 85-95) to Bishop.

J3   JACKSON, Robert
AIR HEROES OF WORLD WAR II: Sixteen Stories of Heroism in the Air
Arthur Barker, London, 1978
175 pp, hb, cr

This companion volume to J2 narrates in dedicated chapters 16 tales of courage displayed by allied airmen in WW2. One chapter (pages 39-46) entitled *The Bridges at Maastricht* is devoted to the VC action of Fg Off RE Garland and Sgt T Gray. Another chapter (pages 155-161) entitled *The Last VC*, concerns the VC deed of Lt RH Gray.

J4   "JACKSTAFF" (pseudonym for BENNETT, J.J.)
THE DOVER PATROL: The Straits, Zeebrugge, Ostend including a narrative of the operations in the Spring of 1918
Grant Richards, London, 1919
214 pp, photos, hb, cr

This book is, predominantly, an account of the naval actions against Zeebrugge in April 1918 and Ostend in May 1918 and, in particular, the part played by HMS *Vindictive* which earned its commander (Captain AFB Carpenter) the VC. The eight photographs include a portrait of Carpenter but mainly portray the damage inflicted on *Vindictive*. Some of the other VC deeds associated with the raid are also recalled and include a chapter relating to Lt Sandford's action in command of HM Sub *C3*.

J5   JACOBSEN, Alf R. (translated from Norwegian by COWLISHAW, J. Basil)
X CRAFT VERSUS TIRPITZ: The Mystery of the Missing X5
Sutton Publishing, Stroud, 2006
287 pp, photos, maps, index, hb, cr
[*fp* H. Aschehoug, Oslo, 2003 as *Banesår* (Norwegian text)]

A Norwegian investigative journalist relates the attack by *X5* (Lt Henty-Creer), *X6* (Lt Cameron) and *X7* (Lt Place) on the *Tirpitz*. Henty-Creer and his crew were lost but Cameron and Place were made POW and received the VC. This volume investigates if the *X5* penetrated the anti-submarine defences to lay their charges and whether Henty-Creer and his crew were deserving of posthumous awards.

J6   JACOBSEN, Alf R. (translated from Norwegian by COWLISHAW, J. Basil)
DEATH AT DAWN: Captain Warburton-Lee VC and the Battle of Narvik April 1940
The History Press, Stroud, 2016
229 pp, photos, maps, index, hb, cr
[*fp* Vega Forley, 2011, as *Angrop red dagger* (Norwegian text)]

This book describes the two day first Battle of Narvik in April 1940 in which two German destroyers were sunk and six damaged. Using first hand accounts, including letters from Warburton-Lee to his wife, the author describes the events leading up to the battle and the battle itself. Warburton-Lee delivered a blow to the German Squadron on which was occupying a key iron ore port. During the engagement on 10 April 1940 Warburton-Lee was killed on HMS *Hardy* and was awarded a posthumous VC.

J7   JACOBSEN, Alf R.
ANGREP VED DAGGRY: Narvik, 9 - 10 April 1940
Vega Forlag, Oslo, 2012
245 pp, photos, maps, index, hb, cr

A Norwegian-text full account of the events which culminated in the First Battle of Narvik on 10 April 1940. The book's title means "Attack at Dawn". Captain Bernard Warburton-Lee, on board HMS *Hardy*, was in command of the force which successfully attacked German warships and merchant ships in Narvik harbour. Warburton-Lee won a posthumous VC during the action. His involvement in the operation is described extensively through the book.

J8   JAMES, David
LORD ROBERTS
Hollis & Carter, London, 1954
503 pp, photos, maps, index, hb, cr

A full biography of the life and career of Lord Roberts VC. Also included is a synopsis of his career identifying his promotions, appointments and honours with respective dates.

J9   JAMESON, Rear Admiral Sir William S., KBE CB
SUBMARINERS VC
Peter Davies, London, 1962
208 pp, photos, maps, hb, cr

This book provides a detailed narrative of the circumstances in which the VC was awarded for service in submarines. Separate chapters describe the VC deeds of Holbrook, Boyle, Nasmith, Sandford, Geoffrey S White, Wanklyn, Roberts and Gould, Miers, Linton, Cameron and Place, and Fraser and Magennis.

J10 JAMESON, Rear Admiral Sir William, KBE CB
THE FLEET THAT JACK BUILT: Nine Men Who Made a Modern Navy
Rupert Hart-Davis, London, 1962
344 pp, photos, index, hb, cr

A study of nine admirals who influenced the development of the Royal Navy. Arranged in three parts, the work provides biographical accounts in Part 1 (Forerunners) - Sir Henry Keppel; in Part 2 (The Builders) - Sir Arthur Wilson VC (pages 39-60), Lord Charles Beresford (brother of Lord William Beresford VC), Lord Fisher and Sir Percy Scott; in Part 3 (The Users) – Lord Jellicoe, Lord Beatty, Sir Reginald Tyrwhitt and Lord Keyes (father of Geoffrey Keyes VC).

J11 JARVIS, Enid
LIEUTENANT WILLIAM BARNARD RHODES-MOORHOUSE VC RFC - a Northamptonshire Hero
Spratton Local History Society, Spratton, Northampton, 2015
82 pp, photos, maps, index, sb, cr

A biography of the first airman to be awarded the VC. The book describes his early life in Northamptonshire, his love of cars and his early aviation adventures. There is a detailed description of his last fateful mission which resulted in the award of a posthumous VC. Rhodes-Moorhouse was in an early bombing raid of a rail junction at Courtrai, Belgium on 26 April 1915 and by flying low was hit by small arms fire and died the following day. The volume includes first hand accounts from contemporary sources including accounts from people who knew him.

J12 JEFFERY, David
COMMANDER LOFTUS WILLIAM JONES: Petersfield's only VC
David Jeffery Publications, Petersfield, 2016
74 pp, photos, maps, sb, cr

This biography, which is illustrated within the text, is arranged in three parts. Part 1 relates to Cdr Jones' childhood, schooling and early career. Details of his family and antecedents are supported by a family tree. Part 2 covers his naval career from 1914 to his death at the Battle of Jutland on 31 May 1916 and gives a detailed account of the battle and the action for which he was awarded the VC posthumously. Part 3 relates to his VC award and the numerous memorials for him are featured and supported by photographs.

J13 JENKINS, Herbert (*Publisher*)
HEROES OF THE RAF: The Best Adventure Stories from the "RAF Flying Review"
Herbert Jenkins, London, 1960
142 pp, photos, drawings, hb, cr

A selection of ten stories about RAF heroes of WW2, which first appeared in the *RAF Flying Review* in the late-1950s. Chapter 7 (pages 90-99) relates to the VCs won in Blenheims (Scarf, Edwards, Newton and Malcolm). Chapter 8 (pages 100-111) is devoted to some of the Lancaster VCs (Reid, Jackson, Mynarski, Swales, Bazalgette, Palmer and Nettleton). A chapter on exploits in Hurricanes includes an account of Nicolson's VC action.

J13A   JENSEN, Anne E. and CHRISTENSEN, Ole (*editors*)
OPERATION ALBUMEN: Danskeren Anders Lassen og hans fantastiske commandoraid mod en tysk luftbase i landsbyen Kastelli Pediados pa Kreta. Fortalt af de græsk modstandansfolk, som deltog i aktionen
Imprint Grafisk, Næstved, 2010
24 pp, photos, maps, sb, cr

This Danish-text booklet gives an account of Anders Lassen VC and his exploit during Operation *Albumen* in Crete 1943. The book's subtitle means: "The Dane Anders Lassen and his fantastic commando raid against a German air base in the village Kastelli Pediados in Crete. Told by the Greek resistance fighters who took part in the action". The booklet contains extracts from Giorgos Kalogerakis' book about Operation *Albumen*.

J14   JERROLD, Walter
SIR REDVERS H. BULLER VC: The Story of His Life and Campaigns
[1] S. W. Partridge, London, 1901 (*updated*); (fp 1899)
257 pp, photos, hb, cr
[2] W. A. Hammond, London, 1913 (*updated*)
270 pp, photos, hb, cr

A biography of Sir Redvers Buller VC covering his ancestral background and military career. His involvement in the campaigns in Canada, Ashanti, Zululand and Transvaal, Egypt and South Africa are documented. The 1913 edition is expanded with a Chapter XII covering the period 1901 up to his death in 1908.

J15   JERROLD, Walter
[1] LORD ROBERTS OF KANDAHAR VC: The Life-Story of a Great Soldier (*original title*)
S. W. Partridge, London, 1901 (*updated*) (fp 1900)
254 pp, photos, line drawings, hb, cr
[2] FIELD-MARSHAL EARL ROBERTS VC: The Life-Story of a Great Soldier (*later title*)
W. A. Hammond, London, 1913
237 pp, photos, line drawings, hb, cr

A concise biography of Field Marshal Earl Roberts and his military career up to 1900. The 1901 edition incorporates an additional chapter (XIII) which concludes Roberts' service in South Africa. The 1913 edition is expanded further, with a Chapter XIV covering the period 1901 onwards.

J16   JERROME, Edward George
TALES OF THE VICTORIA CROSS (AIR)
Blackie, London, 1959
25 pp, drawings, sb, cr

A children's book in Blackie's *True Adventure* Series (No. 22) featuring three air VC winners: Ball (pages 1-8), Esmonde (pages 9-16) and Gibson (pages 17-25).

J17   JERROME, Edward George
TALES OF THE VICTORIA CROSS (ARMY)
Blackie, London, 1959
26 pp, drawings, sb, cr

A children's book in Blackie's *True Adventure* Series (No 21) featuring three army VC winners: Martin-Leake (pages 1-8), Upham (pages 9-19) and Keyes (pages 20-26).

J18   JERROME, Edward George
TALES OF THE VICTORIA CROSS (NAVAL)
Blackie, London, 1959
26 pp, drawings, sb, cr

A children's book in Blackie's *True Adventure* Series (No 20) featuring three naval VC winners: Bythesea (pages 1-8), Cornwell (pages 9-16) and Magennis (pages 17-26).

J20   JOHNS, Captain W.E.
THE AIR VCs
John Hamilton, London, nd (c1935)
181 pp, photos, hb, cr

All 19 air VCs of WW1 are featured in this work. A separate chapter is devoted to each recipient and provides a short biographical sketch and details the exploits leading to the award of the VC. In some cases, the exploit is supported by the VC citation in full or as an extract. The author, who had served as an observer in the RFC, also wrote the 'Biggles' books.

J21   JOHNSON, David
ONE SOLDIER AND HITLER, 1918: The Story of Henry Tandey VC DCM MM
Spellmount (The History Press), Stroud, 2012
188 pp, photos, index, hb, cr

A full biography of Henry Tandey VC DCM MM who won his VC on 28 September 1918 at Marcoing, France. Hitler commented in 1938 that Tandey had spared his life in the battle. This statement took Tandey by surprise. The author demonstrates from extensive research that this event never happened as Hitler was not present in the location on the date described.

J22   JOHNSON, Barry C.
RORKE'S DRIFT AND THE BRITISH MUSEUM: The Life of Henry Hook VC
np, London, 1986
64 pp, photos, line drawings, maps, sb, cr

A biography of Henry Hook who received his VC for action at Rorke's Drift and later worked at the British Museum. It chronicles his early life and his military career and, in particular, his service in the Kaffir and Zulu Wars. The second half of the book examines Hook's employment at the British Museum, his life in retirement and his death. Source notes are included at the end of each chapter. (See also J23). Reviewed in V54.

J23   JOHNSON, Barry C.
HOOK OF RORKE'S DRIFT: The Life of Henry Hook VC: 1850-1905
Bartletts Press, Hall Green, Birmingham, 2004
294 pp, photos, line drawings, maps, index, hb, cr

This is a full biography of Henry Hook who achieved fame by winning the VC at Rorke's Drift. The book covers his family background, army career, VC action and his employment at the British Museum. The book has detailed notes at the end of each chapter, corrects myths about Hook and includes many previously unpublished photographs. This is an expansion of an earlier work by the author (see J22). Reviewed in V54.

J24 JOHNSON, Carl and BARNES, Andrew (*compiler and editor*)
JACKA'S MOB: A Narrative of the Great War by Edgar John Rule
Military Melbourne, Prahran, Victoria, Australia, 1999
283 pp, photos, index, sb, cr

This work, which was originally published as R85, reflects the experiences of Captain Edgar Rule MC MM whilst serving in the 14th Bn, 1st Australian Infantry Force along with Albert Jacka VC. Using the original drafts of the 1933 book together with other manuscript material held by the Australian War Memorial, it identifies most of the aliases used in the original text. It also includes a nominal roll of the 5,500 men who served in the 14th Bn between 1914 and 1919 and photographic sections containing portraits of a large number of personnel mentioned in the text and who served in the battalion.

J25 JOHNSON, George 'Johnny'
THE LAST BRITISH DAMBUSTER: One man's extraordinary life and the raids that changed history
Ebury Press, London, 2014
306 pp, photos (some colour), hb, cr

An autobiography by George 'Johnny' Johnson DFM, the last surviving British member of the RAF to take part in the Dams Raid. The book was compiled by Johnson's son, Morgan Johnson, following extensive interviews. Johnson was bomb aimer on Lancaster ED 825 'T-Tommy', piloted by Flt Lt Joe McCarthy on the raid. The book covers Johnson's early years, wartime service, post war service and post war career as a teacher. Reprinted as sb in 2015.

J27 JOHNSON, Robin
CAPTAIN JACK GRAYBURN VC: Arnhem 17th-20th September 1944
Privately published, Chalfont St Giles, 1994
10 pp, photo, sb, cr

This booklet was published as part of a 50th anniversary tribute to Captain Jack Grayburn VC, and all who served at Arnhem, by the residents of his home village of Chalfont St Giles. The booklet relates Grayburn's early life and military service and describes the incident which won him a posthumous VC at the Arnhem bridge.

J28 JOHNSON, Stephen (*compiler*)
SHEFFIELD VC GC : The men of Sheffield and the men connected with Sheffield who were awarded the Victoria and George Crosses (*sic*)
Privately published, Sheffield, 2005
21 pp, photos, sb, cr

This A4 photocpied comb-bound publication contains brief biographies of VC and GC recipients with a Sheffield link. Some links are very distant including Carton de Wiart whose only link is that he commanded a Brigade which included the Hallamshire Battalion. Biographies are short varying from half a page to one page. Other VCs featured are G Lambert, J Firth, JC Raynes, AH Proctor, WB Allen, A Loosemore, JB Daykins and JW Harper.

J31 JONES, Alan Baynham and STEVENSON, Lee
RORKE'S DRIFT: By those who were there
Lee Stephenson Publishing, Brighton, 2003
292 pp, photos, index, sb, cr

A compilation of official records, reports, first-hand accounts, newspaper cuttings and reminiscences about the defence of Rorke's Drift on 22/23 January 1879.

J33   JONES, Flt Lt Ira, DSO MC DFC MM
KING OF AIR FIGHTERS: The Biography of Major "Mick" Mannock VC DSO MC
Ivor Nicolson & Watson, London, 1934
303 pp, photos, index, hb, cr

This biography details the early life and WW1 combat experiences of Britain's greatest fighter ace. It reveals Mannock's character and describes his achievements in aerial warfare. Extracts from Mannock's war diary and letters intersperse the text. Republished by Thackwell Publishing, London (*facsimile*), 1986.

J35   JOYNT, W.D., VC
SAVING THE CHANNEL PORTS: 1918 After the breach of the 5th Army
Wren Publishing, Australia, 1975
233 pp, photos, maps, hb, cr

Lt Col Joynt VC describes the decisive role played by Australian forces when the British 2nd and 5th Armies were close to collapse following the German Spring offensive in 1918. The author's personal diary for this period is replicated in full to add immediacy to the account.

J36   JOYNT, W.D., VC
BREAKING THE ROAD FOR A REST
Hyland House, Melbourne, Australia, 1979
206 pp, photos, maps, index, hb, cr

An autobiography of Lt Col Joynt VC describing his childhood, WW1 service (VC) and return to civilian life in Australia where he established a photographic business. Joynt also describes his visits to three VC reunion celebrations.

K1 KALOGERAKIS, Giorgos
TO ASPRADI TOU AVGOU - EPIHIRISI ALBUMEN
Publisher unknown, Iraklion, 2009
263 pp, photos, maps, sb, cr

This Greek-text well-illustrated book gives a detailed account of Operation *Albumen* in Crete in 1943. The significant role played by Anders Lassen VC in this operation is featured prominently throughout the book which is based partly on interviews and eyewitness accounts from local resistance fighters.

K1A KAPOOR, Lieutenant Colonel R.K. (*editor*)
PREM BHAGAT: Commemorative Issue, The Bombay Sappers 23 May 1976
BEG Printing Press, India, 1976
92 pp, photos, sketches, maps, sb, cr

An issue of *The Bombay Sappers* journal devoted to Lt Gen Premindra Singh Bhagat VC, who died in 1975. It comprises a compilation of articles, appreciations and accounts by his comrades, relatives and friends describing his life and career.

K2 KARK, Leslie
THE FIRE WAS BRIGHT
MacMillan, London, 1943
143 pp, hb, cr

This book comprises 15 chapters of reminiscences about the RAF during WW2. One chapter (11 pages) is devoted to Flt Sgt RH Middleton VC. The foreword is by Group Captain Hughie Edwards VC.

K3 KARSLAKE, Lieutenant General Sir Henry, KCB CMG DSO
LEADERS OF THE ARMY
Hutchinson, London, nd (c1940)
128 pp, sb, cr

This book, No. III in the series *Leaders of Britain*, comprises biographical sketches of three contemporary British Army commanders: General Sir Edmund Ironside (Inspector-General), General The Viscount Gort VC KCB (C-in-C BEF France) and General Sir Walter Kirke (C-in-C Home Front).

K4 KAUSHALA, R.S.
TIGER SONS OF INDIA: India's Winners of the Victoria Cross
Standard Publishing, Ambala City, India, nd (c1948)
75 pp, photos, hb, cr

A collection of biographical sketches of the 17 soldiers of the Indian Army who were awarded the VC in the two world wars. Eleven VCs are featured for WW1, five for WW2 and one in Waziristan. Most recipients covered feature a portrait photo. The publication gives no explanation for the VCs selected.

K5   KAVANAGH, T. Henry, VC
HOW I WON THE VICTORIA CROSS
Ward & Lock, London, 1860
219 pp, line drawing, hb, cr

This book, which is one of the earliest written by a VC recipient, is devoted to Kavanagh's experiences during the Indian Mutiny. His account of his VC action is described in Chapters 11 and 12.

K5A   KAVANAGH, T.H., VC
MEMORIALS OF THE CIVIL AND MILITARY SERVICES OF T.H. KAVANAGH ESQ.
W.S. Kirkland, London, 1860
33 pp, sb, cr

A compilation of memorials and letters to and from Kavanagh VC, including correspondence in relation to his VC (pages 31-33).

K6   KAVANAGH, T.H., VC
GUILTY OR NOT GUILTY OF CONDUCT UNBECOMING AN OFFICER AND A GENTLEMAN?
American Methodist Mission Press (printer), Lucknow, 1876
54 pp, sb, cr

A compilation of letters and papers relating to a charge against the author when he was Deputy Commissioner of Oudh. (See K7).

K7   KAVANAGH, T.H., VC
THE VERDICT
American Methodist Mission Press, Lucknow, 1877
27 pp, sb, cr

A follow-up publication to K6 with memorials, correspondence and papers relating to the author's removal from office as the Deputy Commissioner of Oudh.

K8   KEAN, T. (*compiler*)
617 SQUADRON FROM LANCASTERS TO TORNADOES 1943-1993: The Story of Wing Commander GP Gibson VC DSO DFC
Lisek Publications, 1993 (supplement issued 1994)
13 pp, supplement 5 pp, photos, sb, cr

This typed and photocopied booklet relates predominantly to Guy Gibson's RAF service and, in particular, his participation in the Dams Raid.

K9   KEAN, T.J. (*compiler*)
NICOLSON'S STORY: The Story of Wing Commander James Brindley Nicolson VC DFC (1917-45)
Lisek Publications, 1993
7 pp, photos, sb, cr

A typed and photocopied booklet describing briefly the WW2 service of Wing Commander JB Nicolson VC.

K10   KEAN, T.J. (*compiler*)
THE FORGOTTEN HERO: The Story of Albert Mackenzie VC
Lisek Publications, 1997
5 pp, sketch, sb, cr

A typed and photocopied booklet about Able Seaman AE McKenzie (incorrectly spelt "Mackenzie") who won his VC at Zeebrugge.

K11   KEAN, T.J. (*compiler*)
THE D-DAY VICTORIA CROSS: The Story of Sergeant-Major Stanley Hollis VC
Lisek Publications, 1997
9 pp, photos, maps, sb, cr

A typed and photocopied booklet about CSM Hollis VC.

K12   KEEGAN, John (*editor*)
CHURCHILL'S GENERALS
Weidenfeld & Nicolson, London, 1991
368 pp, photos, index, hb, cr

An examination of the careers of twenty key British generals of WW2. For each general, a critical appraisal of the strategies, abilities and expertise is given and is followed by a biographical chronology. Chapter 2 (pages 34-50) relates to FM Lord Gort VC. Chapter 17 in part (pages 323-349) concerns Lt Gen Sir Adrian Carton de Wiart VC.

K13   KELLEHER, J.P. (*compiler and editor*)
ELEGANT EXTRACTS: The Royal Fusiliers Recipients of the Victoria Cross
The Royal Fusiliers Association, London, nd (c 2001)
20 pp, photos, sb, cr

This booklet briefly describes the 20 VC recipients of the Royal Fusiliers awarded between 1854 and 1919. One page is dedicated to each recipient with a photograph, the full LG citation and brief biographical details. There are also details of the location of each VC and medal group and a sale history.

K14   KEMP, Lieutenant Commander P.K.
HM SUBMARINES
Herbert Jenkins, London, 1952
224 pp, photos, sketches, index, hb, cr

The book covers Royal Navy submarine operations in the Dardanelles, Heligoland and the Baltic during WW1 and operations in the various theatres during WW2. VC recipients covered are: Boyle, Wanklyn, Gould, Roberts, Linton, Miers, Nasmith, Cameron, Place, Fraser and Magennis.

K15   KEMP, Paul
UNDERWATER WARRIORS
Arms & Armour Press, London, 1996
256 pp, photos, sketches, index, hb, cr

This comprehensive study of midget submarine warfare, from its inception up to the present day, provides a detailed description of the various types of midget submarines and human torpedoes and the operations in which they were involved. Chapters 10 and 11 (pages 128-157) relate to the development of *X-craft* and the attack on the *Tirpitz* resulting in the VC award to Cameron and Place. Chapter 14 (pages 176-182) concerns the *XE craft* attack in which Fraser and Magennis won their VCs.

K15A   KEMP, Ross
WARRIORS: British Fighting Heroes
Random House, London, 2010
328 pp, photos, index, hb, cr

The author has compiled an assorted number of British heroes and includes the following VCs: A Ball, NG Chavasse, ESF Fegan, SE Hollis, NC Jackson, JN Randle and MD Wanklyn.

K16   KEMPTON, Chris
VALOUR AND GALLANTRY: HEIC & Indian Army Victoria Crosses and George Crosses 1856 – 1946
The Military Press, Milton Keynes, 2001
280 pp, photos, maps, index, hb, cr

This major reference work provides details of the 162 VC recipients and 21 GC winners of the HEIC and Indian Army. The major part of the book is divided into wars or time periods: Persian War, Indian Mutiny, Campaigns 1859-1904, WW1, India 1915-1936 and WW2. The background to each campaign is briefly described. The full LG citation and date is then given for each recipient with biographical details. The entry for each VC recipient varies from half a page to two pages. The following section covers the awards of 21 GC winners including transfers from the AM and EGM. Subsequent sections include a listing of awards by Regiment and Corps and a recipients' index for all awards. The appendices provide a roll of AM/EGM recipients who did not exchange to the GC, a chronological roll with name, place/date of action and LG date for each decoration. There is also a short listing of VC recipients who subsequently served in the Indian Army. Reviewed in V57.

K16A   KENDALL, Paul
THE ZEEBRUGGE RAID 1918: 'The Finest Feat of Arms'
Spellmount (The History Press), Stroud, 2009
351 pp, photos, maps, index, hb, cr

This volume describes the raids at Zeebrugge and Ostend which attempted to block the German submarines at Bruges. A total of 11 VCs were awarded and their actions are described in the text. VCs were awarded to Carpenter, Sandford, PT Dean, Bamford, Finch, AE McKenzie, GN Bradford, AL Harrision, Crutchley, Drummond and Bourke. In 2018, the centenary of the action, the book was republished by Frontline Books in the *Voices from the Past* series.

K16B   KENDRICK, Michael
GREATER LOVE: Memories of Soldier Boys from the Great War of 1914-18: Look into their eyes and see the holy glimmer of goodbyes.
Michael Kendrick, Old Woodhouse, Leicestershire, 2007
296 pp, maps, photos (some in colour), sb, cr

This A4 size, well-illustrated book contains stories about many of the men from the Loughborough area, where the author lives, who fought in the Great War. It includes William Bees VC (6pp), Philip Bent VC (7pp) and Bernard Vann VC (2pp).

K17   KENNEALLY, John Patrick VC
[1] KENNEALLY VC: The True Story of a Remarkable Life (*original edition*)
Kenwood, Huddersfield, 1991
204 pp, photos, sb, cr
[2] THE HONOUR AND THE SHAME [*updated and reformatted edition*]
Headline Review, London, 2007
245 pp, photos, hb, cr

Kenneally reveals an eventful life in this frank autobiography. He describes vividly his unsettled childhood as the illegitimate son of a wealthy Jewish family. Following his desertion from the Honourable Artillery Company at the outbreak of WW2, he changed his name to Kenneally and joined the Irish Guards. He chronicles his military career and experiences in the Guards and, latterly, in the Parachute Regiment. Kenneally died in 2000. The republished edition was issued in 2008. Reviewed in V60.

K18   KENNEDY, Billy (*editor*)
STEADFAST FOR FAITH AND FREEDOM: 200 Years of Orangeism
Grand Lodge of Ireland, Belfast, 1995
104 pp, hb, cr

This work contains a six-page chapter (by Greg Hopkins) on Orange VCs: G Richardson, Acton, Quigg, Hanna, JW Foote. For each recipient, biographical details, a short description of the VC action and a photographic portrait is included.

K19   KENNEDY, Ludovic
MENACE: The Life and Death of the Tirpitz
Sidgwick & Jackson, London, 1979
176 pp, photos, maps, index, hb, cr

This profusely-illustrated work describes the operational activities of the German battleship *Tirpitz* and the attempts by the British forces to destroy her. Chapters 6 and 7 (pages 106-133) relate specifically to the *X-craft* attack (Operation *Source*) for which Lt D Cameron and Lt BCG Place were awarded the VC.

K19A   KEOHANE, Leo
CAPTAIN JACK WHITE: Imperialism, Anarchism and the Irish Citizen Army
Merrion Press, Dublin, 2014
283 pp, photos, index, hb, cr

A biography of Captain Jack White DSO (1879-1946), son of Field Marshal Sir George White VC. The book is based on the White family papers are previously unpublished archives. White had a conventional upbringing and was educated at Winchester and Sandhurst before being commissioned in the Gordon Highlanders. In the Boer War he won a DSO for escaping from captivity and saw much action. Later he was ADC to his father in Gibraltar. White became disillusioned with British foreign policy and became a founder member and first Commandant of the Irish Citizen Army. He wrote an autobiography charting his change of direction in life declaring himself to be an anarchist.

K20   KERNAHAN, Coulson
IN GOOD COMPANY: Some personal recollections Swinburne, Lord Roberts, Watts-Dunton, Oscar Wilde, Edward Whymper, S.J. Stone, Stephen Phillips
Books for Libraries Press, Freeport, New York, USA, 1917
278 pp, hb, cr

A collection of personal recollections in essay format featuring celebrities of the second half of the 19th century: Algernon Charles Swinburne, Lord Roberts VC, Theodore Watts-Dunton, Oscar Wilde, Edward Whymper, Samuel John Stone and Stephen Phillips.

K20A   KERR, Rex
A SHIP, A MAN AND A BOY: The story of the Otaki Scholar
Black Pony Press, Otaki, New Zealand, 2012
138 pp, illustrations (some colour), maps, hb, cr

This book describes a Scottish-based scholarship which marks a heroic sea battle in World War 1 between the New Zealand Shipping Company's SS *Otaki* and a *Moewe*, a heavily armed German raider in the North Atlantic. The *Otaki* was skippered by a former pupil of Robert Gordon's College in Aberdeen, Archibald Bisset Smith. In the battle the *Otaki* was seriously damaged and Captain Smith ordered his crew to abandon ship before he went down with his ship. Captain Smith was awarded a posthumous Victoria Cross. In 1937 the captain's family presented the Otaki Shield to the school's head boy as part of a scholarship that is now funded in part by the New Zealand government. It is awarded to the head boy of Robert Gordon's College to reward an outstanding pupil with a seven-week trip to travel through New Zealand. A recipient has travelled to New Zealand every year since 1937, except for the war years 1940-46.

K21   KERR, Rodney E.
REAL CANADIAN HERO: A Biography of John Chipman Kerr VC
Valley Publishing, Summerland, British Columbia, Canada, 2002
148 pp, photos, maps, sb, cr

A biography of JC Kerr VC who won his VC at Courcelette on the Somme on 16 September 1916 while serving with the 49th Canadian Infantry Battalion. The text covers his early years in Canada, service in both world wars and his final days.

K22   KESBY, Joanne, HARPER, Jane and KIDDY, Leanne
A BIOGRAPHY OF JOHN HURST EDMONSON VC
Hurlstone Agricultural High School, NSW, Australia, 1984
42 pp, photos, sketches, sb, cr

A short biography of Cpl Edmonson VC, written by students of his old school, which also published the booklet. His early life is documented fully, following which an account is given of his military service culminating in his posthumous VC action. Additionally, two poems written in his honour are included.

K23   KEY PUBLISHING (BRIDGEWATER, Stephen (*editor*))
VALOUR IN THE AIR
Key Publishing, Stamford, Lincolnshire, 2017
114 pp, photos (some colour), index, sb, cr

An A4 format magazine focusing entirely on the aviation VCs of WW1 and WW2. The publication is profusely illustrated with an artist's profile in colour of each VC's aircraft and markings in their VC action. Pages 6 to 31 cover the 19 WW1 recipients. Pages 34 to 111 give more in-depth profiles of the 32 WW2 recipients with an average of 2 to 3 pages per recipient.

K24   KEYES, Elizabeth
GEOFFREY KEYES VC OF THE ROMMEL RAID
George Newnes, London, 1956
278 pp, photos, maps, index, hb, cr

A full biography of Lt Col Keyes VC MC, written by his sister. Keyes won his posthumous VC for leading an unsuccessful raid on Rommel's HQ in North Africa in November 1941. An appendix includes an eyewitness account of Keyes' death by a German soldier present. The commander of the submarine *Torbay* which transported Keyes and his party to the North African coast was Commander ACC Miers DSO who was awarded the VC in 1942.

K24A   KIERAN, Dr Brian L.
THE NEW ZEALAND CROSS: The Rarest Bravery Award in the World
Authorhouse (self published), New Zealand, 2016
316 pp, coloured illustrations, maps, sb, cr

This volume is a comprehensive history of the New Zealand Cross (NZC) which resembles the VC. The author explores the development of the creation and inauguration of the award, a listing of all the recipients and an outline of the New Zealand Wars from 1860 to 1872. The VC and other decorations were being awarded to Imperial troops but settlers in the Volunteers and Militia were not being recognised for carrying out similar acts of bravery. The NZC was instituted on 10 March 1869 by Sir George Bowen, the Governor of New Zealand, under the mistaken impression that colonial troops were not eligible for the VC unless under command of British troops. A total of 40 NZCs were awarded between 1869 and 1910. Charles Heaphy VC features prominently in the book. He was a member of the militia who was awarded the VC in 1867 for an action in 1864.

K25   KIERNAN, R.H.
CAPTAIN ALBERT BALL VC, DSO (two bars), MC, Croix de Chevalier, Légion d'Honneur, Russian Order of St George: A Historical Record
John Hamilton, London, 1933
223 pp, photos, index, hb, cr

A study of the brief, yet exceptional, life of Captain Ball. Based on Ball's letters and personal records and on official combat reports, aerial diaries and operations books, the study provides a detailed account of his combat experiences and of his last patrol on which he was killed. There are significant mentions of three other air VCs: Bishop, Mannock and McCudden.

K25A KILDUFF, Peter
BILLY BISHOP VC - LONE WOLF HUNTER: The RAF Ace Re-examined
Grub Street, London, 2014
192 pp, photos, maps, index, hb, cr

This book sheds new light on the 72 victories claimed by Billy Bishop VC DSO DFC MC. His victories are steeped in controversy and there is uncertainty about some of the victories he claimed. The author uses records held by the Germans to assess the veracity of the claims made.

K26 KING, David
THE PITY OF WAR
Privately published, 2016
? pp, photos, maps, sb, cr

This A5-sized booklet is a centenary commemoration of three men from the Allerdale district in Cumbria who were awarded the VC in WW1: James Alexander Smith VC of Workington, Abraham Acton VC of Whitehaven and Ned Smith VC DCM of Maryport. It features a collection of poems, sonnets and diary entries.

K27 KINGSMILL, Suzanne
FRANCIS SCRIMGER: Beyond the Call of Duty
Hannah Institute & Dundurn Press, Toronto, Canada, 1991
112 pp, photos, index, hb, cr

Written by the wife of Francis Scrimger's grandson, this monograph is No. 5 in the *Canadian Medical Lives* series. It is a detailed biography of Lieutenant-Colonel FAC Scrimger who won the VC in the Canadian Army Medical Corps in WW1 and in peacetime became a distinguished surgeon. Numerous photographs from the family collection, together with a family tree, are included. There is also a list of his medical publications.

K30 KINGSTON, William Henry Giles
MEMOIR OF LIEUT. CHARLES DUNCAN HOME (*sic*)
Griffith & Farran, London, 1863
22 pp, line drawings, hb, cr

This brief memoir of Lt Duncan Charles Home, one of the Delhi VCs, was written to immortalise his memory. It first appeared in a magazine and annual edited by the author.

K31 KINGSTON, William Henry Giles
OUR SAILORS: Anecdotes of the Engagements and Gallant Deeds of the British Navy during the Reign of Her Majesty Queen Victoria
Griffith & Farran, London, 1863 (revised and updated: Griffith Farran Browne, London, 1865, 1882 and 1900)
(1865 edition: 282 pp.; 1882 edition: 326 pp.), line drawings, hb, ncr

A collection of anecdotes relating to acts of heroism performed in actions during the reign of Queen Victoria from the war on the coast of Syria (1840) to the China War (1900). In many cases, from the Crimean War onwards, the anecdotes focus on VCs relating to naval actions. The 1882 and 1900 versions include revisions and updates by GA Henty. VC recipients receive only brief mentions. See K32.

AUSTRALIAN WINNERS
OF THE
VICTORIA CROSS
IN THE
GREAT WAR
1914-19

SYDNEY 1919

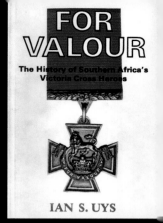

FOR
VALOUR
The History of Southern Africa's
Victoria Cross Heroes

IAN S. UYS

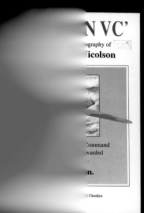

N VC'
...graphy of
...icolson

Command
...warded

Cheshire

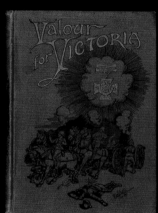

Valour
for Victoria

V.C
RO
JO

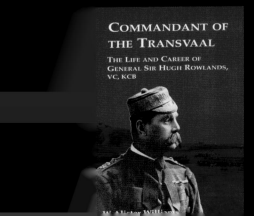

COMMANDANT OF
THE TRANSVAAL
THE LIFE AND CAREER OF
GENERAL SIR HUGH ROWLANDS,
VC, KCB

W. Alister Williams

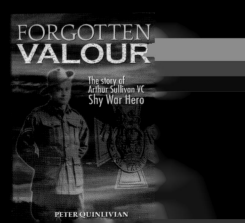

FORGOTTEN
VALOUR
The story of
Arthur Sullivan VC
Shy War Hero

PETER QUINLIVIAN

The Story of
GURKHA VCs

In Honour of Brave Men

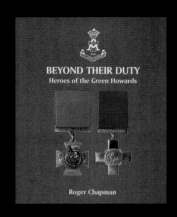

BEYOND THEIR DUTY

Heroes of the Green Howards

Roger Chapman

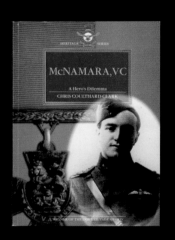

HERITAGE SERIES

McNAMARA, VC

A Hero's Dilemma

CHRIS COULTHARD-CLARK

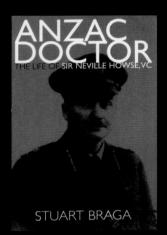

ANZAC DOCTOR

THE LIFE OF SIR NEVILLE HOWSE, VC

STUART BRAGA

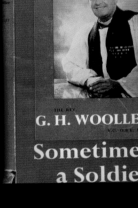

THE REV.
G. H. WOOLLE
VC OBE

Sometime
a Soldie

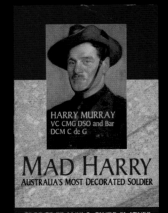

HARRY MURRAY
VC CMG DSO and Bar
DCM C de G

MAD HARRY

AUSTRALIA'S MOST DECORATED SOLDIER

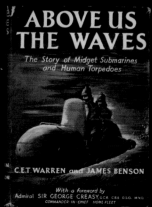

ABOVE US
THE WAVES

The Story of Midget Submarines
and Human Torpedoes

C.E.T. WARREN and **JAMES BENSON**

With a foreword by
Admiral **SIR GEORGE CREASY** GCB CBE DSO MVO
COMMANDER-IN-CHIEF HOME FLEET

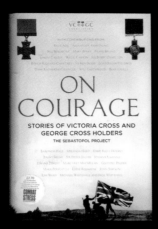

ON COURAGE

STORIES OF VICTORIA CROSS AND
GEORGE CROSS HOLDERS
THE SEBASTOPOL PROJECT

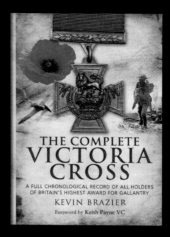

THE COMPLETE VICTORIA CROSS

A FULL CHRONOLOGICAL RECORD OF ALL HOLDERS
OF BRITAIN'S HIGHEST AWARD FOR GALLANTRY

KEVIN BRAZIER

Foreword by Keith Payne VC

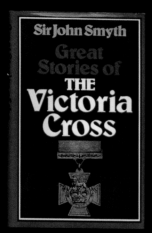

Sir John Smyth

Great Stories of THE Victoria Cross

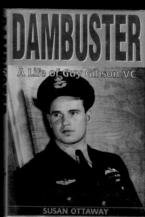

DAMBUSTER

A Life of Guy Gibson VC

SUSAN OTTAWAY

FROGMAN V.C.

Ian Fraser

VENTURER COURAGEOUS

GROUP CAPTAIN LEONARD TRENT VC, DFC

A Biography
by
James Sanders

Foreword by Laddie Lucas

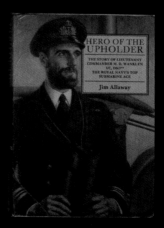

HERO OF THE UPHOLDER

THE STORY OF LIEUTENANT
COMMANDER M. D. WANKLYN
VC, DSO**
THE ROYAL NAVY'S TOP
SUBMARINE ACE

Jim Allaway

'Wonderful. The best single book on the Victoria Cross.'
RICHARD HOLMES

BRAVEST
OF THE BRAVE
THE STORY OF THE
VICTORIA
CROSS
JOHN GLANFIELD

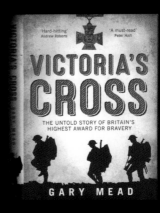

MY MYSTERY SHIPS
by ADMIRAL CAMPBELL

THIS
CLASSIC STORY
OF 'Q' BOAT
COURAGE

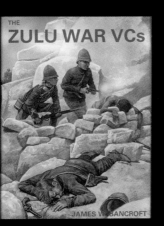

THE
ZULU WAR VCs

JAMES W. BANCROFT

The
LAST ELEVEN?
Winners of the Victoria Cross
since the Second World War
MARK ADKIN

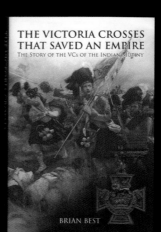

'Hard-hitting' Andrew Roberts   'A must-read' Peter Hart

VICTORIA'S
CROSS

THE UNTOLD STORY OF BRITAIN'S
HIGHEST AWARD FOR BRAVERY

GARY MEAD

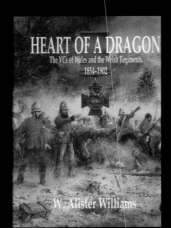

HEART OF A DRAGON
The VCs of Wales and the Welsh Regiments
1854-1902

W. Alister Williams

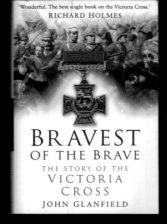

THE VICTORIA CROSSES
THAT SAVED AN EMPIRE
THE STORY OF THE VCs OF THE INDIAN MUTINY

BRIAN BEST

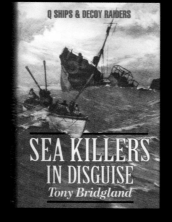

Q SHIPS & DECOY RAIDERS

SEA KILLERS
IN DISGUISE
Tony Bridgland

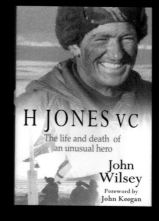

H JONES VC
The life and death of
an unusual hero

John
Wilsey

Foreword by
John Keegan

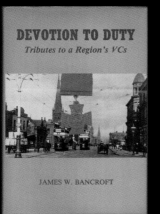

DEVOTION TO DUTY
Tributes to a Region's VCs

JAMES W. BANCROFT

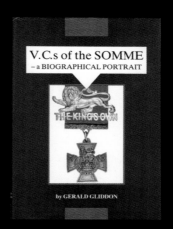

V.C.s of the SOMME
– a BIOGRAPHICAL PORTRAIT

THE KING'S OWN

by GERALD GLIDDON

THE SAPPER VCs

YORKSHIRE
VCs

ALAN WHITWORTH

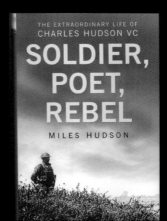

THE EXTRAORDINARY LIFE OF
CHARLES HUDSON VC

SOLDIER,
POET,
REBEL

MILES HUDSON

GEOFFREY KEYES V.C.
OF THE ROMMEL RAID

by
ELIZABETH KEYES

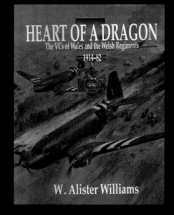

HEART OF A DRAGON
The VCs of Wales and the Welsh Regiments
1914-82

W. Alister Williams

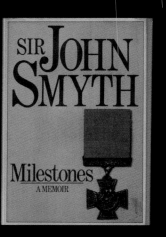

SIR JOHN
SMYTH

Milestones
A MEMOIR

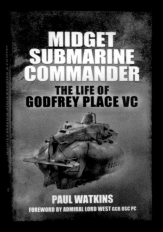

MIDGET
SUBMARINE
COMMANDER
THE LIFE OF
GODFREY PLACE VC

PAUL WATKINS
FOREWORD BY ADMIRAL LORD WEST GCB DSC PC

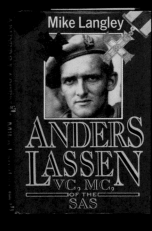

Mike Langley

ANDERS
LASSEN
VC, MC,
OF THE
SAS

Warneford, VC

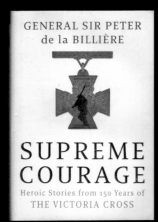

GENERAL SIR PETER
de la BILLIÈRE

SUPREME
COURAGE

Heroic Stories from 150 Years of
THE VICTORIA CROSS

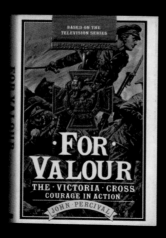

BASED ON THE
TELEVISION SERIES

·FOR·
VALOUR

THE·VICTORIA·CROSS
COURAGE IN ACTION

JOHN·PERCIVAL

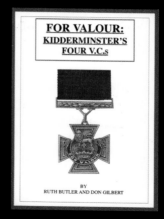

FOR VALOUR:
KIDDERMINSTER'S
FOUR V.C.s

BY
RUTH BUTLER AND DON GILBERT

AN EXHIBITION OF IMPORTANT
BRITISH GALLANTRY AWARDS, 1800–1950

TUESDAY 28TH MAY TO FRIDAY 5TH JUNE 1992

SOTHEBY'S

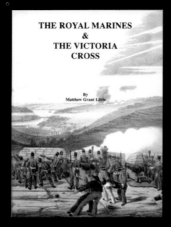

THE ROYAL MARINES
&
THE VICTORIA
CROSS

By
Matthew Grant Little

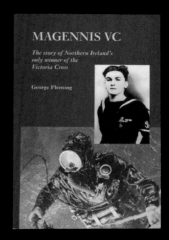

MAGENNIS VC

The story of Northern Ireland's
only winner of the
Victoria Cross

George Fleming

ALBERTA'S VICTORIA CROSS WINNERS

WITH HIS PLANE ON FIRE, SQUADRON LEADER BAZALGETTE
BATTLED ON TO MARK THE TARGET IN ONE OF THE MOST
GLORIOUS DEEDS OF THE R.A.F. PATHFINDERS!

THE
VICTOR

EVERY
MONDAY

No. 103
FEB. 9th
1963

The MASTER BOMBER

BAZALGETTE VC
ALBERTA PATHFINDER

Terry MacDonald

BRITAIN'S
ROLL OF GLORY
OR
THE VICTORIA CROSS
ITS HEROES AND
THEIR VALOUR

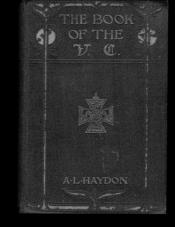

THE BOOK
OF THE
V. C.

A·L·HAYDON

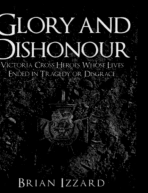

GLORY AND
DISHONOUR

VICTORIA CROSS HEROES WHOSE LIVES
ENDED IN TRAGEDY OR DISGRACE

BRIAN IZZARD

THE
GREAT
WAR
1914-1918

VICTORIA CROSS   FREEMASONS

Granville Angell

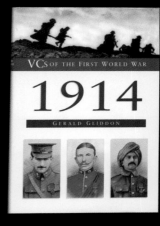

VCs OF THE FIRST WORLD WAR

1914

GERALD GLIDDON

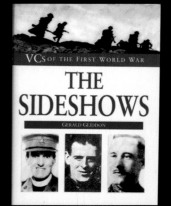

VCs OF THE FIRST WORLD WAR

THE
SIDESHOWS

GERALD GLIDDON

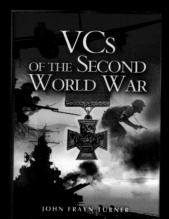

VCs
OF THE SECOND
WORLD WAR

JOHN FRAYN TURNER

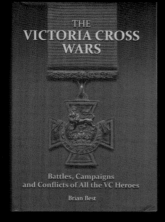

THE
VICTORIA CROSS
WARS

Battles, Campaigns
and Conflicts of All the VC Heroes

Brian Best

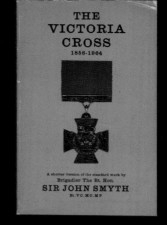

THE
VICTORIA
CROSS
1856-1964

A shorter version of the standard work by
Brigadier The Rt. Hon.
SIR JOHN SMYTH
Bt. VC. MC. MP

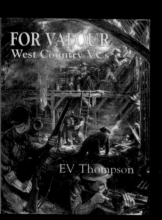

FOR VALOUR
West Country VCs

EV Thompson

C.E. LUCAS PHILLIPS
VICTORIA
CROSS BATTLES
OF THE SECOND WORLD WAR

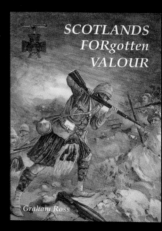

SCOTLANDS
FORgotten
VALOUR

Graham Ross

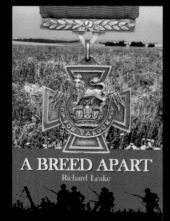

A BREED APART
Richard Leake

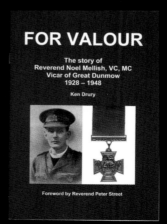

FOR VALOUR

The story of
Reverend Noel Mellish, VC, MC
Vicar of Great Dunmow
1928 – 1948

Ken Drury

Foreword by Reverend Peter Street

AMAZING STORIES OF VICTORIA CROSS AND GEORGE CROSS RECIPIENTS

EXTRA**ORDINARY**
HEROES

FOREWORD BY LORD ASHCROFT, KCMG

RUTH SHEPPARD

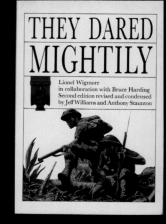

THEY DARED MIGHTILY

Lionel Wigmore
in collaboration with Bruce Harding
Second edition revised and condensed
by Jeff Williams and Anthony Staunton

Against the Odds

The Life of
Group Captain
Lionel Rees VC

W. Alister Williams

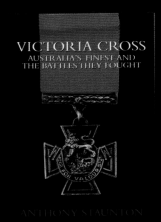

VICTORIA CROSS
AUSTRALIA'S FINEST AND
THE BATTLES THEY FOUGHT

ANTHONY STAUNTON

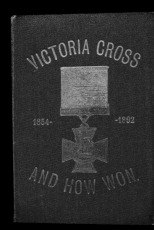

VICTORIA CROSS

1854-   -1892

AND HOW WON.

WHERE
THE
PRIZE
IS
HIGHEST

The stories of the
New Zealanders who won the Victoria Cross

G. BRYANT

BRITANNIA'S
CALENDAR OF HEROES

KATE STANWAY

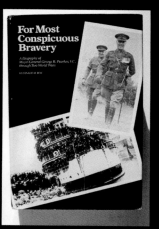

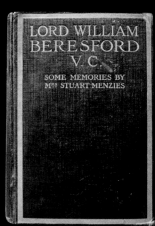

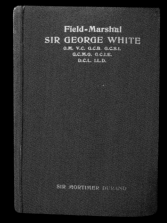

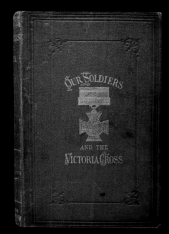

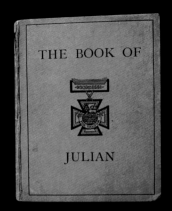

THE BOOK OF

JULIAN

THE VICTORIA CROSS
The Empire's Roll of Valour

A COMPLETE RECORD OF ALL THOSE WHO HAVE WON THE
VICTORIA CROSS, FROM ITS INSTITUTION TO THE PRESENT
DAY, ARRANGED BY REGIMENTS, ETC. WITH CHRONOLOGICAL
AND ALPHABETICAL INDICES AND CONQUERED FRONTISPIECE

Compiled by
LIEUT.-COL. RUPERT STEWART, M.V.O.

KENNETH SANDFORD

Mark of the Lion

The story of
Capt. Charles Upham
V.C. and Bar

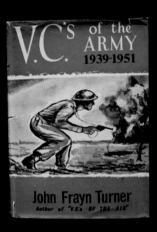

V.C.'s of the ARMY
1939-1951

John Frayn Turner
Author of "V.C.s OF THE AIR"

Whom the Gods Love

BY PATRICK COGHILL

Pro Valore
CANADA'S VICTORIA CROSS

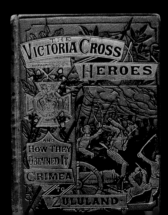

THE VICTORIA CROSS
HEROES

AND
HOW THEY
OBTAINED IT
CRIMEA
TO
ZULULAND

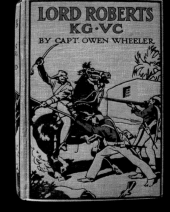

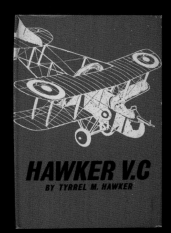

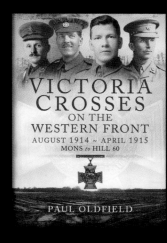

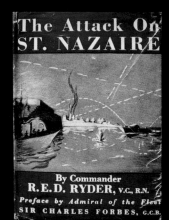

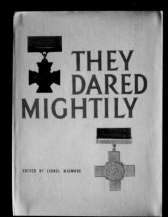

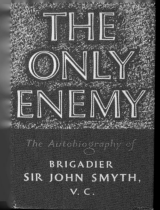

THE
ONLY
ENEMY

The Autobiography of

BRIGADIER
SIR JOHN SMYTH,
V. C.

V.C.s of the AIR

A
NATIONAL
RECORD IN
PICTURE &
PROSE OF
THE MEN
OF THE
AIR FORCE
AWARDED
THE
VICTORIA
CROSS
FOR
VALOUR

EDITED BY
Lieut. Gilbert
Barnett
WITH
16 PAINTINGS
Dudley Tennant

ED. J. BURROW & Cº. LTD.
LONDON
SUBSCRIBER MEMORIAL HALL LONDON & Cº.
4 Stationers Hall Court, E.C.

5/-
NET

OLD
MEMORIES

GENERAL SIR HUGH GOUGH

Kenneth Hare-Scott

For Valour

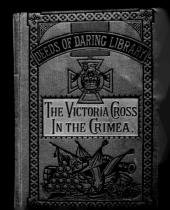

DEEDS OF DARING LIBRARY

THE VICTORIA CROSS
IN THE CRIMEA.

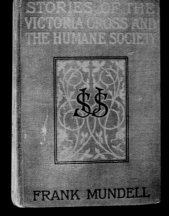

STORIES OF THE
VICTORIA CROSS AND
THE HUMANE SOCIETY

SS

FRANK MUNDELL

DEEDS OF DARING LIBRARY

THE VICTORIA CROSS
IN AFGHANISTAN.

THE BOY HERO
OF THE AIR
WALTER A BRISCOE

GUY Edmund Burke
GIBSON V.C.

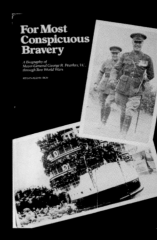

For Most
Conspicuous
Bravery

A Biography of
Major-General George R. Pearkes, V.C.
through Two World Wars

REGINALD H. ROY

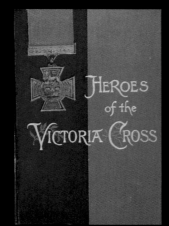

HEROES
of the
VICTORIA CROSS

OLD
MEMORIES

GENERAL SIR HUGH GOUGH

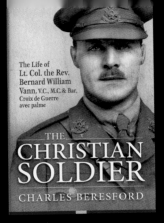

The Life of
Lt. Col. the Rev.
Bernard William
Vann, V.C., M.C. & Bar,
Croix de Guerre
avec palme

THE
**CHRISTIAN
SOLDIER**

CHARLES BERESFORD

THE·BOY·HERO
OF·THE·AIR
WALTER·A·BRISCOE

The VICTORIA
CROSS

India's V.C.s in two World Wars
PRICE: EIGHT ANNAS

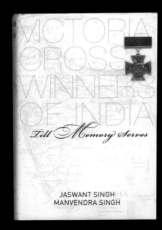

VICTORIA
CROSS
WINNERS
OF INDIA
Till Memory Serves

JASWANT SINGH
MANVENDRA SINGH

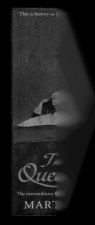

'This is history as

T.
Que
The extraordinary
MART

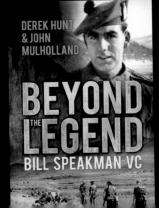

DEREK HUNT
& JOHN
MULHOLLAND

**BEYOND
THE
LEGEND**

BILL SPEAKMAN VC

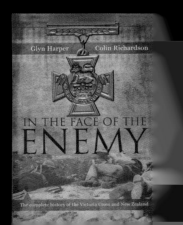

Glyn Harper   Colin Richardson

IN THE FACE OF THE
ENEMY

The complete history of the Victoria Cross and New Zealand

K32   KINGSTON, William Henry Giles
OUR SOLDIERS: Anecdotes of the Campaigns and Gallant Deeds of The British Army during the reign of Her Majesty Queen Victoria
Griffith & Farran, London, 1863 (revised and updated: Griffith Farran Browne, London, 1870 and nd [c1902])
284 pp, (revised c1902 edition: 374 pp.), line drawings, hb, ncr

Principally a book describing some of the British army campaigns in the reign of Queen Victoria. In the first edition, campaigns from 1837 to South Africa 1850-53 are covered in pages 1-140. Many VC actions are covered in the chapters on the Crimea (pages 141-192), Persia (pages 193-200), Indian Mutiny (pages 201-271) and ends with the Second China War 1856-60 (pages 272-282). The new revised edition was updated to the end of the Second Boer War by William Moxon. Although VC actions are covered extensively, each recipient receives only a brief mention. A third edition was published in 1870 with 312 pages. It was the same as the 1863 edition but with the following additions: pages 284-291 relating to the New Zealand War of 1865 and pages 292-310 relating to the Abyssinian Expedition of 1867-1868. See K31.

K33   KING'S OWN ROYAL REGIMENTAL MUSEUM (*publisher*)
THE VICTORIA CROSS AND THE KING'S OWN ROYAL REGIMENT
King's Own Royal Regimental Museum, Lancaster, 1994 (expanded 1998)
18 pp, drawing, sb, cr

This booklet gives the LG citation and brief biographical details of each of the nine men who won the VC whilst serving in the King's Own Royal Regiment or its forebears (H Christian, JA Collin, T Grady, A Halton, J Hewitson, TF Mayson, J Miller, T Neely and J White). The 1998 edition has a page on WRF Addison.

K34   KIPLING, Rudyard
SEA WARFARE
MacMillan, London, 1916
222 pp, hb, cr

This book is a collection of three series of articles and poems written for the Ministry of Information for publication in British and American newspapers in 1915 and 1916. A chapter entitled *Tales of the Trade* (pages 72-84) describes the exploits of Lt Cdr ME Nasmith and Lt Cdr EC Boyle for which they were awarded the VC.

K35   KIPLING, Rudyard
LAND AND SEA TALES FOR SCOUTS AND SCOUTMASTERS
Ward, Lock & Co., London, 1897
322 pp, illus., hb, ncr

Written in a patriotic style, this book for the younger reader includes a chapter (Chapter 1) entitled *Winning the Victoria Cross* (24 pages). A selection of VC deeds are recalled, but generally, without referring to the recipients by name.

K36   KIPLING, Rudyard
LAND AND SEA TALES FOR SCOUTS AND GUIDES
MacMillan, London, 1923
282 pp, hb, ncr

Written in a similar style to K35, this book also includes (as Chapter 1) the Chapter entitled *Winning the Victoria Cross* (20 pages).

K37   KIPLING, Rudyard
WINNING THE VICTORIA CROSS
CreateSpace Independent Publishing Platform, 2014
32 pp, sb, ncr

Originally published in *Youth's Companion* and the *Windsor Magazine* in June 1897, one page of text was added during the Great War. In recalling tales of heroism in India, Afghanistan and South Africa in the latter half of the 19th Century, Kipling provides numerous examples reflecting the different types of individual awarded the VC and the differing circumstances that led to its award. Generally, recipients' names are not stated.

K38   KIRBY, Henry L.
PRIVATE WILLIAM YOUNG VC: One of Preston's Heroes of the Great War
THCL Books, Blackburn, 1985
16 pp, photos, map, sb, cr

A biographical sketch of the short life of Pte William Young VC, who died of war wounds in 1916. The eight full-page plates include a cabinet photograph of him. See K39.

K39   KIRBY, Henry L.
A VISIT TO FONCQUEVILLERS
THCL Books, Blackburn, 1998
11 pp, photos, maps, sb, cr

This comb-bound book supplements the author's previous work on Private William Young VC (see K38) and is his physical survey of the area around the French village of Foncquevillers where Young's VC action occurred. He identifies the approximate location of the action and supports his claim with photographs.

K40   KIRBY, H.L. and WALSH, R.R.
THE FOUR BLACKBURN VCs
THCL Books, Blackburn, 1986
40 pp, photos, line drawings, sb, cr

A biographical sketch of each of the four VCs from Blackburn: J Pitts, WH Grimbaldston, J Schofield, PT Dean. Each sketch describes their family background, early years, war service and a detailed description of their VC action.

K41   KIRBY, H.L. and WALSH, R.R.
DRUMMER SPENCER JOHN BENT VC
THCL Books, Blackburn, 1986
52 pp, photos, map, sb, cr

A biographical sketch of CSM Bent VC MM, who won his VC in 1914 and died in 1977. His entire life and, in particular, his military service and exploits are documented. The work concludes with a full transcript of the thanksgiving service for him. The 28 photographs (12 in colour) include some of him wearing his VC and medals in old age.

K42   KIRBY, Henry L. and WALSH, R. Raymond
THE SEVEN VCs OF STONYHURST COLLEGE
THCL Books, Blackburn, 1987
135 pp, photos, maps, hb, cr

Biographical sketches of each of the seven VC recipients who had attended the Jesuit public school in Lancashire: Costello, PA Kenna, Dease, JA Liddell, Coury, Jackman and Ervine-Andrews. Their military career and campaign service is chronicled and a full account of their VC deed is given. The numerous photographs include colour plates of the portraits of the seven VCs, which hang in the refectory at the College. The foreword was written by Lt Col HM Ervine-Andrews VC.

K43   KIRBY, Henry L. and WALSH, R. Raymond
ANDREW MOYNIHAN VC
THCL Books, Blackburn, 1993
42 pp, photos, line drawings, maps, sb, cr

A biographical account of the life and military career of Capt Andrew Moynihan who received his VC for service in the Crimea. His distinguished family history is recorded and his great-grandson, the late and infamous 3rd Baron Moynihan, wrote the Foreword. Battle maps (including one drawn by Moynihan in 1855) support the detailed description of his VC deed and his other services in the Crimean War. The photographs include one of his VC and medal group.

K44   KNIGHT, Ian and CASTLE, Ian
RORKE'S DRIFT
Pen and Sword Books, Barnsley, 2000
141 pp, photos, maps, index, sb, cr

This well-illustrated publication, in the *Battleground South Africa* series, features an insight into four battles of the Zulu War in 1879: Rorke's Drift (35 pages); Ntombe (17 pages); Hlobane (21 pages) and Khambula (20 pages). Many of the VC actions relating to these battles are covered briefly. More detailed VC accounts are given for A Booth, RH Buller and J Chard. The services of Col HE Wood VC at Hlobane and Khambula are featured in depth.

K45   KNIGHT, Ian and CASTLE, Ian
THE ZULU WAR - THEN AND NOW
Battle of Britain Prints International, London, 1993
280 pp, photos, sketches, line drawings, maps, index, hb, cr

This profusely-illustrated volume in the *After the Battle* series is a detailed history of the Zulu War battles, the scenes of which are compared photographically 'then and now'. Significant coverage is given to the VC recipients of the war.

K46   KNIGHT, Ian
RORKE'S DRIFT 1879: 'Pinned like rats in a hole'
Osprey, London, 1996
96 pp, photos, maps, drawings, sb, cr

This volume (No 41 in the Osprey *Campaign* series) is a concise account of the action at Rorke's Drift in January 1879 in which 11 VCs were won. Following an examination of the origins of the battle, the forces involved and the campaign strategies of both the British and the Zulu commanders, a detailed narrative of the fight is then given. The VC deeds are chronicled in the context of the battle. The text is supported by more than 90 illustrations including numerous artists' impressions of the deeds performed, coloured three-dimensional battle maps and photographs of the men and of the site.

K47   KNIGHT, Ian
NOTHING REMAINS BUT TO FIGHT: The Defence of Rorke's Drift, 1879
Greenhill Books, London, 1993
167 pp, photos, maps, index, hb, cr

This profusely-illustrated reassessment of the defence of Rorke's Drift details what really happened in the action and attempts to dispel the myths. Chapter 4 covers the VC deeds performed in the battle. Chapter 5 (pages 115-161) gives biographical information on the 11 VCs and includes their portraits and photographs of their memorials.

K48   KNIGHT, Ian
ZULU: Isandlwana and Rorke's Drift 22nd-23rd January 1879
Windrow & Green, London, 1992
136 pp, photos, line drawings, maps, hb, cr

This well-illustrated large format book tells the story of the British defeat at Isandlwana and also the defence of Rorke's Drift. Although there are brief references to and photographs of the VCs, the predominant focus in the Rorke's Drift chapter is on Chard's involvement in the defence. Overall, there is much less detail on Rorke's Drift than in K47 but 150 photographs, drawings and maps supplement the text.

K49   KNIGHT, Ian
BRAVE MEN'S BLOOD: The Epic of the Zulu War, 1879
Greenhill Books, London, 1990
199 pp, photos, sketches, maps, index, hb, cr

A comprehensive and profusely-illustrated history of the Zulu War of 1879. Each of the actions that resulted in the award of the VC, particularly those relating to Rorke's Drift, is described briefly in the context of the battle but extensive references to the services of RH Buller VC and HE Wood VC are also made.

K49A   KNIGHT, Ian
BY ORDERS OF THE GREAT WHITE QUEEN: Campaigning in Zululand through the Eyes of the British Solder, 1879
Greenhill Books, London, 1992
272 pp, hb, ncr

This book presents first-hand witness accounts by participants in the Anglo-Zulu War of 1879. Some material is based on later memoirs of officers present at Isandlwana, Rorke's Drift, Hlobane and Ulundi. The book also describes the mundane life of day-to-day campaigning.

K49B   KNIGHT, Ian
ZULU RISING: The Epic Story of Isandlwana and Rorke's Drift
Macmillan, London, 2010
697 pp, photos, maps, index, hb, cr

This book is a very detailed description of the causes of the Zulu War and the opposing forces and strategies employed by both sides which culminated in the defeat of the British at Isandlwana and the defence of Rorke's Drift. The text uses extensive eye-witness accounts of the fighting and brings new light to a well-documented subject. The three VCs associated with Isandlwana and the 11 VCs of Rorke's Drift are covered. Reviewed in V66.

K50 KNOLLYS, Major W.W., FRGS
THE VICTORIA CROSS IN THE CRIMEA
Dean, London, nd (c1877)
128 pp, line drawings, index, hb, cr

This work, within the *Deeds of Daring Library* series, describes the VC deed of every recipient of the Crimean War. Each act of gallantry is covered in the context of the main battles and campaigns of the war. The accounts of the individual deeds vary in length and are arranged within separate chapters on the battles of Alma, Balaklava, Inkerman and Sebastopol, the assault on the Redan, the Naval Brigade, the defence of Kars and the Baltic.

K51 KNOLLYS, Major W.W., FRGS
THE VICTORIA CROSS IN THE COLONIES
Dean, London, 1877
78 pp, line drawings, hb, cr

This work, within the *Deeds of Daring Library* series, describes the VC deed of acts performed in the colonies and elsewhere, covering Persia 1856-7, China 1860, Bhootan 1864-6, New Zealand 1863-6, Abyssinia 1868, Andaman Islands 1867, Ashantee 1873-4. A total of 33 VC deeds are described in the context of the campaigns. The accounts of each recipient vary in length.

K52 KNOLLYS, Major W.W., FRGS
THE VICTORIA CROSS IN INDIA
Dean, London, nd (c1878)
142 pp, line drawings, index, hb, cr

This work, within the *Deeds of Daring Library* series, describes every VC deed performed in the Indian Mutiny campaigns. The VC deeds, the accounts of which vary in length, are narrated in the context of the main battles, actions and expeditions.

K53 KNOLLYS, Lieutenant Colonel W.W. FRGS and ELLIOTT, Major W.J.
HEROES OF THE BATTLEFIELD
Dean, London, 1895
440 pp, line drawings, maps, hb, cr

This volume comprises the full text and illustrations of K51, E11 and E12 (Vol 1) but also contains an additional chapter concerning the Egyptian campaign (1882). The work is not part of the *Deeds of Daring Library* series.

K54 KNOLLYS, Lieutenant-Colonel W.W. and ELLIOTT, Major W.J.
GALLANT DEEDS OF OUR HEROES OF THE VICTORIA CROSS: The Victoria Cross Heroes and How They Obtained It - Crimea to Zululand
Dean, London, 1882
871 pp, line drawings, hb, ncr

An omnibus edition replicating in full, as separate sections, the text and illustrations of E11, E12, K50, K51 and K52. An addendum extends the text of E12 to include the first Boer War. Republished by Naval & Military Press.

K65 KNOX, Collie
HEROES ALL
Hodder & Stoughton, London, 1941
319 pp, index, hb, cr

A selection of accounts of the heroic deeds of British servicemen, servicewomen and civilians during the first twelve months of WW2, many of which resulted in a gallantry award. The 14 VC actions of the period are detailed in Chapter I (Warburton-Lee and Mantle), Chapter III (Fegen), Chapter IV (Stannard), Chapter XII (Ervine-Andrews, Nicholls, Wilson, Annand and Gristock) and Chapter XVIII (Garland and Gray, Learoyd, Hannah and Nicolson).

K70 KOFOD-HANSEN, Mogens (*Translator:* SPINK, Reginald)
'ANDY' - et portraet af danskeren major Anders Lassen somefter at vaere faldet i anden verdenskrig - blev tildelt Victoriakorset (*original Danish edition*)
'ANDY'- a portrait of Major Anders Lassen, the Dane who was posthumously awarded the Victoria Cross in the Second World War (*English edition*)
Friends of the Freedom Museum, Copenhagen, 1990 (Danish edition); 1991 (*English edition*)
Danish edition: 62 pp.; English edition: 66 pp, photos, sb, cr

This biographical sketch of Major Anders Lassen VC MC and two bars recalls his early years and his experiences as a seaman but mainly focuses on his wartime exploits in the Special Boat Service, which culminated in his posthumous VC action in April 1945.

K75 KRASNOFF, Stan
WHERE TO? FOR VALOUR: A true story of Keith Payne VC
Shala Press, Australia, 1995
242 pp, photos, maps, sb, cr

A biography of WO Keith Payne focusing on the story of his service in the Vietnam War, in which he won the VC. The work also describes Payne's awakening to the betrayal perpetrated by the politicians and his attempt to come to terms with the aftermath of the war.

L1   LA GIORGIA, Giancarlo
CANADIAN WAR HEROES
Folklore Publishing, Canada, 2005
145 pp, sb, cr

This publication profiles the courage of nine Canadian war heroes. There are short chapters on Alexander Dunn VC and Billy Bishop VC.

L1A   LAFFIN, John
RAIDERS: Great Exploits of the Second World War
Sutton Publishing, Stroud, 1999
194 pp, photos, index, hb, cr

This volume has 22 short chapters on various raids carried out by allied special forces and others in WW2. A number of VC recipients are covered including Beattie, Cameron, Place, Ryder, Savage, Porteous, Magennis, Fraser, Newman, Lassen, Keyes, Durrant and Freyberg.

L2   LAFFIN, John
BOYS IN BATTLE
Abelard-Schuman, London, 1966
192 pp, photos, index, hb, cr

An anthology of accounts describing gallantry performed by boys, aged 18 years and under, in campaigns ranging from the earliest times up to the Korean War. In the latter half of the book, which covers the Indian Mutiny onwards, particular emphasis is given to winners of the highest gallantry decorations of the major nations. Their deeds are recalled by campaign. VC recipients covered include ESt J Daniel, A Fitzgibbon, DG Boyes, BJD Guy, JT Cornwell, W Jackson, J Richardson, T Ricketts, AA McLeod and J Hannah.

L3   LAFFIN, John
BRITISH VCs OF WORLD WAR 2: A Study in Heroism
Sutton Publishing, Stroud, 1997
258 pp, photos, index, hb, cr

This book describes the 106 British VC actions of WW2 and is arranged into three parts - one covering each service within which the arrangement is by theatre of operation or other category. The full VC citation is given for each winner and is accompanied by brief biographical information and a portrait photograph. The two appendices list dominion and colonial VCs of WW2 and the surviving VC recipients in 1997.

L4   LAKE, Colonel Atwell, CB
KARS AND OUR CAPTIVITY IN RUSSIA: With letters from General Sir W.F. Williams KCB, Major Teesdale CB and the late Captain Thompson CB
Richard Bentley, London, 1856
367 pp, line drawings, index, hb, cr

A graphic eye-witness account of the Siege of Kars in the Crimean War based on letters by officers prominent in its defence, including Major CC Teesdale who was later awarded the VC for his services in the action.

L5 LAKE, Deborah
THE ZEEBRUGGE AND OSTEND RAIDS 1918
Leo Cooper, Barnsley, 2002
208 pp, photos, maps, index, hb, cr

Drawing on previously unpublished material from both Allied and German sources, the author provides a full account of the background, planning and execution of raids in Zeebrugge and Ostend in April and May 1918. The deeds in the raids that led to the award of eleven VCs are woven into the account.

L5A LAKE, Deborah
SMOKE AND MIRRORS: Q Ships Against U-Boats in the First World War
Sutton Publishing, Stroud, 2007
241 pp, photos, maps, index, hb, cr

This book tells the story of *Q* ships and their war against German U-boats. The text covers the *Q* ship operations by following the careers of eight men who were awarded the VC: G Campbell, W Bonner, N Stuart, E Pitcher, W Williams, W Sanders, T Crisp and H Auten.

L6 LANGLEY, Mike
ANDERS LASSEN VC MC OF THE SAS: The story of Anders Lassen and the men who fought with him
New English Library, Hodder & Stoughton, Sevenoaks, 1988
254 pp, photos, maps, hb, cr

A detailed and complete biography of Major Anders Lassen VC MC and two bars - the only VC winner of the SAS. The book is based partly on interviews with Lassen's contemporaries and eyewitness accounts of his exploits.

L7 LANGMAID, Captain Kenneth, DSC RN
BEAT TO QUARTERS! Ten Outstanding Naval Exploits
Jarrolds, London, 1968
207 pp, photos, index, hb, cr

Three of the ten Royal Navy exploits covered in this work are VC actions. Chapter 4 (pages 69-87) concerns *Q* ships in WWI but focuses on Gordon Campbell VC. Chapter 7 (pages 126-161) relates specifically to Augustus Agar's VC action in *CMB4* in Russia. Chapter 8 (pages 162-173) recalls the raid on St Nazaire but concentrates on the involvement of HMS *Campbeltown* and of Cdr RED Ryder VC and Lt Cdr SH Beattie VC.

L8 LANGMAID, Captain Kenneth, DSC RN
THE BLIND EYE
Jarrolds, London, 1972
166 pp, photos, drawings, index, hb, cr

Each of this book's nine chapters recalls a historically important situation in which a British naval officer chose to act daringly and independently. Apart from Chapter 1, which concerns Admiral Nelson, all other chapters relate to WW1 or WW2 actions. Chapter 2 (pages 19-33) and Chapter 4 (pages 44-68) are devoted to the *Q* ship exploits of Gordon Campbell VC and to the VC deed of Augustus Agar, respectively.

L9   LASSEN, Suzanne (*translator*: Inge Hack)
[1] ANDERS LASSEN: Sømand og Soldat (*original Danish publication*)
[2] ANDERS LASSEN VC: The Story of a Courageous Dane (*English publication*)
Gyldendalske Boghandel, Kobenhavn, 1949 / Frederick Muller, London, 1965
Danish edition: 228 pp.; English edition: 244 pp, photos, index, hb, cr

This biography of Lassen is written by his mother, who throughout the war received only sparse and occasional news of her son. As a professional writer, the author undertook the research carefully, visited the scenes of her son's exploits and interviewed those who knew him.

L10   LAVERTON, Ronald H.
GENERAL GORT
Pilot Press, London, 1940
94 pp, photos, hb, cr

A short biographical sketch of General Gort VC. The book is Volume 16 in the series *How They Did It Life Stories*.

L11   LAWRENCE, Alenka (*interviewer and compiler*)
[1] LEONARD CHESHIRE: WHERE IS GOD IN ALL THIS?
St Paul's Publications, Slough, 1991
229 pp, photos, hb, cr
LAWRENCE, Alenka (translated by CAVICCHIOLI, Carlo)
[2] C' È DIO IN TUTTO QUESTO? (*Italian edition*)
San Paolo, Milan, Italy, 1994
172 pp, photos, sb, (*Italian text*)

This unusual book is a direct transcript of an interview with Lord Cheshire VC, which was conducted in his home by Alenka Lawrence of the BBC World Service. Cheshire's detailed and spontaneous responses give a vivid insight into his thinking and deep faith. The transcript is structured into the various aspects of his life and experiences, covering how he found faith, his war-time service, subsequent views about war, services to the disabled, family life, suffering, prayer and his attitudes towards travel and work.

L12   LAWRIWSKY, Michael
HARD JACKA: The Story of the Gallipoli Legend
Mira Books, Chatswood, New South Wales, 2010
421 pp, photos, maps, index, sb, cr

A full biography of Albert Jacka VC MC* who served with the AIF at Gallipoli and on the Western Front. While keeping to historical facts, the author includes fictional conversations between Jacka and others.

L12A   LAWRIWSKY, Michael
RETURN OF GALLIPOLI LEGEND: Jacka VC
Mira Books, Chatswood, New South Wales, 2010
528 pp, photos, map, index, sb, cr

This book is a novel about Albert Jacka VC MC* and the men of the 14th AIF in WW1. It is based on fact but much is fictional narrative focusing on Jacka's return to Australia after WW1.

L13   LEAKE, Richard
A BREED APART: The story of the remarkable men of the Yorkshire Regiment, both winners of the Victoria Cross, Second-Lieutenant Oswald Bell and Captain Archie White
Great Northern Publishing, Scarborough, 2008
128 pp, photos, maps, index, sb, cr

This book contains the biographies of two officers of the Green Howards who were awarded the VC in WW1: 2nd Lt. DS Bell VC and Capt. ACT White VC MC. The volume is profusely illustrated with good quality photographs. There is also a short chapter on two other Green Howards who were awarded the VC in 1916: W Short and SW Loudoun-Shand.

L14   LE QUESNE, Walter J
THE LE QUESNES OF JERSEY
Channel Islands Family History Society, St Helier, Jersey, 1995
134 pp, photos, index, sb, cr

A book tracing eight branches of the Le Quesne family and including details on Lt Col FS Le Quesne VC.

L15   LEASK, G.A., MA
VC HEROES OF THE WAR (*original title*)
HEROIC DEEDS OF THE GREAT WAR (*1917 title*)
George Harrap, London, 1916
301 pp, photos, hb, cr

This book describes 50 VC deeds of WW1 that occurred during 1914/1915. Sixteen of the twenty-two chapters relate to an individual VC or a specific VC action. The remaining chapters concern, typically, the various VCs of particular battles. Artist's impressions of eight VC deeds are included.

L16   LEASK, G.A.
GOLDEN DEEDS OF HEROISM: A Popular Book of Bravery and Devotion in the Great War
Joseph Johnson, London, nd (c1919)
246 pp, sketches, hb, cr

Accounts of valour set in the context of the campaigns and events of WW1. Thirteen of the 17 chapters relate to actions in which VCs were awarded and 46 VC deeds are described in detail. There are also brief references to many more VC recipients.

L21   LEE, Philip H.
THE VICTORIA CROSS
Preston Brothers and Co. (Printers), Huddersfield, 1912
25 pp, line drawing, sb, ncr

This small booklet gives a summary history of the VC from the Crimean War to the Tibet campaign of 1904. Short chapters typically cover the Royal Warrants, a description of the Cross and its monetary value. No individual VC recipient is covered in a significant way.

L22   LEEK, Alan
FREDERICK WHIRLPOOL VC: Australia's Hidden Victoria Cross
Big Sky Publishing, Newport, New South Wales, Australia, 2018
313 pp, index, sb, cr

This is a detailed biography of Frederick Whirlpool VC who won his award in the Indian Mutiny. He arrived in Australia in 1859 and became a volunteer rifleman and teacher. His VC was presented to him in Melbourne in 1861. The book describes his true identity and early life in Ireland before joining the HEIC, his service in the Indian Mutiny and his chequered life in Australia till his death in June 1899. Republished by Pen & Sword Military.

L23   LEEMING, John F.
ALWAYS TOMORROW
George Harrap, London, 1951
188 pp, photos, maps, hb, cr

The author describes the POW experiences he shared with Air Marshal Boyd, Generals Neame VC, Carton de Wiart VC and O'Connor and other high-ranking officers during their time in captivity in Italy. The story is told of their day-to-day life, firstly in a villa at Sulmona and latterly in the fortress of Vincigliata. (See also H28.)

L25   LENNOX, Lord William (*compiler*)
THE VICTORIA CROSS: The Rewarded and Their Services
John Mitchell, London, 1857
64 pp, hb, ncr

This book, which is the first published work about the VC, is a compilation of all VC citations relating to the Crimean War. It is arranged in separate sections for the Royal Navy, Royal Marines and the Army.

L27   LEONARD CHESHIRE FOUNDATION (*subsequently* LEONARD CHESHIRE)
[1] **THE STORY OF LEONARD CHESHIRE INCLUDING THE HISTORY OF THE LEONARD CHESHIRE FOUNDATION**
Leonard Cheshire Foundation, London, nd (c1995)
20 pp, photos, sb, cr
[2] **THE STORY OF LEONARD CHESHIRE**
Leonard Cheshire, London, nd (c1998)
20 pp, sb, cr

A small booklet which describes the life of Leonard Cheshire VC and how he established the homes for the disabled which bear his name. The text includes a short section on his war service and how he won the VC. The text is taken mainly from B91 and S87.

L30   LETHBRIDGE, J.P.
BIRMINGHAM HEROES
Newgate Press, Birmingham, 1993
46 pp, sb, cr

Short biographical sketches of 20 VCs associated with Birmingham. Each sketch records the recipient's family background and early years, the VC citation and brief details of any subsequent career. The booklet also contains details of Birmingham's eight George Cross recipients and a selection of seven other personalities from Birmingham. Reviewed in V51.

L31   LETT, Brian, QC
THE SMALL SCALE RAIDING FORCE
Pen & Sword Books, Barnsley, 2013
216 pp, photos, index, hb, cr

A history of the Small Scale Raid Force and its raids in WW2. Its formation in February 1942 is described along with raids using adapted motor torpedo boats. Key members of the Force are described including Anders Lassen VC.

L33   LEWIS, Robert, and GURRY, Jim
IN SEARCH OF JACKA: Investigating the Life of a Famous World War I Australian Soldier Through Evidence
ANZAC Day Commemoration Committee (Queensland) Inc., Victoria, Australia, 2002
25 pp, photos, maps, sb, cr

An educational tool to help schoolchildren conduct their own investigations into the life of Albert Jacka VC. The aim is to examine the evidence and develop conclusions about the life of soldiers in the First World War and the attitudes and actions of participants.

L35   LEYLAND, Eric
FOR VALOUR: The Story of the Victoria Cross
Edmund Ward, London, 1960
144 pp, line drawings, hb, cr

This book for boys tells the story of the VC by describing some of the VC deeds performed in the main conflicts from the Crimean War through to the Korean War. An appendix lists living holders of the VC as at November 1959.

L37   LIDDLE, Dr Peter
CAPTURED MEMORIES 1900 - 1918: Across the Threshold of War
Pen & Sword, Military, Barnsley, 2010
313 pp, photos, index, hb, cr

This publication is a series of transcripts of interviews the author conducted with soldiers and sailors over a number of decades. Three chapters cover interviews with VC recipients: Grimshaw, Holbrook and JG Smyth.

L38   LIDDLE, Dr Peter
CAPTURED MEMORIES 1930-1945: Across the Threshold of War - The Thirties and the War
Pen & Sword Military, Barnsley, 2011
395 pp, photos, index, hb, cr

The Liddle Collection of Second World War archives in the University of Leeds was founded by the author in 1999. In this Volume II in the *Captured Memories* series, the author has selected transcripts of interviews he conducted with 42 individuals, eight representing the 1930s and 34 from WW2. Two VC recipients are featured: Flt Lt W Reid (pages 122-130) and Col ECT Wilson (pages 163-167).

L40   LIMBU, Lieutenant (QGO) Rambahadur, VC
MY LIFE STORY
Gurkha Welfare Trusts, London, nd (c1982)
20 pp, photos, sb, cr

This booklet is an autobiography of Limbu VC as told to WO2 Kulbahadur Rai of 10th Princess Mary's Own Gurkha Rifles. The narrative includes details of his VC action in Sarawak in November 1965. A full colour portrait of Limbu in uniform wearing his VC and medals appears on the front cover.

L41   LINDEMANN, Kelvin (*editor*)
MED EVENTYRERNE OVER ALLE GRAENSER
Boghallen, København, 1963
235 pp, sketches, hb, cr

A book in Danish, whose title means *With Adventurers Across All Frontiers*. It is a compilation of accounts written by members of the Adventurers' Club of Denmark. Thirteen pages contain the wartime recollections of Thomas Dinesen VC, including his account of the action for which he was awarded the VC.

L42   LINDSAY, Sid
MERSEYSIDE HEROES: A Collection of Biographical Notes
Privately published, Liverpool, 1988
208 pp, sketches, sb, cr

This comb-bound book with typescript text contains biographical sketches and a description of the VC deed of the 64 VC winners who had a connection with Merseyside. The work was privately published as a limited edition restricted to 30 copies (many of which were distributed to local libraries). See C77, C78, C79 and C80.

L45   LITTLE, Matthew G.
THE ROYAL MARINES VICTORIA CROSSES
Royal Marines Museum, Eastney
1) 1st edition: 1986, 47 pp, photos, sb, cr
2) Revised edition: 2002, 54 pp, photos, sb, cr

This booklet provides short biographies and a portrait photograph of each of the ten Royal Marines VC winners. An updated version was published in 2002 with the title *The Royal Marines and the Victoria Cross*. Reviewed in V52.

L46   LITTLE, Paul
WILLIE APIATA VC: The Relucant Hero
Viking (Penguin Group (NZ)), Auckland, New Zealand, 2008
255 pp, photos, hb, cr

A full biography of Willie Apiata, the first recipient of the Victoria Cross for New Zealand. The volume covers his family background and his service in the New Zealand Army as a peacekeeper and the action in Afghanistan resulting in the award of the VC. His father was Maori, making him the second Maori to be awarded the VC, the first being Ngarimu in N Africa in WW2. Reviewed in V63.

L47   LITTLEWOOD, Arthur (*editor*)
INDIAN MUTINY AND BEYOND: The Letters of Robert Shebbeare VC
Pen & Sword, Barnsley, 2007
144 pp, photos, maps, index, hb, cr

Robert Shebbeare went to India at the age of 17 and after a spell of regimental duties saw action in the Indian Mutiny. He escaped from Delhi, where he was attached to the Guides and took part in many actions during the summer of 1857. He was wounded six times and awarded the VC for the storming of the city on 14 September. This book reproduces his letters to his family between 1844 and 1860. It also makes use of letters of fellow officers to provide a context. At the age of 33, Shebbeare died at sea on his way home on leave. Reviewed in V60.

L50   LLOYD, W.G.
JOHN WILLIAMS VC: A Biography
WG Lloyd, Cwmbran, Gwent, 1993
117 pp, photos, map, hb, cr

A full and well illustrated biography of Private John Williams VC (whose real name was John Fielding). It provides a detailed account of his family background, early life, military service in the Kaffir and Zulu wars, later life and his death in 1932. His Rorke's Drift VC action is well documented and is supported by appendices that contain transcripts of letters written to the press by several participants in the defence of Rorke's Drift. A list is provided identifying the reference sources which are mainly contemporary newspaper articles.

L51   LOCK, Ron
BLOOD ON THE PAINTED MOUNTAIN: Zulu Victory and Defeat - Hlobane and Kambula, 1879
Greenhill Books, London, 1995
224 pp, photos, line drawings, maps, index, hb, cr

An examination of the British defeat at Hlobane and the British victory at Kambula on the following day. There is extensive text on Lt Col Redvers Buller (who won his VC at Hlobane) and on Col Evelyn Wood VC who commanded the column at Hlobane.

L52   LOCKHART, Thomas Glen
LAST MAN STANDING: The Life of Smokey Smith, VC, 1914 - 2005
Friesens Press, Victoria, British Columbia, 2012
102 pp, photos, hb, cr

'Smokey' Smith VC was the sole surviving Canadian VC until his death in 2005, giving rise to this biography's title. The volume describes his early life in New Westminster, Canada and his time in the Depression. His WW2 service, during which he destroyed multiple tanks at Cesna on 21/22 October 1944 and was awarded the VC, is covered in depth. Chapter 9 describes his funeral and Appendix D featuring a transcript of the Service of Thanksgiving and Remembrance.

L53   LOCKWOOD, Kim
WWII HEROES: The Bravest of the Brave
Wilkinson Publishing, Melbourne, Victoria, Australia, 2016
128 pp, photos (some colour), artist drawings, sb, cr

This lavishly-illustrated book (No 10 in the publisher's *Military Series*) recalls the deeds of 51 heroes of WW2, including 19 VCs and 18 US Medal of Honor recipients. The stories are arranged in six categories: Army, Navy, US Marine Corps, Air Force, Behind the Lines and Largely Unsung.

L54 LOCKYER, Keira Quinn
KEYSOR VC: Gallipoli's Quiet Hero
High Tech Printing Services, Ballarat, Victoria, Australia, 2014
301 pp, photos, sb, cr

The author's great uncle was Leonard Keysor VC who was born into a Jewish family in London in 1885. He spent ten years in the Manitoba prairies before moving to Australia in 1914 and was one of the first to enlist in the AIF on the outbreak of War. He served at Gallipoli and won the VC at Lone Pine and later was sent to the Western Front. The remaining chapters cover the Keysor family history.

L55 LODWICK, John
[1] **THE FILIBUSTER**
Methuen, London, 1947
201 pp, maps, hb, cr
[2] **FRIBYTTERNE og Anders Lassen** (*Danish translated version*)
J.H. Schultz Forlag, Denmark, 1958
201 pp, maps, hb, cr

An account of the Special Boat Service and its role in WW2. Major Anders Lassen VC MC** is featured prominently in this book and many of his wartime exploits in the SBS are described. The book's Danish title means *The Filibuster and Anders Lassen*.

L56 LOFTUS, Ian
THE MOST FEARLESS AND GALLANT SOLDIER I HAVE EVER SEEN: The Story of Martin O'Meara, Australia's only Irish-born Victoria Cross recipient of the First World War
Privately published, Applecross, Western Australia, 2016
274 pp, maps, photos, index, sb, cr

A biography of the Irish-born VC recipient Pte M O'Meara who served in the 16th AIF in WW1. O'Meara won his VC at Poziéres on the Somme between 9 and 12 August 1916 for bringing in wounded men and moving ammunition under heavy fire. He survived the war but suffered severe mental health trauma for the rest of his life. He died in Australia in 1935.

L58 LOVELL, Mark
ROBERTS OF KANDAHAR
London Publishing Company, London, 1900
16 pp, sb, cr

A short biography of Lord Roberts VC and No. 1 in the series *Soldiers of the Queen Library*. See B118 and B119.

L59 LOVELL, Nicholas
VCs OF BROMSGROVE SCHOOL: The Stories of five Victoria Crosses won by Old Bromsgrovians
Bromsgrove School Enterprises, Bromsgrove, 1996
17 pp, photos, line drawings, sb, cr

This booklet summarises the life and achievements of each of the five Old Bromsgrovian VCs: PT Dean, E Jotham, NG Leakey, FB Wearne and Sir G White.

L60   LOW, Charles Rathbone, IN FRGS
MAJOR-GENERAL SIR FREDERICK S. ROBERTS Bart VC GCB CIE RA: A Memoir
WH Allen, London, 1883
405 pp, photo, hb, cr

A comprehensive biography of General Roberts VC up to 1882. It describes the services of his distinguished father, General Sir Abraham Roberts and traces FS Roberts' life from childhood. A chronicle of his military career up to the aftermath of the Afghan War is covered extensively. Reviewed in V51.

L61   LOW, Charles Rathbone
SOLDIERS OF THE VICTORIAN AGE
Chapman & Hall, London, 1880
Two volumes - 793 pp. (Vol 1: 347 pp.; Vol 2: 446 pp.), hb, cr

Volume 1 includes biographical sketches of Henry Clifford VC and of Sir H Evelyn Wood VC. Detailed accounts of their VC actions are documented.

L62   LOWE, Charles, MA
OUR GREATEST LIVING SOLDIERS
Chatto & Windus, London, 1900
178 pp, photos, hb, cr

The ten chapters of this book appeared originally as a series of articles in newspapers. Eight chapters are devoted to individual generals. Chapters II, III, IV and V (pages 20-85) relate the biographical sketches of Sir Redvers Buller VC, Lord Roberts VC, Sir Evelyn Wood VC and Sir George White VC, respectively. The other four dedicated chapters are in respect of Viscount Wolseley, Sir Donald Stewart, Lord Kitchener and Sir Hector MacDonald. The final two chapters concern the royal dukes and other generals.

L63   LOWTHER, W.W.
CYRIL JOE BARTON VC
Wear Books, Sunderland, 1994
66 pp, photos, sketches, maps, sb, cr

A well-illustrated and full account of the short life of Pilot Officer CJ Barton VC, based on family memories and eye-witness reports. Following a description of his formative years the book then focuses on his RAF service. In-depth coverage is given to the raid on Nuremburg in which Barton won the VC posthumously and is supplemented by photographs, maps and the official report on the raid. Appendix II is a list of memorials to Barton. Appendix III is a facsimile of pages from the 21 June 1975 issue of the boys' comic *The Victor* featuring Barton's VC deed.

L69   LUCAS, Laddie (*editor*)
THANKS FOR THE MEMORY: Unforgettable Characters in Air Warfare 1939-45
Stanley Paul, London, 1989
450 pp, photos, index, hb, cr

A compilation of reminiscences of 93 Allied and Axis airmen of WW2 who recall the most memorable air force personality they met during the conflict. Many of these first-hand accounts have been written by, or are in respect of, legendary names. The following four VCs are written about: Leonard Cheshire (pages 19-27), Guy Gibson (pages 359-364), Sir Hughie Edwards (pages 378-383) and Leonard Trent (pages 389-391). Additionally, Cheshire contributed his reminiscences of ACM Sir Ralph Cochrane, his former AOC.

L70   LUCAS PHILLIPS, C.E.
VICTORIA CROSS BATTLES OF THE SECOND WORLD WAR
Heinemann, London, 1973
292 pp, photos, sketches, maps, index, hb, cr

This book focuses on a selection of battles in different theatres of WW2 in which VCs were awarded. A total of 34 VC recipients are covered in separate chapters on Crete, Battle of the Atlantic, Operation *Crusader*, Gazala, Rueisat, Wadi Akarit, *X-craft* and Imphal. The VC deeds are described in the context of the related battle, which is chronicled fully. A roll of WW2 VCs is included in an Appendix.

L71   LUCAS PHILLIPS, C.E.
THE GREATEST RAID OF ALL
Heinemann, London, 1958
288 pp, photos, sketches, maps, hb, cr

With the help of Lt Col Newman VC and Capt Ryder VC, the author has provided a comprehensive account of the St Nazaire raid. Detailed sketch maps and many photos relating to the action are included, together with a list of those who died in the operation and a list of the awards made. The deeds of the VC recipients (Ryder, Savage, Beattie, Newman and Durrant) are described fully. Republished by White Lion Publishers, 1973.

L80   LUCIUK, Lubomyr K. and SOROBEY, Ron
KONOWAL
Kashtan Press, Kingston, Ontario, Canada for The Royal Canadian Legion Branch 360, 1996
18 pp, photos, sb, cr

This trilingual (English/French/Ukrainian) biographical sketch of Cpl Filip Konowal VC, a Ukrainian-Canadian, summarises his service in the Canadian Expeditionary Force, during which he was awarded the VC in 1917. It also recalls his subsequent life, including his connection with the Royal Canadian Legion and describes and illustrates (with photographs) the memorials to him. Other photographs include his medal group and Army Record of Service.

L86   LUMMIS, Lieutenant W.M.
THE ROLL OF THE VICTORIA CROSS
Privately published, Belgaum, India, 1925
137 pp, hb, ncr

This book records the campaigns for which the VC was awarded up to 1920, a summary of awards, the surviving holders of the VC, forfeitures, a nominal roll of recipients arranged in order of date gazetted, a list of recipients arranged according to service or unit and a chronological list by date of VC deed. (Lummis had 20 copies of the work printed in Belgaum, India where he was based at the Army School of Education, in 1926. Five copies were bound in India and subsequently seven copies were bound in Ipswich. The remaining copies were left unbound).

L87   LUMMIS, Canon William M., MC
PADRE GEORGE SMITH OF RORKE'S DRIFT
Wensum Books, Norwich, 1978
94 pp, photos, line drawings, index, hb, cr

Whilst this book is a biography of Padre Smith, it contains a chapter on the Rorke's Drift action, in which Smith participated, and describes some of the VC deeds. Appendix III (pages 84-94) entitled *The Victoria Cross Heroes of Rorke's Drift* contains biographical details of each VC recipient.

L88   LUMMIS, Canon William Murrell, MC
VICTORIA CROSS BIBLIOGRAPHY
Privately published, Suffolk, 1956
22 pp, sb, ncr

A typewritten document listing the VC books in the library of Canon Lummis while he was serving at St Mary's Vicarage, Bungay, Suffolk. The document was circulated by the National Book League during the VC Centenary year, and lists nearly 200 titles.

L100   LUNT, James
CHARGE TO GLORY!: A Garland of Cavalry Exploits
Heinemann, London, 1961
265 pp, map, hb, cr

Chapter 10 (pages 217-237) of this book, entitled *Moreuil Wood 30 March 1918*, describes the VC action of Lt GM Flowerdew, who died of wounds the day after his famous cavalry charge and was awarded a posthumous VC. The chapter includes the painting by Sir Alfred Munnings titled *The Charge of Flowerdew's Squadron*.

L110   LYMAN, Robert
INTO THE JAWS OF DEATH: The True Story of the Legendary Raid on Saint-Nazaire
Quercus, London, 2013
384 pp, photos, maps, index, hb, cr

An account of Operation *Chariot*, the audacious raid on the dry dock at St Nazaire on 28/29 March 1942. The book describes the planning, the raid itself, the cost, effects and aftermath. A total of five VCs were awarded including the leader of the operation, RED Ryder VC.

M1 McALEER, Anthony. J.
'GREAT COURAGE AND INITIATIVE': The Heroic Life of George Ingram VC MM
Vic Wandin and District Historical Museum Society, Wandin North, Australia, 2015
187 pp, photos, maps, hb, cr

This biography of Captain G Ingram VC MM includes his country childhood in Bagshot and Seville and describes his service with the Australian Garrison Artillery and the Tropical Forle's Matupi Battery. He served with the 24th Battalion AIF on the Western Front where he was decorated with the MM and VC. His was the last Australian VC recipient of the war. After WW1 he became a solder settler and in WW2 served with the Royal Australian Engineers.

M1A McALLISTER, Heyden (*editor*)
FLYING STORIES
Octopus Books Ltd, Australia, 1982
304 pp, illustrations, hb, cr

A children's book covering aviation stories. Pages 32 to 49 cover WW1 ace JTB McCudden VC. Pages 204 to 215 describes the flight by RH Middleton resulting in his death and a posthumous VC.

M1B MacBRIDE, Sam
THE BRAVEST CANADIAN - FRITZ PETERS VC: The Making of a Hero of Two World Wars
Granville Island Publishing, Vancouver, British Columbia, 2012
209 pp, photos, maps, index, sb, cr

A full biography of FT Peters VC DSO DSC*, one of Canada's most decorated officers. The author had access to a substantial number of letters from and about Peters as well as access to family members and their archives. Peters won a DSO in WW1 on anti-submarine patrols and a VC in WW2 for the attack on the Vichy held port of Oran in North Africa during Operation *Torch*. He died in a flying accident shortly after the operation.

M1C McCAFFERY, Dan
BILLY BISHOP: Canadian Hero
James Lorimer, Toronto, 1988
227 pp, photos, hb, cr

This re-examination of Bishop's 75 aerial victories in WW1 attempts to redress the criticisms of false claims purported in the National Film Board of Canada's controversial documentary *The Kid Who Couldn't Miss* (see C36). The author has uncovered much new information which counters some long-held misconceptions about Bishop. His victory log is contained in an appendix.

M1D McCAFFERY, Dan
AIR ACES: The Lives and Times of Twelve Canadian Fighter Pilots
James Lorimer, Toronto, 1990
234 pp, photos, hb, cr

Separate chapters relate to each of the 12 Canadian aces selected who include three VCs: Alan McLeod, William Barker and Billy Bishop. At the end of the book is a list of Canadian aces of WW1, WW2 and the Korean War.

M2   McCLINTOCK, Mary Howard
THE QUEEN THANKS SIR HOWARD: The Life of Major-General Sir Howard Elphinstone VC KCB CMG
John Murray, London, 1945
273 pp, photos, index, hb, cr

Told through his letters, this biography focuses largely on Elphinstone's experiences in the court of Queen Victoria. A genealogical table tracing the Elphinstone family is included. There are also numerous references to Major AF Pickard VC and his service to the Royal Household.

M3   McCOMBIE, Frank
GALLIPOLI: THE FINAL CHANCE: General Kenna and the Yeomen at Suvla Bay
University Library, Newcastle-Upon-Tyne, 1990
107 pp, maps, sb, cr

This desk-top published work provides a detailed description of the 2nd Mounted Division's actions at Gallipoli in August 1915, during which Brig-Gen PA Kenna VC led the 3rd (Notts and Derby) Brigade until his death at the hands of a Turkish sniper. It also chronicles Kenna's service between August 1914 and August 1915.

M4   McCRERY, Nigel
FOR CONSPICUOUS GALLANTRY: A Brief History of the Recipients of the Victoria Cross from Nottinghamshire and Derbyshire
JH Hall, Derby, 1990
87 pp, photos, index, sb, cr

A collection of biographical sketches of the 37 VC recipients from Nottinghamshire and Derbyshire. A portrait photograph and full VC citation accompanies each sketch.

M4A   McCRERY, Nigel
THE FINAL SEASON: The Footballers who Fought and Died in the Great War
Random House Books, London, 2014
262 pp, photos, index, hb, cr

During WW1, over 200 professional football players fell in action on the battlefield or were so badly injured they would never play again. For many of these men, the author recalls their achievements on the football pitch and their heroic conduct on the battlefield. Three VC recipients (two of whom were killed) are featured: W Angus (pages 54-59); DS Bell (pages 19-21 and 129-140); and BW Vann (pages 235-249).

M5   McCUDDEN, Major James VC DSO MC MM
[1] **FIVE YEARS IN THE ROYAL FLYING CORPS** (*original title*)
Aeroplane and General Publishing, London, 1918
348 pp, photos, hb, cr
[2] **FLYING FURY** (*later title*)
Aviation Book Club, London, 1939 (*reformatted*)
270 pp, photos, hb, cr
[3] **FLYING FURY: Five Years in the Royal Flying Corps** (*subsequent title*)
Bailey Brothers and Swinfen, London, 1973 (*expanded*)
356 pp, photos, hb, cr

McCudden describes this autobiography as a faithful personal record of his service in the Royal Flying Corps and relates his experiences as a mechanic, observer and pilot in France. He was killed in a flying accident a few days after completing the manuscript. (The original publication was edited by CG Grey, editor of *The Aeroplane* magazine. Some later editions of the books [from 1968] were edited by Lt Col S Ulanoff).

M6   McCULLOUGH, Colleen
[1] **RODEN CUTLER, VC: The Biography** (*Australian edition*)
Random House, Australia, 1998
416 pp, photos, maps, index, hb, cr
[2] **THE COURAGE AND THE WILL: The Life of Roden Cutler VC** (*UK edition*)
Weidenfeld and Nicolson, London, 1999
416 pp, photos, maps, index, hb, cr

This full biography of Sir Roden Cutler VC traces his early years (pages 9-57), his military service (pages 59-214), his subsequent distinguished career as a diplomat and long-serving Governor of New South Wales (pages 215-397) and life in retirement. A chapter is devoted to his VC deed.

M7   McDONALD, Gabrielle
JACK HINTON VC: A Man Amongst Men
David Ling Publishing, Auckland, New Zealand, 1997
192 pp, photos, maps, index, sb, cr

A full biography of Jack Hinton VC who, in September 1939, was one of the first New Zealanders to volunteer for war service. The book describes his VC action, includes details from official Army records and features the recollections of those who knew him personally, including fellow soldiers and POWs.

M7A   McDONALD, Penelope J.
MAHONEY: A Canadian Hero
The Royal Westminster Regiment Association, British Columbia, Canada, 2001
14pp, photos, sb, cr

A short biography of Canadian WW2 hero, Major JK Mahoney VC. His award was for taking a bridgehead in Italy in May 1944. The booklet describes his early life in New Westminster, his military service in WW2 and his post war career in the Canadian army.

M8   MacDONALD, W. James
A BIBLIOGRAPHY OF THE VICTORIA CROSS
W James MacDonald Publishers, Baddeck, Nova Scotia, Canada, 1994
15 pp, sb, ncr

The books listed in this non-annotated bibliography are arranged under the following headings: history of the Victoria Cross, biographies and autobiographies of VC recipients and books written by VC recipients. A total of 288 titles are recorded.

M8A MacDONALD, Terry
BAZALGETTE VC: Alberta Pathfinder
Terry MacDonald and Bunker to Bunker Publishing, Calgary, Alberta, 2002
84 pp, photos, maps, sb, cr

This is a profusely illustrated short biography of Squadron Leader IW Bazalgette VC DFC who was awarded a posthumous VC for a pathfinder raid in August 1944. Over half the book has photos, documents, maps and a reproduction of two articles from the boys' comic *The Victor*. Reviewed in V51.

M8B MACDONALD, Donald
HOW WE KEPT THE FLAG FLYING: The Story of the Siege of Ladysmith
Ward, Lock & Co, Melbourne, 1900
289 pp, photos, map, hb, cr
1999 reprint of this book published by Covos Books, Roodepoort, South Africa. (Anglo-Boer War Centenary edition)

The author was the war correspondent for the Melbourne Argus and was in Ladysmith for the entire siege. Sir George White VC, the commandant of the garrison is mentioned frequently. Sir Redvers Buller VC is also mentioned, although less frequently. (See G66).

M9 MacDONNELL, J.E.
VALIANT OCCASIONS
Constable, London, 1952
262 pp, hb, cr

An account of 19 naval engagements of WW2 involving the Royal Navy and the Royal Australian Navy. Three chapters relate to specific VC actions. Chapter 7 (pages 78-90) describes HMS *Glowworm*'s attack on *Hipper* (Roope VC). Chapter 10 (pages 120-134) covers the *X-craft* attack on the *Tirpitz* (Cameron VC and Place VC). Chapter 17 (pages 214-224) is an account of HMS *Jervis Bay*'s VC action against the *Admiral Scheer* (Fegen VC).

M10 MacDONNELL, J.E.
FOR VALOUR
Horwitz Publications, Sydney, 1971
125 pp, sb, cr

A dramatic account of three separate gallant naval actions of WW2 for which the ships' captains were awarded the VC. The first account (pages 9-59) relates to HMS *Glowworm* (Roope VC); the second account (pages 60-106) concerns HMS *Jervis Bay* (Fegen VC); the third account deals with the St Nazaire action of HMS *Campbeltown* (Beattie VC), but the other VC winners in the raid are mentioned only briefly.

M10A McENTEE-TAYLOR, Carole
HERBERT COLUMBINE VC
Pen and Sword Military, Barnsley, 2013
172 pp, photos, index, hb, cr

A biography of Herbert Columbine who was killed in the action on 22 March 1918 for which he was awarded the VC. The book describes his early life in which his father was killed in the Boer War and traces his military service till the time of his death. Reviewed in V72.

M11 MACFARLANE, Major A.M., RA
143RD (TOMBS'S TROOP) BATTERY, ROYAL ARTILLERY: A Short History
Royal Artillery Printing Press, Woolwich, nd (c1968)
64 pp, photos, sb, cr

The Honour Title *Tombs's Troop* was named after Major General Sir Henry Tombs VC KCB in 1926, being allocated to 56 Field Battery RE (which eventually became 143 Light Battery RA). Major (later Colonel) Tombs commanded its early predecessor, 2 Troop 1 Brigade Bengal House Artillery from 1856-62 during which command he won the VC. Chapter II in this booklet relates to Tombs' service in the Indian Mutiny. Chapter III is devoted to the VC deeds of Tombs and Lt Hills (later Lt Gen Sir J Hills-Johnes). The 13 annexures include a biography of Tombs (Annexure F) and a description of *The Tombs Memorial Scholarship* (Annexure G).

M11B MACFARLANE, John
TRIQUET'S CROSS: A Study in Miltary Heroism
McGill-Queen's University Press, Montreal, Quebec, Canada, 2009
250 pp, photos, maps, index, hb cr

A full and detailed biography of the French-Canadian officer, Paul Triquet, who was awarded the VC for gallantry in Italy in 1943. The book is in three parts: Part 1 covers his early life and service to 1943. Part 2 covers the period March 1943 to August 1944 including the award of the VC. Part 3 covers post war years to 1980 including the pressure felt by Triquet to resign from the Army to escape the public and political expectations that the award entailed. Reviewed in V64.

M12 McGOVERN, Joseph Henry
HOW ONE OF THE McGOVERN OR McGAURAN CLAN WON THE VICTORIA CROSS IN THE INDIAN MUTINY WITH A SKETCH OF ITS TRIBAL HISTORY
Daily Post & Echo, Liverpool, 1889
39 pp, hb, cr

A total of 18 pages is devoted to the action for which Sgt John McGovern, 1st Bengal Fusiliers, was awarded the VC.

M12B McGREAL, Stephen
ZEEBRUGGE & OSTEND RAIDS
Leo Cooper (Pen & Sword Books), Barnsley, 2007
216 pp, photos, maps, index, sb, cr

Published as part of the *Battleground Europe* series, this well-illustrated volume describes the raids on Zeebrugge and Ostend in April and May 1918. Eight VCs were awarded for the attack on Zeebrugge and three VCs for Ostend.

M13 MacGREGOR, James
MacGREGOR VC: Goodbye Dad – Biography of the man who won more prestigious awards for valour than any other Canadian soldier
The Victoria Publishing Co., Victoria, British Columbia, Canada, 2002
260 pp, photos, maps, hb, cr

A full biography of John MacGregor VC MC and bar DCM of 2nd Canadian Mounted Rifles, 1st Central Ontario regiment, who won his VC near Cambrai for gallantry between 29 September and 3 October 1918. The book, written by his son, includes two colour portraits and two colour maps.

M14   MACHUM, Lieutenant Colonel George C.
CANADA'S VCs: The Story of Canadians who have been awarded the Victoria Cross
McClelland & Stewart, Toronto, 1956
208 pp, sketches, index, hb, cr

Produced as a VC Centenary Memorial, this publication records, chronologically by *London Gazette* date, the 94 Canadian VCs. A short biographical account and the full LG citation is given for each recipient. A drawn portrait (based on photographs/original drawings) illustrates each account. Analyses by birthplace and by regiment/corps/service are contained in the appendix.

M14B   MACINTYRE, Alasdair
NINE VALIANT ACADEMICALS: Edinburgh Academical Holders of the Victoria Cross
Alan Fyfe, Ratho, Scotland, 2007
73 pp, photos, maps, sb, cr

Short biographies of nine old boys of the Edinburgh Academy who were awarded the VC: Cadell, Hills, Tytler, Dundas, J Cook, E Brown, Brodie, Ker and Miers. The author is the son of DL Macintyre VC CB. Reviewed in V61.

M15   MACINTYRE, Captain Donald, DSO** DSC RN
NARVIK
Evans Brothers, London, 1960
224 pp, photos, maps, index, hb, cr

The full story of the naval battles fought by the Royal Navy in the Norwegian Sea and fjords in 1940 in which three VCs were awarded to the commanding officers of HMS *Glowworm* (Lt Cdr Roope), HMS *Hardy* (Capt Warburton-Lee) and HMS *Arab* (Lt Stannard). Their VC exploits are fully documented in the context of the battles. In addition, there are numerous references to the General commanding the BEF in Norway, Maj Gen Carton de Wiart VC.

M16   MACINTYRE, Captain Donald, DSO** DSC RN (Rtd)
FIGHTING SHIPS AND SEAMEN
Evans Brothers, London, 1963
192 pp, photos, hb, cr

An account of 16 naval actions of WW1 and WW2, each of which is recalled in a separate chapter. Seven chapters concern the VC exploits of: HMS *Lion* and *Shark* (Chap 1); *E11* and *E14* (Chap 2); Q5, *Pargust* and *Dunraven* (Chap 3); *Hardy* (Chap 6); *Campbeltown* (Chap 10); *Onslow* (Chap 13); and *X6* and *X7* (Chap 14).

M16A   McLAUGHLIN, Dennis and McLAUGHLIN, Leslie
FOR MY COUNTRY: Black Canadians on the Field of Honour
National Defence of Canada, Ottawa, Canada, 2004
52 pp. (*French*)/52pp. (*English*), photos, sb, cr

This bi-lingual publication describes the contribution of black soldiers in the Canadian forces. Pages 9 to 15 cover William Hall VC.

M17   MACLEOD, J.R. (*compiler*)
PORTRAIT OF A SOLDIER: Sgt John Meikle, VC MM
Dingwall Museum Trust, Dingwall, 1992
20 pp, photos, maps, sb, cr

This short booklet is a biography of Sgt John Meikle VC MM of the Seaforth Highlanders. It includes eight photographs and reproduces a number of documents and letters.

M17A   McLEOD, Murray
FOR VALOUR: The air VCs of World War II
CreateSpace Independent Publishing Platform, Australia, 2012
80 pp, coloured paintings, sb, cr

This work, which the author has illustrated with his paintings of the respective aircraft types and portraits of the VC recipients, is arranged by aircraft type and recalls the deeds of 31 air VCs of WW2. Two pages are devoted to each aircraft type and to each recipient (except Aaron and Cruickshank for whom only brief mention is given).

M17B   McLEOD, Murray
AIR VCs OF WORLD WAR ONE
CreateSpace Independent Publishing Platform, Australia, 2018
80 pp, photos, coloured drawings, sb, cr

This book contains brief biographies of the 19 air VCs of WW1. Each biography, which provides basic information about the recipient's early life, concentrates on his military service and, in particular, his VC deed. A portrait painting and full colour aircraft side profile drawing, both illustrated by the author, form part of each biography.

M17C   MACKLIN, Robert
JACKA VC: Australian Hero
Allen and Unwin, Crow's Nest, New South Wales, Australia, 2006
298 pp, photos, maps, index, sb, cr

A full biography of Albert Jacka VC MC*. Most of the volume covers Jacka's extraordinary wartime service at Gallipoli and France. He was the first Australian-born man to win the VC for defending a trench at Gallipoli on 19/20 May 1915 when all his men were killed or wounded. He later won an MC and bar on the Western Front. The author describes Jacka's strained relationships with his superior officers and his commitment to the men under his command. The last 50 pages cover his post-war business career and death.

M17D   MACKLIN, Robert
BRAVEST: How some of Australia's greatest war heroes won their medals
Allen and Unwin, New South Wales, Australia, 2008
278 pp, photos, index, sb, cr

In this account of Australian war heroes who were awarded the VC or the GC, numerous recipients are mentioned briefly, but the focus is on thirteen VC and two GC recipients whose life and deeds are described in detail. The VCs are: CGW Anderson, PJ Badcoe, AR Cutler, TC Derrick, HI Edwards, N Howse, A Jacka, E Kenna, FH McNamara, J Maxwell, H Murray, K Payne and R Simpson. Pages 258-260 list (at the time of writing) the 96 Australian VC winners recording their unit and place and date of VC deed.

M17E   McKELVEY, Ben
THE COMMANDO: The Life and Death of Cameron Baird VC MG
Hachette Australia, Sydney, New South Wales, Australia, 2017
341 pp, photos, index, hb, cr

A biography of Corporal Cameron Baird VC MG who won a posthumous VC (for Australia) for his actions in Afghanistan on 22 June 2013. He was with the 2nd Commando Regiment Special Forces when he led his platoon into an unknown Taliban stronghold. In a prolonged fire fight Baird was mortally wounded but his leadership was responsible for clearing and securing the area.

M18   McKEAN, Captain G.B., VC MC MM
SCOUTING THRILLS
Humphrey Milford, Oxford University Press, London, 1919
235 pp, sketches, hb, cr

A personal narrative of the adventures and bravery of scouts in the author's Canadian infantry battalion in France and Belgium in WW1. The author served as a Scout Officer and recounts in Chapter IX (pages 155-180) his VC action. The book is aimed at boys and was written to promote the Boy Scouts movement. The Foreword is written by Lt Gen Sir REW Turner VC KCB KCMG DSO.

M19   McKEAN, Captain G.B., VC MC MM
MORE SCOUTING THRILLS
Privately published, Norwich, 1925
132 pp, sketches, hb, cr

This continuation of M18 describes scouting raids behind German lines in WW1.

M20   McKEE, Alexander
AGAINST THE ODDS: Battles at Sea, 1591-1949
Souvenir Press, London, 1991
272 pp, photos, paintings, hb, cr

The author has selected 26 sea battles to illustrate naval courage spanning four centuries, from Sir Richard Grenville's action off the Azores in 1591 to the Yangtse incident in 1949 involving HMS *Amethyst*. Six of the 26 chapters relate specifically to VC deeds: Chapter 14 - Holbrook, Boyle and Nasmith; Chapter 18 – Sandford; Chapter 19 - Dobson, Agar and Steele; Chapter 20 - Roope and Warburton-Lee; Chapter 21 - Fegen; and Chapter 24 - Cameron and Place.

M21   McMILLAN, Doug
MAJOR CHARLES HEAPHY VC AND THE WARRANT OF 1867
Words & Pix, Brisbane, Australia, 1990
21 pp, photos, sketches, maps, sb, cr

A brief description of the Waikato War, the skirmish at Waiari and the action at the Mangapiko for which Heaphy was awarded the VC. Heaphy was the first colonial soldier to be awarded the VC. The VC was won on 11 February 1864 but the announcement was not made in the LG until 8 February 1867. The last chapter of the book, *The Battle for the Cross,* describes the precedent set by Heaphy's award for colonial soldiers, not under British command, to be awarded the VC.

M22   MACMILLAN, Norman
       OFFENSIVE PATROL: The Story of the RNAS, RFC and RAF in Italy 1917-18
       Jarrolds, London, 1973
       264 pp, photos, maps, index, hb, cr

Wg Cdr Macmillan presents a detailed narrative of the involvement of the British aerial forces in Italy during 1917-1918. In addition to the historical perspective, the work describes many of the exploits performed by pilots of 28, 66 and 139 Squadrons. An appendix summarises the victories of individual pilots. Extensive coverage is given to William Barker who served in all three squadrons in Italy and who later won the VC in France. Chapter 7 (pages 96-106) is devoted to a critical appraisal of Lt Alan Jerrard's VC action (he was sole VC of the air campaign).

M22A   McNEILL, Major Ian
       THE TEAM: Australian Army Advisers in Vietnam 1962-1972
       University of Queensland Press/Leo Cooper/Secker and Warburg, London, 1984
       534 pp, photos, sketches, maps, index, hb, cr

A highly detailed and well-researched history of the Australian Army Training Team Vietnam (AATTV) from its origination in 1962 to its withdrawal from Vietnam in 1972. It documents thoroughly the actions that resulted in four VCs for its members (Wheatley, Badcoe, Simpson and Payne).

M22B   McVEIGH, Tom and SIEBENHAUSEN, Ron
       OUR RESTLESS WARRIOR: Private John Leak, Queensland's First Victoria Cross Recipient
       Publisher unknown, Australia, 2015
       192 pp, photos, maps, sb, cr

An A4-sized biography of Pte John Leak VC who was born in 1892 in Portsmouth, England. The volume describes his early life, emigration to Australia and military service in the AIF in WW1. He arrived in Gallipoli in June 1915 and later won his VC for actions at Pozières on the Somme in July 1916. After WW1 he returned to Australia where he worked and died there at the age of 80.

M22C   MACE, Martin
       THE DUNKIRK EVACUATION IN 100 OBJECTS: The Story Behind Operation *Dynamo* in 1940
       Frontline Books, inprint of Pen & Sword, Barnsley, 2018
       242 pp, photos (some colour), maps, index, hb, cr

This volume contains 100 short chapters describing objects relted to Dunkirk evacuation. A six page (pages 112-117) chapter (Object No 46) titled *Dunkirk's VC,* has photos and eye-witness accounts of the action in which Capt. HM Ervine-Andrews was awarded the only VC for Dunkirk.

M23   MACE, James
       CRUCIBLE OF HONOUR: The Battle of Rorke's Drift
       Legionary Books, Meridian, Idaho, USA, 2017
       418 pp, photos, drawings, maps, sb, cr

An account of the defence of Rorke's Drift on 22/23 January 1879 for which 11 VCs were awarded. Part of the text is factual based on real events. Part is fictional where the author invents dialogue between the principal characters.

M23A   MADDEN, Michael C.
THE VICTORIA CROSS : Australia Remembers
Big Sky Publishing, New South Wales, Australia, 2018
512 pp, photos (some colour), hb, cr

This volume is a limited edition and provides profiles of 100 Australian VC recipients. The families and friends of the recipients provide their contribution on how the VC has affected them and how families coped after the fighting had ended. The author travelled around the world to interview the families, peers and friends of the recipients. The book proceeds were given to the Totally and Permanently Incapacited Ex-Servicemen and Women's Association of Victoria Inc.

M24   MAGARA, Dalabak-adura Puna
MEMOIRS, ESSAYS AND REAL STORIES OF GORKHA VC HOLDERS
Publisher unknown, Nepal, 2000
177 pp, photos, sb, cr

A short introduction to Gurkas awarded the VC in WW1 and WW2.

M25   MAITLAND, Major General Gordon L.
TALES OF VALOUR FROM THE ROYAL NEW SOUTH WALES REGIMENT
Playbill, Pymble, Australia, 1992
245 pp, photos, maps, hb, cr

This book relates specifically to the 24 VC recipients of the RNSW Regiment. Following an illustrated overview of the particular conflict and theatre of operation, a biographical sketch of each VC recipient (accompanied by a portrait) and an account of the VC deed is given. The VCs included are: L Keysor, J Hamilton, AJ Shout, W Jackson, HW Murray, TJB Kenny, GJ Howell, J Carroll, CS Jeffries, PV Storkey, WE Brown, BS Gordon, G Cartwright, WM Currey, AH Buckley, AC Hall, MV Buckley, J Ryan, J Maxwell, JH Edmonson, AR Cutler, CGW Anderson, A Chowne, E Kenna. The work was published as a limited edition of 2000 copies.

M27   MAJOR, E. Mabel F.
IN EASTERN GARDENS
The Religious Tract Society, London, nd (c1923)
192 pp, photos, hb, cr

The story of missionary work in Ceylon (now Sri Lanka) and includes a chapter on Sepoy Khadadad Khan, the first Indian VC recipient.

M28   MALONE, Michael J. and LUTLEY, Peter D.
SIMMO: A biography of Ray Simpson VC DCM, One of Australia's Greatest Soldiers
Imprimatur Books, North Perth, Australia, 2015
266 pp, photos, map, index, hb, cr

A full biography of Ray Simpson VC who served in WW2, Korea, Malaya and Vietnam where he won the VC on 6 May 1969. The volume covers Simpson's early life, extensive military career and post-service life.

M29   MANNING, Stephen
EVELYN WOOD VC: Pillar of Empire
Pen & Sword Military, Barnsley, 2007
265 pp, photos, index, hb, cr

A full biography of Sir Evelyn Wood VC who began his career in the Royal Navy in the Crimea before transferring to the cavalry. He won his VC in India and became a member of Wolseley's select Ashanti Ring which helped his career. His greatest victory at Kambula was preceded a day earlier by a crushing defeat at

Hlobane which he covered up. He went on to become Adjutant-General and a Field Marshal. Reviewed in V65.

M30   MANSON, James A.
VALOUR FOR VICTORIA: Stirring deeds that won the Queen's Cross
George Newnes, London, 1901
150 pp, sketches, hb, cr

A selective narrative describing some of the Victorian campaigns in which the VC was awarded. Sixteen representative VC actions are described in the context of the campaigns (Baltic, Crimea, Persia, Indian Mutiny, Zulu War, Afghan War, Sudan and South Africa). Brief references to some other VCs of these campaigns are mentioned. Artists' impressions of various VC actions support the text.

M32   MANTLE, Jonathan
THE STORY OF LEONARD CHESHIRE DISABILITY
James & James, London, 2008
96 pp, photos, sb, cr

This volume describes the charity founded by Leonard Cheshire VC. It was initially devoted to the care of disabled servicemen. Since then it has become a leading institution for the care of people with any disability and for raising awareness of their needs.

M35   MARLING, Colonel Sir Percival, Bt VC CB
RIFLEMAN AND HUSSAR
John Murray, London, 1931
412 pp, photos, maps, hb, cr

An autobiography describing Marling's early years and, through reference to his diary, his long and active life as a regimental officer, sportsman and country gentleman. He served with the 60th Rifles and later 18th Hussars, winning the VC at Tamai, Eastern Sudan, 1884. His 30 years military service spanned six campaigns, including acting as an interpreter in WW1.

M36   MARQUIS, T.G.
[1] EARL ROBERTS VC, LORD KITCHENER AND THE GREAT BOER WAR
Roberts & Kitchener Publisher, London, nd (c1902)
541 pp, photos, line drawings, maps, index, hb, cr
[2] EARL ROBERTS VC: From Cadet to Commander-in-Chief
Sampler's edition: The Bradley-Garretson Co, Detroit, USA and Linscott Publishing, London
294 pp, photos, line drawings, maps, index, hb, cr

This book is, predominantly, a detailed biography of Lord Roberts VC. The text up to page 396 describes his early years and military career in India. Pages 396-489 and 528-541 concern his Boer War command. Pages 513-527 are devoted to the life of Lord Kitchener. The work contains in excess of 100 half-tone engravings and photographs.

M37   MARRIOTT, Janice
SOLDIER IN THE YELLOW SOCKS: Charles Upham, Our Finest Fighting Soldier
HarperCollins (New Zealand), Auckland, New Zealand, 2006
48 pp, drawings, sb, cr

A children's book describing WW2 and exploits of Charles Upham VC* in Crete and North Africa and as a POW. It is illustrated by Bruce Potter.

M38   MARSHMAN, John Clark
MEMOIRS OF MAJOR-GENERAL SIR HENRY HAVELOCK KCB
Longman, Green, Longman & Roberts, London, 1860 (1890 edition: Longmans, Green & Co., London)
462 pp. (1890 edition: 457 pp.), photos, maps, hb, cr

This comprehensive biography of Major-General Havelock written by his brother-in-law chronicles Havelock's campaigns in India and Afghanistan. It also includes a genealogical account of the Havelock family. During the Indian Mutiny, his son Lt HM Havelock (later Lt Gen Sir Henry Havelock-Allan) was awarded the VC on the recommendation of his father. An account of the ensuing controversy is described in Chapter VIII (pages 359-363).

M39   MASON, Peter D.
'NICOLSON VC': The full and authorised biography of James Brindley Nicolson
Geerings of Ashford, Ashford, Kent, 1991
164 pp, photos, maps, index, hb, cr

A biography of JB Nicolson VC DFC, the only VC of the Battle of Britain. The book chronicles Nicolson's RAF service from 1936 up to his death on active service in 1945. It is supported by numerous family and service photographs. A record of service lists all his service appointments, promotions, postings, honours and awards and aircraft flown.

M40   MASON, David
RAID ON ST NAZAIRE
Purnell, London, 1970
159 pp, photos, sketches, maps, sb, cr

This volume, Battle Book No. 14 in *Purnell's History of the Second World War*, is a well-illustrated account of the raid for which five VCs were awarded. Introduced by Lt Col Newman VC OBE, the book describes the VC actions of Newman, Beattie, Ryder, Savage and Durrant in the context of the operation.

M41   MASON, Ian
PRIVATE 'BILLY' CLARE VC
Chatteris Museum, Chatteris, Cambridgeshire, 2016
? pp, sb, cr

A short biography of Pte GWB Clare VC who came from Chatteris in Cambridgeshire. The author is Curator of Chatteris Museum who produced the publication to commemorate the centenary of the award of Clare's posthumous VC for the action at Bourlon Wood, France on 28/29 November 1917.

M42   MASTERS, David
"UP PERISCOPE": The Immortal Record of His Majesty's Submarines
Eyre & Spottiswoode, London, 1942 (revised and enlarged: 1943)
176 pp. (1943 edition: 200 pp.), photos, index, hb, cr

The author recalls (in the 1943 edition) the exploits of twenty-two British submariners in WW2 focusing on the actions for which their captain and crew were decorated for gallantry. Chapter XXII (pages 191-198) is devoted to Lt Cdr Wanklyn VC and his command of HM Submarine *Upholder*.

M43   MASTERS, David
"I.D." - New Tales of the Submarine War
Eyre & Spottiswoode, London, 1935
297 pp, photos, index, hb, cr

A collection of accounts recalling the heroism and ordeals of Britain's merchant seamen in WW1 and, in particular, their struggle against the U-boat. The stories are based on the author's study of Lloyd's submarine records and on first-hand reminiscences obtained from survivors of the actions. Three of the chapters are specific to the VC actions of Lt Cdr WE Sanders (Chap V - 22 pages), Skipper T Crisp (Chap XVIII - 12 pages) and Skipper J Watt (Chap XXV - 7 pages), all of whom were serving in the RNR.

M44   MASTERS, David
SO FEW: The Immortal Record of the Royal Air Force
Eyre & Spottiswoode, London, 1941 (enlarged & revised: 1943; further revised: 1946)
256 pp, photos, index, hb, cr

A selection of tales of RAF aircrew whose actions in WW2 resulted in the award of a gallantry decoration. Chapter XII (pages 94-98) is devoted to the VC deed of Sgt Hannah. Chapter XXXII (pages 222-232) which relates specifically to RAF VCs, covers briefly the actions of Nettleton, Edwards, Ward, Middleton and Gibson. Learoyd's VC deed is outlined elsewhere.

M45   MATHIESON, William D.
BILLY BISHOP VC
Fitzhenry & Whiteside, Markham, Ontario, Canada, 1989
64 pp, photos, sketches, index, sb, cr

A brief biographical account of Bishop's early life, air force service spanning two world wars, his business ventures and his death in 1956. The text is interspersed with photographs depicting his family and service life and portraying his awards.

M46   MATHIESON, William D.
MY GRANDFATHER'S WAR: Canadians Remember the First World War 1914-1918
MacMillan of Canada, Toronto, Ontario, Canada, 1981
338 pp, photos, index, hb, cr

Chapter 9 (pages 178-206) titled *For Valour* gives an account and includes a portrait of the following Canadian WW1 VC winners: Strachan, Bishop, Learmouth, TW Holmes, Pearkes, McLeod, Dinesen, Rutherford, CN Mitchell and Barker.

M47　MALET de CARTERET, Ned
MY FAMILY IN THE GREAT WAR
Reveille Press, Eastbourne, 2014
196 pp, photos (some colour), maps, sb, cr

The author traces the lives of three ancestors who served in the Great War. The author's great-uncle, Midshipman PR Malet de Carteret, heir to St Ouen's Manor in Jersey saw action at the Falklands and Gallipoli in HMS *Canopus* before losing his life on 31 May 1916 at Jutland on HMS *Queen Mary* at the age of 18. His Australian cousin Midshipman John Malet Armstrong joined battle cruiser HMAS *Australia* in 1918 and saw no action but later became one of Australia's most decorated Captains in WW2. The author's great-grandfather, Captain Harold Ackroyd VC MC, served as a medical officer with the 6th Bn, Royal Berkshire Regiment and won the MC at Delville Wood in 1916 but was killed at Passchendaele in August 1917, winning the Victoria Cross. The biographies of all three men are told through their letters home and the volume includes many previously unpublished photographs. Reviewed in V74.

M49　MAUDE, Colonel Francis Cornwallis, VC CB and SHERER, John W., CSI
MEMORIES OF THE MUTINY
Remington, London, 1894
Two volumes - 569 pp, photos, maps, hb, cr

This work concerns mainly the events involving Havelock's column. Maude had no kind words for Henry Havelock VC or Frederick Roberts VC. Chapter XV includes *Muddling the VC* in which Maude describes a ballot for the VC. The appendix includes a letter from Henry Havelock to Col Fraser-Tytler and one from Maude regarding Fraser-Tytler's bravery at Lucknow. Maude applied to the War Office for a loan of a Cross to replace the one he himself sold. (See C145, pages 194-5).

M52　MAXWELL, Charlotte
FRANK MAXWELL, BRIG-GENERAL, VC CSI DSO*: A Memoir and Some Letters
John Murray, London, 1921
228 pp, photos, sketches, index, hb, cr

This biography of Brig-Gen Maxwell VC, by his widow, is based on his letters. The book gives an insight into Maxwell's campaigns on the Indian Frontier (DSO), South Africa (VC), India and WW1 in France (bar to DSO) in which he commanded the 27th Brigade (9th Division). He was killed in action in September 1917.

M53　MAXWELL, Charlotte (*only mentioned in signed postscript*)
I AM READY
Hazell Watson & Viney, London, 1955
212 pp, photos, hb, cr

I Am Ready (the motto adorning the family crest) is a compilation of extracts from the diaries of Brig-Gen FA Maxwell VC CSI DSO and bar assembled by his widow for the benefit of his children. These extracts cover the period 1900 to 1917 when he was killed. Pages 182-196 record his military service, obituary notices, extracts from war histories and his decorations and medals (including citations). There is a photograph of his VC and medal group and 13 other photographs portraying Maxwell and his family.

M55 MAXWELL, J., VC MC DCM
HELL'S BELLS AND MADEMOISELLES
Angus & Robertson, Sydney, 1932
267 pp, hb, cr

This book relates the WW1 reminiscences of Lt J Maxwell VC MC and bar DCM. Whilst he writes about those who fought with him in the war he mentions little of his own exploits. This modesty led the writers of the Foreword to include a biographical summary of Maxwell which also describes the actions that resulted in his four gallantry awards. The final chapter of the book describes the presentation of the VC to Maxwell by King George V.

M70 MAY, Philip R.S., GC (*editor*: COWLEY, Richard)
BEYOND THE FIVE POINTS: Masonic Winners of the Victoria Cross and the George Cross
Twin Pillars Books, Kettering, Northamptonshire, 2001
358 pp, photos, drawings, hb, cr

Brief biographical accounts of the 105 VC winners and 13 GC winners who were Freemasons. The accounts also include details of their Masonic career. The author, also a Freemason and one of the book's subjects, died in 1994 before completing his research which was continued by the editor.

M80 MEAD, Gary
THE VICTORIA CROSS: The Untold Story of Britain's Highest Award for Bravery
Atlantic Books, London, 2015
326 pp, photos, index, hb, ncr

This volume follows the theme of Crook (C145) and Smith (S51) in describing the evolution of the history of the VC from its institution to the present. It examines the changing nature of warfare and the changing preferences of the monarch, government, the military, the civil service and public opinion in the bestowal of the award. The author expresses his views on the VC being partly used as a political tool to deflect public attention from military disasters, as a means of boosting morale or addressing unpopular wars. The author expresses his views on the lack of any VC awarded to a woman, the meaning of the 'in the presence of the enemy', VCs which should have been GCs and vice versa. The idea of a quota is examined and poses questions why so many VCs were issued in Vietnam and so few in Korea relative to the troops deployed and engaged. There are 50 pages of notes and a number of VCs are cited briefly as a means of illustrating a particular point or argument. Reviewed in V76.

M90 MELVILLE, Colonel C.H., CMG
THE LIFE OF GENERAL THE RIGHT HON SIR REDVERS BULLER VC GCB GCMG
Edward Arnold, London, 1923
Two volumes - 653 pp. (Vol 1: 328 pp.; Vol 2: 325 pp.), photos, maps, index, hb, cr

A full biography of Buller written by the author at the request of Buller's daughter. Volume 1 details his family history, early life and his military service prior to the South African War. Volume 2 relates to his service in South Africa and the controversy which led to his retirement and concludes with a character assessment of him (pages 290-310). The author did not wish to create more controversy so, with the consent of Buller's daughter, he wrote a series of explanatory notes on the more controversial points. These notes were not published but left in the family's possession.

M95   MELVILLE, Douglas A.
CANADIANS AND THE VICTORIA CROSS
Vanwell Publishing, St Catharines, Ontario, Canada, 1987
93 pp, photos, sketches, maps, index, hb, cr

This book, in the *Vanwell History Project Series* for juveniles, contains a brief biographical account, description of VC action and photograph of 32 Canadian VC recipients selected from the 94 winners. The obverse and reverse of AHL Richardson's VC is portrayed on the front cover.

M98   MENPES, Mortimer
LORD ROBERTS
A & C Black, London, 1915
63 pp, drawings, sb, cr

This volume in the *Portrait Biographies* series is a concise account of the life of Earl Roberts VC. It is illustrated with eight watercolour portraits of Lord Roberts painted by the author.

M99   MENZIES, Mrs Stuart
LORD WILLIAM BERESFORD VC: Some Memories of a Famous Sportsman, Soldier and Wit
Herbert Jenkins, London, 1917
336 pp, photos, index, hb, cr

A biography of Beresford by a friend. It deals in depth with Beresford's early days, military career and sporting memories. A detailed account of his VC action is narrated. A significant portion of the text relates to his services as Military Secretary to the Viceroy of India and to his achievements in horseracing circles both in India and in England.

M100   MILBERRY, Larry and HALLIDAY, Hugh A.
AVIATION IN CANADA: Fighter Pilots and Observers 1915-1939
CANAV Books, Toronto, Ontario, Canada, 2018
184 pp, photos, index, hb, cr

This lavishly-illustrated work, Volume 8 in the *Aviation in Canada* series, honours Canada's pioneers of aerial warfare. It tells the stories of individual aviators, well-known and lesser-known, and their aircraft. Accounts are drawn from official combat reports, letters, diaries and newspapers. VC recipients featured are: WG Barker, WA Bishop and AA McLeod.

M101   MILES, Alfred H. and PATTLE, Arthur John
FIFTY-TWO STORIES OF THE INDIAN MUTINY: And the Men who saved India
Hutchinson, London, 1895
449 pp, sketches, hb, cr

This book, written for younger readers, contains a series of stories arranged chronologically to describe the main incidents in the rise, progress and suppression of the Indian Mutiny. Seven stories relate specifically to VC actions, as follows: Powder Magazine VCs at Delhi (pages 77-80), H Tombs and Hills (pages 96-97), Cashmere Gate VCs (pages 106-107), Mangles and McDonell (pages 178-180), WA Kerr (pages 217-220), medical VCs (pages 350-358) and Kavanagh (pages 394-400). Several other stories contain very brief accounts of associated VC actions.

M102   MILES, Alfred Henry (*editor*)
        THE BRAVEST DEED I EVER SAW: Stories of Personal Experience
        Hutchinson, London, 1905
        364 pp, photos, hb, cr

Stories of personal experience as told by Major-General Baden-Powell, Admiral Sir Richard Vesey Hamilton, Winston Churchill and others. Of the 44 unnumbered chapters, three have a specific focus on the VC: *At the Sikandarbargh* (pages 9-24) by Field Marshal Earl Roberts VC; *How Vice-Admiral Sir Arthur Knyvet Wilson VC boxed the Fuzzy-Wuzzies at El Teb* (pages 41-50) by Frank Scudamore and *Through the Enemy's Camp* (pages 171-183) by Sir Charles Wyndham concerning Kavanagh VC. Many other chapters have brief references to VC actions and recipients.

M102A   MILES, Alfred H.
        HEROES OF HISTORY
        Raphael Tuck & Sons, London, nd (c1916)
        112 pp, sketches, hb, cr

This book contains as separate chapters short biographies of British heroes including Drake, Raleigh, Sidney, Nelson, Wellington, Havelock, Gordon and Rhodes. There is an 11-page chapter on Lord Roberts VC.

M102B   MILLER, Frederic P., VANDOME, Agnes F. McBREWSTER, John (*editor*)
        FRANK HUBERT McNAMARA
        VDM Publishing, Mauritius, 2010
        184 pp, photos, sb, cr

A biography of Air Vice Marshal FH McNamara VC CB CBE who was the only Australian airman to win a VC in WW1. He later became a senior commander in the RAAF.

M102C   MILLER, Frederic P., VANDOME, Agnes F. McBREWSTER, J. (*editor*)
        VICTORIA CROSS: Victoria Cross for Australia, Victoria Cross (Canada), Dickin Medal, George Cross, Richard Ernest William Turner
        Alphascript Publishing, Mauritius, 2009
        59 pp, photos, sb, cr

This book is a compilation of material from published books and the internet. There is a two page description of REW Turner VC, and a description of the award of the VC for Canada and the VC for New Zealand.

M102D   MINISTRY OF DEFENCE
        WE WERE THERE
        Directorate General Media and Communication, Ministry of Defence, 2007
        64 pp, photos, sb, cr

This publication is based upon the *We Were There* exhibition which was jointly launched by the Ministry of Defence and the Commission for Racial Equality on 12 October 2006. The A4 booklet was published by the Ministry of Defence, in January 2007, to accompany an exhibition highlighting "the significant but little known contribution made by Britain's ethnic minorities to defence over the past two hundred and fifty years." It contains photos and details of several VC recipients: William Hall, WJ Gordon, Khudadad Khan, Kamal Ram, Gian Singh, Abdul Hafiz and Johnson Beharry. The front cover has 49 small photos of the people featured inside, including several VC recipients: Hall, Khan, Ram, Singh, Hafiz, and Beharry.

M103   MITCHELL, Alan W.
NEW ZEALANDERS IN THE AIR WAR
George Harrap, London, 1945
192 pp, photos, hb, cr

In this book the author recalls in 24 dedicated chapters the WW2 exploits of 17 pilots of the RNZAF or New Zealanders in the RAF and of seven RNZAF units serving in the European theatre. Chapter 7 (pages 57-65) is devoted to Sgt Plt JA Ward and his posthumous VC action. Chapter 18 (pages 143-146) concerns Flg Off LA Trigg VC DFC. In Chapter 9 (pages 73-85) the exploits of 487 (RNZAF) Squadron are recalled and in particular the deeds of Sqn Ldr LH Trent that led to his VC award, which had not been gazetted at the time of the book's publication.

M104   MITCHELL, Pamela
TIP OF THE SPEAR: The Midget Submarines
Richard Netherwood, Huddersfield, 1993
232 pp, photos, index, hb, cr

This book traces the evolution and development of the British midget submarine and contains a chapter for each of the significant midget submarine operations in two of which four VCs were won. Chapters 12 and 13 (pages 70-103) relate to Cameron VC and Place VC and Operation *Source*. Chapters 23 and 24 relate to Fraser VC and Magennis VC and Operation *Struggle*.

M104A   MITCHELL, Peter
FROM ENGLAND TO NEW ZEALAND: The Life of Samuel Mitchell VC
Published by author, Christchurch, New Zealand, 2003
108 pp, photos, sketches, maps, sb, cr

This book was written by the great-grandson of Samuel Mitchell VC and provides a biography of his ancestor. There are 13 chapters, one of which describes his VC action at the Battle of Gate Pa in April 1861. It describes his journey back to England and his life on his return to New Zealand. Chapter 10 describes the loss and return of his VC.

M104B   MOLTKE-LETH, Nicolai
JO, DU KAN
Aschehoug , København, 1996
257 pp, photos, sb, cr

In this Danish-text book (the title means "Yes, You Can") the author describes his life in the Danish Jaeger Corps (a special forces unit). The book is dedicated to Major Anders Lassen VC MC**, and a chapter (pages 230-254) is devoted to Lassen's life story.

M105   MONTELL, Hugh (*editor*)
A CHAPLAIN'S WAR: The Story of Noel Mellish VC MC
Serendipity, London, 2002
276 pp, photos, maps, sb, cr

Rev Noel Mellish, the first chaplain to be awarded the VC in WW1, was ordained in 1912 and commissioned as Chaplain to the Forces in 1915. He wrote an account of his experiences of trench warfare in WW1 but locked it away and it was not discovered until after his death in 1962. The editor has used this and a later draft by Mellish covering his early years in South Africa, together with extracts from Mellish's letters to his future wife, to write a full biography. See D30. Reviewed in V53.

M106   MOODIE, William (*compiler*)
THE CROWN OF HONOUR: Being Stories of Heroism, Gallantry, Magnanimity, and Devotion from the Great War of 1914-18
James Clarke & Co., London, nd (c1925)
239 pp, index, hb, cr

A record of numerous individual deeds and detached incidents performed by, or relating to, the British Empire and her Allies in the Great War. Many of the brief accounts are extracts of published works. Others are extracts from contemporary press reports. A ten-page chapter devoted to the VC recalls the deeds of 15 VC recipients. The deeds of a further 20 VC recipients are narrated elsewhere in the book.

M107   MOORHEAD, Murray
THE QUEEN'S HEROES: Victoria and New Zealand Crosses
Zenith Publishing, New Plymouth, New Zealand, 2005
233 pp, map, sketches, sb, cr

This book is divided into two parts: the first describes the criteria for the award of the VC, the perceived inequalities of the criteria and how the New Zealand Cross originated. The second part provides biographical descriptions of 15 VC recipients and the 23 men awarded the New Zealand Cross. The text is supplemented by sketches by the author who is also an artist.

M109   MOORHOUSE, Geoffrey
HELL'S FOUNDATIONS: A Town, its Myths and Gallipoli
Hodder & Stoughton, London, 1992
256 pp, photos, maps (on end papers), index, hb, cr

This book focuses on the town of Bury, regimental home to the Lancashire Fusiliers, and the local battalion's service in Gallipoli in which 1600 local men failed to return. Chapter 6 (pages 124-140) tells the story of the *Six VCs Before Breakfast* and the dreadful casualties sustained by the battalion. The following VCs are covered: C Bromley, JE Grimshaw, WS Keneally, AJ Richards, FE Stubbs, RR Willis and J Lynn.

M111   MORGAN, Mike
D-DAY HERO: CSM Stanley Hollis VC
Sutton Publishing, Stroud, 2004
174 pp, photos, maps, index, hb, cr

A biography of CSM Stanley Hollis VC who was awarded the only VC for the D-Day landings on 6 June 1944. The book includes memories from Hollis's son and daughter and includes a chapter on Hollis from C46. There is also a transcript from a tape of a talk given by Hollis after the war to officers attending the Camberley Staff College battlefield tours in Normandy. Most of the photographs are previously unpublished.

M112   MORLEY, Mike and HUNTER, Jack
LOUIS McGUFFIE VC: The Story of Wigtown's War Hero
Royal Burgh of Wigtown and District Community Council, Wigtown, Scotland, 2018
66 pp, photos, map, sb, cr

This is a biography of Sergeant Louis McGuffie VC who won his VC with the KOSB on 28 September 1918 near Wytschaete in Belgium but was killed six days later. The publication describes his family and upbringing in Wigtown and includes a short description of the town and its history. His military service is covered in detail until his death in October 1918.

M113   MORRIS, Donald R.
THE WASHING OF THE SPEARS: The Rise and Fall of the Zulu Nation
Jonathan Cape, London, 1965 / Konecky & Konecky, New York, USA, 1965
655 pp, photos, sketches, maps, index, hb, cr

A detailed history of the rise of the Zulu nation under Shaka and its fall in the Zulu War of 1879. The following VC recipients receive coverage: Buller, D'Arcy, Melvill, Coghill, HE Wood, Bromhead, Chard, Fielding, Beresford and Lysons.

M115   MORRIS, Richard with DOBINSON, Colin
GUY GIBSON
Viking, London, 1994
400 pp, photos, maps, index, hb, cr

A biography of Wg Cdr Guy Gibson VC DSO* DFC*, leader of the Dams Raid and veteran of over 170 operations. The author re-examines the Gibson legend against the backdrop of daily life in wartime Bomber Command. There is a reappraisal of the events surrounding the Dams Raid. Appendices cover Gibson's awards and citations, his North America Tour 1943 and his operational record.

M116   MORRIS, Richard
CHESHIRE: The Biography of Leonard Cheshire, VC OM
Viking, London, 2000
530 pp, photos, index, hb, cr

An extensive biography of Gp Capt Lord Cheshire VC OM DSO** DFC. It examines thoroughly his family history, time as an Oxford undergraduate, distinguished wartime service and his life-long campaign for the relief of suffering. It also reveals his personality and beliefs. Sources used include a very wide range of previously unpublished letters and documents. The book is illustrated with 60 photographs.

M116A MORRIS, Richard (*editor*)
BREACHING THE GERMAN DAMS: Flying into History
Newsdesk Communications, London, on behalf of the Royal Air Force Museum, 2008
78 pp, photos, drawings, maps, sb, cr

This well-illustrated 'bookazine' tells the full story of Operation *Chastise*, 617 Squadron's Dams Raid on 16/17 May 1943 led by Wg Cdr Gibson. Coverage is given to the Squadron's formation, the training, planning and preparation for the raid, Lancaster modifications and technical aspects, tactics and execution and the effects and costs of the raid. The measures taken by British dams in case of German reprisals are examined. A chapter is devoted to Gibson's involvement in the post-raid public relations. The final chapter records the fate of the unused *Upkeep* mines and the *Upkeep* Lancasters.

M117   MORTIMER, Gavin
FIELDS OF GLORY: The Extraordinary Lives of 16 Warrior Sportsmen
André Deutsch, London, 2001
272 pp, photos, index, hb, cr

This volume provides short biographies of sixteen sportsmen who gave distinguished service in the armed forces between 1900 and 1945. A chapter is dedicated to each man and five of the chapters cover VC recipients: R Johnston, TJ Crean, DS Bell, J Harrison and FMW Harvey.

M118 MORTIMER, Gavin
THE DARING DOZEN: 12 Special Forces Legends of World War II
Osprey, London, 2012
304pp, photos, maps, hb, cr

This book contains biographies of 12 special forces commanders from WW2 including Anders Lassen VC MC.

M118A MORTIMER, Gavin
KILL ROMMEL!: Operation *Flipper* 1941
Osprey, Oxford, 2014
80 pp, photos, maps, artist's impressions, maps, index, sb, cr

This book, No 43 in Osprey's *Raid* Series recounts the unsuccessful raid led by Lt Col GCT Keyes on 16-18 November 1941 to kill General Erwin Rommel at his suspected headquarters at Beda Littoria, Cyrenaica. The operation's plan and conduct are documented in detail and analysed. Keyes and his party were landed by submarine HMS *Torbay* commanded by Lt Cdr ACC Miers (who won the VC in March 1942).

M119 MOSDELL, S.G.
ALFRED ERNEST IND VC
Privately published, Tetbury, Gloucestershire, 1990
8 pp, sb, cr

A short biography of Shoeing Smith Ind VC produced as a limited edition of 100 copies. Ind was born in Tetbury in 1872 and the publication covers his early life prior to joining the RHA in 1891. His service in India and the Boer War is described including the VC action on 20 December 1901 for which he received the VC. He left the army in 1906 and died in 1916.

M120 MOSES, Harry
THE FIGHTING BRADFORDS - NORTHERN HEROES OF WORLD WAR ONE
County Durham Books, Durham, 2003
125 pp, photos, sb, cr

This is the story of the four Bradford brothers: two were awarded posthumous VCs, one an MC and one a DSO. The DSO was awarded to Thomas, who was the only brother to survive WW1 and was later knighted. George Bradford was awarded his VC for the attack on Zeebrugge on 23 April 1918. Roland became the youngest Brigadier-General in the British Army and received his VC for fighting on the Somme on 1-2 October 1916. See A32. Reviewed in V54.

M121 MOYNIHAN, Michael (*editor*)
A PLACE CALLED ARMAGEDDON: Letters from the Great War
David and Charles, Newton Abbot, 1975
191 pp, photos, hb, cr

The book contains seven chapters, each of which focuses on letters home from soldiers, sailors and an airman. The material is drawn from the archives of the Imperial War Museum. Chapter 3 (pages 61-76) features Midshipman Drewry VC and includes, in full, one of his letters from Gallipoli dated 12 May 1915.

M122 MUDDOCK, J.E.
"FOR VALOUR": The VC
Hutchinson, London, 1895
292 pp, line drawings, index, hb, ncr

This book describes the first VC Investiture in Hyde Park in June 1857 and also the origins of the Crimean War. There are very brief accounts of VC actions in the Indian Mutiny (pages 196-262) and in the Zulu War, particularly Rorke's Drift (pages 263-288). Reviewed in V51.

M124 MULHOLLAND, John and JORDAN, Alan
VICTORIA CROSS BIBLIOGRAPHY
Spink, London, 1999
217 pp, drawings, index, hb, ncr

The first edition of this volume, listing 640 titles in Part 1 and 167 titles in Part 2.

M125 MUNDELL, Frank
STORIES OF THE VICTORIA CROSS
Sunday School Union, London, nd (c.1895)
160 pp, line drawings, hb, cr

A selection of stories about how the VC was won, which are described in the context of the battle or campaign. Apart from Chapter XI (pages 69-76) dedicated to Kavanagh, all other chapters contain only brief accounts of 17 VC winners. There are, in addition, passing references to many other recipients. This work is also a constituent of M126.

M126 MUNDELL, Frank
STORIES OF THE VICTORIA CROSS AND THE HUMANE SOCIETY
Sunday School Union, London, 1907
356 pp, photos, sketches, hb, cr

This book comprises two parts. The first part (pages 1-176) relates to the VC and is a direct transcript of item M125 (above) but incorporating an additional chapter covering the VCs of the South African War. The second part (comprising 180 pages) narrates stories of the Royal Humane Society and lists all Silver Medals awarded between 1884 and 1907.

M126A MUNDY, Terence
SGT THOMAS J HARRIS V.C., M.M. 1892-1918: a record of Military Service
Produced by MHS Homes for the Official Opening of Thomas Harris Close, Halling, Kent on 6 October 2008
31 pp, photos, maps, hb, cr

This work, specially-produced work to commemorate the opening of Thomas Harris Close, contains: a summary of Sgt Thomas Harris' service; a detailed account of his VC action; a transcript of his platoon commander's letters written to his parents following his VC action; and details of the opening of Harris House in Halling. The Appendices include: a transcript of the War Diary of The Queen's Own (Royal West Kent Regiment) during the period in which Harris won his MM and VC and related contemporary maps; Battalion Orders and *London Gazette* promulgations for Harris; and copies of his service records.

M127   MUNROE, R.D.
A WARRIOR IN PEACETIME: The Non-Wartime Career of Bernard Freyberg VC
Published by the author, New Zealand, 1992
77 pp, photos, sb, cr

The author, who served under Freyberg, charts his earlier life and family move to New Zealand and includes his time as Governor General of New Zealand from 1946 to 1952.

M128   MURFETT, Malcolm H. (*editor*)
THE FIRST SEA LORDS: From Fisher to Mountbatten
Praeger Publishing, London, 1995
328 pp, hb, cr

This volume comprises 18 studies by naval historians including Goldrick, Hattendorf, Lambert and Schurman covering the First Sea Lords. There is a chapter on Sir Arthur Kynvett Wilson VC who was First Sea Lord in 1910/11. Drawing on primary source material these essays provide portrayals of the individual Sea Lords and the impact they had upon the Admiralty's administrative and strategic domains.

M129   MURPHY, James
LIVERPOOL VCs
Pen & Sword Military, Barnsley, 2008
243pp, photos, maps, index, hb, cr

This volume contains biographies of 23 VCs who were born or buried in Liverpool. The criteria applied by the author excludes Noel Chavasse VC and bar MC, and others with close associations with Liverpool. Appendix A has brief details on Patrick Mylott VC and Charles Anderson VC. The VCs are listed in chronological order of the award, starting with Joseph Prosser VC (1828 - 67) and ending with Frank Lester VC (1896 - 1918). Twelve of the 23 recipients won their VCs in the Great War. Approximately 10 pages are devoted to each VC. (See C77, C78, C79 and C80). Reviewed in V62.

M130   MURPHY, Ralph
CAPTAIN JOHN NORWOOD VC: A Man of Kent
Self-published, 2017
187 pp, photos, maps, sb, cr

A biography of Captain John Norwood of the 5th Dragoon Guards who won his VC in 1899 at Ladysmith, South Africa. His South African service, including his VC action, is well covered. He had previously served in Sudan and India, and he rejoined his regiment at the outbreak of WW1. Norwood was killed in the Battle of the Marne on his 38th birthday on 8 September 1914. The author was able to draw on Norwood's diary and letters he sent to his wife.

M132   MURRAY, Iain R.
DAM BUSTERS: Owners' Workshop Manual - A guide to the weapons technology used against the dams and the special targets of Nazi-occupied Europe
Haynes Publishing, Sparkford, Yeovil, Somerset, 2011
160 pp, photos, drawings, maps, index, hb, cr

This profusely-illustrated volume provides an insight into the weapons technology used by Avro Lancaster bombers from 1943 onwards. Chapters 1 and 2 (pages 7-37) deal with Barnes Wallis' selection of dams as targets and the development of his *Upkeep* bouncing bomb for use against the dams. The modifications made to Lancasters and equipment in preparation for the Dams Raid are examined in detail and supported by technical drawings and photographs. Chapter 3 (pages 39-67) relates to Operation *Chastise*, the Dams Raid led by Wg Cdr Gibson, which is described fully. Later chapters concern the development and use of Barnes Wallis' earthquake bombs. Appendix 1 tabulates 617 Sqn crews on the Dams Raid.

M134   MURRAY-OLIVER, Anthony
A FOLIO OF WATERCOLOURS BY CHARLES HEAPHY VC, 1821-1881
Avon Fine Prints, Christchurch, New Zealand, 1981
62 pp, colour plates, hb, cr

A folio of 62 coloured plates plus two unnumbered pages which presents Heaphy's life through his paintings. This work is a limited edition of 1000 copies.

M135   MUSCIANO, Walter A.
LT COL WILLIAM BARKER: Canada's All-Around Ace
Hobby Helpers Publisher, New York, 1973
55 pp, photos, sketches, sb, cr

A biographical sketch of Lt Col William Barker VC DSO and bar MC and two bars - one of the highest scoring air aces of WW1. The text describes briefly Barker's aerial combat achievements and is supplemented by 22 photographs. Additionally, there are 11 scale drawings profiling the specific aircraft that he flew (RE8, Camel, F2B).

N1   NADLER, John
VALOUR ROAD
Viking, Penguin Group (Penguin Canada Books), Toronto, 2014
360 pp, photos, index, hb, cr

Of the 71 Canadians who were awarded the VC in WW1, three of them were from the same street: Pine Street, Winnipeg, Manitoba. This book provides biographies of the three VCs: LB Clarke, FW Hall and R Shankland. The street was renamed Valour Road and a statue erected with three WW1 soldiers silhouetted on a horizon.

N2   NAPIER, Gerald
THE SAPPER VCs: The Story of Valour in the Royal Engineers and its Associated Corps
Stationery Office, London, 1998
342 pp, photos, maps, drawings, index, hb, cr

Colonel Napier, late Director of the Royal Engineers Museum, provides a profusely-illustrated and detailed account of the 55 Sapper VCs and the events that led to their VC award. Of these recipients, 31 were on the strength of the RE at the time of their VC action, 13 were in corps that subsequently were absorbed into the RE, five were former Royal Engineers, two were future Royal Engineers and four were from Dominion engineer corps. The work is arranged by conflict and the VC actions are set in the context of the particular campaign or battle. A biographical account of each respective recipient, up to the award of the VC, is then given and is followed by details of their subsequent career. Annex A contains an alphabetical list of the recipients which, in addition to recording their VC citation and associated information, also identifies their last resting place. Notes on visiting sites at which some of the VCs were won are provided in Annex B.

N3   NASH, Norman S.
VALOUR IN THE TRENCHES!: 'Bombo' Pollard VC MC* DCM HAC in The Great War
Pen & Sword Military, Barnsley, 2011
246 pp, photos, maps, index, hb, cr

This biography of Alfred 'Bombo' Pollard concentrates mainly on his military experiences in the First World War in the Honourable Artillery Company, a period in which he was awarded the DCM, MC & bar and the VC. The author has used material from a number of sources including many quotes from Pollard's own book *Fire-Eater: The Memoirs of a VC* (see P40). After the war Pollard became a successful author and wrote over 60 books. (See Part 2 Sections A and B).

N5   NATIONAL ARMY MUSEUM (*publisher*)
THE VICTORIA CROSSES AND GEORGE CROSSES OF THE HONOURABLE EAST INDIA COMPANY AND INDIAN ARMY 1856 - 1945
National Army Museum, London, 1962
46 pp, (plus 10 pp. plates), sb, ncr

This booklet describes very briefly, by campaign, the deeds of the 164 VC recipients of the HEIC and the Indian Army. It also contains an alphabetical listing of these recipients which records their highest rank in addition to basic details appertaining to the award. A similar list concerns the 32 EGM / GC recipients of the Indian Army.

N9   'P.N.' (NEAME, Lieutenant Colonel P., VC DSO)
AN INCIDENT OF BATTLE NEAR NEUVE CHAPELLE, DECEMBER, 1914
Voile & Robertson, Faversham, Kent, 1919 (2nd edition)
15 pp, sb, cr

The incident to which the title of this book refers is the author's VC action on 18/19 December 1914 near Neuve Chapelle, at which time he was a Lieutenant commanding No. 1 Section, 15 Fld Coy RE. The account concerns, predominantly, Neame's participation in the attack and the exploits that won him the VC.

N10   NEAME, Lieutenant General Sir Philip, VC KBE CB DSO
PLAYING WITH STRIFE: The Autobiography of a Soldier
George Harrap, London, 1947
352 pp, photos, index, hb, cr

This autobiography was written by Neame when he was a POW in Italy in WW2. The manuscript was hidden and recovered after the war. The book chronicles his early life and his distinguished career as a Royal Engineer from 1908 through WW1 (VC) and WW2, culminating in his successful escape and return home in December 1943. Carton de Wiart VC was a fellow POW and is mentioned in the text in several instances.

N12   NEW ZEALAND RETURNED SERVICES ASSOCIATION (*publisher*)
50TH ANNIVERSARY OF THE END OF WORLD WAR II 1945-1995: THE VICTORIA CROSS
New Zealand Returned Services Association, New Zealand, 1995
10 pp, photos, sb, cr

This Official RSA Commemorative Folder (in a limited edition of 1500) was published in tribute to the eight New Zealanders who won the Victoria Cross during WW2: Elliot, Hinton, Hulme, Ngarimu, Trent, Trigg, Upham and Ward. For each recipient, their VC citation is reproduced in full and is accompanied by a portrait photograph. A Telecom New Zealand Victoria Cross phonecard and a Charles Upham 80c (franked 'First Day of Issue 4 Oct 1995') are incorporated on the inside covers.

N12A   NEW ZEALAND POST OFFICE (*publisher*)
VICTORIA CROSS: The New Zealand Story
New Zealand Post, Auckland, New Zealand, 2011
106 pp, photos, maps, paintings, stamps and stamp sheets, hb, cr

This lavishly-illustrated volume was published in conjunction with New Zealand Post's 2011 issue of a set of 22 60c postage stamps commemorating New Zealand's 22 VC recipients. Each stamp depicts a recipient's portrait, except for Apiata who is represented by an image of the VC. The text of the book commences with a brief history of the VC and is followed by biographies of the 22 recipients. Miniature sheets comprising three stamps intersperse the biographies and a miniature sheet containing all 22 stamps precedes a Roll of Honour listing all other VC recipients who had an association with New Zealand.

N13   NEWNES, George (*publisher*)
BRITAIN'S GREAT MEN
George Newnes, London, nd (c1914)
90 pp, photos, artists' impressions, hb, cr

This work, comprising three 30-page sections, provides an illustrated biographical account of three Field Marshals: Lord Kitchener, Sir John French and Lord Roberts VC and describes their campaign service. The contents of the book are identical to the *Britain's Great Men* section in item N14.

N14   NEWNES, George (*publisher*)
FAMOUS MEN AND BATTLES OF THE BRITISH EMPIRE
George Newnes, London, nd (c1914)
212 pp, photos, artists' impressions, hb, cr

The book comprises two main sections. A three-part section entitled *Britain's Great Men* covers individually Field Marshals Kitchener, French and Roberts VC. A four-part section entitled *Our Fighting Forces* covers the Empire's Armies. The 30-page part devoted to Lord Roberts VC, summarises his life, career and campaigns and is supported by photographs of him and artists' impressions of key events. The *Britain's Great Men* section was also published separately as item N13. Additionally, variations exist to the composition of the main work which whilst still featuring two sections may contain fewer parts.

N15   NEWNES, George (*publisher*)
THE ROMANCE OF THE VICTORIA CROSS
George Newnes, London, nd (c1899)
80 pp, line drawings, maps, sb, cr

A 15-chapter publication in the *Tit-Bits Citizens Library* briefly covering VC actions during the Crimean War, India Mutiny, Afghanistan, Rorke's Drift and minor campaigns up to 1898. Some chapters include first-hand accounts by VC recipients.

N16   NEWNES, George (*publisher*)
"BOBS": The Stirring Life Story of Field Marshal Lord Roberts
George Newnes, London, nd (c1900)
80 pp, sketches, sb, cr

A brief account of life and military career of Lord Roberts VC up to 1900. The book is a companion volume to N17 and is uniform with the *Tit-Bits Monster Series*.

N17   NEWNES, George (*publisher*)
BULLER: The Life and Campaigns of Sir Redvers H Buller
George Newnes, London, nd (c1900)
80 pp, sketches, maps, sb, cr

A brief account of the life and military career of Buller VC up to 1900. The book is a companion volume to N16 and is uniform with the *Tit-Bits Monster Series*.

N18   NGATA, A.T. (Sir Apirana)
THE PRICE OF CITIZENSHIP – NGARIMU VC
Whitcomb & Tombs Ltd., New Zealand, 1943
82 pp, sb, cr

This booklet is a tribute to the gallant service of the 28th (Maori) Battalion of the 2nd NZEF in WW2. One of its members, Moana-nui-a-Kiwa Ngarimu, won the VC posthumously. Chapter 1 is devoted to him and includes his full VC citation in both English and Maori. The rest of the booklet records the Battalion's service from 1939 to 1943 and is supplemented by a nominal roll of all officers, NCOs and men who embarked from New Zealand with the Battalion and reinforcements.

N25　　NICE, James, and HAYWARD, James (*editor*)
FOR VALOUR: VC Winners 1914-45
CD41 Publishing, Dereham, Norfolk, 2007
8 pp, photos, sb, cr

This audio book CD has 15 original wartime recordings by VC recipients or those closely associated with them. One is from WWI: Sgt Edward Dwyer VC who was awarded his VC for action at Hill 60. The recording, made in 1915, was used as a recruiting tool and sold as a gramophone. It is the only surviving spoken-word recording made by a serving soldier in the Great War. Dwyer was killed in 1916. The other 14 recordings were made by WW2 VC recipients: Learoyd, Nicolson, Upham, Ward, Ryder, Smythe, Middleton, Place/ Cameron, Nand Singh, Jefferson, Mahony, Hollis, Norton and Thompson.

N30　　NISBET, James (*publisher*)
THE LATE CAPTAIN H.E. HARINGTON VC OF HM BENGAL ARTILLERY
James Nisbet, London, 1879
96 pp, sb, cr

This work was written in the form of a memorial, compiled from letters by Lt HE Harington VC to his parents and from his friends. It provides vivid accounts of the fighting in the Indian Mutiny and reveals much about the attitudes of British officers.

N40　　NORMAN, Terry (*editor*)
ARMAGEDDON ROAD: A VC's Diary 1914-1916, Billy Congreve
William Kimber, London, 1982
223 pp, photos, sketches, maps, index, hb, cr

Edited transcripts of entries in Major William La Touche Congreve's personal diaries from 31 July 1914 to 17 January 1916 form the basis of this book. The editor provides background text to set Congreve's story in the context of the war in France. He also narrates the period from 18 January 1916 to Congreve's death in July 1916, during which time Congreve did not compile a diary.

N50　　NOTTINGHAM & NOTTINGHAMSHIRE VICTORIA CROSS COMMITTEE
NOTTINGHAMSHIRE VICTORIA CROSS HOLDERS
Nottingham & Nottinghamshire Victoria Cross Committee, Nottingham, 2012
51 pp, photos (some colour), drawing, sb, cr

This well-illustrated book commemorates the 20 VCs who were born in Nottinghamshire or were laid to rest within the county. Two pages are devoted to each recipient and biographical details, in a standard format comprise details of: birth, family background, military service, VC citation, *London Gazette* date, VC investiture, medal entitlement, death, burial, memorials and commemorations. Each biography is supported by a portrait photograph and colour photographs of the recipients' graves and other memorials. A photograph shows the Nottingham & Nottinghamshire Victoria Cross Memorial which lists the 20 VCs and was unveiled on 7 May 2010.

O3 O'BRIEN, Giles
WORLD FAMOUS WAR HEROES
Parragon, Robinson Publishing, London, nd (c1990s)
184 pp, photos, sb, cr

This title contains ten chapters, each of which focuses on a particular war hero (seven are covered) or a particularly gallant action (three are covered). Chapter Six (pages 113-126) is devoted to Col 'H' Jones VC and concentrates on his posthumous VC action in the Falklands conflict. Other chapters in this vein relate to Alexander the Great, Horatio Nelson, Audie Murphy, Douglas Bader, James Wolfe and John Paul Jones. Chapter Five (pages 95-112) concerns the 'Glorious Glosters' at the Battle of the Imjin River and concentrates on the VC actions of Lt Col Carne and Lt Curtis. The front cover shows the author as Giles O'Brien but the title page shows Wynn Wheldon as author.

O5 O'BYRNE, Robert W. (*editor*)
[1] THE VICTORIA CROSS: An Official Chronicle of Deeds of Personal Valour achieved in presence of the Enemy during the Crimean and Baltic Campaigns, the Indian Mutinies and the Persia, China and New Zealand Wars (*original title*)
O'Byrne Brothers, London, 1865
184 pp, index, hb, ncr
[2] THE VICTORIA CROSS: An Official Chronicle of Deeds of Personal Valour achieved in presence of the Enemy during the Crimean and Baltic Campaigns, the Indian, Persian, Chinese, New Zealand and African Wars (*updated title*)
W. H. Allen, London, 1880
185 pp, index, hb, ncr

This work records the citation of every VC awarded up to 1864. Entries are arranged by service and in respect of the Army, by regiment. Footnotes provide brief biographical details for commissioned recipients. The book also describes the arrangements relating to the VC's inauguration ceremony in Hyde Park in 1857 and lists the sequence in which the VCs were presented by Queen Victoria. The 1880 edition extends the citation narratives to include the awards made up to 1880 and the subtitle is expanded to show *African Wars*. The work has also been reset and excludes the biographical footnotes.

O9 ODHAMS PRESS (*publisher*)
FIFTY AMAZING STORIES OF THE GREAT WAR
Odhams Press, London, 1936
767 pp, sketches, hb, cr

This collection of true accounts taken from published works includes five VC-related stories. Pages 85-95 concern *How Trooper Potts won the VC on Burnt Hill*, taken from *In the Line of Battle* by Walter Wood. The other four stories are written by the following VCs and taken from their memoirs: Pollard (*Fire-Eater*), pages 114-121; Auten (*Q Boat Adventures*), pages 293-303; Carpenter (*The Blocking of Zeebrugge*), pages 449-482; and G Campbell (*My Mystery Ships*), pages 666-674.

O10 ODHAMS PRESS (*publisher*)
FIFTY WORLD FAMOUS HEROIC DEEDS
Odhams Press, London, nd (c1935)
703 pp, sketches, hb, cr

This companion volume to O9 includes three VC stories, as follows: *John Travers Cornwell, VC* by Alastair MacLean (pages 351-362); *Mick Mannock, VC* by Eric Sanderson (pages 395-404); and *An Early Air VC* by AJ Insall (pages 686-692) which concerns the author's brother, G Insall VC.

O11   ODHAMS PRESS (*publisher*)
EPIC STORIES OF THE SECOND WORLD WAR
Odhams Press, London, 1957
318 pp, hb, cr

This anthology of heroic deeds of WW2 contains edited extracts from 26 published works, three of which relate to the VC: *Enemy Coast Ahead* by Guy Gibson VC (pages 68-80); *The Dambusters* by Paul Brickhill (pages 81-99); and *No Passing Glory* by Andrew Boyle which relates to Cheshire VC (pages 173-183).

O13   OLDFIELD, Paul
VICTORIA CROSSES ON THE WESTERN FRONT: August 1914 - April 1915
Mons to Hill 60
Pen & Sword Military, Barnsley, 2014
362 pp, photos, maps, index, hb, cr [Vol 1]

This book is the first in a series of nine volumes on the VCs of the Western Front. Pages 1 to 154 contain six chapters describing chronologically the context of each VC action illustrated with contemporary and modern maps and photographs. Chapter 1 starts with *The Retreat from Mons* and Chapter 6 ends with *Summer Operations 1915*. Pages 155 to 312 provide biographies of each of the 59 VC recipients who are arranged in alphabetical order by surname. On average each VC is covered in two to three pages.

O14   OLDFIELD, Paul
VICTORIA CROSSES ON THE WESTERN FRONT: April 1915 – June 1916
Second Ypres to the Eve of the Somme
Pen & Sword Military, Barnsley, 2015
476 pp, photos, maps, index, hb, cr [Vol 2]

This volume covers the VCs between 22 April 1915 and 30 June 1916. Pages 1 to 183 contain seven chapters describing chronologically the context of each VC action illustrated with contemporary and modern maps and photographs. Chapter 1 starts with the *Second Battle of Ypres 1915* and Chapter 7 ends with *Prelude to the Somme*. Pages 184 to 437 provide biographies of each of the 64 VC recipients who are arranged in alphabetical order by surname. On average each recipient is covered in four pages.

O15   OLDFIELD, Paul
VICTORIA CROSSES ON THE WESTERN FRONT: SOMME 1916
1 July 1916 - 13 November 1916
Pen & Sword Military, Barnsley, 2016
528 pp, photos, maps, index, hb, cr [Vol 3]

This volume covers the Somme VCs between 1 July and 13 November 1916. Pages 1 to 173 contain six chapters describing chronologically the context of each VC action, illustrated with contemporary and modern maps and photographs. Chapter 1 starts with *Battle of Albert* and includes VCs of 1 July 1916 and Chapter 6 concludes with *Transloy Ridges and the Ancre*. Pages 174 to 488 provide biographies of each of the 51 VC recipients who are arranged in alphabetical order by surname. On average each recipient is covered in six pages.

O16   OLDFIELD, Paul
VICTORIA CROSSES ON THE WESTERN FRONT: 1917 to Third Ypres
27th January 1917 – 27th July 1917
Pen & Sword Military, Barnsley, 2016
556 pp, photos, maps, index, hb, cr [Vol 4]

This volume covers the VCs between 27 January and 27 July 1917. Pages 1 to 208 contain five chapters describing chronologically the context of each VC action, illustrated with contemporary and modern maps and photographs. Chapter 1 starts with *Local Operations Winter 1917* and Chapter 5 concludes with *Battle of Messines and Prelude to Third Ypres*. Pages 209 to 499 provide biographies of each of the 50 VC recipients who are arranged in alphabetical order by surname. On average each recipient is covered in six pages.

O17   OLDFIELD, Paul
VICTORIA CROSSES ON THE WESTERN FRONT: THIRD YPRES 1917
31ˢᵗ July 1917 to 6ᵗʰ November 1917
Pen & Sword Military, Barnsley, 2017
828 pp, photos, maps, index, hb, cr [Vol 5]

This volume covers the Third Ypres VCs between 31 July and 6 November 1917. Pages 1 to 238 contain nine chapters describing chronologically the context of each VC action, illustrated with contemporary and modern maps and photographs. Chapter 1 starts with *Battle of Pilkem Ridge* and Chapter 9 concludes with *The Battles of Passchendaele.* Pages 239 to 753 provide biographies of each of the 70 VC recipients who are arranged in alphabetical order by surname. On average each recipient is covered in seven pages.

O18   OLDFIELD, Paul
VICTORIA CROSSES ON THE WESTERN FRONT: CAMBRAI TO THE BATTLE OF ST QUENTIN
20ᵗʰ November 1917 to 23ʳᵈ March 1918
Pen & Sword Military, Barnsley, 2018
553 pp, photos, maps, index, hb, cr [Vol 6]

This volume covers the VCs between 20 November 1917 and 23 March 1918. Pages 1 to 157 contain four chapters describing chronologically the context of each VC action, illustrated with contemporary and modern maps and photographs. Chapter 1 starts with *The British Attack at Cambrai* and Chapter 4 concludes with *First Battles of the Somme 1918 – Battle of St Quentin*. Pages 158 to 491 provide biographies of each of the 38 VC recipients who are arranged in alphabetical order by surname. On average each recipient is covered in nine pages.

O19   OLDFIELD, Paul
VICTORIA CROSSES ON THE WESTERN FRONT: CONTINUATION OF THE 1918 GERMAN OFFENSIVE
24th March - 24th July 1918
Pen & Sword Military, Barnsley, 2019
? pp, photos, maps, index, hb, **tbc** [Vol 7]

To be published.

O20   OLDFIELD, Paul
VICTORIA CROSSES ON THE WESTERN FRONT: ALBERT TO THE HINDENBURG LINE
August-September 1918
Pen & Sword Military, Barnsley, 2019?
? pp, photos, maps, index, hb, **tbc** [Vol 8]

To be published.

O21   OLDFIELD, Paul
VICTORIA CROSSES ON THE WESTERN FRONT: THE HINDENBURG LINE AND THE FINAL ADVANCE
September-November 1918
Pen & Sword Military, Barnsley, 2020?
? pp, photos, maps, index, hb, **tbc** [Vol 9]

To be published.

O35   ORTZEN, Len
STORIES OF FAMOUS SUBMARINES
Arthur Barker, London, 1973
170 pp, hb, cr

Accounts of the gallantry, self-sacrifice and endurance of British, German and Italian submariners in times of war and peace. Each of the 13 chapters in the book relates to a famous submarine or submarine operation, four of which are VC-associated: Chapter 2 (pages 23-41) concerns HM Sub *E11* and Nasmith VC; Chapter 9 (pages 116-129) - HM Sub *Upholder* and Wanklyn VC; Chapter 10 (pages 130-143) - the VC action of Cameron and Place; and Chapter 12 (pages 154-159) - the VC action of Fraser and Magennis.

O40   OTTAWAY, Susan
[1] **DAMBUSTER: The Life of Guy Gibson VC DSO* DFC***
Leo Cooper, London, 1994
196 pp, photos, index, hb, cr
[2] **GUY GIBSON VC: The Glorious Dambuster** [*reformatted and updated edition*]
Speedman Press, Hampshire, 2009
210 pp, photos, index, hb, cr

This biography of Wg Cdr Gibson describes his family background, early years and distinguished RAF service. It chronicles his wartime operations in Fighter Command and Bomber Command and, in particular, as leader of the Dams Raid for which he received the VC. The author examines Gibson's temperament and character and the difficulties he experienced in handling his fame. She also portrays his private life. Appendices include important dates in Gibson's life; aircraft flown by him in operations between 1939 and 1944; citations for his awards; and the results of the Dams Raid of 16/17 May 1943.

O45   OUGHTON, Frederick
THE ACES
Neville Spearman, London, 1961
390 pp, photos, index, hb, cr

The story of aerial combat in WW1 revealed through the exploits of some of the great aces. Chapters are devoted to Mannock VC (Chapters 14-16, pages 157-188), Ball VC (Chapters 17-19, pages 189-216) and Bishop VC (Chapters 26-28, pages 276-303), which in addition to describing their combats also assesses their characters.

O50   OUGHTON, Frederick and SMYTH, Commander Vernon
        ACE WITH ONE EYE: The Life and Combats of Major Edward Mannock VC DSO (2 bars)
        MC (1 bar), Royal Flying Corps and Royal Air Force
        Frederick Muller, London, 1963
        308 pp, photos, index, hb, cr

        A full biography of the formative years, service career and death of Mannock VC, who despite being partially
        sighted in one eye, is officially credited with shooting down 73 enemy aircraft in WW1 until he himself was
        shot down and killed in 1918. Many of his aerial combats are narrated.

O55   OUGHTON, Frederick (*compiler*)
        THE PERSONAL DIARY OF MAJOR EDWARD 'MICK' MANNOCK VC DSO (2 bars)
        MC (1 bar)
        Neville Spearman, London, 1966
        221 pp, photos, index, hb, cr

        In 1963 the compiler located Mannock's diary which had been unlocated for 44 years. In this book, Mannock's
        diary for the period 1 April 1917 to 5 September 1917 appears in facsimile and the associated transcription is
        printed on the facing pages. The diary section is preceded by a biographical sketch of Mannock up to March
        1917 (pages 11-24) and is followed by detailed explanatory notes to the Diary (pages 148-168). The main
        text concludes with Mannock's biographical sketch from September 1917 up to his death in July 1918 and
        tributes to him (pages 169-204).

O60   OWEN, Ann
        THE LASCELLES OF PENMAEN DYFI
        Privately published, Merionethshire, Wales, 1962
        16 pp, photos, sb, cr

        The book covers the Lascelles family when they were resident in North Wales between the 1890s and 1920s.
        There is significant mention of AM Lascelles VC (including two photographs). The author and her family
        were employed by the Lascelles.

O65   OWEN, R.J.
        MISSION FOR A PILOT: The Story of Leonard Cheshire
        Religious Education Press, Exeter, 1980
        28 pp, photos, sketches, sb, cr

        This booklet in the *Faith in Action* series, designed for the religious education of children, is a brief account
        of the life of Group Captain Cheshire VC and his foundation of the Cheshire Homes.

O66   OWEN, Robert
        HENRY MAUDSLAY DAM BUSTER
        Fighting High, Hitchin, 2014
        364 pp, photos, index, hb, cr

        This biography of Squadron Leader Henry Eric Maudslay DFC recalls his early years and schooling and
        his service in the RAFVR from 1940. Promoted to Squadron Leader, he was posted to 617 Sqn on 25 Mar
        1943 and appointed 'B' Flight Commander. He took part in the Dams Raid on 16/17 May 1943 and piloting
        Lancaster AJ-Z attacked the Eder Dam but on the way home his damaged aircraft was shot down and he and
        his crew were killed. Pages 250-316 document the Dams Raid and the aftermath.

O67   OWEN, Robert, DARLOW, Steve, FEAST, Sean and THORNING, Arthur
DAM BUSTERS: FAILED TO RETURN
Fighting High, Hitchen, 2013
128 pp, photos (some colour), hb, cr

This book describes the losses on the Dams Raid on 16/17 May 1943 in which Guy Gibson won the VC. The book documents the eight Lancaster aircraft lost in the raid and the 53 aircrew who were killed and three who were captured. The book draws upon family archives, official documents, wartime memoirs and letters, flying logbooks and relative and witness recollections.

O68   OWEN, Dr Robert and CHESHIRE, Leonard
BOMBER PILOT: Bomber Command Pilot Leonard Cheshire's Classic Second World War Memoir
Fighting High Ltd, Hitchin, 2019
208 pp, photos, hb, cr

This publication contains Leonard Cheshire's autobiography (see C51) with the original text supplemented with additional commentary by Dr Robert Owen, aviation historian and Official Historian to 617 Sqn. The commentary provides a broader context of the Bomber Offensive and includes a full record of Cheshire's operations and wartime awards.

O70   OXFORDSHIRE COUNTY COUNCIL & THE VALE OF DOWNLAND MUSEUM (*publisher*)
ROBERT LOYD-LINDSAY, LORD WANTAGE OF LOCKINGE: Soldier, Civic Leader and Local Benefactor
Oxfordshire County Council Department of Leisure and Arts and the Vale of Downland Museum, 1994
19 pp, photos, sb, cr

This booklet is a short biographical account of Lord Wantage VC KCB. Pages 2-7 give a chronology of the key aspects of his life. The main text traces his military career, describes the VC Gallery containing the Desanges collection of VC paintings which he purchased for Wantage, and then documents his achievements in public life.

P1   PACHAI, Bridglal
WILLIAM HALL: Winner of the Victoria Cross
Four East Publications, Tantallon, Nova Scotia, Canada, 1995
40 pp, photos, sketches, maps, sb, cr

This well-illustrated book is a biography of William Hall - a black Canadian hero who came from a humble background in rural Nova Scotia. He had a distinguished career in the Royal Navy, receiving the VC for action in the Indian Mutiny. A poem dedicated to Hall is on the back cover.

P2   PADFIELD, Peter
WAR BENEATH THE SEA: Submarine Conflict During WWII
John Murray, London, 1995
560 pp, photos, maps, index, hb, cr

This book gives comprehensive coverage of submarine warfare in WW2. It includes descriptions of Allied submarines and German U-boats, key figures and significant actions. Wanklyn VC and Miers VC are covered in detail. Other VCs included are Fraser, Magennis, Place, Cameron and Linton.

P3   PAGNAMENTA, Peter, and WILLIAMS, Momoko
SWORD AND BLOSSOM: A British Officer's Enduring Love for a Japanese Woman
Century, London, 2006
318 pp, photos, index, hb, cr

The true story of a British army officer, Arthur Hart-Synnot, son of RC Hart VC, who was posted to Japan in 1904 to study Japanese and learn about the Japanese army. He fell in love with a Japanese woman, Masa Suzuki, and they had two sons from their secret affair. In May 1918 he was badly wounded in France and had both legs amputated. Brigadier General Hart-Synnot CMG DSO* was invalided from the army in 1920 and later married his nurse. This book is a moving love story based on 800 letters written between 1904 and the early 1930s. The volume provides useful family background to RC Hart VC. Republished by Arrow in 2007. This title has also been published with the title *Falling Blossom*.

P4   PAGE, Bette (*compiler and editor*)
MYNARSKI'S LANC: The story of two famous Canadian Lancaster Bombers KB726 & FM213
Boston Mills Press, Erin, Ontario, Canada, 1989
192 pp, photos, sketches, index, hb, cr

The editor, a member of the Canadian Warplane Heritage Museum, tells the operational story of the Lancaster bomber built in Malton, Ontario and focuses on the career of two Lancasters. KB726 was piloted by Plt Off Mynarski, who won a posthumous VC. FM213, restored into flying condition and owned by the Heritage Museum, has been given the identity KB726 and named *The Mynarski Memorial Lancaster*. This profusely illustrated book traces the restoration work on FM213 and describes its inaugural flight and the ceremony dedicating it as *Mynarski's Lanc*. A biographical sketch of Mynarski includes a description of other memorials in his name.

P4A PAGE, Brian J, and PEWSEY, Stephen
MOST CONSPICUOUS BRAVERY: The Life of Edgar Kinghorne Myles VC - A Forgotten Essex War Hero
Troy Novant Press, Dagenham, Essex, 1995
41 pp, photos, drawings, maps, sb, cr

This short biography of Captain EK Myles VC DSO, recalls his childhood in East Ham followed by his employment with the Port of London Authority before joining the army in 1914. His military service, including his VC action, is narrated in detail and supported by Appendix 1 which provides a comprehensive listing of all his army promotions and appointments from 1914 up to 1945 when he left the Regular Army Reserve. The text concludes with what is known of his later life. His birth certificate is replicated in the Appendices.

P4B PAGET, Julian
NO PROBLEM TOO DIFFICULT: A History of the Forces Help Society and Lord Roberts Workshops
Privately published, Lymington, Hampshire, 1999
134 pp, photos, index, hb, cr

This book is a detailed history of the society and workshops created to assist disabled ex-servicemen and of which Lord Roberts VC was a staunch supporter. Formed as the Soldiers and Sailors Help Society in 1899 (renamed Soldiers, Sailors and Airmen's Help Society in 1918), the Society's Workshops were named in 1914 in memory of Lord Roberts following his death while visiting troops in France. The Society's name changed in 1948 to the Forces Help Society and Lord Roberts Workshops and on amalgamation in 1997 became SSAFA/Forces Help. Appendix D provides details of the 13 Lord Roberts Workshops and Appendix H is a chronology of the Society and Workshops.

P4C PALMER, Tom
THE LAST TRY
Kingston Press (imprint of Hull City Council), Hull, 2014
68 pp, photos, sb, cr

This account of the later years in the life of Jack Harrison VC from 1912 up to his death and posthumous award of the VC in 1917 is based on research of historical records and newspapers. The story uses fictional characters in addition to identifiable real characters.

P4D PANNETT, Doreen and Robert
THE MILITARY EXPLOITS OF CAPTAIN JOHN JAMES CROWE VC
Reveille Press, (Tommies Guides), Brighton, 2013
106 pp, photos, sb, cr

This biography of JJ Crowe VC is co-authored by his grand-daughter. It traces his upbringing in an army family before following his father into the Worcestershire Regiment as a private. He took part in the Gallipoli campaign and served on the Western Front and was promoted to RSM before being commissioned as Captain and Adjutant. In this rank he won the VC during the Spring Offensive of 1918. Reviewed in V74.

P5   PARRY, D.H.
BRITAIN'S ROLL OF GLORY: Or the Victoria Cross - Its Heroes and Their Valour (*original title*)
THE VC - ITS HEROES AND THEIR VALOUR (*1913 title*)
Cassell, London, 1895 (revised: 1898, 1899, 1906; expanded and reset 1913)
368 pp. (1899 edition: 404 pp; 1906 edition: 519 pp.; 1913 edition: 520 pp.), sketches, hb, cr

This book provides in 29 of its 32 chapters, a narrative of the VC deed of 167 recipients. Each chapter, which usually relates to several VCs, describes the VC action in the context of the conflict or battle and is based on personal accounts, official records or regimental tradition. The work includes an alphabetical list of all VCs and records their VC citation. It also contains a description of the first presentation ceremony. The scope of the 1895 edition is up to the Chitral campaign. Subsequent editions update the awards.

P6   PATERSON, Patsy, VARNAM, Harold and MOUNT, Penny
TIGERS' TALES: The story of two young men from Countesthorpe
Matador Publishing, Kibworth Harcourt, Leicester, 2016
39 pp, photos (some colour), sketchessb, cr

This richly illustrated book describes the lives of two men from Countesthorpe, Leicestershire in WW1. The story of William Buckingham VC is told by Penny Mount. It describes his early life and his military service including winning the VC. Buckingham was then sent to the UK on a recruitment drive before returning to France where he was killed on the Somme in September 1916. The other man featured in the book is an un-named soldier referred to as 'Lucky Jim' and his story is written by Harold Varnam. Patsy Paterson provides a brief historical account of Countesthorpe.

P6A   PARRY, Simon
BATTLE OF BRITAIN COMBAT ARCHIVES 16-18 August 1940 Volume 5
Red Kite, Walton-on-Thames, 2017
144 pp, photos, (some colour), maps, sb, cr

This publication is part of a series of 12 volumes detailing combats and casualties in the Battle of Britain. Pages 591 to 595 detail the VC action of Flt Lt EJB Nicolson, the only VC of the Battle of Britain. Included is a full page artist's impression in colour of the VC action with Nicolson's Hurricane on fire. It also features on the front cover. Details are also provided of the Luftwaffe pilot who is thought to have shot down Nicolson.

P6B   PEACOCK, A. J. (*editor*)
DONALD SIMPSON BELL VC
AJ Peacock, York, nd (c1995)
64, pp, photos, maps, sb, cr

This monograph (GUN FIRE: A Journal of the First World War History No 31) has pages 2 to 16 devoted to DS Bell VC.

P7   PEACOCK, A..J. (*editor*)
RELUCTANT HERO: Harry Blanshard Wood of York (and Bristol). A Great War VC
AJ Peacock, York, nd (c1994)
84 pp, photos, maps, sb, cr

This monograph (GUN FIRE: A Journal of First World War History No 28) has a 60-page biographical sketch of L/Sgt HB Wood VC MM (pages 2-62),. Pages 63-84 are *Notes and Queries* on other Great War VCs. which includes numerous photographs. The remaining pages contain notes relating to some other WW1 VCs.

P7A   PEACOCK, A. J. (*editor*)
THE DIARY OF JOB H. C. DRAIN
AJ Peacock, York, nd (c1998)
72 pp, sb, cr

This monograph (GUN FIRE: A Journal of First World War History No 45) has pages 2 to 13 devoted to Drain VC.

P8   PEACOCK, A.J. (*editor*)
THE QUEST FOR THE REAL ARTHUR EVANS, VC: Some Notes
AJ Peacock, York, nd (c1999)
84 pp, maps, sb, cr

This monograph (GUN FIRE: A Journal of First World War History No 49) is wholly devoted to a detailed examination of the life and career of Sgt Arthur Evans (alias Walter Simpson), VC DCM. It compares and contrasts information from primary and secondary sources and attempts to resolve the various anomalies in the records and published material relating to him. The author cites the appropriate evidence.

P8A   PEACOCK, Kenneth R.
JOHN HURST EDMONDSON VC: A Hero in the Mould of Other Days
Published by the author, 2014
130 pp, photos, maps, sb, cr

A biography of John Hurst Edmondson VC. Chapter 1 covers his early life. Chapters 2 to 5 cover his military career and death at Tobruk. These chapters include photos of Edmondson in the Western Desert. The final chapter covers other members of the Edmondson family, some of whom served in WW1.

P9   PEARCE, Charles E.
STIRRING DEEDS IN THE GREAT WAR: Our Boys' History of British Heroism
Stanley Paul, London, 1919
308 pp, sketches, hb, ncr

A selection of brief accounts of heroism described in the context of various battles and actions during WW1. Many of these accounts relate to VC deeds, some of which are supported by an artist's impression of the deed.

P10   PEARCE, Lance Sergeant (later Sergeant) L.
A SHORT HISTORY OF THE REGIMENT'S VICTORIA CROSS HOLDERS (*original title*)
A HISTORY OF THE COLDSTREAM GUARDS VICTORIA AND GEORGE CROSS HOLDERS (*republished title*)
RHQ Coldstream Guards, London, 1988 (republished: 1995)
35 pp. (1995 edition: 34pp.), photos, sb, cr

This booklet gives a biographical sketch and summary of the military career of all 13 VC recipients of the Coldstream Guards. A photograph of the recipient and of his grave is included. The 1995 edition, which has been produced to a higher quality, has reformatted contents and includes a photograph of the VC and medal group of each recipient. It also incorporates information and photographs of the sole GC of the Regiment and provides a summary of the history of the VC and GC Association.

P11   PECK, Edward
CY PECK VC: A Biography of a Legendary Canadian
Privately published, Winnipeg, Canada, 2008
211 pp, photos, maps, index, sb, cr

A biography of Colonel CW Peck VC DSO*, partly based on his diaries and letters. The author, Peck's son, focuses the majority of the book on WW1 and traces Peck's war service in France and Belgium between 1915 and 1918 culminating in the award of the VC for most conspicuous bravery on 2 September 1918. An earlier version of this book was published by the author in 2007.

P12   PEEL, Wallis
FOR VALOUR: The Gloucestershire VCs
Giete, Milverton, Somerset, 2012
60 pp, sb, cr

Following a ten-page overview of the history of the VC, 34 pages are devoted to alphabetically-arranged biographical sketches of 28 VC recipients who had a connection with Gloucestershire, by birth, education, residence, death or burial in the county, or service in the Gloucestershire Regiment.

P13   PEELAN, Theo
DRIFTING INTO DEATH: The Full Story of John D Baskeyfield VC
Privately published, Rheden, Holland, 1986
114 pp, photos, sketches, maps, sb, cr

The author, a retired WO1 in the Royal Dutch Army, has assembled in this work, photocopies of articles, press cuttings and photographs relating to L/Sgt Baskeyfield and his posthumous VC deed in the battle of Arnhem in September 1944, the tributes to him and the search for his burial place. Typewritten text by the author narrates Baskeyfield's life and the part played by the South Staffordshire Regiment at Arnhem. The book, privately published for limited circulation, also contains transcripts of the author's interviews with Baskeyfield's former comrades.

P14   PEELAN, Theo and A. L Vann Vliet
ZWEVEND NAAR DE DOOD: Arnhem 1944
Uistgave Drukkerij Ter Hoven, BV Te Velp, 1975
360 pp, photos, maps, sketches, index, hb, cr

This book, in Dutch, describes the Arnhem operations in 1944. Chapter 4 is devoted to John Baskeyfield VC (pages 90 - 106).

P15   PEILLARD, Léonce
SINK THE TIRPITZ!
G.P. Putnam's Sons, New York, 1968
360 pp, photos, maps, index, hb, cr

A French account of British attempts to sink the *Tirpitz*. First published as *Coulez le Tirpitz* in 1965 and translated and published in 1968 by Jonathan Cape Ltd. Cameron and Place received the VC for their attacks on the *Tirpitz* and their exploits are covered in detail.

P16   PENGELLY, Colin
ALBERT BALL VC: The Figher Pilot Hero of World War 1
Pen & Sword, Barnsley, 2010
224 pp, photos, index, sb, cr

A full biography of WW1 fighter ace, Albert Ball VC DSO** MC. The book covers Ball's childhood and family background in Nottingham. Ball enlisted in the 2/7th Bn Sherwood Foresters in 1914 and was later commissioned. He joined the RFC and in 15 months rose to the top ranks of fighter pilots achieving 44 confirmed victories. He was awarded a posthumous VC and was also decorated with DSO** and MC. Appendices 1 and 2 cover the Austin-Ball Scout which was Ball's outline plan for a new fighter aircraft. Appendix 3 lists 56 Sqn pilots to 7 May 1917. Appendix 4 lists Ball's victories.

P19   PENTREATH, Michael
GENERAL SIR REDVERS BULLER VC GCB GCMG: The People's General
Published by the author, 2008
24 pp, photos, index, sb, cr

A short biography of Sir Redvers Buller VC.

P19A   PEPPER, Eric
ARNHEM TRIBUTE
Frank Cassidy, Droylsden, Manchester, 1999
40 pp, photos, drawing, map, sb, cr, (fp 1981,

This brief account of 271 Squadron's participation in the airborne assault at Arnhem in Sep 1944 focusses on the posthumous VC action of Flt Lt Lord, captain of Dakota KG374. Two pages, comprising a biographical sketch and portrait photograph, are devoted to each of Lord's crew members who were killed along with him when his Dakota crashed (Plt Off REH Medhurst, Off AF Ballantyne, Cpl PE Nixon, Dvr J Ricketts, Dvr A Rowbotham and Dvr LS Harper). Eight pages are devoted to Lord's navigator, Off HA King, who was the sole survivor.

P19B   PEPPER, Eric *(original author unknown)*
FLT LT DAVID S. A. LORD VC DFC 1915-1944
Author-published, date unknown
13 pp, photos, sb, cr

This brief sketch of Flt Lt Lord focusses primarily on his WW2 service with 31 Squadron on supply-dropping missions in Burma where he won the DFC and with No 271 Squadron with which unit he flew re-supply missions at Arnhem until killed in action on 19 Sep 1944 (awarded the VC posthumously).

P20   PERCIVAL, John
FOR VALOUR: The Victoria Cross, Courage in Action
Thames Methuen, London, 1985
257 pp, photos, index, hb, cr

The author of this book was the producer of a Thames Television series of programmes on the Victoria Cross (see T7). The book contains chapters on sea, land and air VCs and a history of the VC. The focus is then turned to chapters on some recipients still alive when the series was made: Ganju Lama, Elliott, Cutler, Parkash Singh, Tilston and Cheshire.

P21   PERCY, Algernon (*editor*)
A BEARSKIN'S CRIMEA: Colonel Henry Percy VC and his brother officers
Leo Cooper (Pen & Sword Books), Barnsley, 2005
238 pp, photos, maps, index, hb, cr

This book is framed around the letters of Henry Percy who was awarded the VC for the Crimea. The letters are interspersed with letters written by other officers including Henry Clifford VC. There are also letters which Percy received from relatives while on campaign. Percy was one of 62 recipients to be decorated at the first VC investiture on 26 June 1857. As the senior officer he was in command of the other 61 recipients and his account of the day forms the last chapter. Reviewed in V56.

P23   PEREPECZKO, Andrzej
VICTORIA CROSS KAPITANA ROOPE'A
Cypniew Sp.zo.o, Lodz, Poland, 1997
124 pp, photos, maps, sb, cr

A Polish account of the duel between HMS *Glowworm* and the German cruiser *Admiral Hipper* in the North Sea on 8 April 1940. The CO, Lieut-Commander GB Roope, was awarded a posthumous VC for the action.

P24   PERKINS, Roger
THE KASHMIR GATE: Lieutenant Home & the Delhi VCs
Picton Publishing, Chippenham, 1983
161 pp, photos, line drawings, maps, index, hb, cr

An in-depth account of the blowing of the Kashmir Gate during the storming of Delhi on 14 September 1857 and of the four VCs awarded for the action (Lt Duncan Home, Lt Philip Salkeld, L/Cpl Henry Smith and Buglar Robert Hawthorne). There is also a chapter devoted to each of these VCs, which provides a biographical sketch. An appendix contains a chronologically-arranged list of, and full VC citations for, the 43 VCs won in operations in the Delhi area.

P25   PERKINS, David (*compiler and editor*)
CC DOBSON VC DSO RN
Seaboots Enterprise, Nova Scotia, 1991
28 pp, photos, map, sb, cr

A comb-bound booklet describing the life and career of CC Dobson VC DSO. There is a record of service from his entry in May 1900 to the Britannia Naval College as a cadet to his retirement as Rear-Admiral in 1936 and his death in 1940. The book describes how Dobson sank *U23* (DSO) on 20 July 1915 and a detailed account of the Kronstadt raid which resulted in his award of the VC. Included is a picture of Dobson with Alexander Graham Bell at Baddeck, Nova Scotia where he met his future wife, who was Bell's secretary.

P26   PERRETT, Brian
HEROES OF THE HOUR: Brief Moments of Glory
Cassell, London, 2001
224 pp, photos, maps, index, hb, cr

The author has selected 12 military heroes of their time, some of whom faded into obscurity, others of whom were later disgraced. One chapter (pages 167-176) relates to Lieutenant Walter Hamilton who fought to the death at the Kabul Residency during the Afghan War of 1879-80 and was awarded the VC.

P28   PERRETT, Brian
FOR VALOUR: Victoria Cross and Medal of Honor Battles
Weidenfeld & Nicolson, London, 2003
378 pp, photos, index, hb, ncr

The author has selected numerous acts of gallantry that resulted in the award of the Victoria Cross or the USA's Medal of Honor. These acts are retold within the context of the battle. VC actions are covered under: Crimean War (Alma, Balaclava and Inkerman), Indian Mutiny (Delhi Arsenal, Siege of Delhi, Storming of Delhi and Second Relief of Lucknow), campaigns between 1860 and 1900 (Taku Forts, Rorke's Drift, Nilt Forts, Colenso and Boxer Rising), WW1 (Mons/Le Cateau/The Aisne, Gallipoli, Jutland, the Somme and Zeebrugge/Ostend) and WW2 (Tobruk, St Nazaire, Dieppe, Alamein, Anzio, Burma and Arnhem).

P29   PERRIN, Dr Les
THE MYSTERY OF THE LEICHHARDT SURVIVORS: The Story of the Men Who Sought to Solve It
Published by author, Stafford, Queensland, Australia, 1990
162 pp, photos, maps, sb, cr

A chronicle of the search in 1874 for a survivor of Ludwig Leichhardt's expedition, that went missing in the Australian outback in 1848, who was alleged to be living wild with outback Aborigines. Timothy O'Hea VC, who arrived in Australia in 1874 following recent service with the New Zealand Armed Constabulary, was a member of the three-man search party on which the book focuses. His fate remains a mystery. Chapter 9 (pages 82-94) is a biographical account of O'Hea. Substantial references are made to him throughout the book.

P30   PETERSON, Leonard
BILLY BISHOP AND THE RED BARON
Simon and Pierre, Toronto, Canada, nd (c1975)
62 pp, photos, sb, cr

A one-act play featuring the Canadian VC recipient Billy Bishop.

P31   PHILPOTT, Bryan
FAMOUS FIGHTER ACES
Patrick Stephens, Wellingborough, 1989
160 pp, photos, index, hb, cr

A collection of short biographical accounts of 50 well-known fighter aces from both sides in the two world wars. A chapter is devoted to each pilot, five of whom were awarded the VC: Albert Ball, William Barker, Lanoe Hawker, James McCudden and Mick Mannock. There is also a chapter relating to Fg Off William Rhodes-Moorhouse DFC, the son of the WW1 VC.

P32   PICKARD, Lieutenant A.F., VC RA
OPERATIONS OF THE ROYAL ARTILLERY DURING THE CAMPAIGNS IN NEW ZEALAND IN 1861, 1863-1864
Extracted from the Proceedings of the Royal Artillery Institution Vol IV, London, 1865
23 pp, folding maps, sketches, sb, cr

A detailed and professional study tracing the career of Captain Mercer's battery of the 4th Brigade, RA. Pickard details the costly action at Rangiriri, New Zealand, in which he won the VC in 1863. The drawings and maps of Maori fortifications are very detailed.

P33   PIGOTT, Peter
       FLYING CANUCKS: Famous Canadian Aviators
       Hounslow Press, Toronto, Canada, 1994
       178 pp, photos, sb, cr

A collection of biographical accounts of 37 aviators in Canada's history in wartime and in peacetime, many of whom served in the RFC, RAF or RCAF. Six of the biographies relate to Canadian airmen who won the VC: WG Barker, IW Bazalgette, WA Bishop, RH Gray, DE Hornell and AC Mynarski.

P35   PILLINGER, Dennis and STAUNTON, Anthony
       VICTORIA CROSS LOCATOR
       Privately published, Queanbeyan, New South Wales, Australia, 1991 (revised and updated: 1997)
       58 pp, sb, ncr

This work identifies the location of every VC held publicly (by museums, regiments and other public bodies). Chapter 1 lists all VC recipients alphabetically and shows the location of the VC if held by a public body. Chapter 2 contains the same information but lists VC recipients according to Service, Regiment and Country. Chapter 3 lists VCs held by each public body. Chapter 4 lists VCs sold publicly by advert or auction from 1879 onwards, and shows date of sale, sum realised and auction house. Also included is a list of VCs who were alive at the time of publication. The 1997 edition of the work updates the original lists and incorporates the extensive changes resulting from the reorganisation of the British Army. Part 4 has been expanded to include a chronological listing of VC sales. See P36.

P36   PILLINGER, Dennis and STAUNTON, Anthony
       VICTORIA CROSS PRESENTATIONS AND LOCATIONS
       Privately published, Maidenhead, Berkshire and Woden, Australia, 2000
       74 pp, sb, ncr

This work is an updated reprint of P35. The VC location and sales lists are in the same format as the earlier work but brought up to date to 1 June 2000. A new 22-page chapter (Chapter 1) is an alphabetical list (by recipient's surname) of VC presentations recording the presentation date, by whom and the presentation location. A continuation of records of VC sales from 2000 can be found on http://www.victoriacross.org.uk (See Part 3).

P37   PITT, Barrie
       ZEEBRUGGE: St George's Day, 1918
       Cassell, London, 1958
       237 pp, photos, sketches, maps, index, hb, cr

A full account of Admiral Keyes's expeditions against Zeebrugge and Ostend in April 1918 and against Ostend in May 1918. For these operations 11 VCs were awarded (Carpenter, Sandford, PT Dean, Bamford, Finch, AE McKenzie, GN Bradford, AL Harrison, Crutchley, Drummond, and Bourke). Their VC deeds are detailed within the context of the operation and their *LG* citations are contained in an appendix.

P38   PLATT, Frank C. (compiler)
        GREAT BATTLES OF WORLD WAR I: In the Air
        Weathervane Books, New York, USA, 1966
        206 pp, maps, hb, cr

The compiler focuses on the exploits and writings of two influential pilots to narrate the story of aerial combat in WWI. The first section (up to page 82) relates to 'Billy' Bishop VC and comprises accounts of him written by Capt Roy Brown (pages 9-24) and by Alan Hynd (pages 25-72). This section is concluded with a ten-page article written by Bishop (when a Lt Col) titled *Chivalry in the Air*. The rest of the book concerns the exploits of General William ('Billy') Mitchell and includes a chapter written by him about Eddie Rickenbacker, the American ace.

P39   POLLARD, Captain A.O., VC MC DCM
        EPIC DEEDS OF THE RAF
        Hutchinson, London, 1940
        287 pp, photos, index, hb, cr

Dedicated to Fg Off DE Garland and Sgt T Gray, who were awarded posthumous VCs, this book describes the operational activities of the RAF during the first twelve months of WW2. For each theme, the author narrates a selection of heroic deeds that resulted in the award of the VC, DSO, DFC or DFM. The VC actions described relate to Garland and Gray (pages 184-185), Learoyd (pages 268-270) and Hannah (pages 276-277).

P40   POLLARD, Captain A.O., VC MC DCM
        FIRE EATER: The Memoirs of a VC
        Hutchinson, London, 1932
        278 pp, photos, index, hb, cr

This memoir is a detailed account of Pollard's military life from the outbreak of WW1 to his demobilisation in 1919, during which period he was awarded the VC, MC and DCM. Throughout the war, he served in the HAC and saw extensive action in France and Belgium which he narrates vividly. He also describes the actions for which he was decorated and recalls the presentation of his VC. An account of the VC deed of his fellow HAC officer, 2nd Lieutenant RL Haine, is provided, together with a portrait photograph of him in uniform. Reprinted by Naval & Military Press in 2009. Reviewed in V56.

P41   POLLARD, Captain A.O., VC MC DCM
        THE ROYAL AIR FORCE: A Concise History
        Hutchinson, London, nd (c1934) (revised and expanded: c1939)
        288 pp. (1939 edition: 276 pp.), photos, maps, index, hb, cr

This work chronicles the development of the RAF from its inception as the Royal Flying Corps and the Royal Naval Air Service and, predominantly, focuses on the period up to Armistice 1918. In describing the main events in British aerial warfare development and the struggle for air supremacy in WW1, the author recalls numerous notable individual actions. In addition, an 18-page chapter narrates the deeds of the air VCs of this period. The history concludes with an account of the RAF's activities in the aftermath of the war and up to 1934. The 1939 edition of the book updates the account and describes the RAF's rearmament and expansion programme in the 1930s.

P47   POLLOCK, George
THE JERVIS BAY
William Kimber, London, 1958
206 pp, photos, hb, cr

The story of HMS *Jervis Bay*, an armed merchant cruiser tasked with escorting Atlantic convoys. Commanded by Captain ESF Fegen RN, she was sunk by the German pocket-battleship *Admiral Scheer* on 5 November 1940 in a gallant action for which Fegen was awarded a posthumous VC. The book chronicles the war service of the *Jervis Bay* but substantial text is devoted to the VC action, which is reconstructed with the help of the surviving crew.

P49   POLLOCK, J.C.
WAY TO GLORY: The Life of Havelock of Lucknow
John Murray, London, 1957
270 pp, photos, maps, index, hb, cr

A full biography of Maj Gen Sir Henry Havelock Bt KCB, of Lucknow fame. There are extensive references to the life, character and career of his son, Lt Gen Sir Henry Havelock-Allan, who won the VC during the Indian Mutiny. A genealogical table of the Havelock family is included.

P50   POLLOCK, Major A.W.A.
WITH SEVEN GENERALS IN THE BOER WAR: A Personal Narrative
Skeffington, London, 1900
300 pp, photos, sketches, maps, hb, cr

The author served in the Boer War with Prince Albert's Somersetshire Light Infantry Regiment and was also a special correspondent for *The Times*. Chapter IX (pages 91-108) is entitled *Montmorency's Operations about Dordrecht* and is followed by a significant mention of de Montmorency and his post-VC career.

P51   POPE, Dudley
73 NORTH: The Battle of the Barents Sea
Weidenfeld & Nicolson, London, 1958
320 pp, photos, maps, index, hb, cr

A full account of how four convoy escort destroyers of the Royal Navy held off the might of the German High Seas Fleet in the Barents Sea on 31 December 1942. One of these destroyers, HMS *Onslow*, was captained by Capt R St V Sherbrooke DSO, who won the VC during the action. His role and deeds in the battle are described extensively throughout the book. An appendix lists, by ship, the gallantry awards that resulted from the battle.

P52   POSTLETHWAITE, Mark, with SHORTLAND, Jim
DAMBUSTERS IN FOCUS: A photographic album of 617 'Dambuster' Squadron at War 1943-1945
Red Kite, Walton-on-Thames, 2017
128 pp, photos, drawings, map, sb, cr

This profusely-illustrated history of 617 Sqn in WW2 contains over 200 photographs relating to its operations, men and aircraft. Pages 5-43 concern the forming of the Squadron in March 1943 under Wg Cdr Guy Gibson, and its preparation for, and execution of, Operation *Chastise* in May 1943. Details of the individual crews are given. Pages 44-127 record each of the Squadron's 59 targets from 15 July to 25 April 1945 and include loss reports for those aircraft and crews that failed to return. Pages 59-89 concern the period Leonard Cheshire (later VC) was Squadron Commander. Page 92 records the attack on 31 July 1944 at Rilly-La-Montagne, France and related loss report for Flt Lt Reid VC's aircraft. A map plotting the Squadron's 60 targets is shown on page 128.

P53 POTTER, John Deane
FIASCO: The Break-out of the German Battleships
Heinemann, London, 1970
235 pp, photos, maps, index, hb, cr

The story of the 'Channel dash' of the German battleships *Scharnhorst* and *Gneisenau* and heavy cruiser *Prinz Eugen* in February 1942 and the attacks on them by the RAF, Fleet Air Arm and ships of the Royal Navy. An attack in a Swordfish earned Lt Cdr E Esmonde a posthumous VC. His involvement in the operation and his VC deed are described fully.

P54 POWELL, Ted
[1] **THE CHANNEL DASH HEROES** (*1st Edition*)
Fleet Air Arm Association, Whitstable, Kent, nd (c.1995)
34 pp, photos, sketches, map, sb, cr
[2] **CHANNEL DASH HEROES** (*2nd Edition and 60th Anniversary Edition*)
J & KH Publishing, Hailsham, East Sussex, 2002
64 pp, photos, sketches, map, sb, cr (*accompanied by audio tape*)
[3] **CHANNEL DASH HEROES** (*3rd Edition, 65th Anniversary Edition*)
John Hodges, location not known, 2007
52 pp, sb, cr

This booklet is a brief account of 825 Sqn's Swordfish attack on the German battleships *Scharnhorst* and *Gneisenau* and heavy cruiser *Prinz Eugen* on 12 February 1942 in the Straits of Dover. It describes the actions and fate of the 18 aircrew who participated in the attack, one of whom, Lt Cdr E Esmonde, won a posthumous VC. It also documents the search for, the burial of, and the dedications to, the 13 participants killed in the action.

P55 POWELL, Geoffrey
BULLER: A SCAPEGOAT?: A Life of General Sir Redvers Buller VC
Leo Cooper, London, 1994
245 pp, photos, sketches, maps, index, hb, cr

A biography of Sir Redvers Buller VC whose generalship and command in the Boer War ended in controversy. The author has incorporated fresh material revealing how a near conspiracy of the press, politicians, landed interests and military rivals succeeded in destroying Buller's career and denigrating his reputation.

P56 PRINCE, Stephen
THE BLOCKING OF ZEEBRUGGE: Operation *Z-O* 1918
Osprey, Oxford, 2010
64 pp, photos, drawings, maps, index, sb, ncr

This No 7 title in Osprey's *Raid* series is an account of the raids on the German-held Belgian ports of Zeebrugge and Ostend (Operation *Z-O*), which resulted in the award of 11 VCs. In addition to describing the raids, the book also traces its origins and documents the Admiralty's strategy and Vice Admiral Keyes' plan. An analysis of the raids concludes the work.

P57   PRINGLE, Patrick
       FIGHTING PILOTS
       Evans Brothers, London, 1961
       207 pp, photos, hb, cr

Stories of air warfare in the two world wars, describing the deeds of a selection of heroic pilots. Three of the sixteen chapters (4, 10 and 11) relate specifically to the VC deeds of WL Robinson (pages 31-39), Gibson (pages 125-135) and Cheshire (pages 136-149).

P58   PRINGLE, Patrick (*editor*)
       FIGHTING MEN
       Evans Brothers, London, 1964
       191 pp, photos, hb, cr

The editor has selected 12 true stories of great daring and achievement from both world wars. All accounts are summarised extracts from published books. Three stories relate to VC actions: *Zepp Sunday* by Kenneth Poolman (pages 29-44) is based on his book *Zeppelins over England* and relates to WL Robinson; *Motor-boat against Battleship* by Augustus Agar (pages 45-50) is from his memoirs *Footprints in the Sea*; and *The Dam Busters* (pages 78-94) by Paul Brickhill relates to his classic work on Gibson VC's raid on the Ruhr dams.

P59   PRINGLE, Patrick
       FIGHTING MARINES
       Evans Brothers, London, 1966
       192 pp, photos, hb, cr

This companion volume to P57 and P58 recalls the notable achievements and gallant exploits of the Royal Marines from its origination. Chapters 3 and 4 (pages 41-59) concern the RM VC actions up to 1918. Chapter 5 (pages 60-77) relates to the Zeebrugge raid on 23 April 1918 and focuses on the RM and RN VCs won.

P65   PRINS, François (e*ditor*)
       DAM-BUSTERS: The Amazing Story of Operation Chastise
       Kelsey Publishing Group, Cudham, Kent, 2013
       130 pp, photos, drawings, maps, sb, cr

This profusely-illustrated account of the Dams Raid on 16/17 May 1943 led by Wg Cdr Gibson documents the operation's planning and preparation, the attack, and the aftermath. Separate chapters are devoted to Barnes Wallis, Guy Gibson, Roy Chadwick and the development of the Lancaster and MRAF Sir Arthur Harris. A chapter on the making of *The Dam Busters* film includes the cast list. Complete listings of Operation *Chastise* aircrew (by aircraft) and of those crews who failed to return from the raid are provided.

P70   PUGH, Peter
       BARNES WALLIS - Dambuster
       Icon Books, Thriplow, Cambridge, 2005
       200 pp, photos, index, hb, cr

A biography of Barnes Wallis, inventor of the bouncing bomb which was used by 617 Sqn in breaching the dams on 16/17 May 1943 for which Guy Gibson won the VC. Chapter 3 describes the planning of the raid. Chapter 4 describes the raid and Chapter 5 the aftermath. All this other noteable contributions and achievements are covered.

Q3   QUIGG, Leonard
SERGEANT ROBERT QUIGG VICTORIA CROSS: A Bushmills Hero
Impact Printing, Coleraine and Ballycastle, Northern Ireland, 2015
104 pp, photos, maps, index, hb, cr

This is a short biography of Robert Quigg VC which covers historical detail of where he was born and raised including a chapter on the political turbulence in Ireland in 1912 to 1914. The book covers Quigg's VC action in which he repeatedly ventured into No Man's Land to rescue wounded comrades. Later chapters cover his hero's return home on leave and further service in Mesopotamia and Egypt before his discharge in June 1919. A bronze statue of Quigg was unveiled by HM The Queen on 28 June 2016.

Q5   QUILIVIAN, Peter
FORGOTTEN VALOUR: The Story of Arthur Sullivan VC, Shy War Hero
New Holland, New South Wales, Australia, 2006
304 pp, photos, maps, index, sb, cr

A full biography of Arthur Sullivan VC, an Australian who served in the First World War and then fought in the Russian Civil War in 1919 when he was awarded the VC. Pages 159-162 cover the public statement by Lieutenant-Colonel Sherwood-Kelly VC CMG DSO on the conduct of the North Russian campaign which led to his court martial. The second half of the book covers Sullivan's post-war career to his death on 9 April 1937. Sullivan was one of the Australian Coronation contingent outside Wellington Barracks, London during the ceremonies.

Q10   QUINN, Tom
THE MILITARY'S STRANGEST CAMPAIGNS AND CHARACTERS: Extraordinary but true tales from military history
Robson Books, London, 2006
321 pp, sb, cr

The book's content is reflected in its title and sub-title. It has brief coverage of the following VCs: Lucas, Coltman and Nanjit Singh.

R1   RABY, Paul
ZULU: The Truth Behind the Film
York Publishing Services, York, 2009
103 pp, photos, sb, cr

This book describes the 1964 film *Zulu* which depicts the defence of Rorke's Drift on 22/23 January 1879 for which 11 VCs were awarded. The book describes the actors including Stanley Baker (Chard VC) and Michael Caine (Broomhead VC). The book then charts each scene of the film and highlights how the film conforms or departs from actual events. It also describes historical inaccuracies regarding uniforms, medals and fictitious characters. It corrects a number of myths about Rorke's Drift which the film created.

R3   RALPH, Wayne
BARKER VC: The Life, Death and Legend of Canada's Most Decorated War Hero
Doubleday, Toronto, Canada, 1997 / Grub Street, London, 1997
308 pp, photos, maps, index, hb, cr

A full biography of Lt Col WG Barker VC DSO*, MC **, Croix de Guerre (France), Italian Silver Medal for Valour (twice) and MID (thrice) - who was credited with 50 aerial combat victories. The book describes Barker's family background and early years. It then chronicles his distinguished military career and war service as a machine gunner in the Canadian Mounted Rifles and as a highly successful combat pilot. Following the Armistice, he co-founded a flying venture with Bishop VC (Bishop-Barker Aeroplanes Ltd) prior to becoming a founder member of the Canadian Air Force, in 1922. The author then describes how Barker, as a civilian again, felt humiliated until joining Fairchild Aircraft Ltd with whom he was killed in a flying accident. The book concludes with an extensive list of reference sources used by the author. A 10th anniversary edition was published in 2007 by John Wiley & Sons Canada Ltd with additional photos interspersed within the text.

R5   RAMSDEN, John
THE DAM BUSTERS
I.B. Tauris, London, 2003
128 pp, photos, sb, cr

This volume in the *British Film Guide* series investigates the background, context and making of the legendary 1955 film *The Dam Busters*. It then focuses on the film itself and the critical and popular reception it received. It concludes with an appraisal of the accuracy portrayed by the film. A complete list of film credits is included. See F2.

R6   RAMSLAND, John, Professor Emeritus
VENTURING INTO NO MAN'S LAND: The Charmed Life of Joseph Maxwell VC World War 1 Hero
Brolga Publishing Pty Ltd, Melbourne, Australia, 2012
343 pp, photos, maps, index, sb, cr

This is a full and detailed biography of Joseph Maxwell VC MC* DCM, the second highest decorated Australian soldier of the Great War. Most of the 12 chapters focus on his wartime service in Gallipoli and France. There are references to other VCs including A Jacka, H Murray, P Storkey and H Throssell.

R8   RAMSEY, Winston G. (*editor*)
BATTLE OF BRITAIN THEN AND NOW
After The Battle Magazine, London, 1980
816 pp, photos, drawings, maps, index, hb, cr

In the first and subsequent editions of this profusely illustrated book, there is a chapter dedicated to James Nicolson – the only Battle of Britain fighter pilot to be awarded the VC. The chapter (pages 306-313) is written by Andy Sanders and includes a detailed map and obverse and reverse photographs of his VC. In addition to this chapter there are a number of other references to Nicolson throughout the book.

R9   RAMSEY, Winston G. (*Editor*)
THE BLITZ THEN AND NOW VOLUME 1
After The Battle Magazine, London, 1987
336 pp, photos, drawings, maps, index, hb, cr

Within this book is a chapter by Andy Sanders on JF Mantle VC. The chapter, *The Foylebank VC* (pages 116-119), is well illustrated with maps and photographs including one of Mantle's grave.

R10   RAPIER, Brian J.
HALIFAX AT WAR
Ian Allan, London, 1987
127 pp, photos, drawings, maps, hb, cr

A profusely illustrated history of the Handley Page Halifax examining its various roles and theatres of operation in WW2. Chapter 8 (pages 70-77) is devoted to the posthumous VC action of Pilot Officer CJ Barton in the Halifax raid on Nuremburg on 30 March 1944, which is recalled by Fg Off HD Wood, Barton's mid-upper gunner.

R11   RAW, David
IT'S ONLY ME: A life of The Reverend Theodore Bayley Hardy VC DSO MC, 1863-1918
Frank Peters Publishing, Gatebeck, Cumbria, 1988
105 pp, photos, maps, sb, cr

A comprehensive and detailed biography of the most highly decorated chaplain of WW1, the Rev TB Hardy VC DSO MC, who was killed in 1918. Letters, maps and a range of photographs support the text. (See R12 and H25).

R12   RAW, David
THEODORE BAYLEY HARDY VC DSO MC
Pen & Sword Military, Barnsley, 2018
150 pp, photos, maps, hb, cr

This is an expanded and updated version of R11 covering the life of the most highly decorated chaplain of WW1, the Rev TB Hardy VC DSO MC.

R15   REED, A.H.
HEROES OF PEACE AND WAR IN EARLY NEW ZEALAND
AH & AW Reed, Wellington, New Zealand, 1959
128 pp, photos, hb, cr

This title contains biographical portraits of early settlers in New Zealand and recalls their contribution. Those described include Father Rolland, Marsden, Brunner and Charles Heaphy VC.

R16   REED, Paul
GREAT WAR LIVES
Pen & Sword, Barnsley, 2010
224 pp, photos, hb, cr

This book provides guidance to family historians on how to research servicemen of WW1. Each chapter provides a specific individual and this illustrates how archive sources can build up a picture of a particular individual. Chapter 5 covers Sapper William Hackett VC of the Royal Engineers.

R17   REEVE, Lieutenant D.W. and STARK, Lieutenant J.P.
THE MURPHY AND MORLEY VICTORIA CROSS RESEARCH
Royal Corps of Transport, Aldershot, 1984
60 pp, sb, cr

This photocopied transcript work, written by the commanders of the Murphy and Morley Troops of the Junior Leaders Regiment, RLT, is a biographical account of Michael Murphy VC and Samuel Morley VC. Both men were awarded the VC for the same action, near Azimgurh on 15 April, 1858, during the Indian Mutiny. In 1872 Murphy forfeited his VC for theft at Aldershot. he was demoted but served until 1875 and died in abject poverty in 1893. Morley served time for various military offences and died in 1888. The authors have researched this work using original sources.

R18   REID, Elizabeth
THE SINGULAR JOURNEY OF O'HEA'S CROSS: A Unique Victoria Cross
Leamcon Press, Yale, British Columbia, Canada, 2005
142 pp, photos, maps, sketches, index, sb, cr

The author attempts to unravel the mysterious travels of Timothy O'Hea's VC and its location at the time of publication. O'Hea was awarded the VC for putting out a fire on an ammunition railway car at Danville, Quebec. O'Hea's VC was the only one to be awarded in the New World and, unusually, was for valour not in the presence of the enemy. Reviewed in V59.

R19   REID, D.I.
THE VICTORIA CROSS 1856-1981: A Select Bibliography
School of Library & Information Studies, Ealing College of Higher Education, London, 1981
11 pp, sb, ncr

A typewritten script in the *Ealing Miscellany* series listing 81 key titles relating to the VC.

R20   REID, P.R.
WINGED DIPLOMAT: The Life Story of Air Commodore "Freddie" West VC CBE MC
Chatto & Windus, London, 1962
219 pp, photos, index, hb, cr

A detailed biography of Air Cdre West VC. The book spans West's boyhood in Milan through to him working for the Rank Organisation in 1947. It describes his unorthodox student life in Italy and Switzerland. It then details his WW1 experiences in trench warfare and as an RFC pilot winning the VC. His RAF career in the inter-war years included appointments as Air Attaché to various British legations and embassies. During WW2, West was Air Attaché to the British Embassy in Berne, Switzerland and was responsible for helping allied airmen escape. The author was Assistant Military Attaché during this period after his escape from Colditz Castle in late 1942.

R21   REID, Richard
FOR VALOUR: Australians and the Victoria Cross
Sprintpak, a Division of Australian Post, Australia, 2000
40 pp, photos, sb, cr

This profusely illustrated book, researched and written by Dr Reid of Australia's Department of Veterans' Affairs, accompanied the issue on 24 July 2000 of the set of five Australian postage stamps commemorating the Centenary of the first Australian VC. The contents are arranged by conflict and recount the VC deeds of a selection of Australian recipients. Main features include two-page accounts of the deeds of each of the four recipients depicted on the stamps (Sir Neville Howse, Sir Roden Cutler, Edward Kenna and Keith Payne). A table lists all the Australian VCs, and indicates their birthplace, age, battalion, date of award, location of action and place of burial or commemoration.

R25   REVELL, Alex
JAMES McCUDDEN VC
Albatross Publications, Berkhamstead, Herts, 1987
28 pp, photos, sketches, sb, cr

This well-illustrated booklet, No 3 in the series *Aces and Aeroplanes*, chronicles the life and death of McCudden. An appendix logs his 57 aerial combat victories. Three colour paintings of his aircraft are included.

R27   REVELL, Alex
VICTORIA CROSS: WW1 Airmen and Their Aircraft
Flying Machines Press, Stratford, Connecticut, USA, 1997
96 pp, photos, drawings, sb, cr

This well-illustrated work gives a biographical account of each of the 19 air VCs of WWI and focuses on their active service. An appendix details the particular aircraft they flew in their VC action and supplements the coloured profile drawings of these aircraft. Numerous black and white portraits and other photographs intersperse the text. A second expanded edition was published by Aeronaut Books in 2016, softback with 156 pages and colour illustrations of aircraft flown by the VCs integrated into the text profile for each recipient. On average each recipient is covered in 8 pages with many photographs.

R28   REVELL, Alex
HIGH IN THE EMPTY BLUE: The History of 56 Squadron, RFC/RAF 1916 to 1920
Flying Machines Press, Mountain View, California, USA, 1995
448 pp, photos, drawings, colour profiles, maps, index, hb, cr

This is a comprehensive and profusely-illustrated history of 56 Sqn RFC/RAF during WW1. Chapters 1 to 21 (pages 1-392) chronicle the Squadron's service and the 21 Appendices provide extensive details on the Squadron's organisation, locations, aircraft, personnel, victories, casualties and other aspects. There are many references to its aces, particularly: A Ball VC and JTB McCudden VC, both of whom scored significant victories while flying with the squadron. Appendix 15 documents the death of Albert Ball.

R29   REVELL, Alex
THE HAPPY WARRIOR: James Thomas Byford McCudden
Aeronaut Books, USA, 2015
304 pp, photos, drawings, maps, index, sb, cr

A full and highly detailed biography of Major JTB McCudden VC DSO* MC* MM CdG of the RFC/RAF who achieved 56 confirmed victories. The book contains 275 rare photographs.

R30   REYNOLDS, Quentin
THEY FOUGHT FOR THE SKY: The Story of the First War in the Air
Cassell, London, 1958
298 pp, photos, index, hb, cr

A general history of air fighting in WW1 with a focus on the well-known aces on both sides. Set in the context of the development of air fighting, the exploits of the following VCs are given significant coverage: Ball, Bishop, McCudden and Mannock.

R31   RHODES-MOORHOUSE, Linda
KALEIDOSCOPE, 1886-1960: The story of a family in peace and war
Arthur Barker, London, 1960
180 pp, photos, maps, hb, cr

This autobiography of the widow of Capt W Rhodes-Moorhouse VC (the first air VC), includes 30 pages relating to her husband. Their son, Fg Off W Rhodes-Moorhouse DFC was killed in action during the Battle of Britain.

R32   RIACH, Margaret
FROM LIEUTENANT TO FIELD-MARSHAL: A Life of Lord Roberts
Wells Gardner, London, 1915
184 pp, photos, hb, cr

A concise biography of Lord Roberts VC. It relates his early days, his distinguished military career and campaign service and his death in 1914.

R33   RICHARDS, Jeff
BILLY BISHOP
Canadian Library Association, Ottawa, Ontario, Canada, 1986
22 pp, sb, cr

This small booklet on the life of AM Bishop VC was produced as an aid to improving adult literacy and is, therefore, written in a simple style.

R34   RICHARDS, Miriam M. (Lieutenant Colonel, Salvation Army)
IT BEGAN WITH ANDREWS: The Saga of a Medical Mission
Salvationist Publishing & Supplies, London, 1971
185 pp, photos, hb, cr

The story of a medical mission which began in an amateur dispensary in a bathroom in Nagercoil, India in 1893. The Catherine Booth Dispensary (later Hospital) was founded by HJ ('Harry') Andrews, who won the VC posthumously in 1919. Chapter 1 is devoted to his life and, in particular, describes his work in India and also his VC action in Waziristan.

R35   RICHARDS, Walter
HEROES OF OUR DAY: or Recent Winners of the Victoria Cross
Hutchinson, London, nd (c.1882) (updated: Virtue, London, 1892)
230 pp, sketches, hb, ncr

This book narrates brief accounts of the VC actions of many recipients (from the Crimean War up to the First Boer War in 1881). These accounts are described in the context of the conflict. The updated 1892 version covers the campaign in Sudan in 1884-85.

R37   RICKSON, P.A. and HOLLIDAY, A.
MISSION ACCOMPLISHED
William Kimber, London, 1974
244 pp, photos, sketches, maps, index, hb, cr

An account of three great air operations of WW2. Pages 1-85 describe Operation *Chastise*, the Dams Raid of 617 Squadron for which Wg Cdr Gibson was awarded the VC; pages 87-148 concern Operation *Jericho*, the raid on Amiens prison; and pages 149-236 describe Operation *Thunderbolt*, the Luftwaffe air operation supporting the 'Channel Dash' of *Scharnhorst*, *Gneisenau* and *Prinz Eugen*. An account of the VC actions of Fg Off K Campbell and Lt Cdr E Esmonde in attacking the ships is given.

R38   RIDLEY, John Cotch, MC
FOR VALOUR: Or the First VC, Captain B. A. Warburton-Lee
Brown, Prior, Anderson Pty, Melbourne, Australia, 1940
15 pp, sb, cr

The author, who served in the AIF, has written this short religious booklet as No 17 in the *J. G. R Series*. The author has connected the first VC (Lucas) and the first VC of WW2 (Warburton-Lee) to Jesus Christ. He writes that there is a heavenly VC which can be won and will eclipse the glory of the VC as the light of the Sun eclipses the twinkle of a star.

R39   RILEY, Milton E. MC
MIGHTY IN BATTLE: A Memorandum of 1918 of Major-General C. Coffin VC CB DSO Bar
Privately Published, 1971
30 pp, sb, cr

An account of the exploits of Major General Coffin in holding back the German offensive in March 1918 and the author's part in the battle. Some details are provided of Coffin's ancestry. A copy is in the IWM.

R40   RIMELL, Raymond Laurence
THE AIRSHIP VC: The Life of Captain William Leefe Robinson
Aston Publications, Bourne End, Buckinghamshire, 1989
128 pp, photos, hb, cr

A biographical portrait of one of WW1's most popular heroes, who was awarded the VC for shooting down the first Zeppelin over England. This well-illustrated book details his life, service career, POW experiences and death. His VC exploit is documented thoroughly and is supported by appendices which replicate key documents. Extensive sources used by author are recorded.

R41 RITCHIE, Carson I.A.
Q SHIPS
Terence Dalton, Lavenham, Suffolk, 1985
216 pp, photos, sketches, index, hb, cr

A detailed and well-illustrated study of the Royal Navy's *Q* ships in WW1, recalling their development and operations. Dr Ritchie consulted *Q* ship archives, which had been previously withheld by the Official Secrets Act, to narrate many of the *Q* ship actions. In particular, the services performed by Gordon Campbell VC are well documented.

R45 RIVAZ, Squadron Leader R.C., DFC
TAIL GUNNER
Jarrolds, London, 1943 (reissued 1996, Sutton Publishing, Stroud, hb, 128 pp.)
96 pp, photos, hb, cr

A first-hand account of Bomber Command's offensive between August 1940 and December 1941. The author flew as tail gunner to Leonard Cheshire VC who wrote the Foreword. His experiences include flying missions in Whitleys and Halifax bombers in 102 and 35 Squadrons.

R50 ROBERTS OF KANDAHAR, Field Marshal Lord, VC GCB GCSI GCIE
FORTY ONE YEARS IN INDIA: From Subaltern to Commander-in-Chief
[1] Richard Bentley, London, 1897
Two Volumes: 1033 pp, (Vol 1 511 pp.; Vol II 522 pp.), hb cr
[2] Macmillan, London, 1914
Single Volume 601 pp, hb, cr
[3] EINUNDVIERZIG JAHRE IN INDIEN: Vom Subaltern-Offizier bis zum Ober-Befehishaber
Verlag de Holbuchhandlung Karl Siesmund, Berlin, 1994
Two Volumes: 764 pp. (Band I 380 pp.; Band II 384 pp.), hb, cr

A comprehensive memoir of Lord Roberts' military service in India from 1852 to 1893. He narrates, in detail, his participation in numerous campaigns. Volume 1 covers his early days in India, the Indian Mutiny and his service up to the 1860s. Volume 2 continues with the Umbeyla Expedition of 1868, the Abyssinian Expedition, the Lushai Expedition, the Afghan War and the Burma Expedition. The work concludes with his farewell to India. The appendices include extracts from some of his official reports. A German translation entitled "Einundvierzig Jahre in Indien vom Subaltern-Offizier bis zum Ober-Betehlsha von Feldmarschall Lord Roberts of Kandaha euebersetzung von Ritter von Borosini" was published in 1904 by K. Siegismund, Berlin.

R51 ROBERTS, Fred (later Field Marshal Earl, KG VC)
LETTERS WRITTEN DURING THE INDIAN MUTINY
Macmillan, London, 1924
169 pp, photos, maps, index, hb, cr

Countess Roberts, the daughter of FM Earl Roberts VC, assembled for this work a selection of 30 family letters written by him as a young subaltern during the Indian Mutiny. They narrate his experiences and adventures in the Mutiny. They also describe his views (which he modified in his memoirs - see R50) of the operations and participating officers. This volume was reprinted a number of times up till 2005 by Mittal Publications in Delhi.

R53   ROBERTS, Captain T.G.D. (*editor*)
THIRTY CANADIAN VCs: 23rd April 1915 to 30th March 1918
Skeffington, London, 1919
96 pp, hb, cr

An authoritative account of Canada's 30 VCs of WW1, which is based on official records of the Canadian War Records Office. The VC deed of each recipient is told in the context of the operation or battle.

R53A   ROBERTSON, Stuart
COMMAND AND VALOUR: The Grand Strategy of D-Day and the Battle of Normandy and How 21 Heroic Deeds Helped Enable Victory
Sabrestorm, Devizes, Wiltshire, 2019
208 pp, photos, maps, index, hb, cr

A 13 chapter book covering D-Day and the battle for Normandy. Chapter 1 covers a history of the Medal of Honor and the Victoria Cross. The following VCs for Normandy are covered: SE Hollis, S Bates, D Jamieson, T Watkins and DV Currie.

R54   ROBERTSON, Terence
CHANNEL DASH: The Drama of Twenty-four Hours of War
Evans Brothers, London, 1958
208 pp, photos, index, hb, cr

The story of the breakout of the German warships *Scharnhorst*, *Gneisenau* and *Prinz Eugen* from Brest, in 1942, their passage through the Straits of Dover and the attempts by the British forces to sink the ships. One such attack by Swordfish, led by Lt Cdr E Esmonde, earned him a posthumous VC. This action is described in detail. Additionally, extensive references to Esmonde are made throughout the text and describe his life, career and death. An account of the presentation of his VC is given.

R55   ROBINSON, Peter (*editor*)
THE LETTERS OF MAJOR GENERAL PRICE DAVIES VC, CB, CMG, DSO: From Captain to Major General, 1914-18
Spellmount, Stroud, 2013
255pp, photos, index, sb, cr

Major General Llewellyn Alberic Emilius Price-Davies was a prolific letter writer and his letters, mostly to his wife, and diary entries have been brought together in this book. They have been edited and supported by copious notes. There are five chapters, covering the years 1914 to 1918, with short chapters before and after these dates, but the war years are the main focus of the book.

R56   ROBSON, Brian (*editor*)
ROBERTS IN INDIA: The Military Papers of Field Marshal Lord Roberts 1876-1893
Alan Sutton for the Army Records Society, Stroud, 1993
478 pp, photo, index, hb, cr

A selection of 273 military papers written by, or to, Lord Roberts VC during the period 1876 to 1893 which illustrate both his career in India and the interreaction between British and Indian policies. Additionally, they reveal the personality of Lord Roberts. Extensive notes (28 pages) and a bibliography (7 pages) support the text. Pages 449-456 provide biographical summaries of personalities referred to in the papers which include 6 VC Generals: SJ Browne, CJ Gough, HH Gough, J Hills, HT MacPherson and GS White.

R57   ROBSON, Brian
FUZZY WUZZY: The campaigns in the Eastern Sudan 1884-85
Spellmount, Tunbridge Wells, 1993
228 pp, photos, maps, index, hb, cr

A detailed study of campaigns conducted by Lt Gen Sir Gerald Graham VC. Using original War Office records and unpublished personal accounts, the author has reconstructed the campaigns fought by Sir Gerald Graham, in the Eastern Sudan. Amongst the extensive references to Graham is a description of his career. Also within the text, the services of Sir Redvers Buller VC, Sir William Hewett VC, Sir John McNeill VC and Sir Arthur Wilson VC are described in relation to the campaign. (See also D11).

R58   ROBSON, Michael Charles
FOR VALOUR: The Complete History of the Victoria Cross
Volume 1: Where it all started, The Crimean War
Uniform (Unicorn Publishing Group), London, in association with the Victoria Cross Trust, 2017
328 pp, photos, maps, index, hb, cr

This is Volume 1 of an eight-volume series published between 2017 and 2020, in association with The Victoria Cross Trust. Each volume is divided into two parts: Part 1 titled *Wars, Battles and Deeds* contains descriptions of each war, campaign, battle or engagement that resulted in the award of a VC. The deeds are described within the context of the engagement in which they occurred. Part 2 titled *Portraits of Valour* contains biographical details of each VC recipient. Volume 1 covers the Crimean War and contains a short history of the VC and the warrants governing its award. The foreword is by Lord Ashcroft.

R59   ROBSON, Michael Charles
FOR VALOUR: The Complete History of the Victoria Cross
Volume 2: The Indian Mutiny (1857-1859)
Uniform (Unicorn Publishing Group), London, in association with the Victoria Cross Trust, 2017
525 pp, photos, maps, index, hb, cr

This Volume 2 in the eight-volume series described in R58 covers VC recipients of the Indian Mutiny.

R60   ROBSON, Michael Charles
FOR VALOUR : The Complete History of the Victoria Cross
Volume 3: The Colonial Wars (1860-1889)
Uniform (Unicorn Publishing Group), London, in association with the Victoria Cross Trust, 2018
420 pp, photos, maps, index, hb, cr

This Volume 3 in the eight-volume series described in R58 covers VC recipients of the campaigns between 1860 and 1889.

R61   ROBSON, Michael Charles
FOR VALOUR: The Complete History of the Victoria Cross
Volume 4: The Victorian Wars from 1896
Uniform (Unicorn Publishing Group), London, in association with the Victoria Cross Trust, 2019
? pp, photos, maps, index, hb, **tbc**

This Volume 4 in the eight-volume series described in R58 covers VC recipients from 1896 to 1913. Due to be published in 2019.

R62   ROBSON, Michael Charles
FOR VALOUR: The Complete History of the Victoria Cross
Volume 5: The First World War - Part 1
Uniform (Unicorn Publishing Group), London, in association with the Victoria Cross Trust, 2019
? pp, photos, maps, index, hb, **tbc**

This Volume 5 in the eight-volume series described in R58 covers the first half of VCs awarded in WW1. Due to be published in 2019.

R63   ROBSON, Michael Charles
FOR VALOUR: The Complete History of the Victoria Cross
Volume 6: The First World War - Part 2
Uniform (Unicorn Publishing Group), London, in association with the Victoria Cross Trust, 2019
? pp, photos, maps, index, hb, **tbc**

This volume in the eight-volume series described in R58 covers the second half of VCs awarded in WW1. Due to be published in 2019.

R64   ROBSON, Michael Charles
FOR VALOUR: The Complete History of the Victoria Cross
Volume 7: The Second World War
Uniform (Unicorn Publishing Group), London, in association with the Victoria Cross Trust, 2020
? pp, photos, maps, index, hb, **tbc**

This Volume 7 in the eight-volume series described in R58 covers the VC awarded in WW2. Due to be published in 2020.

R65   ROBSON, Michael Charles
FOR VALOUR: The Complete History of the Victoria Cross
Volume 8: Between the Wars and Modern Day
Uniform (Unicorn Publishing Group), London, in association with the Victoria Cross Trust, 2020
? pp, photos, maps, index, hb, **tbc**

This Volume 8 in the eight-volume series described in R58 covers VCs awarded between WW1 and WW2 and post WW2. Due to be published in 2020.

R69   ROCA GONZÁLEZ, Carlos (Translated from Spanish by HOPWOOD, Sally-Ann)
RORKE'S DRIFT: The Inmortal (*sic*) **Anglo-Zulu War** (*English Edition*)
Alcañtiz y Fresno's SA, Valladolid, Spain, 2008
318 pp, photos, paintings, engravings, map, hb, cr
[fp Quirón Ediciones, Valladoid, 2007 as *Rorke's Drift: La Inmortal Batalla Anglo-Zulu* (Spanish text)]

This volume, which features over 120 illustrations, provides a comprehensive account of the Battle of Rorke's Drift on 22/23 January 1879. Following a historical narrative of events leading up to the battle, a detailed chronicle of the action is interwoven with evidence sourced from official records, contemporary news reports and statements from Rorke's Drift survivors. Later chapters feature Rorke's Drift in literature and painting, the film *Zulu*, Rorke's Drift today and an analysis of the battle. The eleven Appendices include the sequence of events at the hospital (App II), VC and DCMs awarded ((App IV), press articles, testimonials, interview and letters (App V) and Robert Jones' service record (App VI).

R70   ROE, F. Gordon
       THE BRONZE CROSS: A Tribute to Those who Won the Supreme Award for Valour in the years 1940-45
       PR Gawthorn, London, 1945
       124 pp, photos, sketches, index, hb, cr

This book is divided into two parts. Pages 1-48 cover the institution of the VC and narrates a selection of key VC deeds from the first VC up to 1945. Some recipients' photographs and artists' impressions of various VC actions accompany the text. Pages 50-114 show, chronologically by VC deed, portraits (or other photographs) of WW2 VC recipients. Adjacent to each photo is a brief description of the VC action. A photograph is not portrayed for nine VCs. As the book was published in December 1945, the nine WW2 VCs gazetted after this date are not included.

R71   ROGERS, Stanley
       GALLANT DEEDS OF THE WAR
       Blackie, London, 1941
       223 pp, sketches, hb, cr

An anthology of acts of heroism and self sacrifice performed by Britain's armed forces in the early years of WW2. Amongst the episodes related are separate accounts (each up to eight pages in length) of the deeds of eight VCs: Warburton-Lee, Mantle, Nicholls, Ervine-Andrews, Annand, Garland, T Gray and Hannah. The book is a companion volume to R72.

R72   ROGERS, Stanley
       MORE GALLANT DEEDS OF THE WAR
       Blackie, London, 1942
       223 pp, sketches, hb, cr

A companion volume to R71, this work describes more acts of heroism performed by Britain's armed forces and Civil Defence during WW2. The deeds of six VCs (Fegen, Wilson, Edmonson, Nicolson, Learoyd and Ward) are recalled in dedicated chapters.

R73   ROGERS, David, Major
       WALTER MILLS VC
       Privately printed
       ? pp, photos, maps, sb, cr

This biography of Walter Mills VC is available at Oldham Local Studies Library for reference purposes only. Another copy is in the Manchester Regiment archive based in the Tameside Archive Centre. The publication describes Walter Mills' service in the 10th Bn, Manchester Regiment and his VC action at Givenchy on 11 December 1917.

R73A   ROSS, Al
       ANATOMY OF THE SHIP: The Destroyer CAMPBELTOWN
       Conway Maritime Press, London, 1990 (revised 2014)
       127 pp, photos, drawings, hb, ncr

This monograph of destroyer HMS *Campbeltown*, formerly USS *Buchanan*, is arranged in three parts. The Introduction (pages 7-14) relates the ship's design history, technical details and service history. The alterations made for the St Nazaire Raid are described and a brief account of the raid is given. Photographs (all full-page plates) on pages 15-40 depict the ship in USN and RN service, culminating in her rammed in the lock at St Nazaire. Pages 41-127 contain detailed design drawings of the ship, reproduced to 1/256 scale.

R74   ROSS, Graham
SCOTLAND'S FORGOTTEN VALOUR
McLean Press, Isle of Skye, 1995
99 pp, photos, index, sb, cr

This book gives an overview of the deeds of Scotland's 158 VC recipients, arranged by campaign. Two appendices list Scottish born recipients alphabetically and by regiment or service. Appendix 3 identifies and describes, briefly, the VC deed of recipients with close Scottish connections.

R75   ROWBOTHAM, Commander W.B., RN (*editor*)
THE NAVAL BRIGADES IN THE INDIAN MUTINY, 1857-1858
Navy Records Society, 1947
332 pp, map, index, hb, cr

An exhaustive study of all the Naval Brigades (*Shannon*, *Pearl*, *Pelonis*) engaged in the Indian Mutiny based on official documents and private letters, including the Mutiny correspondence of Lt Nowell Salmon who won his VC at Lucknow (Appendix H, 21 pages). In addition, some 50 pages replicate correspondence from or to Capt Sir William Peel VC KCB who, at the time, commanded HMS *Shannon*'s Brigade.

R76   ROWE, Douglas
LIEUTENANT COLONEL BERNARD Wm VANN VC MC & BAR, MID, CROIX DE GUERRE
Privately published, location unknown, 2009
50 pp, photos, map, sb, cr

An account of the life of Lt Col the Rev Bernard Vann, one of Wellingborough's two VCs. One page is devoted to the other recipient, Mick Mannock. Pages 4-12 trace Vann's family background and describe his early years, schooling and university education leading to his ordination. His sporting achievements are also covered. Pages 13-42 provide a detailed account of his service and exploits in WW1 and War Diary narratives are supported by eight maps. Memorials to him are depicted in some of the book's 38 photographs.

R77   ROWLEY, Squadron Leader Clive, MBE RAF (Retd)
DAMBUSTERS: The most daring raid in the RAF's history
Mortons Media Group, Horncastle, Lincolnshire, 2018
132 pp, photos, artwork, drawings, sb, cr (fp 2013)

This profusely-illustrated bookazine was republished to commemorate the 75th anniversary of the Dams Raid by 617 Squadron on 16/17 May 1943. Following a 24-page account of the raid and its results, detailed coverage is given to Barnes Wallis, *Upkeep* (the bouncing bomb), Guy Gibson VC (pages 49-57) and the aircrews. From page 86, the Squadron's operations for the rest of the war are documented. Pages 102-109 are devoted to the Squadron's two other VCs: Bill Reid (won serving with 61 Sqn) and Leonard Cheshire. Other features include the film *The Dam Busters* and commemorative flypasts over the Derwent.

R78   ROY, Reginald H.
FOR MOST CONSPICUOUS BRAVERY: A Biography of Major General George R Pearkes VC, through Two World Wars
University of British Columbia Press, Vancouver, Canada, 1977
388 pp, photos, maps, index, hb, cr

This comprehensive biography of Maj Gen Pearkes VC PC CC CB DSO MC CD relates his life as a distinguished Canadian soldier and statesman. Following a period in the Royal North West Mounted Police, he served throughout WW1 in the Canadian Mounted Rifles (VC, DSO, MC) and retired as GOC-in-C Pacific Command towards the end of WW2. His service is chronicled extensively and his VC action is detailed. The author then examines Pearkes' life as an MP, as Minister of National Defence and as Lieutenant Governor of British Columbia. Extensive notes relating the sources used by the author conclude the book.

R79   ROYAL REGIMENT OF WALES MUSEUM (*publisher*)
BETH A DDIGWYDDODD I'R ARWYR?: Brywdran Isandhlwana & Rorke's Drift / WHAT HAPPENED TO THE HEROES?: The Battles of Isandhlwana & Rorke's Drift
Royal Regiment of Wales Museum, Brecon, 2005
50 pp, illustrated, sb, cr (*Welsh and English text*)

This well-illustrated bilingual work provides a brief account of the 24th Regiment's involvement in the Anglo-Zulu War of 1879 but its principal focus is a biographical sketch of all those VCs won at Isandhlwana (three) and Rorke's Drift (eleven) on 22/23 January 1879. Two pages are devoted to each VC, including W Griffiths VC of the 24th, who won his VC in 1867 but was killed at Isandhlwana.

R80   ROYAL ARMY MEDICAL CORPS (*publisher*)
THE MEDICAL VICTORIA CROSSES
Royal Army Medical Corps Historical Museum, Aldershot, 1983 (reformatted: 1988)
89 pp. (1988 edition: 115pp.), artist's impressions, sb (1988 edition: hb), cr

This book covers the 39 VC recipients of the Army Medical Services of the British Army and Forces of the Crown. It provides for each recipient a biographical sketch, incorporating the VC citation, and an artist's impression of the VC deed which, in the 1988 hardback version of the book, is a full-sized colour plate.

R83   ROYAL COMMISSION OF THE WAR IN SOUTH AFRICA
EVIDENCE OF GENERAL THE RIGHT HON. SIR REDVERS BULLER VC GCB GCMG
Royal Commission on the War in South Africa, 1904
157 pp, sb, cr

A full transcript of the proceedings of the Royal Commission on the War in South Africa in taking evidence from General Buller in his preparation and conduct of the war. The transcript was prepared following the thirty-sixth day of proceedings on 17 Feb 1903. [The Commission comprised the Earl of Elgin and Kincardine (Chairman), the Viscount Esher, the Lord Strathcona and Mount-Royal, Sir George Dashwood Taubman-Goldie, Fld Mshl Sir Henry Wylie Norman, Sir Frederick Matthew Darley, Adm Sir John Ommanney Hopkins, Sir John Edge and Sir John Jackson].

R85   RULE, E.J., MC MM
        JACKA'S MOB: The Story of Albert Jacka's Victoria Cross
        Angus and Robertson, Sydney, 1933
        346 pp, hb, cr

        A memoir of an Australian farmer who served as a private, NCO and officer in the same battalion as Albert Jacka VC. Taken from notes made at the time of the action the book makes a tribute to the ANZAC soldier and Jacka VC. See also J24.

R86   RUNDELL, Anthony J.
        KARS: Victory into Defeat
        Impress, Nether Wescote, 2005
        220 pp, photos, hb, cr

        This book includes a selection of writings of Christopher Charles Teesdale, RA, who as a young lieutenant took part in the siege of Kars under Colonel William Fenwick Williams. Teesdale was awarded the VC for his exploits during the Russian assault on the town on 29 September 1855. Reviewed in V57.

R87   RUSSELL, Ernest
        LORD ROBERTS OF KANDAHAR AND WATERFORD F.M., VC, KP, GCB, GCSI, GCIE
        Henry J. Drane, London, 1901
        92 pp, frontis portrait, hb, cr

        A brief biography of Lord Roberts VC in *The Bijou Biographies Series*.

R88   RUSSELL, Jesse and COHN, Ronald
        HMNZS CHARLES UPHAM
        Bookvita Publishing (Lennox Corp), Edinburgh, 2012
        88 pp, sb, cr

        This print-on-demand publication describes a sea-lift vessel operated by the Royal New Zealand Navy and named after Charles Upham VC*. The ship was commissioned in 1995 but not deemed to be a success. It was decommissioned in May 1998 and sold to civilian service in 2001.

R89   RUSSELL, Wilfred
        NEW LIVES FOR OLD: The Story of the Cheshire Homes
        Victor Gollancz, London, 1963 (expanded 1969 and revised 1980)
        224 pp. (1969 edition: 246 pp.), photos, hb, cr

        The author, who was closely concerned with the Cheshire Foundation, describes the inception (in 1948) and evolution of the Cheshire Homes. There are many significant references to Leonard Cheshire's involvement with the Foundation and to his influence, as a visionary, in extending the work world-wide. The 1969 expanded version of the book contains a new chapter to cover the period 1963-68. An appendix lists all Cheshire Homes in existence or planned.

R90   RYAN, Mark
THE FIRST VCs: The Moving True Story of First World War Heroes Maurice Dease and Sidney Godley
The History Press, Stroud, 2014
223 pp, photos, map, index, hb, cr

Detailed biographies of the first two VCs of the Great War: Lt. Maurice Dease and Pte Sidney Godley who served with the 4th Royal Fusiliers and won their VCs in the first main British action of the war at Mons on 23 August 1914. Dease died of his wounds and Godley, also wounded, was made a POW. The author had access to photographs, letters and records from the families of the two recipients.

R91   RYDER, Commander R.E.D., VC RN
THE ATTACK ON ST NAZAIRE: 28th March, 1942
John Murray, London, 1947
118 pp, photos, sketches, maps, index, hb, cr

Ryder tells the story of Operation *Chariot*, the combined operation which he commanded against the dry dock facility in the port of St Nazaire, on 28 March 1942. He describes the rationale, planning and preparation for the attack and then gives a detailed account of the attack itself, which resulted in the award of five VCs (the author, Newman, Beattie, Savage and Durrant). The actions of Newman and Beattie are recalled. Ryder then assesses the outcome of the raid. An appendix lists, by ship, all naval personnel who took part in the operation.

R95   RYDER, Sue (Baroness Ryder of Warsaw, CMG OBE)
CHILD OF MY LOVE: An Autobiography
Collins Harvill, London, 1986 (revised, Harvill Press, 1997)
624 pp. (1997 edition: 656 pp.), photos, index, hb, cr

This autobiography is a record of the life and achievements of a remarkable woman who, following her wartime service in the Polish Section of the SOE, formed the Sue Ryder Foundation in 1953, devoting her life to the relief of suffering on the widest scale. She was created a Life Peer in 1978 for her humanitarian work. In 1959 she married Group Captain Leonard Cheshire VC DSO** DFC, who in 1948 originated the Cheshire Foundation. The work contains numerous references to Leonard Cheshire. Chapter 10 relates to their partnership. In the 1997 edition, this chapter has an additional 13 pages which are devoted to her remembrances of him and the tributes to him received by her following his death in 1992.

S2   SÆLEN, Frithjof
UNGE ANDERS LASSEN
John Griegs Forlag, Bergen, Norway, 1950
371 pp, photos, hb, cr (*Danish text*)

A Norwegian-text full biography of Major Anders Lassen VC MC**. Written in a fictional style, this book is mainly based on Suzanne Lassen's biography: *Anders Lassen: Sømand og Soldat*. (See L9).

S5   SANDERS, James
NEW ZEALAND VC WINNERS: The Story of New Zealand Servicemen Who Won the Greatest Honour for Valour on the Battlefield
Wilson & Horton, Auckland, New Zealand, 1974
48 pp, photos, drawings, maps, sb, cr

This well-illustrated magazine format book provides brief biographical accounts of each of the 21 VC recipients of the New Zealand forces. There is a also a list of the six other New Zealanders who won the VC serving in non-NZ forces and 18 other VCs who had other associations with New Zealand.

S6   SANDERS, James
VENTURER COURAGEOUS: Group Captain Leonard Trent VC DFC
Hutchinson, Auckland, New Zealand, 1983
266 pp, photos, sketch, index, hb, cr

A biography of Group Captain Trent who, as a RNZAF Squadron Leader, led an ill-fated attack on Amsterdam on 3 May 1943 for which he was awarded the VC. Following an account of his early years, the work then concentrates on Trent's service in the RNZAF and the RAF to which he transferred. It chronicles his war service, in detail, including his VC action, his capture and time as a POW in Stalag Luft III and his unsuccessful participation in the *Great Escape*. The book then recounts his post-war appointments up to his retirement from the RAF in the 1960s.

S15   SANDFORD, Kenneth
MARK OF THE LION: The Story of Capt Charles Upham, VC and bar
Hutchinson, London, 1962
287 pp, photos, hb, cr

A full biography of Charles Upham, the only man to win a VC and bar in WW2. Whilst its scope is from his birth in 1908 to the VC centenary celebrations, it concentrates on his WW2 service in the New Zealand Military Forces and his subsequent exploits as a POW. Following his numerous escape attempts, Upham was transferred to Colditz from where he was repatriated at the end of the war. In retirement, he became a sheep farmer.

S16   SANDFORD, Christopher
ZEEBRUGGE: The Greatest Raid of All
Casement Publishing, Oxford, 2018
181pp, photos (some colour), maps, index, hb cr

An account of the Zeebrugge raid on 22/23 April 1918 with eye witness accounts. Two of the author's great uncles took part in the operation: one was RD Sandford who won the VC. The eight VCs awarded for the action are included: Carpenter, Sandford, PT Dean, Bamford, Finch, AE McKenzie, GN Bradford and AL Harrison.

S17 SARKAR, Dilip
GUARDS VC: Blitzkrieg 1940
Ramrod Publications, Worcester, 1999
255 pp, photos, maps, index, hb, cr

This profusely-illustrated book tells the story of the 1st Guards Brigade between September 1939 and June 1945 from both British and German perspectives. In particular it gives a description of the action of 3rd Bn Grenadier Guards on 21 May 1940 in which L/Cpl Harry Nicholls was awarded the VC. It also recalls the VC deed of CSM George Gristock, 2nd Bn Royal Norfolk Regiment, which occurred on the same day. The work includes many previously unpublished British and German photographs.

S18 SASKATCHEWAN HERITAGE FOUNDATION (*publisher*)
"FOR VALOUR": Saskatchewan Victoria Cross Recipients
Saskatchewan Heritage Foundation, Canada, 1995
40 pp, photos, drawings, maps, sb, cr

This book was produced to celebrate the 16 Saskatchewan VC recipients on the 90th anniversary of the founding of the Province and the 50th anniversary of the end of WW2. Two pages are dedicated to each VC and contain a line-drawn portrait, a short description of their VC deed and a map showing the location of their memorial plaque in Saskatchewan.

S19 SATTERTHWAITE, Sue
BONNER VC: The Biography of Gus Bonner: VC and Master Mariner
SR Print Management Company, Aldridge, 2008
130pp, photos, hb, cr

This A5-sized book, which has 88 illustrations, describes the life of Q-Ship hero Gus Bonner VC DSC. The author had access to family archives, letters, documents and photographs to provide a detailed biography of a modest man whose career began in the merchant navy and after WW1 was involved in many naval salvage operations. There are a number of references to G Campbell VC, RN Stuart VC and W Williams VC. Reviewed in V63.

S20 SAWARD, M.H.
MEMOIR OF MAJOR-GENERAL SIR HENRY TOMBS VC KCB RA
Royal Artillery Institution, Woolwich, 1875
92 pp, photos, hb, cr

A comprehensive yet concise account of the life and military career of Maj Gen Tombs VC. Chapter 1 provides an ancestral history. The memoir then concentrates on describing his distinguished military career. The book concludes with an account of his death, the tributes to him and the founding of the Tombs Memorial Scholarship. Several portraits of Tombs and family members are provided. The appendix, which is updated periodically, is a list of winners of the Tombs Memorial Scholarship from its foundation in 1877. A leather-bound copy of the book was issued annually to the winner of the scholarship.

S21 S.B.
THE YARN OF THE VC SHIPS: Being the Adventures of Captain Gordon Campbell RN VC DSO in "Q" Ships
HH Tetley, Bradford, 1920
19 pp, photos, hb, cr

This small book describes the actions for which Gordon Campbell was awarded the VC and DSO while commanding Q ships. Other Q ship VCs covered are: Stuart, W Williams, Bonner and Pitcher.

S23   SCOTT, Carolyn
THE PILOT WHO CHANGED COURSE: Leonard Cheshire
Lutterworth Educational, London, 1972
36 pp, drawings, sb, cr

In this juvenile literature from the series *Biography for the Day*, the author gives an overview of the main events in Cheshire's life from his Oxford days through to his Foundation work.

S24   SCOTT, Michael
CEMETERIES AND MEMORIALS IN THE AREA OF THE BATTLES OF THE SOMME WHERE VCs ARE BURIED OR COMMEMORATED (Military Fact Sheet No. 6)
The Western Front Association, 1995
8 pp, sb, ncr

This publication has two tables with brief details of VC recipients with memorials for the Somme area. The first has the names in alphabetical order with name, rank, unit, brigade, division and the cemetery/memorial. The second table lists the cemeteries/memorials in alphabetical order with the name of the VC, the date and place of action and the date of death. (See C32, S25 and S26).

S25   SCOTT, Michael
CEMETERIES AND MEMORIALS IN FRANCE WHERE VCs ARE BURIED OR COMMEMORATED PART II: EXCLUDING THE SOMME (Military Fact Sheet No. 8)
The Western Front Association, 1996
8 pp, sb, ncr

This publication has two tables with brief details of VC recipients in France excluding the Somme area. The first has the names in alphabetical order with name, rank, unit, brigade, division and the cemetery/memorial. The second table lists the cemeteries/memorials in alphabetical order with the name of the VC, the date and place of action and the date of death. (See C32, S24 and S26).

S26   SCOTT, Michael
CEMETERIES AND MEMORIALS AROUND THE WORLD WHERE VCs ASSOCIATED WITH WORLD WAR ONE ARE BURIED OR COMMEMORATED (Military Fact Sheet No. 12)
The Western Front Association, 1998
9 pp, sb, ncr

This publication has two tables with brief details of VC recipients with memorials for WW1 not on the Western Front. The first has the names in alphabetical order with name, rank, unit, brigade, division and the cemetery/memorial. The second table lists the cemeteries/memorials in alphabetical order with the name of the VC, the date and place of action and the date of death. (See C32, S24 and S25).

S27   SCOTT, Stuart R.
BATTLE-AXE BLENHEIMS: No 105 Squadron RAF at War 1940-41
Sutton Publishing, Stroud, 1996
235 pp, photos, maps, sketch, index, hb, cr

The scope of this RAF squadron history is the period Aug 1940 - Oct 1941, during which the squadron was commanded by Wg Cdr HI Edwards (May-Oct 1941). The substantial references to Edwards include a chapter (pages 75-87) relating to his VC action in a raid on Bremen in July 1941. Additionally, Appendix 1 (pages 203-206) is a biographical sketch of him which, in particular, charts his distinguished flying career.

S28   SCOTT, Stuart
CHARLES DON'T SURF BUT AUSSIES DO: Tall tales and true from the Peter Badcoe Club
Watson, Ferguson & Co, Salisbury, Queensland, Australia, 2009
127 pp, sb, cr

During the Vietnam War some Australian servicemen set up a recreational centre which featured surfing. This facility is described by those who were there. It is named after one of the four Australians awarded the VC in Vietnam: Peter Badcoe VC. It was located at Vung Tau in South Vietnam.

S30   SEATON, Derek
A TIGER AND A FUSILIER: Leicester's VC Heroes
Published by author, Botcheston, Leicestershire, 2001
80 pp, photos, maps, index, sb, cr

This A4-sized book describes the lives of two Leicester VC winners: Robert Gee VC MC and William Buckingham VC. Both VC recipients, as young boys, were in the care of Leicester Board of Guardians and the Leicester Union Workhouse. Buckingham was killed in WW1 and Gee went on to become a Conservative MP. The book is profusely illustrated with pages 1-28 dedicated to Buckingham and pages 29-73 to Gee. Reviewed in V50.

S31   SEATON, Derek
THIS GALLANT STEELBACK: William Ewart Boulter VC
Published by author, Leicester, 2010
78 pp, photos, maps, index, sb, cr

This A4 format publication is a profusely illustrated biography of WE Boulter VC who won his VC as a Sergeant at Trones Wood on 14 July 1916. He served in the RAF in WW2 and died in 1955. Reviewed in V67.

S32   SELLAR, Edmund Francis
THE STORY OF LORD ROBERTS
TC & EC Jack, London, 1914
120 pp, coloured paintings, hb, cr

This small volume in *The Children's Heroes Series* gives a concise account of the life and career of Lord Roberts. Half of the book focuses on the Indian Mutiny. Subsequent chapters cover the campaigns in Abyssinia, Afghanistan and South Africa.

S33   SELLERS, Leonard
THE HOOD BATTALION, Royal Naval Division: Antwerp, Gallipoli, France 1914-1918
Leo Cooper, London, 1995
334 pp, photos, maps, index, hb, cr

The story of the Hood Battalion, RND from its formation in 1914 up to its disbandment at the end of WW1. There are substantial references to Freyberg VC (later Lt Gen and Baron) who served with the Battalion as a company commander from 1914 to 1915 and its commanding officer from 1915 to 1917 during which appointment he won the VC in France. The book includes an extensive list of reference sources used by the author.

S35   SELLWOOD, A.V.
           [1] **STAND BY TO DIE**
           New English Library, London, 1961
           128 pp, hb, cr
           [2] **HMS L1 WO: The Most Decorated Small Ship in the Navy**
           Amberley Publishing, Stroud, 2015
           158 pp, maps, sb, cr

The story of HMS *Li Wo*, a former Yangtse river steamer, and its gallant attack on an escorted Japanese convoy in the Java Sea in 1942 which earned its master, Lt Wilkinson, a posthumous VC. First-hand accounts of some of the ship's survivors have been used to describe the detail of this epic naval action.

S36   SHANKLAND, Peter and HUNTER, Anthony
           DARDANELLES PATROL
           Collins, London, 1964
           192 pp, photos, maps, hb, cr

The story of the operational service of HM Submarine *E11* and of her commander, Lt Cdr Nasmith (later Admiral Sir Martin Dunbar-Nasmith), in the Dardanelles in 1915. The book chronicles the patrol for which Nasmith was awarded the VC. It also provides an account of the services of the other submarines that participated in the operations which includes HM Submarine *E14*, commanded by Lt Cdr Boyle who was also awarded the VC for a preceding incident.

S37   SHANNON, Stephen D.
           BEYOND PRAISE: The Durham Light Infantrymen who were awarded the Victoria Cross
           County Durham Books, Durham, 1998
           60 pp, photos, sb, cr

This booklet provides brief biographical accounts of each of the 11 VC recipients of the Durham Light Infantry beginning with the Crimean War and ending with WW2. The text is supplemented with 32 photographs and a fact file on each recipient at the end of the volume. The Foreword was written by Capt RW Annand VC.

S38   SHARKEY, Lieutenant-Colonel A.J., CStJ TD
           FORGOTTEN HEROES: THE MILLERS OF RADWAY AND THEIR LINKS WITH THE BATTLE OF EDGEHILL, WATERLOO, AND A ROYAL ARTILLERY CRIMEA VC
           Edgehill Enterprises, Hampton in Arden, West Midlands, 2003
           48 pp, photos, sb, cr

A family history of the Millers of Radway which includes a 12-page chapter on Lt Frederick Miller VC, who won his award for action in the Crimean War. There is an account of why his award was so late in appearing in the LG. The remainder of the book deals with family genealogy.

S39   SHAW, John F. (*publisher*)
           VALOUR AND VICTORY
           John F Shaw, London, nd (c1900)
           256 pp, photos, drawings, hb, cr

This book contains, in its two 128-page parts, 20 factual and fictional stories relating to the Boer War and its personalities. Pages 22-37 (in Part 2) relate the story of Lord Roberts VC (who is also referred to elsewhere in the book). Pages 92-103 (Part 2) concern Sir George White VC and Sir Redvers Buller VC at Ladysmith.

S39A SHARP, Iain
HEAPHY
Auckland University Press, Auckland, New Zealand, 2008
232 pp, photos, drawings, paintings, maps, index, hb, cr

This scholarly work traces the life and career of Major Charles Heaphy VC, artist, explorer, surveyor and soldier, and is lavishly-illustrated with Heaphy's paintings, drawings and maps. The volume's six chapters document his early years, service with the New Zealand Company, experiences as an explorer, service as an MP, Commissioner of Native Reserves and government official in Auckland, his military service and award of the VC and his later years. Extensive notes support the text.

S40 SHEPPARD, Ruth
EXTRAORDINARY HEROES: The Amazing Stories of Victoria Cross and George Cross Recipients
Osprey, Oxford, 2010
120 pp, photos, sb, cr

This book was written to coincide with the opening of Lord Ashcroft Gallery at the Imperial War Museum in November 2010. On display at the time were over 160 VCs from the Lord Ashcroft Collection and the VCs and GCs already held by the Museum. The book typically devotes one or two pages to each VC and GC recipient. As in the exhibition, the book follows seven themes: boldness, aggression, leadership, skill, sacrifice, initiative and endurance. Each recipient is allocated to one of these categories. The Appendices list the VCs in the Lord Ashcroft Collection, VCs in the IWM collection and the GCs in the IWM collection as at November 2010.

S41 SHERRIFF, Marc J.
ARTYVICS: The Victoria Cross and The Royal Regiment of Artillery
Royal Artillery Heritage Trust, location not specified, 2006
74 pp, photos, index, sb, cr

This volume provides biographical information on the 62 VC recipients of the Royal Artillery. Arranged alphabetically (by surname), the biographies are in a standard format (typically a single page) identifying: rank (VC and highest), unit/service, date and location of VC action, event, *London Gazette* date, medal group composition, place and date of birth, place and date of death, grave location, VC inscriptions (Cross and suspender) and VC citation. The 'Contents' page lists the recipients chronologically by VC deed date and the 'Recipient Index' lists alphabetically by surname. Coloured photographs show six RA VC medal groups.

S41A SHERWOOD, Martyn
THE VOYAGE OF THE TAI-MO-SHAN
Rupert Hart-Davis, London, 1957
202 pp, photos, diagram, map, hb, cr (*fp* 1935)

This volume chronicles the planning and voyage of the 20-ton ketch *Tai-Mo-Shan* from Hong Kong to Dartmouth, England in 1933-34. The crew, all naval officers serving with the British China Squadron, comprised Lt Cdr MB Sherwood (the book's author), Lt RED Ryder (who won the VC in 1942), Lt PS Francis, Lt GS Salt and naval doctor Surg-Lt C Ommaney-Davis. They had the ketch built in Hong Kong and having been granted leave on half-pay, they set sail from Hong Kong on 31 May 1933. Taking the east-about route via Japan, Aleutian Islands, the west coast of North and Central America, and through the Panama Canal to the West Indies, they ran aground in the Bahamas. Refloated after two weeks, they sailed across the Atlantic Ocean, arriving at Dartmouth on 30 May 1934. Ten appendices provide navigational, technical and logistical data and narratives.

S42 SHIRLEY, Rachel, SHIRLEY, Raymond and ROWLEY, Christine
WINDOWS ON THE ZEEBRUGGE RAID 1918: With Rare Photographs of the Mole
CreateSpace Independent Publishing Platform, 2016
72 pp, photos, sb, ncr

This publication describes the Zeebrugge Raid in April 1918 for which eight VCs were awarded. It includes photographs taken by German naval officers of the Mole after the raid. Some of the photos were salvaged from craft fairs and flea markets.

S42A SHORTLAND, Jim
THE STORY OF THE DAMS RAID: A souvenir booklet to commemorate the 50th Anniversary of the 'Dambusters' 16th - 17th May 1943
Lincolnshire's Lancaster Association, Lincoln, 1993
24 pp, photos, sb, cr

This booklet provides a brief account of Operation *Chastise* for which Guy Gibson was awarded the VC. Following a biography of Barnes Wallis, coverage is given to the formation of 617 Squadron, its crewing, training and preparations, the attacks on the dams, the casualties and recognition.

S43 SIMS, Anthony
JOHN J SIMS VC: From Bloomsbury to Sevastopol
Fastprint Publishing, Peterborough, 2013
229 pp, photos (some colour), maps, index, sb, cr

A detailed biography of John Sims VC of 34th Regiment, who was awarded the VC for bravery at Sebastopol, aged 19. He received his award from Queen Victoria at the first VC investiture on 26 June 1857. The A5 sized volume charts Sims' background and includes a family tree. His army service is described in detail including the VC action. The author shares the surname of the recipient but is not related. Reviewed in V72.

S44 SIMPSON, Geoff
GUY GIBSON: Dam Buster
Pen & Sword Aviation, Barnsley, 2013
191 pp, photos, index, hb, cr

This is a well-researched and detailed biography of Guy Gibson VC who received his award for leading 617 Sqn on the Dams Raid in May 1943. The book is both concise and detailed, bringing to light new material and insights on a much written about Gibson. It traces his early life, service career to the Dams Raid, the raid itself and Gibson's search for a purposeful role after the raid. Gibson's fatal crash in September 1944 is covered in detail which the author concludes his death was "early and needless". Reviewed in V72.

S45 SINGH, Jaswant, and SINGH, Manvendra
TILL MEMORY SERVES: Victoria Cross Winners of India
Rupa & Co., New Delhi, India, 2007
198 pp, photos, maps, hb, cr

This book provides short biographies of the 40 VCs associated with the Indian Army between 1914 and 1945. At the beginning of the book is a reproduction of the first VC warrant followed by a chapter introducing the Victoria Cross. Each theatre of operations or campaign is described followed by brief biographies (typically three pages) of each VC recipient. The full citations from the *London Gazette* are shown in full for each recipient.

S46 SINGH, Lieutenant General Baljit
A TALE OF TWO VICTORIA CROSSES
Pentagon Press, New Delhi, India, 2017
82 pp, photos, drawings, hb, cr

The author recalls the life and exploits of two Indian Army subalterns, Lt JG Smyth of the 15th Ludhiana Sikhs and Lt Karamjeet Singh Judge of the 4th Bn, 15th Punjab Regiment, who won the VC thirty years apart, in 1915 and 1945. Their VC deeds are described in detail.

S47 SINGLETON-GATES, Peter
GENERAL LORD FREYBERG VC: An Unofficial Biography
Michael Joseph, London, 1963
328 pp, photos, index, hb, cr

A full biography of the life and career of Lt Gen Freyberg VC, under whom the author served in WW1. Following an account of his early years, the book then concentrates on Freyberg's distinguished military service. For most of WW1 he served in the RND's Hood Battalion and, whilst its commanding officer, was awarded the VC. During the inter-war years he remained in the British Army until 1938, when he retired. Recalled on the outbreak of WW2, he soon became commander of the NZ military forces and served with distinction in North Africa and in Crete. The book concludes with recalling his service as Governor-General of New Zealand and his death in 1963.

S48 SLATER, Guy (*editor*)
MY WARRIOR SONS: The Borton Family Diary 1914-1918
Peter Davies, London, 1973
228 pp, photos, index, hb, cr

The editor has assembled transcripts of the diaries of Lt Col Arthur Borton, compiled between 1914 and 1918. Whilst the diaries refer to various members of the Borton family they concentrate on the WW1 achievements and experiences of his two sons, Air Vice Marshal Amyas Borton CB CMG DSO AFC who had been recommended for (but was not awarded) the VC, and Lt Col Arthur Borton VC CMG DSO who won his VC in 1917. The editor has annotated many diary entries to provide background information or details not known or recorded by the diarist.

S49 SMITH, Adrian
MICK MANNOCK, FIGHTER PILOT: Myth, Life and Politics
Palgrave, Basingstoke (in association with King's College, London), 2001
211 pp, photo, index, hb, cr

A reappraisal of the life and war service of Major Edward Mannock VC DSO MC, examining how he has been portrayed factually and fictionally. It also traces the development of his socialist beliefs and how these influenced his approach to collaboration in air combat. The book is part of a series of *Studies in Military and Strategic History*.

S50   SMITH, M.
THE STAFFORDSHIRE REGIMENT 80TH FOOT AT THE INTOMBI RIVER DRIFT 1879
np, nd
12 pp, photos, map, sb, cr

This A4-sized volume is devoted wholly to the action at Intombi River Drift in March 1879 in which the 80th Foot were attacked by over 5,000 Zulus. Out of the Regiment's 105 officers and men, two officers and 43 men were killed and 17 were missing. In addition to an in-depth account of the battle, based on historical records and statements from those men who took part, a detailed account of the VC action of Sgt Booth is given. The 80th's casualties are listed on pages 10-12.

S51   SMITH, Melvin Charles
AWARDED FOR VALOUR: A History of the Victoria Cross and the Evolution of British Heroism
Palgrave Macmillan, Basingstoke, 2008
281 pp, index, hb, ncr

An examination of the history and evolution of the VC from the Crimea to the present day. The author analyses the complex interactions between civilian culture, governmental and military policy and the changing face of warfare in setting the standards required for the bestowal of the VC. The volume contains 14 statistical tables, particularly for WW1, categorizing the VC acts in order to make comparisons. An Appendix contains all the VC Warrants from 1856 to 1961. There are full source notes for each chapter and a detailed bibliography. A total of 266 VCs are mentioned briefly but usually as means of illustrating a particular point. (See C145). Reviewed in V61.

S56   SMITHERS, A.J.
WONDER ACES OF THE AIR: The Flying Heroes of the Great War
Gordon & Cremonesi, London, 1980
212 pp, photos, index, hb, cr

The author has selected ten of the greatest Allied fighter aces of WW1 and, in a chapter for each ace, recalls their life, character and career. Four VCs are covered: Ball (pages 47-60), McCudden (pages 61-82), Bishop (pages 83-95) and Mannock (pages 96-113).

S57   SMY, W.A., and FERGUSON, A.F.D.
INTERESTING TIMES: A Biography of G.T. Lyall VC
Privately published, Canada, nd
121 pp, photos, maps, sb, cr

A biography of Colonel GT Lyall who won his VC in the Great War and died in active service in North Africa in November 1941. Lyall's life is covered in six chapters (pages 1 to 58) with 10 appendices. Appendix 9 covers his VC and medals.

S58   SMY, Lieutenant Colonel William A., OMM CD UE with FERGUSON, Alexander F. D.
FOR VALOUR: Colonel Graham Thomson Lyall VC
Published privately, Fort Erle, Ontario, Canada, 2009
178 pp, sb, cr

A biography of GT Lyall VC covering his early years, military service including his VC action as a Lieutenant in the CEF on 27 September 1918 near Cambrai. His inter-war life is described and service in the RAOC in WW2 and death on active service in Egypt in November 1941.

S59 SMYTH, Brigadier Sir John, Bt VC MC MP
RETREAT FROM BURMA 1942
Army Publishers, Delhi, nd (c1957)
135 pp, photos, map, hb, cr

This book was published in India under arrangements of Cassell, London who published S60. It contains a description of the retreat of 17th Division, under the command of the author, following the Japanese invasion of Burma in 1942. According to the author his Division received a cold reception on their return and were treated with contempt because their defeat resulted in the loss of Burma to the Japanese.

S60 SMYTH, Brigadier Sir John, Bt VC MC MP
BEFORE THE DAWN: A Story of Two Historic Retreats
Cassell, London, 1957
220 pp, photos, maps, index, hb, cr

The book describes, fully, two major retreats of WW2 - Dunkirk in 1940 and Burma in 1942 - as seen through the eyes of the author. Smyth commanded 127th Infantry Brigade at Dunkirk and the 17th Division in Burma. It is a story of bitter fighting under the most difficult circumstances and Smyth assesses where he believes the responsibility lies for each failure.

S61 SMYTH, Brigadier Sir John, Bt VC MC MP
THE ONLY ENEMY: An Autobiography
Hutchinson, London, 1959
352 pp, photo, index, hb, cr

This memoir describes the five main stages in the author's life: before WW1; service in WW1 (during which he was awarded the VC); soldiering in the inter-war years; his WW2 military commands, forced retirement and new career in journalism; and his political life and interests in the post-war years. S70 is an updated account of Smyth's life.

S62 SMYTH, Brigadier Rt Hon Sir John, Bt VC MC MP
THE STORY OF THE VICTORIA CROSS 1856-1963
Frederick Muller, London, 1963
496 pp, photos, index, hb, ncr (except author)

The book reviews the history of the VC in five main phases: 1854-1914; 1914-1919; 1920-1939; 1939-1945; after 1945. For each phase, a selection of VC deeds is described (by conflict for the 1854-1914 part and by year for 1914-1919 and 1939-1945). At the end of each chapter is a comprehensive list of associated VC recipients showing rank, unit, action location/date and LG date. A further chapter describes the VC centenary and the birth of the VC and GC Association. The appendices include statistical data of VC awards, transcripts of extracts of *London Gazette* VC warrants and a list of VC recipients (and their relatives) who attended the 1962 Garden Party at Buckingham Palace.

S63 SMYTH, Brigadier Rt Hon Sir John, Bt VC MC MP
THE VICTORIA CROSS 1856-1964: A Shorter Version of the Standard Work
Frederick Muller, London, 1965
221 pp, photos, index, sb, ncr (except author)

An abridged version of S62, which contains a similar but slightly shorter narrative and omits the lists of awards appended to each chapter.

S64 SMYTH, Brigadier Rt Hon Sir John, Bt VC MC
THE VALIANT
AR Mowbray, London, 1970
236 pp, photos, index, hb, cr

A selection of 20 gallant actions performed by units of Britain and her Empire spanning the period 1758 to 1945. A chapter is devoted to each action, five of which relate specifically to the VC deeds of: Grenfell, G Campbell, Roope, Gibson, D Cameron, Place, IE Fraser and Magennis. Brief accounts of other VC actions are included in some other chapters.

S67 SMYTH, Brigadier Rt Hon Sir John, Bt VC MC
LEADERSHIP IN WAR 1939-1945: The Generals in Victory and Defeat
David & Charles, London, 1974
247 pp, photos, index, hb, cr

An examination of the achievements and leadership qualities of 66 British and Empire, Allied and Axis military leaders in WW2 in the context of four theatres of war. Five VC generals are covered: Chapter 1 (Dunkirk and Battle of Britain) covers Gort VC and Neame VC; Chapter 2 (North Africa - 1st phase) Neame VC, Carton de Wiart VC and Freyberg VC; Chapter 3 (North Africa – 2nd phase) Freyberg VC; Chapter 4 (Far East) JG Smyth VC (ie the author). This work is a companion volume to S68.

S68 SMYTH, Brigadier Rt Hon Sir John, Bt, VC MC
LEADERSHIP IN BATTLE 1914-1918: Commanders in Action
David & Charles, Newton Abbott, 1975
191 pp, photos, maps, index, hb, cr

An assessment of WW1 as it was experienced by some British leaders, at all levels, and by two French generals. The work concerns, primarily, the campaigns in France, Gallipoli and Palestine. The author, who had first-hand experience of WW1 (VC), also examines the qualities that make great commanders. There are numerous brief accounts of VC deeds to illustrate leadership in battle. This work is a companion volume to S67.

S69 SMYTH, Brigadier Rt Hon Sir John, Bt VC MC
GREAT STORIES OF THE VICTORIA CROSS
Arthur Barker, London, 1977
192 pp, photos, index, hb, cr

The author has selected 32 thematic or specific VC actions to narrate the story of the VC from the Crimean War to the end of WW2. A brief description is given of the VC deed of many recipients. One chapter is dedicated to Gordon Campbell VC.

S70 SMYTH, Brigadier Rt Hon Sir John, Bt, VC MC
MILESTONES: A Memoir
Sidgwick & Jackson, London, 1979
304 pp, photos, index, hb, cr

A full autobiography written in Smith's eighty-sixth year and four years before his death. The book covers his family background and early days, his service career in WW1 (VC), the interwar years (MC), and WW2 and the post-war years as author, politician and Chairman of the VC and GC Association. There is a chapter relating to his career as an author and in which he describes all the books he had written. (S61 is his earlier autobiography, written in 1959.)

S74   SNELLING, Stephen
COMMANDO MEDIC: Doc Harden VC
Spellmount, Stroud, 2012
240 pp, photos, maps, index, hb, cr

This biography of (Henry) Eric Harden records his life from his childhood in Northfleet, Kent through the Second World War and his death in action while rescuing wounded men under enemy fire while he himself was wounded. This was the deed in Holland in January 1945 for which he was awarded his posthumous VC. Before the war Harden was a butcher by trade and a member of St John Ambulance Brigade in his spare time. During the Blitz he was an ambulance driver. He joined the Royal Artillery in 1942 but was soon transferred to the RAMC and attached to a Royal Marine Commando unit, where he took part in the D-Day landings and the liberation of NW Europe. See H22.

S75   SNELLING, Stephen
VCs OF THE FIRST WORLD WAR: GALLIPOLI
[1] Alan Sutton Publishing, Stroud, 1995
264 pp, photos, maps, index, hb, cr
[2] The History Press, Stroud, 2010
274 pp, photos, maps, index, sb, cr

This book covers the 39 VCs awarded for action at Gallipoli in 1915. A chapter is devoted to each VC recipient or group of recipients for multiple-award actions. Each account contains information about the recipient's family background, early years, military career, post-service life (if applicable) and death. It also describes their VC deed in the context of the campaign. The text is accompanied by over 100 illustrations and the extensive sources used by the author are listed to conclude the work. The book is part of the series *VCs of The First World War*. See G31 annotation, second paragraph.

S76   SNELLING, Stephen
VCs OF THE FIRST WORLD WAR: PASSCHENDAELE 1917
[1] Sutton Publishing, Stroud, 1998
280 pp, photos, maps, index, hb, cr
[2] The History Press, Stroud, 2012
303 pp, photos, maps, index, sb, cr

This book covers the 61 VCs awarded in 3rd Battle of Ypres in 1917. A chapter is devoted to each VC recipient or group of recipients for multiple-award actions. Each account contains information about the recipient's family background, early years, military career, post-service life (if applicable) and death. It also describes their VC deed in the context of the campaign. The text is supported by many photographs and maps. The book is part of the series *VCs of The First World War*. See G31 annotation, second paragraph.

S77   SNELLING, Stephen
VCs OF THE FIRST WORLD WAR: THE NAVAL VCs
[1] Sutton Publishing, Stroud, 2002
280 pp, photos, index, hb, cr
[2] The History Press, Stroud, 2010
280 pp, photos, index, sb, cr

This book covers the 42 naval VCs of WW1 but excludes VCs awarded to RNAS and Royal Naval Division. A chapter is devoted to each VC recipient or group of recipients for multiple-award actions. Each account contains information about the recipient's family background, early years, service career, post-service life (if applicable) and death. It also describes their VC deed in the context of the operation. The text is supported by many photographs and maps. The book is part of the series *VCs of The First World War*. See G31 annotation, second paragraph. Reviewed in V50.

S78   SNELLING, Stephen

THE WOODEN HORSE OF GALLIPOLI: The Heroic Saga of SS *River Clyde*, a WWI icon told through the accounts of those who were there

Frontline Books, (Pen and Sword Books), Barnsley, 2017

408 pp, photos, maps, index, hb, cr

Part of *Voices from the Past* series this book tells the story of the SS *River Clyde* which was beached at Gallipoli to land attacking troops. It describes how the plan was devised, the men who sailed and their bravery in establishing a bridgehead at Gallipoli despite fierce resistance from the opposing Turkish forces. CHM Doughty-Wylie VC is covered in a chapter and there is significant coverage of others awarded the VCs in the action: E Unwin, GL Drewry, W St A Malleson, W Williams, G McK Samson and AW St C Tisdall.

S79   SNOOK, Lieutenant Colonel Mike

LIKE WOLVES ON THE FOLD: The Defence of Rorke's Drift

Greenhill Books, London, 2006

302 pp, photos, diagrams, index, hb, cr

A highly illustrated description of the defence of Rorke's Drift in January 1879 for which 11 VCs were awarded. The deeds of each VC recipient are covered.

S79A   SNOW, Richard

ALL FOR VALOUR: The Story of Captain John Brunt VC MC

The Marketing Solution, Paddock Wood, Kent, nd, (c2006)

144 pp, photos, map, sb, cr

A biography of John Brunt from his birth in 1922 to his death in action in 1944. The author traces his early life in Shropshire and service history in the army including his part in the Italian campaign. Brunt was awarded the MC for his actions on 13/14 December 1943 and the VC for action on 9 December 1944. He was killed in action the following day.

S79B   SNOW, Richard

TEN BRAVE MEN AND TRUE: The Victoria Cross Holders from the Borough of Tunbridge Wells

Menin House Publishers (Tommies Guide), Brighton, 2012

344 pp, photos (some colour), index, sb, cr

This A4-sized book provides biographies of 10 VC recipients connected to Tunbridge Wells. The recipients covered are: C Lucas, W Temple, JD Grant, Douglas Belcher, W Addison, L Queripel, John Brunt, MC Dixon, ES Dougall and HW Clark-Kennedy. The author interviewed a number of the descendants of the VCs. This book includes a number of previously unpublished photographs. Reviewed in V71.

S79C   SØRENSEN, Bent

JENSEN OG VERDENSKRIGEN; En fortælling om en dreng fra Løgstør, der under Første Verdenskrig tradte ind i den australske hær og vandt Victoriakorset

Forlaget Krejl, Løgstør, 2006

111 pp, photos, drawing, maps, index, sb,

A Danish-text biography of Jørgen Christian Jensen VC. The title means: "Jensen and the World War: An account of a boy from Løgstør who during WW1 joined the Australian army and won the VC". The book describes Jensen's life and military career from his birth in Løgstør in Denmark until his death in Australia in 1922.

S80   SOTHEBY'S (*publisher*)
AN EXHIBITION OF IMPORTANT BRITISH GALLANTRY AWARDS, 1800-1950
Sotheby's, London, 1992
76 pp, photos, sb, cr

A publication to accompany a special exhibition (in May/June 1992) of British gallantry awards, to mark the 50th anniversary of the Orders and Medals Research Society. The work comprises a biographical sketch, a photographic portrait (or artist's impression) and a photograph of the medal group of 35 gallant men and women including 17 VC recipients. Despite the period covered by the catalogue (1800-1950), Bill Speakman (whose VC action in Korea was in November 1951) is also featured.

S85   SOUTHDOWN PRESS (*publisher*)
FOR VALOUR: The Story of the Victoria Cross
Southdown Press, Melbourne, Australia, nd (post-1967)
39 pp, photos, maps, sb, cr

A magazine-format account of 16 ANZAC VC winners: Jacka, Freyberg, Partridge, Heaphy, FH McNamara, Upham, J Maxwell, CGW Anderson, Newton, Badcoe, Cutler, Howse, HW Murray, Derrick, McCarthy, HI Edwards. The text is supplemented by their portraits and illustrations of their VC deed. The citations of all 119 ANZAC VC winners are also recorded.

S86   SOWARD, Stuart E.
A FORMIDABLE HERO: Lt R.H. Gray VC DSC RCNVR
Canav Books, Toronto, Canada, 1987
187 pp, photos, index, hb, cr

The biography of Lt RH Gray, whose VC action was on 9 August 1945. The book focuses on his naval service which commenced with the RCNVR in 1940. It chronicles his training for war, as a pilot flying Corsairs, and his operational service which culminated in carrier-borne operations in the Pacific. Lt Cdr Soward describes, in detail, Gray's last flight which resulted in the award of a posthumous VC. The epilogue contains photographs, tributes and memorials to Gray. Transcripts of tribute letters are in the appendix.

S87   SPATH, Frank
HOW THE CHESHIRE HOMES STARTED
Leonard Cheshire Foundation, London, 1977
31 pp, photos, sb, cr

The author, in collaboration with Group Captain Leonard Cheshire VC, gives an account of the founding and development of the Cheshire Homes.

S88   SPIES, S.B.
[1] ROBERTS AND KITCHENER AND CIVILIANS IN THE BOER REPUBLICS, January 1900 - May 1902
PhD Thesis for University of Witwatersrand, South Africa, 1973
494 pp, hb, cr
[2] METHODS OF BARBARISM? Roberts and Kitchener and Civilians in the Boer Republics: January 1900 – May 1902
Human & Rousseau, Cape Town and Pretoria, South Africa, 1977
416 pp, photos, index, hb, cr

An examination of the policies of Field Marshal Lord Roberts VC and General Lord Kitchener towards non-combatants in the Boer territories between January 1900 and May 1902. It also assesses the policy and personality clashes between Sir Alfred Milner (Governor of the Cape and British High Commissioner in South Africa) and Roberts and Kitchener. Professor Spies sourced this work from a significant array of private and public papers. The text of the book is substantially the same as that which he used previously for his 494-paged PhD thesis, which had been approved by the University of Witwatersrand in 1973.

S88A   SPOONER, Tony, DSO DFC
SUPREME GALLANTRY: Malta's Role in the Allied Victory 1939-1945
John Murray, London, 1996
358 pp, photos, maps, index, hb, cr

This full account of the attacks made from Malta against the Axis forces during WW2 contains extensive reference to the exploits of HMS *Upholder* commanded by Lt Cdr MD Wanklyn VC DSO and two bars. In particular, Chapter 4 (pages 44-73) entitled *Success and a VC* concerns the period April-October 1941.

S89   SPRINGMAN, Michael (*editor*)
SHARPSHOOTER IN THE CRIMEA
Pen and Sword, Barnsley, 2005
228 pp, photo, maps, index, hb, cr

This book is based on 60 letters written by Gerald Goodlake VC between March 1854 and May 1856. The principal subject matter is divided into six chapters which cover different phases of the campaign together with chapters on the origin and reasons for the Crimean War. Reviewed in V56.

S90   STANDARD ART BOOK COMPANY (*publisher*)
DEEDS THAT THRILL THE EMPIRE: True Stories of the Most Glorious Acts of Heroism of the Empire's Soldiers during the Great War
[1] Standard Art Book Company, London, nd (c.1917)
888 pp, artist's impressions, index, hb, cr
[2] Naval & Military Press, c2001 (*facsimile*)
Two volume set
903 pp, artist's impressions, index, hb, cr

This classic work describes many deeds of WW1 that resulted in the award of the VC, DSO, MC, DCM, DSM, IOM or CB. Each chapter is devoted to a recipient and is supported by an artist's impression of the deed. In this format, 56 VCs are covered. The VC deeds of many other recipients are illustrated by captioned artists' impressions. The work was issued as a weekly magazine but, subsequently, was bound (with decorative boards) in sets of two to five volumes.

S92   STANISTREET, Allan
BRAVE RAILWAYMEN
Token Publishing, Grayshott, Surrey, 1989
141 pp, photos, hb, cr

This book provides illustrated biographical sketches of the 21 railwaymen who were awarded either the VC, GC, Albert Medal or Sea Gallantry Medal. The five VC recipients covered are: J Rivers, E Sykes, JA Christie, W Wood and J Meikle. Photographs and details of the locomotives named after Wood, Sykes and Christie are included.

S93   STANISTREET, Allan
'GAINST ALL DISASTER: Gallant Deeds Above and Beyond the Call of Duty
Picton Publishing, Chippenham, 1986
197 pp, photos, index, hb, cr

Since Sir John Smyth VC published his works on the VC in 1963 (see S60), and on the GC in 1968 (see Part 2), additional awards have been made and the Edward and Albert Medals have been exchanged for the George Cross. This book chronicles the seven VCs awarded since 1963 (Limbu, Badcoe, Wheatley, Payne, Simpson, "H" Jones and McKay), the 13 GCs awarded between 1968 and 1986 and the 132 awards exchanged for the GC. A brief biographical account of each recipient is provided.

S95   STANNUS, Lieutenant General Henry James
CURIOSITIES OF THE VICTORIA CROSS
William Ridgway, London, 1882
40 pp, hb, cr

Unlike other books on the Victoria Cross, this work denounces the criteria for the award of the VC and circumstances in which the VC was awarded, particularly in the Afghan War. Although no VC recipient is mentioned by name, the circumstances described provide a clue to their identity.

S100   STANWAY, Kate (*compiler*)
BRITANNIA'S CALENDAR OF HEROES
George Allen, London, 1909
412 pp, photos, sketches, index, hb, ncr

This unusual book gives, by date of anniversary, a brief account of the heroic deeds that resulted in the awards of the VC, EM, AM, KPM, NZC and the gallantry medals of various British societies and institutions. Of the 522 VCs awarded to 1909 and recorded in the book, the compiler has included a facsimile signature of 160 recipients, which she has arranged according to the month of the VC deed.

S101   STANWAY, Kate
SONS OF VALOUR: A Complete Record of Victoria Cross Heroes From Its Institution to the Present
Henry J Drane, London, 1907
142 pp, index, hb, ncr

This book contains citations or very brief accounts of the deeds of all VC recipients from 1854 to 1904. A complete listing of all 522 VC recipients appears at the end of the volume.

S110   STARR, Alison
NEVILLE HOWSE VC: Biography of an Authentic Australian Hero
Les Baddock, Sydney, 1991
105 pp, photos, map, hb, cr

Written by his daughter, this book narrates the life and achievements of Surg Gen Hon Sir Neville Howse VC KCB KCMG who, after a distinguished medical career in the Australian forces, became a cabinet minister in the Australian government. It describes his family background and early years and then concentrates on his military career and campaigns in the Boer War (VC) and WW1. The book concludes with an account of his political career and his death in 1930.

S115   STATIONERY OFFICE, THE (*publisher*)
THE BOER WAR: LADYSMITH AND MAFEKING, 1900
The Stationery Office, London, 1999
212 pp, map, sb, cr

An abridged version of five Command Papers of 1901 and 1902 relating to the despatches covering the Siege and Relief of Ladysmith and the Siege and Relief of Mafeking. The despatches include those of Lord Roberts VC, Sir Redvers Buller VC and Sir George White VC.

S118   STAUNTON, Anthony
VICTORIA CROSS: Australia's Finest and the Battles they Fought
Hardie Grant Books, Prahan, Victoria, Australia, 2005
358 pp, photos, maps, index, sb, cr

This is a revised and updated version of W70. Pages 1 to 289 cover each of the 96 Australian VC recipients with a full-page photograph and approximately 1000 words of text including the full LG citation. The chapters chronologically cover wars and campaigns from the Boer War to Vietnam. Pages 290 to 339 cover 21 Australian recipients of the George Cross, both direct and exchange awards, in the same format as that for the VCs. One of the appendices lists other VC and GC recipients who had some association with Australia including those who died there. Reviewed in V57.

S123   STEVENS, Major General W.G., CB CBE
FREYBERG VC: THE MAN 1939-1945
AH & AW Reed, Wellington, New Zealand, 1965
130 pp, photos, hb, cr

The author's personal memoir of Lt Gen Lord Freyberg VC, on whose staff he served for the duration of WW2. Maj Gen Stevens provides an intimate insight into the character of Freyberg as a leader and as a man.

S124   STEVENSON, Lee
THE RORKE'S DRIFT DOCTOR: James Henry Reynolds, VC and the Defence of Rorke's Drift, 22nd-23rd January 1879
Lee Stevenson Publishing, Brighton, 2001
284 pp, photos, map, index, sb, cr

A full biography of JH Reynolds who was awarded his VC for bravery at Rorke's Drift. The book covers his family and ancestry. His part in the action at Rorke's Drift is covered in detail as well as biographical details both before and after his military service. Details are included of the patients at Rorke's Drift and information on the Army Medical Department, one of the forerunners of the RAMC.

S125   STEWART, Charles H.
A RECORD OF VALOUR: Canadian Recipients of the Victoria Cross and Medal of Honor
Privately published, Toronto, 1987
133 pp, index, sb, cr

This publication records the full LG citation for each of the 93 awards of the VC to Canadians and gives brief biographical details of each recipient. It also includes the citations of the 55 Canadian recipients of the Medal of Honor of the USA.

S126   STEWART, William F.
THE EMBATTLED GENERAL: Sir Richard Turner and the First World War
McGill-Queen's University Press, Montreal, Quebec, 2015
374 pp, maps, photos, index, hb, cr

This book focuses on the WW1 service of Lieutenant General Sir Richard Turner VC in which he commanded a Canadian Infantry Brigade and later the 2nd Canadian Division. The controversy over his leadership in the field is examined and his move to become GOC of Canadian Forces in England in 1916-18. In this position he was able to reform an administration in chaos. Turner won his VC in the Boer War on 7 November 1900.

S128   STEWART, Major Rupert (*compiler*)
THE BOOK OF THE VICTORIA CROSS
Hugh Rees, London, 1916
555 pp, photo, sketches, index, hb, ncr

A complete record of those who were awarded the VC from its institution up to 1916. Arranged by service and by regiment or corps, it reproduces the LG citation for each award. An alphabetical index by recipient is included. (See S129).

S129   STEWART, Lieutenant Colonel Rupert, MVO (*compiler*)
THE VICTORIA CROSS: The Empire's Roll of Valour
Hutchinson, London, 1928
469 pp, one photo, index, hb, ncr

A complete record of those who were awarded the VC from its institution up to 1928. Arranged by service and by regiment or corps, it reproduces the LG citation for each award. Chronological and alphabetical indexes are included. (See S128).

S130   STINGLHAMBER, Colonel G.M., DSO (*translated by* LANGDALE, Major C.S.)
THE STORY OF ZEEBRUGGE WITH AN ACCOUNT OF THE BLOCKING OF ZEEBRUGGE
Zeebrugge Museum, Belgium, 1932
48 pp, photos, maps, sb, cr

After a short history of the port of Zeebrugge, the book concentrates on the blocking of Zeebrugge action on 23 April 1918 and the follow-up attack on Ostend. The associated VC exploits are described in the context of the action. The final part of the book describes the restoration of the harbours and the development of the Zeebrugge Museum and the memorials to the attack. The author was the manager of the Zeebrugge Museum at the time of publication.

S132   STOCK, James W.
ZEEBRUGGE 23 April 1918
Ballantine Books, New York, 1974
159 pp, photos, maps, sb, cr

This *Battle Book No.* 3 in Ballantine's *Illustrated History of the Violent Century* series is a detailed and well-illustrated account of the naval raid on Zeebrugge in April 1918 and on Ostend in May 1918. It recounts in the context of the operations the associated VC deeds, particularly the role played by Capt AFB Carpenter.

S133   STONE, A.G., OBE
THE CAMPAIGNS AND MEDALS OF THE HONOURABLE EAST INDIA COMPANY AND THE INDIAN ARMY; THE VICTORIA CROSS OF THE HONOURABLE EAST INDIA COMPANY AND THE INDIAN ARMY
Military Press International, London, 1997
73 pp, hb, ncr

This work comprises two sections. The first section (pages 4-44), which is a reprint of a 1974 publication by the author, lists every campaign in which the HEIC or Indian Army participated and records the associated medals and clasps issued. The second section (pages 45-73) is a complete alphabetical listing of the VCs relating to these forces. The list records the recipient's rank and unit at the time of the VC deed, the location and date of deed, *LG* date, final rank, other decorations and date of death.

S134   STOSSEL, Katie
A HANDFUL OF HEROES: Rorke's Drift - Facts, Myths and Legends
Pen & Sword Military, Barnsley, 2015
201 pp, photos, drawings, index, hb, cr

A collection of material relating to Rorke's Drift. The book includes letters from Augustus Hammar, a young Swedish friend and visitor of the Rev Otto Witt, whose mission had been requisitioned by the British. Hammar retreated to the hills and watched as the British were defeated at Isandlwana. He headed back to Rorke's Drift but was again forced into the hills and from there watched the attack on the Mission. There is a detailed and critical analysis of Chard's report after the action and the bravery of VCs not at Rorke's Drift are also covered: Melvill, Coghill and Wassall. Reviewed in V77.

S135   STRANG, Herbert
STORIES OF THE INDIAN MUTINY
Henry Frowde, Hodder and Stoughton, London, nd (c1912)
160 pp, artist's impressions, map, hb, cr

A collection of narratives of striking episodes in the Indian Mutiny, based on contemporary records and eye-witness accounts. The chapter entitled *Lucknow Kavanagh* (pages 114-139) is Kavanagh's own account of his VC action at Lucknow (see K5). He also wrote the following chapter (pages 140-160) describing the relief of Lucknow and his personal involvement in the episode.

S136   SURRIDGE, Keith Terrance
MANAGING THE SOUTH AFRICAN WAR, 1899-1902: Politicians -v- Generals
The Boydell Press, Woodbridge, Suffolk (for the Royal Historical Society), 1998
205 pp, maps, index, hb, cr

This work examines the disputes that arose between the British Government and Sir Alfred Milner, the High Commissioner for South Africa, and the three leading British generals, Lord Wolseley, Lord Roberts VC and Lord Kitchener, over whether the politicians or generals should control the strategic management of the war in South Africa (1899-1902). The outcomes of the disputes are appraised. There are a number of references to Sir Redvers Buller VC.

S138   SUTHERLAND, Ivan Lorin George
THE NGARIMU HUI: VC Investiture Meeting, 1943
Polynesian Society, Wellington, New Zealand, 1949
40 pp, photos, sb, cr

This booklet, *Polynesian Society Memoir No 28*, commemorates 2nd Lt Moana-Nui-a-Kiwa Ngarimu, the only Maori to be awarded the VC. Following a full transcript of his VC citation, the work contains a nine-page account of his posthumous VC investiture in 1943. Pages 14-40 are illustrated with photographs of the preparation for the investiture and of Maori life in the locality of his village.

S140   SUTTON, Chris
FOR KING & COUNTRY: Smethwick's Two VCs of the First World War
Smethwick Heritage Centre, Smethwick, West Midlands, 2012
56 pp, photos, sb, cr

This book provides biographies of two WW1 recipients from Smethwick: H James and HG Colley. Lt James VC was with the Worcestershire Rgt when he won his VC at Gallipoli in 1915. Sergeant Colley VC won his VC at Martinpuich on 25 August 1918 but was killed on 22 October 1918. Reviewed in V70.

S141   SUTTON, Chris
FROM SMETHICK TO ST NAZAIRE: The Life of Bill Savage VC
Smethwick Heritage Centre, Smethwick, West Midlands, 2012
76 pp, photos, sb, cr

A short biography of Able Seaman WA Savage VC who won a posthumous VC for his actions on the raid on the dry dock at St Nazaire on 27/28 March 1942. The author accessed material from Savage's family and interviewed a survivor of MGB*314*. This vessel was used by Commander Robert Ryder VC, the commanding officer of the raid and there is detail on life aboard the vessel before the raid as well as the raid itself. Ryder recommended Savage for his award. Reviewed in V71.

S142   SWEETMAN, John
OPERATION CHASTISE: The Dams Raid: Epic or Myth (*original title*)
THE DAMBUSTERS RAID (*1990 title*)
Jane's Publishing, London, 1982 (revised and retitled: Arms and Armour Press, London, 1990)
218 pp. (1990 edition: 219 pp.), photos, index, hb, cr

Dr Sweetman, Head of the Department of Defence and International Affairs, at Sandhurst, re-examines Operation *Chastise* - the Dams Raid for which Wg Cdr Gibson was awarded the VC. With the benefit of newly-released official reports he reassesses the impact of the raid. Gibson's involvement in establishing 617 Squadron is chronicled. An extensive bibliography concludes the work.

S143   SWEETMAN, John
THE OFFICIAL DAMBUSTERS EXPERIENCE
Carlton Books, London, 2013
64 pp, plus enclosures, hb (boxed), cr

This publication is a boxed edition with enclosures and facsimile documents relating to the dambuster raid of 16/17 May 1943 to commemorate the 70th anniversary. It includes extract from log books, flight plans, eye-witness accounts on the damage inflicted on the dams and other material relating to the raid.

S144   SWEETMAN, John, COWARD, David and JOHNSTONE, Gary
THE DAMBUSTERS
Time Warner Books, London, 2003
192 pp, photos, maps, index, hb, cr

This well-illustrated book accompanied the Channel 4 Television's major documentary commemorating the 60th anniversary of the Dams Raid in May 1943. The book provides a very detailed account of the 1943 operation from its planning to its execution and also reveals the challenges faced by a specially selected modern RAF aircrew who attempt to emulate their predecessors who participated in the Dams Raid.

S145   SWETTENHAM, John (*editor*)
VALIANT MEN: Canada's Victoria Cross and George Cross Winners
Hakkert, Toronto, 1973
234 pp, photos, index, hb, cr

This *Canadian War Museum Historical Publication No. 7* covers every Canadian recipient of the VC or GC. For each recipient, there is a related photograph and an account of the VC or GC deed, based on the LG citation or an extract from a published work. The biographical detail is minimal. There is also a list of other VC and GC recipients who had an association with Canada.

S150   SWIFT, Eric
THE BRAVE AND THE PREJUDICED: Together they won an Empire
Springfield, Chelmsford, 1982
151 pp, photos, maps, sb, ncr

This book narrates the history of India under the control of the Honourable East India Company and under British Crown rule. In the context of the key events from the Indian Mutiny awards, it gives a brief account of the VCs awarded on the Indian sub-continent or won by the Indian Army in conflicts elsewhere. A roll of honour of Indian Army VCs (reproduced from N5) appears as the appendix.

S155   SYMONS, Julian
BULLER'S CAMPAIGN
Cresset Press, London, 1963
312 pp, photos, sketches, maps, index, hb, cr

An assessment of General Sir Redvers Buller VC and his campaign in the Boer War. It commences with an account of the struggle in 1895 for the position of C-in-C of the Army by the 'Wolseley Ring' and the 'Roberts Ring'. It then examines the political and diplomatic issues and the preparation for war. Buller's command, which led to an inquest and the demise of his career, is covered in detail. There are chapters and extensive text elsewhere on Lord Roberts VC and Sir George White VC. Colonel Wood VC's involvement in the campaign also receives significant coverage.

S160   SYMONS, Captain William Penn
RORKE'S DRIFT DIARY: An account of the Battles of Isandlwana and Rorke's Drift Zululand 22nd January 1879
Uniform, in association with the Victoria Cross Trust, London, 2018
96 pp, photos, sb, ncr

An account of the battles of Isandlwana and Rorke's Drift written by Captain WP Symons of 2nd 24th Regt, who survived Isandlwana. Included are eye-witness accounts from Pte Williams, groom to Colonel Glynn, Pte Bickley and Pte Wilson, band members, Capt Gardener (14th Hussars), Lt Cochrane (32nd Regt), Lt Smith-Dorrien (95th Regt) and Lt Curling (RA). Lt H Smith-Dorrien was later General Sir Horace Lockwood Smith-Dorrien GCB GCMG DSO ADC who commanded 11 Corps at the battles of Mons and Le Cateau in 1914. The author was killed at Talana Hill during the second Boer War.

T1   TAMELANDER, Michael
DAMBUSTERS: Historien om operational Chastise, 1943
Prisma, Stockholm, 2009
318 pp, drawings, maps, hb, cr

This Swedish-text describes Operation *Chastise* in 1943 - the attack on the Ruhr dams for which Wg Cdr Guy Gibson was awarded the VC. The book describes Gibson's command of 617 Squadron, from its formation and details the preparation for the attack on the dams. The role played by Gibson is described extensively throughout the book which is written in a fictional style.

T1A   TAMESIDE METROPOLITAN BOROUGH COUNCIL (*publisher*)
A TRIBUTE TO THE MEN OF TAMESIDE AWARDED THE VICTORIA CROSS
Tameside Leisure Services, Tameside Metropolitan Borough Council, Ashton-under-Lyne, nd (c1995)
17 pp, photos, sb, cr

A collection of biographical sketches, portraits and accounts of the deeds of the eight VC recipients from Tameside, Greater Manchester. The following VCs are covered: J Buckley, AH Proctor, WT Forshaw, J Kirk, HN Schofield, A Hill, A Moynihan and E Sykes.

T2   TANGYE, Derek (*editor*)
WENT THE DAY WELL... : Tributes to men and women who died for freedom when Britain stood alone in the first two years of the Second World War
George Harrap, London, 1942 (reissued: Michael Joseph, London, 1995)
239 pp. (1995 edition: 243 pp.), hb, cr

Re-issued to coincide with the 50th anniversary of VE Day, this 1942 book pays tribute to men and women who sacrificed their life whilst in or with Britain's armed services or civilian services during the early years of WW2. The biographical tributes are arranged into 42 chapters, each of which is written by a close friend of the subject concerned. Chapters I (pages 7-17), VI (pages 41-45) and XXX (pages 179-185) are devoted to Sgt Plt JA Ward VC RNZAF, Subadar Richpal Ram VC and A/Capt ESF Fegen VC RN, respectively, and include a detailed account of their posthumous VC deeds.

T3   TANNER, John (*editor*)
FIGHTING IN THE AIR: The official combat technique instructions for British fighter pilots, 1916-1945
Arms and Armour Press, London, 1978
307 pp, photos, sketches, hb, cr

This book, Volume 7 in the *RAF Museum Series*, is a compilation of official instructions on aerial combat techniques. *Fighting in the Air* by Major LWB Rees (later VC), RFC and RA, is reproduced in full on pages 7-39 and is based on his personal combat experiences. A short note *Fighting the SE, January, 1918* by Captain JTB McCudden VC is featured on pages 80-82.

T4   TEMPLE, Arthur
OUR LIVING GENERALS: Twelve Biographical Sketches of Distinguished Soldiers
Andrew Melrose, London, 1898 (revised and updated 1899)
198 pp. (1899 edition: 202 pp.), photos, hb, cr

This book contains 12 biographical sketches of Victorian generals including four VC recipients: Lord Roberts (pages 29-49); Sir Redvers Buller (pages 64-80); Sir Evelyn Wood (pages 81-96) and Sir George White (pages 97-111). These sketches were thoroughly revised and updated in the 1899 edition. Reviewed in V56.

T5   TERRY, C. Sanford, LittD (*editor*)
OSTEND AND ZEEBRUGGE APRIL 23: MAY 10, 1918: The Despatches of
Vice-Admiral Sir Roger Keyes, KCB KCVO And other Narratives of the Operations
Oxford University Press - Humphrey Milford, London, 1919
224 pp, photos, maps, index, hb, cr

Admiral Keyes' despatches of 9 May and 15 June 1918 provide an authentic and detailed record of the naval raids on Zeebrugge and Ostend in April and May 1918. The deeds in the raids that led to the award of the VC are documented fully in respect of eight of the eleven recipients.

T6   THACKERAY, Colonel E.T., VC
BIOGRAPHICAL NOTES OF OFFICERS OF THE ROYAL (BENGAL) ENGINEERS
Smith & Elder, London, 1900
288 pp, photos, hb, cr

Arranged chronologically into five periods, this history uses 34 brief biographies to highlight the history of the Corps. There is a chapter each on P Salkeld VC and DC Home VC.

T7   THACKERAY, Colonel E.T., VC
TWO INDIAN CAMPAIGNS IN 1857-8
Royal Engineers Institute, Chatham, 1896
130 pp, maps, hb, cr

An account of the siege of Delhi, the taking of Lucknow and the campaign in Romilcund, which is based mainly on letters written by Thackeray, as a subaltern, to friends in England. He also makes use of the reports and diaries of Baird Smith, Chief Engineer of the Delhi Field Force, and articles in the *Journal of the Royal United Service Institution* for the operations at Alum Bagh.

T8   THACKERAY, Colonel Sir Edward, VC, KCB, Late RE
REMINISCENCES OF THE INDIAN MUTINY (1857-58) AND AFGHANISTAN (1879)
Smith, Elder & Co, London, 1916
181 pp, index, hb, cr

This work comprises, principally, seven papers which had been published originally in the *Cornhill Magazine*, the *Bengal Engineers Journal* and the *Royal Engineers Journal*. It commences with a 47-page account of Col Thackeray's recollections of the Siege of Delhi. He then recalls the capture of Lucknow, which he supplements with an eight-page memoir of Lt Gen JJMcL Innes, VC CB. He concludes with a paper on his experiences in the Afghan War and with notes on the natural history of Upper Assam. Other papers included are the memoirs of Gen Sir A Taylor GCB, Lt Hodson (Hodson's Horse) and Col Brasyer (Brasyer's Sikhs).

T9   THAMES TELEVISION (*publisher*)
       FOR VALOUR: A history of the Victoria Cross from its inception to the present day
       Thames Television, London, nd (c1985)
       24 pp, photos, sb, cr

This booklet, which was produced in association with the Royal British Legion, accompanied the Thames Television series on the VC (see also P20). It gives an overview of the history of the VC told through the deeds of 16 VC recipients, portrait photographs of whom are included. A 43-paged typescript *document For Valour – A VC Project* was issued with the booklet and is intended for educational purposes. It includes a data template for VC research and a county-arranged directory of VC recipients who are buried or were cremated in the UK. The directory, which is not comprehensive, contains biographical data extracted from T10 (1st edition).

T9A   THE FRIENDS OF KENSAL GREEN CEMETERY
       PATHS OF GLORY
       The Friends of Kensal Green Cemetery, London, 1997
       107 pp, photos + illustrations, maps, sb

This publication is a history of Kensal Green Cemetery containing a guide to the location of monuments and a selected list of persons of note commemorated. This edition has shorter biographies than those given in V155 and omits Davies GC, James VC, Lenon VC and Manners-Smith VC which V155 includes.

T10   THIS ENGLAND BOOKS (*publisher*)
       THE REGISTER OF THE VICTORIA CROSS
       [1] This England Books, Cheltenham, 1981 (1st Edition)
       303 pp, photos, index, hb, ncr
       [2] This England Books, Cheltenham, 1988 (2nd Edition)
       352 pp, photos, index, hb, cr
       [3] This England Books, Cheltenham, 1997 (3rd Edition)
       352 pp, photos, index, hb, cr

This reference work on the VC was compiled by Nora Buzzell of *This England* and contains biographical data for every VC recipient, which in nearly all cases is accompanied by a portrait. Each entry gives the name, rank, unit, place/date of deed, place/date of birth, place/date of death, place of memorial, town/county connections and remarks. Also included is an alphabetical index of VC recipients showing the *LG* citation date and an alphabetical listing of towns and counties with which VCs had a connection. The 1988 edition of the work also incorporates for each recipient's entry the LG citation date and a short account of the VC deed. The 1997 edition corrects and updates the previous editions. Also the quality of the portrait photographs is improved. A two page (loose) addendum was issued to include VC recipients: Beharry, Budd, Apiata and Donaldson. No further editions are planned by the publisher.

T11   THOMAS, Lieutenant General Matthew, PVSM, AVSM, VSM (Ret'd) and MANSINGH, Jasjit
       LT GEN PS BHAGAT PVSM VC: A Biography
       Lancer International, New Delhi, 1994
       517 pp, photos, index, hb, cr

A comprehensive account of the life of Premindra Singh Bhagat, who had the distinction of being the first Indian commissioned officer to be awarded the VC and became one of the Indian Army's most outstanding generals. It chronicles his 35 years' service in the Indian Army from the 1930s, through WW2 (VC), to his eventual commands in the Indo-Pakistan Wars. It then describes his subsequent business career and his death in 1975. The appendix is an account written by Bhagat expressing his views on the Chinese threat.

T11A   THOMAS, Roy Digby
TWO GENERALS: Buller and Botha in the Boer War
AnchorHouse, Bloomington, Indiana, USA, 2012
246 pp, two portrait photos, maps, index, hb, cr

A reappraisal of how General Sir Redvers Buller and General Louis Botha, the commanders of the British and Boer armies, confronted each other in the Boer War in 1899-1900. In comparing and contrasting them, their personalities, attitudes and services are fully examined. Subsequent chapters deal with the Boer War operations under their leadership, which are appraised impartially from both their perspectives. The work concludes with accounts of their later lives.

T12   THOMPSON, E.V.
FOR VALOUR: West Country VCs
Truran Books, Truro, Cornwall, 2004
86 pp, photos, sb, cr

This book contains short chapters on 22 VC recipients who had connections with Devon and Cornwall. The author, a novelist living in Cornwall, does not claim the list is comprehensive. In fact the four Mutiny VCs featured were Irish but served in the DCLI. Typically each chapter has three or four pages with the recipient's photograph. The front cover is a colour reproduction of a painting of the VC action at the Dunkirk perimeter where Captain Ervine-Andrews won his VC. Reviewed in V54.

T13   THOMPSON, Dave
I LAUGHED LIKE BLAZES! The Life of Private Thomas 'Todger' Jones VC DCM
Mailbook Publishing, Widnes, Cheshire, 2002
44 pp, photos, map, sb, cr

A profusely illustrated biographical portrait of 'Todger' Jones, from Runcorn, who, in 1916, won the VC whilst serving in the Cheshire Regiment. After tracing his family background and childhood years, the book focuses on his WW1 service and particularly his heroism. It recalls the many tributes to him during his homecoming to receive the VC and includes a full transcript of his interview by a local newspaper. An account of his post-WW1 life and experiences is concluded with the final tributes and memorials to him following his death in 1956. Reviewed in V51.

T14   THORNICROFT, N.J.
THE VCs OF GLOUCESTERSHIRE AND NORTH BRISTOL
Wedderburn Art, Gloucester, nd (c2005)
197 pp, photos, maps, sb, cr

This well-illustrated book gives a biographical account of each of the 77 VC recipients who, by birth, residence, education or burial place are linked with the county of Gloucestershire, including the Bristol area north of the River Avon. In addition to photographs of the recipients, there are numerous photographs depicting associated memorials and residences. Reviewed in V60.

T14A THORNING, Arthur G.
THE DAMBUSTER WHO CRACKED THE DAM: The Story of Melvin 'Dinghy' Young
Pen & Sword Aviation, Barnsley, 2008
178 pp, photos, maps, index, hb

This biography of Squadron Leader Henry Melvin Young DFC* recalls his early years, his time as an undergraduate at Oxford and his service in the RAFVR from Aug 1939. Posted to 617 Sqn on 10 Apr 1943, he served as 'A' Flight Commander under Wg Cdr Gibson and took part in the Dams Raid on 16/17 May 1943. Piloting Lancaster AJ-A in the first wave, led by Gibson, Young attacked the Möhne Dam causing a small breach and, after observing the breach of the Eder Dam, he was shot down and killed as his aircraft headed for home. Chapters 9 and 10 (pages 112-162) document the Dams Raid and the aftermath.

T15 THORNTON, Lieutenant Colonel L.H., CMG, DSO and FRASER, Pamela
THE CONGREVES: Father and Son - General Sir Walter Norris Congreve VC, Bt-Major William La Touche Congreve VC
John Murray, London, 1930
337 pp, photos, sketches, index, hb, cr

This biography comprises two parts. Part 1 (written by Lt Col Thornton) contains a family history and then concentrates on the life, career and death of Sir Walter Congreve VC KCB. It documents his campaign service in the Boer War (VC) and in WW1 and his various peacetime appointments, culminating in his position as Governor of Malta. Part 2 (written by Pamela Fraser) relates to William Congreve VC DSO MC and describes his early years, his military service in WW1 and his death in action. Extracts from his diaries are used extensively.

T15A THORNTON, Neil
RORKE'S DRIFT: A New Perspective
Fonthill Media, Stroud, 2016
208 pp, photos, illustrations, maps, index, hb, cr

An account of Rorke's Drift which focuses on the 11 VCs and those awarded the DCM. It includes previously unpublished accounts, specially commissioned art work and provides a new perspective on the fighting within the hospital.

T16 THORPE, Barrie
PRIVATE MEMORIALS OF THE GREAT WAR ON THE WESTERN FRONT
The Western Front Association, Reading, 1999
118 pp, photos, maps, index, sb, cr

After the Great War many bereaved families and friends erected private memorials to their loved ones. Most of these were in the UK, but a number were on the battlefields of France and Flanders. This book lists 40 such memorials and includes brief biographical details, how the person commemorated died, the history of the memorial and how the land was purchased, etc and a photo of the memorial. Two VC recipients have private memorials: A Ball (3pp) and A Poulter (3pp).

T17   THROSSELL, Ric
FOR VALOUR
Currency Press, Sydney, Australia, 1976
110 pp, photos, sketches, sb, cr

This book is the author's response to memories of his father, Captain H Throssell VC, and of the ANZACs. After an examination of Australia's 1914-18 repatriation programme, he gives an 11-page character study of his father, and includes a comrade's reminiscences. The rest of the book contains the script of a 1960 play, *For Valour*, which was directed by Ric Throssell and featured a fictitious VC, Harry Cordell.

T18   THROSSELL, Ric
MY FATHER'S SON
William Heinemann, Richmond, Australia, 1989
414 pp, photos, index, hb, cr

The book, by the son of Captain H Throssell VC is divided into three parts. Part 1 describes the life of his father, who won the VC at Gallipoli. The last two parts are an autobiography. The author's early life was overshadowed by his father's suicide. His subsequent career in the Australian Government's Department of Foreign Affairs was subjected to suspicion, prejudice and controversy.

T19   THWAITES, Lieutenant Michael, RNVR
THE JERVIS BAY AND OTHER POEMS
Putnam, London, 1943
59 pp, sb (1943), hb (1945), cr

An anthology of 11 war poems and 18 other poems by Lt Thwaites, who received the Royal Medal for Poetry in 1939. The first poem (on pages 3-16) is entitled *The Jervis Bay* and is about the armed merchant cruiser HMS *Jervis Bay* and her gallant fight against the *Admiral Scheer*, for which ESF Fegen won the VC posthumously.

T20   TICKLER, Harry
MIDGET SUBMARINES
np, Grimsby (*printer*), nd (c1944)
12 pp, hb, cr

A slim volume to commemorate the attack on the *Tirpitz* by midget submarines *X7* and *X6* commanded by Place and Cameron respectively who both won the VC. The author was Place's father-in-law. The text reproduces the LG citations and the text of a broadcast on the subject given by Rear Admiral CB Barry in February 1944.

T21   TIDESWELL, Anthony G.
WILLIAM COLTMAN: The Story of Two Crosses
Sovereign Bookcare, Stoke-on-Trent, 2008
86 pp, photos, sb, cr

A short biography of the most decorated other rank of WW1: William Coltman VC, DCM* MM*. As a conscientious objector he worked as a stretcher bearer with the North Staffordshire Regiment on the Western Front. He was driven by his Christian faith and felt unable to take up arms but was prepared to save his comrades. Between the wars he worked as a gardener in Burton-on-Trent's public gardens. In WW2 Coltman served in ACF in Burton. He died in 1974.

T22   TIDEY Iain
[1] EAST GRINSTEAD'S VC HERO: SIDNEY FRANK GODLEY VC
Privately published by Iain W. Tidey, 2012
38 pp, photos (some colour), map, sb, cr
[2] SIDNEY FRANK GODLEY, VC: The First Private to be awarded the Victoria Cross in World War One
Privately published by Iain W. Tidey, 2015
76 pp, photos (some colour), map, sb, cr

This is a well-illustrated A4-sized document describes the story of Sidney Godley and how he with Lt Maurice Dease won the first VCs of WW1 at Mons on 23 August 1914. A limited number of copies of the first edition were desk-top produced and comb-bound. The second edition was A5-sized and a perfect-bound book.

T22A   TILDESLEY, Janet
SECOND LIEUTENANT FREDERICK BIRKS VC MM
The Buckley Society, Buckley, Flintshire, Wales, nd (c2017)
28 pp, photos (some colour), map, sb, cr

This biography of Frederick Birks VC MM was published for the centenary of his death in 2017. It was based on an earlier account, published in 2014, by the author who is Birk's grand niece. The A5 booklet describes his early life, his emigration to Australia in 1913, his military service including at Gallipoli and on the Western Front with the AIF. A short description is given of his MM award and the action at Glencorse Wood near Ypres on 20 September 1917 where he was killed and resulted in the award of a posthumous VC.

T22B   TIMES, THE (*publisher*)
GREAT MILITARY LIVES
Times Books/HarperCollins Publishers, London, 2008
335 pp, hb, cr

A collection of 50 military obituaries previously published in *The Times*, from the Duke of Wellington (in 1852) to Admiral of the Fleet Lord Fieldhouse (in 1992). The back cover has a large colour picture of the VC, but despite this there is only one VC obituary: FM Lord Roberts VC (19pp). Foreword by William Hague MP and Introduction by Major General Michael Tillotson.

T23   TISDALL, Arthur Walderne St Clair VC
VERSES, LETTERS & REMEMBRANCES OF ARTHUR WALDERNE St CLAIR TISDALL VC, Sub Lt RNVR
Sidgwick & Jackson, London, 1916 (republished: The Naval & Military Press, London, 1992)
158 pp, photos, line drawings, hb, cr

The life of Sub Lt Tisdall VC is told through letters from persons who knew him in his schooldays, in his time as an undergraduate at Cambridge University and during his WW1 active service in the RNVR and RND. Accounts of his posthumous VC action on V Beach, Gallipoli in 1915 are given. A collection of verses written by Tisdall between 1909 and 1912 concludes the book.

T24   TONKIN, Keith
NEW ZEALANDERS IN ACTION IN WORLD WAR TWO
Gilt Edge Publishing, Pentone, Wellington, New Zealand, 2006
26 pp, photos, map, index, sb, cr

This short highly-illustrated booklet features four New Zealanders who distinguished themselves in WW2: Upham VC and bar, Ngarimu VC, Keith Park and Nancy Wake.

T25   TOOMEY, T.E.
HEROES OF THE VICTORIA CROSS
George Newnes, London, 1895
260 pp, photos, index, hb, ncr

This book contains photographic portraits of 228 VC recipients and provides a short account of their VC deed. Typically, the portraits show the recipients in uniform and wearing their medals. A roll of VC recipients by year and campaign is included.

T26   TOOMEY, T.E.
VICTORIA CROSS AND HOW WON: 1854-1889
Alfred Boot, London, 1889
67 pp, photo, sketches, hb, ncr

The introductory chapter of this book identifies superlatives and notabilities relating to VC recipients and gives an account of the first VC investiture. The book then lists alphabetically all the recipients and gives a short description of their VC deed. The book concludes with various analyses and lists of VCs awarded.

T27   TOOTAL, Stuart
DANGER CLOSE: The True Story of Helmand from the Leader of 3 PARA
John Murray, London, 2009
337 pp, photos (colour), maps, index, hb, cr

The author commanded 3 Para who were the first British unit deployed in the Helmand province in Afghanistan. They endured many actions which resulted in a posthumous VC for Bryan Budd. The regiment lost 15 men and had 46 wounded. Tootal describes his frustrations with other Nato soldiers who declined to engage the enemy and the lack of care of the wounded once they were back in the UK.

T28   TOOWOOMBA STATE HIGH SCHOOL
CORPORAL J. A. FRENCH VC
Toowoomba State High School, Queensland, Australia, nd (c1982)
55 pp, photos, map, sb, cr

This publication is the work of students of the Crow's Nest and District School in Queensland, Australia to honour Cpl JA French and his VC action on 4 September 1942 at Milne Bay, New Guinea. The book also commemorates a new library named in honour of Cpl French which was officially opened on 18 July 1958 by the Governor-General, FM Sir William Slim.

T29   TORSIN, René H.
THEY STAYED WITH US: The Victoria Crosses of Belgium
Privately published, 1992
35 pp, sb, ncr

A photocopied transcript (in English) recording the 67 VC recipients whose VC action occurred in Belgium or who had a close association with the country. Some RAF VCs of WW2 are included. Details of the VC burial locations in Belgium and of the winners who served in Belgium in WW1 are also provided.

T29A TOUT, Ken
HOW MODEST ARE THE BRAVEST!: Courage from the Beaches of Normandy and Beyond
Helion & Co, Warwick, 2018
208 pp, photos, maps, sb, cr

The author recalls the life and deeds of 22 war heroes decorated for gallantry in North West Europe during the period from D-Day to VE Day. Their character and motivation are also examined. Seven VCs are featured in separate chapters (Stan Hollis, Ian Bazalgette, Robert Cain, Ted Chapman, George Eardley, Jack Harper and Fred Tilston). Eleven other heroes with individual chapters are from the UK (4), Canada (1), France (1), Germany (2), Poland (1), and the USA (2). A single chapter concerns four Belgium, Dutch and French resistance fighters.

T30 TREMBLAY, Jack
BILLY BISHOP: Hero of the Air
Brunswick Press, Fredericton, New Brunswick, Canada, 1967
22 pp, sketches, sb, cr

This *Beaver Book for Young Canadians*, No 2 in the series *Story of Canada*, is a biographical sketch of the life and achievements of Air Marshal Bishop VC.

T31 TREW, Peter
THE BOER WAR GENERALS
Sutton Publishing, Stroud, 1999
274 pp, photos, index, hb, cr

An in-depth study of the principal British and Boer commanders in the Boer War 1899-1902. Chapters are devoted to each of the three British C-in-Cs: Buller VC (pages 16-44), Lord Roberts VC (pages 45-87) and Kitchener (pages 88-136), and to three Boer generals (Botha, De Wet and De La Rey) as well as Smuts. In addition to describing their background and career, the author examines in detail their role in the war and their personality, abilities and contrasting command styles. He also documents their lives after the war.

T32 TRUESDALE, David and YOUNG, John
HEROES, ROGUES & VAGABONDS: Irish VCs in the Crimean War
Helion & Co., Warwick, 2019
136 pp, photos, maps, sb, cr

This volume provides short biographies of 30 men from Ireland who were awarded the VC in the Crimean War.

T33 TUCKER, Alan (*compiler*)
THE LIFE OF GEORGE RAVENHILL VC
Privately published, Birmingham, 2006
12 pp, photos, sb, cr

This typescript document describes the life of George Ravenhill VC and reproduces documents and newspaper articles covering family background, army career, VC action, forfeiture of VC following a conviction for theft in 1908, his death and funeral. This is available in City of Birmingham Reference Library along with a similar research file on Ravenhill compiled by Nigel J Mussett MBE MA FLS in 2017.

T34 TUCKER, Squadron Leader Nicholas G., RAF
IN ADVERSITY: Exploits of Gallantry and Awards to the RAF Regiment and its associated forces 1921-1995
Jade Publishing, Oldham, 1997
337 pp, photos, maps, index, hb, cr

This book gives details of all recipients of awards to the RAF Regiment, its predecessors and its associated units. It also includes information on the six VC winners who later served with the regiment: MA James (page 300), F Luke (page 301), GI McIntosh (page 302), FW Palmer (page 303), LWB Rees (pages 304-305), STD Wallace (page 306). Each VC entry includes a photograph, LG citation and biographical details with an emphasis on their service with the RAF Regiment.

T35 TURNER, John Frayn
VC's (*sic*) OF THE AIR
George Harrap, London, 1960
187 pp, photos, hb, cr

This book details, in its 31 chapters, the VC deed of the 32 air VCs of WW2 and in some cases, brief biographical information is given. A photograph of each recipient is included. This work is a companion volume to T36 and T37. See also T38.

T36 TURNER, John Frayn
VC's (*sic*) OF THE ARMY 1939-1951
George Harrap, London, 1962
224 pp, hb, cr

This companion volume to T35 and T37 narrates, in its 22 chapters, the deeds of 127 army VCs of WW2 and Korea. The description of the deeds is modelled mainly on the LG citation. In most cases, biographical information is not included. See also T38.

T37 TURNER, John Frayn
VC's (*sic*) OF THE ROYAL NAVY
George Harrap, London, 1956
192 pp, photos, hb, cr

This book narrates, in its 19 chapters, the VC deeds of the 24 WW2 VCs of the Royal Navy, Royal Canadian Navy and the Royal Marines. In many cases no biographical information is included. This work is a companion volume to T35 and T36. See also T38.

T38 TURNER, John Frayn
VCs OF THE SECOND WORLD WAR
Pen and Sword Military, Barnsley, 2004
309 pp, photos, hb, ncr

This is an omnibus edition combining the author's earlier works T35, T36 and T37 under one cover. The book covers every VC of WW2. Reviewed in V54.

T39   TURNER, John Frayn
FAMOUS AIR BATTLES
Arthur Barker, London, 1963
215 pp, sketches, hb, cr

A collection of 17 notable air actions of WW1 and WW2. The six chapters on WW1 relate specifically to the VC deeds of Warneford, Ball, Robinson, Bishop, McLeod and Barker. Two of the eleven WW2 chapters relate to the VC exploits of Gibson and Cheshire.

T40   TURNER, John Frayn
PERISCOPE PATROL: The Saga of Malta Force Submarines
George Harrap, London, 1957 (republished: Airlife Publishing, Shrewsbury, 1997)
218 pp. (1997 edition: 152 pp.), photos, drawing, map, hb (1997 edition: sb), cr
Republished Pen & Sword Maritime, Barnsley, 2018
218 pp, hb, cr

An account of the operational activities of the 10th Submarine Flotilla, which operating from Malta, attempted to stop enemy supplies from reaching North Africa. HM Submarine *Upholder*, commanded by Lt Cdr MD Wanklyn VC DSO**, accounted for 21 enemy vessels (128,353 tons) out of 71 vessels (390,660 tons) sunk by the Flotilla. Extensive coverage (including five dedicated chapters) is given to Wanklyn's patrols and successes.

T60   TYQUIN, Michael B.
NEVILLE HOWSE: Australia's First Victoria Cross Winner
Oxford University Press, South Melbourne, Australia, 1999
212 pp, photos, index, hb, cr

A full biography of Maj Gen Sir Neville Howse VC KCB KCMG, who was the first soldier to be awarded the VC while serving with an Australian unit. Following his distinguished service in the Australian Medical Services that led to his promotion to Surgeon General, he was elected to the Australian Federal Parliament and in due course held several Cabinet portfolios. His medical, Army and political careers are documented thoroughly. See W3.

U2 ULSTER-SCOTS COMMUNITY NETWORK
'FOR VALOUR': Ulster VCs of the Great War
Ulster-Scots Community Network, nd (post 2006)
39 pp, photos, sb, cr

The booklet contains a biographical sketch of each of the 23 WW1 VC recipients who were born in Ulster, or were of Ulster parentage, or who served in the 36th (Ulster) Division. Typically, each biography includes a portrait photograph.

U3 UNITED STATES SPECIAL OPERATIONS COMMAND (USSOCOM) PUBLIC AFFAIRS OFFICE (*Publisher*)
SPECIAL OPERATIONS RECIPIENTS OF THE MEDAL OF HONOR AND THE VICTORIA CROSS
Ussocom Public Affairs Office, MacDill Air Force Base, Florida, USA, 1997
109 pp, photos, drawings, sb, cr

A record of the recipients of the Medal of Honor or the Victoria Cross whose deed was performed whilst on special operations associated with the US forces. For each recipient, the award citation is given and, typically, is accompanied by a full plate portrait photograph. The MoH recipients are arranged as follows: US Navy Seals (3 recipients); US Army Special Operations – Indian Scouts (16); Army Special Operations Forces (22); and US Air Force Commandos (5). The VC recipients relate to Australian Special Operations in Vietnam and are: WO2 K Payne, WO2 RS Simpson and WO2 KA Wheatley.

U5 USBORNE, Vice Admiral C.V., CB, CMG
SMOKE ON THE HORIZON: Mediterranean Fighting 1914-1918
Hodder & Stoughton, London, 1933
327 pp, photos, maps, index, hb, cr

A selection of accounts relating to minor naval actions of WW1. Chapter I (pages 1-19) details Holbrook's VC deed when commanding submarine *B11*. Chapter VI (pages 124-139) describes Lt Cdr Boyle VC and his exploits on submarine *E14* in the Dardenelles, Chapter VII (pages 140-167) entitled *The River Clyde* provides a detailed account of Unwin's VC deed together with some minor references to other VCs of the action. Chapter VIII (pages 168-183) concerns submarine *E11*'s adventures in the Sea of Marmora earning its commander, Nasmith, the VC. Detailed maps support the text.

U10 UYS, Ian S.
FOR VALOUR: The History of Southern Africa's Victoria Cross Heroes
Privately published by author, Johannesburg, 1973
398 pp, photos, sketches, maps, index, hb, cr

This well-illustrated book provides biographical accounts of the 44 VC recipients with a connection to southern Africa. An account of their VC deed is narrated in the context of the battle or campaign. At the end of each chapter is a full LG citation, a listing of the recipient's awards and additional biographical information. The appendices contain statistical analyses and listings of the awards under various criteria (including other VCs who had associations with southern Africa).

U11   UYS, Ian S.
VICTORIA CROSSES OF THE ANGLO-BOER WAR
Fortress Financial Group (Pty) Ltd., Knysna, South Africa, 2000
127 pp, photos, map, index, sb, cr

An account of each of the six VCs of the First Anglo-Boer War (1881) and the 78 VCs of the Second Anglo-Boer War (1899-1902). The biographical sketch of each recipient also includes their VC citation details and the composition of their medal group. Associated lists and analyses are contained in the seven appendices.

V1   VACHON, S.
LE CAPITAINE JEAN BRILLANT CV CM: Par Ses Amis
np, Rimouski, Quebec, 1920
50 pp, photo, sketch, sb, cr

This French-text work is a biographical sketch of Capt J Brillant VC MC, a French-Canadian who won a posthumous VC during WW1. It also contains transcripts of numerous letters written by him to his family and also written as tributes to him after he was killed in action.

V5   VALENTINE, L.
HEROES OF THE BRITISH ARMY
Frederick Warne, London, nd (c1899)
280 pp, sketches, hb, cr

In this companion volume to V6 (see also V7), Mrs Valentine gives an account of the life and exploits of 14 famous British soldiers, which spans the period 1759 (General Wolfe) to 1900 (Sir George White VC). The remaining six chapters relate to specific battles and recall some of their heroic participants. Two chapters focus on the life and VC deed of Col Sir Charles Russell VC (pages 142-148) and of Lt Chard VC (pages 232-238). A further chapter (pages 260-276) relates to Sir George White VC at Ladysmith. The final chapter (pages 277-280) concerns some of the VCs won at Colenso in 1899.

V6   VALENTINE, L.
HEROES OF THE BRITISH NAVY
Frederick Warne, London, nd (c1900)
280 pp, drawings, hb, cr

This companion volume to V5 tells the story of 18 heroic British naval commanders from Sir Francis Drake (d.1595) to Sir Richard Strachan (d.1828). Additionally, there is a section (pages 265-270) relating to Capt Burgoyne VC and also a section (pages 271-277) devoted to the deeds of other naval VCs of the Crimean War and Indian Mutiny. (See also V5 and V7).

V7   VALENTINE, L.
HEROES OF THE UNITED SERVICE
Frederick Warne, London, nd (c1900)
504 pp, line drawings, photos, hb, cr

This work is an omnibus edition of V5 and V6. The first part (248 pages) relates to "Heroes of the British Army" up to the reconquest of the Sudan. The second part, *Heroes of the British Navy*, comprises 256 pages and, in particular, omits the chapters in V6 relating to Capt Burgoyne VC and to the VCs of the Crimean War and Indian Mutiny. VC coverage in the first part concerns, predominantly, Sir Charles Russell VC and William Peel VC in the Crimea (pages 142-148) and Chard VC at Rorke's Drift (pages 232-238).

V8   (1) VAN DEN DRIESSSCHEN, Jan
DE DAMMEN BREKERS: De roemruchte aanval van Guy Gibson en zijn 'Dam Busters' op de stuwdammen in het Ruhrgebied tijdens de Tweede Wereldoolog
Van Holkema & Warendorf, Bussum, Netherlands, 1979
124 pp, photos, drawings, hb, cr (*Dutch text*)
 (2) VAN DEN DRIESSSCHEN, Jan, with GIBSON, Eve
WE WILL REMEMBER THEM: Guy Gibson and the Dam Busters
The Erskine Press, Quidenham, Norfolk, 2004
163 pp, photos, maps, hb, cr

Originally published in Dutch in 1979, this first English edition (2004) contains much new information, particularly new chapters written by Guy Gibson's widow, Eve. It also includes a detailed account of Operation *Chastise*, the Dams Raid, and it also documents Gibson's death and memorials to him.

V10   VANDERBILT, Gloria and FURNESS, Thelma, Lady
DOUBLE EXPOSURE
Frederick Muller, London, 1959
364 pp, photos, index, hb, cr

An autobiography of high society American twins, one of whom married into British high society, becoming step-mother to C Furness VC. Several references to him are made within the text.

V12   VARMA, Ashali
THE VICTORIA CROSS: A Love Story
Dorling Kindersley (Indian) Pvt Ltd, India, 2013 (Third Edition published by author, 2014)
243 pp, photos, map, sb, cr

Written by his daughter, this memoir of Lieutenant General Premindra Singh Bhagat PVSM VC recalls his heritage, early life, distinguished army career and chairmanship of the Damodar Valley Corporation up to his death in 1975. It is also a memoir of his wife, Mohini and reveals their devotion to each other. The narrative is interspersed with correspondence transcripts and the plates comprise over 40 photographs.

V14   VERNEY, Lieutenant Edmund Hope, RN
THE SHANNON BRIGADE IN INDIA: Being Some Account of Sir William Peel's Naval Brigade in the Indian Campaign of 1857-1859
Saunders, Otley and Co., London, 1862
153 pp, drawings, maps, hb, cr

A personal account of General Campbell's march to the relief of Lucknow. HMS *Shannon*'s Naval Brigade was commanded by Captain William Peel VC. The VC exploits of Lt Salmon and Lt Young are described. (See V15).

V15   VERNEY, Major General G.L., DSO MVO
THE DEVIL'S WIND: The Story of the Naval Brigade at Lucknow
Hutchinson, London, 1956
176 pp, photos, maps, index, hb, cr

An account of HMS *Shannon*'s Naval Brigade (commanded by Captain William Peel VC) in the campaign in India 1857-58, which is based on the letters of Edmund Hope Verney and other papers. Peel is referred to extensively throughout the book and detailed accounts of the VC deeds of Lt Salmon and Lt Young are given.

V20 VETCH, Colonel R.H., CB
LIFE, LETTERS AND DIARIES OF LIEUT-GENERAL SIR GERALD GRAHAM VC GCB RE
William Blackwood, Edinburgh, 1901
492 pp, photos, sketches, maps, index, hb, cr

This memoir of the life of Lt Gen Graham VC is based on the correspondence and diaries he compiled throughout his military service. Col Vetch has interspersed the transcripts with much biographical text, which also concludes the memoir. The first half of the book covers campaigns in the Crimea and China. The second half covers the Egyptian campaign. There are 100 pages of appendices which contain extracts from some of Graham's despatches.

V30 VIBART, Colonel Henry M.
THE LIFE OF GENERAL SIR HARRY N.D. PRENDERGAST RE VC GCB (The Happy Warrior)
Eveleigh Nash, London, 1914
445 pp, photos, sketches, maps, index, hb, cr

A full biography of Sir Harry Prendergast VC from his early years to his death in 1913. Several references are made to his contemporary, Lord Roberts VC.

V40 VICKERS, Roy
LORD ROBERTS: The Story of His Life
C Arthur Pearson, London, 1914
128 pp, photo, hb, cr

A concise account of the life of Field Marshal Earl Roberts VC. The book concentrates on his distinguished military service from entering Sandhurst up to his death in France in 1914.

V45 VICTORIA CROSS AND GEORGE CROSS ASSOCIATION
ON COURAGE: Stories of Victoria Cross and George Cross Holders - The Sebastapol Project
Constable, London, 2018
390 pp, photos, maps, index, hb, cr

This volume, an initiative by the VC and GC Association, provides short biographies of 38 VC recipients, four GC holders, Malta GC and Tom Crean AM. Each biography is introduced by celebrities such as famous actors, TV and sports stars, journalists and others. The identity of the authors of each biography is shown in the Notes and includes Saul David, Tom Bromley, Paul Garlington, Spencer Jones and James Holland. Full LG citations for each recipient are included in the Appendix.

V50 VICTORIA CROSS SOCIETY (*editor:* BEST, Brian)
JOURNAL OF THE VICTORIA CROSS SOCIETY Volume 1
Crowborough, East Sussex, October 2002
44 pp, photos (some colour), maps, sb, cr

This inaugural edition contains articles on the first VC investiture on 26 June 1857, the Zulu War VCs, James Gorman VC, William Hall VC, Maurice Dease VC, Albert Jacka VC, Thomas Wilkinson VC and HMS *Li Wo* (Part 1 of 2), James Stokes VC, Kevin Wheatley VC, Valentine Bambrick VC and Anders Lassen VC. Includes book reviews of H52, S77 and S30.

V51   VICTORIA CROSS SOCIETY (*editor:* BEST, Brian)
JOURNAL OF THE VICTORIA CROSS SOCIETY Volume 2
Crowborough, East Sussex, March 2003
58 pp, photos (some colour), maps, sb, cr

This edition contains articles on George Strong VC, Paul Kenna VC (Part 1 of 4), Charles Fitzclarence VC, Gabriel Coury VC (Part 1 of 2), Richard Willis VC, Harry Greenwood VC, Henry Tandey VC, Theodore Cooke VC, James Nicolson VC, Thomas Wilkinson VC and HMS *Li Wo* (Part 2 of 2), Tommy Gould VC, Richard Kelliher VC and Nand Singh VC. There is also an article titled *The first award to the Army Medal Department, the Netley Victoria Cross*. Includes book reviews of W95, L60, M122, L30, G61, T13, M8A and H108.

V52   VICTORIA CROSS SOCIETY (*editor:* BEST, Brian)
JOURNAL OF THE VICTORIA CROSS SOCIETY Volume 3
Crowborough, East Sussex, October 2003
62 pp, photos (some colour), maps, sb, cr

This edition has articles on the unveiling and dedication of the VC and GC Memorial at Westminster Abbey (14 May 2003), NV Carter VC, C Bushell VC, Bill Speakman VC, JA Wood VC, William Beresford VC, Paul Kenna VC (Part 2 of 4), Neville Howse VC, Donald Bell VC, Archie White VC, William Mariner VC, David Findlay VC, Fred Fisher VC, John Carroll VC, Gabriel Coury VC (Part 2 of 2), Bruce Kingsbury VC and Fred Tilson VC. Includes book reviews of L45, C46, H9, F42 and C21.

V53   VICTORIA CROSS SOCIETY (*editor:* BEST, Brian)
JOURNAL OF THE VICTORIA CROSS SOCIETY Volume 4
Crowborough, East Sussex, March 2004
64 pp, photos (some colour), maps, sb, cr

This edition has articles on Jack Harrison VC, Thomas Ricketts VC, Wantage VC paintings, William Goat VC, Thomas Lane VC (Part 1 of 2), Paul Kenna VC (Part 3 of 4), Frank Young VC, Eustace Jotham VC, JW Jackson VC, Hugh Malcolm VC (Part 1 of 2), JA French VC, Norman Jackson VC, George Eardley VC and George Knowland VC. There is also an article titled *Colonial VCs of the Zulu War*. Includes book reviews of I40, H126 and M105.

V54   VICTORIA CROSS SOCIETY (*editor:* BEST, Brian)
JOURNAL OF THE VICTORIA CROSS SOCIETY Volume 5
Crowborough, East Sussex, October 2004
55 pp, photos (some colour), maps, sb, cr

This edition has articles on Charles Lucas VC, the Light Brigade VCs, Henry Clifford VC, Henry Hook VC, Thomas Lane VC (Part 2 of 2), Frederick Dugdale VC, Paul Kenna VC (Part 4 of 4), ET Towner VC, Stanley Boughey VC, Hugh Malcolm VC (Part 2 of 2), Stanley Hollis VC, and an obituary of David Harvey (see H52). Includes book reviews of A61, J23, G36, M120, T12, E2 and T38.

V55   VICTORIA CROSS SOCIETY (*editor:* BEST, Brian)
JOURNAL OF THE VICTORIA CROSS SOCIETY Volume 6
Crowborough, East Sussex, March 2005
56 pp, photos (some colour), maps, sb, cr

This edition has articles on Charles Lucas VC, Robert Loyd-Lindsay VC, Sir James Mouat VC, Joseph Trewavas VC, Richard Fitzgerald VC, Samuel Wassall VC, Randolph Nesbitt VC, Charles Parker VC, Arthur Borton VC, Oliver Brooks VC, Thomas Durrant VC, Edwin Swales VC, Robert Cain VC, James Baskeyfield VC and James Magennis VC. There are also articles on the 1929 VC dinner and funeral of Richard Annand VC. Includes book reviews of D13 and E10A.

V56   VICTORIA CROSS SOCIETY (*editor:* BEST, Brian)
JOURNAL OF THE VICTORIA CROSS SOCIETY Volume 7
Crowborough, East Sussex, October 2005
56 pp, photos (some colour), maps, sb, cr

This edition has articles on Johnson Beharry VC, the VCs for the Great Redan (1855), Charles Lumley VC, William Connolly VC, John Paton VC, Samuel Shaw VC, Frederick Corbett VC, Walter Congreve VC, Wilbur Dartnell VC, Augustus Agar VC (Part 1 of 3), Gobar Singh Negi VC, John Harman VC, Richard Annand VC, Philip Curtis VC and James Carne VC. Includes book reviews of G37, D20, P40, D23, T4, P21 and S89.

V57   VICTORIA CROSS SOCIETY (*editor*: BEST, Brian)
JOURNAL OF THE VICTORIA CROSS SOCIETY Volume 8
Crowborough, East Sussex, March 2006
71 pp, photos (some colour), maps, sb, cr

This edition has articles on Christopher Teesdale VC, Patrick Roddy VC, Thomas Byrne VC, William House VC, James Collis VC, William Cosgrove VC, William Leefe Robinson VC, H Ackroyd VC, Cecil Sewell VC, Augustus Agar VC (Part 2 of 3), HE Harden VC and Maurice Rogers VC. There is a full list of VC recipients on parade at the 1956 VC Centenary and an article on the celebrations. There are articles by John Glanfield examining the gun-metal from which VCs are manufactured (see G29) and one titled *Chavasse Farm - The Great War and nine VCs*. Includes book reviews of G28, D10, S118, G38, D31, B83, K16 and R86.

V58   VICTORIA CROSS SOCIETY (*editor*: BEST, Brian)
JOURNAL OF THE VICTORIA CROSS SOCIETY Volume 9
Crowborough, East Sussex, October 2006
56 pp, photos (some colour), maps, sb, cr

This edition has articles on the VC 150th anniversary commemoration service, CW Buckley VC, R Buller VC, AK Wilson VC, S Shaw VC, W Boulter VC in *Chavasse Farm - The Great War and nine VCs*, American Unknown Soldier VC, E Robinson VC, AJ Shout VC, A Agar VC (part 3 of 3), CC Dobson VC, G Roope VC, D Currie VC, D Cameron VC and G Place VC. Includes book reviews of B79, W7 and H30.

V59 VICTORIA CROSS SOCIETY (*editor*: BEST, Brian)
JOURNAL OF THE VICTORIA CROSS SOCIETY Volume 10
Crowborough, East Sussex, March 2007
64 pp, photos (some colour), maps, sb, cr

This edition has articles on CW Buckley VC, American Unknown Soldier VC, BJ Budd VC, Sheesh Mahal Museum VC Collection, John Buckley VC, William Raynor VC, James Hills Johnes VC, Thomas Kavanagh VC (Part 1 of 2), David MacKay VC, CF Hancock, manufacturer of the VC, JW Adams VC, Henry Pennell VC, EW Costello VC (Part 1 of 2), AO Pollard VC, J Sayer VC, J Brunt VC and Ian McKay VC. Includes book reviews of H94, R18, W79, A65 and B36.

V60 VICTORIA CROSS SOCIETY (*editor*: BEST, Brian)
JOURNAL OF THE VICTORIA CROSS SOCIETY Volume 11
Rutland, October 2007
65 pp, photos (some colour), maps, sb, cr

This edition has articles on WH Apiata VC, T Watkins VC, EWD Bell VC, JW Adams VC, CD Lucas VC, WD Steuart VC, F Maude VC, F Whirlpool VC, T Kavanagh VC (Part 2 of 2), AC Booth VC, EW Costello VC (Part 2 of 2), WA Bishop VC, JH Finn VC, F Dancox VC and C Upham VC. Includes book reviews of D26A, L47, C78, T14 and K17.

V61 VICTORIA CROSS SOCIETY (*editor*: BEST, Brian)
JOURNAL OF THE VICTORIA CROSS SOCIETY Volume 12
Rutland, March 2008
64 pp, photos (some colour), maps, sb, cr

This edition has articles on Bhanbhagta Gurung VC (obituary), William Hewett VC, Edward Robinson VC, Evelyn Wood VC, Joseph Farmer VC, WD Wright VC, H Dalziel VC, Charles Stone VC, B Cloutman VC, John Kenneally VC and HM Ervine-Andrews VC. Included is an article on Crimea VCs including J Bythesea, W Johnston, J Trewavas, J Sullivan, J Craig, John Byrne, V Bambrick, DG Boyes and J McGuire, seven of whom committed suicide. There are also articles on the VC Guard of Honour by 74 VC recipients at the unveiling of the tomb of the Unknown Soldier on 11 November 1920 and the VC paintings of the artist Terence Cuneo. Includes book reviews of C25, S51, M14B and W60.

V62 VICTORIA CROSS SOCIETY (*editor*: BEST, Brian)
JOURNAL OF THE VICTORIA CROSS SOCIETY Volume 13
Rutland, October 2008
64 pp, photos (some colour), maps, sb, cr

This edition has articles on Ian Fraser VC (obituary), Luke O'Connor VC, Hanson Jarrett VC, WF McDonell VC, Michael Murphy VC and Samuel Morley VC, William Bankes VC, William Trevor VC and James Dundas VC, Isaac Lodge VC, J Sherwood Kelly VC, EB Smith VC, Noel Mellish VC, Peter Badcoe VC and Christopher Teesdale VC. There are also articles on the Royal VC Garden Party of 1920 and a description and appraisal of the Victoria Crosses for Australia, New Zealand and Canada instituted by these Commonwealth countries. Includes book reviews of W80, H52, F13, M129 and D30.

V63 VICTORIA CROSS SOCIETY (*editor*: BEST, Brian)
JOURNAL OF THE VICTORIA CROSS SOCIETY Volume 14
Rutland, March 2009
64 pp, photos (some colour) maps, sb, cr

This edition has an article on the award of the Victoria Cross for Australia to Mark Donaldson including investiture photographs. Also featured are Eric Wilson VC (obituary), Anthony Palmer VC and Alfred Ablett VC, James Dalton VC, Walter Hamilton VC, M Meiklejohn VC, A Wilkinson VC, AE Chowne VC, AC Newman VC, RED Ryder VC, S Beattie VC, Ian Liddell VC, H Nichols VC and W Apiata VC. There are also articles on the gun metal used to manufacture the VC (Part 1) and on the 15 VCs for Palestine in WW1. Includes book reviews of L46 and S19.

V64 VICTORIA CROSS SOCIETY (*editor*: BEST, Brian)
JOURNAL OF THE VICTORIA CROSS SOCIETY Volume 15
Rutland, October 2009
64 pp, photos (some colour), maps, sb, cr

The edition has a focus on Gurkha VCs and contains articles on Edward Kenna VC (obituary), JD Grant VC, Kulbir Thapa VC and Karanbahadur Rana VC, Tulbahadur Pun VC and Lachhiman Gurung VC, FG Blaker VC, Rambahadur Limbu VC, TJ Young VC, FHS Roberts VC, AS Cobbe VC (Part 1 of 3), DL Macintyre VC, JH Knight VC and D Donnini VC. In addition there are artcicles on Public School VCs (Part 1). VC Gunmetal (Part 2) and the Redan Medical VCs featuring TE Hale VC and H Sylvester VC with a description of the rejection of a VC to Acting Assistant Surgeon George Fair. Includes book reviews of A12B and M11B.

V65 VICTORIA CROSS SOCIETY (*editor*: BEST, Brian)
JOURNAL OF THE VICTORIA CROSS SOCIETY Volume 16
Rutland, March 2010
64 pp, photos (some colour), maps, sb, cr

This edition has articles on Timothy O'Hea VC, HG Moore VC, F Aylmer VC, GH Boisragon VC, J Manners Smith VC, B Guy VC, J Collis VC, AS Cobbe VC (Part 2 of 3), W Rhodes-Moorhouse VC, C Coffin VC, Joseph Maxwell VC, SF Godley VC, George Evans VC, G Meynell VC, George Thompson VC, Richard Burton VC and TJ Young VC. In addition there is an article in Public School VCs (Part 2). Includes book reviews of C100, I60 and M29.

V66 VICTORIA CROSS SOCIETY (*editor*: BEST, Brian)
JOURNAL OF THE VICTORIA CROSS SOCIETY Volume 17
Rutland, October 2010
56 pp, photos (some colour), maps, sb, cr

This edition has articles on E Towse VC, R Ryder VC, R Hart VC, W Bees VC, AS Cobbe (Part 3 of 3), CH Coverdale VC, F Greaves VC, WM Currey VC, T O'Hea VC and K Muir VC. In addition there were articles in the Sidi Rezegh VCs (J Campbell, J Beeley and GW Gunn), the miniature VC group to A Mountain VC and the Tirah VCs (HLS MacLean, R Adams and Viscount Fincastle). There is also a one page article on the Lord Ashcroft VC Gallery at the IWM. Includes book review of K49B.

V67   VICTORIA CROSS SOCIETY (*editor*: BEST, Brian)
JOURNAL OF THE VICTORIA CROSS SOCIETY Volume 18
Rutland, March 2011
52 pp, photos (some colour), maps, sb, cr

This edition has articles on B Roberts-Smith VC (announcing award of VC), Lachhiman Gurung VC (obituary), GF Day VC, J Tytler VC, R Warneford VC, T Dresser VC, TR Colyer-Ferguson VC, CJ Kinross VC, T O'Hea VC, J Mantle VC, Sefanaia Sukanaivalu VC, R Rattey VC and J Nettleton VC. In addition there are articles on the Morosi Mountain VCs (P Brown, R Scott and E Hartley), a three page article with colour photos on the opening of the Lord Ashcroft VC Gallery at the IWM, an article on the Fjords 1940 VCs (G Roope, B Warburton-Lee and R Stannard) and Public School VCs (Part 3). Includes book reviews of B1, S31 and C149.

V68   VICTORIA CROSS SOCIETY (*editor*: BEST, Brian)
JOURNAL OF THE VICTORIA CROSS SOCIETY Volume 19
Rutland, October 2011
52 pp, photos (some colour), maps, sb, cr

This edition focuses on the Royal Navy with articles on *Shannon* VCs (W Peel, N Salmon, John Harrison and E Daniel), I Harding VC, H Rowlands VC, T Flawn VC, F Fitzpatrick, AHL Richardson VC, Jutland VCs (FJW Harvey, EBS Bingham, J Cornwell and LW Jones), G Prowse VC, Lord Gort VC (Part 1 of 2), J Kirk VC, Kronstadt VCs (G Steele, A Agar and C Dobson) and AL Aaron VC. There are also two articles on VCs held by National Museum Collections and Public School VCs (Part 4).

V69   VICTORIA CROSS SOCIETY (*editor*: BEST, Brian)
JOURNAL OF THE VICTORIA CROSS SOCIETY Volume 20
Rutland, March 2012
52 pp, photos (some colour), maps, sb, cr

This edition has articles on the Gough family VCs (CJS Gough, HH Gough and JE Gough), T Cadell VC, Medical VCs of NZ Wars (W Temple, WGN Manley and J Mouat), CT Kennedy VC, A Martin-Leake VC*, T Veale VC, GT Lyall VC, E Swales VC, H Auten VC, Lord Gort VC (Part 2 of 2), W Sidney VC, J Purcell VC and I Harding VC. There is also an article on the VCs commemorated by the CWGC. Includes book review of I15.

V70   VICTORIA CROSS SOCIETY (*editor*: BEST, Brian)
JOURNAL OF THE VICTORIA CROSS SOCIETY Volume 21
Rutland, October 2012
52 pp, photos (some colour), maps, sb, cr

This edition has an Olympic Games focus as the Games in 2012 were held in London. There are articles on J Prettyjohn VC, HH Gough VC, the four VCs of 32nd Regiment at Lucknow (W Oxenham, SH Lawrence, W Dowling and H Gore-Browne), EH Lenon VC, W Maillard VC, HG Columbine VC, P Neame VC (Part 1 of 2), C McCorrie VC, F Jefferson VC, P Gardner VC and R Simpson VC. Includes book reviews of C81, S140, W52 and C113D.

V71 VICTORIA CROSS SOCIETY (*editor*: BEST, Brian)
JOURNAL OF THE VICTORIA CROSS SOCIETY Volume 22
Rutland, March 2013
52 pp, photos (some colour), maps, sb, cr

This edition announces the award of VCs to DA Keighran and J Ashworth. It has articles on GL Goodlake VC, P Marling VC, GM Ingram VC, JE Gough VC, FAC Scrimger VC and P Neame VC (Part 2 of 2). There is also an 11 page article titled *Victoria Cross at Auction* by Oliver Pepys of Spink charting the history of VCs at auction between 1879 and 2011. There is also a list of the progression of world record prices of VCs at auction between 1884 and 2011. Includes book reviews of S141, S79B and W21.

V72 VICTORIA CROSS SOCIETY (*editor*: BEST, Brian)
JOURNAL OF THE VICTORIA CROSS SOCIETY Volume 23
Rutland, October 2013
52 pp, photos (some colour), maps, sb, cr

This edition focuses on Air VCs and includes articles on F West VC, W Barker VC, James Ward VC, G Gibson VC, J Cruickshank VC and WE Newton VC. In addition there are articles on the renovated grave of A Moynihan VC, the Benares VCs (P Gill, M Rosamund and John Kirk), WE Brown VC, H Ackroyd VC and R Sandford VC. Includes book reviews of H128, S44, S43 and M10A.

V73 VICTORIA CROSS SOCIETY (*editor*: BEST, Brian)
JOURNAL OF THE VICTORIA CROSS SOCIETY Volume 24
Rutland, March 2014
52 pp, photos (some colour), maps, sb, cr

This edition has articles on H Raby VC, FS Roberts VC (Part 1 of 3), G Hinkley VC, RH Buller VC, G Graham VC, C Robertson VC, JJ Dwyer VC, W Elstob VC, A Sullivan VC, S Pearse VC, E Charlton VC and RH Gray VC. This volume also announced the VC award to CS Baird.

V74 VICTORIA CROSS SOCIETY (*editor*: BEST, Brian)
JOURNAL OF THE VICTORIA CROSS SOCIETY Volume 25
Rutland, October 2014
52 pp, photos (some colour), maps, sb, cr

This edition focuses on 1914 to reflect the centenary of the start of WWI and has articles on C Garforth VC, J Leach VC, J Hogan VC, C Yate VC, the Néry VCs (Bradbury, Dorrell and Nelson), Khudadad Khan VC, H Ranken VC and N Holbrook VC. In addition there are articles on FS Roberts VC (Part 2 of 3), HCD D'Arcy VC, the youngest VC (A Fitzgibbon VC and T Flynn VC), VCs buried in the state of Victoria, Australia, a centenary event of the first VCs of WW1 (Dease and Godley) and WW1 VC Commemorative Paving Stones. Includes book reviews of W125, D24, H129, P4D and M47.

V75 VICTORIA CROSS SOCIETY (*editor*: BEST, Brian)
JOURNAL OF THE VICTORIA CROSS SOCIETY Volume 26
Rutland, March 2015
52 pp, photos (some colour), maps, sb, cr

This edition focuses on 1915 VCs and features M O'Leary VC, LG Hawker VC, G Campbell VC, JP Hamilton VC, F Potts VC, M Dunbar-Nasmith VC, G Woolley VC and F Parslow VC. In addition there are articles on Joshua Leakey (announcing VC award), FS Roberts VC (Part 3 of 3), J Robarts VC, HND Prendergast VC (Part 1 of 2) and HM Ervine-Andrews VC. There is a report on the VC Commemorative Paving Stones Project and the National Memorial Arboretum. Includes book reviews of C55 and B84A.

V76   VICTORIA CROSS SOCIETY (*editor*: BEST, Brian)
JOURNAL OF THE VICTORIA CROSS SOCIETY Volume 27
Rutland, October 2015
52 pp, photos (some colour), maps, sb, cr

This edition has articles on JD Grant VC, G Fosbery VC and HW Pitcher VC, HND Prendergast (Part 2 of 2), Edward Boyle VC and Geoffrey White VC, R Bell-Davies VC, P Hansen VC, LJ Keyworth VC, G Peachment VC, Kulbir Thapa VC and B Kingsbury VC. There is also an article by Anthony Staunton titled *Forfeited Victoria Cross Myths*. Includes book reviews of M80 and H13.

V77   VICTORIA CROSS SOCIETY (*editor*: BEST, Brian)
JOURNAL OF THE VICTORIA CROSS SOCIETY Volume 28
Rutland, March 2016
52 pp, photos (some colour), maps, sb, cr

This is the final edition and is titled *1916 Special Edition*. There are articles on F Aikman VC, W Coffey VC, F Wheatley VC, J Lyons VC, HM Havelock VC, J Bergin VC and M Magner VC, JPH Crowe VC and C Teesdale VC, L Halliday VC, N Carter VC, A Carton de Wiart VC, H Firman VC and C Cowley VC, LWB Rees VC, J Leak VC and AS Blackburn VC, M Doyle VC and G Mitchell VC. There is also an article titled *First VC Presentation to Next of Kin by Monarch* covering posthumous awards. Includes book reviews of C37, S134, H12 and B42.

V155   VIVIAN-NEAL, Henry
[1] **HOLDERS OF THE VICTORIA CROSS AT KENSAL GREEN CEMETERY** (*original edition*)
The Friends of Kensal Green Cemetery, London, 2004
6 pp, illustrations, maps, sb, cr
[2] **VALOUR AND GALLANTRY AT KENSAL GREEN CEMETERY: a guide to the monuments to the recipients of the Victoria Cross and the George Cross at the Cemetery of All Souls Kensal Green** (*updated version*)
The Friends of Kensal Green Cemetery, Kensal Green, London, 2009
12 pp, illustrations, maps, sb, cr

This is a short guide to the monuments to holders of the VC and GC and the Cemetery of All Souls Kensal Green. After a short introduction to the VC and GC there are sketches of the memorials with short biographical details of each VC and GC holder. The VCs featured are FR Aikman, GH Biosragon, C Dickson, MC Dixon, HH Gough, NR Howse, WH James, EH Lenon, OEP Lloyd, J Manners-Smith, JC Malcolmson, J Mouat, DM Probyn and WS Trevor. The GC holder featured is Frederick Davies. See T9A.

V157   VOWLES, Alan
'OUR WILF' : The Story of Wilfred Dolby Fuller VC
Avon and Somerset Constabulary History and Heritage Group, 2017
122 pp, photos, hb, cr

A biography of WD Fuller VC who served in 1st Bn Grenadier Guards and won the VC on 15 March 1915 at Neuve Chapelle on the Western Front. His early years and family background are described. His VC action is detailed along with his hero's welcome home to Mansfield when his VC was announced. Before WW1 Fuller was a miner but enlisted in the Grenadier Guards in 1911. After WW1 he joined the Somerset Police before retiring in 1940. He died in Frome, Somerset in 1947.

V160   VULLIEZ, Captain Albert
VICTORIA CROSS: Trois Héros de la Marine Anglaise
André Bonne, Paris, 1949
221 pp, photo, sketches, maps, hb, cr

This book, a French text, gives a detailed account of three naval actions in WW2 for which the VC was awarded. Part 1 (pages 13-171) relates to Roope and Warburton-Lee. Part 2 (pages 175-218) relates to Sherbrooke.

W2   WALDRON, T.J. and GLEESON, James
THE FROGMEN: The Story of the Wartime Underwater Operators
Evans Brothers, London, 1950
191 pp, photos, sketches, hb, cr

An account describing the experimental, training and operational activities of Royal Navy frogmen, charioteers and *X/XE*-Craft submariners in WW2, from the idea's inception by the Italians. Amongst the gallant deeds described in detail are the VC actions of Cameron, Place, Fraser and Magennis. Republished by Elmfield Press, Yorkshire, 1974.

W3   WALES, Murdoch and PEARN, John
NEVILLE HOWSE VC: Soldier, Surgeon and Citizen
Amphion Press, Herston, Queensland, 1997
57 pp, photos, sb, cr

A biography of Major-General Sir Neville Howse VC KCB KCMG KStJ, the only Australian doctor to have been decorated with the VC. Howse was a doctor in New South Wales and volunteered for service in the South African War in 1899. As a Lieutenant he won his VC for rescuing a soldier under fire in 1901. He also served in the senior staff of the Division of Medical Services in WW1. He was active in the St John Ambulance Association and served as a Federal Parliamentarian. See T60.

W4   WALKER, Colin
J. T. CORNWELL VC AND THE SCOUTS 'BADGE OF COURAGE'
Writebooks CPR Ltd, Ferrybridge, West Yorkshire, 2006
75 pp, photos, paintings, sb, cr

This well-illustrated biographical sketch of the short life of Jack Cornwell VC recalls his upbringing, time as a Boy Scout, employment after leaving school, followed by entry into the Royal Navy. Details are given of his naval service and heroism on HMS *Chester* in the Battle of Jutland, for which he awarded the VC and Scouts' Bronze Cross posthumously, and his funeral and reburial in Manor Park. The numerous tributes and memorials to him are recorded and supported by photographs which also depict the range of memorabilia.

W5   WALKER, Frank and MELLOR, Pamela
THE MYSTERY OF X5: Lieutenant H. Henty-Creer's attack on the Tirpitz
William Kimber, London, 1988
239 pp, photos, maps, index, hb, cr

Pamela Mellor was Henty-Creer's sister; Frank Walker an ex-RAN anti-submarine officer. The book commences with Henty-Creer's autobiography. Part 2 (pages 105-148) concerns the preparation and attack on the *Tirpitz* by three midget submarines. During the attack, Henty-Creer's *X5* was lost but the commanders of *X6* and *X7* (Cameron and Place) were awarded the VC. The attack is described fully and contains many references to Cameron and Place. Part 3 describes the search for *X5*. Part 4 is the case for a VC to be also awarded to Henty-Creer. The appendices contain full transcripts of the Admiralty reports on the attack.

W7   WALLACE, Lieutenant-General Sir Christopher, and CASSIDY, Major Ron
FOCUS ON COURAGE: The 59 Victoria Crosses of the Royal Green Jackets
The Royal Green Jackets Museum Trust, Winchester, 2006
233 pp, photos, maps, index, hb, cr

This book describes the feats of 59 VCs to members of the antecedent regiments of The Royal Green Jackets, namely The Oxfordshire and Buckinghamshire Light Infantry, The King's Royal Rifle Corps and The Rifle Brigade. The book includes biographical details and is supplemented by colour and black and white photographs. Reviewed in V58.

W8   WALSH, R. Raymond and WALSH, Jean M.
A SHORT ACCOUNT OF THE LIFE AND SERVICE TO HIS COUNTRY IN THE EAST LANCASHIRE REGIMENT, OF HAROLD MARCUS ERVINE-ANDREWS VICTORIA CROSS
THCL Books, Blackburn, 2000
22 pp, photos, sb, cr

A desktop-published document with acetate covers and a plastic binder. The publication describes the life and service of HM Ervine-Andrews who won the VC in rearguard action at Dunkirk. There are 34 photographs, some in colour. The text focuses mainly on Ervine-Andrews' early days and service prior to 1940. The VC action is described on pages 14-15 by Lt Col Cetre who won an MC in the same action.

W8A   WALSH, Jean M
THE COLONEL AND THE WHEELBARROW
Published by Raymond Walsh, Blackburn, nd (c1996)
7 pp, sb, cr

This is a reproduction of a letter written by the publisher's wife to her brother. It describes an incident in a river near Truro, where an infirm and elderly HM Ervine-Andrews VC was fishing in August 1993. He fell into the river and had to be rescued and brought home in a wheel-barrow.

W9   WALTERS, E.W.
HEROIC AIRMEN AND THEIR EXPLOITS
Charles H. Kelly, London, 1917
270 pp, photos, drawing, hb, cr

Stories of some of the pioneering aviators. Three chapters are devoted to VCs: Chap IX (pages 61-74) - Flt Cdr WL Robinson; Chap XIII (pages 104-107) – Lt Warneford; Chap XVII (pages 127-129) - Flt Cdr Ball.

W10   WALTERS, Ian
DASHER WHEATLEY AND AUSTRALIA IN VIETNAM
Northern Territory University, Darwin, Northern Territory, Australia, 1998
179 pp, photos, tables, index, sb, cr

This book, written by an anthropologist, examines in detail the life and death of WO2 KA Wheatley who was awarded a posthumous VC for his actions on 13 November 1966 at Long Tan, Vietnam. The author examines, from a contemporary perspective, the significance of these events in Australian life and culture.

W11   WANTAGE, Lady Harriet S.
LORD WANTAGE VC KCB: A Memoir
Smith, Elder & Co, London, 1908
474 pp, photos, index, hb, cr

A full biography of Brig-Gen Lord Wantage (RJ Loyd-Lindsay) by his wife. His family background and early years are narrated followed by a detailed description of his service with the Scots Guards in the Crimea (VC), his subsequent election to Parliament and his Red Cross work. His business ventures are described as is his service commanding a volunteer brigade. Lady Wantage concludes the memoir by recording tributes to him on his death.

W12   WAR OFFICE (INTELLIGENCE BRANCH OF QUARTERMASTER-GENERAL'S DEPARTMENT) (Author now known to be Captain J.S. Rothwell, RA)
NARRATIVE OF THE FIELD OPERATIONS CONNECTED WITH THE ZULU WAR OF 1879
Her Majesty's Stationery Office (*printer*), London, 1881; facsimile reprint: Greenhill Books, London, 1989
174 pp, maps, hb, cr

This contemporary official history of the Anglo-Zulu War of 1879, prepared from military intelligence sources, documents fully the background and conduct of the campaign, from both military and political perspectives. Throughout the book, extensive references are made to the parts played by Evelyn Wood VC and Redvers Buller (who won his VC in the campaign). Additionally, there is significant coverage of the services of Hugh Rowlands VC.

W13   WAR OFFICE (*publisher*)
ALPHABETICAL LIST OF THE RECIPIENTS OF THE VICTORIA CROSS FROM THE INSTITUTION OF THE DECORATION IN 1856 TO 1ST AUGUST 1914
War Office (MS3), London, 1920
11 pp, sb, ncr

This 'for official use only' publication lists, alphabetically (by surname), all VCs gazetted between 1856 and 1914.

W14   WAR OFFICE (*publisher*)
ALPHABETICAL LIST OF THE RECIPIENTS OF THE VICTORIA CROSS DURING THE WAR, 1914-20
War Office (MS3), London, 1920
16 pp, sb, ncr

This 'for official use only' publication lists, alphabetically (by surname), all VCs gazetted between August 1914 and 30 April 1920 and records their service number, initials, gazetted rank, corps or unit, LG date, theatre in which the VC was won and the date of deed.

W15   WAR OFFICE (*publisher*)
       LIST OF RECIPIENTS OF THE VICTORIA CROSS
       War Office (MS3), London, 1953
       28 pp, sb, ncr

       This publication lists every VC gazetted up to December 1951 and is arranged in five parts covering 1856 to
       Aug 1914; WW1 to 1920; the inter-war years; WW2 and post-WW2. The lists are alphabetical by surname
       and record the recipient's service number, rank, unit or service, LG date, theatre in which the VC was won
       and the date of VC deed. Part VI provides general notes and statistics relating to the VC.

W16   WARD, Chris, LEE, Andy and WACHTEL, Andreas
       DAMBUSTERS: The Definitive History of 617 Squadron at War 1943-1945
       Red Kite Publishing, Walton-on-Thames, 2003
       288 pp, photos, maps, drawings, hb, cr

       This volume documents in detail 617 Squadron's entire wartime record and is profusely illustrated with
       over 350 original photographs. Each raid is described fully and all participating aircraft and pilots are
       identified. There is significant coverage of Guy Gibson and Leonard Cheshire who both were awarded the
       VC commanding the Squadron.

W17   WARD, Chris and WACHTEL, Andreas
       **DAMBUSTER CRASH SITES: 617 Dambuster Squadron Crash Sites in Holland and
       Germany**
       Pen & Sword Aviation, Barnsley, 2007
       115 pp, photos, maps, sb, cr

       This book reveals the crash sites of 617 Squadron Lancasters that failed to return from raids on the Möhne,
       Eder and Sorpe Dams on 16/17 May 1943 (eight aircraft) and on the Dortmund-Ems Canal on 14/15 & 15/16
       Sep 1943 (six aircraft). A chapter is devoted to each aircraft and, in addition to providing information about
       its crew and the part it played, describes the circumstances of the crash and reveals the crash site. Typically,
       chapters include then-and-now photographs of the crash site and a map showing its location, as well as
       photographs of related memorials.

W18   WARD, Chris with LEE, Andy and WATCHEL, Andreas
       DAMBUSTERS: The Forging of a Legend
       Pen & Sword Aviation, Barnsley, 2009
       298 pp, photos, hb, cr

       This comprehensive wartime history of 617 Squadron, from 1943 up to the end of WW2, examines in detail
       every operation the Squadron undertook. Pages 1-90 relate to Wg Cdr Gibson's command of the Squadron
       from its formation at RAF Scampton in Mar 1943 up to Aug 1943, during which period he led the raid on the
       Möhne, Eder and Sorpe Dams in May 1943 and was awarded the VC. Pages 140-187 concern the operations
       under Wg Cdr Cheshire's command of the Squadron from Nov 1943 to Jul 1944 (he was awarded the VC
       in Sep 1944). Appendices include the Squadron's roll of honour, list of commanders and locations, statistics
       and aircraft histories.

W19　WARNER, Philip
THE ZEEBRUGGE RAID
William Kimber, London, 1978
238 pp, photos, maps, index, hb, cr

A historical account of the raid by the Royal Navy on the ports of Zeebrugge and Ostend in April and May 1918 for which eleven VCs were awarded. Part 1 describes the background to the raid. Part 2 is a detailed account of the actual operations. Pages 41-100 concern HMS *Vindictive* and the VC deed of its commander, Capt Carpenter. The other VC deeds are recounted in the context of the operation. The appendices contain the VC citations and a comprehensive list of awards appertaining to the raids.

W20　WARREN, C.E.T. and BENSON, James
ABOVE US THE WAVES: The Story of Midget Submarines and Human Torpedoes
George Harrap, London, 1953
256 pp, photos, maps, hb, cr

This book chronicles the evolution and operations of the Royal Navy's midget submarines and human torpedoes in WW2. Amongst the exploits of the many decorated submariners and charioteers recalled in detail are the VC deeds of Cameron, Place, Fraser and Magennis. Numerous photos support the text. The appendices include a list of officers and men decorated for *X-craft* and chariot operations.

W21　WATKINS, Paul
MIDGET SUBMARINE COMMANDER: The Life of Rear Admiral Godfrey Place VC CB CVO DSC
Pen & Sword, Barnsley, 2012
244 pp, photos, maps, index, hb, cr

A detailed biography of Godfrey Place who won his VC in command of *X7* midget submarine for the attack on the *Tripitz* in 1943. The volume covers Place's family background, education and early naval career culminating in the award of the VC, his time as a POW and post war service flying with 801 Squadron in the Korean War and serving on aircraft carriers at Suez, Nigeria and Aden. Detailed notes are given for each chapter. Reviewed in V71.

W22　WATSON, Edward Spencer
A NAVAL CADET WITH HMS SHANNON'S BRIGADE IN INDIA: Journal of Edward Spencer Watson
WE and J Goss, Kettering, nd (c1859) (facsimile edition: London Stamp Exchange, 1988)
131 pp, hb, cr

The Journal's writer joined the Royal Navy as a 13-year-old cadet aboard HMS *Shannon* on 11 September 1856. He was promoted to Midshipman two years later, serving as one of two ADCs to Captain William Peel VC who was commanding *Shannon*'s Naval Brigade. The Journal commences on 18 August 1858 with the embarking of the Naval Brigade at Calcutta and gives a day-by-day account of its operations and service during the Indian Mutiny up to 17 September 1859 when *Shannon* sailed for home. Extensive references are made to Captain Peel VC (who died in command) and to Lieutenants Salmon and Young who both won the VC at Lucknow.

W23   WEATE, Mark
BILL NEWTON VC: The Short Life of a RAAF Hero
Australian Military History Publications, Loftus, Australia, 1999
91 pp, photos, maps, index, hb, cr

A full and well-illustrated biography of Flt Lt WE Newton VC RAAF, who, following being shot down in action over Papua New Guinea, which was to lead to his posthumous award of the VC, was executed by the Japanese. The work documents his early years, his two years' Army service and his three years' service in the RAAF culminating in his captivity and death. There is a detailed account of his VC action, which is supplemented by both a full transcript of the recommendation for the award of the VC and his citation. An appendix provides his record of service including promotions, postings, medals awarded and memorials to him.

W24   WESSELS, André (*editor*)
LORD ROBERTS AND THE WAR IN SOUTH AFRICA
Sutton Publishing Ltd., Stroud, 2000
368 pp, photo, map, index, hb, cr

This work, published as Vol 17 in the Army Records Society series (and a companion volume to R68) reproduces in full 111 letters, mostly previously unpublished, written by or to Lord Roberts VC during the Anglo-Boer War (1899-1902), and includes correspondence between him and Queen Victoria, Lord Landsdowne, Lord Kitchener and Ian Hamilton. Pages 267-342 comprise extensive notes in connection with the correspondence and the persons mentioned in the text.

W25   WHARNCLIFFE HISTORY MAGAZINES (*publisher*)
DAMBUSTERS: The Raid Sixty-Five Years On
Wharncliffe History Magazines (in association with Pen & Sword Military Books), Barnsley, 2009
98 pp, photos, drawings, map, sb, cr

The profusely-illustrated 'bookazine' reviews Operation *Chastise,* the Dams Raid led by Wg Cdr Gibson on 16/17 May 1943. With chapters written by notable authors of Dambusters books, coverage is given to 617 Sqn's formation, planning, preparation and execution of the operation and the aftermath. Individual chapters are devoted to Guy Gibson (p36-44 and 90-97), Flt Lt David Maltby and Sqn Ldr 'Dinghy' Young. A tribute to those crews who failed to return and details of their crash sites are provided.

W26   WHARNCLIFFE HISTORY MAGAZINES (*publisher*)
FIGHTER ACES: Combat Pilots of the Great War
Wharncliffe History Magazines (in association with Pen & Sword Military Books), Barnsley, 2009
99 pp, photos, colour drawings, map, sb, cr

This profusely-illustrated 'bookazine' traces the evolution of the fighter ace in WW1 and has individual chapters on a selection of notable RFC/RAF, French and German aces. Each chapter includes a biographical sketch, a narrative on the individual's combat record and photographs depicting the ace and his aircraft. The RFC/RAF aces covered are VC recipients: Lanoe Hawker (p36-42), Albert Ball (p56-63), James McCudden (p64-68), John Anthony McCudden (p70-73), Edward Mannock (p78-83) and Billy Bishop (p84-87). The other aces are Immelmann, Boelcke, Von Richtofen and Voss from Germany and Guynemer from France. A half-page is given to each of the top fighter aces with 50 or more victories (including VCs Beauchamp-Proctor and Barker). A two-page map plots all the Allied and German aerodromes on the Western Front in WW1.

W27   WHEATLEY, Kris (*author*) and BANCROFT, James W (*editor*)
HEROES OF RORKE'S DRIFT
House of Heroes, Eccles, 2009
60 pp, photos, sb, cr

This book describes the defence of Rorke's Drift and the men who were decorated for bravery.

W28   WHEELER, Harold F.B., FRHistS
THE STORY OF LORD ROBERTS
George Harrap, London, 1915
272 pp, photos, maps, index, hb, cr

This volume in the *Told through the Ages* series of books, is a biographical account of the life and military career of Lord Roberts VC from his early years up to his death in 1914. It also describes the tributes to him.

W30   WHEELER, Captain Owen
LORD ROBERTS KG VC
Ward, Lock & Co., London, nd (c1915)
299 pp, photos, sketches, maps, hb, cr

This book for boys is a biography of Lord Roberts from his boyhood to his death in 1914. It focuses mainly on the military campaigns in which he served.

W35   WHETTON, Douglass
MANNOCK, PATROL LEADER SUPREME
Ajay Enterprises, Falls Church, Virginia, USA, 1977
47 pp, photos, map, sb, cr

A biographical sketch of Major 'Mick' Mannock VC DSO** MC*, relating his distinguished RFC/RAF service in WW1 culminating in his death. The text provides a narrative account of his many aerial combats and describes his service with 40, 74 and 85 Sqns. The appendices list his aerial victories and record the citations of his six gallantry awards.

W40   WHETTON, Douglass
PROCTOR, ACE OF THE 84 SQUADRON, RFC/RAF
Ajay Enterprises, Falls Church, Virginia, USA, 1978
43 pp, photos, index, sb, cr

This book, which is No. 3 is a series on WW1 aces, is a short biographical account of Flt Lt Beauchamp-Proctor VC DSO MC* DFC. It chronicles his flying career and describes his aerial combats. Full citations of his gallantry awards and lists of his aerial victories and of the aircraft flown by him during 1917-18 are included.

W42   WHIPPLE, Dr Sally MA (Oxon) LRCP MCRS (*compiler*)
**CATALOGUE, LORD WANTAGE VICTORIA CROSS CENTENARY PAINTINGS
EXHIBITION: Masonic Hall, Wantage, 21ˢᵗ October to 26ᵗʰ November 2000**
Published by author, Wantage, 2001
64 pp, plates, sb, cr

This catalogue was produced to commemorate the centenary exhibition of the Desanges paintings held in
Wantage in 2000. Following a seven-page introduction, a total of 45 images are featured. Of these nine are
in black and white, and the rest in colour. However, the images of A Henry VC, JR Roberts VC, JJ Sims VC
and GF Day VC are missing. For each individual VC featured the full LG citation is given along with brief
biographical details. Also details of each picture are given including current location (if known), size and
current condition. The document is desktop-published and comb-bound. (See also C150, D15, D16 and H15).

W45   WHITE, A.J. (*publisher*)
THE VICTORIA CROSS ALMANAC 1901
AJ White, Montreal, Canada, 1901
32 pp, sketches, sb, cr

Internally titled *Mother Seigal's Victoria Cross Almanac 1901*, the booklet has four pages devoted to the VC
and its recipients, particularly Lord Roberts, Sir George White, Sir Redvers Buller, Sir Evelyn Wood, WN
Congreve and W Babtie. Nine other VC recipients are mentioned briefly. Twelve pages list (by month) the
leading battles of the world, each page headed by a drawing depicting a military action but none ascribed
to the VC. Most other pages relate to the range of Mother Seigal's medication supplied by AJ White, the
booklet's producer.

W46   WHITE, A.J. (*publisher*)
THE VICTORIA CROSS AND HOW IT HAS BEEN WON
AJ White, London, nd (c1902)
33 pp, sketches, sb, ncr

This book comprises similar information to W45 but has an additional section on some VCs of the RN and
Royal Marines.

W49   WHITEHOUSE, Arch
EPICS AND LEGENDS OF THE FIRST WORLD WAR
Frederick Muller, London, 1964
352 pp, photos, maps, index, hb, cr

The author, a former RFC fighter pilot, describes and reappraises many of the battles on land, at sea and in
the air in WWI. He also recalls numerous tales of individual heroism performed in these battles, some of
which resulted in the award of the VC. A detailed description of the VC deeds of Holbrook, Boyle, Nasmith,
Rhodes-Moorhouse, WL Robinson, FH McNamara and Ball is given.

W50   WHITFORD, Jan
FOUR MEN OF HUON: The Victoria Crosses of World War 1
Franklin Historic Society, Tasmania, Australia, 2014
38 pp, photos (some colour) sb , cr,

This publication commemorates the lives of four men from Huon who were awarded the VC in WW1: PH
Cherry, JJ Dwyer, SR McDougall and JW Whittle.

W51 WHITMAN, Captain J.E.A.
GALLANT DEEDS OF THE WAR: Stories of the BEF on the Western Front and of the RAF in the Battles of France and Britain
Oxford University Press, Oxford, 1941
202pp, photos, drawings, hb, cr

A selection of stories, based on material supplied by the Ministry of Information, describing heroic deeds of British servicemen during the first year of WW2. Part I covers gallantry in the BEF in France, Belgium and Norway and in land operations elsewhere. A chapter (pages 13-21) narrates the VC actions of Annand, Gristock, Ervine-Andrews, Nicholls and Wilson. Part II concerns the deeds of RAF aircrew and two chapters (pages 145-161) include the VC actions of Learoyd, Hannah and Garland and Gray.

W51A WHITTON, F. E., Lieutenant Colonel CMG
THE ZULU WAR 1979 XXIV: Rorke's Drift
Reliance Printing Works, Halesowen, West Midlands (*printer*), nd (c1979)
14 pp, sb, cr

An account of the action of Rorke's Drift by Lt Col FE Whitton, whose account was "generally acknowledged as the most factual and authorative", first published in *Blackwood's Magazine* in February 1934 and republished for the centenary in 1979.

W52 WHITWORTH, Alan and ARTHUR, Max
YORKSHIRE VCs
Pen & Sword, Barnsley, 2012
221pp, photos, maps, index, hb, cr

This volume briefly describes 68 VCs who were born in Yorkshire or had a close association with the county. Pages 3 to 89 is a brief history of modern British campaigns by Max Arthur, largely reproduced from A61. Pages 90 to 196 cover the 68 VCs arranged alphabetically by surname. Coverage ranges from less than half a page to five pages per recipient. An Appendix provides details of LG entries. See W53. Reviewed in V70.

W53 WHITWORTH, Alan
VCs OF THE NORTH: Cumbria, Durham and Northumberland
Pen & Sword, Barnsley, 2015
162pp, photos, index, hb, cr

This volume has an eight page Preface charting the history of the VC followed by a six page listing titled *British Army Campaigns 1600 - 2000* listing dates, wars, campaigns and a selected list of associated campaign medals. The book is then divided into three parts providing brief biographical details of VCs associated with Cumbria, Durham and Northumberland. Pages 3 to 33 include 12 VCs from Cumbria listed alphabetically. Pages 37 to 122 lists 23 VC recipients from Durham. Finally pages 125 to 152 lists 11 VC recipients from Northumberland. On average each recipient is covered in three pages and the volume follows the format for W52.

W54 WHYBRA, Julian
THE DEFENCE OF RORKE'S DRIFT 22/23 JANUARY 1879
Allen Publishing Co., Hull, nd (c1990)
20 pp, drawings, maps, sb, cr

This booklet is a constituent of a similarly-titled 'British Archives Publication' portfolio and gives a brief account of the Rorke's Drift action during which 11 VCs were won. The portfolio also includes a 10-page facsimile of the personal narrative of Sgt Henry Hook VC, which was edited by Walter Wood and appeared in the February 1905 issue of *The Royal Magazine* (pages 339-348). It also contains facsimile pages from seven contemporary newspapers (Jan-Mar 1879) reporting the Rorke's Drift action, as well as copies of selected prints and maps.

W54A WICKS, W. Oliver
MARLING SCHOOL 1887 TO 1987
Privately published, Stroud, 1986
253 pp, photos, drawings, index, hb, cr

Marling School in Stroud, Gloucestershire, was founded in 1887 by Sir William Henry Marling, 2nd Baronet and his brothers in honour of their father, Sir Samuel Stephens Marling, 1st Baronet, the grandfather of Sir Percival Scrope Marling VC CB 3rd Baronet. This detailed school history features a biographical sketch of Sir Percival (pages 29-31) and his contributions and legacy are narrated elsewhere. Pages 52-56 are devoted to Eugene Paul Bennett VC MC, an Old Marlingtonian, after whom the School's Bennett Prize is named. The book depicts over 60 photographs.

W55 WIGMORE, Lionel (*editor*) and HARDING, Bruce (*in collaboration*)
THEY DARED MIGHTILY
Australian War Memorial, Canberra, 1963
317 pp, photos, maps, hb, cr

This book narrates the gallant deeds of Australia's 92 VC recipients and 12 GC recipients (prior to the Vietnam War). The VC section is arranged chronologically by conflict and date of deed. For each recipient, a biographical sketch is provided which contains a transcript of the award citation, a narrative of the deed in the context of the operation and details relating to their background, life, service career and death. Photographic plates depict their portrait. The appendices provide separate lists of VC recipients by unit, rank, occupation and by Australian State on enlistment, and also replicate the VC warrants. (See also S118, W56 and W70.)

W56 WIGMORE, Lionel (*editor*) and HARDING, Bruce (*in collaboration*)
THEY DARED MIGHTILY: The War in Vietnam 1962-1973
Australian War Memorial, Canberra, nd (c1980)
40 pp, photos, maps, sb, cr

This publication, produced without covers, is intended to be inserted in W55 which it supplements. The contents are in a similar format and cover the four Australian VCs for Vietnam and three GCs awarded between 1965 and 1978 (Rogers, Emanuel and Pratt). (See also S118 and W70.)

W60 WILKINS, Philip A.
THE HISTORY OF THE VICTORIA CROSS
Archibald Constable, London, 1904 (reprinted: Benchmark Publishing, 1970 and by Naval & Military Press 2007)
443 pp, photos, index, hb, ncr

An account of how the VC was won by 520 of its recipients. Brief biographical information is provided in respect of commissioned officers. A portrait photograph of the recipient is included in 392 cases; typically the subject is depicted in uniform and wearing the VC and medals. The appendices include transcripts of several official reports which relate to Kavanagh's VC deed, the Rorke's Drift VC action (written by Chard VC and Reynolds VC) and the posthumous VC deeds of Coghill and Melvill. Also included is a list of VCs by service or regiment. Reviewed in V61.

W61 WILKINSON, Major General Osborn, CB and WILKINSON, Major General Johnson
THE MEMOIRS OF THE GEMINI GENERALS: Personal anecdotes, sporting adventures and sketches of distinguished officers
AD Innes, London, 1896
441 pp, hb, cr

Part 1 (pages 3-132) and Part 2 (pages 133-201) of this book are the autobiographical accounts of the authors who were twin brothers and who both saw extensive service in India. Part 3 (page 203 onwards) contains, in separate chapters, biographical sketches of 26 British generals, five of whom were VC recipients: Lord Roberts, Sir Henry Tombs, Sir Henry Havelock-Allan, Sir William Olpherts and Sir Dighton Probyn.

W62 WILKINSON, Major General Osborn, CB
HEROES IN RHYME AND OTHER RANDOM VERSES
Richard Clay and Sons, London and Bungay, 1900
253 pp, hb, cr

A collection of verses written by Maj Gen Wilkinson. The first of the three sections in this book relates to verses about heroes. Over 50 pages are devoted to his verses about nine distinguished VC recipients who were personal friends. They are: Lord Roberts, Rev JW Adams, Sir Hugh Gough, Sir Charles Gough, Sir John Watson, Sir Sam Browne, Sir George White, Sir James Hills-Johnes and Sir Dighton Probyn. In addition, there are two verses on his general reflections about the VC and how it was won.

W63 WILLEY, Harry (*editor*)
150 YEARS OF THE VICTORIA CROSS 1857-2007 CRIMEA TO AFGHANISTAN
Printing Services (*Printer*), University of Technology, Sydney, Australia, 2007
175 pp, photos, sb, cr

This book is a miscellany of articles and information on the VC from an Australian perspective. Articles include an account of Hancocks, the manufacturer of the VC, a list of all VC recipients and a list of the 72 Australians who were denied a VC following a recommendation for one. There are ten stories out of these 72 described in more detail. The author is related to James Gorman VC and a 15 page biography is included. There are 4 to 6 page biographies on 21 VC recipients and Kipling's article on *Winning the Victoria Cross*.

W67 WILLIAMS, Beverley
LIEUT JRM CHARD VC RE AND THE DEFENCE OF RORKE'S DRIFT
Royal Engineers Museum & Library, Chatham, 1993 (partially revised: 1995)
18 pp, photos, sketches, maps, sb, cr

This comb-bound publication, *RE Museum and Library Information Sheet No. 3*, summarises the family background, education and military career of Lt Chard who won the VC leading the defence of Rorke's Drift. An assessment of his character is followed by details of his illness and death. The booklet also contains a list of items, file papers and photographs relating to Chard that are held in the collection of the RE Museum. A detailed bibliography relating to Chard and Rorke's Drift concludes the work.

W68 WILLIAMS, Charles
THE LIFE OF LIEUTENANT-GENERAL SIR HENRY EVELYN WOOD VC GCB GCMG
Sampson, Low & Marston, London, 1892
309 pp, photo, index, hb, cr

A full biography of the life and the naval and military career of Sir Evelyn Wood VC up to 1891. It describes his extensive campaign service in the Crimean War (recommended for the VC), Indian Mutiny (VC), Ashanti War, Kaffir War, Zulu War, first Boer War and the campaign in Egypt. The appendix is a 53-page transcript of Wood's report on the Autumn manoeuvres in 1891.

W69 WILLIAMS, Charles
BRADMAN: An Australian Hero
Little, Brown and Company, London, 1996
336 pp, photos, index, hb, cr

Australian cricket hero Donald Bradman met Alexander Hore-Ruthven VC, Earl of Gowrie, on numerous occasions when Gowrie was Governor of South Australia and Governor-General of Australia. There are several references to Gowrie, including his involvement in the "bodyline" controversy.

W70 WILLIAMS, Jeff and STAUNTON, Anthony
THEY DARED MIGHTILY
Australian War Memorial, Canberra, 1986
191 pp, photos, index, sb, cr

This book is a revised, condensed and reformatted version of W55 and W56. Its text and portrait photographs relate specifically to the 96 Australian VCs awarded up to the end of the Vietnam War whilst the GC recipients are only listed in an appendix. The content of the biographical sketches, compared with the original work, is much reduced and the LG citations are omitted. (See also S118).

W75 WILLIAMS, W. Alister
THE VCs OF WALES AND THE WELSH REGIMENTS
Bridge Books, Wrexham, 1984
115 pp. (text) and 47 pp. (plates), photos, hb, cr

This publication contains biographical details of 81 VC recipients who were Welsh or who otherwise had served in a Welsh regiment. The information is recorded under the following headings: name, place/date of birth, parental details, education, service record, decorations/medals, marriage/children, place/date of death, burial location, location of VC and full LG citation. The 47 pages of plates contain 167 photographs relating to the recipients. See W79.

W76   WILLIAMS, W. Alister
AGAINST THE ODDS: The Life of Group Captain Lionel Rees VC OBE MC AFC
Bridge Books, Wrexham, 1989
283 pp, photos, sketch, maps, sb, cr

A full biography of LWB Rees who was awarded his VC in WW1 whilst serving with the RFC. He was Britain's first official fighter pilot. The book covers his childhood, military service and his post-service life. It relates his aerial combat experiences in WW1, his continued service in the RAF in the inter-war years and eventual recall during WW2. It also describes his passion for sailing, particularly in the West Indies where, eventually, he settled.

W76A   WILLIAMS, W. Alister
REES VC: The first of the original 'Few'
Bridge Books, Wrexham, 2017
339 pp, photos, maps, drawings, index, sb, cr

The author has brought up-to-date his earlier biography of Gp Capt Rees (see W76) in this much expanded, revised and reformatted edition. Appendix III provides a full transcript of the Gordon-Shephard Memorial Prize Essay 1929 submitted by Rees for which he was awarded second prize.

W77   WILLIAMS, W. Alister
ROWLANDS VC: The Life and Career of General Sir Hugh Rowlands VC KCB
VC Books, Wrexham, 1992
70 pp, photos, sketches, maps, sb, cr

This comb-bound and laser-printed biographical sketch of General Rowlands details his family background, military career and life in retirement. A genealogical table tracing the Rowlands family from Madog (a descendant of a Prince of Powys) is included. (See W78).

W78   WILLIAMS, W. Alister
COMMANDANT OF THE TRANSVAAL: The Life and Career of General Sir Hugh Rowlands VC KCB
Bridge Books, Wrexham, 2001
192 pp, photos, maps, sb, cr

A reformatted and much expanded version of the author's earlier biography of Sir Hugh Rowlands (see W77). Additionally the author unravels the complex details of the operations in the Transvaal in 1878-9 and throws new light on the political manipulations carried out by some of the senior officers.

W79   WILLIAMS, W. Alister
HEART OF A DRAGON: The VCs of Wales and the Welsh Regiments 1854-1902
Bridge Books, Wrexham, 2006
229 pp, photos, maps, hb, cr

This detailed volume covers the period 1854 to 1902 and provides biographical accounts of VC recipients with a Welsh connection including being born in Wales or serving in a Welsh regiment. A total of 39 VCs fall in this category. Entries range from two to nine pages. An Appendix includes short biographical details of nine VC recipients who had an indirect connection with Wales. Reviewed in V59. (See W80).

W80   WILLIAMS, W. Alister
HEART OF A DRAGON: The VCs of Wales and Welsh Regiments 1914 - 82
Bridge Books, Wrexham, 2008
480pp, photos, maps, hb, cr

This substantial and well illustrated book is the second volume of *Heart of a Dragon* (See W79) covering the period 1914 to 1982 and includes awards of 42 VCs who were born in Wales, of Welsh parentage, died in Wales or gained the award serving in a regiment associated with Wales. The recipients featured are listed in order of the VC awarded date. Appendix 1 includes shorter biographies of six VCs who had an indirect connection with Wales. Appendix 2 contains updates and corrections to W79. Reviewed in V62.

W81   WILLIS, Christopher J. and ROGERS, David Fletcher
FOR VALOUR: HMS Conway, HMS Worcester
Conway Club & the Association of Old Worcesters, 1984
29 pp, illus, sb, cr

This booklet contains biographical sketches of the following naval VC recipients who had been cadets on the training ships *Conway* and *Worcester*: E Unwin, CH Cowley, CJ Bonner, PE Bent, GC Steele, IE Fraser. An account of each VC action is also given.

W82   WILLISTON, Floyd
THROUGH FOOTLESS HALLS OF AIR: The Stories of a Few of the Many who Failed to Return
General Store Publishing House, Burnstown, Ontario, Canada, 1996
310 pp, photos, maps, index, sb, cr

This book chronicles the lives of six airmen from Atlantic Canada, based in Britain, who died during WW2. Five of the airmen flew with Bomber Command. One of these was F/O Fred Mifflin who was the skipper of the bomber on which Norman Jackson won the VC.

W84   WILSEY, John (General Sir)
H JONES VC: The Life and Death of an Unusual Hero
Hutchinson, London, 2002
335 pp, photos, maps, index, hb, cr

A full biography of 'H' Jones who won a posthumous VC leading 2 Para during the battle at Goose Green in May 1982. The author had full access to the papers and letters of Sara Jones. The biography takes 281 pages to meticulously describe the decisive moments of the battle leading to Jones's death. The author also explores the controversies and rumours arising from the events at Goose Green.

W85   WILSON, Michael
DESTINATION DARDANELLES: The Story of HMS E7
Leo Cooper, London, 1988
194 pp, photos, maps, index, hb, cr

Based on the diaries of Lt Oswald Hallifax, this book chronicles the exploits of HM Submarine *E7* in the Dardanelles in WW1. Additionally, it chronicles the involvement of the other British submarines in the operations including those commanded by Boyle, Holbrook and Nasmith, all of whom were awarded the VC.

W86   WILSON, Michael and KEMP, Paul
MEDITERRANEAN SUBMARINES
Crecy Publishing, Wilmslow, Cheshire, 1997
219 pp, photos, maps, index, hb, cr

A well-illustrated chronicle of submarine warfare in the Mediterranean Sea during WW1. Many of the submarine operations of the navies of the Allies and the Central Powers are documented. Chapter Six (pages 74-93) is devoted to the exploits of British submarines in the Sea of Marmara in 1915 and in particular those of HM Submarines *E11* (Lt Cdr ME Nasmith) and *E14* (Lt Cdr EC Boyle) for which their commanders won the VC. A four-page account of Lt Holbrook's VC deed in HM Submarine *B11* is contained in Chapter 2.

W87   WILSON, Patrick
DUNKIRK – 1940: From Disaster to Deliverance
Leo Cooper, Pen and Sword Books, Barnsley, 1999
192 pp, photos, maps, index, sb, cr

This book, part of the *Battleground Europe* series of battlefield guides, covers a series of actions by the BEF on the road to Dunkirk in May 1940 and the evacuation. Chapter 4 covers the defence of the perimeter around Dunkirk and includes a detailed description of the rearguard action on 1 June 1940 by the East Lancashires (pages 87-92) resulting in the award of the VC to Capt HM Ervine-Andrews.

W88   WINGATE, John, DSC
HMS CAMPBELTOWN (USS BUCHANAN): Flush Decker Destroyer ('4-stacker') 1918-1942
Profile Publications Ltd., Windsor, Berkshire, 1971
24 pp. (pages 97-120), photos, plans, maps, sb, cr

This publication, No 5 in the *Warship Profile* series, traces the history of the Destroyer HMS *Campbeltown*. Built as USS *Buchanan* in 1918, she was transferred to the Royal Navy in 1940. After service as an escort destroyer on Atlantic convoy duty, she was converted into an expendable vessel for use in the St Nazaire raid in March 1942. Her role in this raid is the main feature of the profile which also documents the services for which her CO, Lt Cdr SH Beattie, and the Senior Naval Officer, Cdr RED Ryder, won the VC. Illustrations include coloured profile plans of *Campbeltown* and 33 black and white photographs.

W89   WINTON, John
HURRAH FOR THE LIFE OF A SAILOR!: Life on the lower-deck of the Victorian Navy
Michael Joseph, London, 1977
320 pp, photos, index, hb, cr

In this history of the British 'bluejacket' in the nineteenth century, Chapter 8 (pages 123-138) is devoted to the VC deeds of the Navy in the Crimean War and Chapter 9 (pages 139-150) relates to Capt W Peel VC and his Naval Brigade in the Indian Mutiny. Short accounts of the various naval VCs are given within chapters recalling the associated campaigns.

W90 WINTON, John
THE VICTORIA CROSS AT SEA
Michael Joseph, London, 1978
256 pp, photos, index, hb, cr

This work contains a biographical account of each of the 124 VC recipients from the Royal and Dominion Navies, the Fleet Air Arm, Royal Marines and RAF Coastal Command and spans the period 1854 to 1945. Each account records the recipient's family background, pre-service years, naval career, post-service life (where relevant) and death. Additionally, each VC deed is described in detail.

W93 WOOD, Eric
THRILLING DEEDS OF BRITISH AIRMEN
George Harrap, London, 1917
318 pp, sketches, hb, cr

A collection of true stories describing some heroic deeds performed by the RFC and RNAS. There are separate chapters on five VCs (Rees, Warneford, Rhodes-Moorhouse, Bell Davies and Ball). There is a further chapter covering four other WW1 air VCs (Hawker, Liddell, Insall, Mottershead). Leefe Robinson's deed is included elsewhere in the book.

W95 WOOD, Field Marshal Sir Evelyn, VC GCB GCMG
FROM MIDSHIPMAN TO FIELD MARSHAL
Methuen, London, 1906 (two volumes); single volume: 1907
Two volumes: 621 pp. (Vol I: 322 pp.; Vol II: 299 pp.); single volume: 423 pp, photos, maps, index, hb, cr

An autobiography of FM Sir Evelyn Wood VC. He began his career as a midshipman in the Royal Navy and served in the Naval Brigade in the Crimean War. He was then commissioned into the Army and saw campaign service in the Indian Mutiny, Ashanti War, Gaika Expedition, Zulu War, Boer War 1880-81, Egypt 1882 and Sudan 1884-85. He documents fully both his short naval service and his distinguished military career. Volume 1 covers his family background and spans the period up to 1878. Volume 2 continues from 1878 and ends with his appointment, in 1903, as a Field Marshal. Reviewed in V51.

W96 WOOD, Field Marshal Sir Evelyn, VC GCB GCMG DCL
WINNOWED MEMORIES
Cassell, London, 1917
408 pp, photos, index, hb, cr

The author has assembled a selection of his personal memories spanning sixty years and covering diverse topics such as his sporting experiences, military anecdotes, after-dinner speeches, authorship addresses, military correspondence and memorials and obituaries.

W100 WOOD, General Sir Evelyn, VC GCB GCMG
THE CRIMEA IN 1854 AND 1894
Chapman & Hall, London, 1896
400 pp, sketches, maps, index, hb, cr

Sir Evelyn Wood describes his experiences in the Crimean War in which he served as a midshipman. His recollections are based on contemporary records and his personal correspondence. In revisiting the Crimea, in 1894, he tested the validity of his earlier views and impressions and incorporated into this book any modifications he considered necessary. The plans and illustrations are taken from sketches taken on the spot by Colonel the Hon WJ Colville, CB.

W106   WOODHOUSE, Peter, and POND, Chris
LIFE IN LOUGHTON 1926-1946
Loughton and District Historical Society, Loughton, 2003
58 pp, photos, sb, cr

The second edition of this publication has a short section on Lt RB Stannard VC RNR who won his VC in April 1940 in the campaign in Norway. Before and after WW2 he lived in Loughton in Essex before emigrating to Australia where he died in 1977.

W110   WOODS, Rex
ONE MAN'S DESERT: The Story of Captain Pip Gardner VC MC
William Kimber, London, 1986
208 pp, photos, maps, index, hb, cr

This profusely-illustrated biography of Captain Gardner tells the full story of his life and achievements. Serving as a tank officer in North Africa (VC, MC), he was eventually captured. His subsequent escape and evasion is described. Recaptured, he was transported to a POW camp in Germany where he remained until repatriation in 1945. His subsequent patronage of the Brunswick Boys' Clubs concludes the memoir.

W115   WOOLLEY, The Reverend Geoffrey Harold, VC OBE MC MA
SOMETIMES A SOLDIER
Ernest Benn, London, 1963
196 pp, photos, index, hb, cr

The autobiography of Rev Woolley who won a VC as a subaltern on the Western Front in 1915. He was later ordained into the Church of England, became Chaplain of Harrow School and served as a Chaplain to the Forces in WW2. The book relates his early years, military service in WW1 (VC and MC), his inter-war time as a schoolmaster at Rugby and Chaplain of Harrow School, his chaplaincy in WW2 and his post-war years as a vicar.

W125   WRIGHT, Christopher J. OBE and ANDERSON, Glenda (*compilers*), Hywel-Jones, Lt. Col., Ian, MBE MC (*project co-ordinator*)
THE VICTORIA CROSS AND THE GEORGE CROSS: The Complete History
Methuen and Co. and the VC and GC Association, London, 2013
Volume I   1854 - 1914, 634 pp. plus extensive notes I - CCXIV
Volume II   1914 - 1918, 864 pp. plus extensive notes I - LXXXVI
Volume III   1919 - 2013, 946 pp. plus extensive notes I - LXXVIII
photos, maps, index, hb, cr

This very significant publication is the fruit of 14 years research organised by the VC and GC Association into the history of Britain's two most senior gallantry awards. Each volume is printed on high quality paper and bound in dark blue cloth with images of the VC and GC embossed in gilt on the front cover. There are no dust wrappers but there is a slip case to contain the three volumes.

Volume I begins with Charles Lucas VC and Volume III ends with James Ashworth VC but since publication in 2013, two further VCs have been awarded to Cameron Baird and Joshua Leakey. The first award of the Albert Medal to be converted to the George Cross was to Thomas McCormack and the last GCs covered are to Staff Sergeants Olaf Schmid GC and Kim Hughes GC for mine-clearing work in Afghanistan in 2009.

The volumes are arranged chronologically by date of action, within each chapter. There is a selected chronology of significant events and an overview of each war or period and shorter descriptions of specific campaigns or actions where the VC or GC/Albert Medal/Edward Medal/Empire Gallantry Medal was awarded. Each entry has a small black and white portrait of the recipient (where available) and the full citation from *The London Gazette*, followed by biographical information in note form (similar to *Who's Who* entries). This includes details of birth, family, education, marital status, career, VC/GC action, final rank, death, commemoration, other awards, investiture and current location of the decoration (if known). The size of the entry depends on the length of LG citation and how much is known about the individual; Patrick Mahoney VC (Indian Mutiny) has half a page while recent recipients such as Corporals Benjamin Roberts-Smith VC and Daniel Keighran VC each have two and a half pages.

As the three volumes can be obtained individually, each contains the same preliminary notes, including a Foreword by HRH The Prince of Wales, as President of the VC and GC Association, acknowledgements, a brief history of the VC and the GC, the history of the VC and GC Association and the Royal Warrants for both decorations. Each volume contains a chronological list of awards for the period covered by that volume, many pages of maps, abbreviations and an index.

Volume III contains 27 appendices, covering 200 pages; listing elected and forfeited awards, posthumous VCs and GCS, a breakdown of awards to individual regiments, a list of location of actions and other useful data. Each volume has a comprehensive bibliography. Reviewed in V74.

W130   WRIGHT, Matthew
FREYBERG'S WAR: The Man, the Legend and Reality
Penguin Books, Camberwell, Melbourne, Australia, 2005
288 pp, photos, maps, index, sb, cr

Lieutenant-General Sir Bernard Freyberg led the 2nd NZEF from 1939 to 1945. In his in-depth study the author addresses the criticisms of Freyberg in handling the loss of Crete and the destruction of the monastery above Cassino in 1944. The author draws on previously unpublished material to shed new light on these controversies. After WW2 Freyberg became Governor General of New Zealand.

Y2   YOUNG, John
THEY FELL LIKE STONES: Battles and Casualties of the Zulu War, 1879
Greenhill Books, London, 1991
240 pp, engravings, index, hb, cr

This book describes the main engagements of the Anglo-Zulu War of 1879 and provides a full casualty list of British troops killed or wounded, both officers and men. There is an estimate of the Zulu casualties. Citations are included for all awards and honours.

Y5   YORKE, Edmund J.
RORKE'S DRIFT, 1879: Anatomy of an Epic Zulu War Siege
Tempus Publishing, Stroud, Gloucestershire, 2002
160 pp, photos, maps, plans, index, sb, cr

The story of the action at Rorke's Drift at which 11 VCs were won. In addition to constructing an analytical detailed narrative of the action and its prelude and aftermath, the author has also focused upon the personalities, tactics and battle experiences of both sides, deploying extensively contemporary eyewitness accounts. Later published in paperback with the title *Zulu!: The Battle for Rorke's Drift 1879*.

Z2   ZETTERLING, Niklas and TAMELANDER, Michael
TIRPITZ: The Life and Death of Germany's Last Super Battleship
Casemate, Newbury, Berkshire, 2009
360 pp, photos, maps, hb, cr

An account of the German battleship *Tirpitz* from its conception, design, launch, service in WW2 and its demise at the hands of the RAF. The attempts by *X-craft* to sink her are described which resulted in VCs for Cameron and Place.

PART 2

Books written by VC recipients on non-VC subjects

Section A   Non-fiction

Section B   Fiction

AYLMER, Major General F.J., VC CB
PROTECTION IN WAR
Hugh Rees, London, 1912
478 pp., plans, index, hb, cr

A doctrine of measures to prepare an army for readiness in protecting itself in time of war.

AYLMER, Sir F.J., VC
THE AYLMERS OF IRELAND
Mitchell, Hughes and Clarke, London, 1931
393 pp., photos, map, hb, cr

Genealogy of the Aylmer family.

AYLMER, Major General F.J., VC
FRENCH VIEWS ON THE TACTICAL EMPLOYMENT OF FIELD ARTILLERY
H. Rees, London, 1911
21 pp., plans, sb, cr

A booklet describing drills and tactics of deploying French Army artillery in field and mountain terrain.

AYLMER, Fenton John, VC
NOTES ON BRIDGING
W & J Mackay, Chatham, 1894
17 pp., sb, cr

A booklet describing drills on building military bridges.

BATTEN-POOLL, A.H., VC MC FLS
SOME GLOBETROTTING WITH A ROD
Spottiswoode, Ballantyne and Co., Eton, 1937
123 pp., hb, cr

A record of the author's impressions of various places around the world he had toured, particularly on fishing excursions. In addition to describing his angling activities, he also notes the flora and fauna observed. The chapters focus separately on his trips to Yugoslavia, the South Sea Islands, New Zealand, the Amazon, Iran and Russia.

BHAGAT, P. S., PVSM VC
MY LAND DIVIDED
No further details known. (c1945-6)

BHAGAT, Brigadier P.S., PVSM VC
[1] FORGING THE SHIELD: A Study of the Defence of India and South East Asia (*original edition*)
The Statesman, Calcutta & New Delhi, 1965
102 pp., hb, cr
[2] DEFENCE OF INDIA AND SOUTH EAST ASIA (Forging the Shield) (*expanded version*)
EBD Publishing and Distributing Co., Dehra Din, 1967
143 pp., hb, cr

Following his service on a board of enquiry into India's poor performance in the 1965 conflict with Pakistan, Bhagat wrote this book to record the lessons learned so that an effective defence could be organised against future aggression.

BHAGAT, Lieutenant General P.S., PVSM VC
THE SHIELD AND THE SWORD: India 1965 and After: The New Dimensions
Vikas Publishing House, New Delhi, 1974
115 pp., maps, index, hb, cr

The author continues the theme of Forging the Shield, proposing that India's defensive policy against Pakistan and China must include bold offensive action by India's armed forces.

BHAGAT, Lieutenant General P.S., PVSM VC
WIELDING OF AUTHORITY IN EMERGING COUNTRIES
Lancer International, New Delhi, 1986
cr

This book was completed in 1974 but published posthumously in 1986. The author deals with questions such as 'How is authority exercised by those in power?', 'Who lays down policy and executes it?', 'What should be the image of those in authority?' No further details known.

BHAGAT, Lieutenant General P.S., PVSM VC
AN ARMY COMMANDER'S RED DIARY
Lancer International, New Delhi, 1986
99 pp., sketches, hb, cr

A set of personal instructions covering how a commander or senior staff officer should brief his subordinates for detailed implementation of policies.

CAMPBELL, Vice Admiral Gordon, VC DSO MP
BRAVE MEN ALL: Tales of Great Courage
Hodder & Stoughton, London, 1935
307 pp., photos, maps, index, hb, cr

A selection of stories about heroism at sea in peace time. Chapters include lifeboat rescue, men-of-war to the rescue, shipwrecks, ships out of control and fires on ships. Many of the acts of heroism covered resulted in the award of a gallantry medal. Background information about some of these awards (for example, the Albert Medal and the awards of the RNLI, Lloyds' and the Royal Humane Society) is included in Chapter 1.

CAMPBELL, Vice Admiral Gordon, VC DSO
CAPTAIN JAMES COOK RN FRS
Hodder & Stoughton, London, 1936
320 pp., photos, maps, index, hb, cr

A description of Captain Cook's three major voyages and his untimely death. A list of logs and journals describing Captain Cook's travels is included.

CAMPBELL, Vice Admiral Gordon, VC DSO
ABANDON SHIP!
Hodder & Stoughton, London, 1938
318 pp., sketches, maps, hb, cr

Accounts of a selection of 18th- and 19th-century shipwrecks, namely East Indiaman Antelope; HMS Alceste; HMS Prospective; HMS St George and HMS Defence; and HMS Litchfield.

CAMPBELL, Vice Admiral Gordon, VC DSO
SAMARITANS OF THE SEA
Hutchinson, London, nd (c1939)
cr

The story of England's lifeboatmen. No further details known.

CAMPBELL, Vice Admiral Gordon, VC DSO and EVANS, I.O., FRGS
THE BOOK OF FLAGS
Oxford University Press, London, 1950 (revised and updated periodically)
120 pp. (1969 edition: 123 pp.), drawings, index, hb, cr

This book is an illustrated guide (in colour and black and white) to the national flags of the world, flags of Britain's armed forces, Britain's official and civic flags, and house flags and funnels of Britain's merchant navy. The origin, design and heraldic significance of these flags are described.

CHESHIRE, Group Captain Leonard, VC
THE HOLY FACE: An Account of the Oldest Photograph in the World
RH Johns, Newport, Monmouthshire, nd (c1960s) (*fp* 1954)
11 pp. (*fp* 16 pp.), photos, sb, cr

A history and description of the Turin Shroud.

CHESHIRE, Group Captain G.L., VC DSO DFC
PILGRIMAGE TO THE SHROUD
Hutchinson, London, 1956
72 pp., photos, hb, cr

An account of Cheshire's pilgrimage to the Shroud of Turin on which he was accompanied by an 11-year old girl who was dying.

CHESHIRE, Group Captain Leonard, VC
DEATH
Catholic Truth Society, London, 1978
22 pp., sb, cr

Cheshire's theological reflections on death and dying.

CREAGH, General Sir O'Moore, VC GCB GCSI
INDIAN STUDIES
Hutchinson, London, nd (c1918)
320 pp., hb, cr

A collection of 17 authoritative studies by the author, who saw extensive service in India. These studies cover six main themes: the Indian races, the various tiers of government in India, the land arrangements at village and state levels, the army in India, India intelligentsia and constitutional reform.

DINESEN, Thomas (VC)
ØKSEN: En Laegmands Livssyn
Jespersen og Pios Forlag, København, Denmark, 1959
158 pp., sb, cr (*Danish text*)

A Danish text in which the author gives an account of his outlook on life. The first chapter contains reflections on war and warriors with references to his participation in WW1. In other chapters he reflects on science, faith, religion (as a non-believer), ethics and morals, life and death. Later published in English under the title The Axe.

DINESEN, Thomas (VC)
BOGANIS: Min fader, hans slaegt, hans liv og hans tid
Gyldendal, København, Denmark, 1972
136 pp., photos, sb, cr (*Danish text*)

This Danish text is a detailed history of Thomas Dinesen's family which traces his forebears back to the seventeenth century. The principal subject of the book is his father, Captain Wilhelm Dinesen, soldier, politician, writer and adventurer, who wrote his well-known Letters from the Hunt under the pseudonym 'Boganis'. There are numerous photographs of the family and family residences.

DINESEN, Thomas, VC
[1] **TANNE, MIS SOSTER KAREN BLIXEN** (*original Danish edition*)
Gyldendal, København, Denmark, 1974 (*Danish text*)
125 pp., photos, sb, cr
[2] **MY SISTER, ISAK DINESEN** (*English edition*)
Michael Joseph, London, 1975
127 pp., photos, hb, cr

Thomas Dinesen's memoir about his famous elder sister, Karen Christentze Dinesen, alias Isak Dinesen, alias Karen Blixen, who was known affectionately by her family as "Tanne". She became one of Denmark's foremost authors. The memoir recalls her family background and her early years in Denmark. It then focuses on her years in Africa between 1914 and 1931 where she lived on her farm. It concludes with an account of her return to Denmark and her literary success which brought her world-wide fame. Karen Blixen was the author of Out of Africa which was later made into an Oscar-winning film.

DINESEN, Thomas (VC)
ANNE MARGRETHE: Dage of naetter l oldemores liv
Gyldendal, København, Denmark, 1976
128 pp., sb, cr (*Danish text*)

A biography of the author's maternal great-grandmother, Anne Margrethe (she died in 1849), who married Generalløjnant Wolfgang von Haffner.

DINESEN, Thomas (VC)
DAG BUG FRA SAFARI: Masai-Reserve 28 Februar – 15 April 1922
Gyldendal, København, Denmark, 1982
106 pp., cr (*Danish text*)

This book, published posthumously in 1982, is based on the diary the author kept of his experiences in 1922 on safari in the Masai Reserve in Kenya. The author was staying with his sister, Tanne (or Isak), on her Kenyan farm. She was the well-known author, Karen Blixen. The book describes big game hunting, the animals, hunting methods, the country and the people he visited as well as his outlook on life.

FREYBERG, Colonel B. C., VC CMG DSO
A STUDY OF UNIT ADMINISTRATION
Gale and Polden, Aldershot, 1933 (Second Edition 1940)
72 pp. (2nd Ed 73 pp.), specimen graphs & proformae, hb, cr

Written for the guidance of Regimental Officers serving with units on the home establishment, the book deals primarily with the peacetime ration and the peacetime system of accounting. To assist the wartime officer, a Second Edition, which Maj Gen Freyberg produced in 1940 while commanding the NZEF in Egypt, incorporated additional guidance. The text is supported by specimen layouts of eleven graphs and three proformae.

GOUGH, General Sir Charles, VC GCB and INNES, Arthur D., MA
THE SIKHS AND THE SIKH WARS: The Rise, Conquest and Annexation of the Punjab State
AD Innes, London, 1897
304 pp., photos, maps, index, hb, cr

The co-author Sir Charles Gough VC was a great nephew of Hugh, Lord Gough (1779-1869), whose diary and memoranda were referred to in the compilation of this history of the Punjab. Unpublished notes and diaries of officers who took part in the Sikh Wars were also sourced.

GRAHAM, General Sir Gerald, VC GCB RE
LAST WORDS WITH GORDON
Chapman & Hall, London, 1887
64 pp., hb, cr

Part of the text of this book appeared originally in the Fortnightly Review in January 1887. It was then published separately later that year and included additional text and appendices. General Graham was a close friend of Major General Charles Gordon, who died at Khartoum on 26 January 1885. Graham's last period with Gordon was aboard a Nile steamer destined for Khartoum. On the voyage the two men had a number of significant conversations, which provided the material for this book which was published after Gordon's death.

HART, Lieutenant R.C., RE
PARIS 1870-1871
R Williams, Station Press, Simla, India, nd (c1875)
33 pp., sb, cr

A lecture delivered at Simla on 1 July 1875 when Hart was an Assistant Garrison Instructor, being a chronological account of military operations in Paris during 1870-71. Hart later won the VC on 31 January 1879 in Afghanistan.

HART, Brigadier-General Sir Reginald Clare, VC KCB
REFLECTIONS ON THE ART OF WAR
William Clowes, London, 1894 (enlarged: 1897 and 1901)
236 pp. (1897 and 1901 editions: 364 pp.), index, hb, cr

General Hart VC compiled these notes for his "own instruction" and to aid his brother officers in their study of the art of war. Following an appraisal of the great generals in history, he discusses the theory and practice of war, its moral effects, strategies and tactics and various other facets. He then examines, in a historical context, the offensive and defensive roles of armies, the contributions by the cavalry, engineers and outposts and the operational and logistical requirements. The 1901 edition includes an additional chapter relating to mountain warfare.

HART, Brigadier-General R.C., VC CB
SANITATION AND HEALTH
William Clowes, London, 1894
57 pp., hb, cr

This work, which was authorised by the War Office for use in all army schools, evolved from a lecture delivered to the troops at Ranikhet, India, by Col Hart, VC. At that time, sickness among the troops within the district he was commanding was rife. He explains the health hazards to which troops in India were exposed and describes the precautions, particularly dietary and sanitary, that needed to be taken. Later editions were revised by Brigade Surgeon Lt Col T.H. Hendley.

HART, Brigadier-General R.C., VC CB
REPORT ON SINGLE STAFF RIDE, UNDER THE DIRECTION OF BRIGADIER-GENERAL R.C. HART, VC, CB
Samachar Press (*printer*), Belgaum, India, 1899
47 pp., maps, hb, cr

This volume was produced as an instruction manual following a military exercise under the command of Brigadier General Hart in March 1899. A key element of the text includes staff duties and the issuing of orders for military action against an imaginary enemy created for the purpose of the exercise. Detailed maps are included.

HART, Lieutenant General Sir Reginald, VC KCB
A VICTORIA CROSS MAN AND TEMPERANCE
Church of England Temperance Society, London, nd (c1912)
15 pp., sb, cr

A lecture to soldiers, given by General Hart, on the problems of alcohol and the benefits of temperance.

HARTIGAN, Henry (VC) (*Editor*: N.T. Walker)
STRAY LEAVES FROM A MILITARY MAN'S NOTEBOOK: Description of Men and Things Regimental at Home and Abroad
TS Smith, Calcutta, 1877
296 pp., hb, cr

An assortment of reminiscences of people and places by Sgt Henry Hartigan who won a VC with the 9th Lancers in the Indian Mutiny. Some of this material had previously been published in The Indian Daily News.

HAVELOCK, Captain H.M., VC
THREE MAIN MILITARY QUESTIONS OF THE DAY: (i) A Home Reserve Army; (ii) The more economic Tenure of India; (iii) Cavalry as affected by Breach-loading Arms
Longmans Green, London, 1867
209 pp., maps, hb, cr

Part of the book consists of two long essays contrasting the relative failure of British cavalry pursuing mutinous sepoys during the Indian Mutiny with the successes of federal mounted riflemen in the operations after the fall of Richmond during the American Civil War.

HEAPHY, Charles (VC)
NARRATIVE OF A RESIDENCE IN VARIOUS PARTS OF NEW ZEALAND TOGETHER WITH A DESCRIPTION OF THE COMPANY'S SETTLEMENT
Smith, Elder & Co., London, 1842 (facsimile editions: Hocken Library, University of Otago, Dunedin, New Zealand, 1968; and Capper Press, New Zealand, 1972)
142 pp., hb, cr

Charles Heaphy (later a Major and a VC) was appointed artist and draughtsman to the New Zealand Company in 1839 when he was only 17 years old. This volume is a description of the delights and hazards facing potential immigrants for whom the work was intended. This lively and compelling account of pioneering days gives an insight into Heaphy's character. Heaphy explored, studied and surveyed New Zealand and his local knowledge later helped to earn him a VC in 1864.

HUDSON, Charles Edward, VC CB DSO MC
POEMS
Privately published, nd (c1990)
32 pp. (unnumbered), line drawings, sb, cr

A compilation by the author's son of 16 poems by CE Hudson VC. There are seven line drawings by Veronica Hudson including a sketch of Hudson's VC and 17 other orders, decorations and medals. See H115 and H116.

INNES, J.J. McLeod, RE VC
ROUGH NARRATIVE OF THE SIEGE OF LUCKNOW
? , Calcutta, 1857
cr

No further details known.

INNES, Lieutenant General (J.J.) McLeod, RE VC
LUCKNOW & OUDE IN THE MUTINY - A NARRATIVE AND A STUDY
AD Innes, London, 1895
340 pp., sketches, maps, hb, cr

In the Preface, Innes states that this work is "...not an account of my private experiences or reminiscences... except to support my various statements and news...'. This volume is concerned principally with the defence of Lucknow in which Innes participated as a young engineer officer.

INNES, Lieutenant General (J.J.) McLeod, RE VC
THE SEPOY REVOLT: A Critical Narrative
AD Innes, London, 1897
319 pp., maps, index, hb, cr

This history of the Indian Mutiny re-examines its origins, development and eventual suppression. General Innes concludes with a summary and his comments, which are based on his personal experiences in the revolt.

INNES, Lieutenant General J.J. McLeod, RE VC
SIR HENRY LAWRENCE: The Pacificator
Clarendon Press, Oxford, 1898
208 pp., photo, index, hb, cr

A biography of Sir Henry Lawrence KCB, administrator in India, whose eminent services included the pacification and administration of the Punjab after its annexation. Subsequently, he prepared Lucknow for defence during the ensuing mutiny. He was mortally wounded in the Residency building.

INNES, Lieutenant General J.J. McLeod, RE VC
THE LIFE AND TIMES OF GENERAL SIR JAMES BROWNE RE KCB KCSI ('BUSTER BROWNE')
John Murray, London, 1905
371 pp., photos, maps, index, hb, cr

This memoir of Maj Gen Browne relates his life and, in particular, his extensive military service in India from 1859 up to 1896. As a military engineer, he participated in numerous wars and campaigns including North West Frontier 1860-63, Umbeyla, Afghan War 1878, Egypt 1882, Black Mountain and Zhob Valley. He died in post in 1896.

JONES, Lieutenant Colonel A.S., VC
WILL A SEWAGE FARM PAY? OR, THEORY COMBINED WITH PRACTICE
Longman's Green, London, 1874
39 pp., sb, cr

Written while the author was managing a sewage farm near Wrexham. The text (pages 1-27) explores the technical and economic aspects of sewage treatment. The appendix (pages 29-39) contains detailed financial accounts.

JONES, Lieutenant Colonel A.S., VC and ROECHLING, H. Alfred
NATURAL AND ARTIFICIAL SEWAGE TREATMENT
E & FN Spon, London, 1902
96 pp., hb, cr

This book is in two parts: Part 1 is by AS Jones VC (pages 1-27) and covers the technical aspects of sewage treatment. Included is a letter from Sir Redvers Buller VC congratulating him on his efficient operation of a sewage plant at Aldershot. Part 2 (pages 28-96) is by HA Roechling.

JOYNT, Colonel William Donovan, VC
TO RUSSIA AND BACK THROUGH COMMUNIST COUNTRIES
Lothian Publishing, Melbourne and Sydney, 1971
100 pp., photos, hb, cr

A description of the author's tours in Eastern Europe in 1962 and 1968.

KERR, W.A., VC
RIDING: Practical Horsemanship
George Bell and Sons, London, 1894
222 pp., photos, drawings, hb, cr

A practical guide of equestrian skills. Captain Kerr (an Indian Mutiny VC) had been second-in-command of the 2nd Regiment, South Maharatta Horse. This book was combined with the author's related work Riding for Ladies (see below) to form an omnibus edition entitled Riding.

KERR, W.A., VC
RIDING FOR LADIES
George Bell and Sons, London, 1894 (?)
? pp., photos, drawings, hb, cr

A practical guide to horse riding for ladies. (See Riding: Practical Horsemanship, above.)

KERR, W.A., VC
RIDING
George Bell and Sons, London, 1891
313 pp., photos, drawings, hb, cr

An omnibus edition of Riding: Practical Horsemanship and Riding for Ladies.

KERR, W.A., VC
DRIVING
George Bell and Sons, London, 189**?**
? pp., hb, cr

No further details known.

KERR, W.A., VC
PEAT AND ITS PRODUCTS: An Illustrated Treatise on Peat and its Products as a National Source of Wealth
Begg, Kennedy and Elder, Glasgow, 1905
318 pp., photos, drawings, hb, cr

A study of the development of the peat industry and the use of peat as a national resource, particularly in Great Britain and Ireland. The author evaluates the numerous products derived from peat and also discusses the working and reclamation of peat bogs.

LENNOX, Lieutenant Colonel W.O., VC (*compiler*)
THE ENGINEERS' ORGANIZATION IN THE PRUSSIAN ARMY FOR OPERATIONS IN THE FIELD 1870-1
? pp., London, 1878
cr

No further details known.

LENNOX, General Sir Wilbraham Oates, VC (*Editor*)
SERIES OF SEVEN TRANSLATIONS FROM PRUSSIAN MANUALS PRODUCED FOR PRIVATE CIRCULATION AMONG THE OFFICERS OF THE CORPS OF ROYAL ENGINEERS
2 volumes, Chatham and Portsmouth, 1874-80, hb, cr

This work comprises seven Prussian manuals translated by the Royal Engineer Institute and classified as "confidential", which were only issued to serving officers of the Royal Engineers. The manuals are:
Proposed Prussian Organisation for the Duties of Troops at Sieges, 26 pp., 1874
Prussian Sapping Regulations, 40 pp., 1874
Prussian Etappen Regulations, 72 pp., 1875
Elements of Fortress Warfare, 72 pp., 1875
Principles of Fortification, 210 pp., 1876
Prussian Pontoon Regulations, 76 pp., 1877
Fortification Atlas, 66 pp., 1880

MacINTYRE, Major General Donald, VC
HINDU-KOH: Wanderings and Wild Sport on and beyond the Himalayas
William Blackwood, Edinburgh and London, 1889
464 pp., photos, sketches, hb, cr

A book recounting the author's travels and big game hunting in the Himalayas. He describes the animals, hunting methods and a description of the country and the peoples of the areas he visited.

ALEXANDER, R.D.T., DSO OBE TD and MARTIN-LEAKE, A., VC VD
SOME SIGNPOSTS TO SHIKAR
Bengal Nagpur Railway Magazine, Calcutta, 1932
128 pp., photos, line drawings, hb, cr

The authors recall their experiences in tracking and shooting wild animals in India and Burma which they supplemented with a series of their excursions for gathering additional material to advise the would-be game hunter. Martin-Leake provided the line drawings and photographs that illustrate the book. More details of the book appear on pages 209-210 of his biography C76.

MAUDE, Colonel Francis Cornwallis, VC CB
FIVE YEARS IN MADAGASCAR with Notes on the Military Situation
Chapman & Hall, London, 1895 (*reprinted* Negro University Press, New York, 1969)
285 pp., drawings, maps, hb, cr

Col Maude recalls his experiences of his 58-month residency in Madagascar between 1888 and 1893. His mission was to procure some modifications in the terms imposed by the Potentate, when granting a concession for cutting timber in the north-east of the island, and in this capacity he became Director of the Madagascar Timber Company. Additionally, he gives his detailed observations on many aspects of Madagascan life and on the political and military situation.

MAUDE, Colonel Francis Cornwallis, VC CB
BACON OR SHAKESPEARE? Enquiries as to the authorship of the plays of Shakespeare
Robert Banks and Son (*printer*), London, 1895
72 pp., hb, cr

An examination of the authenticity of the authorship of the plays of William Shakespeare (spelt "Shakspere"; Francis Bacon's pseudonym was "Shake-speare"). Colonel Maude based the text of his book on his notes he read to a meeting of the Literary Society of the Goldsmith's Institute on 22 January 1895.

MAUDE, Colonel Francis Cornwallis, VC CB
INVASION OF THE BRITISH ISLES
cr

No further details known.

MELLISS, Captain C.J. (later Major General Sir Charles John, VC KCB)
LION HUNTING IN SOMALILAND, ALSO AN ACCOUNT OF "PIGSTICKING" THE AFRICAN WARTHOG
Chapman & Hall, London, 1895 (*facsimile edition*: St Martin's Press, New York, 1991)
186 pp., photos, line drawings, hb, cr

Maj Gen Sir Charles Melliss wrote this book whilst he was a captain serving with the 9th Bombay Infantry. He provides a vivid account of an African hunting adventure in which he survived a number of close calls in his quest for lions and warthogs.

NEAME, Brevet Lieutenant Colonel Philip, VC DSO
GERMAN STRATEGY IN THE GREAT WAR
Edward Arnold, London, 1923
132 pp., maps, hb, cr

This book is based on a series of the author's lectures delivered at the Staff College, Camberley between 1920 and 1923. He discusses the strategic operations of each phase of the war, outlining the plans of the General Staff and indicating the causes of success or failure. The characters of different commanders are examined. A total of 17 coloured maps support the text.

PEEL, Captain W., RN
A RIDE THROUGH THE NUBIAN DESERT
Longman, Brown, Green & Longmans, London, 1852
135 pp., map, hb, cr

A personal account of the journey made by Capt Peel (who later won the VC in the Crimean War) and Joseph Churi who left England in August 1851. The excursion, via Cairo, took them up the Nile, across the desert to Khartoum and on to El Obeid. Their journey was curtailed when both travellers suffered a severe attack of fever and had to return home.

PERCY, Captain Lord Henry Hugh Manvers
EXPLANATIONS OF THE MANOEUVRES OF A BRIGADE OF INFANTRY
Parker, Furnivall & Parker, London, 1852
69 pp., plans, hb, cr

This pocket reference manual was written before the author was awarded the VC. The book's aim was to assist young officers in acquiring the knowledge of posts and duties in Brigade Drill.

PERCY, Captain (Brevet Lieutenant Colonel) Lord Henry Hugh Manvers
CAUTIONS FOR COMPANY AND BATTALION DRILL
? pp., London, 1855
cr

This pocket manual was published after the author won the VC but before it was gazetted. The text gives concise guidance to regimental officers on drill procedures without having to consult larger reference manuals. No further details known.

POLLARD, Captain A.O., VC MC DCM
THE BOY'S ROMANCE OF AVIATION
George Harrap, London, 1935 (revised 1939)
327 pp. (1939 edition: 320 pp.), photos, sketches, index, hb, cr

The story of the evolution of manned flight and its advancement from earliest times to the 1930s. It describes pioneering developments in ballooning, aircraft and aircraft engine design and construction, civil and military aviation and air pilotage. The 1939 edition updates the text to reflect developments that occurred during the 1930s.

POLLARD, Captain A.O., VC MC DCM
ROMANTIC STORIES OF AIR HEROES
Hutchinson, London, 1937
300 pp., photos, sketches, hb, cr

A collection of 19 stories of famous pioneers in aviation from de Rozier's balloon ascent in 1783 to Charles Scott's record-breaking flights in 1936. The author recalls famous air races and pioneering flights across the English Channel, Atlantic Ocean, North and South Poles and what were to become the Imperial air routes.

POLLARD, Captain A.O., VC MC DCM
LEADERS OF THE ROYAL AIR FORCE
Hutchinson, London, nd (c1940)
130 pp., sb, cr

This book, No. II in the series Leaders of Britain, comprises biographical sketches of five contemporary RAF commanders: ACM Sir Cyril Newall (Chief of Air Staff), ACM Sir Edgar Ludlow-Hewitt (AOC in C Bomber Command), ACM Sir Hugh Dowding (AOC in C Fighter Command), ACM Sir Frederick Bowhill (AOC in C Coastal Command) and AM AS Barratt (AOC in C British Air Force in France).

POLLARD, Captain A.O., VC MC DCM
BOMBERS OVER THE REICH
Hutchinson, London, 1941
208 pp., photos, hb, cr

A description of the offensive activities of Bomber Command, Coastal Command and the Fleet Air Arm against the German war machine. Illustrative examples of the human aspect of these operations are included.

POLLARD, Captain A.O., VC MC DCM
THE ARMY OF TODAY
Raphael Tuck, London, nd (c1942)
48 pp., photos, sketches, sb, cr

A small booklet describing the life and training of the typical soldier of Britain and the Commonwealth.

ROBERTS, Field Marshal Lord, VC
THE RISE OF WELLINGTON
Sampson, Low & Marston, London, 1895
198 pp., sketches, maps, index, hb, cr

A reproduction of articles, published originally in Pall Mall Magazine, detailing the life and campaigns of The Duke of Wellington. (See Woods's Cavalry in the Waterloo Campaign later in Part 2.)

ROBERTS, Field Marshal Earl, VC
NOTES ON THE CENTRAL ASIAN QUESTION AND THE COAST AND FRONTIER DEFENCES OF INDIA, 1877-1893
War Office, London, 1902
326 pp., hb, cr

A series of 75 papers written by Roberts while QMG in India and from 1886-1893 as C-in-C. Roberts promoted a forward policy in India including the close control of border areas to prevent Russian invasion. These papers give a good insight into Roberts' thinking on policy issues relating to India.

ROBERTS, Field Marshal Earl, VC KG
DEFENCE OF THE EMPIRE: Field Marshal Earl Roberts' Appeal to the Nation
Spottiswoode (for the Lads' Drill Association), London, 1905
55 pp., sb, cr

This booklet was a compilation of articles and speeches given by Lord Roberts in 1905. One letter and one speech covered the importance of rifle shooting. A speech to the House of Lords covered national defence. The longest text (pages 25-45) covers a speech to the London Chamber of Commerce on imperial defence. The last section covers press extracts reporting on Lord Roberts' activities to promote national defence.

ROBERTS, Field Marshal Earl, VC KG
A NATION IN ARMS
John Murray, London, 1907
222 pp., hb, cr

A compilation of speeches delivered by FM Earl Roberts on the requirements of the British Army.

ROBERTS, Field Marshal Earl, VC KG
NATIONAL SECURITY: Speech delivered in the House of Lords on 23 November 1908
np, 1908
16 pp., sb, cr

Transcript of a speech delivered by Lord Roberts to the House of Lords describing the need for Britain to re-arm its forces.

ROBERTS, Field Marshal Earl, VC
FALLACIES AND FACTS: An Answer to Compulsory Service
John Murray, London, 1911
247 pp., hb, cr

An analysis of conscription into the armed services. The book is divided into three parts: The Nation's Peril, The Military and Naval Situation and The Argument from History.

ROBERTS, Field Marshal Earl, VC KG
LORD ROBERTS' MESSAGE TO THE NATION
John Murray, London, 1912
54 pp., sb, cr

On 25 October 1912, Lord Roberts made a speech in Manchester advocating national service in Britain. He pointed out the probability of a war with Germany and the fact that the British Empire was founded on war and conquest. Much controversy followed the speech and the booklet expands Roberts' argument. (Also see title below).

ROBERTS, Field Marshal Earl, VC KG
LORD ROBERTS' CAMPAIGN SPEECHES: A Continuation of "The Message to the Nation"
John Murray, London, 1913
53 pp., sb, cr

A continuation of the debate initiated by the title above.

ROBERTS, Field Marshal Earl, VC KG
LORD ROBERTS AND THE NEW CAMPAIGN: The Bristol Speeches, February 14th, 1913
National Service League, location not stated, 1913
20 pp., photo in full dress on cover, sb, cr

Published following the inauguration of Lord Roberts' campaign for National Service on his formal visit to Colston Hall, Bristol. The booklet features a full transcript of his speech and the introductory oration by Sir Arthur Lawley.

SMYTH, Brigadier J.G., VC MC
DEFENCE IS OUR BUSINESS
Hutchinson, London, 1945
93 pp., cr

An examination of Britain's post-war defence policy with an assessment of the lessons learnt from the war in 1939-45 and how they should be applied to post-war defence. Topics discussed include administration and supply, personnel training, leaders and leadership, propaganda, weapons and research and demobilisation.

SMYTH, Brigadier J.G., VC MC MP (*Editor*)
THE WESTERN DEFENCES
Wingate, London, 1951
144 pp., cr

A collection of nine essays, contributed by experts in various fields, on the need for a united defence of Western European countries against the increasing threat posed by the Soviet Union. In his six-page introduction, Brig Smyth discusses the key issues relating to the threat and proposes a Western European Defence Force to combat any Soviet aggression.

SMYTH, Brigadier J.G., VC MC MP
LAWN TENNIS
Batsford, London, 1953
240 pp., photos, index, hb, cr

This volume in the British Sports: Past & Present series is a concise history of lawn tennis from its beginnings up to the present day (1953). The author incorporates his own views on the greatest players of each generation and of all time and also his views on the contemporary developments of the professional game.

SMYTH, Brigadier Sir John, Bt VC MC MP
THE GAME'S THE SAME: Lawn Tennis in the World of Sport
Cassell, London, 1956
104 pp., photos, hb, cr

A study of the style, strokes and court behaviour of leading tennis players from the 1920s onwards.

SMYTH, Brigadier Sir John, Bt VC MC MP
SANDHURST
Weidenfeld & Nicholson, London, 1961
301 pp., photos, index, hb, cr

A history of the Royal Military Academy, Woolwich and the Royal Military College, Sandhurst from their foundation in the eighteenth century, through their amalgamation in 1947 to form the Royal Military Academy, Sandhurst and up to 1961. The author also examines the reforms of the Victorian era and the contribution made by ex-cadets during the two world wars. One of the eight appendices lists the 37 Woolwich and 90 Sandhurst cadets who, subsequently, were awarded the VC.

SMYTH, Brigadier Rt Hon Sir John, Bt VC MC MP
BELOVED CATS
Frederick Muller, London, 1963
84 pp., photos, sketches, hb, cr

A character study of a pair of Siamese cats owned by Sir John and Lady Smyth.

SMYTH, Brigadier Rt Hon Sir John, Bt VC MC MP
BLUE MAGNOLIA
Frederick Muller, London, 1964
80 pp., photos, sketches, hb, cr

A companion volume to Beloved Cats, describing the integration of two Siamese kittens, one named Blue Magnolia, into the cat family of Sir John and Lady Smyth.

SMYTH, Brigadier Rt Hon Sir John, Bt VC MC MP as told by MACAULAY, Lieutenant Colonel A.D.C., OBE
BEHIND THE SCENES AT WIMBLEDON
Collins, London, 1965
320 pp., photos, index, hb, cr

Col Macaulay, late Secretary of the All England Lawn Tennis Club, recounts the highlights of each Wimbledon tournament from 1922 to 1964 and reveals the workings of the tournament.

SMYTH, Brigadier Rt Hon Sir John, Bt VC MC MP
MING: The Story of the Cat Family
Frederick Muller, London, 1966
96 pp., photos, sketches, hb, cr

The sequel in the trilogy of books about the author's cats, including a new addition to the family – a Burmese named Ming.

SMYTH, Brigadier Rt Hon Sir John, Bt VC MC
THE REBELLIOUS RANI
Frederick Muller, London, 1966
223 pp., photos, maps, hb, cr

An account of the Rani of Jhansi who, during the Indian Mutiny, was responsible for the brutal murder of 60 men, women and children to whom she had promised safe conduct. It is also a study of the military campaigns of General Sir Hugh Rose in Jhansi and Gwalior and includes brief accounts of some of the VCs won in the campaign.

SMYTH, Brigadier Rt Hon Sir John, Bt VC MC
BOLO WHISTLER: The Life of General Sir Lashmer Whistler GCB KBE DSO DL: A Study in Leadership
Frederick Muller, London, 1967
270 pp., photos, index, hb, cr

A biography of General "Bolo" Whistler who was commissioned in 1917 and survived trench warfare in WW1. During WW2, he commanded a battalion at Dunkirk, a brigade in North Africa and Italy and a division in Normandy. Smyth regarded him as one of Britain's most able commanders of the war.

SMYTH, Brigadier Rt Hon Sir John, Bt VC MC
THE STORY OF THE GEORGE CROSS
Arthur Barker, London, 1968
208 pp., photos, index, hb, cr

Written in the same style as The Story of the Victoria Cross (S60), the book covers 139 GC recipients from 1940 to 1968. Section 6 details the Empire Gallantry Medallists who were authorised to exchange their EGM for the GC. An appendix reproduces the Royal Warrants for the GC. Sir John Smyth was, at the time of writing, the Chairman of the VC and GC Association.

SMYTH, Brigadier Rt Hon Sir John, Bt VC MC
IN THIS SIGN CONQUER: The Story of the Army Chaplains
AR Mowbray, London, 1968
362 pp., photos, index, hb, cr

The history of the Royal Army Chaplains' Department, its predecessors and its Dominion equivalents in WW2. It is also an account of many of its padres who performed gallant or noble service. A brief description of the VC deed of JW Adams, WRF Addison, TB Hardy, EN Mellish and JW Foote is included within the text relating to the particular conflict. Additionally, an account of the VC action of GH Woolley, who later became a padre, is given.

SMYTH, Brigadier Rt Hon Sir John, Bt VC MC
THE WILL TO LIVE: The Story of Dame Margot Turner DBE RRC
Cassell, London, 1970
176 pp., photos, index, hb, cr

A biography of Brigadier Turner, which focuses on her distinguished career in military nursing from 1937 to 1969, when she became Colonel Commandant of the QARANC. Between 1964 and 1968 she was Matron-in-Chief and Director of the Army Nursing Service. The author also recalls fully her capture during the fall of Singapore and her consequent internment in a Japanese POW camp which lasted three-and-a-half years. He provides a vivid account of her experiences as a POW and of life in her camp.

SMYTH, Brigadier Rt Hon Sir John, Bt VC MC
PERCIVAL AND THE TRAGEDY OF SINGAPORE
Macdonald, London, 1971
304 pp., photos, maps, index, hb, cr

A biography of Lieutenant General Arthur Ernest Percival, CB DSO OBE MC DL, who was General Officer Commanding Malaya at the time of the fall of Singapore in 1942 and was blamed for the capitulation. Much of the book concerns this period and his subsequent three years in Japanese captivity.

SMYTH, Brigadier Rt Hon Sir John, Bt VC MC
THE LIFE STORY OF BRIGADIER TOOSEY, CBE DSO TD DL JP
np (printer: James Lever Printing Co, Liverpool), nd (c1973)
161 pp., photos, hb, cr

This biography, printed for private circulation, was written at the request of Brigadier Toosey, who asked for it not to be published commercially during his lifetime. In particular, it documents his WW2 service thoroughly, which covered action at Dunkirk and in the Far East. Captured by the Japanese in 1942, Col Toosey was Senior British Officer in the building of the notorious bridge over the River Kwai. Following completion of the bridge, he became the base hospital commandant at the POW camp. His POW experiences are described vividly. Post-war, he was a driving force behind the Far East Prisoners of War Federation and became its National President (the author was its Honorary Vice-President).

SMYTH, Sir John, VC
JEAN BOROTRA: The Bounding Basque – His Life of Work and Play
Stanley Paul, London, 1974
239 pp., photos, maps, index, hb, cr

A biography of the French Basque tennis star, Jean Borotra, who won six Wimbledon titles during the inter-war years. It also recalls his service in the French Army in WW1 for which he won the CdeG, and his two-and-a-half years' imprisonment by the Gestapo in WW2 after which he was awarded the Legion of Honour.

STEELE, Lieutenant Gordon C., VC and WILSON-BARKER, Sir David
NAVIGATION: Theory and Practice
Charles Griffin & Company's Nautical Series, London, 1923 (4th edition)
158 pp., hb, cr

Sir David Wilson-Barker was the author of the first edition of this book on navigation at sea, which was published in 1896 and revised in 1904 and in 1913. The fourth edition was revised by Lieutenant Gordon Steele VC.

STEELE, Captain Gordon C., VC RNR
[1] ELECTRICAL KNOWLEDGE FOR THE MERCHANT NAVY OFFICER (*1950 title*)
[2] ELECTRICAL KNOWLEDGE FOR SHIPS' OFFICERS (*1954 title*)
Brown, Son & Ferguson, Glasgow, 1950
256 pp. (1954 edition: 290 pp.), photos, line drawings, maps, index, hb, cr

This book is an introduction to electrical equipment on ships to equip ships' officers with a basic understanding of the subject. The expanded 1954 edition includes additional chapters on fire detection systems, direction finding and navigational aids.

STEELE, Commander Gordon, VC RN
THE STORY OF THE WORCESTER
George Harrap, London, 1962
256 pp., photos, index, hb, cr

This book was written to commemorate the HMS Worcester's proud achievements during one hundred years of service to the Merchant Navy as a training ship. The author served on her as a cadet (1907-1909) and as her Captain Superintendent (1929-1957).

STEELE, Gordon, VC
TO ME, GOD IS REAL
Stockwell, Ilfracombe, 1973
199 pp., hb, cr

A devotional book aimed at bringing the reality of God to a new generation by a reasoned argument for Christian belief.

STEELE, Gordon, VC
ABOUT MY FATHER'S BUSINESS
Stockwell, Ilfracombe, 1974
109 pp., hb, cr

This devotional book of 29 short unnumbered chapters was written in support of orthodox Christianity. Each chapter gives a reasoned explanation for Christian belief.

STEELE, Gordon, VC
IN MY FATHER'S HOUSE
Stockwell, Ilfracombe, 1975
74 pp., hb, cr

A devotional book consisting of 25 short unnumbered chapters aimed at promoting Christian discipleship with discourses on the nature of heaven.

STEELE, Gordon, VC
WHERE GOD STEPS IN
Privately published, Winkleigh, Devon, 1976
55 pp., sb, cr

This book is similar to other religious books by the author. Although printed by Stockwell it is privately published by the author. The book encourages Christian believers to harness God's power when facing life's difficulties.

STEELE, Gordon, VC
ONE IN ALL AND ALL IN ONE
Stockwell, Ilfracombe, 1977
40 pp., sb, cr

A devotional booklet aimed at promoting Christian discipleship. A total of 17 unnumbered chapters, each following a spiritual theme or thought to guide the reader on their pilgrimage of life.

THACKERAY, Lieutenant-Colonel E.T., VC
VIEWS OF KABUL AND ITS ENVIRONS FROM PICTURES TAKEN BY THE PHOTOGRAPHIC SCHOOL OF THE CORPS OF BENGAL SAPPERS AND MINERS
Privately printed, 1881
? pp., photos, hb, cr

The title describes the book's content which includes 30 photographic plates and includes a short description of Kabul and its buildings. See T6.

VICKERS, Sir Geoffrey (VC)
VALUES AND DECISION-TAKING
University of Toronto, Toronto, 1956
34 pp., sb, cr

A series of three papers on sociology delivered by the author to the University of Toronto in November 1956.

VICKERS, Sir Geoffrey (VC)
THE UNDIRECTED SOCIETY: Essays on the Human Implications of Industrialization in Canada
University of Toronto Press, Toronto, 1959
162 pp., cr

A collection of essays on the human aspects of industrialization in Canada.

VICKERS, Sir Geoffrey (VC)
THE IMPACT OF AUTOMATION ON SOCIETY
Ontario Woodsworth Memorial Foundation, Toronto, 1964
12 pp., illus, sb, cr

A text of the address on the social impacts of automation given at the Conference on Automation and Social Change held in Toronto in September 1963.

VICKERS, Sir Geoffrey (VC)
THE ART OF JUDGEMENT: A Study of Policy Making
Chapman & Hall, London, 1965 (expanded Sage Publications, Thousand Oaks, California, USA, 1995)
242 pp. (1995 edition: 284 pp.), index, hb, cr

A text on policy decision-making for executives in public administration. Republished in 1995 as a Centenary Edition to commemorate the birth of Sir Geoffrey Vickers, this version includes a 12-page preface reappraising Vickers' thoughts on public policy-making. It also contains a 20-page chapter entitled The Life of Sir Geoffrey Vickers which recalls his early years, military service (VC) and distinguished and varied civilian careers spanning the law, civil service, management and authorship. An expanded bibliography lists the associated works, written by Vickers, including 25 academic papers and 58 articles in professional journals.

VICKERS, Sir Geoffrey, (VC)
INDUSTRY, HUMAN RELATIONS AND MENTAL HEALTH
Tavistock Publications, London, 1965
14 pp., sb, cr

An address on industrial relations and sociology delivered at the 17th annual meeting of the World Federation for Mental Health at Berne on 4 August 1964.

VICKERS, Sir Geoffrey (VC)
TOWARDS A SOCIOLOGY OF MANAGEMENT
Chapman & Hall, London, 1967
206 pp., index, hb, cr

A collection of papers for administrators and businessmen to stimulate thinking about the purpose, structure and values of organisations. Two specific themes explored are the methods of control and the importance of social/human factors when setting performance targets in organisations.

VICKERS, Sir Geoffrey (VC)
VALUE SYSTEMS AND SOCIAL PROCESS
Tavistock Publications, London, 1968
217 pp., hb, cr

A text book on social sciences.

VICKERS, Sir Geoffrey (VC)
FREEDOM IN A ROCKING BOAT: Changing Values in an Unstable Society
Allen Lane/The Penguin Press, Harmondsworth, 1970
215 pp., hb, cr

A social sciences text book covering the relationship of technology to civilization.

VICKERS, Sir Geoffrey (VC)
SCIENCE AND THE REGULATION OF SOCIETY
Institute for the Study of Science in Human Affairs, Columbia University, New York, 1970
56 pp., sb, cr

A paper covering science, civilization and the state as part of a series of Occasional Papers for Columbia University.

VICKERS, Sir Geoffrey (VC)
MAKING INSTITUTIONS WORK
Associated Business Programmes, London, 1973
187 pp., hb, cr

A study of economic policy, social institutions and social values.

VICKERS, Sir Geoffrey (VC)
RESPONSIBILITY: Its sources and limits
Intersystems Publications, Seaside, California, USA, 1980
137 pp., hb, cr

A text book on responsibility and systems analysis. Portions of the book had been previously published in two journals on behavioural science.

VICKERS, Sir Geoffrey (VC)
HUMAN SYSTEMS ARE DIFFERENT
Harper & Row, London, 1983
188 pp., index, hb, cr

A text book on social systems, social evolution and system theory.

VICKERS, (Sir) Geoffrey (VC)
MOODS AND TENSES: Occasional Poems of an Old Man
Privately published, 1983
71 pp., sb, cr

An anthology of the author's poems published after his death.

VICKERS, Sir Geoffrey (VC)
THE VICKERS PAPERS
Harper & Row, London, 1984
379 pp., index, sb, cr

The collected social science papers of Sir Geoffrey Vickers edited by the Open Systems Group.

VICKERS, Sir Geoffrey (VC)
POLICYMAKING, COMMUNICATION AND SOCIAL LEARNING: Essays of Sir Geoffrey Vickers
Transaction Books, New Brunswick, USA, 1987
202 pp., hb, cr

A collection of edited essays published after the author's death. The essays cover policy sciences, communication, social values and the professions.

VICKERS, Sir Geoffrey (VC) and LOWE, Adolph
RETHINKING THE FUTURE: The Correspondence between Geoffrey Vickers and Adolph Lowe
Transaction Publications, New Brunswick, USA, 1991
239 pp., index, hb, cr

This correspondence between two eminent social scientists was edited by Jeanne Vickers and published after the death of the authors.

VICKERS, Sir Geoffrey (VC)
RETHINKING PUBLIC POLICY-MAKING: Questioning Assumptions, Challenging Beliefs: Essays in honour of Sir Geoffrey Vickers on his centenary
Sage Publications, London, 1995
232 pp., photos, index, hb, cr

A collection of essays by Sir Geoffrey Vickers VC edited by Margaret Blunden and Malcolm Dando, originally published as a special issue of the American Behavioural Scientist (Vol 18, No. 1 September/October 1994) to commemorate the centenary of the author's birth.

WHITE, Colonel A.C.T., VC
THE STORY OF ARMY EDUCATION 1643-1963
George Harrap, London, 1963
286 pp., photos, index, hb, cr

This history of the Royal Army Educational Corps and its predecessors examines the development of army education from 1643.

WILSON, Lieutenant Colonel Eric, VC
STOWELL IN THE BLACKMORE VALE
Privately published, Stowell, Somerset, 1986 (*reprinted 1999*)
40 pp., photo, sketches, sb, cr

A history of the village of Stowell, in Somerset, in which the author lived for over 50 years. Glimpses of various aspects of Stowell and its inhabitants over the centuries have been chronicled from local history sources.

WOOD, General Sir Evelyn, VC
CAVALRY IN THE WATERLOO CAMPAIGN
Sampson, Low & Marston, London, 1895 (*facsimile edition*: Worley Publications, Felling, Tyne and Wear, 1998)
203 pp., photos, sketches, maps, index, hb, cr

A reproduction of a number of articles published originally in the Pall Mall Magazine and which describe the role of cavalry in the Waterloo campaign.

WOOD, General Sir Evelyn, VC GCB GCMG
ACHIEVEMENTS OF CAVALRY
George Bell, London, 1897
260 pp., maps, index, hb, cr

A narrative of the achievements of cavalry in twelve battles ranging from Villers-en-Cauchies, in 1794, to Rezonville, in 1870. There is also a chapter describing the achievements of cavalry.

WOOD, Field Marshal Sir Evelyn, VC GCB GCMG
THE REVOLT IN HINDUSTAN 1857-59
Methuen, London, 1908
367 pp., sketches, maps, index, hb, cr

The contents of this book first appeared in The Times in October 1907. The author, who participated in the Indian Mutiny, rewrote some of the chapters that had been republished in book form in 1908. Major events, such as the sieges of Delhi, Lucknow and Cawnpore, are chronicled in detail. There are brief descriptions of a number of VC actions.

WOOD, Field Marshal Sir Evelyn, VC (*editor*)
BRITISH BATTLES ON LAND AND SEA
Cassell, London, 1915
Two volumes - 1130 pp. (Vol 1: 583 pp.; Vol 2: 547 pp.), photos, sketches, maps, index, hb, cr

This profusely-illustrated two-volume work commences in Volume 1 with a 183-page history of how the fighting services helped to create the Empire up to 1902. Volume 1 then narrates the story of 23 battles from 1797 to 1813 and 28 earlier battles from 1066 to 1591. Volume 2 continues these two themes with 27 battles from 1815 to 1900 and 27 earlier battles from 1642 to 1794. In the 'modern' battles section of this volume there are brief references to numerous VCs and their deeds or commands. Wood recounts his own experiences in the Crimea, Ashanti, first Boer War and Zulu War. The work contains 24 colour plates and 500 other illustrations.

WOOD, Field Marshal Sir Evelyn, VC GCB GCMG DCL
OUR FIGHTING SERVICES: And How they Made the Empire
Cassell, London, 1916
616 pp., sketches, maps, index, hb, cr

This monumental work covers the period 1066 to 1902 and describes, in detail, all the major battles in wars and campaigns including the English Civil War, Peninsular War, Waterloo Campaign, and Zulu War. The book has numerous maps illustrating the major battles.

WOOLLEY, The Rev Geoffrey Harold, VC OBE MC
EPIC OF THE MOUNTAINS
Blackwell, Oxford, 1929
13 pp., sb, cr

The author describes this work as an attempt in Miltonic verse to trace the story of evolution and man's struggle to reach truth in such a way that the modern scientist facing the evidence would have to admit that his own discoveries compelled him to recognize the mind and purpose of God, and not merely material causes or accident, behind the Universe and in human life.

WOOLLEY, The Rev Geoffrey Harold, VC OBE MC
FEAR AND RELIGION
Benn, London, 1930
32 pp., sb, cr

A pamphlet written in the series Affirmations by a Church of England committee, of which the author was a member. They were concerned with promoting religious renewal through special training initiatives with clergy.

WOOLLEY, The Rev Geoffrey Harold, VC OBE MC
A JOURNEY TO PALESTINE
Blackwell, Oxford, 1935
15 pp., sb, cr

While travelling in Palestine, the author recorded his impressions of places like Bethlehem, Nazareth, the Garden of Gethsemane and Emmaus in the form of short poems, generally sonnets. At the request of his fellow travellers the jottings were published in this book.

WOOLLEY, The Rev Geoffrey Harold, VC OBE MC
A POCKET BOOK OF PRAYERS
Student Christian Movement Press, London, 1940
63 pp., sb, cr

A short volume of prayers for members of the armed forces.

WOOLLEY, The Rev Geoffrey Harold, VC OBE MC
THE HILLTOP AND OTHER POEMS
?
? , cr

Woolley turned to the study of sonnets as one means of solace following the loss of many of his friends in WW1. Later he suffered from his war memories and decided to counter them by writing poetry and sonnets. They were published in this volume after Tubby Clayton asked the author to allow him to publish them for distribution to Toc H.

BISHOP, W.A., VC DSO MC and STUART-WORTLEY, Major Rothesay
    THE FLYING SQUAD (1929)

CAMPBELL, Vice Admiral Gordon, VC, DSO
    A SON OF THE SEA (1936)
    WITCH OF THE WAVE (1937)
    TWO CADETS (1938)
    DOG-NELSON, A.B. (1938)
    THE GREAT BLUFF (1938)

DINESEN, Lieutenant Thomas, VC
    SYRENBUSKEN (original Danish version) (1951)
    SYRENBUSKEN (Norwegian translated version) (1951)
    SYRENBUSKEN (Swedish translated version) (1951)
    SYRENBUSKEN (Finnish translated version) (1951)
    ZEVEN NACHTEN OP DE RODE ZEE (Dutch translated version) (1952)
    TWILIGHT ON THE BETZY (English translated version) (1952)

McKEAN, Captain G.B., VC MC MM
    MAKING GOOD: A Story of North-West Canada (1921)

POLLARD, Captain A.O., VC MC DCM
    PIRDALE ISLAND (1930)
    RUM VALLEY (1931)
    MURDER AND HIDE-AND-SEEK (1931)
    CIPHER FIVE (1931)
    THE DEATH FLIGHT (1932)
    THE HAVENHURST AFFAIR (1932)
    THE RIDDLE OF LOCH LEMMAN (1933)
    THE PHANTOM PLANE (1934)
    MURDER IN THE AIR (1935)
    THE SECRET OF CASTLE VOXZEL (1935)
    UNOFFICIAL SPY (1935)
    THE DEATH GAME (1936)
    HIDDEN CIPHER (1936)
    THE MURDER GERM (1937) Reissued in 1947
    FLANDERS SPY (1937)
    BLACK-OUT (1938)
    AIR REPRISAL (1938)
    THE SECRET FORMULA (1939)
    MURDER OF A DIPLOMAT (1939)
    THE SECRET PACT (1940)
    A.R.P. SPY (1940)
    SECRET WEAPON (1941)
    WANTED BY THE GESTAPO (1942)
    INVITATION TO DEATH (1942)
    THE DEATH SQUADRON (1943)

GESTAPO FUGITIVE (1944)
THE FIFTH FREEDOM (1944)
BLOOD HUNT (1945)
DOUBLE CROSS (1946)
A DEAL IN DEATH (1947)
THE DEATH GAME (1947)
THE IRON CURTAIN (1947)
DAVID WILSHAW INVESTIGATES (1950)
THE DEATH CURSE (1950)
THE SECRET VENDETTA (1950)
DEAD MAN'S SECRET (1950)
RED HAZARD (1950)
THE POISONED PILOT (1950)
THE DEATH PARADE (1951)
THE GOLDEN BUDDHA (1951)
DEATH INTERVENED (1951)
COUNTERFEIT SPY (1952)
THE DEAD FORGER (1952)
CRIMINAL AIRMAN (1953)
THE BUCKLED WING (1953)
HOMICIDAL SPY (1954)
THE MISSING DIAMOND (1955)
SINISTER SECRET (1955)
SMUGGLERS' BUOY (1958)
THE SECRET PACT (1958)
WRONG VERDICT (1960)
FORGED EVIDENCE (1962)

SMYTH, Brigadier Sir John Smyth, Bt VC MC
PARADISE ISLAND (1958)
TROUBLE IN PARADISE (1959)
ANN GOES HUNTING (1960)

VICKERS, Geoffrey, VC
SECRET OF TARBURY TOR (1925)

PART 3

Other Sources of Information

INTRODUCTION

Part 3 aims to highlight other sources of printed and electronic material, not within the scope of this bibliography.

AUCTION CATALOGUES

The UK has some of the world's most eminent auction houses for coins and medals. For example, Spink, the publishers of this volume, were established in 1666. Since 1879 auction houses and dealers have been listing VCs for sale in the catalogues which can be a useful source of information. In recent years these catalogues have included many photographs, some in colour, as well as information not previously published. *Victoria Cross Presentations and Locations* (P36) by Dennis Pillinger and Anthony Staunton was published in 2000. In Chapter 6 there is a list of public sales of VCs from February 1879 to May 2000. This shows the name of the VC recipient, whether sold or withdrawn, sale value in local currency, the name of the auction house or dealer and the date of sale. This is invaluable data for identifying useful catalogues. This good work has been continued by Iain Stewart on his VC website **www.victoriacross.org/uk/aaauctio.htm** with VC sales from May 1998 to the present. So Stewart's list overlaps with that of Pillinger and Staunton's between May 1998 and May 2000.

Stewart's list has rank, first name, surname, war/campaign, auctioneer name, sale date and sale amount in local currency. It also shows the buyer's identity, if known. By clicking on the surname further details of the sale are usefully shown.

WEBSITES

There are a number of websites covering the VC and its recipients. The quality varies but some are listed here:

http://victoriacross.org.uk (Iain Stewart's site referred to above)
http://www.vconline.org.uk
http://victoriacrosstrust.org
https://en.wikipedia.org/wiki/Victoria_Cross
https://www.hancocks-london.com/the-victoria-cross/
https://www.thegazette.co.uk/awards-and-accreditation/content/100077
Websites can change regularly and as they are not a permanently accessible body of knowledge. They are not a printed source therefore are not included in the Bibliography.

ARTICLES IN JOURNALS AND MAGAZINES

There are thousands of articles on the VC and its recipients in journals and magazines dating back to the institution of the VC. Some are very well researched and detailed in content. Others are short articles often using only published sources with no primary research and therefore often offering little or no new information.

As a team we decided to omit journal articles from the Bibliography as no extensive search had been made to compile a comprehensive list. As library and archive indexes are increasingly being digitized these articles can be more easily located than in the past. However, more obscure journals, no longer being published, are hard to trace without physically visiting a library. A worthy future project is for researchers to conduct a comprehensive world-wide search of journals and magazine articles on the VC and its recipients with a similar cross reference index, as used in this volume. Such a project is likely to identify over ten thousand such articles which would probably require two or three volumes the size of this bibliography.

NEWSPAPERS

These can be a useful source of printed literature particularly with a name search facility to identify articles on individual VC recipients. National newspaper libraries in the UK, Canada, Australia, New Zealand, India, South Africa and the USA can be a useful source but often involving paying an annual subscription or via a pay-per-view facility. An example is: **https://www.britishnewspaperarchive.co.uk**

The National Newspaper Collection for newspapers for New Zealand, Australia and the Pacific can be found at: **https://natlib.govt.nz/collections/a-z/national-newspaper-collection**
In addition to the libraries mentioned above World Catalogue is a useful site to identify which libraries hold printed and electronic volumes. Their website is **https://www.worldcat.org/**

Their advanced search engine will indicate which libraries hold the title entered.

MUSEUMS

Museums around the world often have extensive archives on VC recipients. In the UK The National Archives, Imperial War Museum, National Army Museum, RAF Museum and the National Maritime Museum have much primary data. The Imperial War Museum also has extensive oral archives some of which were used to produce Roderick Bailey's volume *Forgotten Voices of the Victoria Cross* (B1).

Regimental museums provide good sources of information but they usually need to be visited to access data.

INDEX

Recipient	Gazette Date	Item Number in Part 1 / Part 2
Aaron, A.L.	5 Nov. 1943	B12 B23 B89 C55 K23 L3 L53 M17A R70 T35 V68 W52 W125
Abdul Hafiz	27 Jul. 1944	A16 A66 B44 I6 I10 K16 M102D R70 S40 S45 T36 W125
Ablett, A.	24 Feb. 1857	B15A C62 C130 C150 D17 G15 K50 K54 G63 R58 V63 W42 W125
Ackroyd, H.	6 Sep. 1917	A65 C80 C130 L42 M47 O17 R80 S76 V57 V72 W125
Acton, A.	18 Feb. 1915	B143 C130 G31 H140 K18 K26 O13 W53 W125
Adams, J.W.	26 Aug. 1881	B43 C130 C150 D17 E11 K16 K53 K54 P5 R60 S62 S95 V59 V60 W62 W125
Adams, R.B.	9 Nov. 1897	A65 B43 C130 K16 P5 V66 W125
Addison, H.	2 Sep. 1859	B42 C130 K52 K54 R59 W7 W79 W125
Addison, W.R.F.	26 Sep. 1916	A25 A26 A27 A28 C59 C130 G37 I15 K33 M70 S62 S79B W63 W125
Adlam, T.E.	25 Nov. 1916	B1 C130 G30 O15 W125
Agansing Rai	5 Oct. 1944	A16 A65 B44 B50 I10 K16 L70 M24 R70 S45 T36 W125
Agar, A.W.S.	22 Aug. 1919	A10 A11 A12 B1 B43 B95 C112 C130 D23 F13 H56 L7 L8 M20 P58 V56 V57 V58 V68 W90 W125
Aikman, F.R.	3 Sep. 1858	B42 B134 C130 C150 D17 K16 R59 T9A V77 V155 W42 W125
Aitken, R.H.M.	16 Apr. 1863	B42 C130 K16 K52 K54 R59 W125
Albrecht, H.	8 Aug. 1902	A12B C130 U10 U11 W125
Alexander, E.W.	18 Feb. 1915	A65 A67 C77 C130 G31 H140 L42 M129 O13 S41 U2 W125
Alexander, J.	24 Feb. 1857	B15A C130 G39 G63 K50 K54 R58 T32 W125
Algie, W.L.	31 Dec. 1919	A65 B69 B114 C130 G35 G39 M14 S125 S145 W125
Ali Haidar	3 Jul. 1945	A16 A65 I10 K16 R70 S45 T36 W125
Allan, H.M. Havelock: see Havelock, H.M.		
Allen, W.B.	26 Oct. 1916	C130 G30 O15 R80 W52 W125
Allen, W.W.	2 May 1879	A61 B9 B11 B13 B15 B15B B15D B15E C130 E12 G24 G27 G41 G60 G60A G60B H5 H92 J31 K45 K46 K47 K49B K53 K54 L87 M13B M30 R6 R60 R69 R79 S79 S134 T15A W27 W51A W53 W54 W75 W79 W125 Y2 Y5
Allmand, M.	26 Oct. 1944	B44 B50 B152 I10 K16 L3 R70 T36 W125
Amey, W.L.	31 Jan. 1919	B86A C130 D1 G35 L30 W125
Anderson, C.	11 Nov. 1862	B42 B44 C130 K52 K54 L42 R59 W53 W75 W77 W79 W125
Anderson, C.G.W.	13 Feb. 1942	B76A B116 H90 M17D M23A M25 R70 S85 T36 W55 W70 W125
Anderson, E.	29 Jul. 1943	B24A B45 L3 L70 R70 T36 W52 W125
Anderson, J.T.McK.	29 Jun. 1943	B45 L3 R70 T36 W125
Anderson, W.	May 22, 1915	B28 C46 C130 G62 H140 L15 O13 W125
Anderson, W.H.	3 May 1918	C130 G32 W125
Andrew, L.W.	6 Sep. 1917	A27 A28 A58 B140 C40 C130 H30 N12A O17 S5 S76 W125
Andrews, H.M. Ervine-: see Ervine-Andrews, H.M.		
Andrews, H.J.	9 Sep. 1920	A13 A66 B1A C130 K16 R34 R80 W125
Angus, W.	29 Jun. 1915	B28 B134 C130 H12 H140 L15 L35 M4A M106 O14 S90 W125
Annand, R.W.	23 Aug. 1940	A15 A61 A66 B1 H55 K65 L3 L53 R70 R71 S37 T36 V55 V56 W51 W53 W125
Anson, A.H.A.	24 Dec. 1858	B42 C130 R59 W75 W79 W125
Apiata, W.H.	2 Jul. 2007	C34 L46 N12A V60 V63 W125

Recipient	Gazette Date	Item Number in Part 1 / Part 2
Archibald, A.	6 Jan. 1919	A27 A28 A36 C130 G35 N2 W125
Arthur, T.	24 Feb. 1857	B15A C130 G63 K50 K54 R58 S41 W125
Ashford, T.E.	7 Oct. 1881	C130 E11 K13 K53 K54 R60 W125
Ashworth, J.	22 Mar. 2013	V71 W125
Atkinson, A.	8 Aug. 1902	C46 C130 C145 U11 W52 W125
Auten, H.	14 Sep. 1918	A80 B95 B121 C48 C130 L5A O9 R41 S77 V69 W90 W125
Axford, T.L.	17 Aug. 1918	B76A B116 C125 C130 E82 G32 G52 M23A W55 W70 W125
Aylmer, F.J.	12 Jul. 1892	B43 C130 D23 K16 N2 V65 W125 (also see Part 2 Section A)
Babtie, W.	20 Apr. 1900	A25 C130 P5 R80 U11 W45 W125
Badcoe, P.J.	13 Oct. 1967	A5 B76A B116 B116A C34 M17D M22A M23A S28 S85 S93 W56 W70 V62 W125
Badlu Singh	27 Nov. 1918	A13 A65 C18 C130 G37 K4 K16 W125
Baird, C. S.	18 Feb. 2014	B76A M17E M20A M23A V73
Baker, C.G.	25 Feb. 1862	B42 C130 K16 K52 K54 R59 W125
Ball, A.	8 Jun. 1917	A61 B1 B21 B25 B89 B94 B115 B125 C9 C108 C108A C114 C130 D13 D24B E10 F32 F43 G57 G64 G80 H10 H12 H55 I20 J2 J16 J20 J30 K15A K23 K25 L16 L35 M4 M17B N50 O45 P16 P20 P31 P41 P57 R3C R27 R29 R30 S56 T9 T16 T39 W9 W26 W49 W93 W125
Bambrick, V.	24 Dec. 1858	A61 B42 B43 C130 I61 K52 K54 R59 V50 V61 W7 W125
Bamford, E.	23 Jul. 1918	B95 C21 C95 C130 H85 H102 K16A L5 L45 M12B P37 P59 S16 S77 W19 W90 W125
Bankes, W.G.H.	24 Dec. 1858	B42 C130 K52 K54 R59 V62 W125
Barber, E.	19 Apr. 1915	A75 B28 C59 C130 G15 H140 O13 W125
Barker, W.G.	30 Nov. 1918	B25 B26 B69 B76 B89 B114 C9 C113A C114 C119 C130 D21 D28 E6A E7 G39 H10 H12 H36 J2 J20 K23 M1D M13 M17B M22 M46 M95 M100 M135 P31 P33 P41 R3 R27 S125 S145 T39 V72 W125
Barratt, T.	6 Sep. 1917	C130 D1 G33 H35 H98 O16 W125
Barrett, J.C.	14 Dec. 1918	C130 G34 G39 T14 W125
Barron, C.F.	11 Jan. 1918	A27 A28 A36 B69 B114 C130 M14 M70 O17 R53 S76 S125 S145 W125
Barry, J.	8 Aug. 1902	A65 C130 D23 U11 W125
Barry, M.: see Magner, M.		
Barter, F.	29 Jun. 1915	B28 C130 H140 S90 O14 W75 W80 W125
Barton, C.J.	27 Jun. 1944	B89 C33 C55 C101 K23 L3 L63 M17A R10 R70 T35 W125
Baskeyfield, J.D.	23 Nov. 1944	L3 H98 P13 P14 R70 T36 V45 V55 W125
Bassett, C.R.G.	15 Oct. 1915	A27 A28 A58 B140 C40 C130 H30 M70 N2 N12A S5 S75 W125
Bates, S.	2 Nov. 1944	B1 B31 L3 R53A R70 T36 W125
Batten-Pooll, A.H.H.	5 Aug. 1916	B15C B29 C130 G36 O14 W125 (also see Part 2 Section A)
Baxter, E.F.	26 Sep. 1916	A65 B84 B160 C78 C130 G36 L42 O14 W125
Baxter, F.W.	7 May 1897	C130 P5 U10 W125
Bazalgette, I.W.	17 Aug. 1945	B66 B67 B69 B89 B114 C55 D26 G51 J13 K23 L3 M8A M14 M17A P33 R70 S125 S145 T29A T35 W125
Beach, T.	24 Feb. 1857	B15A C130 G63 K50 K54 R58 W125
Beak, D.M.W.	15 Nov. 1918	A65 C80 C130 G34 H12 L42 P12 T14 W90 W125

Recipient	Gazette Date	Item Number in Part 1 / Part 2
Beal, E.F.	4 Jun. 1918	B103 C46 C130 G32 G62 O18 W125
Beatham, R.M.	14 Dec. 1918	B76A B116 C125 C130 G34 H98 M23A W55 W70 W125
Beattie, S.H.	May 21, 1942	B115 C110 C113C D25 L1A L3 L7 L53 L71 L110 M10 M16 M40 R70 R91 T12 T37 V63 W75 W80 W88 W90 W125
Beauchamp-Proctor, A.F.W.	30 Nov. 1918	A19 A66 B25 B89 C114 C130 F43 F44A J20 J30 K23 M17B R27 U10 W40 W125
Beeley, J.	21 Apr. 1942	B12 B45 D1 L3 L70 R70 T36 V66 W125
Bees, W.	17 Dec. 1901	C130 E16 K16B M4 U11 V66 W125
Beesley, W.	28 Jun. 1918	C130 G32 W7 W125
Beet, H.C.	12 Feb. 1901	C130 M4 N50 S18 U11 W125
Beharry, J.G.	17 Mar. 2005	A65 A66 B36 B37 B43 C34 C148 H94 M102D S40 V56 W63 W125
Belcher, D.W.	23 Jun. 1915	A27 A28 B28 C59 C130 L15 M70 O14 S79B W7 W125
Bell Davies, R.	1 Jan. 1916	B25 B38 B89 C114 C130 G64 J20 K23 L16 M17B P41 R27 S75 V76 W90 W93 W125
Bell, D.	17 Dec. 1867	C130 K51 K53 K54 R60 W75 W79 W125
Bell, D.S.	9 Sep. 1916	A61 C46 C130 G30 G62 H12 H37 L13 M4A M117 O15 P6B V45 V52 W52 W125
Bell, E.W.D.	24 Feb. 1857	B15A B35 C130 C150 D17 G63 K50 K54 M70 P5 R58 T14 T32 V60 W42 W75 W79 W125
Bell, E.N.F.	26 Sep. 1916	C60 C78 C130 G30 L42 O15 U2 W125
Bell, F.W.	4 Oct. 1901	B76A B116 B122 C130 G52 G62A H90 M23A T14 U11 W55 W70 W125
Bell, M.S.	20 Nov. 1874	C130 K51 K53 K54 N2 R60 W125
Bellew, E.D.	May 15, 1919	B28 B69 B114 C130 F41 G39 M14 M95 O14 S125 S145 T14 W125
Bennett, E.P.	30 Dec. 1916	A27 A28 C130 G30 H12 O15 T14 W54A W125
Bent, P.E.	11 Jan. 1918	B69 B79 B114 C79 C130 E80 G39 H83 K16B L42 M14 O17 S76 S125 S145 W81 W125
Bent, S.J.	9 Dec. 1914	A25 A27 A28 A65 A67 C130 G31 H12 H127 H140 K41 L15 M70 O13 S90 W125
Beresford, W.L. de la P.	9 Sep. 1879	A69 B13 C130 F27 G60A G60B K45 M70 M99 M113 R60 V52 W125 Y2
Bergin, J.	28 Jul. 1868	B43 C130 H89 K51 K53 K54 R60 V77 W125
Berryman, J.	24 Feb. 1857	B15A B43 C130 G63 H35 K50 K54 M30 P5 R58 V54 W125
Best-Dunkley, B.	6 Sep. 1917	B43 C130 F25 O17 S76 W52 W125
Bhagat, P.S.	10 Jun. 1941	A16 B45 I10 K1A K4 K16 N2 R70 S45 T11 T36 V12 W125 (also see Part 2 Section A)
Bhanbhagta Gurung	5 Jun. 1945	A16 A61 B44 B50 I10 K16 M24 R70 S45 T36 V61 W125
Bhandari Ram	8 Feb. 1945	A16 B44 I10 K4 K16 R70 S45 W125
Bingham, E.B.S.	15 Sep. 1916	B63 C60 C130 D23 L16 S77 U2 V68 W90 W125
Birks, F.	8 Nov. 1917	B76A B116 C125 C130 M23A O17 S76 T22A W55 W70 W75 W80 W125
Bisdee, J.H.	13 Nov. 1900	B76A B116 C121 C130 H90 M23A M70 U11 W55 W70 W125
Bishop, W.A.	11 Aug. 1917	B2 B22 B25 B27 B69 B70 B71 B72 B73 B89 B114 C9 C36 C113A C114 C119 C130 D21 D28 F32 F43 G39 G56 G59 G61 G64 H10 H12 H36 J2 J20 K23 K25 L1 L16 M1C M1D M14 M17B M45 M46 M95 M100 O45 P25 P33 P38 P41 R7 R27 R28 R30 R33 R53 S56 S125 S145 T30 T38 V60 W26 W125 (also see Part 2 Section B)

Recipient	Gazette Date	Item Number in Part 1 / Part 2
Bissett, W.D.	6 Jan. 1919	C130 G35 W75 W80 W125
Bissett-Smith, A.	May 24, 1919	B121 C130 S77 W90 W125
Blackburn, A.S.	9 Sep. 1916	A27 A28 B76A B116 C121 C125 C130 F8 G30 H90 M23A O15 V77 W55 W63 W70 W125
Blair, J.	25 Feb. 1862	B42 C130 K16 R59 W125
Blair, R.	18 Jun. 1858	B42 C130 K52 K54 W75 W79 W80 W125
Blaker, F.G.	26 Sep. 1944	B44 B50 I10 K16 L3 R70 T36 V64 W125
Bloomfield, W.A.	30 Dec. 1916	A27 A28 C130 G37 M70 U10 W125
Bogle, A.C.	2 Sep. 1859	B35 B42 C130 R59 T14 W125
Boisragon, G.H.	12 Jul. 1892	B50 C130 K16 T9A V65 V155 W125
Bonner, C.G.	2 Nov. 1917	C10 C47 C79 C130 D1 E80 H35 L5A L42 S19 S21 S77 W81 W90 W125
Booth, A.C.	24 Feb. 1880	B13 B43 B86B C130 D1 G60A G60B H35 H96 H97 H98 K44 K45 M4 N50 R60 V60 W125 Y2
Booth, F.C.	8 Jun. 1917	C130 G37 P12 T14 U10 W125
Borella, A.C.	16 Sep. 1918	B76A B116 C121 C125 C130 G32 H90 M23A S50 W55 W70 W125
Borton, A.D.	18 Dec. 1917	B43 C130 G37 I15 S48 V55 W125
Boughey, S.H.P.	13 Feb. 1918	B80 C130 G37 V54 W125
Boulger, A.	18 Jun. 1858	B42 C130 K52 K54 R59 W125
Boulter, W.E.	26 Oct. 1916	C130 G30 O15 S31 V58 W125
Bourchier, C.T.	24 Feb. 1857	B15A C130 G63 K50 K54 R58 W7 W125
Bourke, R.R.L.	28 Aug. 1918	A65 B69 B114 C95 C130 G39 H102 K16A L5 M12B M14 M95 P37 S77 S125 S145 T5 W90 W125
Boyd-Rochfort, G.A.	1 Sep. 1915	B28 C130 D23 G15 O14 W125
Boyes, D.G.	21 Apr. 1865	A65 A67 B43 C130 I61 K54 L2 R60 S40 T14 V61 W90 W125
Boyle, E.C.	May 21, 1915	C22 C111 C130 G58 H140 J9 K14 K34 M16 M20 P12 S36 S75 S77 S90 T14 U5 V76 W49 W85 W86 W90 W125
Bradbury, E.K.	25 Nov. 1914	B12 B104 C130 G31 H140 L15 O13 S40 S41 S90 V74 W125
Bradford, G.N.	17 Mar. 1919	A32 A65 C21 C95 C130 D13 H85 H102 K16A L5 M12B M120 P37 S16 S77 T5 W19 W53 W90 W125
Bradford, R.B.	25 Nov. 1916	A32 A65 B1 C130 D13 G30 H12 M120 O15 S37 W53 W125
Bradley, F.H.	27 Dec. 1901	A66 B111 C130 S41 U11 W125
Bradshaw, J.	24 Feb. 1857	B15A C130 G63 K50 K54 P5 R58 T32 W7 W125
Bradshaw, W.	18 Jun. 1858	B35 B42 C130 C150 D17 R59 R80 W42 W125
Brennan, J.C.	11 Nov. 1859	B42 C130 K16 R59 S41 W125
Brereton, A.P.	27 Sep. 1918	A67 B69 B114 C130 G34 G39 M14 S125 S145 W125
Brillant, J.	27 Sep. 1918	B69 B114 C130 G34 G39 M14 S125 S145 V1 W125
Brodie, W.L.	12 Dec. 1914	A27 A28 A36 C130 G31 H140 L16 M14B O13 W125
Bromhead, G.	2 May 1879	B9 B11 B13 B15 B15B B15D B15E B39 B40B C130 G24 G41 G60 G60A G60B H5 H89 H92 H96 J31 K45 K46 K47 K49B K51 K53 K54 L87 M13B M30 M70 M113 R6 R60 R69 R79 S79 S134 T15A W27 W51A W54 W75 W79 W125 Y2 Y5
Bromley, C.	15 Mar. 1917	A27 A28 C130 H12 M70 M109 S75 V45 W125
Brooke, J.A.O.	18 Feb. 1915	C130 G31 H140 O13 S90 U2 W125
Brooks, E.	27 Jun. 1917	C130 G33 O16 W7 W125
Brooks, O.	28 Oct. 1915	B28 C130 G15 H12 H108 H125 H127 H129A O14 P10 V55 W125

Recipient	Gazette Date	Item Number in Part 1 / Part 2
Brown, D.F.	14 Jun. 1917	A58 B135 B140 C40 C130 G30 H30 N12A O15 S5 W125
Brown, E.D.	15 Jan. 1901	B6 C130 M14B U11 W125
Brown, F.D.M.	17 Feb. 1860	B42 C130 D23 K16 R59 W125
Brown, H.W.	17 Oct. 1917	B69 B114 C35 C130 G36 G39 M14 M95 O17 R53 S125 S145 W125
Brown, P.	12 Apr. 1880	B43 C130 R60 U10 V67 W125
Brown, W.E.	17 Aug. 1918	A27 A28 B26 B76A B116 C121 C125 C130 D7 G32 H90 M23A M25 M70 V72 W55 W63 W70 W125
Browne, E.S.	17 Jun. 1879	B13 B15 C130 G24 G60A G60B K45 R60 W75 W79 W125 Y2
Browne, H.G. Gore-: see Gore-Browne, H.G.		
Browne, S.J.	1 Mar. 1861	B42 B137 C130 K16 R56 W62 W125
Bruce, W.A.McC.	4 Sep. 1919	A13 C130 G31 K16 O13 W125
Brunt, J.H.C.	8 Feb. 1945	L3 I15 M4 R70 S79A S79B T36 V59 W125
Bryan, T.	8 Jun. 1917	A65 C130 G33 G44 H35 O16 W52 W125
Buchan, J.C.	May 22, 1918	C130 G32 O18 W125
Buchanan, A.	26 Sep. 1916	A66 C130 G37 P12 T14 W75 W80 W125
Buckingham, W.	28 Apr. 1915	B28 C130 P6 S30 O13 W125
Buckley, A.H.	14 Dec. 1918	B76A B116 C125 C130 G34 M23A M25 W55 W70 W125
Buckley, C.W.	24 Feb. 1857	A65 B15A C130 C150 D17 G63 K50 K54 R58 T14 V58 V59 W42 W90 W125
Buckley, J.	18 Jun. 1858	A65 B12 B40B B42 C130 H89 K16 K52 K54 P5 R59 T1A V59 W125
Buckley, M.V.	14 Dec. 1918	B76A B116 B116A C121 C125 C130 G34 M23A M25 W55 W70 W125
(alias Sexton, G.)	8 Aug. 1919	
Budd, B.J.	14 Dec. 2006	B43 B74 C34 C148 T27 V59 W125
Bugden, P.J.	26 Nov. 1917	B24B B76A B116 C125 C130 M23A O17 S76 W55 W70 W125
Buller, R.H.	17 Jun. 1879	A12B A35 A69 A73 B13 B19A B40B B118 B155 C86 C118 C130 D38 F35 G60A G60B G66 H96 I61 J14 K44 K45 K49 L51 L62 M8B M36 M70 M90 M113 N17 P19 P55 R57 R60 R83 S39 S115 S136 S155 T4 T11A T12 T31 V5 V58 V73 W7 W12 W45 W125 Y2
Burges, D.	14 Dec. 1918	C130 G37 T14 W80 W125
Burgoyne, H.T.	24 Feb. 1857	B15A C130 C150 D17 E14 G63 K50 R58 T32 V6 W42 W90 W125
Burman, W.F.	26 Nov. 1917	C130 O17 S76 W7 W125
Burslem, N.G.	13 Aug. 1861	C130 K51 K53 K54 R60 W125
Burt, A.A.	22 Jan. 1916	B28 C130 O14 W125
Burton, A.S.	15 Oct. 1915	A65 A76 B76A B116 B116A C125 C130 H90 H98 M23A S75 W55 W70 W125
Burton, R.H.	4 Jan. 1945	L3 R70 T36 V65 W125
Bushell, C.	3 May 1918	A67 C79 C130 G32 I15 L42 O18 V52 W125
Butler, J.F.P.	23 Aug. 1915	C130 G31 G37 T14 W7 W125
Butler, T.A.	6 May 1859	B35 B42 C130 C150 D17 K16 K52 K54 R59 W42 W125
Butler, W.B.	17 Oct. 1917	A66 C130 G36 O17 W52 W125
Bye, R.J.	6 Sep. 1917	C130 G15 M4 N50 O17 S76 W75 W80 W125
Byrne, James	11 Nov. 1859	B42 C130 K52 K54 R59 W125
Byrne, John	24 Feb. 1857	B15A C130 D13 G63 I61 K50 K54 R58 S37 V61 W75 W79 W125
Byrne, T.	15 Nov. 1898	B43 B123 C130 D23 I15 M30 P5 V57 W125

Recipient	Gazette Date	Item Number in Part 1 / Part 2
Bythesea, J.	24 Feb. 1857	A66 B15A B32 C130 G63 J18 K50 K54 N15 R58 S40 V61 W90
Cadell, T.	29 Apr. 1862	A36 B42 C130 K16 K52 K54 M14B R59 W125
Cafe, W.M.	17 Feb. 1860	B42 C130 K16 K52 K54 R59 W125
Caffrey, J.	22 Jan. 1916	B28 B103 C130 M4 N50 O14 W125
Cain, R.H.	2 Nov. 1944	C148 H26 H98 L3 R70 T29A T36 V55 W125
Cairns, G.A.	20 May 1949	B44 B114 I15 L3 T36 W125
Cairns, H.	31 Jan. 1919	B69 C130 G35 G39 H98 M14 S18 S125 S145 W53 W125
Caldwell, T.	6 Jan. 1919	A27 A28 A36 B134 C130 G35 V69 W125
Calvert, L.	15 Nov. 1918	A65 C130 G34 W52 W125
Cambridge, D.	23 Jun. 1857	A1 B15A C130 G63 K50 K54 R58 S41 T32 W125
Cameron, A.S.	11 Nov. 1859	B42 C130 R59 W125
Cameron, D.	22 Feb. 1944	B1 B75 B115 B134 C110 C111 E6 F11 F47 G2 G71 H55 H104 J5 J9 K14 K15 K19 L1A L3 L70 M9 M16 M20 M104 N25 O35 P2 P15 R70 S64 T20 T37 V58 W2 W5 W20 W21 W90 W125 Z2
Campbell, F.W.	23 Aug. 1915	B28 B69 B114 C130 G39 L16 M13 O14 R53 S125 S145 W125
Campbell, G.	21 Apr. 1917	A80 B95 B115 B121 C10 C11 C12 C48 C110 C112 C130 H12 H56 H127 L5A L7 L8 L35 M16 O9 R41 S19 S21 S64 S69 S77 V75 W90 W125 (also see Part 2 Sections A and B)
Campbell, J.C.	3 Feb. 1942	B45 L3 L70 R70 S41 T36 V66 W125
Campbell, J.V.	26 Oct. 1916	C130 G15 G30 L42 O15 P10 P12 T14 W125
Campbell, K.	13 Mar. 1942	B20 B65 B89 C114A E60 K23 L3 L70 M17A R37 R70 T35 W90 W125
Campbell, L.MacL.	8 Jun. 1943	B24A B45 L3 R70 T36 W125
Carless, J.H.	17 May 1918	B95 C130 D1 H35 S77 W90 W125
Carlin, P.	26 Oct. 1858	B42 C130 R59 W125
Carmichael, J.	17 Oct. 1917	A27 A28 B134 C130 H98 N2 O17 S76 W125
Carne, J.P.	27 Oct. 1953	A5 C19 C20 C34 F5 O3 P12 T12 T14 T36 V56 W125
Carpenter, A.F.B.	23 Jul. 1918	B95 B126 C7 C12 C21 C95 C130 D12 H85 H102 H126 J4 K16A L5 M12B O9 P12 P37 S16 S40 S77 S130 S132 T5 T14 W19 W90 W125
Carroll, J.	2 Aug. 1917	B76A B116 C121 C125 C130 G33 G52 M23A M25 O16 V52 W55 W70 W125
Carter, H.A.	9 Dec. 1904	C130 K16 M70 W125
Carter, N.V.	9 Sep. 1916	C130 G36 O14 V52 V77 W125
Carton de Wiart, A.	9 Sep. 1916	B43 C25 C130 G30 H12 H28 H98 K12 J28 L23 M14 N10 O15 S67 S80 T14 V77 W125
Cartwright, G.	14 Dec. 1918	A27 A28 B76A B116 C125 C130 G34 H90 M23A M25 M70 S40 W55 W70 W125
Cassidy, B.M.	3 May. 1918	A65 C130 G32 W125
Castleton, C.C.	26 Sep. 1916	B76A B116 C125 C130 G30 H90 M23A O15 W55 W70 W125
Cates, G.E.	11 May 1917	C130 D19 G33 O16 W7 W125
Cather, G.StG.S.	9 Sep. 1916	C60 C130 D23 G30 O15 U2 W125
Cator, H.	8 Jun. 1917	A27 A28 A65 C130 G33 M70 O16 W125
Chafer, G.W.	5 Aug. 1916	C130 G36 O14 W52 W125
Champion, J.	20 Jan. 1860	B42 C130 R59 T14 W125

Recipient	Gazette Date	Item Number in Part 1 / Part 2
Channer, G.N.	14 Apr. 1876	A66 B43 B50 C130 E14 K16 K51 K53 R60 T14 W125
Chaplin, J.W.	13 Aug. 1861	C130 H89 R60 W125
Chapman, E.T.	13 Jul. 1945	A66 B1 E8 L3 R70 T29A T36 W75 W80 W125
Chard, J.R.M.	2 May 1879	A19 A65 A67 B7 B9 B11 B13 B15B B15D B15E B39 B40B C130 E12 G24 G41 G60 G60A G60B H5 H58 H89 H92 H93 H96 J31 K44 K45 K46 K47 K48 K49B K53 K54 L87 M13B M30 M70 M113 N2 R6 R60 R69 R79 S40 S79 S134 T14 T15A V5 V7 W27 W51A W54 W67 W79 W125 Y2 Y5
Charlton, E.C.	2 May 1946	B12 G15 L3 T36 V73 W125
Chase, W.StL.	7 Oct. 1881	C130 E11 K16 K53 K54 L35 R60 W125
Chatta Singh	21 Jun. 1916	A13 C18 C130 G37 K4 K16 S45 W125
Chavasse, N.G. Bar	26 Oct. 1916 14 Sep. 1917	A61 A65 A66 C75 C77 C79 C130 D13 D27A G30 G75 H12 K15A L42 O15 O17 R80 S40 S76 T14 W125
Cherry, P.H.	11 May 1917	B26 B76A B116 B116A C121 C125 C130 D7 G33 M23A O16 W50 W55 W70 W125
Cheshire, G.L.	8 Sep. 1944	A55 A61 A65 B18 B30 B40 B41 B88A B89 B91 B92 B99 B100 B105 B115 B120 B151 C50 C51 C52 C53 C55 C116 C148 D29 F24 F62 G4 H10 H26 H82 H100 H120 H123 K23 L3 L11 L27 L53 L69 M17A M32 M116 O11 O65 068 P20 P52 P57 R45 R70 R77 R89 R95 S23 S40 S87 T35 T39 V45 W16 W18 W125 (also see Part 2 Section A)
Chhelu Ram	27 Jul. 1943	A16 B45 I10 K16 R70 S45 T36 W125
Chicken, G.B.	27 Apr. 1860	A66 A67 B42 C130 K16 K52 K54 R59 W53 W90 W125
Chowne, A.	6 Sep. 1945	B44 B76A B116 C104 H90 M23A M25 R70 T36 V63 W55 W70 W125
Christian, H.	3 Mar. 1916	B28 C130 K33 O14 W53 W125
Christie, J.A.	27 Feb. 1918	A27 A28 B12 C130 G37 S92 W7 W125
Clamp, W.	18 Dec. 1917	B134 C46 C130 G62 O17 S76 W125
Clare, G.W.B.	11 Jan. 1918	C130 G36 M41 O18 W125
Clark-Kennedy, W.H.	14 Dec. 1918	A27 A28 B69 B114 C130 G34 G39 M14 M70 S79B S125 S145 W125
Clarke, J.	6 Jan. 1919	A65 B12 C130 G35 W125
Clarke, L. B.	26 Oct. 1916	B69 B114 C130 G30 G39 L16 M14 N1 O15 R53 S125 S145 W125
Clarke, W.A.S.	29 Jun. 1943	B12 B45 C80 G10 L3 L42 R70 T36 W125
Clements, J.J.	4 Jun. 1901	A65 A67 C130 U10 U11 W125
Clifford, H.H.	24 Feb. 1857	B15A C82 C130 F20 G60B G63 K50 K54 L61 P21 R58 V54 W7 W125
Clogstoun, H.M.	21 Oct. 1859	B42 C130 K16 R59 W125
Cloutman, B.M.	31 Jan. 1919	C130 G35 N2 V61 W125
Cobbe, A.S.	20 Jan. 1903	C130 K16 P5 V64 V65 V66 W79 W125
Cochrane, H.S.	24 Dec. 1858	B42 C130 R59 W125
Cockburn, H.Z.C.	23 Apr. 1901	B69 B114 C130 M14 M95 S125 S145 U11 W125
Coffey, W.	24 Feb. 1857	B15A C130 G1 G63 K50 K54 M4 R58 V77 T32 W79 W125
Coffin, C.	14 Sep. 1917	C130 N2 O17 R39 S76 V65 W125
Coghill, N.J.A.	2 May 1879 15 Jan. 1907	A26 B13 B15 C90 C130 E12 G24 G60A G60B H92 K45 K48 K49B K53 K54 M30 M70 M113 P5 R60 R69 R79 S134 W75 W79 W125 Y2 Y5

Recipient	Gazette Date	Item Number in Part 1 / Part 2
Coghlan, C.: see Coughlan, C.		
Coleman, J.	24 Feb. 1857	B15A C130 G63 K50 K54 R58 W125
Colley, H.J.	22 Oct. 1918	C130 D1 G34 H35 L30 S140 W125
Collin, J.H.	28 Jun. 1918	C130 G32 K33 W53 W125
Collings-Wells, J.S.	24 Apr. 1918	A27 A28 C130 G10 G32 M70 S140 W125
Collins, J.	18 Dec. 1917	C130 G37 T14 W75 W80 W125
Collis, J.	16 May 1881	A66 B43 C130 E11 I61 K53 K54 N15 P5 R60 S41 S95 T9 V57 V65 W125
Coltman, W.H.	6 Jan. 1919	C130 G35 H12 H98 Q10 T21 W125
Columbine, H.G.	3 May 1918	A33 C130 G32 M10A O18 V70 W125
Colvin, H.	8 Nov. 1917	B1 C130 D23 K16 O17 S76 U2 W125
Colvin, J.M.C.	20 May 1898	C130 N2 P5 W125
Colyer-Fergusson, T.R.	6 Sep. 1917	C130 I15 O17 S76 V67 W125
Combe, R.G.	27 Jun. 1917	B69 B114 C130 G33 G39 H69 M14 O16 R53 S18 S125 S145 W125
Commerell, J.E.	24 Feb. 1857	A65 A67 B15A B79 C130 G63 K50 K54 M70 P5 R58 S40 W90 W125
Congreve, W.N.	2 Feb. 1900	A12B B6 C79 C107 C130 H98 I15 L42 M30 P5 T15 U11 V5 V45 V56 W7 W45 W125
Congreve, W.LaT.	26 Oct. 1916	C79 C107 C130 G30 H12 L42 N40 O15 T15 V45 W125
Conker, F.: see Whirlpool, F.		
Connolly, W.	3 Sep. 1858	B42 C77 V79 C130 K16 K52 K54 L42 R59 S41 V56 W125
Connors, J.	24 Feb. 1857	B15A C130 G63 K50 K54 R58 T32 W125
Conolly, J.A.	5 May 1857	B15A C130 G63 K50 K54 M129 P10 R58 T32 W125
Cook, J.	18 Mar. 1879	A65 B50 C130 E11 K16 K53 K54 M14B P5 R60 W125
Cook, W.	18 Jun. 1859	B42 C130 R59 W125
Cooke, T.	9 Sep. 1916	B76A B116 B140 C40 C125 C130 G30 H12 H30 H98 M23A O15 V51 W55 W70 W125
Cookson, E.C.	21 Jan. 1916	C79 C130 H140 L16 L42 S77 S90 W90 W125
Cooper, E.	14 Sep. 1917	A27 A28 C117B C130 M70 O17 P20 S76 T9 W7 W52 W53 W125
Cooper, H.	24 Feb. 1857	A65 B15A C130 G63 K50 K54 R58 W90 W125
Cooper, J.	17 Dec. 1867	C130 D1 K51 K53 K54 L30 R60 W75 W79 W125
Cooper, N.B. Elliot-: see Elliot-Cooper, N.B.		
Coppins, F.G.	27 Sep. 1918	B69 B114 C130 G34 G39 M14 S125 S145 W125
Corbett, F.	16 Feb. 1883	B43 C130 I61 R60 V56 W7 W125
Cornwell, J.T.	15 Sep. 1916	A65 B95 C35 C43 C130 D19 E9 G43 H12 H55 H87 J18 L2 L16 M106 O10 P20 S40 S77 T9 V68 W4 W90 W125
Cosens, A.	22 May 1945	B29 B114 C113A D26 F40 F41 G51 M14 R70 S125 S145 T36 W125
Cosgrove, W.	23 Aug. 1915	C130 C148 D23 S40 S75 V57 W125
Costello, E.W.	9 Nov. 1897	C130 D23 F15 G36 K16 K42 P5 V59 V60 W125
Cotter, W.R.	30 Mar. 1916	A66 C130 I15 O14 W125
Coughlan, C.	11 Nov. 1862	B42 C130 K52 K54 R59 W125
Coulson, G.H.B.	8 Aug. 1902	C130 U11 W125
Counter, J.T.	22 May 1918	B84 C35 C79 C130 G32 L42 W125
Coury, G.G.	26 Oct. 1916	B1 C77 C78 C130 G30 K42 L42 M129 O15 V51 V52 W125

Recipient	Gazette Date	Item Number in Part 1 / Part 2
Coverdale, C.H.	18 Dec. 1917	B12 B84 C92 C130 S76 O17 V66 W52 W125
Cowley, C.H.	2 Feb. 1917	B43 B95 C78 C130 L42 S77 V77 W81 W90 W125
Cox, C.A.	11 May 1917	C130 G33 H9 H12 O16 S40 W125
Craig, J.	20 Nov. 1857	B15A C130 G15 G63 K50 K54 R58 V61 W125
Craig, J.M.	2 Aug. 1917	C130 D19 G37 W125
Crandon, H.G.	18 Oct. 1901	B6 B12 B15C C130 U11 W125
Creagh, O'M.	17 Nov. 1879	C130 C131 E11 K16 K53 K54 M70 R60 W125 (also see Part 2 Section A)
Crean, T.J.	11 Feb. 1902	C130 D23 M117 R80 U10 U11 W125
Crichton, J.	15 Nov. 1918	A58 B140 C40 C130 G35 H30 N12A S5 U2 W125
Crimmin, J.	17 Sep. 1889	B15C B43 C130 K16 P5 R60 R80 W125
Crisp, T.	2 Nov. 1917	B121 C23 C130 L5A M43 R41 S77 W90 W125
Croak, J.B.	27 Sep. 1918	B69 B79 B114 C30 C130 G34 G39 M14 S125 S145 W125
Cross, A.H.	4 Jun. 1918	C130 G32 W125
Crowe, J.J.	28 Jun. 1918	C130 G32 P4D W125
Crowe, J.P.H.	15 Jan. 1858	B42 C130 R59 U10 V77 W125
Cruickshank, J.A.	1 Sep. 1944	A60 A61 B1 B43 B65 B89 F32 H55 K23 L3 M17A R70 R74 T35 V72 W90 W125
Cruickshank, R.E.	21 Jun. 1918	A27 A28 B114 C130 D19 G37 G39 W125
Crutchley, V.A.C.	28 Aug. 1918	A65 B95 C95 C130 H102 K16A L5 M12B P37 S77 T5 W90 W125
Cubitt, W.G.	18 Jun. 1859	B42 C130 C150 D17 E14 K16 K52 R59 W42 W125
Cumming, A.E.	20 Feb. 1942	B44 I10 K4 K16 L3 R70 T36 W125
Cuninghame, W.J.M.	24 Feb. 1857	B15A C130 G63 K50 K54 R58 W7 W125
Cunningham, J. (Pte.)	13 Jan. 1917	C35 C130 G30 O15 W52 W125
Cunningham, J. (Cpl.)	8 Jun. 1917	C130 G33 O16 W125
Cunyngham, W.H. Dick-: see Dick-Cunyngham, W.H.		
Currey, W.M.	14 Dec. 1918	A27 A28 B76A B116 C121 C125 C130 G34 H90 M23A M25 V66 W55 W70 W125
Currie, D.V.	27 Nov. 1944	A61 B69 B114 C113A D26 F41 G51 M14 M95 R53A R70 S18 S125 S145 T36 V58 W125
Curtis, A.E.	15 Jan. 1901	A65 A67 A12B C130 U11 W125
Curtis, H.	24 Feb. 1857	A65 B15A A67 C130 G63 K50 K54 R58 W90 W125
Curtis, H.A.	6 Jan. 1919	A65 C130 G35 W125
Curtis, P.K.E.	1 Dec. 1953	A5 B1 B43 C19 C20 C34 O3 P12 T12 T36 V56 W125
Cutler, A.R.	28 Nov. 1941	B45 B76A B116 B116A H52 H90 M6 M17D M23A M25 P20 R21 R70 S41 S85 T9 T36 W55 W70 W125
Dalton, J.L.	17 Nov. 1879	B7 B9 B11 B13 B15B B15D B15E B39 B43 C130 D32 E12 G24 G41 G60 G60A G60B H5 H92 J31 K45 K46 K47 K49B K53 K54 L87 M13B M30 R6 R60 R69 R78 R79 S79 S134 T15A U10 V63 W27 W51A W53 W54 W63 W125 Y2 Y5
Dalziel, H.	17 Aug. 1918	B76A B116 C125 C130 G32 M23A V61 W55 W70 W125
Danagher, J.: see Danaher, J.		
Danaher, J.	14 Mar. 1882	B43 C130 R60 U10 U11 W125
Dancox, F.G.	26 Nov. 1917	C130 O17 S76 V60 W125

Recipient	Gazette Date	Item Number in Part 1 / Part 2
Daniel, E.StJ.	24 Feb. 1857	A61 A65 B15A C130 I61 G63 K50 K54 L2 R58 R75 S80 T14 V15 V68 W90 W125
Daniels, H.	28 Apr. 1915	A25 A27 A28 B28 C130 H140 L15 M70 O13 S90 W7 W52 W125
D'Arcy, H.C.D.	9 Oct. 1879	B13 B43 C130 D5 G60A G60B H30 I61 K45 M113 R60 U10 V74 W125 Y2
Dartnell, W.T.	23 Dec. 1915	B76A B116 C121 C125 C130 G37 K13 M23A U10 V56 W55 W63 W70 W125
Darwan Sing Negi	7 Dec. 1914	A13 C18 C130 G31 H12 K4 K16 O13 S45 W125
Daunt, J.C.C.	25 Feb. 1862	A65 B42 C130 K16 K52 K54 R59 W125
Davey, P.	17 Aug. 1918	B76A B116 B116A C121 C125 C130 G32 M23A W55 W70 W125
Davies, J.J.	26 Sep. 1916	C130 D1 G30 H12 H35 O15 W75 W125
Davies, J.L.	6 Sep. 1917	C130 O17 S76 W75 W125
Davies, J.T.	22 May 1918	C79 C130 G32 L42 W80 W125
Davies, L.A.E. Price-: see Price-Davies, L.A.E.		
Davies, R. Bell: see Bell Davies, R.		
Davis, G.	23 Jun. 1857	B15A C130 G63 K50 K54 R58 S41 W125
Davis, J.	27 May 1859	A65 B28 C130 L16 R59 W125
Dawson, J.L.	7 Dec. 1915	B28 C130 N2 O14 W125
Day, G.F.	24 Feb. 1857	B15A B35 C130 C150 D17 G63 K50 K54 P5 R58 V67 W42 W90 W125
Day, S.J.	17 Oct. 1917	C130 G36 O17 W125
Daykins, J.B.	6 Jan. 1919	C130 G35 J28 W125
Dean, D.J.	14 Dec. 1918	A27 A28 C130 C149 D19 G34 I15 M70 W125
Dean, P.T.	23 Jul. 1918	A65 B95 C21 C95 C130 H85 H102 K16A K40 L5 L59 M12B P37 S16 S77 T5 W19 W90 W125
Dease, M.J.	16 Nov. 1914	A61 A65 C130 D23 G31 H56 H140 K13 K42 O13 R90 S90 T14 T22A V45 V74 V50 W125
de L'Isle, Viscount: see Sidney, W.P.		
de Montmorency, R.H.L.J.	15 Nov. 1898	B69 B114 B123 C130 M30 P5 P50 W125
Dempsey, D.	17 Feb. 1860	B42 C130 K52 K54 R59 W125
de Pass, F.A.	18 Feb. 1915	A13 C130 G31 G67 K16 O13 W125
Derrick, T.C.	23 Mar. 1944	B44 B76A B116 F4 H26 H90 M17D M23A R70 S85 T36 W55 W70 W125
Devereux, J.: see Gorman, J.		
Devine, J.: see Divane, J.		
de Wind, E.	15 May 1919	B69 B114 C60 C130 G32 G39 H2 M14 O18 S18 S125 S145 U2 W125
Diamond, B.	27 Apr. 1858	B42 C130 K16 K52 K54 R59 S41 W125
Diarmid, A.M.C. McReady-: see McReady-Diarmid, A.M.C.		
Dick-Cunyngham, W.H.	18 Oct. 1881	C130 C150 D17 E11 K53 K54 R60 T14 W125
Dickson, C.	23 Jun. 1857	B15A C130 G63 K50 K54 R58 S41 T9A V155 W125
Digby-Jones, R.J.T.	8 Aug. 1902	A12B C130 N2 U11 W125
Dimmer, J.H.S.	19 Nov. 1914	A27 A28 B103 C130 D19 G31 H140 L16 M70 O13 S90 W7 W125
Dinesen, T.	26 Oct. 1918	A66 B69 B114 C130 D20 G34 G39 H10 L41 M14 M46 S125 S145 W125 (also see Part 2 Sections A and B)
Divane, J.	20 Jan. 1860	B42 C130 D23 K52 K54 R59 W7 W125

Recipient	Gazette Date	Item Number in Part 1 / Part 2
Dixon, M.C.	21 Jan. 1860	A66 B15A C130 G63 I15 K50 K54 R58 S79B T9A V155 W125
Donaldson, M. G	22 Jan. 2009	B76A B116A C34 D24 M23A V63 W125
Dobson, C.C.	11 Nov. 1919	A10 A12 B79 C130 F13 H56 I15 M20 P25 T14 V58 V68 W90 W125
Dobson, F.W.	9 Dec. 1914	C130 G15 G31 H140 L15 O13 P10 W53 W125
Donnini, D.	20 Mar. 1945	L3 R70 T36 V64 W53 W125
Donohoe, P.	24 Dec. 1858	B42 C130 R59 W125
Doogan, J.	14 Mar. 1882	C130 H127 I15 R60 U11 W75 W79 W125
Dorrell, G.T.	16 Nov. 1914	A27 A28 C130 G31 H140 L15 O13 S40 S41 S90 V74 W125
Dougall, E.S.	4 Jun. 1918	C78 C130 G32 I15 L42 S41 S79B W125
Doughty-Wylie, C.H.M.	23 Jun. 1915	C130 H107 H140 S75 S78 S90 W75 W80 W125
Douglas, C.M.	17 Dec. 1867	B15C B43 B69 B114 C113A C130 E14 K51 K53 M14 R60 R80 S18 S125 S145 W75 W79 W125
Douglas, H.E.M.	29 Mar. 1901	C70 C130 R80 U11 W125
Douglas-Hamilton, A.F.	18 Nov. 1915	B28 C130 O14 W125
Dowell, G.D.	24 Feb. 1857	B15A C130 G63 K50 K54 L45 N15 P59 R58 W90 W125
Dowling, W.	21 Nov. 1859	B42 C78 C130 K52 K54 L42 M129 R59 T12 V70 W125
Down, J.T.	22 Sep. 1864	B35 C130 M107 R60 W125
Downie, R.	25 Nov. 1916	C130 D23 G30 O15 W125
Doxat, A.C.	15 Jan. 1901	A65 C130 U11 W125
Doyle, M.	31 Jan. 1919	A61 A65 C130 D23 G34 H12 I61 V77 W125
Drain, J.H.C.	25 Nov. 1914	A65 A66 C35 C130 G31 H140 L16 O13 P7A S40 S41 S90 W125
Drake, A.G.	22 Jan. 1916	A65 A67 B28 C130 O14 W7 W52 W125
Dresser, T.	27 Jun. 1917	C46 C130 G33 G62 O16 V67 W125
Drew, A.M.C. McReady: see McReady-Diarmid, A.M.C.		
Drewry, G.L.	16 Aug. 1915	A65 B95 C130 F3 H12 H140 L16 M121 S40 S75 S77 S78 S90 W90 W125
Drummond, G.H.	28 Aug. 1918	A27 A28 A65 C95 C130 H102 K16A L5 M12B P37 S40 S77 S80 T5 W90 W125
Duffy, J.	27 Feb. 1918	C60 C130 G37 R59 U2 W125
Duffy, T.	18 Jun. 1858	B42 C130 D23 K16 K52 K54 W125
Dugdale, F.B.	17 Sep. 1901	C130 P12 U11 T14 V54 W125
Dunbar-Nasmith, M.E.	25 Jun. 1915	B43 C12 C22 C106 C110 C111 C130 G58 H12 H55 H140 J9 K14 K34 L15 M16 M20 O35 S36 S75 S77 S90 U5 V45 V75 W49 W85 W86 W90 W125
Dundas, J.	31 Dec. 1867	A65 B43 C130 K16 K51 K53 K54 M14B N2 R60 S40 V62 W125
Dunkley, B. Best-: see Best-Dunkley, B.		
Dunlay, J.	24 Dec. 1858	B42 C130 K52 K54 R59 W125
Dunlea, J.: see Dunlay, J.		
Dunley, J.: see Dunlay, J.		
Dunmore, Earl of: see Fincastle, Viscount		
Dunn, A.R.	24 Feb. 1857	B15A B43 B69 B114 C130 G63 K50 K54 L1 M14 M30 M70 M95 P5 R58 S125 S145 V54 W125
Dunsire, R.	18 Nov. 1915	B1 B28 C130 L15 O14 W125

Recipient	Gazette Date	Item Number in Part 1 / Part 2
Dunstan, W.	15 Oct. 1915	A27 A28 A76 B76A B116 B116A C125 C130 H90 H98 M23A S75 W55 W70 W125
Dunville, J.S.	2 Aug. 1917	C60 C130 G33 O16 U2 W125
Durrant, A.E.	18 Oct. 1901	C130 U11 W7 W125
Durrant, T.F.	19 Jun. 1945	B1 C113C D25 I15 L1A L3 L71 L110 M40 N2 R91 T36 V55 W125
Dwyer, E.	22 May 1915	B28 C35 C130 H12 H140 L15 N25 O13 S90 W125
Dwyer, J.J.	26 Nov. 1917	B26 B76A B116 C125 C130 D7 M23A O17 S76 V73 W50 W55 W70 W125
Dynon, D.	25 Feb. 1862	A65 B42 C130 D31 D32 K52 K54 R59 W125
Eardley, G.H.	2 Jan. 1945	A65 A67 D31 D32 E1 E2 E2A E2B L3 R70 S80 T29A T36 V53 W125
Edmonson, J.H.	4 Jul. 1941	B45 B76A B116 H90 K22 M23A M25 M70 P8A R70 R72 T36 W55 W70 W125
Edwards, A.	14 Sep. 1917	A27 A28 A36 C130 M70 O17 S76 W52 W125
Edwards, F.J.	25 Nov. 1916	C130 G30 H12 O15 W125
Edwards, H.I.	22 Jul. 1941	B23 B76A B89 B92 B116 B116A C55 F32 G52 H90 H110 J13 K2 K23 L3 L35 L53 L69 M17A M17D M23A R70 S27 S85 T35 W55 W70 W75 W80 W125
Edwards, T.	21 May 1884	C130 R60 W125
Edwards, W. C.	14 Sep. 1917	C130 O17 S76 W125
Edwards, W.M.M.	13 Feb. 1883	C130 E12 K51 K53 R60 W125
Egerton, E.A.	26 Nov. 1917	C35 C130 H98 M4 O17 S76 W125
Elcock, R.E.	26 Dec. 1918	C35 C130 D1 G35 H35 H98 W125
Elliott, K.	24 Sep. 1942	A58 B45 B140 C40 E15 H30 M70 N12 N12A P20 R70 S5 T36 W125
Elliott-Cooper, N.B.	13 Feb. 1918	C130 G36 K13 O18 W125
Elphinstone, H.C.	2 Jun. 1858	A65 A67 B15A C130 C150 D17 D26A E20 G63 K50 K54 M2 N2 R58 W42 W125
Elstob, W.	9 Jun. 1919	A65 B81 B84 C130 G32 H12 M106 O18 V73 W125
Elton, F.C.	24 Feb. 1857	B15A C130 G63 K50 K54 R58 W125
Embleton, D.: see Corbett, F.		
Emerson, J.S.	13 Feb. 1918	C60 C130 D23 G36 O18 U2 W125
Engleheart, H.W.	5 Oct. 1900	C130 U11 W125
English, W.J.	4 Oct. 1901	A66 C130 M70 U10 U11 W125
Erskine, J.	5 Aug. 1916	C6 C130 G36 O14 W125
Ervine-Andrews, H.M.	30 Jul. 1940	A15 B1 D22 D23 H55 H57 K42 K65 L3 M22C R70 R71 T12 T36 V61 V75 W8 W8A W51 W87 W125
Esmonde, E.K.	3 Mar. 1942	B20 B89 B90 B115 C80 C108 C110 C114A C148 D22 D23 E60 F28 H10 H56 J16 K23 L3 L42 M17A P53 P54 R37 R54 R70 S40 T35 T37 V45 W52 W90 W125
Esmonde, T.	25 Sep. 1857	B15A C130 G63 K50 K54 R58 T32 W125
Evans, A. (alias W. Simpson)	30 Oct. 1918	B12 C78 C130 G34 L42 M129 P8 W125
	31 Mar. 1919	
Evans, W.J.G.	30 Jan. 1920	A27 A28 B12 B84 C130 G30 H127 O15 V65 W125

Recipient	Gazette Date	Item Number in Part 1 / Part 2
Evans, L.P.	26 Nov. 1917	A66 C130 O17 S76 W75 W80 W125
Evans, S.	23 Jun. 1857	B15A C46 C130 G63 K50 K54 R58 W125
Evens, S.: see Evans, S.		
Farmer, D.D.	12 Apr. 1901	A36 B6 C78 C130 L42 M70 M129 R74 U11 W125
Farmer, J.J.	16 May 1881	B43 C130 C150 D17 P5 R60 R80 U11 V61 W125
Farquharson, F.E.H.	16 Jun. 1859	B42 C130 C150 D17 R59 W42 W125
Farrell, J.	20 Nov. 1857	B15A B43 C130 K50 K54 G63 M30 P5 R58 T32 V54 W125
Faulds, W.F.	9 Sep. 1916	C130 G30 H140 O15 U10 W125
Fazal Din	24 May 1945	A16 A66 B44 H26 H55 I10 K16 R70 S45 T36 W125
Fegen, E.S.F.	22 Nov. 1940	A15 B79 D22 D23 D40 E3 F39 H55 K15A K65 L3 L70 M9 M10 M20 P47 R70 R72 T2 T19 T37 W90 W125
Fergusson, T.R. Collyer-: see Collyer-Fergusson, T.R.		
ffrench, A.K.	24 Dec. 1858	B42 C130 D31 D32 K52 K54 R59 W125
Fielding, John: see Williams, John		
Fincastle, Viscount	9 Nov. 1897	C130 F15 P5 W125
Finch, N.A.	23 Jul. 1918	A25 A26 A27 A28 B86A B95 C21 C95 C130 D1 H85 H102 K16A L5 L30 L45 M12B M70 P37 P59 S16 S77 W19 W90 W125
Findlater, G.	20 May 1898	A36 A61 B40B C130 C147 G43 H127 M30 M70 N15 P5 W125
Findlay, G.deC.E.	15 May 1919	C130 G35 N2 W125
Finlay, D.	29 Jun. 1915	B28 C130 H140 O14 S90 V52 W125
Finn, J.H.: see Fynn, J.H.		
Firman, H.O.B.	2 Feb. 1917	B43 C130 S77 V77 W90 W125
Firth, J.	11 Jun. 1901	A65 C130 J28 U11 W52 W125
Fisher, F.	23 Jun. 1915	B28 B69 B114 C130 G39 L15 L16 M14 M95 O14 R53 S125 S145 V52 W125
FitzClarence, C.	6 Jul. 1900	A61 A65 A67 C130 K13 H98 S80 U11 V45 V51 W125
FitzGerald, R.	27 Apr. 1858	B42 C130 K16 K52 K54 R59 S41 V55 W125
Fitzgibbon, A.	13 Aug. 1861	B43 C130 K16 L2 R60 R80 V74 W125
Fitzpatrick, F.	23 Feb. 1880	B43 C130 E12 K53 K54 R60 V68 W125
Flawn, T.	23 Feb. 1880	B43 C130 E12 K53 K54 R60 V68 W125
Fleming-Sandes, A.J.T.	18 Nov. 1915	A27 A28 B28 C130 L16 M70 O14 W125
Flowerdew, G.M.	24 Apr. 1918	B69 B114 C130 G32 G39 G69 L100 M14 M95 R53 S18 S40 S125 S145 W125
Flynn, T.	12 Apr. 1859	B42 C130 D23 H98 V74 W125
Foote, H.R.B.	18 May 1944	B45 D1 L3 L30 L70 R70 T36 W125
Foote, J.W.	14 Feb. 1946	B69 B114 B143 C113A D26 F41 G45 G51 K18 L53 M14 M95 S62 S125 S145 T36 W125
Forbes-Robertson, J.	22 May 1918	B79 C130 G32 M106 P12 T14 W125
Forrest, G.	18 Jun. 1858	B40B B42 C130 H89 K16 K52 K54 P5 R59 W125
Forshaw, W.T.	9 Sep. 1915	B12 B83 B84 C130 L16 S75 T1A W53 W125
Forsyth, S.	22 Oct. 1918	A58 A65 B140 C40 C130 G34 H30 N2 N12A S5 W125
Fosbery, G.V.	7 Jul. 1865	A65 B2A B43 C130 K16 K52 K54 R60 V76 W125
Foss, C.C.	23 Aug. 1915	B28 C79 C130 L42 O13 W125

Recipient	Gazette Date	Item Number in Part 1 / Part 2
Foster, E.	27 Jun. 1917	A65 C130 G33 O16 S80 W125
Fowler, E.J.	5 Apr. 1882	B13 B40B C130 G60A G60B I61 K45 R60 W125 Y2
Fraser, C.C.	8 Nov. 1860	B42 C130 K52 K54 R59 W125
Fraser, I.E.	13 Nov. 1945	A65 A67 B1 B44 B115 C79 C111 E80 F11 F11A F22 F46 H56 I6 J9 K14 K15 L1A L3 L42 L70 M70 M104 O35 P2 R70 S40 S64 S80 T37 V55 V62 W2 W20 W81 W90 W125
Freeman, J.	24 Dec. 1858	A65 B42 C130 I15 K52 K54 R59 W125
French, J.A.	14 Jan. 1943	B44 B76A B116 C103 H90 M23A R70 T28 T36 V54 W55 W70 W125
Freyburg, B.C.	15 Dec. 1916	A26 A27 A28 B17 B33 B85 B140 C26 C40 C130 F50 G30 H12 H30 H75 L1A L16 L70 M70 M127 O15 S33 S47 S67 S85 S123 W125 W130 (also see Part 2 Section A)
Frickleton, S.	2 Aug. 1917	A27 A28 A58 B140 C40 C130 G33 H30 M70 N12A O16 S5 W125
Frisby, C.H.	27 Nov. 1918	B1 C130 G15 G35 P10 W125
Fuller, W.D.	19 Apr. 1915	B15C B28 C130 G15 H140 L15 M4 N50 O13 V157 W125
Fuller, W.C.	23 Nov. 1914	C130 G31 H12 H140 O13 S90 W75 W80 E80 W125
Furness, C.	7 Feb. 1946	L3 G15 T36 V10 W75 W80 W125
Fynn, J.H.	26 Sep. 1916	C130 G37 R59 V60 W75 W80 W125
Gaby, A.E.	30 Oct. 1918	B26 B76A B116 C125 C130 G34 G52 H90 M23A W55 W70 W125
Gaje Ghale	30 Sep. 1943	A16 B44 B50 I10 K16 L70 M24 R70 S45 T36 W125
Ganju Lama	7 Sep. 1944	A16 B44 B50 I10 K16 L70 M24 P20 R70 S45 T9 T36 W125
Gardiner, G.	4 Jun. 1858	B15A C130 G63 K50 K54 R58 T32 W125
Gardner, P.J.	10 Feb. 1942	B45 H56 L70 R70 S40 T36 V70 W110 W125
Gardner, W.	23 Aug. 1858	B42 B134 C130 K52 K54 R59 S40 W125
Garforth, C.E.	16 Nov. 1914	B43 C130 G31 M4 N50 O13 V74 W125
Garland, D.E.	11 Jun. 1940	A15 B23 B89 B152 C55 D22 D23 E60 G64 J3 K23 K65 L3 L53 M17A P39 R70 R71 T35 W51 W125
Garvin, S.	20 Jan. 1860	A66 B42 C130 H98 K52 K54 R59 W7 W125
Geary, B.H.	15 Oct. 1915	A65 B28 B114 C130 H140 O13 S90 W125
Gee, R.	11 Jan. 1918	A27 A28 C130 G36 K13 M70 O18 S30 W125
Gian Singh	22 May 1945	B44 I10 K16 M102D R70 S45 T36 W125
Gibson, G.P.	28 May 1943	A9 A55 A62 B23 B26A B26B B26C B30 B88A B89 B92 B115 B120 B149 B150 C55 C108 C108A C115 C117 C117A D13 D18A E17 E69 E70 E71 E72 F1 F2 F24 F32 F36 F37 F61 G4 G20 G30 G38 H6 H7 H58 H82 H86 H89A H123 J16 J25 K8 K23 L3 L53 L69 M17A M115 M116A M132 O11 O40 O66 O67 P52 P57 P58 P65 P70 R5 R37 R70 R77 T1 T14A T35 S42A S44 S64 S80 S142 S143 S144 T12 T39 V8 V45 V72 W16 W17 W18 W25 W125
Gifford, Lord	28 Mar. 1874	A69 B40B C130 E14 K51 K53 R60 T14 W75 W79 W125
Gill, A.	26 Oct. 1916	A65 B86A C130 D1 G30 L30 O15 W7 W125
Gill, P.	23 Aug. 1858	B42 C130 K16 K52 K54 R59 V72 W125
Glasock, H.H.	26 Jun. 1900	A65 C130 L35 P5 S41 U11 W125
Glenn, J.A.: see Smith, James (Pte.)		
Goat, W.	24 Dec. 1858	C130 K52 K54 P5 R59 V53 W125
Gobar Sing Negi	28 Apr. 1915	A13 B28 C18 C130 K4 K16 O13 V56 S45 W125

Recipient	Gazette Date	Item Number in Part 1 / Part 2
Gobind Singh	11 Jan. 1918	A13 C18 C35 C130 G36 K4 K16 O18 S45 W125
Godley, S.F.	25 Nov. 1914	A65 B1 C130 G31 G39 H56 H140 K13 O13 R90 T22 V65 V74 W125
Good, H.J.	27 Sep. 1918	B69 B79 B114 C130 G34 M14 S125 S145 W125
Goodfellow, C.A.	16 Apr. 1863	B42 C130 D1 K16 N2 R59 R60 W125
Goodlake, G.L.	24 Feb. 1857	B15A C130 C150 D17 E14 G15 G63 K50 P10 R58 S89 V71 W42 W125
Gordon, B.S.	26 Dec. 1918	B26 B76A B116 C121 C125 C130 G34 M23A M25 W55 W70 W125
Gordon, J.H.	28 Oct. 1941	B45 B116 G52 M23A M70 R70 T36 W55 W70 W125
Gordon, W.E.	28 Sep. 1900	C130 U11 W125
Gordon, W.J.	9 Dec. 1892	B43 C130 H98 M102D W125
Gore-Browne, H.G.	20 Jun. 1862	B42 C130 R59 T12 V70 W125
Gorle, R.V.	14 Dec. 1918	A65 C130 G35 S41 U10 W125
Gorman, J.	24 Feb. 1857	A61 B15A C130 G63 K50 K54 M70 R58 V50 W63 W90 W125
Gort, Viscount	27 Nov. 1918	B19 C102 C130 G15 G35 H12 H68 K3 K12 L10 S67 V68 V69 W125
Gosling, W.	14 Jun. 1917	A27 A28 C130 G33 O16 S41 W125
Gough, C.J.S.	21 Oct. 1859	A65 A67 B30 B42 C130 C150 D17 G49 K16 K52 K54 R56 R59 S40 V69 W42 W62 W125 (also see Part 2 Section A)
Gough, H.H.	24 Dec. 1858	A65 B42 C130 C150 D17 G49 K16 K52 K54 R68 T9A V69 V70 V155 W62 W125
Gough, J.E.	15 Jan. 1904	A65 B34 B43 C130 D23 P5 V69 V70 W7 W125
Gould, T.W.	9 Jun. 1942	A61 B1 B45 C111 H41 H55 I15 J9 K14 L3 L35 M70 R70 T37 V51 V69 W90 W125
Gourley, C.E.	13 Feb. 1918	C60 C77 C130 G36 G50 L42 M129 O18 S41 W125
Gowrie, Earl of: see Hore-Ruthven, A.G.A.		
Grady, T.	23 Jun. 1857	B15A C130 E14 G63 K33 K50 R58 T32 W125
Graham, G.	24 Feb. 1857	B15A C130 D11 G63 K50 K54 N2 P5 R57 R58 V20 V73 W125 (also see Part 2 Section A)
Graham, J.R.N.	14 Sep. 1917	C130 G37 M70 W125
Graham, P.	24 Dec. 1858	B42 C130 K52 K54 R59 W125
Grant, C.J.W.	26 May 1891	B43 B50 C130 G68 K16 P5 W125
Grant, J.D.	24 Jan. 1905	A66 B43 B50 C130 I15 K16 S79B T14 V64 V76 W125
Grant, J.G.	27 Nov. 1918	A27 A28 A58 B140 C40 C130 G34 H30 I61 M70 N12A S5 W125
Grant, P.	24 Dec. 1858	B42 C130 K52 K54 P5 R59 W125
Grant, R.	19 Jun. 1860	B42 C130 K52 K54 R59 W52 W125
Gratwick, P.E.	28 Jan. 1943	B45 B76A B116 G52 H90 M23A R70 T36 W55 W70 W125
Gray, R.H.	13 Nov. 1945	B1 B43 B44 B69 B79 B89 B114 D26 G45 G51 J3 K23 M14 M17A P33 R70 S86 S125 S145 T37 V73 W90 W125
Gray, T.	11 Jun. 1940	A15 B23 B89 B152 C55 E60 G64 J3 K23 K65 L3 L53 M17A P39 R70 R71 T35 W51 W125
Grayburn, J.H.	25 Jan. 1945	A61 J27 L3 R70 T36 W125
Greaves, F.	26 Nov. 1917	C130 M4 O17 S76 V66 W125
Green, J.L.	5 Aug. 1916	C130 G30 H98 M4 O15 R80 W125
Green, P.	26 Oct. 1858	B42 C130 H98 K52 K54 R59 W125
Greenwood, H.	26 Dec. 1918	C130 G35 H125 H126 H129 U10 V51 W125

Recipient	Gazette Date	Item Number in Part 1 / Part 2
Gregg, M.F.	6 Jan. 1919	B69 B79 B114 C130 D27 G35 G39 M14 S125 S145 W125
Gregg, W.	28 Jun. 1918	C130 G32 M4 W7 W125
Grenfell, F.O.	16 Nov. 1914	B145 C130 G31 H140 L15 M106 O13 S64 W80 W125
Gribble, J.R.	28 Jun. 1918	C130 G32 G65 O18 W125
Grieve, J.	24 Feb. 1857	B15A C130 G63 K50 K54 P5 R58 W125
Grieve, R.C.	2 Aug. 1917	B76A B116 C125 C130 G33 M23A O16 W55 W70 W125
Griffiths, W.	17 Dec. 1867	C130 G60B K51 K53 K54 R60 R79 W75 W79 W125
Grimbaldeston, W.H.	14 Sep. 1917	A27 A28 C130 K40 L37 O17 S76 W125
Grimshaw, J.E.	15 Mar. 1917	A27 A28 A65 A67 B12 C130 H12 M109 V45 S75 W125
Gristock, G.	23 Aug. 1940	A15 K65 L3 R70 S17 T36 W51 W125
Grogan, G.W.StG.	25 Jul. 1918	C130 G32 W125
Guise, J.C.	24 Dec. 1858	A65 B42 C130 K52 K54 T14 W125
Gunn, G.W.	21 Apr. 1942	B45 C79 L3 L42 L70 R70 S41 T36 V66 W53 W125
Gurney, A.S.	14 Sep. 1942	B45 B76A B116 G52 H90 L70 M23A R70 T36 W55 W70 W125
Guy, B.J.D.	1 Jan. 1901	A65 A67 C130 L2 P5 S40 S80 V65 W53 W90 W125
Hackett, T.B.	12 Apr. 1859	A65 A67 B42 C130 K52 K54 R59 W75 W79 W80 W125
Hackett, W.	5 Aug. 1916	C130 G36 H12 M4 N2 N50 O14 R16 W52 W125
Haine, R.L.	8 Jun. 1917	A27 A28 B1 C130 D19 G33 O16 P40 W125
Hale, T.E.	5 May 1857	B15A C130 G63 K13 K50 K54 R58 R80 V64 W79 W125
Hall, A.C.	14 Dec. 1918	B76A B116 C125 C130 G34 H90 M23A M25 W55 W70 W125
Hall, F.W.	23 Jun. 1915	B28 B29 B69 B114 C60 C130 D23 F41 G39 H12 L15 L16 M14 N1 O14 R53 S125 S145 W125
Hall, W.	1 Feb. 1859	A61 A65 B35 B42 B69 B114 C130 H1 H43 K52 K54 M14 M16A M95 M102D P1 R59 R75 S125 S145 V15 V45 V50 W90 W125
Halliday, L.S.T.	1 Jan. 1901	B43 C130 L45 P5 P59 V77 W90 W125
Halliwell, J.	25 Jul. 1918	B12 C130 G32 W125
Hallowes, R.P.	18 Nov. 1915	A27 A28 B28 C130 D19 H140 M70 O14 S90 W75 W80 W125
Halton, A.	26 Nov. 1917	C130 K33 O17 S76 W125
Hamilton, A.F. Douglas-: see Douglas-Hamilton, A.F.		
Hamilton, J.B.	26 Nov. 1917	B103 B134 C130 O17 S76 W125
Hamilton, J.P.	15 Oct. 1915	A76 B76A B116 C35 C125 C130 H90 M23A M25 S75 V75 W55 W63 W70 W125
Hamilton, T.deC.	24 Feb. 1857	B15A C130 D23 G63 H98 K50 K54 P12 R58 S37 T14 W125
Hamilton, W.R.P.	7 Oct. 1879	A65 B43 C130 D23 E11 H11 K16 K53 K54 M30 P5 P26 R60 S40 V63 W125
Hammond, A.G.	18 Oct. 1881	A65 C130 E11 K16 K53 K54 R60 W125
Hampton, H.	18 Oct. 1901	B6 B84 C79 C130 L42 U11 W125
Hancock, T.	15 Jan. 1858	B42 C130 K52 K54 R59 W125
Hanna, R.H.	8 Nov. 1917	A27 A28 B69 B114 B143 C60 C130 G36 G39 K18 M14 O17 R53 S125 S145 U2
Hannah, J.	1 Oct. 1940	A15 B24 B89 C55 C108 C108A G64 H55 K23 K65 L2 L3 M17A M44 P39 R70 R71 T35 W51 W125
Hansen, P.H.	1 Oct. 1915	C130 H140 L16 S40 S75 S90 U10 V76 W125
Harden, H.E.	8 Mar. 1945	B1 H22 I15 L3 R70 R80 S74 T36 V57 W125

Recipient	Gazette Date	Item Number in Part 1 / Part 2
Hardham, W.J.	4 Oct. 1901	A58 B140 C40 C130 H30 M70 N12A S5 U11 W125
Harding, I.	15 Sep. 1882	A65 B14 B43 C130 R60 S40 V68 V69 W90 W125
Hardy, T.B.	11 Jul. 1918	B75A C130 G32 H25 R11 R12 T12 W63 W125
Harington, H.E.	24 Dec. 1858	B42 C130 K16 K52 K54 N30 R59 S41 W125
Harlock, E.G.: see Horlock, E.G.		
Harman, J.P.	22 Jun. 1944	B1 B43 B44 C8 I15 L3 R70 T14 T36 V56 W125
Harper, J.W.	2 Jan. 1945	J28 L3 R70 T29A T36 W52 W125
Harris, T.J.	22 Oct. 1918	C130 G34 H85 I15 M126A W125
Harrison, A.L.	17 Mar. 1919	C21 C95 C130 G34 H85 H102 K16A L5 M12B P37 S16 S77 T5 T12 V45 W19 W90 W125
Harrison, J. (2/Lt.)	14 Jun. 1917	C130 G33 H37 M117 O16 P4C V53 W52 W125
Harrison, J. (L/Sea.)	24 Dec. 1858	B42 C130 K52 K54 R59 V68 W90 W125
Hart, R.C.	10 Jun. 1879	A65 C130 E11 K16 K53 K54 N2 P3 R60 T14 V66 W125 (also see Part 2 Section A)
Hartigan, H.	19 Jun. 1860	C130 K52 K54 R59 W125 (also see Part 2 Section A)
Hartley, E.B.	7 Oct. 1881	B43 C130 M70 R60 R80 U10 V67 W125
Harvey, F.J.W.	15 Sep. 1916	C130 H91 L45 M15 P59 S77 V68 W90 W125
Harvey, F.M.W.	8 Jun. 1917	B69 B114 C130 G33 G39 G69 M14 M117 O16 R53 S125 S145 W125
Harvey, J.	15 Nov. 1918	A65 C130 G34 S40 W125
Harvey, N.	6 Jan. 1919	C35 C80 C130 G35 L42 N2 U2 W125
Harvey, S.	18 Nov. 1915	B28 C130 M4 N50 O14 W125
Havelock, H.M.	15 Jan. 1858	B42 B43 C130 H89 K52 K54 M38 M49 P5 P49 R59 V77 W61 W125 (also see Part 2 Section A)
Havelock-Allan, H.M.: see Havelock, H.M.		
Hawker, L.G.	24 Aug. 1915	A100 B21 B25 B89 C9 C114 C130 G64 H65 I20 J30 K23 M17B N2 P31 P41 R27 V75 W26 W93 W125
Hawkes, D.	24 Dec. 1858	B42 C130 K52 K54 R59 W7 W125
Hawthorne, R.	27 Apr. 1858	B12 B40B B42 C130 C150 D17 H89 K52 K54 P25 R59 W7 W42 W125
Hayward, R.F.J.	24 Apr. 1918	C130 G32 O18 T14 U10 W125
Heaphy, C.	8 Feb. 1867	A58 B43 B140 C40 C130 G47 H30 K24A M21 M70 M107 M134 N12A R15 R60 S5 S39A S85 W125 (also see Part 2 Section A)
Heathcote, A.S.	20 Jan. 1860	B42 C130 K52 K54 R59 W7 W125
Heaton, W.E.	18 Jan. 1901	B6 B84 C80 C130 L42 U11 W125
Heaviside, M.	8 Jun. 1917	C130 G33 O16 S37 W53 W125
Hedges, F.W.	31 Jan. 1919	C130 G35 W52 W125
Henderson, A.	5 Jul. 1917	A65 C130 G33 O16 W125
Henderson, E.E.D.	8 Jun. 1917	A66 C130 G37 H98 W125
Henderson, G.S.	29 Oct. 1920	B43 B84 C65 C130 W125
Henderson, H.S.	7 May 1897	B43 C130 P5 U10 W125
Heneage, C. Walker-: see Walker-Heneage, C.		
Henry, A.	24 Feb. 1857	B15A C130 C150 D17 G63 K50 K54 R58 S41 W42 W125
Herring, A.C.	7 Jun. 1918	C130 G32 O18 W125
Hewett, W.N.W.	24 Feb. 1857	A25 A26 B15A C130 C150 D17 G63 K50 K54 M70 R57 R58 V61 W42 W90 W125

Recipient	Gazette Date	Item Number in Part 1 / Part 2
Hewitson, J.	28 Jun. 1918	C130 G32 K33 W53 W125
Hewitt, D.G.W.	14 Sep. 1917	C35 C130 O17 S76 W125
Hewitt, W.H.	26 Nov. 1917	C130 P12 S76 T14 U10 W125
Hill, A.R.	14 Mar. 1882	A66 C130 R60 U11 W52 W125
Hill, A.	26 Sep. 1916	B12 C130 G30 O15 T1A W75 W125
Hill, S.	24 Dec. 1858	A65 B42 C130 K52 K54 R59 W125
Hill-Walker, A.R.: see Hill, A.R.		
Hills, J.	27 Apr. 1858	B42 C130 C150 D17 H89 K16 K52 K54 M14B M101 R56 R59 S41 V59 W42 W62 W75 W79 W80 W125
Hills-Johnes, J.: see Hills, J.		
Hinckley, G.	6 Feb. 1863	B43 C77 C130 L42 M129 T12 R60 V73 W90 W125
Hinton, J.D.	17 Oct. 1941	A58 B45 B140 C40 H30 L70 M7 M70 N12 N12A 70 S5 T36 W125
Hirsch, D.P.	14 Jun. 1917	C46 C130 G33 G62 O16 W52 W125
Hitch, F.	2 May 1879	A61 B9 B11 B13 B15 B15B B15D B15E C130 E12 G24 G41 G60 G60A G60B H5 H92 H93 J31 K45 K46 K47 K49B K53 K54 L87 M13A M30 R6 R60 R69 R79 S79 S134 T15A W27 W51A W54 W75 W79 W125 Y2 Y5
Hobson, F.	17 Oct. 1917	B69 B114 C130 G36 G39 M14 O17 R53 S125 S145 W125
Hodge, S.	4 Jan. 1867	B43 C130 H98 K51 K53 K54 R60 W125
Hoey, C.F.	18 May 1944	B69 B44 B114 C113A D26 G51 L3 M14 R70 S125 S145 T36 W125
Hogan, J.	22 Dec. 1914	B12 B84 C130 G31 H140 L16 O13 S90 V74 W125
Holbrook, N.D.	22 Dec. 1914	C22 C106 C111 C130 G31 G43 G58 G90 H55 H91 H140 J9 L15 L37 M20 S77 S90 U5 V74 W49 W85 W86 W90 W125
Holland, E.J.G.	23 Apr. 1901	B69 B114 C130 F41 M14 M95 S125 S145 U11 W125
Holland, J.V.	26 Oct. 1916	C78 C130 G30 L42 O15 W125
Hollis, G.	26 Jan. 1859	B42 C130 K52 K54 R59 T14 W125
Hollis, S.E.	17 Aug. 1944	A61 B136 C46 D37 H26 K11 K15A L3 M111 N25 R53A R70 T29A T36 V54 W52 W125
Holliwell, J.: see Hollowell, J.		
Hollowell, J.	18 Jun. 1858	B42 C130 K52 K54 R59 W125
Holmes, F.W.	25 Nov. 1914	B103 C130 G31 H140 L15 O13 W125
Holmes, J.	18 Jun. 1858	B42 C130 K52 K54 R59 W52 W125
Holmes, T.W.	11 Jan. 1918	B69 B114 C35 C130 C142 G39 M14 M46 M95 O17 R53 S76 S125 S145 W125
Holmes, W.E.	26 Dec. 1918	B1 C130 G15 G35 T14 W125
Home, A.D.	18 Jun. 1858	B35 B42 C130 C150 D17 H89 H95 K52 K54 P5 R59 R80 W42 W125
Home, D.C.	18 Jun. 1858	A61 B40B B42 B43 C130 C150 D17 H89 K16 K30 K52 K54 N2 P25 R59 T6 W42 W125
Honey, S.L.	6 Jan. 1919	B69 B114 C130 G35 G39 M14 S125 S145 W125
Hook, A.H.	2 May 1879	B9 B11 B13 B15 B15B B15D B15E B40B C130 E12 G24 G41 G60 G60A G60B H5 H92 H93 J22 J23 J31 K45 K46 K47 K49B K53 K54 L87 M13A M30 P12 R6 R60 R69 R79 S79 S134 T14 T15A V45 V54 W27 W51A W54 W75 W79 W125 Y2 Y5
Hope, W.	5 May 1857	B15A C130 C150 D17 G63 K13 K50 K54 R58 W42 W125
Hore-Ruthven, A.G.A	28 Feb. 1899	A65 B76 C130 H125 H129 M70 P12 T14 W69 W125
Horlock, E.G.	25 Nov. 1914	C130 G31 O13 S41 W125

Recipient	Gazette Date	Item Number in Part 1 / Part 2
Hornby, E.J. Phipps-: see Phipps-Hornby, E.J.		
Hornell, D.E.	28 Jul. 1944	B69 B79 B89 B114 C108 C108A C113A D26 G45 G51 H10 H26 H56 K23 L70 M14 M17A M95 P33 R70 S125 S145 T35 W90 W125
Horsfall, B.A.	22 May 1918	A27 A28 C130 G32 M70 W125
Horwood, A.G.	30 Mar. 1944	A65 B1 B44 L3 R70 T36 W125
House, W.	7 Oct. 1902	B43 C130 I15 U11 V57 W125
Howell, G.J.	27 Jun. 1917	A27 A28 B76A B116 C121 C125 C130 G33 M23A M25 M70 W55 O16 W70 W125
Howse, N.R.	4 Jun. 1901	B76A B113 B116 B116A C130 H90 M17D M23A R21 R80 S85 S110 T9A T60 U11 V52 V155 W3 W55 W70 W125
Hudson, C.E.	11 Jul. 1918	C130 G37 H12 H115 H116 M4 W125 (also see Part 2 Section A)
Huffam, J.P.	26 Dec. 1918	A27 A28 C130 G34 M70 W125
Hughes, M.	24 Feb. 1857	B15A C130 G63 K13 K50 K54 R58 W52 W125
Hughes, T.	26 Oct. 1916	C60 C130 G30 L16 O15 U2 W125
Hull, C.	3 Mar. 1916	C130 G37 W52 W125
Hulme, A.C.	14 Oct. 1941	A58 B43 B45 B140 C40 H30 I61 L70 N12 N12A R70 S5 T36 W125
Humpston, R.	24 Feb. 1857	B15A C130 G63 K50 K54 M4 N50 R58 W7 W125
Hunter, D.F.	23 Oct. 1918	A27 A28 A36 C130 G34 M70 W125
Hunter, T.P.	12 Jun. 1945	H56 L3 L45 R70 T36 T37 W90 W125
Hutcheson, B.S.	14 Dec. 1918	B69 B114 C130 G34 G39 H130 M14 R80 S125 S145 W125
Hutchinson, J.	9 Sep. 1916	B12 C59 C130 G36 O14 W125
Hutt, A.	26 Nov. 1917	C130 D1 O17 S76 W125
Ind, A.E.	15 Aug. 1902	B6 C130 M119 S41 T14 U1 W125
Ingham, S.: see Meekosha, S.		
Ingouville, G.	24 Feb. 1857	B15A C130 G63 K50 K54 R58 W90 W125
Ingram, G.M.	6 Jan. 1919	B76A B116 C121 C125 C130 G35 H12 M1 M23A V71 W55 W70 W125
Inkson, E.T.	15 Jan. 1901	A12B C130 R80 U11 W125
Innes, J.J.McL.	24 Dec. 1858	B42 C130 K16 N2 R59 T8 W125 (also see Part 2 Section A)
Insall, G.S.M.	23 Dec. 1915	B1 B25 B89 C114 C130 G64 H12 H38 H140 I20 J20 K23 M17B O10 P41 R27 S90 W52 W93 W125
Inwood, R.R.	26 Nov. 1917	B76A B116 B116A C125 C130 M23A O17 S76 W55 W70 W125
Irwin, C.	24 Dec. 1858	B42 C130 D31 D32 K52 K54 R59 W125
Ishar Singh	25 Nov. 1921	A65 B43 C130 C148 K4 K16 S40 S45 W125
Jacka, A.	24 Jul. 1915	A27 A28 A61 A65 A76 B76A B116 B116A C121 C125 C130 D13 G55 H12 H90 H140 J24 L12 L12A L15 L33 M17C M17D M23A R6 R85 S75 S85 S90 V50 W55 W70 W125
Jackman, J.J.B.	31 Mar. 1942	B45 D22 D23 K42 L3 L70 R70 T36 W125

Recipient	Gazette Date	Item Number in Part 1 / Part 2
Jackson, H.	8 May 1918	C130 G32 O18 W125
Jackson, N.C.	26 Oct. 1945	A60 A61 A65 A67 A68 B23 B89 C55 C108 C108A H55 I6 J13 K15A K23 L3 M17A R70 S40 T35 V45 V53 W82 W125
Jackson, T.N.	27 Nov. 1918	C130 G15 G35 P10 W52 W125
Jackson, J.W.A.	9 Sep. 1916	B76A B116 C35 C130 G36 L2 M23A M25 O14 V53 W55 W63 W70 V155 W125
James, H. W.	1 Sep. 1915	B86A C130 D1 L16 L30 S75 S140 W125
James, M.A.	28 Jun. 1918	A65 C130 G32 O18 S40 S80 T14 T34 W125
Jamieson, D.A.	26 Oct. 1944	B1 H52 L3 R53A R70 T36 W125
Jarratt, G.	8 Jun. 1917	C130 G33 K13 K16 O16 W125
Jarrett, H.C.T.	18 Jun. 1859	B42 C130 K52 K54 R59 V62 W125
Jarvis, C.A.	16 Nov. 1914	C130 G31 H140 N2 O13 W125
Jee, J.	8 Nov. 1860	B35 B42 C130 C150 D17 K52 K54 N15 P5 R59 R80 W42 W125
Jefferson, F.A.	13 Jul. 1944	B1 B12 B43 L3 N25 R70 T36 V70 W53 W125
Jeffries, C.S.	18 Dec. 1917	B76A B116 C121 C125 C130 M23A M25 O17 S76 W55 W70 W125
Jennings, E.	24 Dec. 1858	B42 C130 K16 K52 K54 R59 S41 W53 W125
Jensen, J.C.	8 Jun. 1917	B76A B116 C125 C130 G33 H3 M23A O16 S79C W55 W70 W125
Jerome, H.E.	11 Nov. 1859	A66 42 C130 K52 K54 R59 W125
Jerrard, A.	1 May 1918	A66 A68 B25 B89 C114 C130 D1 H98 J20 K23 M17B M22 P41 R27 W125
Johnson, D.G.	6 Jan. 1919	B1 C130 G35 H98 T14 W75 W80 W125
Johnson, F.H.	18 Nov. 1915	B28 C130 N2 O14 W125
Johnson, J.	26 Dec. 1918	C130 G35 W53 W125
Johnson, W.H.	14 Dec. 1918	C130 M4 N50 S90 W125
Johnston, R.	12 Feb. 1901	A12B C130 M14 M117 U10 U11 W125
Johnston, W.H.	25 Nov. 1914	C130 G31 G35 H140 N2 O13 W125
Johnstone, W.	24 Feb. 1857	B15A C130 I61 G63 K50 K54 R58 V61 W90 W125
Jones, A.S.	18 Jun. 1858	B42 C77 C130 L42 M129 R59 W79 W125 (also see Part 2 Section A)
Jones, C. Mansel-: see Mansel-Jones, C.		
Jones, D.	26 Oct. 1916	B84 C130 G30 L42 M129 O15 W125
Jones, H.	11 Oct. 1982	A5 A6 A61 A65 B43 F19 F41A F47 F60 G11 O3 S93 W75 W80 W84 W125
Jones, H.M.	25 Sep. 1857	B15A C130 G63 K13 K50 K54 R58 T32 W125
Jones, L.W.	6 Mar. 1917	A66 B95 C130 J12 L16 M15 S77 V68 W90 W125
Jones, R.B.B.	5 Aug. 1916	C35 C130 G36 I15 O14 W125
Jones, R.	2 May 1879	A65 A67 B9 B11 B12 B13 B15 B15B B15D B15E B40B C130 E12 G24 G41 G60 G60A G60B H5 H92 H93 I61 J31 K45 K46 K47 K49B K53 K54 L87 M30 N15 R6 R60 R69 R79 S40 S79 S134 T15A W27 W51A W54 W75 W79 W80 W93 W125 Y2 Y5
Jones, R.J.T. Digby-: see Digby-Jones, R.J.T.		
Jones, T.A.	26 Oct. 1916	C80 C130 G30 H103 L16 L42 O15 T13 W125
Jones, W.	2 May 1879	B9 B11 B12 B13 B15 B15B B15D B15E B40B C130 D1 E12 G24 G41 G60 G60A G60B H5 H92 H93 J31 K45 K46 K47 K49B K53 K54 L87 M30 N15 R6 R60 R69 R79 S79 S134 T15A W15A W27 W54 W75 W79 W125 Y2 Y5

Recipient	Gazette Date	Item Number in Part 1 / Part 2
Jotham, E.	24 Jul. 1915	A13 B43 B160 C130 G37 H98 K16 L59 V53 W125
Joynt, W.D.	27 Nov. 1918	A27 A28 B76A B116 C125 C130 G34 H98 J35 J36 M23A M70 W55 W70 W125 (also see Part 2 Section A)
Judson, R.S.	30 Oct. 1918	A58 B140 C40 C130 G34 H30 N12A S5 W125
Kaeble, J.	16 Sep. 1918	B69 B114 C130 G32 G39 M14 S125 S145 W125
Kamal Ram	27 Jul. 1944	A16 A65 I10 K16 M102D R70 S40 S45 T36 W125
Karamjeet Singh Judge	3 Jul. 1945	A16 B44 I10 K16 R70 S45 S46 T36 W125
Karanbahadur Rana	21 Jun. 1918	A13 B50 C18 C35 C130 G37 K4 K10 K16 M24 S45 V64 W125
Kavanagh, T.H.	6 Jul. 1859	A26 A61 A65 B35 B40B B42 B43 C130 C150 D17 E14 H89 K5 K5A K6 K7 K16 K52 L35 M30 M70 M101 M102 M125 M126 N15 P5 P20 R59 S135 T9 V59 V60 W42 W125
Keatinge, R.H.	25 Feb. 1862	B42 C130 K16 R59 S41 W125
Keighran, D. A.	31 Oct. 2012	B76A M23A V71 W125
Kellaway, J.	24 Feb. 1857	B15A C130 G63 K50 K54 R58 W90 W125
Kelliher, R.	30 Dec. 1943	A61 B44 B76A B116 B116A D23 H90 M23A R70 T36 V51 W55 W63 W70 W125
Kells, R.	24 Dec. 1858	B42 C130 K52 K54 R59 W125
Kelly, H.	25 Oct. 1916	B3 B12 C130 D23 G30 O15 W125
Kelly, J.D.: see Davis, J.		
Kelly, J. Sherwood-: see Sherwood-Kelly, J.		
Keneally, W.S.	24 Aug. 1915	B12 C130 D23 H12 M109 S75 V45 W125
Kenna, E.	6 Sep. 1945	B44 B76A B116 C104 H90 L53 M17D M23A M25 R21 R70 T36 V64 W55 W70 W125
Kenna, P.A.	15 Nov. 1898	B32 B123 C130 D23 K42 L42 M3 M30 M129 P5 V51 V52 V53 V54 W125
Kenneally, J.P.	17 Aug. 1943	A61 B43 B45 D1 G15 H52 I61 K17 L3 L30 R70 T36 V61 W125
Kennedy, C.T.	18 Oct. 1901	C130 U11 V69 W125
Kennedy, W.H. Clark-: see Clark-Kennedy, W.H.		
Kenny, H.E.	30 Mar. 1916	A65 B28 C130 O14 W125
Kenny, J.	24 Dec. 1858	B42 C130 D31 D32 K52 K54 R59 W125
Kenny, T.	7 Dec. 1915	B28 C130 O14 S37 W53 W125
Kenny, T.J.B.	8 Jun. 1917	B76A B116 C125 C130 G33 H90 M23A O16 M25 W55 W70 W125
Kenny, W.	18 Feb. 1915	C130 D23 G31 O13 W125
Kenny, W.D.	9 Sep. 1920	A65 A67 A13 A67 C130 D23 K16 W125
Ker, A.E.	4 Sep. 1919	A65 C130 G32 M14B O18 W125
Kerr, G.F.	6 Jan. 1919	B69 B114 C130 G35 G39 M14 S125 S145 W125
Kerr, J.C.	26 Oct. 1916	B69 B79 B114 C130 G30 G39 K21 M14 O15 R53 S125 S145 W125
Kerr, W.A.	27 Apr. 1858	A65 B35 B40B B42 C130 C150 D17 H89 I15 K16 K52 K54 M101 P5 R59 W42 W125 (also see Part 2 Section A)
Keyes, G.C.T.	19 Jun. 1942	A65 A67 A72 B45 B115 C45 H26 H55 I60 J17 K24 L1A L3 L35 M118A R70 S40 T36 W125

Recipient	Gazette Date	Item Number in Part 1 / Part 2
Keysor, L.M.	15 Oct. 1915	A76 B76A B116 B116A C125 C130 H90 H140 L16 L54 M23A M25 S75 S90 W55 W70 W125
Keyworth, L.J.	3 Jul. 1915	B28 C130 H140 L15 O14 S90 V76 W125
Keyzor, L.: see Keysor, L.M.		
Khudadad Khan	7 Dec. 1914	A13 A66 C18 C130 G31 K4 K16 M27 M102D O13 V74 W125
Kibby, W.H.	28 Jan. 1943	B45 B76A B116 H90 M23A R70 T36 W53 W55 W70 W125
Kilby, A.F.G.	30 Mar. 1916	A66 B28 C130 H98 O14 P12 T14 W125
Kingsbury, B.S.	9 Feb. 1943	B44 B76A B116 B116A H90 L53 M23A R70 T36 V52 V76 W55 W63 W70 W125
Kinross, C.J.	11 Jan. 1918	B43 B69 B114 C130 D20A G39 M14 O17 R53 S76 S125 S145 V67 W125
Kirby, F.H.	5 Oct. 1900	A65 A67 C130 I15 N2 U11 W125
Kirk, James	6 Jan. 1919	B12 B84 C130 G35 T1A V68 W125
Kirk, John	20 Jan. 1860	B42 C77 C130 K52 K54 L42 M129 R59 V72 W125
Knight, A.J.	8 Nov. 1917	B86A C130 D1 L30 O17 S76 W7 W125
Knight, A.G.	15 Nov. 1918	B69 B114 C130 G34 G39 M14 S18 S125 S145 W125
Knight, H.J.	4 Jan. 1901	A36 B6 B84 C79 C130 L42 M70 U11 V64 W125
Knowland, G.A.	12 Apr. 1945	B1 B44 I15 L3 R70 T36 V53 W125
Knox, C.L.	4 Jun. 1918	C130 G32 N2 O18 U2 W125
Knox, J.S.	24 Feb. 1857	A66 B15A C79 C130 G15 G63 K50 K54 L42 P12 R58 T14 W7 W125
Konowal, F.	26 Nov. 1917	A61 B69 B114 C113A C130 G36 G39 L80 M14 M95 O17 R53 S125 S145 W125
Kulbir Thapa	18 Nov. 1915	A13 B28 B43 B50 C18 C130 K4 K16 M24 O14 S45 V64 V76 W125
Lachhiman Gurung	27 Jul. 1945	A16 B44 B50 I10 K16 M24 R70 S45 T36 V64 W125
Lafone, A.M.	18 Dec. 1917	C78 C130 G37 I15 L42 M129 W125
Laidlaw, D.L.	18 Nov. 1915	B28 C130 D19 H12 L15 L16 O14 V45 W53 W125
Lala	13 May 1916	A13 B24A C18 C130 G37 K4 K16 S45 W125
Lalbahadur Thapa	15 Jun. 1943	A16 B45 B50 I10 K4 L70 M24 R70 S45 W125
Lambert, G.	18 Jun. 1858	B42 C130 J28 K52 K54 R59 W52 W125
Lane, T.	13 Aug. 1861	B43 C130 G60B I61 K51 K53 K54 R60 V53 V54 W125
Lascelles, A.M.	11 Jan. 1918	C130 G10 G36 H12 O18 O60 S37 U10 W75 W80 W125
Lassen, A.F.E.V.S.	7 Sep. 1945	A15A C148 D13 H4 H23 H56 H105 J13 K1 K70 L1A L3 L6 L9 L31 L55 M104B M118 R70 S2 T36 V50 W125
Lauder, D.R.	13 Jan. 1917	A27 A28 A66 B134 C130 S75 W125
Laughnan, T.	24 Feb. 1858	B42 C130 K16 K52 K54 R59 S41 W125
Laurent, H.J.	15 Nov. 1918	A27 A28 A58 B140 C40 C130 G34 H30 M70 N12A S5 W125
Lawrence, B.T.T.	15 Jan. 1901	A65 A67 B160 C130 U11 W125
Lawrence, S.H.	21 Nov. 1859	B42 C130 K52 K54 R59 T12 V70 W125
Lawson, E.	20 May 1898	C130 P5 W53 W125
Leach, E.P.	6 Dec. 1879	C130 E11 K16 K53 K54 N2 R60 W125

Recipient	Gazette Date	Item Number in Part 1 / Part 2
Leach, J.E.	22 Dec. 1914	A66 B12 B84 C130 G31 H140 L16 O13 S90 V74 W53 W125
Leak, J.	9 Sep. 1916	B76A B116 C125 C130 G30 H90 M22B M23A O15 V77 W55 W70 W80 W125
Leake, A. Martin-: see Martin-Leake, A.		
Leakey, J.	26 Feb. 2015	B43 V75
Leakey, N.G.	15 Nov. 1945	B1 B45 L59 R70 T36 W125
Learmonth, O.M.	8 Nov. 1917	B69 B114 C130 G36 G39 M14 M46 M95 O17 R53 S125 S145 W125
Learoyd, R.A.B.	20 Aug. 1940	A15 A55 A60 A65 A68 B1 B24 B89 C55 G38 G64 I15 K23 K65 L3 M17A N25 P39 R70 R72 S40 T35 W51 W125
Lee, B.A.W. Warburton-: see Warburton-Lee, B.A.W.		
Leet, W.K.	17 Jun. 1879	B13 C130 G60A G60B I15 K45 K49 R60 W125 Y2
Leitch, P.	2 Jun. 1858	B15A C130 G63 K50 K54 N2 R58 W125
Leith, J.	24 Dec. 1858	B42 C130 C150 D17 K52 K54 R59 W42 W125
Lendrim, W.J.	24 Feb. 1857	B15A C130 G63 K50 K54 N2 P5 R58 T32 W125
Lennox, W.O.	24 Feb. 1857	B15A C130 G63 K50 K54 N2 R58 W125 (also see Part 2 Section A)
Lenon, E.H.	13 Aug. 1861	C130 C150 D17 R60 V70 V155 W125
Le Patourel, H.W.	9 Mar. 1943	B15C B45 L3 R70 T36 W125
Le Quesne, F.S.	29 Oct. 1889	C130 L14 R60 R80 T14 W125
Lester, F.	14 Dec. 1918	A65 B103 C78 C130 G35 I6 L42 M129 W125
Lewis, H.W.	15 Dec. 1916	A65 C130 G37 H12 I25 W75 W125
Lewis, L.A.	31 Jan. 1919	C130 G34 W75 W80 W125
Liddell, I.O.	7 Jun. 1945	B1 B43 G15 L3 P10 R70 T36 V63 W75 W80 W125
Liddell, J.A.	23 Aug. 1915	A65 A68 B21 B25 B89 C114 C130 D10 J20 K23 K42 L16 M17B P41 R27 W53 W93 W125
Limbu, Rambahadur	21 Apr. 1966	A5 A61 A65 B43 B50 C34 C148 L40 S93 V64 W125
Lindsay, R.J. Loyd-: see Loyd-Lindsay, R.J.		
Linton, J.W.	25 May 1943	A65 B45 C111 I60 J9 K14 L3 P2 R70 S40 T37 W75 W80 W90 W125
Lisle-Phillipps, E.A.	21 Oct. 1859 15 Jan. 1907	A65 B42 C130 K16 R59 S40 W7 W125
Lister, J.	26 Nov. 1917	A65 B12 C130 O17 S76 W125
Lloyd, O.E.P.	2 Jan. 1894	C130 R80 T9A V155 W125
Lodge, I.	26 Jun. 1900	C130 L35 P5 S41 U11 V62 W125
Loosemore, A.	14 Sep. 1917	C130 J28 O17 S76 W52 W125
Lord, D.S.A.	13 Nov. 1945	A65 A67 A68 B1 B89 D23 H26 H150 K23 L3 M17A P19A P19B R70 S40 T14 T35 W75 W80 W125
Loudoun-Shand, S.W.	9 Sep. 1916	A65 C46 C130 G30 G62 L13 O15 W125
Lowerson, A.D.	14 Dec. 1918	B76A B116 C125 C130 G34 H90 M23A W55 W70 W125
Loyd-Lindsay, R.J.	24 Feb. 1857	A36 A65 B15A C130 C150 D16 D17 G15 G63 H15 H89 K50 K54 M70 O70 R58 V55 W11 W42 W125
Lucas, C.D.	24 Feb. 1857	A65 B15A B43 C130 D23 G63 I15 K50 K54 M30 Q10 R38 R58 S78B T9 T32 V54 V55 V60 W90 W125
Lucas, J.	17 Jul. 1861	B35 C80 C130 L42 M107 R60 W125
Luke, F.	25 Nov. 1914	A65 A67 C35 C130 G31 H127 H140 O13 S40 S41 S90 T34 W125

Recipient	Gazette Date	Item Number in Part 1 / Part 2
Lumley, C.	24 Feb. 1857	B15A C130 G63 K50 K54 R58 V56 W75 W79 W125
Lumsden, F.W.	8 Jun. 1917	A27 A28 C130 G33 L45 M70 O16 P59 S57 S58 T14 W90 W125
Lyall, G.T.	14 Dec. 1918	A27 A28 B45 B69 B114 B143 C130 G35 G39 M14 S125 S145 V69 W125
Lyell, The Lord	12 Aug. 1943	G15 H55 L3 R70 T36 W125
Lynn, J.	29 Jun. 1915	B1 B12 B28 C130 H140 M109 O14 S90 W125
Lyons, J.	24 Feb. 1857	B15A C46 C130 G63 K50 K54 R58 T32 V77 W125
Lysons, H.	5 Apr. 1882	B13 B40B C130 G60A G60B K45 M113 P12 R60 T14 W125 Y2
Lyster, H.H.	21 Oct. 1859	A65 B42 C130 K16 R59 W125
MacArthur, T.: see Arthur, T.		
McAulay, J.	11 Jan. 1918	A27 A28 A36 C130 G15 G36 M70 O18 W125
McBean, W.	24 Dec. 1858	B42 C130 P5 R59 W125
McBeath, R.	11 Jan. 1918	A26 A27 A28 C35 C130 G36 O18 W125
McCarthy, L.D.	14 Dec. 1918	B76A B116 C121 C125 C130 G34 G52 M23A S85 W55 W70 W125
McCorrie, C.	24 Feb. 1857	B15A C130 G63 K50 K54 R58 T32 V70 W125
McCrea, J.F.	28 Jun. 1881	A65 A67 B40B B43 C130 R60 R80 U10 W125
McCudden, J.T.B.	2 Apr. 1918	A100 B1 B21 B22 B25 B89 B115 C9 C94 C114 C130 D24B F32 F43 G64 H12 I15 J2 J20 J30 K23 K25 M1A M5 M17B N2 O20 P31 P41 R25 R27 R28 R29 R30 S56 T3 W26 W125
McCurry, C.: see McCorrie, C.		
McDermond, J.	24 Feb. 1857	B15A C130 C150 D17 G63 K50 K54 R58 W42 W125
MacDonald, H.	2 Jun. 1858	B15A C130 C150 D17 G63 K50 K54 R58 W42 W125
McDonell, W.F.	17 Feb. 1860	A65 B42 C130 C150 D17 H89 K16 K52 K54 M70 M101 P12 R59 S40 T14 V62 W42 W125
McDougall, J.L.	13 Aug. 1861	C130 C150 D17 K51 K53 K54 R60 W125
McDougall, S.R.	3 May 1918	A27 A28 B26 B76A B116 B116A C121 C125 C130 D7 G32 M23A W50 W55 W70 W125
MacDowell, T.W.	8 Jun. 1917	B69 B114 C130 G33 G39 M14 M95 O16 R53 S125 S145 W125
McFadzean, W.F.	9 Sep. 1916	C60 C130 D23 G30 O15 U2 W125
McGaw, S.	28 Mar. 1874	A65 C130 K51 K53 K54 R60 W125
McGee, L.	26 Nov. 1917	B26 B76A B116 C121 C125 C130 D7 M23A O17 S76 W55 W63 W70 W125
McGovern, J.	18 Jun. 1859	B42 C130 K16 K52 K54 M12 R59 W125
McGregor, D.S.	14 Dec. 1918	C130 G35 W125
MacGregor, J.	6 Jan. 1919	A26 A27 A28 B69 B114 C15 C130 F41 G35 G39 M14 R74 S125 S145 W125
McGregor, R.	24 Feb. 1857	B15A C130 G63 K50 K54 R58 R74 W7 W125
McGuffie, L.	14 Dec. 1918	C130 G35 M112 W125
McGuire, J.	24 Dec. 1858	B42 C130 D23 I61 K16 K52 K54 R59 V61 W125
McHale, P.	19 Jun. 1860	B42 C130 R59 W125
McInnes, H.	24 Dec. 1858	B42 C130 K16 K52 K54 SR59 41 W125

Recipient	Gazette Date	Item Number in Part 1 / Part 2
McIntosh, G.I.	6 Sep. 1917	A27 A28 A36 A65 C130 O17 S76 T34 W125
Macintyre, D.L.	26 Oct. 1918	C130 G34 V64 W125
MacIntyre, D.	27 Sep. 1872	B43 B50 C130 R60 W125 (also see Part 2 Section A)
McIver, H.	15 Nov. 1918	C130 G34 W125
Mackay, D.	24 Dec. 1858	B42 B134 C130 K16 K52 K54 R59 V59 W125
McKay, I.J.	11 Oct. 1982	A5 A65 C113B C113D S40 S93 V59 W52 W125
MacKay, J.F.	10 Aug. 1900	C130 U11 W125
McKean, G.B.	28 Jun. 1918	B69 B114 C130 D19 G32 G39 M14 M18 M19 S125 S145 W53 W125 (also see Part 2 Section B)
McKechnie, J.	24 Feb. 1857	B15A C130 G15 G63 K50 K54 R58 W125
McKenna, E.	16 Jan. 1864	B35 C130 F59 M107 P5 R60 W52 W125
McKenzie, A.E.	23 Jul. 1918	B95 C21 C95 C35 C95 C130 H85 H102 I6 K10 K16A L5 M12B P37 S16 S40 S77 W19 W90 W125
McKenzie, H.McD.	13 Feb. 1918	B69 B114 C77 C130 G39 M14 M129 O17 R53 S76 S125 S145 W125
Mackenzie, James	18 Feb. 1915	C130 G15 G31 O13 W125
Mackenzie, John	15 Jan. 1901	C130 P5 W125
Mackey, J.B.	8 Nov. 1945	B44 B76A B116 H90 M23A R70 T36 W55 W70 W125
Mackintosh, D.	8 Jun. 1917	C130 G33 O16 W125
Maclean, H.L.S.	9 Nov. 1897 15 Jan. 1907	A65 B43 C130 K16 P5 V66 W125
McLeod, A.A.	1 May 1918	B22 B25 B69 B89 B114 C35 C113A C114 C119 C130 D28 G39 G64 H10 H36 J20 K23 L2 M1D M14 M17B M46 M95 M100 P41 R27 S125 S145 T39 W125
McManus, P.	18 Jun. 1858	B42 C130 H89 K52 K54 R59 W125
McMaster, V.M.	18 Jun. 1858	B35 B42 C130 C150 D17 K52 K54 P5 R59 R80 W42 W125
McNair, E.A.	30 Mar. 1916	A27 A28 C130 G36 M70 O14 W125
McNally, W.	14 Dec. 1918	A65 C46 C130 G37 G62 W53 W125
McNamara, F.H.	8 Jun. 1917	B25 B76A B89 B116 B116A C114 C121 C122 C125 C130 E60 H90 J20 K23 L16 M17D M23A M102B P41 R27 S85 T38 W49 W55 W70 W125
McNamara, J.	15 Nov. 1918	C130 G34 W125
McNeill, J.C.	16 Aug. 1864	A65 A67 B35 C130 H89 K51 K53 K54 M107 P5 R57 R60 R74 W125
McNess, F.	26 Oct. 1916	B43 C130 G15 G30 O15 W52 W125
Macpherson, H.T.	18 Jun. 1858	B35 B42 C130 C150 D17 K52 K54 P5 R56 R59 W42 W125
McPherson, S.	12 Apr. 1859	B42 C130 R59 W125
McPhie, J.	31 Jan. 1919	C130 G35 N2 W125
McQuirt, B.	11 Nov. 1859	B42 C130 H12 M4 R59 W125
McReady-Diarmid, A.M.C.	15 Mar. 1918	C130 G36 O18 T14 W125
McReady-Drew, A.M.C.: see McReady-Diarmid, A.M.C.		
Mactier, R.	14 Dec. 1918	B76A B116 C121 C125 C130 G34 M23A W55 W70 W125
McWheeney, W.	24 Feb. 1857	B15A C130 D23 G63 K50 K54 R58 T32 W125
McWhiney, W.: see McWheeney, W.		
Madden, A.	24 Feb. 1857	B15A C130 G63 K50 K54 R58 T32 W75 W79 W125

357

Recipient	Gazette Date	Item Number in Part 1 / Part 2
Magennis, J.J.	13 Nov. 1945	A65 A67 B1 B44 B115 C111 D22 D23 F11 F11A F22 F46 H56 I6 I61 J9 J18 K14 K15 L1A L3 L53 L70 M104 O35 P2 R70 S40 S64 S80 T37 V55 W2 W20 W52 W90 W125
Magner, M.	28 Jul. 1868	B43 C130 H89 K51 K53 K54 R60 V77 W125
Mahoney, J.K.	13 Jul. 1944	A61 B69 B114 C113A D26 G51 M14 M95 N25 R70 S125 S145 T36 W125
Mahoney, P.	18 Jun. 1858	B42 C130 K16 K52 K54 M7A R59 W125
Maillard, W.J.	2 Dec. 1898	A65 A67 B43 C130 V70 W90 W125
Malcolm, H.G.	27 Apr. 1943	A66 A68 B45 B89 C55 G48 H10 J13 K23 L3 M17A R70 T35 V53 V54 W125
Malcolmson, J.G.	3 Aug. 1860	B35 C130 C150 D17 H89 K16 K51 K53 K54 M30 P5 R60 T9A V155 W42 W125
Maling, G.A.	18 Nov. 1915	B28 C130 G10 I15 O14 R80 W53 W125
Malleson, W.StA.	16 Aug. 1915	A65 B95 C35 C130 H12 H140 S40 S75 S77 S78 S90 W90 W125
Malone, J.	25 Sep. 1857	B5 B12 B15A B43 C130 G63 K50 K54 M30 P5 R58 S80 V54 W125
Mangles, R.L.	6 Jul. 1859	B35 B42 C130 C150 D17 H89 K16 K52 K54 M70 M101 R59 W42 W125
Manley, W.G.N.	22 Sep. 1864	B35 C130 K51 K53 K54 M107 P5 P12 R60 R80 S41 T14 V69 W125
Manners-Smith, J.	12 Jul. 1892	B43 B50 C130 K16 V65 V155 W125
Mannock, E.	18 Jul. 1919	A61 A65 A68 A100 B1 B22 B25 B89 B115 C108A C114 C130 D35 E7 F32 F43 F44 G29 G64 G80 H12 H55 I15 J2 J20 J33 K23 K25 M17B N2 O10 O45 O50 O55 P31 P41 R27 R30 R76 S40 S49 S56 W26 W35 W125
Mansel-Jones, C.	27 Jul. 1900	A12B C130 M70 W79 W125
Manser, L.T.	23 Oct. 1942	A65 A67 A68 B89 B136 C55 L3 K23 M17A R70 T35 W125
Mantle, J.F.	3 Sep. 1940	A15 B1 K65 L3 R9 R70 R71 T37 V67 W90 W125
Mariner, W.	23 Jun. 1915	A61 B12 B28 C130 H12 I61 O14 V52 W7 W54A W125
Marling, P.S.	21 May 1884	A65 A67 C130 M35 M70 P12 R60 T14 V71 W7 W125
Marshall, J.N.	13 Feb. 1919	B1 B86A C130 D1 G15 G35 G53 G54 L30 W125
Marshall, W.T.	21 May 1884	A25 C130 M4 M70 N50 R60 W125
Martin, C.G.	19 Apr. 1915	A27 A28 B28 C130 H140 L15 M70 N2 O13 S90 T14 W125
Martineau, H.R.	6 Jul. 1900	A65 A67 C130 T14 U10 U11 W125
Martin-Leake, A.	13 May 1902	A65 B120 C76 C130 D27A G31 H12 J17 L15 O13 R80 U10 U11
Bar	18 Feb. 1915	V69 W125 (also see Part 2 Section A)
Masters, R.G.	8 May 1918	C78 C79 C130 G32 L42 W125
Masterson, J.E.I.	4 Jun. 1901	A12B C130 D23 U11 W125
Maude, F.C.	18 Jun. 1858	B15A C130 G63 K52 K54 M49 M70 S41 V60 W125 (also see Part 2 Section A)
Maude, F.F.	24 Feb. 1857	B42 C130 K50 K54 R58 R59 T32 W125
Maufe, T.H.B.	2 Aug. 1917	C35 C130 G10 G33 O16 W52 W125
Maxwell, F.A.	8 Mar. 1901	A65 A67 C130 K16 M52 M53 P5 S40 U11 W125
Maxwell, J.	6 Jan. 1919	B76A B116 C121 C125 C130 G35 M17D M23A M25 M55 R6 S85 V65 W55 W63 W70 W125
May, H.	19 Apr. 1915	A27 A28 A36 C130 G31 L15 O13 W125
Maygar, L.C.	11 Feb. 1902	B76A B116 C121 C130 H90 M23A U11 W55 W70 W125
Mayo, A.	25 Feb. 1862	B42 C130 K16 K52 K54 R59 W90 W125

Recipient	Gazette Date	Item Number in Part 1 / Part 2
Mayson, T.F.	14 Sep. 1917	C130 K33 O17 S76 W53 W125
Meekosha, S.	22 Jan. 1916	B28 C130 O14 W52 W75 W80 W125
Meikle, J.	16 Sep. 1918	C35 C130 G32 M17 R74 S92 W125
Meiklejohn, M.F.M.	20 Jul. 1900	A12B A36 B43 C130 M70 U11 V63 W125
Mellish, E.N.	20 Apr. 1916	C59 C130 D30 G36 H12 H140 K13 M105 O14 S62 S90 V62 W63 W125
Melliss, C.J.	15 Jan. 1901	B43 C130 K16 P5 W125 (also see Part 2 Section A)
Melvill, T.	2 May 1879 15 Jan. 1907	A26 A65 B13 B15 C90 C130 E12 G24 G60A G60B H92 K45 K48 K49B K53 K54 M30 M70 M113 P5 R60 R69 R79 S134 T12 T14 W75 W79 W125 Y2 Y5
Melvin, C.	26 Nov. 1917	A27 A28 C130 G37 W125
Merrifield, W.	6 Jan. 1919	B69 B114 C130 G35 G39 M14 S125 S145 W125
Merritt, C.C.I.	2 Oct. 1942	B69 B114 C113A D26 F41 G45 G51 H10 M14 M95 R70 S18 S125 S145 T36 W125
Metcalf, W.H.	15 Nov. 1918	B69 B79 B114 C15 C130 G34 G39 M14 P16 S125 S145 W125
Meynell, G.	24 Dec. 1935	B43 D32 K16 M4 V65 W125
Middleton, R.H.	15 Jan. 1943	B1 B23 B55 B76A B89 B92 B116 C55 F32 H90 K2 K23 M1A M17A M23A N25 R70 T35 W55 W70 W125
Miers, A.C.C.	7 Jul. 1942	A66 A72 B45 C45 C111 H56 I60 J9 K14 K24 L3 M118A M14B R70 R74 T37 W90 W125
Milbanke, J.P.	6 Jul. 1900	C130 M3 U11 W125
Miles, F.G.	6 Jan. 1919	A65 C130 G35 H12 P12 S40 T14 W125
Millar, D.	18 Jun. 1859	B42 C130 H98 R59 W125
Miller, D.: see Millar, D.		
Miller, F.	6 May 1859	A66 B15A C130 G63 K50 K54 R58 S38 S41 W125
Miller, J. (Conductor)	25 Feb. 1862	B42 C130 K16 K52 K54 R59 W125
Miller, J. (Pte.)	9 Sep. 1916	C130 G30 H12 K33 O15 W125
Mills, W.	13 Feb. 1918	B12 B84 C130 G36 O18 R73 W125
Milne, W.J.	8 Jun. 1917	B69 B114 B134 C15 C130 G33 G39 M14 O16 R53 S18 S125 S145 W125
Miner, H.G.B.	26 Oct. 1918	B69 B114 C130 G34 G39 M14 S125 S145 W125
Mir Dast	29 Jun. 1915	B28 C18 C130 K4 K16 O14 S45 W125
Mitchell, C.N.	31 Jan. 1919	B69 B114 C130 G35 G39 M13 M46 N2 S125 S145 W125
Mitchell, G.A.	10 Aug. 1944	C43 L3 R70 T36 V77 W125
Mitchell, S.	23 Jul. 1864	A26 B35 C130 M104A M107 P5 R60 W90 W125
Moffat, M.	26 Dec. 1918	A65 C130 G35 W125
Molyneux, J.	26 Nov. 1917	C80 C130 K13 L42 O17 S76 W125
Monaghan, T.	11 Nov. 1862	B42 C130 K52 K54 R59 W75 W79 W125
Monger, G.	12 Apr. 1859	B42 C130 K52 K54 R59 W75 W79 W125
Moon, R.V.	14 Jun. 1917	B76A B116 C125 C130 G33 M23A O16 W55 W70 W125
Moor, G.R.D.	24 Jul. 1915	C35 C130 P12 S75 T14 W125
Moore, A.T.	3 Aug. 1860	B35 C130 C150 D17 H89 K16 K51 K53 K54 M30 P5 R60 W125
Moore, H.G.	27 Jun. 1879	A19 A66 B43 C130 R60 U10 V65 W125
Moore, M.S.S.	8 Nov. 1917	C130 O17 S76 W125
Moorhouse, W.B. Rhodes-: see Rhodes-Moorhouse, W.B.		
Morley, S.	7 Aug. 1860	B42 C130 K52 K54 M4 N50 R17 R59 V62 W125
Morrell, T.: see Young, T.		

Recipient	Gazette Date	Item Number in Part 1 / Part 2
Morrow, R.	22 May 1915	B28 C60 C130 D23 O13 U2 W125
Mott, E.J.	10 Mar. 1917	C130 G33 O16 W125
Mottershead, T.	12 Feb. 1917	A65 A67 A68 B25 B89 C80 C114 C130 J20 K23 L42 M17B P41 R27 T38 W93 W125
Mouat, J.	2 Jun. 1858	B15A C130 C150 D17 G63 I15 K50 K54 M30 P5 R58 R80 T9A V55 V69 V155 W42 W125
Mountain, A.	7 Jun. 1918	C130 G32 V66 W52 W125
Moyney, J.	17 Oct. 1917	C130 D23 G15 O17 S76 W125
Moynihan, A.	24 Feb. 1857	B15A C79 C130 G63 K43 K50 K54 L42 R58 T1A T32 V72 W52 W125
Mugford, H.S.	26 Nov. 1917	C130 G33 O16 W125
Muir, K.	5 Jan. 1951	A5 A61 C20 C34 C148 L35 V66 W125
Mullane, P.	16 May 1881	B42 C43 C130 E11 K53 K54 P5 R60 S41 W125
Mullin, G.H.	11 Jan. 1918	B69 B114 C130 G39 M14 O17 R53 S18 S76 S125 S145 W125
Mullins, C.H.	12 Feb. 1901	A12B C130 U10 U11 W125
Munro, J.	8 Nov. 1860	B42 C130 I61 K52 K54 R59 W125
Murphy, M.	27 May 1859	B42 C130 I61 K52 K54 R17 R59 V62 W53 W125
Murphy, T.	17 Dec. 1867	C130 K51 K53 K54 R60 W75 W79 W125
Murray, The Rt. Hon. A.E.: see Fincastle, Viscount		
Murray, H.W.	10 Mar. 1917	B26 B76A B116 C121 C125 C130 D7 F42 G33 G52 H60 H90 M17D M23A M25 O16 R6 S85 W55 W70 W125
Murray, James	14 Mar. 1882	B43 C130 R60 U11 W125
Murray, John	4 Nov. 1864	C130 M107 R60 S37 W125
Myles, E.K.	26 Sep. 1916	B103 C43 C130 G37 P4A W75 W80 W125
Mylott, P.	24 Dec. 1858	B42 C78 C130 K52 K54 L42 R59 W125
Mynarski, A.C.	11 Oct. 1946	A65 B69 B89 B114 C55 C113A C119 D26 G45 G51 H10 J13 H1 K23 M14 M17A M95 P4 P33 S125 S145 T35 W125
Namdeo Jadhao	19 Jun. 1945	A16 I10 K16 R70 S45 T36 W125
Nand Singh	6 Jun. 1944	A16 B1 B44 I10 K16 R70 N25 Q10 S45 T36 V51 W125
Napier, W.	24 Dec. 1858	B42 C130 R59 W52 W125
Nash, W.	24 Dec. 1858	B42 C130 K52 K54 R59 W7 W125
Nasmith, M.E. Dunbar-: see Dunbar-Nasmith, M.E.		
Neame, P.	18 Feb. 1915	A27 A28 B1 C25 C130 G31 H12 H28 I15 L23 N2 N9 N10 O13 P12 S67 T14 V70 V71 W125 (also see Part 2 Section A)
Needham, S.	30 Oct. 1918	C130 G37 W125
Neeley, T.	14 Dec. 1918	C78 C130 G35 K33 L42 W125
Nelson, D.	16 Nov. 1914	A27 A28 C60 C130 D23 G31 H140 L15 M70 O13 S40 S41 S90 U2 V74 W125
Nesbitt, R.C.	7 May 1897	B43 B80 C130 P5 U10 V55 W125
Netrabahadur Thapa	12 Oct. 1944	A16 A61 B44 B50 I10 K16 L70 M24 R70 S45 T36 W125
Nettleton, J.D.	28 Apr. 1942	A19 B23 B89 C55 C109 C160 I61 J13 K23 L3 M17A R70 T35 U10 V67 W125
Newell, R.	24 Dec. 1858	A65 B42 C130 K52 K54 R59 W53 W125
Newland, J.E.	8 Jun. 1917	B26 B76A B116 C121 C125 C130 D7 G33 M23A O16 W55 W70 W125

Recipient	Gazette Date	Item Number in Part 1 / Part 2
Newman, A.C.	19 Jun. 1945	A65 B43 C113C D25 I15 L1A L3 L53 L71 L110 M40 M70 N2 R70 R73 R91 S40 T36 V63 W125
Newton, W.E.	19 Oct. 1943	B43 B44 B76A B116 B89 H90 J13 K23 L53 M17A M23A R70 S85 T35 V72 W23 W55 W70 W125
Ngarimu, M-N-a-K.	4 Jun. 1943	A58 B45 B140 C40 E5 H30 L70 N12 N12A N18 R70 S5 S138 T24 T36 W125
Nicholas, H.J.	11 Jan. 1918	A58 B138 B140 C40 C130 G36 G59A H30 N12A O18 S5 W125
Nicholls, H.	30 Jul. 1940	A15 G15 K65 L3 M4 N50 R70 R71 S17 T36 V63 W51 W52 W125
Nickerson, W.H.S.	12 Feb. 1901	B6 B12 B79 B114 C113A C130 H91 R80 U11 W125
Nicolson, E.J.B.	15 Nov. 1940	A15 A61 B1 B24 B89 B93 C108A C148 G64 I17 J13 K9 K23 K65 L3 L53 M17A M38 N25 P6A P20 R8 R70 R72 T9 T35 T38 V51 W125
Noble, C.R.	28 Apr. 1915	B28 C130 H140 O13 S90 W7 W125
Norman, W.	24 Feb. 1857	B12 B15A C80 C130 G63 K13 K50 K54 L42 R58 W125
Norton, G.R.	26 Oct. 1944	H26 L3 N25 R70 T36 U10 W125
Norwood, J.	20 Jul. 1900	C130 I15 M70 M130 U11 W125
Nunney, C.J.P.	14 Dec. 1918	B69 B114 C130 G34 G39 M14 S125 S145 W125
Nurse, G.E.	2 Feb. 1900	B6 C78 C79 C130 L42 M30 M129 P5 S41 U11 V5 W125
Ockenden, J.	8 Nov. 1917	C130 O17 S76 W125
O'Connor, L.	24 Feb. 1857	B15A B43 C130 C150 D17 D23 G63 H89 K50 K54 P5 R58 T32 V62 W42 W75 W80 W125
Odgers, W.	3 Aug. 1860	C130 M107 R60 W90 W125
O'Hea, T.	1 Jun. 1867	B43 B114 C130 H10 K51 K53 K54 P29 R18 R60 V65 V66 V67 W7 W125
O'Kelly, C.P.J.	11 Jan. 1918	B69 B114 C130 G39 M14 M95 O17 R53 S76 S125 S145 W125
O'Leary, M.J.	18 Feb. 1915	B28 B43 B69 B114 C130 C140 D23 G15 G39 H12 H140 I61 L15 M13 O13 S18 S90 S125 S145 V75 W125
Olpherts, W.	18 Jun. 1858	B42 C99 C130 D23 K16 K52 K54 R59 S441 W61 W125
O'Meara, M.	9 Sep. 1916	B76A B116 C125 C130 D23 G30 G52 H90 M23A O15 W55 W70 W125
O'Neill, J.	26 Dec. 1918	B134 C79 C130 G35 L42 W125
O'Niell, J.: see O'Neill, J.		
Onions, G.	14 Dec. 1918	B12 C130 D1 G34 G39 H35 L30 W80 W125
Ormsby, J.W.	8 Jun. 1917	C130 G33 H12 O16 W52 W125
O'Rourke, M.J.	8 Nov. 1917	B69 B114 C130 D24A G36 G39 M14 M95 O17 R53 S125 S145 W125
Osborn, J.R.	2 Apr. 1946	B69 B114 D26 F41 G45 G51 M14 S18 S125 S145 T36 W125
Osborne, J.	14 Mar. 1882	A74 C130 R60 U11 W125
O'Sullivan, G.R.	1 Sep. 1915	A66 C130 L16 S75 W125
O'Toole, E.	9 Oct. 1879	B13 C130 G60A G60B K45 R60 U10 W125 Y2
Owens, J.	24 Feb. 1857	B15A C130 G63 K50 K54 R58 T32 W125
Oxenham, W.	21 Nov. 1859	B42 C130 K52 K54 R59 T12 V70 W125

Recipient	Gazette Date	Item Number in Part 1 / Part 2
Palmer, A.	24 Feb. 1857	B12 B15A C62 C130 C150 D17 G15 G63 K50 K54 R58 V63 W42 W125
Palmer, F.W.	3 Apr. 1917	C130 G33 K13 O16 T34 W125
Palmer, R.A.M.	23 Mar. 1945	B89 C55 F9 I15 J13 K23 L3 M17A R70 T35 W125
Park, James	24 Dec. 1858	B42 C130 K16 K52 K54 R59 S41 W125
Park, John	24 Feb. 1857	B15A C130 G63 K50 K54 R58 T32 W125
Parkash Singh	13 May 1943	A16 B44 I10 K4 K16 P20 R70 S40 S45 T9 T36 W125
Parkash Singh (Jemadar): see Prakash Singh		
Parker, C.E.H.	26 Jun. 1900	C130 D1 L30 L35 P5 S41 U11 V55 W125
Parker, W.R.	22 Jun. 1917	B95 C130 L45 M4 N50 P59 S75 W90 W125
Parkes, S.	24 Feb. 1857	A66 B15A B43 C130 C150 D17 E10A G63 K50 L35 M30 P5 R58 V54 W42 W125
Parslow, F.D.	24 May 1919	C130 S77 V75 W90 W125
Parsons, F.N.	20 Nov. 1900	C130 I15 U11 W125
Parsons, H.F.	17 Oct. 1917	C130 G36 O17 T14 W125
Partridge, F.J.	22 Jan. 1946	A61 B44 B49 B76A B116 H90 H98 M23A S85 T36 W55 W63 W70 W125
Paton, G.H.T.	13 Feb. 1918	C130 G15 O18 T14 W125
Paton, J.	24 Dec. 1858	B42 B112 C130 G36 K52 K54 R59 V56 W63 W125
Pattison, J.G.	2 Aug. 1917	B69 B114 C130 G33 G39 M14 M95 O16 R53 S125 S145 W125
Payne, K.	19 Sep. 1969	A5 A65 B76A B116 B116A C34 C100 C148 K75 M17D M22A M23A R21 S93 U3 W56 W70 W125
Peachment, G.S.	18 Nov. 1915	A65 A67 B12 B28 C35 C130 L16 O14 S40 V76 W7 W125
Pearkes, G.R.	11 Jan. 1918	B69 C15 C130 H1 G39 F41 J1 M14 M18 M46 O17 R53 R78 S18 S76 S125 S145 W125
Pearse, S.G.	23 Oct. 1919	B76A B116 C121 C130 I40 K13 M23A V73 W55 W63 W70 W75 W80 W125
Pearson, James	28 Apr. 1860	B42 C130 K52 K54 R59 W125
Pearson, John	26 Jan. 1859	A65 B42 C130 K52 K54 R59 W52 W125
Peck, C.W.	15 Nov. 1918	A27 A28 B69 B79 B114 C15 C130 G34 G39 M14 P11 S125 S145 W125
Peel, W.	24 Feb. 1857	A65 B15A B35 B40B C130 G63 K50 K54 R58 R75 V7 V14 V15 V68 W22 W89 W90 W125 (also see Part 2 Section A)
Peeler, W.	26 Nov. 1917	B76A B116 C121 C125 C130 M23A O17 S76 W55 W70 W125
Pennell, H.S.	20 May 1898	B43 C130 M4 P5 V59 W125
Percy, H.H.M.	5 May 1857	B15A C130 G15 G63 K50 K54 P21 R58 W53 W125 (also see Part 2 Section A)
Perie, J.	24 Feb. 1857	B15A C130 G63 K50 K54 N2 P5 R58 W125
Peters, F.T.	18 May 1943	A65 A67 B45 B69 B79 B114 D26 G51 L3 M1B M14 R70 S125 S145 T37 W90 W125
Phillipps, E.A. Lisle-: see Lisle-Phillipps, E.A.		
Phillips, R.E.	8 Jun. 1917	C130 D1 G37 H35 W80 W125
Phipps-Hornby, E.J.	26 Jun. 1900	B40B C130 L35 P5 S41 U11 W125
Pickard, A.F.	22 Sep. 1864	A65 B35 C130 K51 K53 K54 M2 M70 M107 P5 P32 R60 S41 W125
Pitcher, E.H.	2 Nov. 1917	A27 A28 A65 A67 B121 C10 C47 C130 L5A S21 S40 S77 T12 W90 W125
Pitcher, H.W.	16 Jul. 1864	A65 B43 C130 K16 R60 V76 W125

Recipient	Gazette Date	Item Number in Part 1 / Part 2
Pitts, J.	26 Jul. 1901	A12B B6 B84 C130 K40 U11 W125
Place, B.C.G.	22 Feb. 1944	B1 B75 B115 B136 C110 C111 C148 E8 F11 F47 G2 G71 H55 H104 J5 J9 K14 K15 K19 L1A L3 L70 M9 M16 M20 M104 N25 O35 P2 P15 R70 S40 S64 T20 T37 V58 W2 W5 W20 W21 W90 W125 Z2
Pollard, A.O.	8 Jun. 1917	C130 G33 N3 O9 O16 P39 P40 P41 V59 W125 (also see Part 2 Sections A and B)
Pollock, J.D.	18 Dec. 1915	A27 A28 B28 C130 O14 W125
Pooll, A.H.H. Batten-: see Batten-Pooll, A.H.H.		
Pope, C.	8 Jun. 1917	B76A B116 C125 C130 G33 G52 M23A O16 W55 W70 W125
Porteous, P.A.	2 Oct. 1942	B1 E8 L1A R70 S41 T36 W125
Potts, F.W.O.	1 Oct. 1915	A27 A28 C130 H56 H140 L3 L15 M70 O9 S40 S75 V75 W125
Poulter, A.	28 Jun. 1918	C130 G32 T16 W52 W125
Prakash Singh	1 May 1945	A16 A61 B44 I10 K16 R70 S45 T36 W125
Premindra Singh Bhagat: see Bhagat, P.S.		
Prendergast, H.N.D.	21 Oct. 1859	B42 C130 C150 D17 K16 N2 R59 V30 V75 V76 W42 W125
Prettyjohn, J.	24 Feb. 1857	B12 B15A C130 E14 G63 K50 L45 P59 R58 T12 V70 W90 W125
Price-Davies, L.A.E.	29 Nov. 1901	C130 D32 R55 U11 W7 W75 W79 W125
Pride, T.	21 Apr. 1865	A65 C130 K51 K53 K54 R60 W90 W125
Probyn, D.MacN.	18 Jun. 1858	B42 B139 C130 C150 D17 H127 K16 K52 K54 R59 T9A V155 W42 W61 W62 W125
Procter, A.H.	5 Aug. 1916	B1 B12 B84 C59 C78 C79 C130 G36 J28 L42 M129 O14 T1A W52 W125
Proctor, A.F.W. Beauchamp-: see Beauchamp-Proctor, A.F.W.		
Prosser, J.	24 Feb. 1857	B15A C78 C130 G63 K50 K54 L42 M129 R58 T32 W125
Prowse, G.	30 Oct. 1918	A65 B95 C130 G34 H108 S80 V68 W75 W80 W90 W125
Pryce, T.T.	22 May 1918	C130 G15 G32 T14 W75 W80 W125
Purcell, J.	15 Jan. 1858	B42 C130 R59 W125
Pye, C.C.	24 Dec. 1858	B42 C130 D31 D32 K52 K54 R59 W125
Queripel, L.E.	1 Feb. 1945	I15 L3 R70 S79B T36 W125
Quigg, R.	9 Sep. 1916	B143 C60 C130 D23 G30 K18 O15 Q3 U2 W125
Raby, H.J.	24 Feb. 1857	A66 B15A C130 G63 K50 K54 R58 V73 W75 W79 W90 W125
Ramage, H.	4 Jun. 1858	B15A C130 G63 K50 K54 P5 R58 S80 W125
Rambahadur Limbu: see Limbu, Rambahadur		
Ram Sarup Singh	8 Feb. 1945	A16 A66 B44 I10 K16 R70 S45 T36 W125
Ramsden, H.E.	6 Jul. 1900	A65 A67 B6 C130 U10 U11 W125
Randle, J.N.	12 Dec. 1944	A65 B1 B44 B100 H26 I6 K15A L3 R70 S40 T36 W125
Ranken, H.S.	16 Nov. 1914	A27 A28 A36 C130 G31 M70 O13 R80 V74 W125
Ratcliffe, W.	2 Aug. 1917	C77 C78 C79 C130 G33 L42 M129 O16 W125
Rattey, R.R.	26 Aug. 1945	B16A B44 B76A B116 H90 M23A R70 T36 V67 W55 W63 W70 W125
Ravenhill, R.A.	4 Jun. 1901	A12B C130 D1 I61 L30 P5 T33 U11 W125

Recipient	Gazette Date	Item Number in Part 1 / Part 2
Rayfield, W.L.	14 Dec. 1918	B69 B114 B143 C130 G34 G39 M14 S125 S145 W125
Raymond, C.	28 Jun. 1945	A61 B44 D23 K16 L3 N2 R70 T36 W125
Raynes, J.C.	18 Nov. 1915	A27 A28 A36 B28 C130 J28 L16 M70 O14 S41 W52 W125
Raynor, W.	18 Jun. 1858	A65 B40B B42 C130 H89 K16 K52 K54 M4 N50 P5 R59 V59 W125
Read, A.M.	18 Nov. 1915	B28 C130 O14 P12 T14 W125
Reade, H.T.	5 Feb. 1861	B42 B69 B114 C130 K52 K54 M14 R59 R80 S125 S145 W125
Readitt, J.	5 Jul. 1917	A65 B12 C80 C130 G37 L42 W125
Reed, H.L.	2 Feb. 1900	A12B A65 C130 M30 S41 U11 V5 W125
Rees, I.	14 Sep. 1917	C130 O17 S41 S76 W75 W80 W125
Rees, L.W.B.	5 Aug. 1916	A66 B21 B25 B43 B89 C130 C148 G64 H12 J20 K23 L16 M17B P41 R27 T3 T34 V77 W75 W76 W76A W80 W93 W125
Reeves, T.	24 Feb. 1857	A65 B15A C130 G63 K50 K54 R58 W90 W125
Reid, O.A.	8 Jun. 1917	B84 C80 C130 G37 L42 U10 W125
Reid, W.	14 Dec. 1943	A26 A60 A61 B1 B23 B88 B89 B134 C55 J13 K23 L3 L38 M17A M70 P52 R70 R74 R77 T35 W125
Rendle, T.E.	11 Jan. 1915	A27 A28 C130 G31 H12 H140 L15 O13 S90 T12 U10 W125
Rennie, W.	24 Dec. 1858	B42 C130 R59 W125
Renny, G.A.	12 Apr. 1859	A66 B42 C130 K16 K52 K54 R59 S41 W125
Reynolds, D.	16 Nov. 1914	A27 A28 A65 C130 G31 H140 M70 O13 P12 S41 S90 T14 W125
Reynolds, H.	8 Nov. 1917	B1 C130 H84 O17 S76 W125
Reynolds, J.H.	17 Jun. 1879	B7 B9 B11 B13 B15B B15D B15E C130 E12 G24 G41 G60 G60A G60B H5 H92 J31 K45 K46 K47 K49B K53 K54 L87 M13A M30 R6 R60 R69 R79 R80 S79 S124 S134 T15A W27 W51A W54 W79 W125 Y2 Y5
Reynolds, W.	24 Feb. 1857	B15A C130 G15 G63 K50 K54 R58 W125
Rhodes, J.H.	26 Nov. 1917	B1 C130 G15 O17 S76 W125
Rhodes-Moorhouse, W.B.	22 May 1915	A65 A67 A68 B21 B25 B89 B140 C114 C130 H30 H140 J11 J20 K23 L16 M17B P33 P41 R27 R31 S40 S80 V65 W49 W93 W125
Richards, A.J.	24 Aug. 1915	A65 C130 H12 M109 S75 V45 W125
Richardson, A.H.L.	14 Sep. 1900	B43 B6 B43 B69 B114 C78 C130 H10 L42 M14 M95 M129 S18 S125 S145 U11 V68 W125
Richardson, G.	11 Nov. 1859	B42 B143 C130 K18 R59 W125
Richardson, J.C.	22 Oct. 1918	B69 B103 B114 B134 C15 C130 G30 G39 H12 L2 M14 M95 O15 S125 S145 W125
Richhpal Ram	4 Jul. 1941	A16 B45 I10 K4 K16 R70 S45 T2 T36 W125
Rickard, W.T.	24 Feb. 1857	A65 A67 B15A C130 G63 K50 K54 P5 R58 S40 W90 W125
Ricketts, T.	6 Jan. 1919	A27 A28 B69 B79 B114 C30 C35 C113A C130 G35 G39 L2 M14 S125 S145 V53 W125
Ridgeway, R.K.	11 May 1880	B43 B50 C130 E11 K16 K53 K54 R60 W52 W125
Riggs, F.C.	6 Jan. 1919	C130 G35 W125
Ripley, J.	29 Jun. 1915	B28 C130 O14 W125
Ritchie, H.P.	10 Apr. 1915	B95 C130 G31 H70 H140 S77 S90 W90 W125
Ritchie, W.P.	9 Sep. 1916	A27 A28 B103 C130 C148 G30 H12 O15 W125
Rivers, J.	28 Apr. 1915	B28 C130 H140 M4 O13 S90 S92 W125
Robarts, J.	24 Feb. 1857	B15A C130 G63 K50 K54 R58 V75 W90 W125
Roberts, F.C.	8 May 1918	C130 G32 O18 S41 W125

Recipient	Gazette Date	Item Number in Part 1 / Part 2
Roberts, F.H.S.	2 Feb. 1900	A12B A65 C86 C130 G38 M30 M36 M70 U11 V64 W7 W125
Roberts, F.S.	24 Dec. 1858	A12B A25 A34 A65 A72 A73 B40B B42 B77 B135 B132 B132 C5 C47 C85 C86 C113 C118 C120 C130 C148 C150 D14 D17 D38 E6 E40 F7 F23 F29 F30 G25 G43 G66 G70 H18 H20 H68 J8 J15 K16 K20 K52 K54 L58 L60 L62 M30 M36 M49 M70 M98 M102 M102A N7 N13 N16 P4B R32 R50 R51 R56 R59 R83 R87 S32 S39 S43 S88 S115 S136 S155 T4 T22B T22C T14 T31 V5 V30 V40 V45 V73 V74 V75 W24 W28 W30 W42 W45 W61 W62 W125 (also see Part 2 Section A)
Roberts, J.R.	24 Dec. 1858	B42 C130 C150 D17 K52 K54 L35 W42 W125
Roberts, P.S.W.	9 Jun. 1942	A65 A67 B1 B45 C111 H41 H55 J9 K14 L3 L35 R70 S40 T12 T37 W90 W125
Roberts-Smith, B	23 Jan. 2011	B76A B116A C34 G52 M23A V67 W125
Robertson, C.G.	9 Apr. 1918	A27 A28 C130 G32 K13 O18 W125
Robertson, C.	18 Dec. 1917	C130 H12 O17 S76 V73 W125
Robertson, J. Forbes-: see Forbes-Robinson, J.		
Robertson, J.P.	11 Jan. 1918	B69 B79 B114 C130 G39 M14 M95 O17 R53 S76 S125 S145 W125
Robertson, W.	20 Jul. 1900	A12B A36 C130 U11 W125
Robinson, E.	24 Dec. 1858	B42 C130 K52 K54 R59 V61 W90 W125
Robinson, E.G.	16 Aug. 1915	A27 A28 C80A C130 S75 S77 V58 W90 W125
Robinson, W.L.	5 Sep. 1916	A65 A67 A68 B1 B22 B25 B60 B89 C58 C108 C108A C114 C130 G64 H12 H56 J20 K23 L16 M17B P41 P57 P58 R27 R40 S40 S80 T39 V45 V57 W9 W49 W53 W93 W125
Robson, H.H.	18 Feb. 1915	C130 G31 O13 W53 W125
Rochfort, G.A. Boyd-: see Boyd-Rochfort, G.A.		
Roddy, P.	12 Apr. 1859	B42 C130 K16 R59 S41 V57 W125
Rodgers, G.	11 Nov. 1859	B42 C130 R59 W125
Rogers, J.	18 Apr. 1902	B76A B116 C121 C130 H90 M23A U10 U11 W55 W70 W125
Rogers, M.A.W.	10 Aug. 1944	B4 R70 T14 T36 V57 W125
Rogers, R.M.	13 Aug. 1861	A66 C130 C150 D17 K51 K53 K54 R60 W42 W125
Rolland, G.M.	7 Aug. 1903	A65 A67 C130 K16 P5 W125
Room, F.G.	17 Oct. 1917	B32 C130 O17 S76 T14 W125
Roope, G.B.	10 Jul. 1945	B43 G71 H10 H56 L3 L53 M9 M10 M15 M20 R70 S64 T37 V58 V67 V160 W90 W125
Rosamund, M.	23 Aug. 1858	B42 C130 K16 K52 K54 R59 V72 W125
Ross, J.	24 Feb. 1857	B15A C130 G63 N2 P5 R58 W125
Roupell, G.R.P.	23 Jun. 1915	B28 C130 H140 O13 S90 W125
Rowlands, H.	24 Feb. 1857	A26 B15A C130 G60B G63 H96 K50 K54 M70 R58 V68 W12 W75 W77 W78 W79 W125
Rushe, D.	24 Dec. 1858	B42 C130 R59 W125
Russell, C.	24 Feb. 1857	B15A C130 C150 D17 G15 G63 K50 K54 R58 V5 V7 W42 W125
Russell, J.F.	11 Jan. 1918	C130 G37 R80 W75 W125
Rutherford, C.S.	15 Nov. 1918	B69 B114 C83 C113A C130 G34 G39 H12 M14 M46 S125 S145 W125
Ruthven, A.G.A. Hore-: see Hore-Ruthven, A.G.A.		
Ruthven, W.	11 Jul. 1918	B76A B116 C125 C130 G32 M23A W55 W70 W125

Recipient	Gazette Date	Item Number in Part 1 / Part 2
Ryan, J. (Pte., Mad. Fus.)	18 Jun. 1858	C130 H89 K16 K52 K54 P5 R59 W125
Ryan, E.J.F. (Pte., A.I.F.)	26 Dec. 1918	B76A B116 C125 C130 G35 M23A M25 W55 W70 W125
Ryan, J. (L/Cpl.)	16 Jan. 1864	B42 C130 M107 R60 W125
Ryan, M.	24 Dec. 1858	B42 C130 K16 K52 K54 P5 W125
Ryder, R.E.	26 Nov. 1916	B79 C130 G30 H12 M4 O15 V66 W125
Ryder, R.E.D.	21 May 1942	B115 C110 C113C C148 D25 H26 H99 L1A L3 L7 L53 L71 L110 M16 M40 N25 R70 R91 S41 S41A S141 T14 T37 V63 W88 W90 W125
Sadlier, C.W.K.	11 Jul. 1918	B76A B116 C125 C130 G32 G52 H90 M23A W55 W70 W125
Sage, T.H.	18 Dec. 1917	C130 O17 S76 W125
Salkeld, P.	18 Jun. 1858	B40B B42 C130 C150 D17 H89 K16 N2 P25 R59 T6 W42 W125
Salmon, N.	24 Dec. 1858	A66 B35 B42 C130 H69 K52 K54 R59 R75 V14 V15 V68 W22 W90 W125
Samson, G.McK.	16 Aug. 1915	A26 A27 A28 A36 A65 A66 B95 C130 H12 H140 L16 M70 S40 S75 S77 S78 W90 W125
Sanders, G.	9 Sep. 1916	C130 G30 O15 W125
Sanders, W.E.	22 Jun. 1917	A80 B43 B121 B140 C12 C40 C47 C110 C130 H12 H30 H55 H101 L5A M43 S5 S77 W90 W125
Sandes, A.J.T. Fleming- see Fleming-Sandes, A.J.T.		
Sandford, R.D.	23 Jul. 1918	B43 B95 B126 C21 C22 C95 C106 C111 C130 G58 H85 H102 H126 J4 J9 K16A L5 M12B M20 P37 S16 S77 T12 V72 W19 W52 W90 W125
Sartorius, E.H.	16 May 1881	A25 C130 E11 K53 K54 M70 R60 S95 W125
Sartorius, R.W.	26 Oct. 1874	B43 C130 K16 K51 K53 K54 M70 R60 W125
Saunders, A.F.	30 Mar. 1916	B28 C130 O14 W125
Savage, D.C.: see Travis, R.C.		
Savage, W.A.	21 May 1942	B115 C113C D1 D25 H26 H35 L1A L3 L30 L71 L110 M40 R91 S80 S141 T37 W90 W125
Sayer, J.W.	9 Jun. 1919	B43 C130 G32 O18 V59 W125
Scarf, A.S.K.	21 Jun. 1946	B44 B89 C55 H10 J13 K23 L3 L53 M17A T35 W125
Schiess, F.C.	29 Nov. 1879	B7 B9 B11 B13 B15B B15D B15E C130 E12 G24 G41 G60 G60A G60B H5 H92 J31 K45 K46 K47 K49B K53 K54 L87 M30 R6 R60 R69 R79 S79 S134 T15A U10 W27 W51A W54 W79 W125 Y2 Y5
Schofield, H.N.	30 Aug. 1901	A12B A65 B6 B12 C130 M30 P5 S41 T1A U11 W125
Schofield, J.	28 Jun. 1918	C130 G32 K40 W125
Scholefield, M.	24 Feb. 1857	A65 B15A C130 G63 K50 K54 R58 W90 W125
Scott, A.	16 Jan. 1878	B43 C130 E11 K16 K53 K54 R60 W125
Scott, R.	26 Jul. 1901	A12B B6 B84 C130 D23 U11 W125
Scott, R.G.	1 Oct. 1880	B43 C130 E12 K53 K54 R60 U10 V67 W125
Scrimger, F.A.C.	23 Jun. 1915	B28 B69 B114 C113A C130 G39 L15 L16 K27 M14 M95 O14 R53 R80 S125 S145 V71 W125
Seagrim, D.A.	13 May 1943	B45 B136 C46 L3 R70 S40 T36 W125
Seaman, E.	15 Nov. 1918	C130 G35 U2 W125

Recipient	Gazette Date	Item Number in Part 1 / Part 2
Seeley, W.H.H.	21 Apr. 1865	C130 R60 W90 W125
Sellar, G.	18 Oct. 1881	C80 C130 E11 K53 K54 R60 W125
Sephton, A.E.	2 Dec. 1941	B45 H35 L3 L42 L70 R70 T37 W90 W125
Sewell, C.H.	30 Oct. 1918	C130 G34 I15 V57 W125
Sexton, G.: see Buckley, M.V.		
Shahamad Khan	26 Sep. 1916	A13 A65 C18 C130 G37 K4 K16 S45 W125
Shand, S.W. Loudon-: see Loudon-Shand, S.W.		
Shankland, R.	18 Dec. 1917	A27 A28 B69 B103 B114 C130 G39 M14 M70 N1 O17 R53 S76 S125 S145 W125
Sharpe, C.R.	29 Jun. 1915	B28 C130 O14 W125
Shaul, J.D.F.	28 Sep. 1900	A65 C130 U11 W125
Shaw, H.	28 Nov. 1865	C130 M107 R60 W125
Shaw, S.(J.)	26 Oct. 1858	B42 C130 K52 K54 R59 V56 V58 W7 W125
Shebbeare, R.H.	21 Oct. 1859	B42 C130 K16 K52 K54 L47 R59 W125
Shepherd, A.E.	13 Feb. 1918	C130 G36 O18 W7 W52 W125
Shepherd, J.: see Sheppard, J.		
Sheppard, J.	24 Feb. 1857	B15A C130 G63 K50 K54 R58 W90 W125
Sherbahadur Thapa	28 Dec. 1944	A16 B50 I10 K16 R70 M24 S45 T36 W125
Sherbrooke, R.StV.	12 Jan. 1943	B1 E4 L3 M4 M16 N50 P51 R70 T37 V160 W90 W125
Sher Shah	8 May 1945	A16 B44 I10 K16 R70 S45 T36 W125
Sherwood-Kelly, J.	11 Jan. 1918	A27 A28 B1 B148 C130 G36 I61 M70 Q5 O18 U10 V62 W125
Shields, R.	24 Feb. 1857	B15A C130 C150 D17 G63 K50 K54 L13 R58 W42 W75 W79 W125
Short, W.H.	9 Sep. 1916	C46 C130 G30 G62 O15 W52 W125
Shout, A.J.	15 Oct. 1915	A65 A76 B43 B76A B116 B140 C40 C121 C125 C130 F12 H30 H90 M23A M25 S75 V58 W55 W63 W70 W125
Sidney, W.P.	30 Mar. 1944	C148 G15 I15 L3 R70 T36 V69 W125
Sifton, E.W.	8 Jun. 1917	B69 B86C B114 C130 G33 G39 M14 M95 O16 R53 S125 S145 W125
Simpson, J.	27 May 1859	B42 C130 R59 W125
Simpson, R.S.	29 Aug. 1969	A5 A61 B43 B76A B116 C34 M17D M22A M23A S93 U3 V45 V70 W56 W70 W125
Simpson, W.: see Evans, A.		
Sims, J.J.	24 Feb. 1857	B15A C130 C150 D17 G63 K50 K54 L30 R58 S43 W42 W125
Sinnott, J.	24 Dec. 1858	B42 C130 R59 W125
Sinton, J.A.	21 Jun. 1916	A13 B114 C60 C78 C130 D23 G37 G39 K16 L42 R80 U2 W125
Skinner, J.	14 Sep. 1917	C130 S76 W125
Sleavon, M.	11 Nov. 1859	B42 C130 N2 R59 W125
Smith, A.	12 May 1885	B43 C130 O17 R60 S41 W125
Smith, A.V.	3 Mar. 1916	C130 H12 S75 W125
Smith, A. Bissett-: see Bissett-Smith, A.		
Smith, C.L.	7 Jun. 1904	C130 P5 W125
Smith, E. B.	22 Oct. 1918	A65 B43 C35 C130 G34 K26 S40 W53 V62 W125
Smith, E.A.	20 Dec. 1944	B69 B114 C113A D26 F41 G45 G51 L52 M14 R70 S125 S145 T36 W125
Smith, F.A.	4 Nov. 1864	A65 C130 H89 M107 P5 R60 W7 W125

Recipient	Gazette Date	Item Number in Part 1 / Part 2
Smith, H.	27 Apr. 1858	B42 C130 H89 K52 K54 P25 R59 W7 W125
Smith, I.	23 Aug. 1915	B28 B84 B84A C130 H12 O14 W125
Smith, J. (Pte.,Mad. Fus.)	24 Dec. 1858	B42 C130 K16 K52 K54 R59 W125
Smith, James (Cpl.)	21 Apr. 1899	C130 I15 P5 W125
Smith, James (Pte.)	18 Feb. 1915	C130 G31 H140 K26 O13 W53 W125
Smith, John (Sgt.)	27 Apr. 1858	B42 C130 K16 M4 N2 P25 R59 W125
Smith, J. Manners-: see Manners-Smith, J.		
Smith, P.	24 Feb. 1857	B15A C130 G63 R58 T32 W125
Smith, B Roberts: see Roberts-Smith, B		
Smyth, J.G.	29 Jun. 1915	A13 A65 B28 C130 C148 H127 H140 K16 L37 O14 S40 S46 S59 S60 S61 S62 S64 S67 S68 S69 S70 W125 (also see Part 2 Sections A and B)
Smyth, N.M.	15 Nov. 1898	B43 C130 W75 W79 W125
Smythe, Q.G.M.	11 Sep. 1942	A19 A65 B45 D36 H56 L70 N25 R70 T36 U10 W125
Somers, J.	1 Sep. 1915	C60 C130 L16 S75 U2 W125
Spackman, C.E.	11 Jan. 1918	C130 G36 W125
Spall, R.	26 Oct. 1918	B69 B114 C130 G34 G39 M14 S125 S145 W125
Speakman, W.	28 Dec. 1951	A5 A61 A65 B12 C20 C34 C148 H128 L35 P12 S80 V52 W125
Spence, D.	24 Dec. 1858	B42 C130 K52 K54 R59 W125
Spence, E.	27 May 1859 15 Jan. 1907	B42 C130 R59 W125
Stagpoole, D.	22 Sep. 1864	B35 C130 D27A M107 R60 W125
Stanlack, W.	24 Feb. 1857	B15A C130 G15 G63 K50 K54 P10 R58 W125
Stanlock, W.: see Stanlack, W.		
Stannard, R.B.	16 Aug. 1940	A15 B136 H56 K65 L3 M15 M70 R70 T37 V67 W90 W106 W125
Starcevich, L.T.	8 Nov. 1945	B44 B76A B116 G52 H90 M23A R70 T36 W55 W70 W125
Statton, P.C.	27 Sep. 1918	B26 B76A B116 C125 C130 D7 G34 M23A W55 W70 W125
Steele, G.C.	11 Nov. 1919	A10 A12 B121 C97 C130 F13 H56 I61 M20 R41 T12 V68 W81 W90 W125 (also see Part 2 Section A)
Steele, T.	8 Jun. 1917	A66 B12 C130 G37 W125
Steuart, W.G.D.: see Stewart, W.G.D.		
Stewart, W.G.D.	24 Dec. 1858	B42 B43 C130 R59 V60 W125
Stokes, J.	17 Apr. 1945	D31 D32 L3 R70 T36 V50 W125
Stone, C.E.	22 May 1918	C130 G32 M4 O18 S41 V61 W125
Stone, W.N.	13 Feb. 1918	C130 G36 K13 O18 W125
Storkey, P.V.	7 Jun. 1918	B76A B116 B140 C40 C125 C130 G32 H30 M23A M25 R6 W55 W70 W125
Strachan, H.	18 Dec. 1917	A27 A28 A36 B69 B103 B114 C130 G36 G39 M14 M46 O18 R53 S125 S145 W125
Stringer, G.	5 Aug. 1916	B12 B84 C130 G37 W125
Strong, G.	24 Feb. 1857	A66 15A C130 G15 G63 K50 K54 P10 R58 V51 W125
Stuart, R.N.	20 Jul. 1917	B79 B95 B121 C10 C47 C77 C130 G43 H56 I15 L5A L42 M15 M129 S19 S21 S77 W90 W125
Stubbs, F.E.	15 Mar. 1917	C130 H12 M109 S75 V45 W125
Sukanaivalu, S.	2 Nov. 1944	A16 B44 R70 V67 W125

Recipient	Gazette Date	Item Number in Part 1 / Part 2
Sullivan, A.P.	29 Sep. 1919	B76A B116 B116A C130 K13 M23A Q5 V73 W55 W63 W70 W125
Sullivan, J.	24 Feb. 1857	B15A C130 G63 K50 K54 V61 R58 T32 W90 W125
Sutton, W.	20 Jan. 1860	B42 C130 I15 K52 K54 R59 W7 W125
Swales, E.	24 Apr. 1945	A19 B89 C55 F9 F10 J13 K23 M17A R70 T35 U10 V55 V69 W125
Sykes, E.	8 Jun. 1917	B12 C130 G33 O16 S92 T1A W52 W125
Sylvester, W.H.T.	20 Nov. 1857	B15A C130 G63 K50 K54 R58 R80 V64 W75 W79 W125
Symons, G.	1 Dec. 1857	B15A C130 G63 K50 K54 R58 S41 W52 W125
Symons, W.J.	15 Oct. 1915	A76 B76A B116 C125 C130 H90 H98 L16 M23A S75 W55 W70 W125
Tait, J.E.	27 Sep. 1918	B69 B114 C130 G34 G39 M14 S125 S145 W125
Tandey, H.	14 Dec. 1918	C46 C130 C148 D1 G35 G62 J21 V51 W125
Taylor, J.	24 Feb. 1857	B15A C130 G63 K50 K54 R58 T14 W90 W125
Teesdale, C.C.	25 Sep. 1857	A66 B15A B43 C130 C150 D17 G63 K50 K54 L4 R58 R86 S41 V57 V62 V77 W42 W125
Temple, W.	22 Sep. 1864	B35 C130 K51 K53 K54 M107 P5 P34 R60 R80 S41 S79B V69 W125
Thackeray, E.T.	29 Apr. 1862	B42 C130 K16 K52 K54 N2 R59 T6 T7 T8 W125 (also see Part 2 Section A)
Thaman Gurung	22 Feb. 1945	A16 B1 B50 I10 K16 M24 R70 S45 T36 W125
Thapa, L. see Lalbahadur Thapa		
Thomas, Jacob	24 Dec. 1858	B42 C130 K16 R59 S41 W75 W79 W125
Thomas, John	13 Feb. 1918	B12 C130 G36 H98 O18 W125
Thompson, A.	27 May 1859	B42 C130 K52 K54 R59 W125
Thompson, G.	20 Feb. 1945	B1 B23 B89 C55 K23 L3 M17A N25 R70 T35 V65 W125
Thompson, J.	20 Jan. 1860	B42 C130 D1 I15 H35 K52 K54 W7 W125
Throssell, H.V.H.	15 Oct. 1915	A27 A28 A61 A76 B76A B116 B116A C121 C125 C130 G52 H12 H13 H90 H98 H140 I61 M23A M70 R6 S75 T17 T18 W55 W70 W125
Tilston, F.A.	22 May 1945	A27 A61 B69 B114 D26 F41 G51 M13 P20 R70 S125 S145 T9 T29A T36 V52 W125
Tisdall, A.W.StC.	31 Mar. 1916	B95 C130 H12 H140 L16 S75 S77 S78 S90 T23 W90 W125
Tollerton, R.	19 Apr. 1915	A27 A28 C130 G31 H12 H140 O13 S90 W125
Tombs, H.	24 Apr. 1858	A61 B42 C80 C130 C150 D17 H89 K16 K52 K54 M11 M101 R59 S20 S41 W42 W61 W125
Tombs, J.H.	24 Jul. 1915	B28 B84 B86A C80 C130 L42 O14 W125
Topham, F.G.	3 Aug. 1945	B69 B114 D26 G45 G51 M14 M95 R70 S125 S145 T36 W125
Towers, J.	6 Jan. 1919	C130 G35 W125
Towner, E.T.	14 Dec. 1918	B76A B116 C121 C125 C130 G34 H90 M23A V54 W55 W70 W125
Towse, E.B.B.	6 Jul. 1900	A36 B40B B43 C130 M30 M70 U11 V66 W125
Toye, A.M.	8 May 1918	A27 A28 C130 D19 G32 N2 W125
Train, C.W.	27 Feb. 1918	C130 G37 W125
Travers, J.	1 Mar. 1861	B40B B42 C130 K16 K52 K54 R59 W125
Travis, R.C.	27 Sep. 1918	A58 B140 C40 C130 G12 G32 H30 N12A S5 W125

Recipient	Gazette Date	Item Number in Part 1 / Part 2
Traynor, W.B.	17 Sep. 1901	A66 C130 D23 I15 M70 U11 W52 W125
Trent, L.H.	1 Mar. 1946	A58 B89 B140 C40 C55 H30 K23 L69 M17A M103 N12 N12A S5 S6 T35 W125
Trevor, W.S.	31 Dec. 1867	B43 C130 K16 K51 K53 K54 N2 R60 T9A V62 V155 W125
Trewavas, J.	24 Feb. 1857	B15A C130 G63 K50 K54 R58 T12 V55 V61 W90 W125
Trigg, L.A.	2 Nov. 1943	A58 A65 A67 A68 B65 B88 B140 C40 H10 H30 K23 L70 M17A M103 N12 N12A R70 S5 S40 T35 W90 W125
Triquet, P.	6 Mar. 1944	B69 B114 C113A D26 F41 G45 G51 G73 H26 M14 M11B M95 R70 S125 S145 T36 W125
Tubb, F.H.	15 Oct. 1915	A76 B76A B116 B116A C125 C130 H90 H98 M23A S75 W55 W70 W125
Tulbahadur Pun	9 Nov. 1944	A16 B44 B50 I10 K16 M24 R70 S45 T36 V45 V64 W125
Turnbull, J.Y.	25 Nov. 1916	C130 G30 O15 W125
Turner, A.B.	18 Nov. 1915	B28 C130 O14 W125
Turner, H.V.	17 Aug. 1944	B44 L3 R70 T36 W125
Turner, R.E.W.	23 Apr. 1901	B69 B114 C130 F41 M14 M95 M102C S116 S125 S145 U11 W125
Turner, S.	20 Jan. 1860	B42 C130 K52 K54 R59 W7 W125
Turner, V.B.	20 Nov. 1942	L3 R70 T36 W125
Turrall, T.G.	9 Sep. 1916	B86A C130 D1 G30 L30 O15 T14 W125
Tytler, J.A.	23 Aug. 1858	B42 B50 C130 K16 M14B R59 V67 W125
Umrao Singh	31 May 1945	A16 B1 B44 I10 K16 R70 S41 S45 T36 W125
Unwin, E.	16 Aug. 1915	A65 B95 C79 C130 E80 F3 H12 H140 I6 L16 L42 S40 S75 S77 S78 S90 T14 U5 W81 W90 W125
Upham, C.H.	14 Oct. 1941	A58 A61 A65 B1 B45 B86 B140 C40 C148 D13 H26 H30 H55
Bar	26 Sep. 1945	H90 J17 N12 N12A L35 L53 L70 M37 N25 R70 R88 S5 S15 S85 T24 T36 V45 V60 W125
Upton, J.	29 Jun. 1915	B28 C59 C130 H140 M4 N50 O14 S90 W125
Vallentin, J.F.	18 Feb. 1915	C130 G31 H98 O13 W125
Vann, B.W.	14 Dec. 1918	A66 B40A C130 G35 K16B M4 M4A R76 V45 W125
Veale, T.W.H.	9 Sep. 1916	C130 G30 H12 H127 O15 T12 V69 W125
Vereker, J. S. S. P: see Gort, Viscount		
Vickers, A.	18 Nov. 1915	B28 B86A C130 D1 H12 L30 O14 W125
Vickers, C.G.	18 Nov. 1915	B28 C130 L15 M4 N50 O14 W125 (also see Part 2 Sections A and B)
Vickery, S.	20 May 1898	C130 P5 W75 W79 W125
Vousden, W.J.	18 Oct. 1881	C130 E11 K16 K53 K54 R60 W125
Wadeson, R.	24 Dec. 1858	B42 C130 K52 K54 R59 W125
Wain, R.W.L.	13 Feb. 1918	C130 G36 H56 O18 W75 W80 W125
Wakeford, R.	13 Jul. 1944	L3 R70 T36 W125
Wakenshaw, A.H.	11 Sep. 1942	B1 B45 L3 R70 S37 T36 W53 W125
Walford, G.N.	23 Jun. 1915	C130 H140 S41 S75 S90 W125

Recipient	Gazette Date	Item Number in Part 1 / Part 2
Walker, M.	2 Jun. 1858	B15A C130 G63 I15 K50 K54 R58 T32 W125
Walker, W.G.	7 Aug. 1903	B50 C130 K16 P5 W125
Walker-Heneage, C.	26 Jan. 1859	B42 C130 K52 K54 R59 W125
Wallace, S.T.D.	13 Feb. 1918	C130 G36 O18 S41 T34 W125
Waller, G.	20 Jan. 1860	B42 C130 K52 K54 R59 W7 W125
Waller, H.	8 Jun. 1917	C130 G33 O16 W52 W125
Waller, W.F.F.	25 Feb. 1862	A65 B42 C130 K16 K52 K54 R59 W125
Walters, G.	24 Feb. 1857	B15A C130 G63 K50 K54 R58 W125
Wanklyn, M.D.	16 Dec. 1941	A14 B1 B45 C111 C126 D13 H26 H40 H55 J9 K14 K15A L3 M42 O35 R70 S88A T37 T40 W90 W125
Wantage, Lord: see Loyd-Lindsay. R.J.		
Warburton-Lee, B.A.W.	7 Jun. 1940	A15 B43 C110 D18 G71 H55 J6 J7 K65 L3 M15 M16 M20 R38 R70 R71 T37 V67 V160 W75 W80 W90 W125
Ward, C.	28 Sep. 1900	C130 M70 U11 W52 W75 W79 W125
Ward, H.	18 Jun. 1858	B16 B35 B42 C130 C150 D17 H89 K52 K54 P5 R59 W42 W125
Ward, J.E.A.	5 Aug. 1941	A58 B1 B89 B140 C40 C55 F32 H10 H30 K23 M103 N12 N12A N25 R70 R72 S5 T2 T35 V72 W125
Ward, J.	26 Jan. 1859	B42 C130 K52 K54 M17A R59 W125
Ware, S.W.	26 Sep. 1916	C130 G37 W125
Waring, W.H.	31 Jan. 1919	C130 G34 W75 W80 W125
Wark, B.A.	26 Dec. 1918	A27 A28 B76A B116 C121 C125 C130 G35 M23A M70 W55 W70 W125
Warneford, R.A.J.	11 Jun. 1915	B25 B89 C108 C108A C114 C130 G23 G43 G64 H12 H140 J20 K23 L15 L16 M17B P41 R27 S90 T39 V67 W9 W90 W93 W125
Warner, E.	29 Jun. 1915	B28 C130 O14 W125
Wassall, S.	17 Jun. 1879	B13 B43 C130 D1 E12 G60A G60B H35 H96 H97 H98 K45 K48 K49B K53 K54 L30 M30 P5 R60 R79 S134 V55 W53 W125 Y2
Waters, A.H.S.	13 Feb. 1919	C130 D1 G35 L30 N2 W80 W125
Watkins, T.	2 Nov. 1944	A66 C148 L3 M70 R53A R70 S40 T36 V45 V60 W75 W80 W125
Watson, J.	16 Jun. 1859	A65 B42 C130 C150 D17 K16 K52 K54 R59 W42 W62 W125
Watson, O.C.S.	8 May 1918	A27 A28 C46 C130 G32 G62 W125
Watson, T.C.	20 May 1898	A61 A66 C130 K16 N2 P5 W125
Watt, J.	29 Aug. 1917	A66 B95 C130 M43 S77 W90 W125
Weale, H.	15 Nov. 1918	C130 G34 W75 W80 W125
Wearne, F.B.	2 Aug. 1917	A65 A67 C130 G33 L59 O16 W125
Weathers, L.C.	26 Dec. 1918	B76A B116 B140 C40 C121 C125 C130 G34 H30 H90 M23A W55 W70 W125
Welch, J.	27 Jun. 1917	C130 G33 O16 W125
Wells, H.	18 Nov. 1915	B28 C130 I15 O14 W125
Wells, J.S. Collings-: see Collings-Wells, J.S.		
West, F.M.F.	8 Nov. 1918	B25 B89 C114 C130 H127 J20 K23 M17B P20 P41 R20 R27 V72 W125
West, R.A.	30 Oct. 1918	A65 A67 B43 C60 C130 D23 G34 H12 P12 T14 U2 U10 W125
Weston, W.B.	15 May 1945	A61 B44 C46 L3 R70 T36 W53 W125
Wheatley, F.	24 Feb. 1857	B15A C130 G63 K50 K54 M4 N50 R58 V77 W7 W125
Wheatley, K.A.	13 Dec. 1966	A5 B76A B116 C34 M22A M23A S55 S93 U3 V50 W10 W63 W70 W125

Recipient	Gazette Date	Item Number in Part 1 / Part 2
Wheeler, G.C.	8 Jun. 1917	A13 B50 C130 G37 H12 K16 W125
Wheeler, G.G.M.	1 Sep. 1915	A13 C130 G37 H12 K16 W125
Whirlpool, F.	21 Oct. 1859	B42 C77 C130 K16 L22 L42 M129 R59 V60 W125
Whitchurch, H.F.	16 Jul. 1895	A66 B43 C130 K16 P5 R80 W125
White, A.	27 Jun. 1917	C77 C130 G33 L16 L42 M129 O16 W75 W80 W125
White, A.C.T.	26 Oct. 1916	C46 C130 G30 G62 L13 L16 O15 V52 W52 W125 (also see Part 2 Section A)
White, Geoffrey S.	24 May 1919	A66 C130 G58 I15 J9 L16 O15 S77 V76 W90 W125
White, George S.	2 Jun. 1881	A12B A73 B40B B119 C84 C86 C130 C150 D17 D38 E11 E14 G66 H68 K19A K53 L59 L62 M8B M70 R56 R60 R83 S39 S95 S115 S155 T4 T11A V5 W45 W62 W125
White, J.	27 Jun. 1917	A27 A28 36 B12 C130 G37 K33 M23A M70 W125
White, W.A.	15 Nov. 1918	A27 A28 A65 C130 G34 H12 W125
Whitfield, H.	8 May 1918	C130 D31 D32 G37 W125
Whitham, T.	6 Sep. 1917	B12 C130 G15 O17 P10 S76 W125
Whittle, J.W.	8 Jun. 1917	A27 A28 B26 B76A B116 C121 C125 C130 D7 G33 M70 O16 W50 W55 W70 W125
Wilcox, A.	15 Nov. 1918	A65 B86A C130 D1 G34 L30 W7 W125
Wilkinson, A.R.	6 Jan. 1919	A65 B12 B84 C130 G35 V63 W125
Wilkinson, T. (Bdr.)	24 Feb. 1857	B15A C130 G63 G39 K50 K54 L45 R58 P59 W52 W90 W125
Wilkinson, T. (Lt.)	17 Dec. 1946	B44 C80 H56 L3 L42 S35 S40 T37 V50 V51 W90 W125
Wilkinson, T.O.L.	26 Sep. 1916	B69 B114 C130 D32 G30 G39 M13 O15 S125 S145 W125
Williams, John	2 May 1879	B9 B11 B13 B15 B15B B15D B15E B40B C130 E12 G24 G41 G60 G60A G60B H5 H92 J31 K45 K46 K47 K49B K53 K54 L50 L87 M13B M30 M113 R6 R60 R69 R79 S79 S134 T15A W27 W51A W54 W75 W79 W125 Y2 Y5
Williams, J.H.	14 Dec. 1918	C130 G35 H12 W75 W80 W125
Williams, W.	20 Jul. 1917	B95 B121 C10 C47 C130 G43 H56 L5A M15 S19 S21 S77 S90 W75 W80 W90 W125
Williams, W.C.	16 Aug. 1915	A65 A67 B95 C130 D32 H12 H140 L16 S40 S75 S77 W75 W80 W90 W125
Willis, R.R.	24 Aug. 1915	A27 A28 C130 H12 M109 P12 S75 T14 V45 V51 W125
Wilmot, H.	24 Dec. 1858	B42 C130 K52 K54 M4 R59 W7 W125
Wilson, A.K.	21 May 1884	A61 B43 B110 C130 H69 H127 J10 M102 M128 R57 R60 V58 W90 W125
Wilson, E.C.T.	14 Oct. 1940	A15 A65 B1 B45 H52 K65 L3 L38 R70 R72 S40 T36 V63 W51 W125 (also see Part 2 Section A)
Wilson, G.	5 Dec. 1914	C130 G31 H140 L15 O13 S90 W125
Wood, H.B.	14 Dec. 1918	C130 G35 H15 H56 P7 T14 W52 W125
Wood, H.E.	4 Sep. 1860	A65 A69 B35 B39 B42 C118 C130 C150 D17 F7 G60B H68 H96 I61 K16 K44 K49 K52 K54 L51 L61 L62 M29 M36 M70 M113 P55 R59 S155 T4 V61 W12 W42 W45 W68 W95 W96 W100 W125 (also see Part 2 Section A)
Wood, J.A.	3 Aug. 1860	A36 B43 C130 K16 M30 P5 R60 V52 W125
Wood, W.	27 Nov. 1918	A27 A28 B12 C130 G37 H12 M70 S92 W125
Woodall, J.E.	28 Jun. 1918	B12 C130 G32 W7 W125
Woodcock, T.	17 Oct. 1917	B12 C130 G15 G76 O17 W125

Recipient	Gazette Date	Item Number in Part 1 / Part 2
Wooden, C.	26 Oct. 1858	A61 B15A B43 C130 C150 D17 G63 I15 K50 K54 M30 P5 R58 V54 W42 W125
Woodroffe, S.C.	6 Sep. 1915	A65 A67 B28 C35 C130 O14 W7 W125
Woods, J.P.	26 Dec. 1918	B76A B116 C121 C125 C130 G34 G52 M23A W55 W70 W125
Woolley, G.H.	22 May 1915	B28 C130 C148 H140 L15 O13 S62 S90 V75 W7 W115 W125 (also see Part 2 Section A)
Wright, A.	24 Feb. 1857	B15A C130 G63 K50 K54 R58 T32 W125
Wright, P.H.	7 Sep. 1944	A66 B1 G15 L3 P10 R70 T36 W125
Wright, T.	16 Nov. 1914	C130 G31 H140 N2 O13 T14 W125
Wright, W.D.	11 Sep. 1903	B43 C130 P5 V61 W125
Wyatt, G.H.	18 Nov. 1915	A27 A28 C130 G15 G31 H140 M70 O13 P10 W52 W53 W125
Wylie, C.H.M. Doughty-: see Doughty-Wylie, C.H.M.		
Wylly, G.G.E.	23 Nov. 1900	B76A B116 C130 H90 M23A M70 U11 W55 W70 W125
Yate, C.A.L.	25 Nov. 1914	B43 C130 D32 G31 H140 O13 S90 V74 W125
Yeshwant Ghadge	2 Nov. 1944	A16 I10 K16 R70 S45 T36 W125
Youens, F.	2 Aug. 1917	B1 C130 G33 O16 S37 W125
Youll, J.S.	25 Jul. 1918	A65 C130 G37 H12 W53 W125
Young, A.	8 Nov. 1901	A65 C130 D23 U10 U11 W125
Young, F.E.	14 Dec. 1918	C130 G34 V53 W125
Young, J.F.	14 Dec. 1918	B69 B114 B160 C130 G34 G39 M14 S125 S145 W125
Young, T.	4 Jun. 1918	C130 G32 S37 W53 W125
Young, T.J.	1 Feb. 1859	B35 B42 C130 K52 K54 R59 R75 V14 V15 V64 V65 W22 W90 W125
Young, W.	30 Mar. 1916	B28 C130 K38 K39 O14 W125
Younger, D.R.	8 Aug. 1902	C130 U11 W125
Zengel, R.L.	27 Sep. 1918	B69 B114 C130 G34 G39 M14 S18 S125 S145 W125